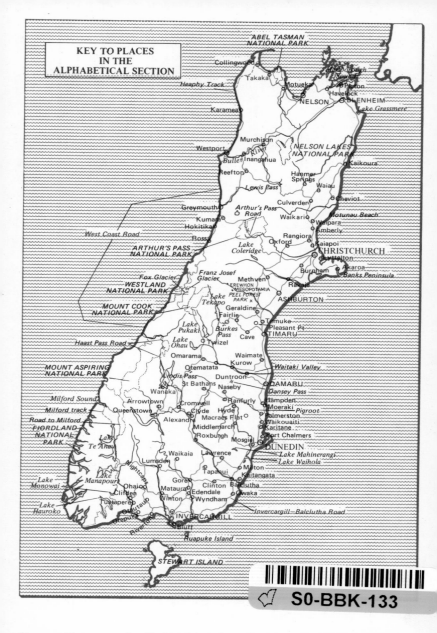

KEY TO PLACES
IN THE
ALPHABETICAL SECTION

discussed in greater detail elsewhere, the reference may be given (*see index*), thus referring the reader to the index at the back of the book; or (*see* △*Westport*), referring the reader to an entry in the Alphabetical Section.

## STARRING SYSTEM

Places and things to see and do have been graded thus:

***—worth a journey  *—interesting
**—worth a detour  no star—see if possible.

These are necessarily subjective assessments, and serve only to guide the traveller who is unfamiliar with an area to the relative strengths of competing claims for his attention.

## ACCOMMODATION

Because of the constantly changing nature of New Zealand's rapidly growing tourist and accommodation industry, details of hotels, motels and camping grounds have not been included. Readers are referred to the annual publications issued by the Automobile Associations.

## PUBLIC RELATIONS OFFICES

Where a place has a public relations office its address and telephone number are given. These generally provide free information on what there is to see and do, will attempt to answer queries of any description and will frequently assist in locating and booking accommodation, and in arranging local tours.

## OVERSEAS VISITORS

THIS BOOK is as much for the New Zealander travelling within his own country as it is for the overseas visitor. It suffices here to note that in area the country is slightly larger than the United Kingdom and its population totals 3,151,700 (January 1978). The population is predominantly of European origin, with one in twelve a Maori and one in seventy a Polynesian Islander. The country lies in the temperate zone of the South Pacific some 1,400 miles (2,250 kilometres) south-east of Australia. Auckland is almost due east of Sydney. The "four main centres", Auckland, Wellington, Christchurch and Dunedin, are evenly spaced along the country's 1,000-mile (1,600-kilometre) length. Centres with populations greater than 20,000 are given "city" status. Of these there are twenty-six, several of which form the Auckland and the Wellington-Hutt urban areas.

Information on such matters as visas, currency, health requirements, travel and package tours is available free of charge from travel offices within New Zealand and from the New Zealand Government Tourist Bureau offices at:

Sydney: *115 Pitt St; tel. 233-6633*
Melbourne: *332 Collins St; tel. 67-6621*
Brisbane: *Watkins Place, 288 Edward St; tel. 221-3722*
London: *New Zealand House, Haymarket*
    *tel. 01-930-8422*
San Francisco: *Suite 970, Alcoa Bldg, 1 Maritime Plaza;*
    *tel. 415-788-7404*
Los Angeles: *Suite 1530, 10960 Wilshire Boulevard;*
    *tel. 213-477-8241*
New York: *Suite 530, 630 Fifth Ave; tel. 212-586-0060*
Toronto: *c/- N.Z. Consulate, Suite 2616, 2 Bloor St East,*
    *Toronto. Ontario - M4W 1A8; tel.*
    *416-961-9797*
Tokyo: *c/- N.Z. Embassy, 20-40 Kamiyana-cho,*
    *Shibuya-ku; tel. 460-8781*
Bonn: *6 Frankfurt am Main, Rathenauplatz la;*
    *tel. 288-189*

First published 1974
Revised 1976, 1978
3rd Revised Edition reprinted 1981, 1983

A.H. & A.W. REED LTD.
68-74 Kingsford-Smith Street, Wellington 3
also
7 Kirk Street, Auckland 2
85 Thackeray Street, Christchurch 2

ISBN 0 589 00998 2

Library of Congress Catalogue Card No. 74-76513

Set by New Zealand Consolidated Press Ltd,
Auckland, New Zealand
in Monotype Plantin
Printed by Dai Nippon Printing Co. (Hong Kong) Ltd.

**Mobil**

# NEW ZEALAND
# TRAVEL GUIDE

# SOUTH
# ISLAND
## AND
## STEWART ISLAND

*by*

*Diana and Jeremy Pope*

REED

# CONTENTS

# ACKNOWLEDGMENTS

THE AUTHORS ARE indebted to the many public relations officers, town and county clerks, and secretaries of local historical societies who provided much helpful information and checked drafts. They acknowledge a particular debt to the late Mr Norman Forrest; also to Miss Patricia Adams who revised the present edition.

Space does not permit the listing of the many people and organisations who have given generously of their time and often of the product of their research, but they include the New Zealand Historic Places Trust, the staff of the Alexander Turnbull Library (Wellington), the Hocken Library (Dunedin), the Canterbury Museum and the Christchurch Public Library.

Government departments who assisted include the New Zealand Railways, the New Zealand Forest Service, the Department of Lands and Survey, the National Parks Authority and the individual park boards, the Ministry of Works and Development, the New Zealand Post Office, the Electricity Department, the Reserve Bank, the Department of Trade and Industry, the Government Statistician, the Department of Agriculture and Fisheries, the Marine Section of the Transport Department, the Ministry of Defence, the Department of Education, the Department of Health, the Internal Affairs Department, State Coal Mines, Mines Department, Customs Department, and the Weather Bureau and Meteorological Service.

The passage quoted from *The History of Gold Mining in New Zealand* by J. H. M. Salmon on page 24 is reproduced by kind permission of the Government Printing Office.

The Art Galleries and Museums Association of New Zealand provided details of museum collections, and the Automobile Associations of Wellington and of Otago provided very many distances.

The publishers wish to thank the Lands and Survey Department for permission to use parts of NZMS 17 (Christchurch, Dunedin, Queenstown), and adapt the basic data in sheets 13 to 26 of NZMS 18 Series. (Lands and Survey Licence No. 1974/16.)

# INTRODUCTION

## THE APPEARANCE OF THE SOUTH ISLAND

THE SOUTH ISLAND has had many names. The Maori called it Te-waka-a-Maui (the canoe of Maui, the mythical figure who drew land from the sea) and also Te Waipounamu (the water of greenstone). Abel Tasman in 1642 named it Staten Landt, a name that in his native Holland became Nieu Zeeland. The British explorer Cook charted the Maori name as Tovypoenammu; the British Government constitutionally designated the island New Munster; and the General Assembly in New Zealand called it The Middle Island. Finally — but only since 1905 — its present simple name was settled on.

The fortunes of the Island, too, have fluctuated. In prehistoric times it had the greater population of the two principal islands, when Moa-hunters stalked their prey predominantly on the tussocklands of the broad Canterbury plains. With the introduction of the *kumara* and the rise of an agrarian economy, the Maori concentrated in the generally warmer climes of the North Island so that in the earliest years of European settlement, the South Island did not have the Maori population nor experience the forceful opposition to land purchases that in the North Island boiled over into the Land Wars. While war raged in the north, goldrushes came to Central Otago and then to the West Coast, disturbing the tranquility of the peaceful South Island and stimulating its economy. The South grew to dominate the country, both in population and in prospects, and could seriously think in terms of its own independence.

As gold waned came the introduction of refrigeration, opening up meat-hungry markets in Britain for the surplus stock of the South Island's multitudinous flocks. But while the innovation revolutionised the sheep industry, it also brought economic viability to the small landowner, most conspicuously the dairyfarmer, who could then export butter and cheese. At the close of the century the populations of both islands were about the same, and the North Island began to move ahead. The principal North Island dairying areas of Taranaki and Waikato were soon closely settled, and to add to the growing imbalance, the Panama Canal opened and gave North Island ports easier access to world shipping routes. Such improved communication, coupled with a growing population, further accelerated the development of the North Island.

Today the South Island has 27.8% of the country's total population (862,600 out of 3.1 million) though it has less than 10% of the Maori population. For the traveller the Island's comparative lack of numbers is reflected in sparse traffic and a more relaxed way of life, and one enjoyed against the unsullied grandeur of a landscape altogether different from that of the North.

**Landforms:** Presumably it was the South Island that earned New Zealand its first name of Aotearoa (long white cloud) as its mountain backbone is frequently covered in cloud. Neither Tasman nor Cook saw the giant peaks now named after them. The Island stretches for some 800 km, lying south-west to north-east, and is divided for almost its entire length by the diagonal Alpine Fault which rises abruptly from the West Coast to create a chain of mountains with heights of up to 3,760 m. The Alps have been continually rising for perhaps 185 million years, though constantly being eroded by wind, ice and rain. During the Ice Ages they were deeply carved by massive glaciers whose remnants still lurk high in the ranges. The glaciers, too, gouged out the long and slender mountain lakes so much a feature of the South Island from Rotoiti to Poteriteri. Technically the term "Alpine Fault" applies only from about Milford Sound to Lake Rotoiti. To the north-east of the Island the line branches to be continued by the Hope, Kekerengu, Clarence, Awatere and Wairau Faults — which cross Cook Strait to re-emerge as major faults on the North Island landscape.

To the west of the Main Divide lie the rain forests of the West Coast; to the east, great rivers have fanned debris eroded from the mountain chain to build the expansive Canterbury plains. These plains have crept out into the Pacific to tie the young volcanic rocks of Banks Peninsula to the mainland. Departed glaciers have clawed fiords into an otherwise unbroken south-west coastline, a topographical feature mirrored to the north-east of the island by the intricate fragments of the Marlborough Sounds. The latter, however, are not glacial in origin but are rather the result of the collapse of large river systems which have been invaded by the sea.

Unlike the wholly volcanic islands of the central Pacific, New Zealand consists of rocks of a wide variety of types and ages. The only young volcanic rocks in the South Island are to be found on Banks Peninsula, the Otago Peninsula, and at Oamaru and Timaru. Old volcanic rock and associated intrusive rocks are found in a band to the east of Lake Te Anau, on the north of Stewart Island, and in a strip to the east of Nelson. As well as serving as a provincial boundary, the Waitaki River marks the division between the greywacke of Canterbury and the schist of the Otago hill country — a rock of similar sedimentary origin to greywacke but compacted by greater heat and pressure into a more stable form. In the main, Southland lies beyond the schist bed, comprising sedimentary rocks from Triassic times (230 to 180 million years old). The south-west and north-west tips of the island contain both the South Island's and New Zealand's oldest rocks, dating from the Precambrian age (over

600 million years ago). As the rocks most resistant to erosion, they have best recorded the shaping action of the glaciers.

Just as the land forms vary, so too does the climate. The West Coast's rain precipitation of up to about 4,000 mm annually is among the world's heaviest. Depleted of its moisture as it rises over the mountains, the prevailing westerly descends to fan the east coast with a warm, föhn-like wind.

**Flora:** The first Polynesian settlers came to a land already undergoing change on a large scale owing to climatic variations. Whereas much of the North Island was devastated by volcanic eruption, the South had been particularly affected by the most recent Ice Age of perhaps 15,000 years ago. Later, as temperatures rose to reach a peak perhaps 5,000 years ago before beginning to fall again, changes took place over a broad spectrum of the Island's flora. The Moa-hunter (as did the later Classic Maori) contributed to this by repeatedly burning off vast areas of forest. The run-holder who succeeded them, too, regularly fired fern and tussock to make it more palatable for his sheep, thereby effectively preventing any forest recovery.

Climatically the South Island ranges from the extremes of very cold to some of the country's hottest regions, and from some of its wettest (4,000 mm per annum) to among its most dry (350 mm annually), giving the Island a wide diversity of flora. Of over 15,000 flowering species, no fewer than 1,300 are endemic, and of these nearly half are unique to the South Island — an extraordinary occurrence when one considers that in Pliocene times Cook Strait did not exist, so that there was a continuous land bridge between what are now two islands. Even though the coastal and lowland vegetation of the southern part of the North Island and that of the northern part of the South are almost identical, the South Island area nonetheless has about 300 native species unknown in the North. From this the broad assumption can be made that many of the South Island species are comparatively young. Even more than Cook Strait, latitude 42° South forms a critical line with regard to distribution.

Over the last 130 years large areas of primeval vegetation have been either replaced with exotic pastures or modified in other ways. Previously the ecology had evolved in the absence of browsing animals. Flightless birds such as the *moa (see index)*, the *kiwi (see North Island index)* and the *weka* took their place. Had a wide variety of plant-destroying mammals not been introduced — sheep, cows, deer and rabbits among them — the country's unique vegetation would be all the more intriguing. As it is, of the rest of the world's significant landmasses only Antarctica shares such a history, for although since Mesozoic times there has been a continuous land surface in New Zealand, the country has been cut off from other land areas at least since the late Mesozoic and early Tertiary eras, times when mammals were spreading over most of the rest of the world.

The native vegetation broadly divides between the rainforests of the West Coast, drenched by moisture-laden winds from the Tasman Sea, and the tussock-grassland to the east of the Main Divide. The rainforest includes both subtropical forests (with a wealth of undergrowth and fern) and subantarctic beech forests (curious by their absence on the West Coast from the Taramakau to the Paringa River, a distance of 160 km).

The tussock-grassland also falls into two categories — tall and low (named by reason of their height). Tall tussock is now virtually confined to the mountains, low tussock dominating the lowland belts to the east of the Divide.

On the mountains themselves are the remarkable open communities established on scree and giant shingle slides. Many of the plants are much the same colour as the stones they cover and are capable of withstanding extremes of both hot and cold, and being temporarily buried in further slips. On the high mountain rocks, the dense cushions of *Raoulia* are of special interest, particularly the "vegetable sheep", *Raoulia eximia* and *Haastia pulvinaris*. They often exceed 2 m in length, 1 m across and 60 cm in height, but grow so close to each other that they appear as an even greater mass.

**Fauna of the south:** In pre-human times even more than they are today, birds were very much the dominant feature of the natural fauna. There were no land mammals other than two species of bat, and these, now scarce elsewhere, survive in their greatest numbers on the natural sanctuary of Stewart Island.

Pre-eminent among the birds was the flightless *moa (see index)*, the largest of the species — also the largest bird the world has known — standing over 3 m high and grazing on native grasses. They lived in their greatest numbers in the South Island, the last surviving species finally succumbing in comparatively recent times to the combined pressures of hunting and climatic change. Survivors of the era of flightless birds include the *kakapo, weka* and *kiwi*. There are three species of *kiwi* — with the *moa* the most ancient of the country's birds — the common *kiwi* (found throughout the country), the little spotted *kiwi* (found only along the western slopes of the South Island), and the great spotted *kiwi* (which occurs from western Nelson to about mid-Westland). In 1948 another contemporary of the *moa*, the unique *takahe (see index)* was rediscovered after being believed extinct for half a century. The far south of the South Island is where the country's wildlife may be observed in a state less disturbed than elsewhere.

A curiosity found on islands in Cook Strait and on the North Island offshore islands of the Bay of Plenty and Northland but not on either mainland, is the *tuatara* (*see index*). A "living fossil", it flourished in past ages when the dinosaur and kindred other reptiles roamed the earth. As the sole surviving reptile of such times, this large lizard attracts the interest of naturalists the world over.

Conspicuous in the South Island are seabirds, with the oceanic families of petrels (70 species) and penguins (11 species) being well represented. They tend to nest on the subantarctic islands to the south of New Zealand, where they breed by the million. Seals also breed there as they recover from the ruthless exploitation of 170 years ago. The world's only known mainland nesting-place of the giant Royal Albatross is at Taiaroa Head on the Otago Peninsula; a breeding ground for the fabled *kotuku* (white heron) is rigidly protected at Okarito (*for both, see index*), and for wading birds, on Farewell Spit.

**Enter the exotics:** The early Polynesian brought his dog and rat with him, the former now extinct. These would have had some impact on nesting birds quite unprepared to cope with such interlopers, but to nothing like the extent of what was to follow. Europeans, seeking to recreate their homeland on a foreign shore, introduced British songbirds (which competed for food) out of sentiment, and game animals for sport, such as pheasant, quail, deer, tahr and chamois. The rabbit, the hedgehog, rats, mice, stoats, weasels and opossums were all introduced to change, irrevocably, the country's flora and fauna. Species of native plants succumbed in the face of browsing sheep, cattle, rabbits and deer; species of native birds became extinct who could not develop mechanisms to counter the depredations of cats, dogs, rats and other rodents.

**Fishing:** Anglers, too, were successful in establishing such fish as brown trout from Europe, rainbow trout from North America, and Atlantic and quinnat salmon. Trout fishing throughout the island in lake and river is uniformly good, and east coast rivers such as the Rakaia and the Waitaki are renowned for their salmon. *Enquire at local sports shops for licences and particulars of any district regulations. Toheroa (see North Island index)*, a prized shellfish delicacy, are taken at points along Foveaux Strait (*the length of the season, if any, and the numbers permitted to be taken both vary annually*).

**Hunting:** The introduction of game animals has created in the South Island some of the world's finest hunting areas. Red deer are found throughout but are in their greatest numbers to the south-west, from Hokitika to Foveaux Strait. Wapiti are found in Fiordland, west of Lake Te Anau, and a minute herd of moose may still be surviving in a small area south-west of Manapouri. The Virginian, or white-tailed, deer is found near Lake Wakatipu and on Stewart Island. There are also widely dispersed pockets of fallow deer, from Nelson to near Balclutha. The keenly-sought tahr is found on the Main Divide from Lake Ohau to Arthur's Pass. The chamois has spread right along the Island's mountain backbone, flourishing most conspicuously in the areas it shares with the tahr.

Distribution of game animals is for ever changing. Herd densities fluctuate as the result of both natural and human influences, more particularly the latter since the venison export trade has caused helicopters to be used to kill deer in large numbers. Specific information on the state of the various herds, on huts, on tracks and on access to hunting areas is available from New Zealand Forest Service offices throughout the country. In addition there are Protection Forest Rangers stationed at Nelson, Murchison, Blenheim, Hokitika, Hanmer Springs, Oxford, Invercargill, Queenstown, Kurow, Te Anau and Harihari (South Westland). Travel agents hold details of high country sheep runs that organise hunting safaris, in the main for the overseas visitor.

**Natural resources:** The Nelson area embraces the most varied rocks of any district in New Zealand, representing virtually every geological period since the Cambrian (600 million years ago). There the rocks contain a wide variety of minerals, both of scientific and of commercial importance — serpentine, dolomite, talc, magnetite, asbestos and marble. On both the West Coast and in Central Otago gold was won in great quantities from fields in which renewed interest is taken as international movements in the price of gold may render them once more "payable". Other metals mined in the South Island at various times include antimony, tungsten, platinum, arsenic and chromium. Tin was for a period mined on Stewart Island.

Bituminous coking coals are found on the West Coast from Westport to Greymouth, sub-bituminous coal at Reefton, Kaitangata and Ohai, and lignite (low-grade non-coking coal) in Canterbury, in North and Central Otago, near Charleston, and throughout Southland. Coal and related shale have been worked at Orepuki. Vast deposits of low-grade shale in Otago's Upper Nevis Valley may yet be worked to distill petroleum. Though traces of petroleum itself have been noted at Murchison and Cheviot, the hopes for important discoveries have not so far been realised.

Uranium has been found in the Buller Valley; small amounts of scheelite have been mined near Queenstown. Titanomagnetite ironsands are on the West Coast north of Westport, and to the south lie quantities of ilmenite sand on which an industry may yet be based. Apart from the ironsands, the only other known source of iron is at Onekaka, near Collingwood.

In addition to its vital ability to grow grass, the most important of the South Island's natural economic resources remain hydro-electric power-generating sites and the vast beech forests of the West Coast. Its most significant industry after those serving the primary sector is probably the aluminium smelter at Bluff, though virtually the only New Zealand contribution to the process there is labour and vast amounts of cheap electricity from the turbines of Lake Manapouri.

**National Parks:** The South Island has a predominance of the country's national parks, in terms of both numbers and area. From north to south these comprise Abel Tasman National Park, Nelson Lakes, Arthur's Pass, Westland, Mount Cook, Mount Aspiring, and Fiordland National Park. (*Each is individually described in the Alphabetical Section.*) In addition there is the Marlborough Sounds Maritime Park and such regions as North-west Nelson Forest Park and Lake Sumner Forest Park, which are being developed as multi-use forestry and recreational areas.

## SOME MAORI MYTHS AND LEGENDS

THE MYTHS AND LEGENDS of the Maori, entertaining though many are (and indeed as some were simply regarded by the Maori himself), served many purposes. They embodied his beliefs on the origin of the universe, of fire, of man, of death. They told of his gods, and by extended genealogies that served as a time-scale linked the present day with the remote past. They also served as colourful ways in which to recount (and so memorise) detailed travelling instructions by melding geographical points into a fanciful tale. Moreover, a Polynesian technique which gave greater impact to a tale was to localise past events, so that some legends appear throughout the Pacific in varying forms yet in each place apply to a particular location with a wealth of supporting detail.

**The Canoe of Maui:** With a number of other islands of Polynesia, New Zealand shares its legendary origin as a fish drawn from the sea by the fabled Maui-tikitiki-a-Taranga. The "Maui cycle" of legends occurs over a wide area, the navigator-explorer living in the twilight time where gods and human beings merge in the borderland between myth and tradition. An embellishment of the Maori legend which describes the origin of Aotearoa (New Zealand) is that the South Island was Te-Waka-a-Maui (the canoe of Maui), Stewart Island, Te-Punga-o-te-waka-a-Maui (the anchorstone of the canoe of Maui), and the Kaikoura Peninsula, Te-Taumanu-o-te-waka-a-Maui (the oarsman's seat of the canoe of Maui). These names give rise to conjecture that Maui (like Abel Tasman) may have discovered the South Island first, sailing round it and climbing the Kaikoura Peninsula whence he first saw Te-Ika-a-Maui (the fish of Maui, the North Island). However any suggestion of the South Island enjoying a greater antiquity was repugnant to North Island tribes, the Ngati Porou of East Cape having their own account which insists that the canoe from which Maui made his fabulous catch is on the slopes of their Mt Hikurangi.

**Kupe and the octopus:** Though the mythical Maui is credited with the drawing up of the land, Kupe is said to have discovered it. (The apparent contradiction is perhaps explained by the way in which the Maui cycle appears in various mythologies throughout Polynesia, suggesting that as groups moved to people other islands they took with them their Maui myths and applied them to the new land.)

Some say Kupe in a dream saw the supreme god, Io, who told him of the new land awaiting discovery. It is, perhaps, more likely that he was persuaded of its existence by the direction and yearly flight of the *kohoperoa* (long-tailed cuckoo) coming from New Zealand to winter in the warmer islands of the central Pacific.

Others, in just one of a variety of conflicting legends, aver that Kupe and his companion Ngahue were fishing out from the Maori's mythical homeland of Hawaiki (probably the Society Islands), when a troublesome *wheke* (octopus) robbed him of his bait. So tiresome was the *wheke* that Kupe determined to kill it, but before he succeeded the *wheke* had led him a merry chase — over the Pacific to a sea-cave on the Wairarapa coast at Castlepoint, then on across Cook Strait and through the Marlborough Sounds before finally meeting its end at Whekenui Bay on Arapawa Island. (Whekenui means big octopus; Arapawa is a corruption of the name given for the *paoa* (downward stroke) with which Kupe administered the fatal blow.) On the West Coast of the South Island, at Arahura, Kupe is said to have killed a *moa* and also to have discovered greenstone. Generally tradition relates that Kupe found uninhabited the land he named Aotearoa (long white cloud) when it was first seen, lying like a cloud on the distant horizon.

On his return to Hawaiki, Kupe was often asked to lead a new expedition to the country he had found, but would only reply with a tantalising, "*E hoki Kupe?*" (Will Kupe return?). He never did.

**The battle of the stones:** A Maori legend that tells of the location of various valuable stones begins with a quarrel on distant shores between Poutini, the guardian of *pounamu* (greenstone), and the whale, Tutunui. Poutini regarded *pounamu* as a fish (the Maoris fossicked pieces of greenstone washed down certain rivers in floods). Tutunui, however, was adamant that *pounamu* was a stone and resisted the suggestion that *pounamu* should share his ocean. Tutunui turned for help to Hine-tu-a-hoanga, the guardian of sandstone which, as an abrasive used in grinding greenstone, was a natural enemy of *pounamu*. Hine drove Poutini out, chasing him all the way to Aotearoa.

Poutini landed at Tuhua (Mayor Island) off the Bay of Plenty coast, and would have stayed there but for the presence of other traditional enemies, Mata (flint) and Tuhua (obsidian), both competing hard rocks. At East Cape opposition was found from Whaiapu (another form of flint). Wherever else *pounamu* landed it was opposed by sandstone until a final confrontation took place on the West Coast of the South Island, at Arahura. There the personifications of *pounamu* and sandstone clashed. *Pounamu* was defeated, some of its "chiefs" were led away as captives, and the rest took refuge in a waterfall on the Arahura River.

> Notes on greenstone appear under Hokitika in the Alphabetical Section.

**The digging of the South Island lakes:** In legend Rakaihautu, a giant among men, arrived in the *Uruao* canoe long before the coming of the canoes of the so-called Fleet. Setting off southward to explore the land on foot, he reached the upper Buller Valley where he seized an enormous *ko* (digging stick) and gouged out the beds of what became Lakes Rotoiti and Rotoroa. As he continued south along the line of the Southern Alps he dug and named a whole series of lakes, his crowning achievement being the creation of Whakatipua (Lake Wakatipu). From there he journeyed north again, to form Waihora (Lake Ellesmere) and Wairewa (Lake Forsyth) before, his work completed, he climbed a hill on Banks Peninsula (Mt Bossu) and there thrust his mighty and much-used *ko* into its summit.

The outline of Mt Bossu is said to resemble a *ko*. There is also a geological link between the lakes and the legend, for the mountain lakes were all formed by glaciers which scraped out their beds as if with a digging-stick. The fable in detail is an example of how a journey of exploration could be described in a colourful, and so a memorable, way.

**The wreck of the Arai-te-uru canoe:** A large number of South Island geographical features are embodied in the legend which tells of the wreck of the *Arai-te-uru* canoe near △Moeraki, north of Dunedin. One of the ancestral canoes of the so-called Fleet, it was on its way to search for greenstone when the mishap occurred. *Kumara* and food-baskets on board were washed ashore, to become respectively irregular rocks and the curious circular Moeraki boulders. The reef at the mouth of the Shag River is said to be the canoe's petrified hull, and a prominent rock nearby, the remains of its navigator, Hipo. Names of passengers who perished in the wreck are given to various hills in the district. The survivors are said to have journeyed overland, north through the Mackenzie country, naming peaks and features as they went. As they reached Mt Cook (the country's tallest at 3,762.9 m) the remark was made that it appeared to be higher than the rest. At that moment a boy with the group was being carried on his grandfather's shoulders and, as he, too, appeared taller than the rest, his name of Aorangi was applied to the peak. Aorangi (occasionally inaccurately rendered "cloud-piercer") means cloud in the sky.

## THE MOA-HUNTER

**The Moa:** It was not until the late 1830s that Europeans became aware of the existence of the *moa* through the discovery and analysis of bones. A member of the order *Dinorthiformes,* unique to New Zealand, the long-extinct *moa*, like the present-day *kiwi*, has uncertain origins extending back at least 15 million years. Though generally thought of as huge (the largest of the species, over 3 m high, was the tallest bird ever to live on earth), most of the twenty-five or so different species were of moderate size. At least nineteen of these species were in the South Island and only two in Stewart Island. Flightless Ratite birds (without the keel that flying birds have to their raft-shaped breastbone), the emu-like *moa* took the place of browsing mammals in the New Zealand ecology, feeding on grass, leaves and fruit. A giant *moa, Dinornis maximus*, taller than any living animal other than the giraffe and the African elephant, would have needed as much grass in a day as does a bullock. His gizzard stones, which helped digest his food, ranged in size from about 1 to 10 cm in diameter and weighed in total almost 3 kg. For a time the small heaps of worn "*moa*-stones" that farmers found as they broke in virgin soil, were thought to be the last remaining vestiges after skeletons had finally disintegrated. It is now known that the *moa* would either vomit or pass the stones out when they had become too worn and smooth to serve their purpose.

The process of extinction was accelerated by the arrival of man, who hunted the *moa* for food, used its bone for tools and ornaments, and its huge eggs for waterbottles (since the Maori had no pottery). In hunting the birds the early inhabitants fired much of the country, accounting for the destruction of vast areas of South Island forest and possibly also for the quantities of *moa*-bone found in swamps. Some consider that the swamp skeletons, with leg-bones still locked in an upright position and with toe-bones still curved in agony, are the result of *moa* in large numbers fleeing to the apparent safety of damp swampland to escape the fires; others aver that there is in some areas too great a quantity of bone for this to have happened, and that the bone accumulated over very long periods of time as, one by one, individual *moa* as they crossed a swamp by a landbridge miscalculated or slipped to become trapped in the mire.

The point at which the *moa* became extinct is still uncertain. Carbon-dating has shown that the large *moa* populations trapped by the Pyramid Valley swamp in North Canterbury were surviving well into the first thousand years of the Christian era — it had previously been postulated that only a solitary genus had survived into times of human occupation. The Wairau Bar site, near Blenheim, has been dated from AD 905 to 1275, and a specimen of the species *Megalapteryx moa* found in the Takahe Valley (near Lake Te Anau) supports the proposition that the *moa* was still extant there in times of early European contact. There have until comparatively recent times been serious suggestions that the *Megalapteryx* might yet be found alive in Fiordland. Though classified as a *moa* the *Megalapteryx* was in fact rather like a large *kiwi*, almost 1 m in height, who could possibly have survived if, again like the *kiwi*, he had been a night-feeder, hiding in the forest by day.

At first treated as a zoological riddle without relevance to human habitation, the *moa* was in the main ignored by early historians such as Sir George Grey as they collected and collated the legends of the Maori. Curiously there is a general absence of references to the birds in Maori tradition. It was the first director of the Canterbury Museum, Sir Julius von Haast, who excavated a number of sites to postulate in 1872 to a sceptical audience the possible existence of a mysterious "*moa*-hunter".

**The Moa-hunter:** Over a century after von Haast first advanced his theory, the questions of who the Moa-hunter was, when he lived and where he originally came from have not been finally answered. Certainly he was of eastern Polynesian extraction, and certainly he was widely established in New Zealand by AD 900. Initially he was thought to have been an itinerant neolithic fisherman, but though he certainly moved about from one food source to another, there has since been discovered evidence to support claims that the Moa-hunter practised the art of agriculture, at least to a limited degree.

The Moa-hunter, too, appears to have been of a peaceful disposition, for apart from the occasional club-shaped stone no weapons have been found. It is possible that he used wooden weapons which, like his clothing, have failed to survive, but his manner of burial (openly in a village) suggests that he had no enemies. The later Classic Maori would hide the bones of his ancestors in remote caves to protect them from desecration by his foes. Apparently, too, cannibalism was not practised. Human bone has not been found in his ovens among the thousands of bones of *moa*, birds, dogs, seals, fish and whales that have been excavated. Nor did he fashion fish-hooks from human bone as the later Maori was wont to do.

He seems to have lived by the coast, in areas plentiful with fish and close to coastal lagoons for fowling and eeling. Campsites (Moa-hunter settlements) have nearly always been found by the mouths of rivers, particularly on the eastern coast of the South Island backing the vast plains where the *moa* would have grazed in his greatest numbers. However campsites have also been found in the North Island, particularly on the Coromandel Peninsula and the west coast between Wanganui and Egmont. As well as trapping their prey on the coast, it seems that the Moa-hunter also brought carcasses of *moa* down by raft from the hinterland after the birds had been killed by being trapped in swamps or driven over cliffs. Traces of Moa-hunter occupation dating from about AD 500 have been found as far inland as near Roxburgh, in Central Otago.

The turning point in New Zealand archaeology came in 1939 when a thirteen-year-old schoolboy fossicking on the Wairau Bar, near Blenheim, found curious remains. The ethnologist, Dr Roger Duff, in recent years director of the Canterbury Museum, was quick to recognise the importance of the site as a rich burial ground where whole collections of contemporary artefacts had been buried along with the dead. The find also laid to rest doubts held in some quarters as to whether the *moa* had still been alive in times of human habitation, for no fewer than eleven graves with *moa* egg bottles were found. It was Duff who first suggested that the later, or Classic, phase of Maori culture grew out of the Moa-hunter or Archaic phase, firmly rejecting the traditional notion that a massive Fleet migration had simply superimposed a superior culture. In place of such an event he advanced the theory that it was the introduction of the *kumara*, a sweet potato, that brought about the transition from the Archaic to the Classic period.

While rejecting a Fleet style invasion, Duff's theory postulates a later migration of some sort as the explanation of the presence of the *kumara*. Other scholars, however, consider that the *kumara* was known to, and introduced by, the original Polynesian migrants. They explain the change from the Archaic to the Classic phases of Maori culture in terms of an adaption to New Zealand conditions.

Whichever theory one follows, there was no sudden and dramatic change of life-style. It would probably have taken some considerable time for the *kumara* to have adapted from its former tropical environment to New Zealand's only marginal climate — passing through experimental and developmental phases before it was systematically planted and harvested.

At the same time, it is assumed, the gradual extinction of the *moa* was taking place. These two processes may explain the eventual concentration of the Classic Maori in the warmer climate of the North Island.

Cook, in 1769 the first European to observe the Maori, formed the view that he was then still generally nomadic, living in temporary *kainga* (unfortified villages) and moving from one food source to another. Certainly the potato which Cook introduced to the Maori would have further consolidated the tendency to stay in one place, while rendering habitable those areas where the less adaptable *kumara* could not be grown.

New Zealand's pre-history studies are still in a state of flux. As work continues, archaeologists have triumphed over the dogged traditionalists, whose theories were based on an often-uncritical acceptance of Maori tradition coupled with a dating system that set arbitrary and biologically unsound age-spans for the generation of each genealogy. Dr Roger Duff's landmark account of *The Moa-Hunter Period of Maori Culture,* though published in 1956 (Government Printer), remains the most definitive work on that era.

**The Moriori:** The term Moriori describes a third limb of Maori culture, one which developed in isolation on the Chatham Islands. There the *kumara* would not grow, and the Islanders lived by fishing, fowling, hunting seals, gathering fruit and shellfish, and feeding on the roots of fern. A dearth of large trees, too, meant that once the canoes they had used to get there had rotted away, they were unable to move on. The Moriori could only build flax rafts, but these would become waterlogged after about twenty-four hours in the sea. Confined to a small area, there was no room for war, and for several hundreds of years after their ancestor Nunuku had persuaded the various families to outlaw fighting, war was unknown. But in 1835 a *heke* of Ngai-Tara under Pomare Ngatata seized a ship visiting Wellington harbour. They forced its captain to sail them to the Chathams, where they fell upon and all but extinguished the simple Moriori.

## MAORI ROCK ART

THE MAORI, like other civilisations the world over, often drew pictures on smooth rock faces. The limestone areas of the South Island contain hundreds of examples of his work. The first recorded discovery was made in the Waitaki Valley, at Takiroa (in North Otago, near △Duntroon), by the surveyor Walter Mantell. In 1852 he noted "rude figures" in an overhang close by the present main road. Since then discoveries have been made in the South Island from Tonga Bay in Abel Tasman National Park in the north, to Clifden, towards the Island's south-western tip. However the vast majority of the country's known drawings lie in North Canterbury, in South Canterbury near Timaru, and in North Otago near the Waitaki River.

The great majority of these are of interest only to the archaeologist and the anthropologist, but examples which travellers should try to see include the Timpendean shelter (*near* △*Waikari*), Takiroa (*near* △*Duntroon*) and those listed under the entry for Timaru. At present some intriguing drawings are not open to the public, among them the famed *taniwha* (water monster) — which has been reproduced on a 20-cent stamp and subsequently on a wide variety of handicrafts.

Just who it was who executed the drawings, and when, is still a matter of conjecture. Julius von Haast was led to suggest that the Timpendean paintings were the work of shipwrecked Indian mariners, carried out in the remote past. Another claimed that he actually knew the group responsible — a band on their way to the West Coast diggings who doodled while delayed by rain. Herries Beattie told of Maori tradition attributing them to the Waitaha Moa-hunters and to the later Ngatimamoe. The floors of the shelters in which rock drawings have been found have often been excavated, occasionally yielding midden bones and artefacts dating back to the time of the Moa-hunter. Indeed one shelter (on Craigmore station, near Timaru) actually contains drawings of the *moa* which are thought to have been carried out while the birds still roamed the tussocklands.

The drawings were mostly made in black, either with dry charcoal or with charcoal mixed in fat or oil. Occasionally *kokowai* (red ochre or oxide of iron) was used, again sometimes mixed with shark oil to form a primitive paint. At times drawings were simply scratched with a sharp tool. Unfortunately many of the more spectacular drawings have been retouched by wellmeaning if misguided enthusiasts, concerned at the drawings' faintness.

No interpretation of the subjects can be made with complete certainty. Some observers have noted a less ornate style in South Island drawings, an element in common with early Maori wood carving. This suggests that many of the drawings here are probably older than those found in the North. Others have seen similarities to drawings in Borneo, on Easter Island and on the island of Lanai in the Hawaiian group. In the meantime one must simply accept the drawings for the creative inventions they are, the oldest being probably carried out to pass the time when hunting parties were forced to take shelter (most of the overhangs in which drawings have been found face north). The rock overhangs were probably on inland com-

Maori life, art and customs are portrayed in *An Illustrated Encyclopedia of Maori Life* by A. W. Reed. *Conflict and Compromise* by Professor I. H. Kawharu (Ed.), also published by A.H. & A.W. Reed, contains essays which represent the pioneering stage in anthropological studies in New Zealand.

munication routes and the widespread nature of the drawings reflects the nomadic existence of the South Island Maori. Some are obviously of great age, depicting birds known to be long extinct; a few drawings show signs of early European contact, incorporating ships and horses'; others incorporate Roman lettering, showing the influence of missionaries. Still more show signs of being carried out towards the end of the nineteenth century.

## THE CLASSIC MAORI IN THE SOUTH ISLAND

IF THE POLYNESIAN explorer Kupe encountered no sign of habitation on his journey here, according to tradition the land had long been peopled by the time Toi-kai-rakau ancestor of a number of Classic Maori tribes, arrived to find *tangata whenua* (people of the land) well settled and in control.

Tradition persists that some several generations after the arrival of Toi (who lived at Whakatane on the North Island's Bay of Plenty), a number of canoes journeyed from Hawaiki, one of which, *Takitimu*, made its landfall perhaps at Tauranga or Cape Runaway before following the coastline south. Tribes claiming descent from *Takitimu* include Ngati-Ranginui of Tauranga, Ngati-Kahungunu of Hawke's Bay and tribes of Poverty Bay and the East Coast. In tradition the canoe travelled the length of the South Island only to be wrecked in Foveaux Strait, near the mouth of the Waiau River, where it was turned into the chain of mountains to this day called Takitimu.

While the Fleet tradition is now generally regarded as fiction, at least insofar as the suggestion of an organised, large-scale migration is concerned, one school of thought holds that an influx of some sort did take place, bringing subtropical plants among them the *kumara* that was to change the life-style of the Moa-hunter.

Not that this change would have taken place either suddenly or uniformly throughout the country. It seems most likely to have taken place very gradually, with both the Moa-hunter (or Archaic Maori) culture and the Classic Maori culture overlapping and co-existing for a while.

Though the South Island appears to have had a predominance of population in Moa-hunter times, the advent or increased use of the *kumara*, plus the dwindling number of *moa*, saw the generally-warmer climes of the North Island attract progressively greater numbers. The *kumara* could not have grown south of the Rakaia River, so that below that point the Maori population was destined to continue as it had in the past — to be itinerant and generally small in number. The West Coast, though a source of greenstone, had a high rainfall, vast forests, little clear land for agriculture and was difficult to journey in — factors which militated against a significant Maori population. The prime area of Classic Maori culture in the South Island was the coastal strip from Banks Peninsula north to Cook Strait, and it is with that area that much of South Island Maori tradition is concerned.

In the shadows of such tradition are Te Rapuwai and Waitaha, possibly Moa-hunters and tribes whose traditions largely perished when the Ngatimamoe invaded from the North Island in about AD 1500. The pattern reoccurs throughout the country where a tribe, dispossessed of its ancestral lands, moved south to conquer and absorb others. On several occasions warparties crossed Cook Strait, driven south to seek new land. This was probably the case in Ngatimamoe, whose pitiless treatment of Waitaha was to be visited upon themselves a century later, at the hands of the stronger and more warlike Ngaitahu. With the conquered tribes perished most of their tradition, explaining the absence in Golden Bay of accounts of Abel Tasman's tumultuous reception in 1642 and in the Marlborough Sounds of Cook's repeated visits from 1770-77.

## THE SOUTH ISLAND MAORI FROM 1800

BY 1800 THE South Island's Maori population was not large. Perhaps less than 5% of the country's total population was living here — mainly on the coastal strip from Banks Peninsula to Nelson — and with Ngaitahu firmly in control. They had slowly but surely conquered the Island from north to south, with the shattered remnants of Ngatimamoe finally fleeing into the mountains and wild forests to become known as the "Lost Tribe of Fiordland". Ngaitahu had crossed to Rakiura (Stewart Island), and held this, too. There were, however, small pockets of Ngati-Apa, Ngati-Kuia and Rangitane in the area of Marlborough Sounds, and to the South of the Island there were more submissive *hapu* of Ngatimamoe, prepared to accept a subservient role.

It was then that a bloodfeud erupted, splitting Ngaitahu, dividing its loyalty and decimating its numbers. What came to be known as the *Kai huanga* (eat relation) feud began when Murihaka, wife of Potahi, put on a dogskin cloak that belonged to the chief Te Maiharanui. Such an invasion of his *tapu* demanded *utu*, which was exacted on a slave belonging to one of Murihaka's relations. Her relations in turn took revenge, but on one of the relatives who had killed the slave. In this unlikely way what began as a comparatively trivial affair quickly escalated. Skirmishes took place on an ever-broadening basis, increasing numbers of battles were fought and by the time Te Rauparaha judged it propitious to invade from the north (an action which inevitably forced the fractured Ngaitahu to reunite) the tribe was depleted to the point of having little chance of defending itself.

**Te Rauparaha comes south:** The *Kai huanga* feud only ended with the arrival on the scene of Te Rauparaha (*c.* 1768–1849), the chief of Ngati Toa who wielded total power from his island fortress of Kapiti. In a remarkable migration, the chief and his tribe had been driven from their Waikato homeland at Kawhia in *c.* 1820, moving south to ally with Te Atiawa, a Taranaki tribe which had also suffered at the hands of the Waikato tribes who had expelled Ngati Toa. Gathering forces as he progressed farther south — and conquering those who would not join him — Te Rauparaha eventually attacked and took Kapiti Island, on the western approach to Cook Strait. There the "Maori Napoleon" established himself as he consolidated his hold on surrounding territory, encouraging the presence of whalers and traders for the guns with which they could supply him.

**The Battle of Niho Manga:** After a combination of tribes from the South Island and from the West Coast of the North Island had joined in an assault on Kapiti Island in *c.* 1828, Te Rauparaha kept the canoes of those who had sought to dislodge him, vowing to wreak vengeance and (as Ngaitahu had been involved) to conquer the South Island. At Kaikoura, a principal centre of Ngaitahu with no fewer than eleven *pa* on the peninsula, the chief Rerewaka heard of Te Rauparaha's threat. But Ngaitahu had been living unmolested for perhaps 150 years and so Rerewaka doubtless felt confident in boasting that should Te Rauparaha attack he would "rip his stomach open with a barracuda tooth (*niho manga*)". (The Maori made sharp cutting knives by attaching shark or barracuda teeth to handles of wood.) The boast was insult enough to the Ngati Toa chief, but was compounded by the choice of weapon — for the barracuda was considered the lowliest of fish whereas the shark was highly respected. In time reports of the boast reached Kapiti and Te Rauparaha, on hearing of the insult, at once set sail for Kaikoura.

The canoes of Ngati Toa approached the Kaikoura Peninsula at dawn. Ngaitahu were ready, but not for this. They were expecting a party of relatives on a friendly visit, and ran to the beaches to welcome them. They were completely caught by surprise and the battle was over almost before it had begun. More than 1,400 were killed and among the captured was Rerewaka, who was taken triumphantly back to Kapiti where he himself was disembowelled — with a knife of barracuda-teeth.

With the conquest of the peninsula complete, *utu* had been exacted and Ngati Toa had accomplished their mission. But one of the Ngati Toa chiefs, Te Pehi (an uncle of Te Rauparaha), insisted on going on to Kaiapohia (*near* △ *Kaiapoi*) to get a greenstone *mere* (club) for his own use. The main body waited at Kaikoura, feasting on the slain, while a hundred or so warriors went on to Kaiapohia, travelling overland. There the visiting chiefs were invited to enter the *pa* by Ngaitahu who knew nothing of the events at Kaikoura, but the ever-alert Te Rauparaha saw the risk as needless. He warned Te Pehi not to go in but rather to barter guns for greenstone outside the *pa*. However some twenty chiefs ignored Te Rauparaha's advice. They entered the *pa* to be feted and feasted — and slain in their beds. Such at least is Ngati Toa tradition as recorded by Tamihana Te Rauparaha, missionary son of the paramount chief.

Ngaitahu, however, have another version. They say that visiting Ngati Toa chiefs came into their *pa* and that while the feasting was taking place a Ngaitahu with Te Rauparaha warned their leader Te Maiharanui that the Ngati Toa planned a surprise attack from within the *pa*. (Their informer had in happier times married a Ngati Toa and, in accordance with custom, gone to live with his wife's people. It would commonly happen that such a person would lose no opportunity to render favours to his original tribe, blood relatives being more precious than those acquired by marriage.)

Any doubt as to Ngati Toa intention was removed by news of what had transpired at Kaikoura. So both in self-defence and in revenge for the barbarism of the battle of Niho Manga, the Ngati Toa chiefs were slain.

**The *Elizabeth* at Akaroa:** The Ngati Toa judged it unwise to retaliate for the loss of their chiefs at once, retreating to bide their time. But come again they did. In *c.* 1830, Ngati Toa at Kapiti Island persuaded the captain of the brig *Elizabeth*, one John Stewart, to take them to Akaroa on Banks Peninsula to exact *utu* (satisfaction) from Te Maiharanui. Stewart agreed, in return for a quantity of dressed flax. He ferried a warparty of Ngati Toa into Akaroa Harbour and, while the *taua* hid below decks, posed as a friendly trader come to do business. He asked for Te Maiharanui, but experienced difficulty in inducing him to come on board. Eventually, however, the chief accompanied the British captain to his cabin. There he was confronted by Te Rauparaha's cousin, Te Hiko, whose father, Te Pehi, the Ngaitahu chief had killed at Kaiapoi. The Ngati Toa chief, without emotion, approached the terrified Te Maiharanui and with a forefinger lifted his upper lip. "So these are the teeth that ate my father," he commented quietly, content in the knowledge that it was for him in his own time to choose the manner of death for the Ngaitahu leader.

To the Maori such a stratagem was perfectly *tika*, for Te Maiharanui had been proved a fool by falling for the ploy. Others on the canoes with the Akaroa chief were also lured on board by the British sailors, where they were thrown in the hold. At dawn the *taua* surged ashore to surprise and devastate the unsuspecting *kainga*. Te Maiharanui was taken back to Kapiti where the widows of the Ngati Toa chiefs he had killed at Kaiapohia "put him to death by slow and nameless torture".

The Maoris gave Stewart short measure when he demanded his flax, and he sailed back to Sydney where the horrified authorities clapped him into gaol. He was eventually released, however, when the prosecution could not proceed for want of witnesses, but the affair so outraged British humanitarians that James Busby was appointed British Resident in New Zealand and the first step was taken towards an assumption of sovereignty by Britain.

**The sacking of Kaiapohia:** With good cause Ngaitahu set to work reinforcing defences, for within two years Ngati Toa had returned yet again. Siege was laid first to the principal Ngaitahu centre of Kaiapohia (*see index*), a siege which for three months proved inconclusive as reinforcements were able to reach the *pa* across a lagoon. Finally Ngati Toa began to construct a trench along the landward approach to the *pa* which zigzagged towards its palisades. At the end of the trench they piled scrub in preparation for a bonfire which would incinerate the stronghold. Defending Ngaitahu were alive to the danger. When at last they proved unable to reduce the size of the pyre by removing branches by night, they themselves set it alight while a strong nor-wester blew to fan the flames away from the palisades. The uncanny warm wind that Cantuarians know so well let down Ngaitahu: a sudden switch to the south saw the fire driven right through the *pa*, kindling the century-old and tinder-dry fortifications. Before the stunned Ngaitahu could redeploy their defences, Ngati Toa poured through the smoke to complete the destruction. After the traditional cannibal feast, Te Rauparaha sailed his canoes south, round Banks Peninsula and into Akaroa Harbour. There he successfully attacked the *pa* of Onawe (*see △Akaroa*), all but annihilating the Maori population of Banks Peninsula.

When European settlers arrived there were barely a dozen Maoris living in the vicinity of Kaiapohia, where once had lived thousands, and Banks Peninsula, too, might have been without any Maori population at all had it not been for Bishop Hadfield's work with Ngati Toa and Te Atiawa at Otaki, near Kapiti Island. As proof of their conversion to Christianity, the northern tribes not only released the slaves they had taken at Kaiapohia and Onawe but accompanied them back to their homelands to ensure their safe return.

Not that Ngaitahu farther south were prepared to see their Canterbury kin go unavenged. Several times *taua* of southern Ngaitahu journeyed north from Otago Peninsula and Foveaux Strait to attempt to exact *utu*. They were never in a position to launch a fullscale assault on Kapiti Island itself, but they assured Ngati Toa of harassment wherever they attempted to occupy the lands they had acquired on the southern side of Raukawa (Cook Strait). In 1833 one of these expeditions, a *taua* which included the renowned "Bloody Jack", Hone Tuhawaiki (*see index*), almost succeeded in taking Te Rauparaha himself. Ambushed by Lake Grassmere as he came to catch ducks, Te Rauparaha was seized by the cloak he was wearing but managed to wriggle out of the garment and swim out to safety.

**The end of the fighting:** The fighting was not yet ended. In 1836 one Te Puoho, a relative of Te Rauparaha and a chief of Ngati Tama recently settled near Collingwood in Golden Bay, led a warparty south along the wild and inhospitable West Coast in one of the most extraordinary outflanking manoeuvres of all time. His party of a hundred or more Ngati Tama took months to make their way down the coast and inland through the difficult Haast Pass. After a miracle of endurance they emerged at Lake Wanaka to take Ngaitahu and the Ngatimamoe they had absorbed completely by surprise. One by one, summer *kainga* in Central Otago were overwhelmed and mercilessly put to the *mere* to keep the presence of the invaders a secret. From Wanaka, Hawea and Wakatipu the *taua* made its way, following the Mataura River downstream from near Kingston to Tuturau (*near △Mataura*) in the heart of Southland. Though they took the Tuturau *kainga* unawares, news reached Tuhawaiki on his Ruapuke Island home in Foveaux Strait. "Bloody Jack" had been gathering arms in anticipation of a showdown with Te Rauparaha. Quickly canoes sped to the mainland, and as Te Puoho's men lay resting from their arduous trek, and sated with both *kanakana* (lamprey) and *kai tangata* (human flesh), they were overwhelmed in the dawn. Many were massacred and a handful taken prisoner. Only one is said to have escaped. Te Puoho himself was shot as he woke from slumber, and suffered the gross indignity of having his head (the most *tapu* part of his body) taken back to Ruapuke in triumph for further desecration there.

So ended the years of hostilities between Ngaitahu and Ngati Toa, between the Maoris of the South Island and those from the North — in an unqualified victory to Ngaitahu all the more sweet for its being overdue.

Undoubtedly the fighting would have continued, but Ngaitahu in Nelson and Canterbury had been crippled by heavy losses while with increasing European contact in the south, *kainga* upon *kainga* was wiped out by measles and other contagious diseases to which the Maori had no resistance. As "Bloody Jack" himself explained to George Clarke, Protector of Aborigines, in 1844: "Look here Karaka, (Clarke) here, and there, and there and yonder; those are all burial places, not ancestral burial places but those of this generation. Our parents, uncles, aunts, brothers, sisters, children, they lie thick around us. We are but a poor remnant now, and the *Pakeha* will soon see us all die out, but even in my time, we Ngaitahu were a large and powerful tribe, stretching from Cook Strait to Akaroa, and the Ngatimamoe to the south of us were slaves. The wave which brought Rauparaha and his allies to the Strait, washed him over to the Southern Island. He went through us, fighting and burning and slaying. At Kaikoura, at Kaiapohia, and at other of our strongholds, hundreds and hundreds of our people fell, hundreds more were carried off as slaves, and hundreds died of cold and starvation in their flight. We are now dotted in families, few and far between, where formerly we lived as tribes. Our children are few, and we cannot rear them. But we had a worse enemy than even Rauparaha, and that was the visit of the *Pakeha* with his drink and disease. You think us very corrupted, but the very scum of Port Jackson shipped as whalers or landed as sealers on this coast. They brought us new plagues, unknown to our fathers, till our people melted away. This (Ruapuke Island) was one of our largest settlements, and it was beyond even the reach of Rauparaha. We lived secure, and feared no enemy; but one year, when I was a youth, a ship came from Sydney, and she brought the measles among us. It was winter, as it is now. In a few months most of the inhabitants sickened and died. Whole families on this spot disappeared and left no one to represent them."

## EXPLORERS FROM EUROPE

**Slaughter at Murderers' Bay:** Accepted as the first European to see New Zealand was the Dutch explorer, Abel Janszoon Tasman (1603-59), sent from Batavia (now Djakarta) by the Dutch East India Company to see if there were commercial openings on the alleged landmass *Terra australis incognita* (the unknown southern continent) of whose existence European geographers of the day were convinced. After rounding Tasmania, the explorer's two small vessels *Heemskerck* and *Zeehaen* crossed the Tasman Sea and, on 13 December 1642, became the first known Europeans to sight New Zealand when they saw land on the South Island's west coast in the vicinity of Hokitika. Tasman followed northwards the shore of the "large land uplifted high" before entering Cook Strait and anchoring in the shelter of Golden Bay. This he did after seeing the first signs of habitation — smoke rising near Cape Farewell. As they lay at anchor, the vessels were inspected by two canoes, whose occupants called out in "a rough loud voice" and blew on an instrument that sounded like a Moorish trumpet. An officer on the *Zeehaen* replied on his own trumpet, and a strange duet developed that was to be the only form of communication between the two groups.

Early on the morning of 19 December, Tasman was still uncertain whether or not to attempt to land. The *Zeehaen*'s cockboat rowed to the *Heemskerck* so that the officers might confer. It was returning to the *Zeehaen* with a crew of seven when two canoes suddenly attacked. Four Dutchmen were killed, but three of the crew swam to safety before, in the face of gunfire, the attackers withdrew unscathed. Tasman elected to leave, "as no friendship could be made with these people, nor water nor refreshments could be obtained". The bay, because of the "detestable deed", he named Moordenaers (or Murderers') Bay. Just as the ships were departing, eleven crowded canoes put out from the shore, but were discouraged by a parting volley of gunfire.

The little vessels sadly sailed northwards, on 6 January 1643 leaving Cape Maria van Diemen and the country they had discovered for Europe but had not even set foot upon. Tasman's lack of enterprise earned him a reprimand, and within weeks of his return to Batavia he had been sent to sea again. New Zealand (or Staten Landt as Tasman had named it) was dismissed as being of no economic consequence.

**Cook's favourite island:** It was nearly 130 years before Europeans were again to sight New Zealand, James Cook (1728-79) arriving in 1769 to circumnavigate the country, claim it for Britain (once in the North Island and again in the South) and disprove the existence of any *Terra australis incognita*.

The Yorkshireman, after landing at Poverty Bay and heading south along the Hawke Bay coastline, turned about to sail round the North Island in an anticlockwise direction. Entering a "very broad and deep bay or inlet" he found "Ship Cove" in "Queen Charlotte Sound" a convenient place in which to careen and overhaul his vessel and to restore the health of his crew. The Maoris at the Sound after "heaving a few stones against the ship" turned friendly. They assured Cook of their practice of cannibalism and even traded the head of a recent victim to his naturalist, Joseph Banks. Cook could find no tradition of Tasman's earlier visit, the Maori perpetrators of the unfriendly reception having been conquered in the meantime. While there he claimed the neighbourhood for his King and named the Sound after his Queen. He then discovered the Strait now named after him. Before turning south to sail down the east coast of the South Island, Cook was induced by his disbelieving officers to first sail up the Wairarapa coastline as far as Cape Turnagain — so completing his circumnavigation of the North Island and completely dispelling their belief that the North Island might be an appendage of the "Unknown Southern Continent".

As he sailed round the South Island, achieving as Banks ruefully noted "the total demolition of our aerial fabrick called continent", adverse and squally weather four times blew his vessel out of sight of land. This resulted in some peculiarities on his chart — Banks Peninsula was shown and named as an island (something it had indeed been in the remote past) and Stewart Island was mistaken for a peninsula (which, again, it had once been — during the last Ice Age). For all his demonstrable errors (the South Island was also shown as being somewhat narrow-waisted), Cook had given New Zealand a sure and defined outline, in less than six months charting over 3,800 km of coastline with unprecedented accuracy. He also took back to Britain a wealth of information about the country and its people — of a rich and beautiful land ideal for European settlement; of splendid timber and abundant fish; of an intelligent and highly-skilled Maori people, but one too greatly divided among themselves to offer united opposition to the settlement of newcomers.

Cook was to come again to the South Island on subsequent voyages, finding Dusky Sound on the Fiordland coast a delightful anchorage, and repeatedly visiting his favourite spot, Ship Cove, which he used as a base from which to explore much of the Pacific. At Ship Cove a number of liberations were made (the country's first sheep among them) in attempts to acclimatise animals. Gardens, too, were established whose cabbages proved invaluable to later visitors. Cook pioneered the importance of greens in the diet of the seamen of the day. Also as part of his efforts to counter scurvy, the first of what was to become the national drink was brewed when in 1773 a makeshift beer was concocted at Dusky Sound.

> From Maori exploration to the surveying of Fiordland in the 1940s and 50s, *Exploration New Zealand* (Reed) by John Pascoe provides an illustrated account of New Zealand history.

**Cook's charts corrected:** After Cook had assiduously mapped the general outline all that remained for later explorers was the tidying up of detail. Cook's contemporaries, the Frenchmen, Jean François Marie de Surville (1717-70) and Marion du Fresne (1714-72) accomplished little, though the latter died at the Bay of Islands in the most violent of the early inter-racial clashes.

George Vancouver (who had sailed as a midshipman on *Resolution* in 1773) charted Dusky Sound in 1791, and William Broughton, whose vessel *Chatham* was with Vancouver's *Discovery*, discovered and named the Chatham Islands.

Then came hordes of sealers as scientific interest gave way to commercial exploitation. Gradually further details were added — Foveaux Strait was discovered, and a startled captain found that land blocked his intended passage to the west of "Banks's Island". The final voyage of discovery was that of Dumont d'Urville in 1826, the year in which the first New Zealand Company proved itself better at discovery than at colonisation, adding to maps by charting Otago Harbour and Port Nicholson (Wellington), but not noticeably adding to the country's population. The Frenchman, Dumont d'Urville (*see index*) corrected charts of Cook Strait, made an epic passage of French Pass, and as a skilled and sympathetic observer compiled valuable accounts of the country and its people.

## THE COMING OF COMMERCE

**Slaughtering the seals:** Within two decades of Cook's last visit, scientific interest gave way to commercial adventure and the scramble for seals had begun. At Fiordland's Dusky Sound a sealing party was established from 1792–93, where Cook had found "great numbers, about the bay, on the small rocks and isles near the seacoast". In ten months they secured 4,500 skins for the China market. Sealskins and oil were among the first of the country's natural resources to appear on world markets, as sealers spread from Fiordland to the islands of Foveaux Strait, Stewart Island and the sub-Antarctic islands of Bounty, Auckland, Macquarie and Campbell. The Chathams, too, were visited and their seals slaughtered. The frenzy of exploitation could not last. In less than thirty years the animals were hounded almost to the point of extinction.

Massacred in their tens of thousands, the seals were skinned for their fur (found only on sub-Antarctic animals); elephant seals and sea lions were then dispatched to the trypots of oiling parties. Unique among the seals is the New Zealand fur seal, thriving and increasing under the protection now afforded to it. Mature bulls are over 2 m long, but cows seldom exceed 1.6 m. They are often seen draped on headlands and reefs, sleeping in seemingly uncomfortable positions. On the approach of man they generally move towards the sea, so that visitors to their colonies should avoid being caught between a seal and the water.

If profitable for the merchants, the sealing trade was arduous in the extreme for members of the sealing parties, who were put ashore on a hostile coast to lead a precarious existence. Occasionally they fell foul of neighbouring Maoris, and occasionally, too, they were either forgotten or abandoned by accident. Parties somehow managed to survive on the Solander Island for fully five years, and another is said to have eked out seven long years on The Snares, south-west of Stewart Island. For all the hardships, the rewards for the sealers themselves seem to have been slight indeed.

**Hounding the whales:** If sealing was comparatively shortlived, whaling was to enjoy a somewhat longer lifespan. As late as 1964 whales were still being taken from Cook Strait, though the station in Tory Channel was persevering in a trade which elsewhere in the country had been virtually moribund for a century or more. The first whales to be taken from New Zealand waters were probably killed by the *William and Ann* in 1791. The number of whales caught slowly increased so that by

1805 vessels were calling regularly at the Bay of Islands in Northland, giving rise to a provisioning and refitting centre there where Maoris could be recruited to make up crews.

The initial quarry was the sperm whale, whose oil was of the highest quality and in whose intestines was found the waxlike ambergris so keenly sought after by the perfume industry. The whaling ships were predominantly American, sailing out of such wellknown whaling ports as Nantucket, New Bedford and New London.

The rugged ships themselves were specially designed for the work, carrying a number of whaling boats and a crew of about thirty. The boats would put off to catch a whale by harpooning it from a distance of about ten metres. Once the whale's death-throes had ceased, the catch was towed back to the ship, where it was made fast and its blubber peeled off. Everything of value would be recovered from the corpse (whalebone from the mouth of the right whale and spermaceti from the head of the sperm whale) before the carcass was simply cast adrift. To win the whale's oil the blubber was boiled in tryworks, a combination of pots (each with a capacity of about 700 l) which sat atop a brick furnace constructed between the fore- and the mainmast, on specially constructed decking. The furnace, though its perimeter was cooled with water, was a constant source of danger, and was known to so scorch the decking as to collapse through the boards, incinerating the whole ship.

The crew was paid in "lays" — a share of the profits — which could range from 1/8th for a master to as little as 1/200th for an ordinary crewman. If a voyage proved successful, rich rewards were reaped. On the other hand, if an ocean whaler caught little or nothing, its crewsmen could and did return to shore only to find themselves in debt to their employers for any clothing they might have had to buy in the course of the voyage.

By the time sperm whaling began to decline (after about 1840), little bay-whaling stations had sprung up round the coast from Foveaux Strait in the south to Cape Runaway. Their technique once a passing whale was sighted was to put out a boat, harpoon the whale and, once it was dead, tow it back to the bay where it would be tryed out on a beach generally littered with the bones and drenched with the oil of past kills. Their quarry was the slower-moving black or right whale, who migrated along the coast each year, coming into sheltered waters such as those of the Marlborough Sounds to calve. A bay-whaling station could be fitted out at far less cost than could a whaling ship, and profits were even more impressive. The stations were often set up by merchants who had ships already trading flax and timber on the New Zealand coast and that could supply the tiny settlements and collect their takings for sale in Sydney. So appeared little pockets of European civilisation on a wild coast. They were not wholly preoccupied with whaling, as out of season the whalers would farm surrounding land and build *whare* for their Maori wives and children.

There were, however, periods of boredom during which the whalers seem to have fully earned their reputation for drunkenness, bawd and depravity. The missionaries were forthright in their condemnation of the bay-whalers — "specimens of human nature at its worst state . . . they practise every species of iniquity without restraint and without concealment . . . The very soil is polluted." If their language and their morals were offensive to the clergy, they at least earned a reputation for hospitality. Most settlements had as their leader a tough and ruthless disciplinarian.

Few died rich, but both Johnny Jones of △Waikouaiti and Captain John Howell of △Riverton left considerable estates, and John Guard's land at Port Underwood is still farmed by his descendants. More typical is Captain Hempleman of Peraki, on Banks Peninsula, who is said to have left an estate comprising no more than his blankets and his personal papers.

The bay-whaling boom could not last. Profit-hungry whalers slew the calves as well as the mother whales as if to guarantee their own early bankruptcy. After reaching a peak in the late 1830s, the catches fell dramatically so that by 1847 only a handful of stations remained. Some whalers came ashore to earn their living from the land; others moved on to the equally uncertain promise of the Californian and Victorian goldfields. The virtual death-knell to the industry came in 1849 with the world's first commercial oil find, in the USA.

## SOVEREIGNTY

**By right of discovery:** Shore-whaling stations were still scattered round the coast in 1840, but activities soon deteriorated to the level of merely supplementing farming. Work was seasonal, and by farming through the off-season a shore station could survive (if not exactly prosper) on a catch of only two or three right whales a season.

These isolated pockets of European population were inconsequential in terms of numbers. In the main, Europeans congregated in the vicinity of the Bay of Islands, where flax and timber trades had flourished based on the Maori's need of firearms and the availability of vast stands of *kauri* forest. It was the concentration of trade in the north that resulted in the tribes there being in the main better equipped with muskets and ammunition to continue the age-old warrior tradition.

With increasing numbers of Europeans came increasing pressure for Britain to annex the country — for she had studiously omitted any reference to New Zealand in published lists of her territories, at times even expressly repudiating British sovereignty. Finally William Hobson was sent to acquire the country for Britain with the "free intelligent consent of the natives, expressed according to their established usages", and thereafter to be its first governor. He planned a series of ceremonial meetings to be held throughout the country, at which chiefs would assemble to have the proposed treaty of annexation read and explained to them (Britain was intent on preserving the fiction that the disunited Maori tribes taken together comprised a fully sovereign state). The first of these was at Waitangi on 6 February 1840. The second, at Mangungu six days later, was also the last. Hobson was crippled by a stroke and copies of the treaty were simply taken far and wide by officials and missionaries as they canvassed signatures from those chiefs who would give them.

Major Thomas Bunbury was sent south on the *Herald* to collect signatures. On 4 June he buried a bottle at Port Pegasus on △ Stewart Island claiming sovereignty by right of discovery, for he apparently feared a hostile reception to the treaty from the Maoris living on Paterson Inlet. A fortnight later he put in to Port Underwood and in a ceremony on Horahora-Kakahu Island he proclaimed the South Island to be British. While Bunbury was away and before he had time to return, Hobson forced the issue. On 21 May 1840 he handed down two proclamations. The first asserted British sovereignty over the North Island as from the date of the Treaty of Waitangi; the second claimed sovereignty over the South Island by right of discovery. His actions were approved by the British Government, who thereupon published the proclamations in the *London Gazette* of 2 October 1840 to put British title to sovereignty over New Zealand beyond question.

**The "race" for Akaroa:** One of the many European land speculators of the day was the Frenchman, Jean Langlois, captain of the whaler *Cachalot* who in 1838 at Port Cooper (Lyttelton) entered into a deed with Ngaitahu whereunder he purchased an area of Banks Peninsula. Back in France he interested merchants in his scheme, and before long some sixty-three migrants were assembled to transplant a little of France to the Southern Seas. The colonising venture was backed by the French Government, who not only gave them a vessel, the *Comte de Paris*, but also the company of a warship, *L'Aube*. The party was already at sea when the Treaty of Waitangi was signed, and their dismay can be imagined when they arrived to find British rule over New Zealand already an accomplished fact. While *L'Aube* was at Waitangi, in the Bay of Islands, Hobson elected to put the matter beyond all doubt, sending Captain Stanley and the *Britomart* to Akaroa, there to land magistrates, hold courts and hoist the British flag. By the time *L'Aube* arrived at Akaroa, British sovereignty was being exercised, albeit by officials who had been there for only five days.

Popular folklore tells of a "race" for Akaroa between *Britomart* and *L'Aube*, a tale long dispelled by historians. However there can be no doubt that the French colonists were dismayed to find that the British had forestalled them. If there was no actual "race", had the French been a little faster and settled Akaroa a little sooner, the French might have established a strong claim to sovereignty.

## SOUTH ISLAND EXPLORATION

AT FIRST commercial interest in New Zealand was almost entirely confined to the coast, so that after Dumont d'Urville's voyage of 1826 the mantle of explorer shifted from seaman to missionary. As the Maori population was concentrated towards the north of the North Island, missionary interest — and exploration — was for years restricted to the northern regions. After the arrival in 1814 of Thomas Kendall (the country's first missionary), various missionaries probed south. The Wesleyan, James Buller, reached Wellington overland from Mangungu in 1839, the same year that Octavius Hadfield became established at Otaki, near Kapiti Island. But while the North Island was being both explored and evangelised, the South Island, mountainous and by then thinly settled by the Maori, remained unknown outside the largely undocumented comings and goings of sealer and whaler.

When the Wesleyan missionary James Watkin established the South Island's first mission station at △Waikouaiti in May 1840, the North Island was scattered with mission settlements from Waikanae (near Wellington) to Kaitaia. Another Wesleyan, Samuel Ironside, from 1840–43 worked with great success at Port Underwood before the Wairau Affray (*see index*) and its consequent evacuation of his converts dictated the end of his mission. At Akaroa, Bishop Pompallier established a Catholic mission to minister to the French settlers there (though for many years this had no incumbent) and in 1843 the North German Missionary Society despatched four Lutheran missionaries to Nelson. Little financial support was sent, so that the Nelson missionaries, and those who followed them, later joined other missions. An exception was the Rev. J. F. H. Wohlers (*see index*), who ventured south to Foveaux Strait where he established a station on △Ruapuke Island.

Settlers at the New Zealand Company's Nelson settlement followed up every rumour of good grazing land, culminating in the great journey of Thomas Brunner (*see index*) who in 1846–48 explored the wild west coast from Westport to the Paringa River. His two-year odyssey ranks as the most arduous in the country's history, but on his return his straightforward account of the perils he had faced impressed Nelsonians far more than did the prospects of the Coast.

Edward Shortland, as a Sub-Protector of Aborigines taking a census of South Island Maoris, in 1844 became the first European to make the overland crossing from Otago to Banks Peninsula — the same year that Charles Kettle penetrated to Central

Otago. The following year William Heaphy became the first European to travel through North Canterbury, from Banks Peninsula to the Waiau River.

Gradually others added to the overall picture of the South Island, some as they explored in the course of Government land purchases, others as they looked for good grazing land. Later came the goldrushes and the opening up of all but the most remote corners of the island.

Passes through the mountain chains were sought, first by the runholders, initially to get their stock from Nelson into Canterbury and later into Central Otago. Passes were then explored for links between the goldfields of Central and the provincial capital of Dunedin, and the gold-rich West Coast and a Christchurch anxious to attract in its direction what trade it could.

By the mid-1860s the combined craving for land, for gold and for scientific knowledge had bared most of the South Island's secrets, leaving only the mountains to be unveiled by mountaineer and prospector. As the century closed there were still isolated pockets of unknown land, principally in Fiordland, as indeed there still are today. But in the 130 years of discovery initiated by Cook, sealer, whaler, missionary, explorer, surveyor, pastoralist, prospector and mountaineer had each in his own way and for his own reasons contributed to a complete understanding of the new land.

Not that much of this work could possibly have been undertaken without the expertise of the Maori, who knew much of the Island's topography and could teach the European something of the consummate skill with which he travelled through the bush. Time and again the *Pakeha* "discoverer" was literally guided to his "find" by the knowledgable Maori, even being shown where canoes were kept for the crossing of perilous rivers. When Nathaniel Chalmers (*see index*) contracted dysentery on his exploration of Central Otago in 1853, it was his Maori companions who placed him on a *mokihi* (raft) and sailed him the length of the Clutha River back to civilisation. The Maori had trails used for war, for trade, for access to seasonal fishing and fowling areas, and for reaching the West Coast where lay the only significant deposits of revered greenstone. Without this fund of knowledge, the exploits of the *Pakeha* would have been more rigorous, less extensive and have taken infinitely longer to achieve.

## EUROPEAN SETTLEMENT

AS THE YEAR 1840 began, there were several European settlements scattered around the coast of the South Island. Some were in the Marlborough Sounds, and others at Waikouaiti (near Dunedin), Riverton, and Bluff. In July was added the party from France which founded Akaroa.

Many *Pakeha* had bought up large areas of land. Some Sydney speculators even claimed to have purchased the entire South Island together with Stewart Island for the princely sum of £100 plus some small annuities. Under the Treaty of Waitangi not only could individuals no longer deal with the Maori direct (the Crown acquired sole right to purchase Maori-owned land) but Hobson set up a Land Commission to enquire into the adequacy of payments made even before the Treaty was signed. The total area of the claimed purchases cannot be estimated. Claims were expressed in round numbers, by millions of acres and by degrees of latitude and longitude, or by the expression "as far as a cannon shot will reach". Obviously many of the claimants had gambled on getting a Crown grant of some description, but by the time the wearying business of sorting out the position had been completed, a number of the few speculators who did receive land were already dead.

Captain John Howell had encouraged whalers to come ashore and settle on his Riverton holdings, and Johnny Jones (a party to the South Island and Stewart Island speculation) landed farmworkers from Sydney at Waikouaiti in March 1840, and in May brought the Rev. James Watkin to act as the South Island's first clergyman and teacher.

**The New Zealand Company:** Among those who had "bought" land prior to the Treaty of Waitangi was Colonel William Wakefield, who claimed to have purchased 8 million ha as agent for the New Zealand Company. The Company, impatient to organise migration from Britain to New Zealand and whose impetuosity had driven a reluctant British Government to annex the country so as to have a measure of control over what was going on, actually "sold" large numbers of "land orders" in London for proposed settlements in New Zealand before it even knew where those settlements were to be. Wellington, New Plymouth and Wanganui were quickly established before the migrants for the first large-scale South Island settlement were embarked. Even when the main body of Nelson settlers arrived in 1841, they found their ultimate destination in doubt. Colonel William Wakefield had wanted Nelson to be established round the present-day port of Lyttelton, Governor Hobson had wanted it near the then-capital of Auckland. Finally the New Zealand Company was forced to found Nelson, however reluctantly (and by today's standards, however felicitously) in Tasman Bay.

Such was the turmoil surrounding land purchases that at each of the New Zealand Company's settlements disputes with the Maoris over land flared into fighting, Nelson suffering in the so-called Wairau Affray.

**Acquiring the Maoris' land:** The British Crown inherited a chaotic situation, with many overlapping and competing claims for land being made by speculators.

They had as often as not made merely token payments and in some cases blatantly swindled chiefs by having them sign documents whose terms bore no relation to what had been agreed. The claims were dealt with by a Land Commission, and future land deals were limited to the Crown by the Treaty of Waitangi. However successive governors had few funds with which to purchase land, leading Governor FitzRoy in 1844 to waive the Crown's right of pre-emption, authorising individuals to buy land direct, subject to paying part of the purchase money to the Crown by way of tax. Governor Grey in 1845 restored the policy of the Crown alone negotiating for Maori land, instituting a system where Land Purchase Commissioners would attend large tribal gatherings at which many Maoris would sign deeds of sale. A multiplicity of signatories was needed to meet the complex and basically-communal nature of Maori land ownership.

**The Wairau Affray:** It took time for the Land Commissioners to adjudicate on the multitude of claims that were made — having to consider not only the arrangement under which land was alleged to have been sold, but the boundaries of such land, the adequacy of payment, the question of whether those Maoris who purported to be selling had in Maori custom any right to do so, and whether they understood the nature of the transaction as there was no place in Maori custom for land to be sold at all.

Nelson settlers, impatient for readily usable land, in 1843 turned to the Wairau plains for solace only to find that Colonel William Wakefield's alleged purchase of the area was keenly contested by Te Rauparaha and Te Rangihaeata, both chiefs of Ngati Toa. Despite warnings — and an abortive plea made by Ngati Toa to the Land Commission to expedite a decision on title to the land — the Nelson settlers pressed on with a survey of the Wairau. When their surveyors were obstructed, the settlers determined to arrest the two chiefs and set out to do so. Their mission ended in tragedy, the result of the settlers either by design or accident contriving to shoot one of a party of Ngati Toa that included Te Rauparaha. By the day's end Nelson had lost its leader, Captain Arthur Wakefield, and some twenty-one others, a number of prominent settlers among them (*see △ Blenheim*).

**An island for sale:** Once land claims by the New Zealand Company, the speculators and early settlers had been examined (and often disallowed in full), the Government embarked on a land purchase programme to "extinguish" native titles, but leaving reserves to satisfy the Maori. Unfortunately for the Maori, the areas he chose to retain often tended to be coastal rivermouths, lagoons, swampland or rocky coastline — excellent for fishing and for fowling but of little commercial value in the society that was to emerge.

The Otago Block of 162,000 ha was bought in 1844 for £2,400 by the New Zealand Company; in 1847 the Government bought land north of the Ashley River from Te Rauparaha and the next year paid the impoverished Ngaitahu some £2,000 for 8 million ha south of the Ashley. In 1851 the purchase of Southland was concluded — 2.8 million ha for £2,000 — to which in 1864 Stewart Island was added, for £6,000. However the most bizarre deal of all involved the West Coast, where in 1860 all of £300 was paid for 3 million ha — land that within a decade was to yield over £12 million in gold.

**The "Wakefield Scheme":** Nelson was the only New Zealand Company settlement in the South Island, but both Canterbury and Otago were promoted along lines dictated by the genius behind the New Zealand Company, Edward Gibbon Wakefield (1796–1862). His idea was that the existing social and economic structure of English society might be preserved by transporting to the colonies a cross-section of that society, excluding only its lowest level. In essence the "Wakefield Scheme" called for large blocks of cheap land to be bought. This was then to be sold at a "sufficient price" — one low enough to encourage wealthy migrants yet high enough to prevent labourers from immediately becoming landowners. The profit on land sales was to be used to ship labourers to the colony, so providing landowners with the workers they would need and to maintain a proper balance between capital and labour. Of the major settlements by 1850, only Auckland, which grew rapidly when proclaimed as the seat of Government, was not a "Wakefield settlement".

The scheme failed to achieve the desired results, "Men of refinement" found little to their liking in the reality of life in the colony, and absentee landowners denied economic stability by speculating in land from afar while failing to provide any capital to employ the labourers. Those landowners who did migrate from Britain too often had too little capital with which to provide much gainful employment. More than anything else, the scheme miscarried because Wakefield failed to recognise the importance of wool, which alone could have been exported profitably. Fortunately for Canterbury and Otago, their early leaders were not so lacking in vision.

**The Scots come south:** After Nelson, the second large-scale South Island settlement to be established was Dunedin, the "Edinburgh of the South", largely motivated by religious turmoil. When in 1843 the celebrated Dr Chalmers (after whom Dunedin's port is named) marched out of the Established Kirk of Scotland to found the Free Church, there was enthusiasm for the idea of transporting the new church to a colony where it might flower in an atmosphere free from the bitterness of the past. Delayed by upheavals within the New Zealand Company, who were helping organise the venture, the first shiploads of colonists landed at Port Chalmers in 1848 (*see* △*Dunedin*).

**The founding of Canterbury:** It was the same spirit of religious purity that prompted the Canterbury settlement of Christchurch, whose eventual site had been arbitrarily denied to the Nelson settlers by Governor Hobson and voluntarily passed over by Frederick Tuckett when he was choosing the site for Dunedin. In the New World, Church and Society might be preserved from the destruction that John Robert Godley saw as inevitable in the northern hemisphere. Wakefield, too, endorsed the notion of an Anglican settlement for the country he had foreseen as "the most Church of England country in the world". At the end of 1850 the "First Four Ships" landed the Canterbury "Pilgrims" who in time were to create "the most English city outside England" on the broad Canterbury plains.

Edward Gibbon Wakefield was insistent that the Wakefield settlements be modelled on English agricultural communities. He was, after all, seeking to create a better England in a new world. Here the land was to be tilled and crops grown, very much to the English pattern.

However, in the South Island at least, Wakefield had miscalculated badly. He wanted the communities to be closeknit agricultural settlements so that the traditional social barriers of class and education and the control of the Church would be preserved. This, however, was to ignore reality: too few men of capital came out who had means enough to employ labour, and in any event the agricultural needs of the infant colony were quite easily met by small farmers whose low prices reflected their need to employ no labour.

It was the switch from an agricultural settlement to a pastoral economy — the leasing at low rentals of vast areas of native grassland — that spelt the end to Wakefield's dream. At the same time it saved many capitalists of moderate means from economic extinction.

## THE RISE OF WOOL

THE CANTERBURY PLAINS should not be seen as once being a boundless sea of dry tussock. Rather the heavy land along the coast was deep swamp; where it was not, it was ribboned by boggy creeks that meandered through the damp of fern, flax, rushes and cutty-grass. On parts of the dry plains, large tracts of *manuka* were higher than a man on a horse, with clumps of cabbage trees signposting better land. Towards the foothills was the thorned *matagouri*, tangled to such an extent that it was impossible to get sheep on to unburnt country, or to find grazing for them when they got there. The runholder's first act was to set fire to his run.

Then came the sheep, basically Merino, to fulfill the legal requirement that the runs be stocked within a set period. Yards were built of timber or sod, and when scab infestation spread from Nelson the sheep were yarded at night to prevent strays from joining them. When wire fences came in the early 1860s, runs were divided into blocks. Runholders continued to increase their flocks as quickly as they could until about 1868, by which time all the runs were fully stocked and surplus sheep had become unsaleable. Some drove their unwanted sheep over cliffs until the practice of boiling-down carcasses for tallow reduced the waste.

The 1870s saw water-races built on the plains, increasing carrying capacity and so making subdivision possible. With the introduction of refrigeration and the opening of a frozen-meat market in Britain the Merino largely made way for halfbred and long-woolled sheep; native tussock steadily gave way to English grasses.
A similar pattern occurred in Central Otago, where the water-races of the goldminers in time came to feed water to the orchards of today.

The runholder was always vulnerable. He held a licence under which any person could buy the freehold and so dispossess him of part or even all of his run. Improvements earned for the runholder a corresponding pre-emptive right of purchase, but this right could be challenged at any time, so that if the runholder did not buy the freehold within a month the challenger could do so — and without compensating the runholder for improvements. The newcomers who bought land out of the runs were contemptuously called cockatoos, an Australian expression since abbreviated to cocky, a colloquial term now commonly applied to all New Zealand small farmers.

To defend their holdings, runholders would where they could indulge in "gridironing" or "spotting" — strategically freeholding key areas such as the homestead block and valley passes, so as to render it quite impracticable for anyone to try to farm the remaining areas by themselves.

## GOLD

WHILE THE LAND WARS were preoccupying the North Island, gold tipped the economic balance in favour of the South and was responsible for an influx of population on such a scale as to alter the South Island's destiny. The miners came at a time when squatters and absentee capitalists seemed likely to perpetuate the South Island as a series of vast sheepruns. The end of the gold and the miners' demand for land brought the goldminers into a head-on conflict with the "squattocracy". With the introduction of universal manhood suffrage the "small men" (of whom the miners were a significant part) achieved the political power necessary to resolve the confrontation in their favour, dissolving many of the great estates and "placing the small man on the land". Curiously, though the New Zealand goldrushes were an extension of the Australian, there is lacking in this country any equivalent claim that the miners were "the Pilgrim Fathers, the first authentic Australians". Certainly the New Zealand soldier was termed a "digger" in the 1914–18 war but, unlike his Australian counterpart, he was no longer so called in the 1939–45 war. The historian J. H. M. Salmon has noted: "New Zealanders seem to have lost the aggressive individualism and suspicious resentment of organised officialdom that Australians claim to inherit from their mining ancestors. When all this is said, something endures in New Zealand attitudes which is part of the legacy received from the formative era of the goldrushes. There remains a vigorous and philistine egalitarianism, an admiration for physical prowess, a mass response to gambling media, and a desire for external conformity — in short, a set of conventions which prevailed in Tuapeka, Thames and the Tara-makau, as they did in Bathurst, Ballarat, and Bendigo. In part at least there are attitudes which stem from the pioneer conditions of nineteenth-century colonial society in general, and not particularly from the mining camp, but they were widened and intensified by the miner when he accepted them from the small frontier settler and the roving pastoral labourer. The small man's distrust of wide-scale capitalist enterprise has much in common with the resentment of the individual alluvial miner who saw his primitive equipment displaced by the stamper battery, the dredge, and the hydraulic elevator."

The rushes to New Zealand were third in a sequence — after the United States (California and Nevada) and Australia (Victoria and New South Wales) but before those of Alaska, Queensland, Western Australia, South Africa and Canada. By 1861 the Californian rushes had waned, and Victorian gold output was dropping. There, capitalists were organising the winning of gold into an industry, and with the sub-stitution of employment contracts for mateship, the displaced independent miner turned to fresh fields to conquer.

These came in 1861 with the discovery by Gabriel Read (typically an Australian who had learned his skill in California) of the fabulous Gabriel's Gully (*see* △*Lawrence*). Read's report electrified Otago just as land troubles in the North Island were driving the land-hungry *Pakeha* into inevitable conflict with his Maori neighbour.

Read's find was by no means the first discovery of gold in New Zealand. The Maoris were aware of its presence long before the advent of the European, and sporadic reports of finds were made in the first years of settlement. At first the economic possibilities of a goldrush were unknown. When they had been illustrated by Californian and Australian experience, a widespread view was that "flour is more necessary than gold"; others felt that the social upheaval and commercial disruption of a goldrush would be more a bane than a blessing. This did not deter "reward committees" from getting together to foster active prospecting and there were shortlived rushes in the North Island to Coromandel and in the South to Golden Bay (*see* △*Collingwood*).

Read's find galvanised Dunedin. "Gold, gold, gold is the universal subject of conversation . . . The fever is running at such a height that, if it continues, there will scarcely be a man left in town." Only months later Hartley and Reilly stunned Dunedin with their 87-pound bags of gold from what swiftly became the Dunstan diggings (*see* △*Clyde*). Then came the Shotover, "the richest river in the world" (*see* △*Queenstown*), and finally, when the game of "hunting the fox" was played out, William Fox and his group were found extracting fortunes from the Arrow River (*see* △*Arrowtown*). Once the town recovered from the stampede to the diggings of most of its ablebodied men, the Dunedin economy boomed as never before, and as never since. It was gold that gave Dunedin and the country a strong economic base — previously wool had been the only export of consequence. Gold spawned Dunedin's noble buildings and earned for the centre the title of "commercial capital of New Zealand". The city, too, had in full measure those traditional Scottish skills of banking and engineering to ensure a ready grasp of the opportunities that presented themselves.

The riches of Otago for a time overshadowed finds on the West Coast, but once the early gold began to dwindle, many Otago miners journeyed overland tempted by reports of rich ground on the Coast. They were not to be disappointed. Thousands more poured in by sea from Australia, and △Hokitika's now-defunct port was for a time the country's busiest.

**The nature of gold deposits:** Most of the gold found in auriferous drifts originally came from quartz reefs. As broken material is washed down rivers and streams, rocks and quartz reefs are subjected to a continual grinding process, with the separated gold quickly sinking through the mass to bedrock. The heavier particles sink first, so that particles of gold become progressively more fine the further they are from their source. When the seabeach is reached only the finest gold is found.

Where glaciers have been the moving force, gold has not been redistributed in this way but irregularly disseminated, requiring the moving of a whole mass to recover gold and not simply tunnelling at bedrock level.

Alluvial goldmining occupied the first two decades of the industry in New Zealand, declining in importance with the introduction of quartz mining and the cyanide process of gold extraction.

**The alluvial goldminer:** Though the tools of the alluvial goldminer were rudimentary — a pick, a shovel, a tin dish, a rocker and a tub — he was not, as fiction would have him, a penniless fortune-seeker. Rather he was an individual who had already acquired some modest capital, for his first requirement was to be able to support himself on the field until he had struck payable dirt, and with soaring transportation costs and profiteering merchants his cost of living was always high and at times astronomical.

At first the ground was simply fossicked over with a knife or pick, some big finds being made where gold had been trapped in crevices, on rock-bottoms and in hollows. The alluvial miner generally needed a rocker or "long-tom" — a box into which auriferous gravel was shovelled and then washed to extract its gold. Towards the end of the 1870s long-toms and sluice-boxes declined in favour of hydraulic alluvial mining. Water-races were constructed to give a plentiful supply of water and a pressure that enabled a jet of water to be slammed onto the side of hills to bring down goldrich gravel. Gravel brought down by the water was washed through long sluice-boxes covered with riffles, plush or matting, to trap the gold. Pressure, too, enabled deep ground to be worked, using the water to scoop out and "elevate" the pay-dirt. It also enabled hitherto unpayable deposits in morainic drifts to be won.

As deposits became harder to work, the solitary miner began to disappear from the scene. As an alluvial goldfield began to settle down, the pioneer miner became progressively less able to pay his way. Organised capital would marshall machinery to win profits, and as wage-earning miners replaced the free partnerships of the pioneers, the free miner moved on to prospect new areas.

**Dredging for gold:** At first gold was won from gullies, riverbanks and from shallow portions of rivers. Gold in deeper parts was taken out by "blind-stabbing" — a miner would wade into a river with a rope tied round his waist and simply grope with a shovel for the goldbearing wash. It was at △Alexandra, on the Clutha River, that a man named Brown made the first "dredge" — an iron ring and an ox-hide bag attached to a long pole which was dragged along the riverbed. The wash obtained was then cradled in an ordinary miner's cradle.

From this unlikely start grew the dredging boom, at first using barges and steam-powered "spoons" to lift the wash, and later "bucket-and-ladder" dredges, where chains of buckets rotated continuously to scrape the river floor and discharge the wash into sluiceboxes. The "tailings" (the processed rubble) were stacked clear of the stern. Soon these moved out of the river and on to dry land, with "paddock dredges" operating on small artificial lagoons that literally moved along with the dredges as they made their way across their claims. Typical of the times was the action of an enterprising Chinese, Sew Hoy, who in 1889 put a dredge on the Shotover River. Though the ground had three times been worked over — twice by Europeans and once by Chinese — the dredge won so much gold that a single £10 share rose to be worth nearly £250.

New Zealand's success with dredging drew worldwide attention, the *Year Book* for 1899 noting that "inquiries are frequently received from Siberia, New Guinea, Borneo, California, British Columbia and the Australasian Colonies". Engineering shops in Dunedin and elsewhere worked night and day to keep pace with demand for new dredges and for improvements to those already in action — not only for New Zealand but for places as far distant as Russia. By the turn of the century there were over 230 dredges operating, principally in Central Otago on the Clutha River but also in Southland and on the West Coast. For the first time since the heady years of 1863–71 annual gold exports (which also reflect a contemporaneous boom in quartz mining) topped the £2 million mark, from 1903–09. Yet dredge numbers were already declining. Many had been set up to work only marginally payable ground (if that), so that whereas by 1910 the number of dredges was down to 104, gold production was actually at a higher level than it had been in 1900. By 1921 only eleven dredges were at work.

In recent times a sole survivor has been cranking its way along the Taramakau River on the West Coast, near Kumara, and a small, new suction dredge at Hartley's Beach has attempted to win further gold from the Clutha River.

**Quartz mining:** The gold sought by the quartz miner was of a different nature from that found in auriferous gravel. Often found in conjunction with other metals, it needs a different treatment to separate it from the quartz and other accompanying minerals. Further, when bedrock is reached on an alluvial field one can be certain that there is no gold further down. In quartz mining, however, a reef may stretch for many kilometres across the country — and descend hundreds of metres below the surface.

The easy riches of the alluvial fields for a time deterred those who might otherwise have attempted the uncertain and costly task of working the reefs. Areas were worked in the North Island, and in the South Island, in Central Otago. Pre-eminent was the △Reefton field on the West Coast, where the Reef Town for some time known as "Quartzopolis" became "the most brisk and businesslike place in the Colony". Within thirty years over £1 million in gold was crushed from Reefton stone.

To extract gold from quartz the "stone" (as the miners termed payable quartz) was fed from a holding bin into mortars where heavy stampers rose and fell on solid cast-steel dies. Water was also fed in to yield a moist crushed powder termed "pulp".

Mercury in the base of the mortars absorbed much of the gold, becoming an amalgam too heavy to wash out. The rest of the pulp passed through a fine wire screen to be washed over amalgamating tables. Fixed over the tables were copper plates silvered over with mercury which absorbed more of the gold as the pulp oozed across them. As a third defence against the loss of gold the remaining paste was processed in a berdan — a large revolving cast-iron bowl with round heavy weights. More mercury was in the berdan, and water was used to swirl the quartz sand into a drain. The sand inevitably still carried a little gold. (Indeed some batteries recovered as little as half of the assayed gold content of the quartz they processed.)

The amalgamating tables were cleaned at regular intervals by scraping and all the amalgam placed in a retort and heated in a furnace. The mercury evaporated — to be condensed for re-use — leaving gold, if not entirely pure, in the bottom of the retort. This process was termed a "clean-up".

The rate of recovery improved with the introduction of the more efficient cyanide process of extraction, though this involved a much finer crushing of the stone. The process was developed by the Cassel Company of Britain, from whom the New Zealand Government shrewdly bought the rights, so enabling a number of companies to use the process who would otherwise have not been able to afford the fee.

Quartz mining never really recovered from the standstill imposed by the 1914–18 war though, in the North Island, Waihi's marvellous Martha Mine closed as recently as 1952 after producing 8 million ounces of gold and 60 million of silver.

**The impact of gold:** The importance of gold to the country's infant economy is illustrated by the following table:

| Year | Wool exports | Grain exports | Flax | Gold | Total value exports |
|------|------|------|------|------|------|
| 1859 | 340,000 | 39,000 | 1,600 | 28,000 | £551,000 |
| 1861 | 524,000 | 2,900 | 40 | 753,000 | £1,370,000 |
| 1863 | 830,000 | 1,200 | 250 | 2,432,000 | £3,485,000 |
| 1866 | 1,354,000 | 7,300 | 1,000 | 2,897,000 | £4,520,000 |

The influx of tens of thousands of migrants drawn by gold resulted in a sharp jump in total population, accelerating national development. Most of the miners who saved some of their winnings were eventually able to buy land and settle on it to help realise the country's agricultural possibilities — conspicuously the fruit-growing potential of Central Otago. In later years, too, the boom in dredging and quartz mining attracted large amounts of foreign capital.

Other industries took some time before they could add demonstrably to the country's wealth — farmers needed time to clear land, grow crops or breed sheep. Gold was an exception, immediately bringing a wealth to the colony that was quickly distributed between miner, merchant, innkeeper, storekeeper, packer and shipmaster. The farmer, too, with increased population had a greater demand for crops and wheat than had previously existed, and the income he gained accelerated the development of his land. As well, the provincial governments were forced to become better organised to administer outlying (and occasionally lawless) areas.

Gold production enjoyed a revival in the Depression years of the 1930s, when the unemployed were encouraged by the Government to reopen old goldworkings. But, as in the past, when living standards began to rise, the fields became progressively less able to fulfill the expectations of the diggers, and again, one by one, they closed.

**Gold exported from New Zealand:**

| Year | oz. (000) | £ (000) |
|------|------|------|
| 1857 | 10·4 | 40·4 |
| 1860 | 45·4 | 17·6 |
| 1862 | 410·9 | 1,591·4 |
| 1864 | 480·2 | 1,857·8 |
| 1866 | 735·4 | 2,844·5 |
| 1868 | 637·5 | 2,504·3 |
| 1870 | 544·9 | 2,157·6 |
| 1875 | 355·3 | 1,407·8 |
| 1880 | 305·2 | 1,227·3 |
| 1885 | 237·4 | 948·6 |
| 1890 | 193·2 | 773·4 |
| 1895 | 293·5 | 1,162·2 |
| 1900 | 373·6 | 1,439·6 |
| 1905 | 520·5 | 2,093·9 |
| 1910 | 478·3 | 1,896·3 |
| 1915 | 422·8 | 1,694·6 |
| 1920 | 213·0 | 883·7 |
| 1930 | 113·7 | 550·7 |
| 1940 | 118·5 | 1,948·3 |
| 1950 | 110·5 | 1,310·8 |
| 1960 | 27·8 | 308·9 |
| 1970 | 0·8 (est) | 14·5 |

**The Yellow Peril:** In contrast with the general benefits brought by most European and Maori goldminers were the activities of the Chinese. The latter would arrive with the sole aim of securing about £500 worth of gold to take back to their native land, where it would ensure them thereafter a comfortable and easy life. They were often content to fossick over previously-worked ground with such meticulous patience and care as to extract fair quantities of gold from claims the Europeans had renounced as unpayable.

With the influx of Australian diggers came wild prejudices against the Asians who, the diggers claimed, were immoral, were a source of disease, and had "clannish propensities" which gave them an advantage in obtaining ground. None of the anti-Chinese riots of Victoria were re-enacted in Otago or on the West Coast, but feeling ran high. Though in terms of population in 1871 the Chinese formed less than 2%, on the goldfields themselves, there was about one Chinese for every three Europeans.

Prejudice spilled over into violence. At Naseby in 1867 the Chinese were physically attacked; the *Dunstan Times* advocated the use of pickhandles against them; and the president of the Arrowtown Miners' Association proclaimed: "We are free men — they are slaves! We are Christians — they are heathens!! We are Britons — they are Mongolians!!!" Unsolved crimes were inevitably blamed on the aliens; Chinese were several times tried (and acquitted) of crimes with which they had undoubtedly had no connection. In 1868 the Government even found it necessary to issue a proclamation that declared the Chinese to be entitled to the same protection of law and to the same civil rights as were British subjects.

Certainly the peasant coolies from Fukien and Kwantung provinces had their vices — gambling at packapoo and fantan, smoking opium and living in shantytowns of packing-cases, old tins and sacking. Yet in those traditional virtues of diligence and honesty they were superior to the bulk of miners — suspicious of a group who did not share their relish for drinking and brawling. A stronger case was made out by those of the miners who protested that the rice-eating coolies provided little custom, brought no money to invest, and took what they won out of the country just as soon as they were able.

In 1871 a special committee was appointed by the Government to investigate the subject. Evidence showed that the typical Chinese had been sent out by a Chinese merchant, who advanced the necessary money to the miner in return for a charge on his earnings. The committee concluded that the Chinese were frugal, industrious and orderly, unlikely to introduce any special infectious diseases and that few would wish to become permanent settlers — as, indeed, was shown by there being virtually no Chinese women in the country. Notwithstanding, particularly on the West Coast, resentment boiled up until finally in 1881 the Government joined Australia in imposing a £10 poll-tax on all Chinese immigrants and restricting their number to one for each ten tons of shipping. Later, fear of a Chinese "invasion" saw the poll-tax increased to £100 and the restriction on entry raised to one Chinese for every 200 tons of shipping. Prime Minister Richard Seddon, himself a veteran of the West Coast goldfields and of Australian origin, passed legislation "in order to safeguard the race purity of the people of New Zealand" and, like Australia, implemented a "White New Zealand" policy. (Since 1920 the immigration of all aliens has been controlled, but the poll-tax was retained for Chinese until 1944.)

With the decline in mining, the Chinese either took up marketgardening or were forced into the towns where they entered the fruit and vegetable trades or ran laundries — occupations where their patient industry was rewarded. From a peak of 5,004 in 1881 (including only nine women) numbers fell to a 1916 low of 2,147 (130 women). There were less than 100 Chinese families in the country in 1935. The Japanese invasion of China led many men in New Zealand to seek permission for their families to join them. Their intended return to China proved difficult so that in the event over 1,400 were allowed to take up permanent residence. Gradually the disparity has closed between numbers of men and those of women and in the 1971 census some 12,818 gave Chinese as their broad ethnic origin.

## FROM WOOL TO MEAT

IT WAS APPROPRIATE that the first sheep to be introduced to the country were brought to the South Island, by Captain Cook in 1773 who set a ram and a ewe ashore at Queen Charlotte Sound. The pair survived only a few days — perhaps an omen of the tribulations to come before the sheep industry achieved a firm foundation.

The move into pastoral farming, begun in the Wairarapa in the early 1840s, was most conspicuous in the South Island with most of the pioneer group in the Wairarapa quickly opting in favour of more promising land to the south of Cook Strait (*see* △*Kaikoura*). Sheep shipped from Australia poured into Nelson, Canterbury and Otago to graze great areas of empty tussockland. At first the sheep were predominantly Merino, excellent for fine wool and introduced to Australia as early as in 1798, so that by the time the sheep country was opening up in New Zealand there was a plentiful supply of stock available across the Tasman. The period from 1850–80, known as the "wool period", saw many Australian squatters arrive to lease large areas of grazing land for their flocks. Disgruntled with Australia's fickle rainfall and here known as the Prophets, they consistently forecast failure for the small agricultural farmlets of the established settlements.

**The scourge of scab:** With the Australian flocks came sheep scab, a parasite which quickly infested South Island flocks. Before long, sheep were being officially inspected, farmers with infested flocks were being fined, and compulsory dipping and a sheep tax were introduced. These measures eventually freed the country of the blight. In the meantime many sheepmen were ruined, thousands of sheep died and tens of thousand were destroyed.

**Runholders and rabbits:** "The man who introduced the rabbit was banqueted and lauded; but they would hang him now if they could get him." So wrote Mark Twain in 1890, twenty years after the rabbit plague had plunged runholders into desolation and, not infrequently, into bankruptcy. Twain's sentiments, if not his history, accurately reflect the mood of the times. None know when the first liberations of rabbits were made — perhaps by missionaries, perhaps by whalers as they stocked the shore with food — but they were established throughout the country in the 1840s, with both the Canterbury and the Otago Acclimatisation Societies later contributing. The rabbit breeds at a prodigious rate, and from the 1860s those in Otago and Southland spread north to meet those coming south from Marlborough. Sheep numbers were spectacularly reduced. Six rabbits eat as much grass as one sheep, and though Moa Flat station (near Roxburgh) at one time had eighty-seven men engaged in rabbiting, its flock diminished from 120,000 to 45,000. In Southland, Castle Rock dropped from 50,000 to 20,000. Vast areas of land were abandoned as runholders simply walked off, having been eaten out. The Government lost over £315,000 in rentals. At the same time the annual exports of rabbit skins soared from 33,000 in 1873 to 9 million in 1882. By 1893 it was a staggering 16 million. Several of the runs ruined and abandoned after defeating a succession of owners are now being successfully farmed by the State, Molesworth (*see index*), near Blenheim, being one example.

For many years farmer and rabbiter were at cross purposes, the farmer wanting the pest exterminated while the rabbiter was secretly leaving enough to breed and so assure him of future livelihood. Not that the rabbiter was alone in this, as low wool and meat prices during the 1880s and 1890s tempted a number of sheep farmers into the realms of rabbitfarming. Only when the rabbit was "devalued" after the 1939–45 war by the prohibition of the sale of both carcass and skin could the battle finally be won — and then only with a nationwide approach to the problem through a Rabbit Destruction Council, large-scale trapping, poison airdrops, and a bounty paid for spring skins to encourage killing during the breeding season. After a century the situation has been brought under control, and it is control rather than destruction that governs present policy.

**Refrigeration revolution:** If rabbits forced a good number of runholders off the land and spelt ruin to many more, an enormous boost was soon to be given to the farming industry with the introduction of refrigeration. Sheep surplus to carrying capacity were valueless once all the runs had been fully stocked, and a small population meant there was little domestic demand for meat. For some years sheepfarmers simply drove unwanted stock over cliffs or into the sea. Boiling-down works placed a slight value on the sheep carcass, but the advent of refrigeration brought the meat-hungry markets of Britain within easy reach. In 1882 the maiden shipment left Port Chalmers (*see* △ *Oamaru*) to open up in good order and sell profitably in London's Smithfield market. Within ten years annual exports reached 1.9 million carcasses.

Prices were low — about 3d per pound — and costs were high, but without refrigeration the sheep industry's plight in a time of depression would have been immeasurably worse. The switch to meat production marked the end of the "wool period" and the emergence of the present three-tiered system of production. The first level is the high country, where pasture production is sufficient only for sheep with slow-growing carcasses and where the Merino and wool remain supreme (e.g. the mountain regions of Marlborough, Canterbury and Otago). At the second level is the hill country, where lambs are bred for sale through saleyards to the third-tier area, the fat-lamb farms. These breed export lambs from stock brought in from the hill country.

In 1973 the country's sheep population was 56.7 million of which 26.7 million were in the South Island.

**Putting the small man on the land:** The advent of refrigeration accelerated the breakup of many of the big runs. After the goldrushes had passed there were many former miners who wanted land; also, after the boom generated by Sir Julius Vogel's free-spending public works policy (which saw the country's railway systems extended and unified) there were many assisted migrants who by then wanted to go on the land. Refrigeration meant that no longer was the need for pastoral runs paramount, for smaller holdings could profitably produce cheese and butter for overseas markets.

Men, as Edward Gibbon Wakefield had noted, tended to migrate out of a desire to better their own condition, yet they saw themselves denied land which was locked up in vast areas by relatively few runholders. In 1890 the Liberal Party under John Ballance came to power with policies pledged to closer settlement by the repurchase of large estates for subdivision by the Crown, the imposition of a land tax to try to force voluntary subdivisions of large holdings, and cheap finance for new farm development. The first major purchase was of "Ready-Money" Robinson's Cheviot estate (*see △Cheviot*). This was followed by others, and between 1892 and 1911 the Government offered 3.5 million hectares for closer settlement. Pledged to "put the small man on the land", the Liberals created over 5,000 new farms and let them to approved applicants. In fact, the new viability of small farming was more greatly felt in the dairying districts of the North Island, so that "put the small man on the land", which began as a South Island catchcry, had a predominantly North Island sequel.

## THE SOUTH ISLAND AND THE CONSTITUTION

AFTER THE ASSUMPTION of sovereignty by Britain, New Zealand was for a time simply administered by a governor responsible to London under the 1840 "Charter for Erecting the Colony of New Zealand". This provided that "the principal Islands, heretofore known as, or commonly called, the 'Northern Island', the 'Middle Island', and 'Stewart's Island', shall henceforth be designated and known respectively as 'New Ulster', 'New Munster' and 'New Leinster'." The designations did not stick, and in 1846 a second royal charter for the first time divided the country into provinces, New Ulster and New Munster — with New Munster taking in Stewart Island as well as the South Island and part of the North to as far as the Patea River. A complex three-tiered system of representative government was planned, but opposition from Governor Sir George Grey persuaded the British Government to wait. The Provincial Council of New Munster had only one legislative session (in 1849) and that of New Ulster had not met at all by the time the New Zealand Constitution Act of 1852 was passed in London.

**Provincial government established:** Under the New Zealand Constitution Act a quasi-federal system of government was introduced. There was to be a central government to attend to national matters, and provincial governments to look after local affairs centred on each of the six main areas of settlement — Auckland, New Plymouth, Wellington, Nelson, Canterbury and Otago. Within limits each province was entitled to legislate for its own area, subject to repeal by the General Assembly, which could also alter boundaries and create new provinces. Hawke's Bay, Marlborough, Southland and Westland came into existence as new provinces between 1858–73 before the entire provincial structure was abolished in 1875.

Though foreseen as having the status of mere municipalities, the provinces fought for real power, in 1856 acquiring the vital right to dispose of Crown Land and so reap the land revenue. In this way each became master of its own destiny, controlling development, immigration, public works, education and hospitals. Contributing factors to the growth of power were the diverse interests and backgrounds of the various settlements, the way in which they were widely scattered, the "off-centre" site of Auckland (the country's capital until 1865) and particularly the lack of easy communication which alone would have hampered any form of centralised administration.

Ultimately it was the steamer services of the 1860s coupled with the introduction of the telegraph in 1862 that undermined the practical need for provincialism. Ease of communication was accompanied by a shift of the capital to Wellington and by opposition to provincialism from settlers in outlying areas. They were vocal in their objection to local land revenue being spent not in the area where it was earned but diverted to the provincial capital for its greater glory. It was this feeling that led Marlborough (1859), Southland (1861) and Westland (1873) to defect from their parent provinces, being the more remote areas of each of the South Island's three original provinces. Marlborough's comic-opera politics entertained the nation, blocked administration and saw its own outlying areas contemplate provincial independence for themselves (*see △Blenheim*); Westland came too late to achieve much before abolition (*see △Hokitika*); and Southland, after nine heady years of independence, was accepted back by Otago as a son prodigal to the point of bankruptcy (*see △Invercargill*). As well, parts of Marlborough, North Otago, South Canterbury and the Buller all at one time or another petitioned for separation and the creation of further new provinces.

The story of provincial government is dominated by the resounding success of both Canterbury and Otago, who were financially sound. Nelson always managed its slender resources prudently, and the trio were the only provinces in the country to discharge their duty of providing adequate public schooling. The canny Scots of Otago and the intellectuals of Canterbury alone could manage on land-sale revenue, the others surviving only on grants from the central government. Finally Sir Julius Vogel's policy of free-spending public works brought the "centralist" and the "provincialist" into an open confrontation that spelt death to provincialism.

**Independence for the South Island?** As Dunedin boomed through the gold era, blossoming from a village to the country's foremost centre and dominating the colony, thoughts inevitably turned towards independence for the South Island. The North Island was wracked by Land Wars with the Maoris, and a gold-rich Otago was progressively less ready to accept direction from a General Assembly whose impoverished members "looked with ill-concealed envy" on the resources of the South. It was, noted the *Otago Colonist*, "the sad but inevitable result of joining by artificial bonds of union countries that Nature [by Cook Strait] designed should be separate". Otago, argued its editor, Julius Vogel (who, ironically, was ultimately to lead the centralists to the abolition of provincialism) was in terms of shipping days three times as far from the capital of Auckland as it was from Victoria or Tasmania, and he looked forward to "a glorious future — the separation of the two islands". A well-attended public meeting in 1862 endorsed the principle of separation — though Southland, which had achieved independence from Dunedin only by appealing to central government, and Canterbury, understanding that Dunedin saw itself as the South Island's capital-to-be, were both unenthusiastic.

The Europeans in the North Island received scant support from the South, Otago in particular being outraged at seeing the fruits of her prosperity wasted on a costly and needless attempt to deprive the Maoris of their land. A Southern Separation League was formed, but Vogel had by then recognised the signs of decay in the provincial system. Seeing that the weaker provinces were heading for insolvency, he opted in favour of centralism — and promptly changed his electorate to stand for a northern seat.

In an attempt to hold her place as a capital of some description, in 1865 Auckland joined forces with Otago to support a resolution in the General Assembly calling for independence for both islands. They lost by 31 votes to 17.

With the passing of the goldrushes, the population drifted north — not to the new capital of Wellington but to Auckland, as the more northern city succeeded to Dunedin's role. Old feelings of independence were given a comparatively recent flourish when the Mount Herbert County Council prepared a memorandum for a local bodies' fact-finding committee. It noted that "intermarriage between Maori and *Pakeha* in the North Island must ultimately result in a brown-skinned Mediterranean-looking race as opposed to fair-haired, blue-eyed Nordic South Islanders" and suggested that "concerning decentralisation, advice might be sought from Scottish Nationalists". The Cook Strait power cable (1965) which provides the North Island with 10% of its electric power also served to arouse the "Mainlanders'" latent resentment of the North.

After decades of near neglect (in 1900 the populations of both islands were about the same) the Labour Government, elected in 1972, embarked on a limited programme of regionalism in an attempt to meet traditional grievances over the drift to the north, but following their subsequent defeat less has been heard of the matter.

> The North Island volume of this travel guide contains notes on the following general topics:
> — The Maori Genesis
> — The Coming of the Maori
> — Maori Culture Periods
> — Classic Maori Society
> — Maori Arts and Crafts
> — Inter-Tribal Wars
> — Missionaries
> — The Land Wars
> — Constitution
> — Party Politics
> — Economic Growth
> — Notes on Place-names
> — Brief Maori Vocabulary

## LIST OF MAPS

# CITIES, TOWNS AND LOCALITIES OF PARTICULAR INTEREST ARRANGED IN ALPHABETICAL ORDER

When looking for a place-name, first look in the index at the back of the book.

In the text the symbol △ denotes a place with its separate entry in this alphabetical section.

Present-day distances, weights and measures are in metric form. In historical notes, values and measures are generally given in pre-metric form.

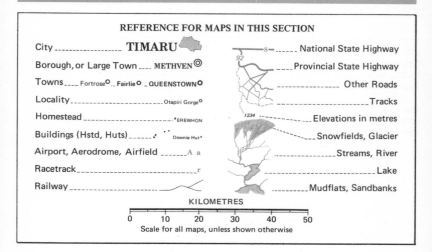

**REFERENCE FOR MAPS IN THIS SECTION**

| | |
|---|---|
| City _____ **TIMARU** | ──8── _____ National State Highway |
| Borough, or Large Town ____ METHVEN ◎ | 92 ____ Provincial State Highway |
| Towns ____ Fortrose○ .. Fairlie ○ _ QUEENSTOWN○ | _____ Other Roads |
| Locality _____ Otapiri Gorge○ | _____ Tracks |
| Homestead _____ •EREWHON | 1234 _____ Elevations in metres |
| Buildings (Hstd, Huts) _____ ⌐̇ ˙˙ Downie Hut • | _____ Snowfields, Glacier |
| Airport, Aerodrome, Airfield _____A a | _____ Streams, River |
| Racetrack _____ ⌐ | _____ Lake |
| Railway _____ ⌐⌐⌐⌐ | _____ Mudflats, Sandbanks |

**KILOMETRES**

0 — 10 — 20 — 30 — 40 — 50

Scale for all maps, unless shown otherwise

---

## ABEL TASMAN NATIONAL PARK***     Maps 26 & 32.    Area: 22,139 ha.

*Totaranui is 31 km E of Takaka. Information offices are at Takaka and Totaranui, where there is also a ranger station. The offices provide details of walks and tracks and issue hunting permits. The "Abel Tasman National Park Handbook" is recommended.*

ABEL TASMAN NATIONAL PARK preserves the native bush and the coastline whose rare beauty stirred to rapturous enthusiasm the French explorer Dumont d'Urville, the first European to see it properly, when he came to describe the peaceful waters that mirror rocky headlands. As the topography ranges from the coastal islands through bush to high country there is a great diversity of plant, insect and bird life.

Proclaimed a National Park in 1942 to commemorate the area's historic associations with Abel Tasman (who anchored near the Tata Islands and would have come ashore but for the killing of several of his crew), the park holds fascination for casual walker, tramper, shooter, skindiver, water-skier and even for the family at the beach for a day. However to appreciate the region fully one should emulate Dumont D'Urville and explore by boat the sandy nooks and rocky crannies of its coastline.

The park includes Harwood's hole and the famous potholes of Canaan are just outside the boundary. (*For both see index.*) Pigs, some goats and a few deer offer the only hunting.

**Totaranui,** reputedly the first place where the Ngaitahu landed on their invasion and migration to the South Island, is the centre of park activity. There is limited camping here, some modest accomodation, a boat ramp and a visitor centre from which information and literature are available. Guided walks leave from the centre in the summer holidays. *31 km from Takaka.*

### SOME HISTORY

**A phantom canoe:** The region was conquered by invading Ngati Toa, Te Atiawa and Ngatirarua under Te Rauparaha in about 1828, who established their own *kainga* (villages) at Totaranui, Marahau and elsewhere along the coast. The defenders had a *pa* (fortified village) at Appleby (SE of Motueka) where they kept a fabulous *waka* (war canoe), *Te Awatea*. The canoe was so admired by the invaders that they took the exquisitely-carved *waka* back to Kapiti Island, first paddling it along the coast from Appleby, past Marahau and Totaranui to Separation Point so that the vanquished might see and bemoan their loss. Over the years tales have been told of the canoe reappearing, silently paddled by ghostly warriors with the only sound being the chant of the *hautu* giving the time for the oarsmen. The apparition is regarded as a prelude to disaster.

**Abel Tasman:** An account of the visit of the Dutch explorer is given under △Nelson.

## SOME WALKS

There are a number of tramps through the park, the most popular being the two- or three-day trek from Totaranui through to Marahau. Short walks, easily accomplished in a day, include:

**From Totaranui:**

**Pukatea Walk:** An easy well-formed path leads through the bush at the northern side of the inlet. The walk passes through vegetation described in a brochure available from the visitor centre. ½ hr. *Follow the road past the homestead to its end, from where the track begins.*

**South:** A track which continues to Marahau follows the beach south passing Skinner Point (½ *hr return*), which separates Totaranui from Goat Bay (*1 hr return*) and Waiharakeke Bay (*3½ hrs return*).

**North:** The track to Separation Point leads over to Anapai Bay (*1½ hrs return*) and the twin beaches of Mutton Cove (*3 hrs return*). Continuing round the coast one reaches Separation Point (*5 hrs return*). *Start from the end of the road beyond the homestead.*

**From Marahau:**

**Torrent Bay:** Torrent Bay itself is a little beyond the capability of the average day walker, but after crossing 2 km of the muddy Marahau Inlet he may choose between Coquille Bay, Apple Tree and Stilwell Bay. The latter two face across the Astrolabe Roadstead to Adele Island. Each is a blissful spot at which to lunch and laze before returning to Marahau.

**Other walks:**

**Wainui waterfall:** A popular walk is the track into a point where the Wainui River heaves over a drop of more than 21 m. *2 hrs return. Start signposted by the roadside at Wainui Inlet on the road to Totaranui.*

**Lookout Rock:** The view from the rock extends only over the forest to Golden Bay (*1½ hrs return*). For wider views, over both Golden Bay and much of Tasman Bay, one must walk on to Gibbs Hill (*405.3 m; allow a good half day*). *Start signposted on the road to Totaranui.*

## BOATING

The coast, delightful as it is, must be treated with respect. Boat owners should obtain information from local residents and have with them the appropriate Marine Department charts. The topography of the park is such that sudden squalls and whirlwinds can occur, particularly near valleys and headlands.

---

**AKAROA***      **Banks Peninsula.    Map 5.    Pop. 639.**

*82 km SE of Christchurch. Information Centre, Beach Road.*

THIS GALLIC-FLAVOURED village dreams by the verdant shores of Akaroa harbour as a precious fragment from the past. Founded on △Banks Peninsula in 1840 as the only French colony in the country, before Nelson had been established and either Christchurch or Dunedin contemplated, the town has traces of its origins in its early architecture, some of its street names and in the name of the hill above the town — L'Aube Hill, called after the French gunboat that accompanied the original colonists.

For all its French beginnings, the village is predominantly late Victorian in style, with a proliferation of quaint cottages that has inspired the formation of a trust in the hope that the now-unique environment can be preserved.

Akaroa corresponds to the northern Whangaroa, meaning long harbour. (In the South Island the Maori consonant "ng" often becomes a distinct "k").

## SOME HISTORY

**Visitors from the north:** Much of the Maori tradition of Banks Peninsula was lost in the fratricide that erupted in the *Kai huanga* (eat relation) feud. This saw Ngaitahu kith fight against kin in a series of costly battles that ended only with the appearance of the Kapiti-based Ngati Toa chief, Te Rauparaha.

After his first abortive raid on Kaiapohia (*see* △*Kaiapoi*), Te Rauparaha vowed to exact *utu* (compensation) for the death there of his uncle, Te Pehi. None but the life of the highest ranking Ngaitahu chief, Te Maiharanui, would suffice. At his base in Cook Strait on the island of Kapiti in 1830 Te Rauparaha arranged with the captain of the trading ship *Elizabeth*, Captain John Stewart, for 170 of his warriors to be taken to Akaroa, in return for about fifty tons of flax. When the *Elizabeth* anchored here the *taua* (war party) hid in the hold until Stewart, posing as a European trader, persuaded Te Maiharanui to come on board. The captain welcomed the Ngaitahu chief, taking him to his cabin where Te Rauparaha seized him and taunted him for his simplicity. Those in the canoes, too, were encouraged to come on board, where they were thrown in the hold. At dawn the *taua* surged ashore to surprise and devastate the *kainga* (village) of Takapueke (Red House Bay) before sailing back to Kapiti. There Te Maiharanui was handed over to the widows of the chiefs killed at Kaiapohia who, in the words of an eyewitness, "put him to death by slow and nameless tortures".

Stewart received short measure when he demanded his flax, and sailed away. Those at Sydney debated whether he had committed any punishable offence; he was arrested but allowed to go free when the prosecution was unable to proceed for want of witnesses. European participation in the affair outraged British humanitarians — "an act of premeditated atrocity on the part of the master and crew of a British vessel, the object of which was to obtain a common article of merchandise". In the wake of their horror, James Busby was appointed British Resident in New Zealand and the first step taken towards an eventual assumption of sovereignty by Britain.

**Slaughter at Onawe:** Fearful of Te Rauparaha's future intentions, the Ngaitahu at Akaroa fortified the pear-shaped peninsula of Onawe. To ensure a copious supply of water, a large number of canoes were beached, filled with water and covered with matting to prevent evaporation. No sooner were the works complete than news came of Te Rauparaha's assault on Kaiapohia (*see △Kaiapoi*). The inhabitants flocked into Onawe, prepared for the worst. Reports of atrocities perpetrated by Te Rauparaha's foraging parties culminated in news of the fall of Kaiapohia. It was not long before a flotilla of canoes entered the harbour, to land Ngati Toa in Barrys Bay and Te Atiawa at the Head of the Bay. The attackers brought with them a number of captives, whose appearance disconcerted the defending Ngaitahu, who were reluctant to risk killing their kinsmen. The captives, partly at the instigation of their conquerors and partly out of a jealous dread that those at Onawe might escape their own certain fate, urged the defenders to surrender. While the Ngaitahu were disconcerted by such unexpected parleying, Te Atiawa warriors slipped inside the gates and began laying about them. Panic gripped the defenders, most of whom were either killed or taken prisoner. There followed on the flats at Barrys Bay a cannibal feast of large proportions.

The capture and destruction of Onawe all but annihilated the Maori population of Banks Peninsula. The area might have been without any real Maori population up to the time of colonisation had it not been for Bishop Hadfield's work with Ngati Toa and Te Atiawa. As proof of the sincerity of their conversion to Christianity, the northern tribes not only released the slaves they had taken but accompanied them back to their homelands.

**The French connection:** The French whaler *Cachalot* put into Port Cooper (Lyttelton) in 1838 where its captain, Jean Langlois, entered into a deed for the purchase of an area of Banks Peninsula for 6,000 francs. Langlois took his deed back to France, where he interested firms in Nantes and Bordeaux and three Parisians in launching the Nanto-Bordelaise Company. Sixty-three migrants were assembled to transplant a little of France to the Southern Seas, a venture backed by the French Government who not only presented them with a vessel, the *Comte de Paris*, but sent a warship, *L'Aube*, under Captain Lavaud to accompany the expedition.

While the party was on its way the Treaty of Waitangi was being concluded, so that when *L'Aube* put into the Bay of Islands in July 1840 its commander was undoubtedly surprised to find that British rule over New Zealand was already an accomplished fact. Lavaud met Hobson, who elected to put the matter beyond all doubt by sending Captain Stanley to Akaroa on HMS *Britomart*, which also took magistrates to hold courts on the Peninsula and to hoist the British flag at Green Point. By the time *L'Aube* arrived at Akaroa on 15 August 1840, British sovereignty was being effectively exercised by resident officials who had arrived from the Bay of Islands only five days earlier.

Popular folklore tells of a "race" for Akaroa between *Britomart* and *L'Aube*, a tale long since dispelled by historians. There can be no doubt, however, that the French colonists were dismayed to find the Union Jack flying at Green Point, and if there was no actual "race" for Akaroa, had the French moved a little faster and settled Akaroa seven months earlier (before Hobson had landed at the Bay of Islands) the French could have established a strong claim to sovereignty. It was not until 1846 that France formally recognised British sovereignty over New Zealand.

**A fragment of France:** Even when the French settlers landed, they were outnumbered by the British population on Banks Peninsula, a fact disguised by the British being sprinkled round the bays while the French were concentrated in one place.

The settlement was intended as a whaling base, where French whalers in the Pacific could put in for supplies, and as a possible penal colony. Though not, it seems, intended as a Wakefield-style agricultural settlement, the French settlers busied themselves on the land. Native bush gave way to the yellow poplars of Normandy, the tangled hedges of Bourbon and willows reputedly grown from slips brought from Napoleon's grave on St Helena; luscious white grapes were cultivated. As English settlers joined the French, the little community was for a time trilingual — English, French and Maori all being in everyday use. A handful of German settlers added further to its cosmopolitan flavour.

In 1849 the French attempt to found a colony was finally abandoned, with Nanto-Bordelaise selling out to the New Zealand Company. A century after the event, descendants of the original French settlers, with names such as Eteveneaux, Le Lièvre, Fleuret and David were to be found not only in Akaroa but throughout the whole country.

## A WALK ALONG THE WATERFRONT

*Allow 3 hrs. Park in Rue Lavaud by the Catholic church.*

**Church of St Patrick** (1864)***: The village witnessed the coming of Catholicism to the South Island when in 1840 Bishop Pompallier established a mission station at Akaroa with Fathers Pezant and Comte. The present picture-book church was the third to be built — the first, erected in 1840, burnt down in 1842 and its replacement collapsed in a violent storm, leaving the Catholics without a church for many years. The present church was built principally of *totara*, black pine and *kauri*, the sacristy and front porch (1886) and the bell-tower (1893) being added later. Pre-eminent among its furnishings is the conspicuously Bavarian east window depicting the crucifixion, given in memory of their Irish mother by members of the Le Lièvre family. *Walk towards the town and turn left up Rue Brittan to pass:*

**Trinity Church** (1886): The first Presbyterian service in the district was held in 1857. The present church is the second on the site. *Continue up Rue Brittan and follow the path up L'Aube Hill to:*

**Old French Cemetery:** The long-neglected resting place of some French colonists was "put in order" in 1925, a well-intentioned act in which the level portion of the hill was cleared and the remains re-interred in a central plot marked by a common monument. This incorporates two inscription plates, those of Captain Edouard Le Lièvre and of Pierre Le Bouffe (Commis de la Marine), the latter being discovered too late for his name to be included on the memorial itself. There is an appealing view from here and an even better prospect from the crest of the hill if one continues up to the Power Board reserve. *Return to Rue Lavaud and continue to:*

**Langlois-Eteveneaux House and Museum***: This conspicuously Gallic two-roomed cottage was probably built between 1841–45 by Aimable Langlois, a supernumerary passenger on *L'Aube* whose brother was the master of the *Cachalot* and instigator of the French settlement. If so, and some doubt lingers, it would be the oldest house in Canterbury province. The building may have been prefabricated in France. From 1858–1906 it was owned by the Eteveneaux family.

The interior of the cottage, furnished in the style of the period in which it was built, may be viewed through windows at the rear. Beside the cottage is a museum with further items from the times of French settlement and before. (*The museum is open from 1.30–5 pm daily in summer; 1.30–4.30 pm in winter; closed Christmas Day, New Year's Day and Good Friday.*) *Immediately turn up Rue Balgueri to reach:*

**St Peter's Anglican Church** (1863: enlarged 1877)* impresses with its straight simple lines: In the grounds is but a single grave, that of the Rev. E. B. Nevill (1835–75), uncle of Bishop Nevill, whose nephew considered he should be buried near the sanctuary where he had celebrated Holy Communion, notwithstanding the fact that the Anglicans had always been buried in their own section of the communal cemetery. The Bishop came to Akaroa secretly, selected the site and engaged a gravedigger.He set to work late at night, in pouring rain, while the Bishop periodically revived him with hot refreshments. By 4 am the grave was ready. Bishop Nevill read the burial service and then returned to Christchurch. In the dawn the local vestry was presented with an accomplished fact. In 1878 a headstone was added after the vestry had be-latedly decided to sanction the burial. Inside the church are memorials to some of those who have lost their lives in Akaroa harbour. *From the church, cross Rue Lavaud and walk to the end of Rue Balgueri. At the foot of Daly's Wharf (conspicuous for its sentry-box style shelter) is the:*

**Early custom house** (pre-1852): This pitsawn timber building once housed the proceedings of solicitors and surveyors as well as custom officers. It is furnished as an early custom house and fitted with a viewing window. (*Open same hours as Museum—see above.*) *Return to Rue Lavaud and turn right to pass the War Memorial. Close by is the:*

**Peraki trypot:** This was used at Peraki by Capt. George Hempleman (*see index*) from about 1837, when he established a shore-whaling station there. *Continue to pass:*

**French Settlers' Memorial:** A stone marks the approximate landing-place of Akaroa's first organised European settlers. Nearby are three more trypots, built into a brick surround as the trypots would have been when used to render blubber at sea on board a whaling ship. Trypots were also used on shore. *Continue along the foreshore to pass the main wharf and reach the:*

**Britomart field-gun:** This 1808 field-gun was on board HMS *Britomart* when she arrived to forestall the French. *After passing the field-gun turn left up Bruce Tce and right into Rue Jolie to reach Akaroa Domain. Walk down through the domain to return to the foreshore. Turn left. After some 250 m the pine-treed entrance to the cemetery is passed. A drive leads up to the point where sheep graze among tombstones old and new. Continue on round the foreshore to the next point, Green Point, and follow the path up to the:*

**Britomart Memorial:** The obelisk here was erected in 1898 to mark the diamond jubilee of Queen Victoria. At a pageant considered of sufficient significance to attract the Earl of Ranfurly (then Governor-General) and Prime Minister Richard Seddon, "The Union Jack was again run up under a salute . . . and the national anthem sung" in the belief that they were re-enacting a dramatic forestalment by Britain of would-be claimants from alien France.

It was in the next bay that pioneer farmers landed cattle a year before the French arrived, and also where stood the *kainga* Takapuneke of the chief Te Maiharanui, sacked in 1830 by Te Rauparaha after its chief had been enticed aboard the brig *Elizabeth (see above)*. The bay was called Red House Bay after W. B. Rhodes in 1839 had built a brightly-painted house there.

### OTHER THINGS TO SEE AND DO

**L'Auberge Suzette\*\*\*:** In keeping with the township's French tradition is the little Victorian cottage where the finest food is served in an intimate restaurant. *17 Rue Balguerie, tel. 219. Reservations essential.* More conventional restaurants are on Beach Road.

**The Kaik:** The little church (1876–78) here, the property of the Onuku *kainga*, stands on a reserve retained by Akaroa Maoris in both the sale to Nanto-Bordelaise and in the later sale of remaining land to the Government. "Kaik" is the South Island equivalent of *kainga* (unfortified village). Onuku (*o* = provision for a journey; *nuku* = to move) has been translated as "coming and going, never staying long". *6.3 km. Follow the road from Akaroa round the foreshore.*

**Some other walks:** Several longer walks may be made in the area — up Purple Peak or along the first 7 km of Lighthouse Road to Flea Bay summit. The stiff climb up Mt Brazenose (*784.2 m*) yields a magnificent view of peninsula, plains and mountains. In tradition Mt Brazenose was a *pa-atua*, an abiding place of the gods and a sacred place where none would venture. Its mists personified the spirits of the dead.

Another good walk, from Wainui on the opposite side of the harbour, is up Mt Bossu (*711.7 m*), named by the French pioneers (*bossu* = hunchback) and where in legend the chief Rakaihautu plunged his *ko* (digging stick) after gouging out the beds of many of the South Island lakes. (*Ask directions locally*).

The Automobile Association has offices throughout the country and offers members a wide range of services, from a breakdown service and legal advice to maps and details of road conditions. Its annual handbooks, listing details of hotels, motels and camping grounds, are the most comprehensive available and are issued free to members.

### SOME POINTS OF INTEREST ON AKAROA HARBOUR

**Duvauchelle** (*10 km from Akaroa*): The locality (pop. 174) is named after Jules and Benjamin Duvauchelle, brothers granted sections by the Nanto-Bordelaise Company.

**Barrys Bay** (*12 km from Akaroa*): The present dairy factory here, now the only one on the peninsula, sells fresh cheese at wholesale prices. Visitors may see the factory during production between 7 am and 2 pm. The level ground in front of the earlier dairy factory witnessed the cannibal feast that followed Te Rauparaha's capture of neighbouring Onawe Peninsula.

**Onawe Peninsula:** Jutting out into the harbour like a stranded whale, the peninsula has obvious natural advantages as a defensive site. A minimum of fortification would render access by land virtually impossible. Traces of the *pa* fortifications have all but vanished under a century of farming. The fact that it is overlooked by higher ground contributed to its downfall, as those besieging the *pa* were able to observe the activities of the defenders within.

**French Farm** (*14 km from Akaroa*): The heights above French Farm were in Maori tradition favoured by the children of the mist, the *patupaiarehe* (fairies) who would gather there both by night and on foggy days to sing their *waiata* (chants) and play their flutes.

**Wainui**\*\* (*20 km from Akaroa*): Wainui (pop. 93) has the largest and most inviting stretch of sand, with the best bathing of all the inner harbour beaches. Occasionally there is surf of modest dimensions.

The open-air chapel at the YMCA camp is of interest. Pews are in a natural setting, surrounded by creeper-tangled bush and canopied by tall native trees. (*Signposted. The chapel is behind the row of huts, to the far left of the entrance.*) There is a good walk from Wainui up the Bossu Road and to the summit of Mt Bossu.

From here one may drive on to return to Christchurch by a most spectacular route (*see "Touring Notes", below*).

## OTHER ENVIRONS

Several of the glorious ocean bays, such as Le Bons, Okains and Little Akaloa, may be explored from Akaroa. *For details see* △ *Banks Peninsula.*

## ORGANISED EXCURSIONS

**NZR Eastern Bay bus route:** The bus leaves at 9.30 am on weekdays (10.15 am Saturday) and returns at about 2.30 pm. The run takes in Pigeon Bay, Little Akaloa, Chorlton, Okains Bay and Le Bons Bay, while mail and freight are delivered. Take your own lunch to picnic at Little Akaloa. *Leaves from the depot in Aubrey St, tel. 85M Akaroa.*

**Trail rides** over the hills round the harbour are organised by Mr W. R. Muller of Mt Vernon (*tel. 180*).

## TOURING NOTES

**Alternative routes to Christchurch:** Instead of Highway 75, two spectacular routes to Christchurch compete for the visitor's attention.

The Summit Road climbs above Akaroa to crisscross the uppermost rim of the volcanic crater, giving superb and alternating views of Akaroa Harbour and of the appealing coves on the peninsula's northern coastline. Highway 75 is rejoined at Hill Top. Alternatively one may continue through Pigeon Bay, Port Levy and Diamond Harbour to Governors Bay.

The second route (*92 km to Christchurch*) covers some of the peninsula's most taxing roads. Skirt the harbour to Wainui and continue along the shore before climbing for magnificent views, first of the heads and then of the length of the harbour as the road snakes round Mt Bossu. A distant view of Peraki is obtained after the Peraki Road turnoff is passed. Follow the crest of the barren hills through tussock for further views as Lake Ellesmere and the Alps come into view. Occasionally the coast may be seen for as far as Timaru. When some 8 km from Lake Forsyth descend to Little River and rejoin Highway 75.

*Refer also to* △*Banks Peninsula.*

> I always love to begin a journey on Sundays, because I shall have the prayers of the church, to preserve all that travel by land, or by water. — Jonathan Swift (*Polite Conversation*).

## ALEXANDRA\*\*\*    Central Otago.    Map 1.    Pop. 4,137.

*192 km NW of Dunedin; 93 km SE of Queenstown; 88 km SSE of Wanaka*

THE FRUITGROWING TOWN of Alexandra is one of contrasts — between the orchards that creep into its centre and great, grey, lifeless dredge tailings; between fertile irrigated valleys and arid, schist-heaped hillsides burnt desert-brown or piled high with snow; and between the greens of summer, the tones of autumn, the skeletons of winter, and the blossoms that each spring draw thousands to Alexandra's annual festival. Known in turn as Lower Township (neighbouring △Clyde was Upper Township), Junction (here the substantial Manuherikia flows in to the Clutha) and Manuherikia, the town was finally named after the then-Princess Alexandra who in 1863 married the Prince of Wales.

## SOME HISTORY

**Taming the Clutha:** Though in conservation terms it is easy to condemn the destruction wrought by gold dredges to large areas of potential orchards and farmland, the town of Alexandra owes if not its existence, certainly its importance, to the dredging boom of the 1890s.

A settlement had sprung up here in 1862, but its twin township on the Dunstan Diggings at Clyde was quickly established as the administrative centre of the goldfields. So much so that for many years Alexandra was bypassed even by the coach route, which on the Clyde-Roxburgh run ran through Earnscleugh and Conroys Gully on the far side of the Clutha River.

# ALEXANDRA AND DISTRICT

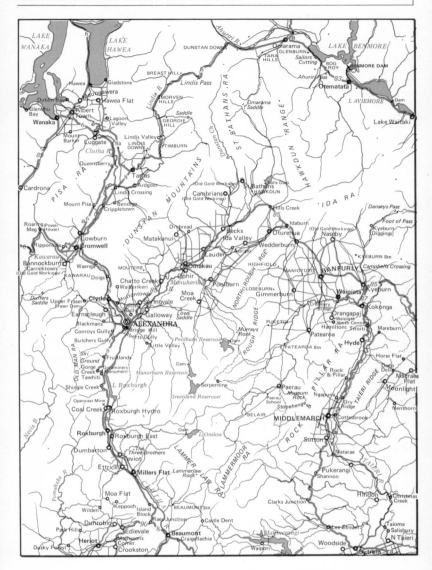

## 1

To overcome this, Alexandra's first borough council made strenuous efforts to have the Clutha bridged at Alexandra, to replace the expensive, erratic and often-dangerous punt. Great was the jubilation when the first bridge opened in 1882. The entire populace roared its approval when Vincent Pyke (*see index*), declaring the bridge officially open, hurled the key of the despised punt far out into the river. The bridge lasted until 1958, when the need for a wider passage led to its replacement by the present arched steel structure. The piers of the old bridge still stand beside the new.

**Dredges on the river:** Gold had generated the town in the first instance (*see △Clyde*) when spectacular finds saw thousands of diggers flock to the Dunstan field. After four hectic years the easily-won alluvial gold was gone and the population here had by 1866 dwindled to 148 Europeans and 100 Chinese.

It was the interest in gold dredging in the 1890s that re-galvanised the town, businesses springing up to service the scores of dredges as they clanked their way, night and day, turning over the riverbeds and much of the flats. Coal was needed to fire the generally steam-driven machines, and much of it came from pits around Alexandra. It is recorded that coalminers, as they toiled below ground, at times could hear the dredges grinding away overhead. A foundry was built, to supply massive dredge buckets and vital bucket pins, which in 1916 could make the surprising claim of being the only workshop in the country that could produce a crankshaft for a motor vehicle.

About the turn of the century the fruitgrowing prospects for the area began to be recognised. Soil rich in potash and phosphoric acid needed only lime and abundant water to realise its potential and as water-rights were abandoned by miners, they were taken up by prospective orchardists.

Several of the dredges have their names perpetuated in Alexandra street names — e.g. *Enterprise*, *Eureka* and *Ngapara*.

**Watson Shennan** (1835–1920): First and foremost of the area's runholders was the Scot, Watson Shennan, who with his brother Alexander arrived at Port Chalmers in 1857. They explored the unknown interior for sheep country until, in the Manuherikia Valley, Alexander enthused: "Here is the country we are looking for, a land well grassed and watered — a very land of promise. Here we will pitch our tent and here we shall stay and make our home for good."

The pair took up two blocks totalling 40,500 ha on either side of the Manuherikia River. The one they named Galloway after their native district in Scotland, the other Moutere (island) as the block was bounded by water on three sides and by mountains on the fourth. To stock the runs and so confirm the leases, the brothers drove sheep from as far away as Balclutha. Over the Lammerlaws they came, where early snow had made conditions difficult. Then, with the sheep high in the mountains, a severe snowstorm led to four desperate weeks — as the hardened Watson said: "I do not think it possible to experience greater hardship and live . . . A journey to the South Pole is nothing to a trip like that." But survive they did and the first sheep were in Central Otago. Nor was it easy to get wool out. Sledges had to be used to travel the 254 km to the coast, and teams were employed for most of the year taking down wool and returning with stores.

As their flock grew, the time came to improve the breed of sheep, and in 1862 Alexander travelled to Germany in search of pure-bred Merinos. There he purchased fifteen rams and twenty-seven ewes from the King of Prussia's celebrated Potsdam stud. To these were added Merinos from other sources and in all eighty-five sheep were safely shipped to Port Chalmers. Once ashore, they had cost almost £2,000. Two failed to survive the voyage of 107 days.

Alexander did not return. He died of rheumatic fever as a medical student, in Edinburgh. His years in Central Otago, exposed to all kinds of weather, had proved too much for him, and his short but useful life ended at the age of only twenty-two years.

Watson sold Galloway in 1863 but retained Moutere, where he founded his famed Puketoi Merino stud, whose strain is found today throughout the world. There, too, he suffered the Dunstan goldrush which he saw as an unmitigated disaster — "It may have been a God send; if it was, I am sure it was sent as a punishment. Anyone visiting that part of the country now has only to open his eyes to see the ruin and desolation brought upon the land through the hunt for gold. A great crime has been committed. 'Gold! Gold! price of many a crime untold', may well be said."

Watson sold Moutere, visited Scotland briefly and then took possession of the Maniototo run of Puketoi (*see* △ *Ranfurly*). He had not disposed of his stud Merinos and there he continued his success, building up the largest stud in the country. He later moved to Conical Hills (*near Tapanui*) before finally retiring to Dunedin, to a mansion complete with ballroom.

> It used to be a good hotel, but that proves nothing — I used to be a good boy. —Mark Twain.

**"The world's best practical joke"**: Today the antics might raise less than a smile, but in the mood of the times and even thirty years later they were regarded as hilarious. It was in the late 1890s that Ah Fook Hu, a Chinese storekeeper, won spectacularly at fantan, withdrew his savings from the bank and set off for his homeland, never to be heard of again. Relatives, suspecting that Ah might have been murdered for his money, posted a reward which attracted the attention of a Swedish miner, John Magnus, then working a claim about 10 km down river from Alexandra. Magnus had little sympathy for the Chinese and could not resist the opportunity to dress a sheep's carcass in the manner described in the reward, complete with pigtail woven from the hair of a black billygoat. Elaborate surgery was carried out on the sheep — its head was covered with inverted sheepskin, teeth were bared and a nose fashioned from a sheep's kidney before the whole "face" was stained with Condys fluid. By the time they had finished the carcass was stinking, which doubtless aided the success of the scheme, for the "body" was placed by the river for another miner to find and rush to Alexandra in all innocence to claim the reward. The local constable, despatched to recover the corpse, was assisted by Magnus's friends to bring it to the town. Here a sergeant and a doctor made a hurried examination before they converted the stables at the Bendigo Hotel into a morgue for the purposes of a post mortem. Ah Fook Hu's brother denied that it was his relative, but others were more certain and positively identified the corpse as being that of the hapless Ah. The post mortem began. Slowly the body was undressed. Eventually, when the trousers were cut to reveal a sheep's leg, the shocked and sombre crowd erupted with mirth. Doctor, police, and mayor all rapidly retreated in a state of embarrassed confusion as Magnus and his friends repaired to the bar of the Bendigo to celebrate. A local resident was paid to bury the corpse but at dawn the next morning it was found propped up against the hotel's front door.

Those taking part were overcome by their hilarity and none seemingly spared a thought for Ah Fook Hu, who had disappeared without trace. *The Bendigo Hotel, scene of the joke's final stages, is still standing in Tarbert St.*

## THINGS TO SEE AND DO

**Tucker Hill Lookout\*\*\***: A road leads across a road/rail bridge over the Manuherikia to the crest of barren Tucker Hill from which there is a panorama of Alexandra and the surrounding district. Below spreads the tree-girt town. To the left the deep green waters of the Clutha emerge from a desert of dredge tailings to meet the meandering Manuherikia. To the right, the orchards of the Manuherikia Valley are a spectacle for all seasons. In the distance can be seen the tips of the Remarkables, and the Pisa Range showing through the Cromwell Gorge. *1.6 km. From Tarbert St on the town's NE exit, turn off where signposted and follow Little Valley Rd.*

Descending the hill to return to the town, a detour may be made along Graveyard Gully Road to pass Shaky Bridge (*at 600 m*). Farther on, above the road, are the remains of a rock overhang walled in to form a miner's hut (*at 1 km*). At Graveyard Gully itself (*1.5 km*) is a memorial to fourteen named pioneers, buried there between 1863 and 1868.

**Sir William Bodkin Museum\*\***: The collection centres on goldmining activities, particularly those of the dredges. Included are a model of a current-wheel dredge (powered by the river's current), photographs, official returns of dredges, and the iron rooster, the "Cock of the River", that was proudly displayed by the dredge that had won the most gold in the preceding week. In a special Chinese section are an opium pipe, an opium bottle and scales, Chinese currency, crockery, chopsticks, sandals, shoulder-yoke and tools. In front of the building is a massive all-steel waterwheel (1879), made in Dunedin and recovered from the higher reaches of the Old Man Range on Earnscleugh station. Each of the forty-five buckets on the 6.84 m wheel holds 136.5 litres. The wheel was probably installed by John Kitching when manager of the Moa Flat estate in an attempt to open up the Alpine Ridge Reef at the head of the Fraser Basin and Campbell Creek — from which remote spot the wheel was recovered in an operation recounted in a booklet on sale at the museum. *Thomson St (signposted off Tarbert St). Open Monday to Friday from 2–4 pm; other times by arrangement (tel. 8139 or 8914).*

**Shaky Bridge** (*c.* 1879): A picturesque suspension bridge once used by wagons and horses but now narrowed to a footbridge, it was once sold for £1 as it was a source of expense to the county. Before the bridge was built the only way of crossing the Manuherikia was by punt, a risky operation when the river was high. The bridge was restored as a pioneer memorial. *At end of Kerry St off Fox St. Signposted from Tarbert St.*

One may cross the bridge and turn right to walk 900 m to reach a stone-walled enclosure in Graveyard Gully (*see above*).

**Hillside clock:** On the Knobbies Range, to the east of and overlooking the town, is a unique illuminated hillside clock. Its diameter of nearly 12 m makes it one of the world's largest. At night the time can be read clearly up to 8 km away.

**Boat Harbour:** A riverside picnic spot and a boat ramp where once gold dredges were built and launched are just upstream from the Clutha bridge. Here the river flows by swiftly on its way to the still waters of Lake Roxburgh. Gold was found on both banks of the river. Though many important relics were lost when the lake formed behind the △Roxburgh dam, there are still interesting sites and ruins along both sides of the gorge. Among them are the stone walls of Nicholas Anderson's hotel and, at Obelisk Creek, Heron's Cottage — the century-old building where the notorious Sullivan gang (*see index*) were fed a meal by Mrs Heron while her husband, pretending to be hoeing potatoes, was burying his gold in the garden. In his anxiety he forgot to mark the spot and was for a worrying night unable to find it. *End of Dunorling St.*

The gorge is presently accessible only to private boatowners.

## A TOUR OF SOME OLD GOLD TOWNS

The suggested route lies by way of the Manuherikia Valley, through △St Bathans, and returns down the Ida Burn and Poolburn Valleys before crossing the Raggedy Range to rejoin the Manuherikia. The round trip of some 174 km takes in a number of old goldtowns and passes two of Central Otago's most historic sheep stations. *Allow a full day.* (The trip may best be shortened by omitting the two sheep stations and driving directly to Omakau.)

*Leave Alexandra north by Highway 85. At 3.7 km one may detour by veering right to wind along Galloway Rd to reach at 8 km the homestead gates of:*

**Galloway station:** The homestead block of the run originally held by Watson Shennan (*see above*). The fine stone buildings were erected by the second owner, W. A. Low, who held the run from 1862 until, in the mid-1870s, he sold out to his partner, Hon. Robert Campbell (*see index*). It was Campbell who brought W. G. Rees (*see index*) to Galloway after the generous Rees had lost his run at Kawarau Falls, so descending from being a runholder to being a run-manager. Cut up in 1916, the Galloway run today extends over 11,340 ha in a thin pinched parcel that stretches from the homestead's irrigated flats back to the steep, rocky broken country east of the Manorburn dam. The flock on several occasions has produced the country's top-selling Merino clip.

The low stone homestead (1865) may be seen from the road. To the right, in order from the road, are the former married couples' quarters, the chaff barn, and the stables, complete with dormer pigeon loft. *Return to Highway 85 and turn right. At 23 km detour left up Moutere Disputed Spur Rd, to stop at 23.5 km outside the entrance to:*

**Moutere station:** The homestead block of the run on the west of the valley, taken up by the Shennan brothers at the same time as Galloway. Merino sheep here are direct descendants of the first of the breed to be introduced to Otago by the Shennan brothers in 1863.

The cob woolshed (early 1870s) was built from clay puddled within its walls. The homestead (1873), also of cob, has been much modernised. The run covers 4,740 ha. *Return to Highway 85 and turn left to reach:*

**Omakau** (pop. 247) (*at 41 km*): A farming centre and station on the Central Otago branch railway. Once called Blacks, the locality was renamed when the railway went through. The Maori name has about fourteen possible meanings, one of which is "a wading place". The story is told of the Rev. T. Knight intending to use the ford here as he rode on his way to Ophir to take service. When he saw a pair in a gig waiting on the other side he called out: "Is the river all right today?" The reply came back: "You go first; Day follows Knight." It was the parish priest, Father Day. *At Omakau turn left to follow the signposted route to:*

**Matakanui** (*at 52 km*): The near-deserted goldtown on the foothills of the Dunstan Mountains was originally named Tinkers. One explanation tells of tinsmiths returning towards Dunstan (Clyde) from plying their trade at the nearby Drybread diggings and deciding to have a prospect here. So great was their success that they abandoned their trade of repairing pans and dishes in favour of using them for washing gold from gravel.

The Newtown Hotel, rebuilt within the century-old stone walls of the original, has lost its liquor licence but caters for the other needs of travellers. Opposite is a mud-brick store, whose antique brass plate proclaims it to be the registered office of the Mount Morgan Sluicing Company Limited. It began life as a goldfields dancehall.

Now flooded, the head of the Deep Lead mine may be seen after a short walk from Sugarpot Rd, a shaft sunk almost 80 m in about 1898 in a determined bid to bottom (*ask direction locally*).

Drybread is so called, it is said, from the reply given by a cagey prospector when asked how his workings there were panning out. Though doing nicely he answered ruefully: "Dry bread, seldom better." *Return once more to Highway 85 and turn left. Bear left again, down Loop Rd, passing through the workings of Cambrians to reach:*

△ **St Bathans**\*\* (*at 97 km*): A crooked line of buildings beside the crater of startling Blue Lake is the very epitome of an old goldtown. *Continue through St Bathans along Loop Rd to rejoin Highway 85 shortly before:*

**Hills Creek** (*at 109 km*): The scattered remains here are of a village that was once a goldmining centre and a stop for wagons and coaches. By the bridge is the shell of the Prince Albert Hotel. *At 109.3 km leave Highway 85 by turning right down the Ida Valley to:*

**Oturehua** (pop. 120) (*at 117 km*): Today a small farming centre, Oturehua was from 1868 the scene of goldmining when reefs in the north-western slopes of the North Rough Ridge were worked, about 2 km to the north-east of the town. The Golden Progress tapped one such reef and some of its equipment — a timber platform at the minehead and the boiler from its battery — can be seen from the main road well up a gully (*from 200 m N of Oturehua School*). There are plans to bring to the local domain the huge "Serpentine" waterwheel from its remote setting between the Manorburn and the Poolburn reservoirs and a good walk from the Old Dunstan Road.

Hayes Engineering Works (1895) still operates, on a limited basis, using water-power. The founder, Ernest Hayes, invented the Hayes parallel wire strainer and the Hayes windmill and produced them along with other farm equipment. The works, now being restored, may be visited. (*Turn right before Hayes Rd, immediately south of the township. Where the roadway forks, bear left to the workshop. The right fork leads past an old stone flourmill building*). Open Sun.-Wed. Tel. Oturehua 801 or 817. *Continue south to pass:*

**Idaburn Dam** (*at 120 km*): A popular winter skating venue. *Continue south, turning right at Poolburn (at 140 km) to rise over the Raggedy Range for superb views, both to the west over the Manuherikia Valley, and back to the east, over the Idaburn and Poolburn Valleys. Descending, turn left to reach:*

**Ophir** (pop. 57) (*at 149 km*): Ophir blazed into life with the finding of gold in April 1863, and in less than three months there were thousands on the field. Hastily-erected huts and tents crystallised into a substantial town, complete with brass band. Its disused courthouse still stands back from the road about 30 m to the left of the

Ophir post office (1886). The post office, today Ophir's main centre of activity, is a delightful pocket-sized stone building seemingly designed to have been built on a grander scale. (*Open 9 am–noon, weekdays*). *Continue through Ophir to cross the picturesque stone-piered suspension bridge over the Manuherikia (1870s), so to rejoin Highway 85. Turn left to return to Alexandra.*

## CONROYS GULLY — CLYDE ROUND TRIP

*30 km.* The run leads through old goldworkings and the mellow village of Clyde. *Leave Alexandra south by Highway 8. Turn right at* **Butchers Dam** *(6.5 km), a source of town water for Alexandra. A detour may be made to* **Conroys Dam.** Conroys (named after its discoverer) and Butchers (presumably named as sheep were slaughtered there) were two rich goldmining areas into which newcomers poured when they found it impossible to drive a wedge between the claims along the Clutha.

*Bear left at Chapman Rd to pass* **Earnscleugh station** *(at 14.5 km; described under △Clyde). Continuing on, one may detour to* **Fraser Domain** *(a pleasant picnic spot) or to the* **Lookout** *(see △Clyde) before crossing the Clutha to enter △***Clyde.**

*Leave Clyde by Hartley Rd, passing the old cemetery. At the locality of Muttontown (22.5 km) turn right down Dunstan Rd to return to Alexandra.*

## ROAD TO ROXBURGH

Highway 8 leads south to Roxburgh passing:

**Butchers Dam** (*5.8 km from Alexandra; 33.5 km from Roxburgh*): A source of town water for Alexandra. *The road then enters the:*

**Fruitlands District** (*12.6 km from Alexandra; 26.7 km from Roxburgh*): In a rich orcharding region, the name of Fruitlands is charged with irony for it was given at a time when the area seemed likely to flourish as a fruit-producing area, but this proved not to be so, and today sheep graze where the trees were planted.

When miners toiled in the valley it was known as Bald Hill Flat. Ground was worked from the flats, with water led more than 20 km from Gorge Creek to the steepest slopes of the Old Man Range, where reefs were located at nearly 3,000 m above sea level to challenge the most intrepid of the waggoners and packmen. *Above the district stands:*

**Old Man Rock:** The Old Man Range takes its name from Old Man Rock, an extraordinary pillar of stone standing some 26.8 m from a base only 8.5 m wide. In Maori legend this is the area where the giant Kopuwai lived, and Old Man Rock is a personification of him (*see △Balclutha*). More recent folklore relates that the rock was first climbed by an enterprising surveyor who flew a kite to get a line over its summit. The kite's string he used to pull a stout cord which, when firmly attached to the ground on the far side, gave him the climbing rope he needed. *The sentinel-like rock is visible over a wide area and is seen from Fruitlands on the ridge to the west of the road, from about 13 km from Alexandra (26 km from Roxburgh). At 12.7 km from Alexandra (26.6 km from Roxburgh) detour west up Symes Rd for 1 km to see, on the right:*

**Mitchell's Cottage** (1876): In this superb example of the Shetland Island stone-mason's craft, the walls are as true as if built of brick, and stone is used even to the window edges. Close by is the solid stone sundial Mitchell carefully left as he hewed out rock for his cottage. *Private property. There is a view of the building from the road. Return to Highway 85 and continue on to pass:*

**Cape Broome Hotel** (*14 km from Alexandra; 25.3 km from Roxburgh*): An old stone hotel, now a barn, with a quaint store behind. *Then are passed:*

**Gorge Creek Goldminers' Memorial** (*17.6 km from Alexandra; 21.7 km from Roxburgh*): 1863 saw the second year of the rushes to Central Otago; it also saw a great snowfall that brought death to an unknown number of ill-prepared and ill-equipped fortune-seekers. Some were working claims locally; others were tackling the 2,000 m range that lies between Central and the Waikaia goldfields of northern Southland. Perhaps as many as thirty nameless diggers perished in the vicinity, but one who survived was a packer who, near death, killed and disembowelled his horse. He huddled in the shelter of the beast's ribs and the next day was found suffering from severe frostbite but nonetheless alive. The common grave of a number of victims is in a roadside picnic area at Gorge Creek. A walk downstream of about 150 m from the monument leads to a miner's stone hut, built into the hillside on the creek's right bank.

**Roxburgh hydro-electric power station** (*31.1 km from Alexandra: 8.2 km from Roxburgh*): *Described under △Roxburgh.*

**Coal Creek Methodist Church** (1869) (*34.5 km from Alexandra; 4.8 km from Roxburgh*): The tiny chapel is to the east of the highway. *The road runs on through orchards to reach △* **Roxburgh** (*39.3 km from Alexandra*).

## TOURING NOTE

**Highway 85 to** △**Ranfurly and** △**Palmerston:** The traveller leaving Alexandra by Highway 85 may wish to follow either section of the round trip suggested above as "A Tour of Some Old Gold Towns".

**Old Dunstan Road:** For notes on a fine-weather route to Styx and so to Dunedin, *see index.*

## AMBERLEY    North Canterbury.   Maps 7, 20 & 21.   Pop. 918.

*28 km N of Kaiapoi; 10 km S of Waipara.*

THE STOCKYARDS of Amberley spread across the main road, handily sited to the railway that spawned the community. The spire of Holy Innocents Church rises with the settlement's trees. The locality was named after Amberley in Derbyshire.

### POINTS OF INTEREST

**Roman Catholic Church of the Most Holy Passion** (1866)*: The simple squat chapel is among the oldest of Canterbury's Catholic churches (only Akaroa's is older). It was originally built on Sir Frederick Weld's Brackenfield run and was moved here in 1955.

Weld (1823–91), who had pioneered the Wairarapa (with his cousin Clifford and his friends Vavasour and Petre) saw the possibilities here in 1850 as he was journeying to Lyttelton to greet the "Pilgrims". In 1864 he became premier and, though in office for less than a year, changed the direction of New Zealand's political development. Appealed to by Governor Sir George Grey "to assist him in saving the country", he did so only on condition that "the system of double government by Governor and ministers was ended". He also introduced the policy of "self-reliance" to the conduct of the Land Wars then raging in the North Island. His health failing, he resigned from office and was in turn appointed Governor of Western Australia (1869–75), of Tasmania (1875–80) and of the Straits Settlements (1880–87). He has been ranked as one of the founders of New Zealand's nationality. Weld, who may even have designed the church, met much of its cost and provided the original stained glass and furnishings. *By Highway 1. Key held locally.*

**Holy Innocents Church** (1877): The building, with the exception of the tower, was blown over in 1890 as the bottom plates of the nave had not been nailed down, presumably because of malpractice on the part of the contractor. It was promptly rebuilt, with the addition of external bracing. Photographs of the church before, during and after the collapse are in the vestry. *Signposted off Highway 1.*

**Amberley Beach,** with a smattering of baches and a domain, is a somewhat exposed stretch of beach on Pegasus Bay. Up the coast Motunau Island (*see index*) may be seen, resembling a millstone. *4 km SE. Signposted.*

Somewhat more developed is **Leithfield Beach** (*5 km S; turn-off from Highway 1 signposted at 3.6 km S*).

> Camping grounds, motels and hotels are listed in the Automobile Association handbooks.

## ARROWTOWN***    Central Otago.   Maps 29 & 36.   Pop. 410.

*20 km NE of Queenstown; 53 km WNW of Cromwell*

THE MELLOW MINING COTTAGES of Arrowtown bunch in a picturesque setting beneath the stark Crown Range, by the river whose gold sparked the settlement. For generations the town hung on as a minute farming centre, but has more recently prospered from a year-round influx of visitors. Particularly in summer they come, and in autumn when its venerable buildings are enhanced by rich colouring. The prospect of Buckingham St, flanked with century-old sycamores and the façades of early buildings, is truly delightful and much beloved of calendar-makers.

### SOME HISTORY

**Hunting the Fox:** For months in 1862 rumours persisted that a group of prospectors were on to rich ground in a secluded gorge and were there making fortunes. Other prospectors roamed far and wide in search of the group, even triggering a rush to the Cardrona as unwittingly they came across a payable field near Lake Wanaka.

Suspicion centred on William Fox (*fl.* 1862), a veteran with both Californian and Victorian experience who was occasionally seen in Dunstan (Clyde), selling large amounts of gold. Attempts to follow him only heightened speculation, as Fox invariably gave his pursuers the slip — on one occasion even abandoning his tent and belongings in the middle of the night. Inevitably, odd miners eventually stumbled on the party that was working in the gorges of the Arrow: generally after a discussion as to whether they should be shot or held prisoner they were sworn to secrecy and allowed to join the group.

The band was well organised and could make its own rules, with Fox as "commissioner". An accomplished fistfighter, the American had no difficulty in enforcing his decisions.

In the end a large group trudging over the Crown Range saw columns of smoke: with rising excitement they hurried towards the campsite, to fall upon about forty men at work. Their eyes goggled. "Are you Fox?" one managed to ask, and the secret was out.

**Discoverer in doubt:** Though Fox is popularly credited with the discovery of gold in the Arrow — and indeed claimed the honour for himself — colour had earlier been found by Jack Tewa, "Maori Jack", one of the hands on William Rees's station at Queenstown. Fox and his mate John O'Callaghan, out of both food and tobacco (they rated the latter predicament the worse), had called at Rees's station and been advised to try the Arrow. There they met a prospector, Peter Stewart, who told them the ground was not payable — an assertion he later claimed he made only to deter the pair. Yet it seems that an earlier duo, John MacGregor and Thomas Low, were already at work higher up the river. Fox was undoubtedly the dominant personality — for a long time the diggings were known as Fox's — and it was probably due to his forceful character that the secret was kept for as long as it was.

**Tipperary Men:** Gone with the secret was the discipline Fox had instilled. As fortune-seekers flocked to the Arrow some claims were jumped while others were re-pegged — Fox had allowed each member of the group to have several times the legal maximum of river frontage. Confusion reigned and revolvers were brandished as men sought to protect their claims from a group of marauding Irishmen known as the Tipperary Men, whose tactics were to force a man off his claim and quickly work it out before he could obtain legal redress. Then the inimitable Sergeant-Major Bracken arrived. "I've been sent to restore order, and by God I will," he is said to have declared, his hand on his revolver.

And he did. His commanding presence and his unofficial system of quick arbitration to settle mining disputes produced order out of chaos so that when in 1863 he retired to become an hotelier in △ Queenstown, the pioneer miners organised a dinner in his honour.

Once he had gone, riot and bloodshed returned to the streets of Arrowtown. There was no gaol, and the stronger prisoners could simply lift up and carry away the logs to which they were chained. To this unruly township was added the presence of the notorious "Bully" Hayes.

**"The Barberous Barber":** One of the most colourful characters to grace the goldfields was the notorious American blackbirder, freebooter and pirate, Captain William Henry ("Bully") Hayes (1827-57). Stories abound of "the scourge of the Pacific", from Riverton to Nelson, as a stay of a few days was enough for him to create a sensation.

After the vessel he had chartered had been seized for debt at △ Port Chalmers, Bully Hayes joined the Buckinghams, a travelling theatrical family who had been passengers on his ship from Australia; one suspects he had designs on the beautiful and talented daughter, Rosie. When the troupe arrived at Arrowtown and the Buckinghams opened the Provincial Hotel, Hayes defected to launch his own Prince of Wales Hotel across the street, taking the precaution of marrying the star performer to assure himself of full houses and a well-patronised bar.

Rumours spread that Hayes's long locks disguised the absence of the lobe of his right ear, removed, the story ran, by a vigilante committee in California to brand him as a cardsharper. Rosie's brother offered a £5 reward to the barber who would "accidentally" snip Hayes's hair. The offer was taken up and, to the delight of most, his ear lobe was indeed found to be missing. The ecstatic Buckinghams promptly staged a nightly farce, *The Barberous Barber, or The Lather and The Shave*, which played to capacity houses while Hayes bandaged his head and wrecked the barber's shop. Public ignominy was more than the pirate could stand. He left Arrowtown for Nelson where, in a boating accident, both the delightful Rosie and her baby were drowned. Typically, Hayes survived. He left the country to roam the Pacific once more, his life ending in a brawl on board ship in the Marshall Islands.

Neither hotel lasted much longer, but the proprietor of the Royal Oak (which still survives) created a sensation in 1864 when he raffled a gold nugget. He did not however, pay out. The matter came to court and was resolved in favour of a German maker of ginger-beer, one Albert Eichardt, who took his winnings to △ Queenstown and there acquired the hotel (now a tavern) which still bears his name.

## THINGS TO SEE AND DO

**The Lakes District Centennial Museum\*\*\*:** This splendid museum is a focal point for visitors to the town. Comprehensive displays detail the history of the Lakes District and the Wakatipu region. The goldmining section is excellent. The older portion of the museum was the early Bank of New Zealand banking chamber (1875). *Buckingham St. Open daily. Allow 1 hr.*

Two blocks away is the old stone **Arrowtown Gaol** (1875) with its ill-ventilated cells, heavy iron doors and a gun rack over the fortunate warder's fireplace. (*Cardigan St. Walk away from the township along Buckingham St. Key available from the museum.*)

**Miner's Monument** lies about 400 m up the Arrow River from the junction with Bush Creek. There are numerous picnic spots in the vicinity and here one may pan for gold not far from the place where William Fox had his claim. *Signposted at N end of Buckingham St. Gold pans and shovels for hire at "The Gold Nugget".*

On the left about 80 m before the main picnic area is an old **Chinese dwelling** with a simple plaque dedicated "In memory of the old Chinese."

**Memorial Hill:** A good viewpoint is the war memorial. It was here that Ben Sutherland and Harry Bowman were resting from their search for Fox's group when they saw two men walk out of the gorge and later return with the carcasses of two sheep. The two were sworn to secrecy and allowed to join the band. *Access from Durham St.*

**Tobin's Track:** One of the earliest roads leads to a viewpoint above the town. *Cross the river at the end of Ford St. Signposted off Buckingham St. Allow 2 hrs.*

**Macetown:** An all-day walk to the traces of an old goldtown whose principal relics are rosebushes, fruit trees, stonework and an old gold battery. The area may be protected as an Historic Park. *26 km return. Enquire locally for detailed directions. Numerous river-crossings are involved.*

## ENVIRONS

For details of environs, see "Arrowtown Round Trip" under △ Queenstown.

> To make the most of your travels you should carry with you the book of Mobil road maps.

## ARTHUR'S PASS NATIONAL PARK***     Map 2.     Area: 98,405 ha.

*154 km from Christchurch and 100 km from Greymouth to Arthur's Pass township. Full information on the park and educational displays are at the park headquarters at Arthur's Pass township. Hunting permits are available from the park headquarters, where climbers and trampers should complete the Intentions Book. The* Arthur's Pass National Park Handbook *is recommended.*

"ARTHUR" was the surveyor-explorer Arthur Dobson and the pass he found across the Main Divide in 1864 was later chosen as the best route for a road from the Canterbury plains to the West Coast goldfields. His brother George, also a surveyor and commissioned to make the final choice of route, declared 'Arthur's pass is the best route', so accidentally giving the pass its name. It had earlier been used by Kaiapohia Maoris on greenstone expeditions to Westland.

The park is one of constrasts. Its 98,405 ha spread over both faces of the Southern Alps, with altitudes ranging from 245 m at the Taramakau River to 2,402 m on the highest peak and dropping again to 610 m to the east of the Main Divide. Annual rainfall varies from 1,780 mm to 5,100 mm. Three-quarters of the park is in Canterbury and the balance in Westland. The park's activities of walking, tramping, climbing, hunting and skiing centre on the alpine village of Arthur's Pass township. On the other side of the Main Divide and with an equally rigorous climate, is the railway settlement of Otira.

**Sir Arthur Dobson** (1841–1934): Arthur Dudley Dobson was a man of great physical resources, of curiosity and invention. He arrived in New Zealand with his father, Edward, on the *Cressy* in 1850. His father, a trained architect, surveyor and engineer, became the Provincial Engineer whose achievements included the Christchurch-Lyttelton rail tunnel, the Lyttelton breakwater, and the planning of the provincial railway system. Arthur and his brother George began surveying under their father, laying out roads, planning drains, prospecting for coal and exploring the ranges. In the course of surveying a block of land on the West Coast Arthur discovered the pass that bears his Christian name. There was public criticism of the rugged terrain over which the road was built but, as one observer noted, not even the combined talents of the Dobson family could reduce the height of the mountains.

Later Arthur's talents blossomed as an engineer, with impressive public works achievements in Victoria and New Zealand. He lived to become a foundation member of the Arthur's Pass Board, in 1929 entrusted with administering the scenic reserve that in 1952 formally became a national park. He was knighted in 1931. *Dobson's portrait is in the park headquarters.*

## SOME GEOLOGY

When the river is not in flood, the broad gravels of the Waimakariri Valley are comparatively dry and wear a deceptive look of stability. In heavy floods, however, the whole mass of gravel and sand to a depth of a metre or more can be set in motion, the rumble of boulders and the shock of collisions being actually felt by the spectator on the riverbank. It was the movement of sand and shingle on such a scale that created the broad Canterbury plains, as the rivers bore vast quantities of gravel waste down from the mountains. The ranges were elevated not separately but in a unified mountain-building process and have been sharpened and cut down by erosion and glacial action.

The glaciers that have shaped the valley walls have all but disappeared, though there are several on Mt Rolleston (*2,270 m*), notable as being the northernmost in the South Island. (*For notes on glaciers, see △ Fox Glacier.*)

Rocks within the park are predominantly greywacke, a hard sandstone of sedimentary origin (i.e. laid down under the sea). Vein quartz, dark-grey argillite, jaspillite of various shades, and conglomerate (quartz pebbles cemented in sandstone) are also found. Notwithstanding the generally sedimentary origin of the rocks, few fossils have been discovered. The rocks are at least 150 million years old, though the mountains they now form have been built by earth movement only in about the last million years.

## FLORA AND FAUNA

The vegetation on either side of the Main Divide is in complete contrast, with mountain beech forest on the east and mixed rain forest to the west. The crossing of the Divide gives a complete and representative cross-section of the flora to be found along the mountain chain. The difference is brought about by a marked climatic change, the Westland slopes having a much higher rainfall and less harsh temperatures. *Information on species found within the park and illustrated booklets for nature walks are available from the park headquarters.*

Native birds commonly seen include the *kea*, the South Island *kaka*, *tui*, bellbird, South Island tomtit, the rifleman and the grey warbler. Throughout the park, but rarely seen, is the large nocturnal grey *kiwi* (or *roa*).

Permits are available from the park headquarters to hunt for red deer, chamois and the occasional tahr. Opossums are widely distributed and menace the scarlet-flowered southern *rata*, in late summer so much a feature of the park.

## SOME WALKS***

**Bridal Veil Walk:** The walk up the east side of the Bealey Valley begins from the highway some 2.2 km towards the pass. The Devil's Punchbowl waterfall is seen, 133.9 m high, tumbling from a glacier-formed hanging valley that was a tributary to the much larger and deeper Bealey Glacier. Signs identify a number of plants as the track leads to the Bridal Veil lookout and continues on to rejoin the highway. *Allow 1¼ hrs from the township. Explanatory booklet available.*

**Devil's Punchbowl Walk:** The track leads to the waterfall. *Allow 1½ hrs. Start at 2.2 km N.*

**Bealey Valley Walk:** An easy walk crosses the Bealey River and passes a typical tarn (small mountain lake). *4 hrs return from the township. 2 hrs return from the highway (starting 2.6 km N of the township).*

**Dobson Nature Walk,** on the summit of Arthur's Pass, is an easy walk that begins by the Dobson Memorial and crosses into Westland. *Allow 1 hr (one way) from the highway or 4 hrs (return) from the township. Start at 5 km N. Boots are advisable when conditions are wet. Explanatory booklet available.*

**Avalanche Peak:** An all-day summer walk for the reasonably fit is steep but yields pleasant views. Two tracks lead up the 1,828.9 m peak, of which Scott's Track is the easier. *Signposted at 700 m N of the township.*

**Mt Bealey Track:** Another all-day walk for the reasonably fit is up Mt Bealey (*1,831 m*). It, too, is quite steep. *Start 300 m S of the township, just over Rough Creek.*

## OTHER POINTS OF INTEREST

**Park headquarters***:** In addition to providing comprehensive information about the park, the headquarters houses a museum which portrays the development of the road and the railway as well as the natural history of the park. *Open daily.*

**Otira Tunnel portal:** The south portal of the first major tunnel to be constructed in New Zealand may be seen from the riverbank. In 1908 contractors began to drill the tunnel at Otira, and the following year at Arthur's Pass township. In 1912 they were forced by expense and difficulties to hand the project over to the Public Works Department (now the Ministry of Works). As the tunnel has a gradient of 1 in 33, rising to the Arthur's Pass township end, most of the work was carried out from the Otira portal. Progress was slow. Four metres was the best average day's progress over twelve consecutive working days, and it was not until 1918 that the breakthrough was made. For fifteen years workmen endured heavy snowfalls and toiled in violent winds and freezing temperatures before the tunnel, 8.6 km in length, finally opened in 1923. At the time it was the seventh longest in the world. Only then did the last of the Cobb & Co coaches make its final journey across the Main Divide. (The coach (1888), once reserved for Prime Minister "King Dick" Seddon's use, is in the park headquarters.)

**Temple Basin Skifield:** The field is administered by the Christchurch Ski Club (*Box 2493, Christchurch for information and bookings for accommodation, which is sometimes available*). Some equipment is for hire. At times it is possible to ski here very early even on January mornings, but few take advantage of the opportunity.

**ARTHUR'S PASS ROAD***     Map 2.    Height: 921.6 m.**

*193 km from Greymouth to Sheffield. Note: Caravans and loads longer than 12 m are not permitted on the section between Otira and Arthur's Pass township. The road can be temporarily closed by wintry conditions but vehicles may be railed through the Otira Tunnel between Otira and Arthur's Pass township.*

AS ALTITUDES RANGE, clear contrasts are afforded between the mixed rainforests and gorges of Westland, the snow and ice of the Main Divide, the broad tawny tussock-lands surrounded by scree-sloped mountains, and the fertile flats and broad shingle riverbeds of Canterbury. The road lies through △Arthur's Pass National Park, into which lead a number of walking tracks.

Though basically an east-west passage, the road over the Main Divide actually lies from north to south. Approached from Westland, the gentle ascent to the summit is abruptly broken when the road narrows to writhe through the Otira Gorge, a ravine particularly splendid in late summer when the scarlet of *rata* mirrors red lichen on river boulders. Similarly, the gentle descent into Canterbury is interrupted by the sharp southern slope of Porters Pass.

## SOME HISTORY

**The building of the road:** A road over the pass was wanted, not by Westland with its busy ports, but by Christchurch, hungry for the trade that would come its way if the flow of gold could be directed through the capital of Canterbury.

In April 1855 work began — the roadmen had, in fact, been waiting at Lake Pearson ready to start work while George Dobson and his father Edward made the final choice of route. At first a bridle track was mooted, but in June the Provincial Council allocated a tentative £20,000 for a coach road and nearly 1,000 men were spread along the line to build it. They toiled in conditions of extreme hardship unlightened by adequate shelter or food. Nor was their lot improved by the procession of miners who trudged through while work continued, for there were no supplies for them on the way and the ill-prepared fortune-seekers were often in need of help from the roadmen. In a remarkable achievement, the entire road was completed in barely a year, albeit at a cost of £145,000. Not that the road was an easy one to use: coaches were jolted so violently that sturdier models had to be specially built for the run; and fully thirteen rivers had to be forded, the Bealey alone being crossed up to twelve times.

The enterprise did not have the desired result. Gold continued to leave the West Coast by sea; the solitary trip by the gold escort ended in humiliation (*see* △*Hokitika*) and the inhabitants of Westland, irate at having to contribute to the cost of a road they had never wanted, soon moved to secede from Canterbury Province. The road did however prove useful as a cattle track, and much stock from east Canterbury was driven across to feed the goldminers on the other side of the Divide.

The story of the road ends in tragedy. George Dobson, having laid the line for the road, stayed on the West Coast to take charge of road construction near Greymouth. In 1866 he was murdered by the infamous Sullivan gang (*see index*).

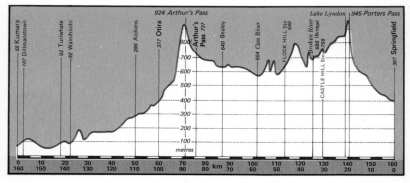

*Profile of the Arthur's Pass Road*

## POINTS OF INTEREST ON THE WAY

*In geographical order, starting from Greymouth.*

Leave Greymouth, south on Highway 6.

**Taramakau River** (*14 km from Greymouth; 173.2 km from Sheffield*): A river famed for the greenstone of its upper reaches is crossed by a narrow combined road-rail bridge. *At Kumara Junction (17.3 km from Greymouth; 169.9 km from Sheffield) turn inland to pass through:*

△**Kumara*** (*24 km from Greymouth; 163.2 km from Sheffield*): An old goldtown, home of the renowned "King Dick", Prime Minister Richard John Seddon. *The road passes through 4 km of pleasant bush to rejoin the Taramakau. There are several pleasant picnic places and viewpoints before:*

# ARTHUR'S PASS ROAD

## 2

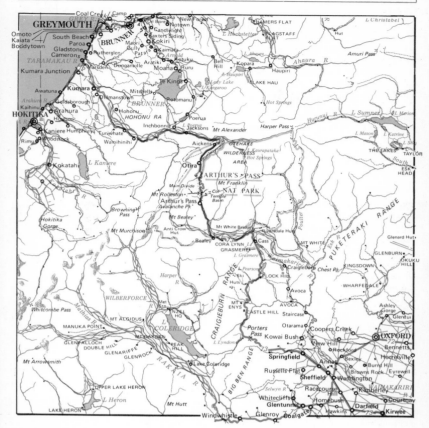

**Jacksons** (*62.6 km from Greymouth; 124.6 km from Sheffield*): The wayside tavern here, refurnished in the style of the coaching inn it once was, is the survivor of five that refreshed horses, passengers and drivers before the rail link was forged through the Alps. For several busy years the locality was both railhead and staging post, but faded when the line was extended up to Otira. Early photographs illustrate the past of the tavern and the departed settlement.

△**Arthur's Pass National Park:** The park is entered at 73.2 km from Greymouth (*114 km from Sheffield*).

**Otira** (pop. 163) (*381 m.a.s.l.*) (*81 km from Greymouth; 106.2 km from Sheffield*): A railway settlement by the river, near the portal to the Otira rail tunnel. In view of the tunnel's considerable length, to overcome ventilation problems trains are pulled through by electric locomotives. Maintenance staff are also housed here. Otira means food for a journey, or out of the sun. *Above Otira the road narrows and bush-framed vistas of the mountains unfold. After crossing and recrossing the Otira River the road climbs steeply to pass a:*

**Lookout** (*88.1 km from Greymouth; 99.1 km from Sheffield*): An awesome alpine viewpoint. After rain the slopes are laced with waterfalls.

**Main Divide** (*921.6 m*): The boundary between Canterbury and Westland. Curiously, the pass at Porters Pass is very slightly higher than this point though not on the Main Divide.

**Arthur Dobson Memorial** (*91.2 km from Greymouth; 96 km from Sheffield*): A memorial to the surveyor/engineer who discovered the pass in 1864. Opposite the monument is the start of a fascinating nature walk (*allow 1 hr one way; illustrated booklet available from the park headquarters*).

**Temple Basin Skifield road** (*91.9 km from Greymouth; 95.3 km from Sheffield*): For details of the field, see △Arthur's Pass National Park (*above*). At the commencement of the road a signpost identifies surrounding peaks.

> Journey all over the universe in a map, without the expense and fatigue of travelling, without suffering the inconveniences of heat, cold, hunger, and thirst. —Miguel de Cervantes.

**Jack's Hut** (*92.6 km from Greymouth; 94.6 km from Sheffield*): An old roadman's hut whose story is told in *Jack's Hut* by Grace Adams (Reed). Opposite, a track gives access to Bealey Chasm (*an easy 20 mins return walk*), Margaret's Tarn, the Bealey Glacier and Mt Rolleston.

**Bridal Veil Walk** (*starts 93.1 km from Greymouth; 94.1 km from Sheffield*): Here one's passengers may follow a track that runs virtually parallel to the road and includes a short detour to the foot of the Bridal Veil Falls. They may rejoin their driver in about ¾ hr at Arthur's Pass township. The nature walk is described in a brochure available at the park headquarters.

**Punchbowl Falls** (*94.6 km from Greymouth; 92.6 km from Sheffield*): Viewed from the road. The 131.2 m falls are seen to greater advantage by making the walk in.

**Arthur's Pass township** (*pop. 131*) (*736 m.a.s.l.*) (*95.2 km from Greymouth; 92 km from Sheffield*): The park headquarters includes a display of the history of the national park. A licensed restaurant serves an informal smorgasbord luncheon, usually from 11 am to 3 pm; there are also picnicking facilities. *For further details of things to see and do at the township, see △ Arthur's Pass National Park. The road passes through the township and follows the Bealey River, passing:*

**Greyneys Flat** (*101.2 km from Greymouth; 86 km from Sheffield*): A pleasant road-side camping and picnic place.

**Klondyke Corner** (*103.2 km from Greymouth; 84 km from Sheffield*): A point just above the confluence of the Bealey and Waimakariri Rivers where coaches once forded the river. The corner takes its name from goldmining days, the Klondyke being an Alaskan goldfield. A hut here accommodated those marooned by the fickle river from the now-vanished Bealey township. A well-bushed camping and picnic area.

**Waimakariri Riverbridge** (*105.5 km from Greymouth; 81.7 km from Sheffield*): Just off the road, at the south end of the bridge and about a kilometre inside the national park boundary, is a tranquil picnicking and camping spot.

**Bealey Spur** (*108.5 km from Greymouth; 78.7 km from Sheffield*): A growing huddle of holiday homes above the road was established after Arthur's Pass township had spread to its limits. There was once a staging settlement on the shingle flats below here. The spur is named after Samuel Bealey, who also has named after him the river, the flat, a glacier, a chasm and a mountain. He was Superintendent of Canterbury in 1865, at the time when Arthur Dobson (an employee of the Provincial Government) named the river.

*The road follows the Waimakariri for a short time before bending round Corner Knob and leaving the river. It is here skirting Mt Horrible (1,233.1 m), a name, like that of adjacent Mt Misery (1,760.8 m), bestowed with feeling by surveyors who endured an uncomfortable time there.*

**Lake Grasmere** (*125.2 km from Greymouth; 62 km from Sheffield*): A tiny lakelet in open tussockland, with brown and rainbow trout. An experimental sheep run is maintained here by the North Canterbury Catchment Board where demonstrations are given and research undertaken.

**Lake Pearson** (*131.2 km from Greymouth; 56 km from Sheffield*): Very much larger than Grasmere, the open lake describes a figure eight. Noted for its brown and rainbow trout, the lake was named after Joseph Pearson, the first European to explore the upper Waimakariri and who took up the Burnt Hill run in 1851. The area from here south is taken up by the Flock Hill run, now administered by the New Zealand Forest Service as a revegetation nursery and an area where shrubs, grasses and clovers are selected for use in the revegetation of eroded mountain lands. The early runholders repeatedly burnt the tussocklands, and only comparatively recently have concerted steps been taken to revegetate the high tops and so check the flow of shingle into the rivers.

**Castle Hill** (*148.4 km from Greymouth; 38.8 km from Sheffield*): Now distinguished by weatherworn rain-smoothed outcrops of limestone, this was once a staging post on the coast route to the West Coast.

**Porters Heights turnoff** (*153.3 km from Greymouth; 33.9 km from Sheffield*): The turnoff to commercial skifields of growing popularity as the closest field to Christchurch. In season tows run every day. Equipment for hire. No accommodation on the field.

**Lake Lyndon** (*156.7 km from Greymouth; 30.5 km from Sheffield*): Unlike Grasmere and Pearson, the lake is generally frozen right over in winter, so attracting ice-skaters, though not in the same numbers as Lake Ida (*see index*). The lakeside lodge is used by skiers from Porters Heights. From here a fine-weather road leads 20 km to △ Lake Coleridge and Lake Ida, lakes more usually approached by way of Windwhistle.

Lake Lyndon lies beneath Mt Lyndon (*1,476.5 m*); to the north-east lies the Torlesse Range. In legend the giant bird Poua-kai settled on the summit of Tawera (Mt Torlesse), snatching wayfarers in the mountains and carrying them off to his nest. Finally Ruru, a noted bird hunter, led an expedition. In a hollow hidden from Poua-kai's view they constructed a cage large enough to hold the group. Ruru then sauntered along the mountainside until he attracted the giant bird's attention. The hunter took refuge in the cage, and though Poua-kai tore at the cage and raked some members of the party with its long talons, others hacked at the giant bird's legs until they severed them from its body. Then those who had survived the ordeal emerged to club the helpless bird to death and to smash the eggs and kill the fledglings that were nesting on the mountaintop. Tawera was renamed Mt Torlesse when it was climbed for the first time by a European, the surveyor Charles Torlesse, a nephew of Edward Gibbon Wakefield. *The road climbs steadily to crest:*

**Porters Pass** (*945.5 m.a.s.l.*) (*159.2 km from Greymouth; 28 km from Sheffield*): Occasionally blocked by snow and a popular tobogganing spot. The pass is somewhat higher than Arthur's Pass itself, on the Main Divide. The telegraph pole here is reputed to be the highest in the country. The pass is named after the family who first took up the Castle Hill run.

*From here the road descends precipitously to fall in with the Kowai River and, accompanied by a lengthy irrigation water race, emerges on to the rich foothills of the Canterbury plains. The road levels out into a series of flat straights, so typical of the plains, passing through:*

**Springfield** (pop. 310) (*178.8 km from Greymouth; 8.4 km from Sheffield*): A little farming community whose earlier name of Kowai Pass is perpetuated in a pleasant domain.

**Sheffield** (pop. 182) (*187.2 km from Greymouth; 60 km from Christchurch*): A railway and farming settlement whose Yorkshire name, like that of Darfield, was given by the Yorkshireman John Jebson, one of the first to work the area's lignite deposits.

Here Highway 72 diverges to pass through △Oxford and △Rangiora. Highway 73 continues through Darfield and West Melton to △Christchurch.

**Darfield** (pop 1,007) (*14 km from Sheffield*): The seat of Malvern County. Over the irrigation channel that has been near the road since the Kowai River, there is at Kirwee (*8.6 km E*) a curious dome erected to commemorate Colonel De Renzie James Brett MLC, Knight of the Medjidieh, Turkey, who persevered to provide a water supply for the Canterbury plains from the Kowai River. It was Brett, a veteran of India, Burma and the Crimea, who bestowed on his run the locality's Indian name.

---

A key to area maps appears on page 2.

---

**ASHBURTON***     **Mid-Canterbury.**     **Maps 3 & 35.**     **Pop. 14,250.**

*87 km SW of Christchurch; 77 km NE of Timaru.*

STATELY TREES on a once desertlike waste beautify Ashburton, the thriving centre of Mid-Canterbury. The trees date back over a century, as do many of the town's substantial brick buildings.

Inland, the abiding impression is of vast tracts of plain which seem to extend to the abrupt line of the Southern Alps — a distant view of many moods and changing colour values. The plains earn for the district the sobriquet of the "Granary of New Zealand".

The town's name comes from the river by which it stands, which was named after Lord Ashburton who, as the Hon. Francis Baring, was prominent in Edward Gibbon Wakefield's New Zealand Association of 1837.

There is magnificent fishing for salmon and sea-run trout in the Rakaia, Rangitata and Ashburton Rivers.

## SOME GEOLOGY

Where a number of streams or rivers emerge from a mountainous area and build fans at their mouths, the fans can link to form a continuous apron along the mountain foot. The Canterbury Plain is a classic example of such a piedmont alluvial plain, or bahada, with a slope away from the mountains and a number of convex areas. The formation is particularly apparent when the broad, braided rivers that ribbon the Plain are seen from the air. The Plain has built up of silt and glacial outwash gravel, in places several hundreds of metres thick. The inland mountains and foothills are of Triassic greywacke and argillite.

## SOME HISTORY

**The Moa-hunter:** A number of Moa-hunter campsites dating back over 500 years have been located in the area, either near a rivermouth or inland on the fringe of the foothills. These show the Moa-hunter as nomadic, moving from place to place as his food requirements demanded, the attraction of the coast being the fish, and of the foothills the birds the forest there had to offer. In rock shelters at Mount Somers and Inverary some primitive rock drawings have been discovered.

For the later Classic Maori, the district seems to have held little appeal and although it was crossed from time to time no permanent settlements appear to have been established.

**The trans-Rakaia "desert":** To early European travellers the area between the Rakaia River and the Ashburton was notorious. The first of such travellers to keep a record of his journey was the missionary, Bishop Selwyn, who in 1844 noted: "We had a tract of twenty-four miles to pass without fresh water over a dry and gravelly plain . . . The want of water is so unusual in New Zealand that I think this is only the second or third time I have been obliged to carry it."

Parts that were not arid were swamp. On the way back, Selwyn crossed the Rangitata to find, "a good hut built there for the convenience of travellers", and filled "several glass bottles . . . left on purpose for this service; [they] had already travelled many times backwards, and forwards, across the space we were about to attempt."

Selwyn described the region as having "no trees in any direction on the plain, the only growth being tufts of grass, stunted fern and 'tutu'." Today it is difficult to visualise the fertile, closely-cropped plains as a vast and treeless expanse of brown-grey tussock, with dense clouds of sand and grit billowing before the perennial nor'westers.

**Turton's Accommodation House:** As runs were taken up in the vicinity, William Turton, his wife and baby daughter, came to the present site of Ashburton, in 1858 leasing 120 hectares as a ferry reserve and building an accommodation house by the river (*the site is indicated by an Historic Places marker by the road bridge*). His liquor licence, like others elsewhere, was conditional upon his providing accommodation for travellers and ensuring the continual presence of a servant to pilot wayfarers across the treacherous riverbed. At this time the only indication of the route from the Rakaia River to the Hinds was a single plough furrow made by Dobson, a Government surveyor, to serve as a guide for travellers — over marshy segments strips of calico were tied to bushes of Wild Irishman. Even when coaches were introduced, the journey was far from being without peril, as Lady Barker (a runholder's wife) recorded in 1867; after dining at the accommodation house she changed coaches: "The moment the groom let go the horses' heads, [the new coachman] stood up on his seat, shook the reins, flourished his long whip, and with one wild yell from him we dashed down a steep cutting into the Ashburton. The water flew in spray over our heads, and the plunge wetted me as effectually as if I had fallen into the river."

**Ashburton emerges:** During the 1860s a smattering of unpainted cottages grew up near the accommodation house but by the time the railway had forged south from Rakaia and the river had been bridged, Ashburton had wrested from South Rakaia the role of principal centre for the plains. With the rail and road bridge came a great leap forward in Ashburton's development and soon a start was made to plant the trees the town then so desperately needed and today so much enjoys.

**John Grigg** (1828–1901): For a long time the mile-wide Rakaia acted as a barrier to agricultural development to the south, giving squatters ample time to secure large blocks of land. The most noteworthy of these was John Grigg of Longbeach, a Cornishman who arrived in the district in 1864 and turned the 13,000-ha property he farmed with his brother-in-law Thomas Russell into "the best farm in the world." While so doing he opened a kiln to produce the field tiles needed for the 240 km of drains that converted almost impassable bog into pasture. After Russell withdrew in 1882, Grigg switched to intensive farming. By 1896 he was cultivating over 1,200 ha of wheat, 285 ha of barley, 723.7 ha of oats, and substantial areas of peas, rape and turnips. As many as 45,000 sheep were fattened annually, 3,000 pigs were raised and butter and ham were exported to Australia. At harvesting times up to 300 men with as many horses were employed. Grigg, whose motto was "The best pays the best", became renowned for his Friesian cattle and Southdown sheep flock, prize rams and ewes being imported in 1901 from King Edward's flock at Sandringham. He also pioneered the frozen meat industry in the province, being prominent in the establishment of the Fairfield freezing works and personally providing half the cargo of the first frozen meat shipment to leave Lyttelton for Britain, early in 1883. It was the profitability of raising sheep for the frozen meat industry which ended the great era of grain production in the district.

**Irrigation:** If Grigg had to drain swamps, others had to combat a lack of moisture, so that today the district is crisscrossed with a water-race system that has made possible the development of small mixed farms.

Even in the 1860s, runholders were cutting channels and water-races but it is Duncan Cameron who is generally credited with being the first to establish a systematic water supply on the dry but otherwise fertile plains of mid-Canterbury. By 1880 he had some 65 km of water-races nurturing his Springfield estate. In that year the local county council became involved in the provision of a comprehensive irrigation scheme, and if a reporter at the time could enthuse that the initial scheme had "to a great extent changed for the better the whole face of Nature in a wide district", time was to remove the hyperbole from his statement. By 1903 the council had constructed some 2,440 km of races supplying water to 243,000 ha, so attracting small farmers to even the driest of areas. The "desert" tag had been dissolved in one of the most effective schemes of any kind initiated by a local body.

Today the irrigation ditches are a familar sight on the plains. At the Winchmore Irrigation Research Station the Department of Agriculture carries out experiments on 300 ha of irrigated land. Large areas have been prepared for border-dyke irriga-

# ASHBURTON AND DISTRICT

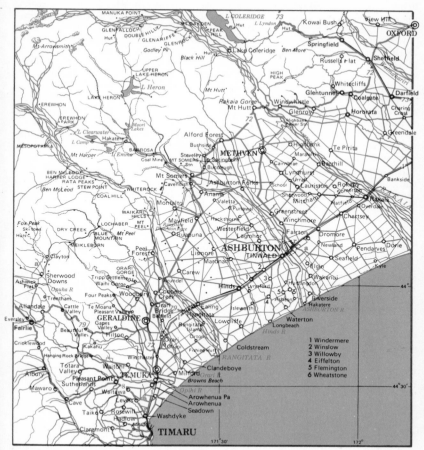

tion, about 500 mm of water being applied each season. Water is led from rivers which, being largely snow-fed, maintain a good summer supply. (*Visits to the Research Station at Winchmore may be made on weekdays by contacting the Station Superintendent. 15 km via Highway 1 and Methven-Dromore Road. Signposted.*

**Balls from space** rained on Ashburton paddocks in 1972, probably from a Russian *Cosmos 482* space probe intended for Venus. In all, five balls were found, automatically welded from an alloy unavailable in New Zealand, but neither Russia nor the USA would claim them, either for fear of compensation claims or to conceal the failure of the mission. Instead the pressure containers were left to become the country's first lost property from space.

## THINGS TO SEE AND DO

**Historical Society Museum:** The collection includes Turton's original hotel licence (1858), a report of a meeting on the need for a school (1868) and items relating to Edward Jerningham Wakefield. *Hours vary. Hakatere College, Cameron St East.*

**Ashburton Domain\*\*:** Massive trees, impeccable gardens and an artificial lake (formed from a mill's water-race) adorn an area where once grew only tussock. A small aviary, children's playground and tree-encircled playing fields round out the domain's appeal. A popular picnic place. No excuse was needed to plant trees, but one giant specimen planted in 1910 is dedicated to the memory of Florence Nightingale. *West St. Across the railway line from the main street, East St.*

**John Grigg's statue:** Shown in old age, bearded and stick in hand, Grigg stands in a garden setting utterly alien to the land as he first saw it. The base records the preoccupations of the district — ploughing, the harvesting of grain and the shearing of sheep. *Baring Sq.*

**Town Clock:** Originally situated in the old Post Office, from which it was removed as an earthquake risk, the town clock was refurbished after many years of gathering dust and installed in a tower especially designed for it, to celebrate 100 years of local government in Ashburton County. *Baring Sq East.*

**Millstone seat:** An old fluted millstone, used in Buchanan's flourmill for shelling oats, now serves as a seat in a small reserve. *Cnr Kermode and West Sts.*

**Edward Jerningham Wakefield's grave:** The only son (1820–79) of Edward Gibbon Wakefield ended his eventful life in Ashburton as an aging alcoholic. When twenty he had come to New Zealand as secretary to his uncle, Col. William Wakefield, the New Zealand Company's representative in New Zealand. Later, in London, he wrote a successful if inaccurate account of contemporary history entitled *Adventures in New Zealand* (1844). After returning to New Zealand with Godley on the *Lady Nugent* he became involved in politics, entering Parliament on the casting vote of the returning officer to represent the Canterbury country districts (*see △ Temuka*). However his overbearing temperament and dominating partisanship militated against success. His grave, like those of many of the town's pioneers, has been grassed, its headstone removed, and his name included on a common memorial. *Cnr Kermode and William Sts.*

**Interesting buildings:** Many of Ashburton's principal buildings are of brick, reflecting the town's once considerable ceramics industry. Noteworthy among these are the Lombardy-styled Catholic Church of the Holy Name (*Sealy St*), the impressive millhouse (*West St*), and four other churches that date from between 1878 and 1885.

**Tinwald Domain:** A pleasant shaded picnic spot, with swimming pool and willowed lake. A segment of the old Mount Somers railway (1880–1967) and two vintage locomotives are preserved by a local railway society. *4.5 km S. At Tinwald.*

### ENVIRONS

**Longbeach Chapel** (1873): The Grigg family chapel with high-pitched shingled roof was dragged here by bullock team from Prebbleton to stand in the homestead garden, well shaded by massive trees. Without are the family graves, and within are memorials (that to John Grigg subscribed to by his late employees). The walk to the chapel lies through part of the 6.8 ha of century-old gardens, themselves an impressive memorial to Grigg. The homestead (1937), the third on the site, has been host to royalty. *23.4 km S of Ashburton. Turn off Highway 1 at 6 km S. Private property.* The route lies through Eiffelton, so called as it was here that John Grigg built his tile-and-brick kiln, whose tall chimney resembled Paris's recently-completed Eiffel Tower.

**Mount Somers** (pop. 263) is a minute settlement with a number of limeworks. In its heyday the locality had a rail link with Ashburton, down which were trucked coal and thousands of tons of quarried stone destined for Melbourne, in the 1870s enjoying a building boom. Many of Melbourne's public buildings of Mount Somers stone remain, but forgotten are the Christchurch merchants who lost heavily when those to whom some of the stone was consigned failed to pay.

The area is renowned for its semi-precious stones, particularly round Barossa and in Petrified Wood Gully (on the Mount Somers estate). In the Clent Hills are jasper, agate, and a plentiful supply of chalcedony with its concentric rings of white, blue and green. A supposed diamond find in Diamond Slips (on Winterslow) once raised high hopes that faded almost immediately. Many fossils have been found in the area.

Sharplin Falls (*13 km from Mount Somers via Staveley*) are reached through a precious expanse of native beech forest (*Not as spectacular as they once were. Allow 1 hr return. First the smaller and then the larger falls are reached. Signposted from Staveley.*) There is an excellent picnic and camping spot by the river at the end of Flynn's Rd (*just beyond the final turnoff to the falls*). *43 km NW of Ashburton.*

**Lake Heron\*\*:** With rainbow trout and landlocked salmon, providing perhaps the best fishing of the lakes in the vicinity, Lake Heron is a wildlife refuge where the rare crested grebe may occasionally be found. There are here groves of mature trees, scarce in the surrounding wilderness of tussock, and attractive if well-used summer camping places. *78 km NW of Ashburton via Mount Somers. Powerboats prohibited.*

**△Erewhon (sheep station):** At Erewhon Park are facilities for those who hunt, climb, fish, tramp or ski. *92 km NNW.*

**△Mesopotamia station:** The memory of Samuel Butler lingers at the run he once held. *100 km NNW.*

**Rakaia Gorge\*\*\*:** The dramatic gorge has for generations been a popular picnicking and camping spot. (*See △Methven*). *48 km N.*

**Mount Hutt:** A recently developed skiing area featuring the longest lift-serviced ski run in the Southern Hemisphere. (*See △ Methven.*) *48 km NNW.*

### TOURING NOTES

**Plane table:** A plane table identifying peaks in the Alps is situated 10.8 km N on Highway 1.

**Tudor House:** A Tudor-styled house in which curiosities are displayed and on sale. *S on Highway 1. Hours vary. Admission charge.* At Winslow (*10 km*) is a lucerne dehydration plant whose output is shipped to Japan through the port of Timaru.

**Christchurch via Rakaia Gorge:** An alternative route to Christchurch is by way of △Methven and the Rakaia Gorge by Highways 77 and 72. The route adds 49 km to the direct route by Highway 1.

# BALCLUTHA AND DISTRICT

**4**

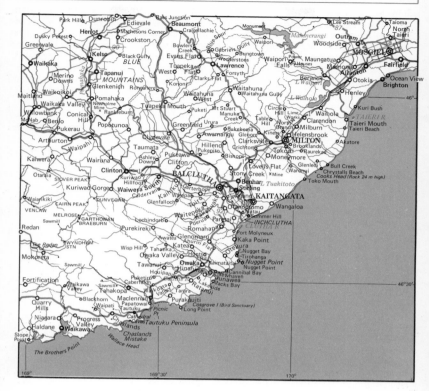

## BALCLUTHA    South Otago.    Maps 4, 9, 14 & 19.    Pop. 4,710.

*80 km SW of Dunedin; 140 km ENE of Invercargill.*

The principal centre of South Otago lies on the banks of the hurrying Clutha River, just before it divides to enclose the flat, fertile island of Inchclutha. As the distribution centre for most of the lower Clutha basin, Balclutha services a rich, predominantly sheepfarming area. Local works annually handle over 1.5 million carcasses. The town's Scottish origins are reflected in its name, Gaelic for "town on the Clyde".

### CLUTHA RIVER

The Clutha River, almost invariably described as the "mighty" Clutha, is named after Scotland's Clyde River, Clutha being Gaelic for Clyde. To the Maori the river was Mata-au (surface current).

Swift and broad, the Clutha is New Zealand's largest river, some 16 km shorter than the Waikato's 354 km but with an average discharge of almost twice the volume. By world standards this is still small, the Amazon's discharge being more than 300 times as great. The river drains about 2.2 million ha of widely varying country, including the lakes of Wakatipu, Wanaka and Hawea, and ranging from mountain peaks to the riverflats of Central Otago with an annual fall as low as 300 mm.

The Clutha and many of its tributaries were rich sources of gold. In 1900 there were no fewer than 187 dredges on the river, working the bed from its source at Lake Wanaka to the sea. Mountainous piles of tailings are much in evidence, particularly near Alexandra and Lowburn.

The only hydro-electric power station presently on the Clutha is at △Roxburgh but there are smaller stations on the Fraser and Teviot tributaries and on Roaring Meg. The river has vast power potential, now being developed amid controversy.

### MAORI LEGEND

**The killing of Kopuwai:** In legend, *kahui tipua* (giants who could step from mountaintop to mountaintop), lived in the hinterland. When bands of eeling and *weka*-hunting Te Rapuiwi went inland from their village on the mouth of the Clutha, none would return. Their disappearance remained a mystery until one day a woman, Kai-amio, returned to tell how she had encountered a *kahui tipua*, one Kopuwai, with ten two-headed dogs. The men she was with he had killed, but she had been kept for him to live with and in time she had become covered in scales from his body. To prevent her escape, Kopuwai had tied a rope around her which he would periodically jerk when she was out of sight.

The cave in which they had been living was close to the river, and as the giant lay sleeping Kai-amio had built a raft from bundles of *raupo*. She had made her escape down the swift flowing river, first tying her end of the tether to uncut *raupo* which, being elastic, prevented the immediate discovery of her flight. When the Kopuwai awoke and found Kai-amio gone, he had traced her footprints to the river's edge and in one mighty draught drank the river dry.

But he was too late, for Kai-amio was by then safe with her people. When she told them her story, her *hapu* (sub-tribe) set out to kill the giant. While he lay sleeping soundly as the warm and soporific north-west wind blew, they collected dry fern and piled it at the entrance to his cave. Once fired there was but one means of escape, through a hole in the roof of the cave. As Kopuwai struggled to get out, Kai-amio's relatives clubbed and battered him to death. Fortunately his dogs were away hunting, for otherwise the giant could never have been killed. Masterless, the animals wandered far afield and were eventually turned into stone in various pools along the river.

The Old Man Range was known to the Maori as Kopuwai after the ogre who once lived there, and Old Man Rock is a manifestation of him. Murihiku Maoris locate this legend on the Waiau River and call caves near △Clifden, Te Rua o te Kai-amio, the caves of Kai-amio.

Canon Stack, who recorded the legend, notes that Kopuwai means water stomach and refers to the immense volume of water carried by the Clutha. He suggests that the legend may recount a "convulsion of Nature" in which a chasm may have opened up and temporarily swallowed the waters of the river.

**A happy ending:** In mythology the river is personified as two people, Koau and his wife Matau, who were journeying to the sea from Lake Wanaka. All went happily until they reached Iwikatea (bleached bones — a name testimony to torrid fighting), now the site of Balclutha. Here they quarrelled and went their separate ways. Koau turned south and after many meanderings stumbled on the place where Matau was waiting to forgive him. From there, together they went singing to the sea.

Matau (right hand) was the name of the north branch as, entering from the sea, a canoe would have to turn right to paddle up it. Koau (shag) was the name of the southern branch and Wai-hakirara (singing water) the name given to the river below the junction. The legend refers to times when the two arms rejoined before entering the sea.

> The whole object of travel is not to set foot on foreign land; it is at last to set foot on one's own land as a foreign land. — G. K. Chesterton.

## SOME HISTORY

**The Ferry:** Thomas Redpath settled on the island of Inchclutha in 1849, though others had preceded him to settle elsewhere in the lower Clutha Valley. The site of Balclutha was given a wide berth, for it lay on an unattractive promontory almost surrounded by the Clutha River, swampy and covered in "great, big flapping flax, ten or twelve feet high".

The eventual town site proved to have the best river crossing. There, at the end of 1852 James McNeil (1799–1875) built a bark hut to become Balclutha's first resident and began a ferry service near the site of today's road bridge. The river's south bank quickly became a stopping place for travellers. The Ferry also achieved a small measure of commercial importance, though interest continued to centre on the fertile flats of Inchclutha, the land with the greatest potential for farming.

Not until the opening of the Otago goldfields and the consequent influx of settlers did The Ferry begin to take the shape of a town. John Barr opened an Accommodation House and then a store, James Rattray began business as a blacksmith and Tom Latta, an Australian, opened a brewery, selling beer by the bucketful for a shilling. In 1867 John Barr subdivided his holding, selling thirty of fifty-five sections offered and at prices sufficiently high to ensure that no time was lost in building on them. Even then the *Bruce Herald* could see that "This sale [has given] a fresh impetus to this spirited little township, which promises to become the centre of a large pastoral and agricultural district of country."

For a time boats steamed up the river, carrying supplies to the goldfields as far as Tuapeka Mouth. The gold temporarily retarded progress as local farmers went to the diggings to earn the money they needed for development. A punt replaced the ferry but as accidents were still commonplace, Balclutha acquired its first road bridge in 1868. It was to last only ten years, but by then the township was firmly established. Balclutha was elevated to borough status and its first mayor was John McNeil (1836–1905), son of the borough's first resident.

**The floods of 1878:** The winter of 1878 was a grim one for much of Otago and Southland. Abnormal snowfalls lay heavy and thick in the hinterland, and thousands of sheep froze to death in the drifts. With the September thaw, runholders, many of them ruined, began to count their losses. With the melting snow came devastation for Balclutha. Three times in a month the river rose to levels never before experienced, inundating the town, sweeping away buildings and silting up the remainder. The whole tract of country from Stirling to Kaitangata and as far north as Lovells Flat was under water. The railway was washed out, a horse and dray could be driven between the piles of the recently completed St Andrew's Church, and roads were scoured so severely that a man drowned in one of the holes.

Stories of narrow escapes abound, but few could match the tale told of the German carpenter, Rehberg. It is said that he was inside his home with his housekeeper when it was struck so heavily by a flood-borne log that it was lifted from its foundations and carried off downriver. All the while shouting for help, Rehberg somehow managed to keep the house upright as he clambered from corner to corner. None heard his cries until the dwelling was passing Inchclutha, where two brothers gave chase in a boat to rescue the couple only twenty minutes before the house was swept into the breakers.

The 1868 roadbridge was another casualty. In 1935 its replacement gave way to the present ferroconcrete structure so much a feature of the town.

The flooding was on such a scale that logic seemed to require the resiting of the town above the flat. This was not to be. A large floodbank was erected round the site and within its lee the town was defiantly rebuilt. The stopbank has withstood many floods, even if on occasions residents have had to work desperately for days on end to strengthen the embankment. Flooding remains a continual menace to both town and district.

**Steamers on the river:** To open up trade with the goldfields, the *Tuapeka* in 1863 began to ply between Port Molyneux on the coast and Tuapeka Mouth. Her replacement, *Clutha*, a side-paddle boat, was not a success, powered apparently by an engine taken from a steam plough and built on the river at Clydevale in 1871. The engine from *Tuapeka* was then used in the *Balclutha*, built at Port Molyneux. A series of ships followed — the *Iona, Matau, Clyde*, and the *Clutha*, the last of the line, which was still operating on the river in the 1940s. (*A telegraph from the* Clyde, *on the river in 1901, is mounted behind the reception desk in the Hotel South Otago*.)

A table of distances between major centres appears inside the back cover.

## A DRIVE TO KAKA POINT AND THE NUGGETS

*50 km return. Leave Balclutha on Highway 92 to reach the:*

**Telford Farm Training Institute** (*7 km*): The Institute was established in 1964 to give theoretical and technical instruction against a background of practical experience to those about to embark on farming careers. Technical training is given on every aspect of farmwork and farm management. Short courses are organised for farmers and others. The Institute has its origins in the gift of the 627 ha farm by descendants of William Telford, who arrived in New Zealand in 1867, acquired several thousand hectares of wasteland and developed it into good farmland. The farm is well suited for mixed farming and so provides students with diverse practical experience. The distinctive stone Otanomomo estate homestead (1869) stands by the roadside. (*To arrange a visit contact the Principal, tel. 81-550; 82-764 after hours*). At the homestead turn left to pass on the right Telfords Bush, in which is:

**Thomas Redpath's grave:** Redpath was buried, as was his wish, near a large tree that the trader was said to climb to watch for expected shipping. (*The reserve is presently closed to the public for conservation reasons.*) At 17.9 km turn right up Roma-hapa Rd and then left at 18.8 km to reach the:

**Port Molyneux cemetery\*\*\*:** The cemetery is a magnificent point from which to see up the coast to Coal Point and the meanderings of the lower Clutha across billiard-flat river plains. Plainly seen is the new-looking sandbar that dams the old south rivermouth and marks the former entry to the vanished harbour of Port Molyneux. Tuhawaiki, "Bloody Jack", (*see index*) was probably born on the tongue of land to the north of the old rivermouth, then part of the island of Inchclutha. Below, cattle now graze on the Octagon, planned as the hub for busy Port Molyneux. Once both port and town, Port Molyneux is today neither.

Cook in 1770 originally named Waikawa as Molineux's Harbour after the master of *Endeavour*, Robert Mollineux — on his death a year later described by Cook as "a young man of good parts, but unhappily given up to intemperance, which brought on disorders which put an end to his life". The name, then pronounced Molinux (with the x sounded) was occasionally so spelt. The name was transferred to the Clutha River where it was applied until the Otago settlers arrived. Cook also noted a considerable Maori population, but with the whalers came measles, and in a single epidemic nearly 2,000 Maoris died in a village near Port Molyneux, leaving but a handful of survivors.

Whaling ships visited the area and a small bay-whaling station operated for a short time in 1838. European settlement dates from 1840 when Thomas Jones, a Sydney wine-and-spirits merchant whose storekeeper brother founded the successful Australian chain of David Jones, sent a small group under George Willsher to protect a block of land he claimed to have bought from Tuhawaiki. For a few whaleboats and guns, some fishing tackle and flour, to a value of £43, Jones received a deed to 103,600 ha — extending 16 km to either side of the Clutha River and some 32 km inland, including the sites of Balclutha and Kaitangata and very nearly those of Waiwera and Milton. Willsher and three others arrived after a foul four-week voyage that took heavy toll of their animals, only a solitary cow surviving. She was in calf, and an anxious time passed before she was delivered of a bull-calf who, mated to his mother, established a successful herd.

When Jones's land claim was disallowed, Willsher was in difficulties but ultimately was personally granted about 8 ha (now part of a reserve that backs Kaka Point).

Frederick Tuckett, in search of a site for the Otago settlement, was highly pleased with the district's fertility and might well have chosen Port Molyneux had he thought the rivermouth possessed sufficient draught for large vessels.

With settlement the port boomed. Pilot station, customs officer, an imposing array of shops, stores and hotels, and an inevitable land boom — over a period of almost thirty years Port Molyneux knew them all.

Then in quick succession fell two crippling blows. First the railway opened from Dunedin to Balclutha, claiming much of the port's freight. Then, only a few months later, came the torrential floods of 1878 when the Clutha so bore down débris that it blocked its outlet and burst two fresh openings to the north.

Port Molyneux, once on a rivermouth, was left with a sandbank where ships had lain at anchor. The port that almost brought the Otago settlement to the Clutha was no more. *Return to the coast road. Straight ahead, at the foot of Romahapa Rd, lies a survivor of Port Molyneux, once its town hall. Turn right to follow the coast road and reach:*

**Kaka Point**\*\* (pop. 162) (*at 21 km*): A favoured seaside holiday place with a fine beach. Near Kaka Point was where the impudent Amy Bock (1864–?) achieved immortality. In 1908 one "Percy Redwood" arrived here and, as a fashionable and wealthy young man, quickly wooed and won the daughter of a Nuggets boarding-house proprietor. It was not until after the wedding, at which a local Member of Parliament proposed the bridal toast, that the "groom" was revealed as none other than Miss Amy Maud Bock, a notorious confidence trickster who had previously confined her activities to small swindles. Amy's greatest exploit ended dismally with her pleading guilty to charges of forgery, false pretences and making a false declaration. She was declared an habitual criminal and imprisoned for two years. *Continue through the settlement to pass the:*

**Willsher cairn** (*22.7 km*): On the corner of Karoro Stream Rd is a memorial to the little group Willsher led to pioneer European settlement in the region. *At the road's end is:*

**The Nuggets Lighthouse:** The distinctive "nuggets" that mark the southernmost end of the bay the Clutha feeds include the point on which the Nuggets Lighthouse stands. The 10-m tower stands some 76 m above sea level. Its light, visible for 35 km, flashes twice each twelve seconds. *The lighthouse may be inspected by arrangement with the keeper.* There are no moorings for the fishing boats whose home is on the point, so that the local fleet are simply winched high and dry on to the sand.

## WAITEPEKA ROUND TRIP

*40 km. The drive leads through varying countryside. Prior arrangements should be made to see the Somerville Museum. Leave Balclutha south on Highway 1, and at 2 km turn left towards Waitepeka. Once 500 m past White Flat Rd detour briefly to the right to reach:*

**Somerville private museum** (*9.1 km*): A small private museum in the huddle of buildings that served an early flourmill. (*To arrange a visit contact E. G. Dix, tel. 80-673.*) *At 10.4 km detour left along Guernsey Rd for a wide low view of the sea and of Kaitangata. Turn right down Waitepeka School Rd (as one turns note the remains of an old sod fence on the left by the corner with Mercer Rd). Bear left in to Hillfoot Rd to see in gum trees to the right the distant:*

**Willowmead homestead** (*c. 1857*) (*seen from the road at about 14 km*): Built of pitsawn timber, predominantly *totara*, the homestead stands on a terrace overlooking undulating country. Built in the style of the period, with twin dormer windows and walls rammed with tussock and clay, the house was the residence of Sir John Larkin Cheese Richardson (1810–78). Richardson retired to New Zealand from India and quickly became embroiled in local politics, succeeding James Macandrew as Superintendent of Otago after leading impeachment proceedings against him. (Macandrew had embezzled public money, and when arrested for debt in 1861 used his powers as Superintendent to declare his own home a prison and a place of detention. The Governor intervened and ordered his temporary removal to the Dunedin gaol.)

Entering national politics Richardson held cabinet rank before becoming Speaker of the Legislative Council (the since-abolished Upper House). Such was his standing that in Invercargill, which looked on Dunedin with no great favour, shops were closed for the day of his funeral. Even Macandrew, whom he had impeached years earlier and who had since enjoyed a remarkable return to popularity that all but led to his becoming prime minister, was moved to declare the occasion a State funeral. It was to Major Richardson that Gabriel Read reported his fabulous find of gold. *Turn up School Rd. At its end, to the left, is:*

**Manning's grave:** In the small cemetery here lies Dr Henry Manning (?1815–?1885), Otago's first doctor, the surgeon on the *John Wickliffe* and a theatrical character who once challenged Justice Stephen to a duel. Always unpredictable, he tended the poor without fee but made up for this with heavy bills to the well-to-do and to those he did not like (that is, in the event of his deigning to treat them at all). Beside the graveyard a tablet marks the site of the first church built in South Clutha (1850). *Return to the foot of the road. Turn left and then right, down Romahapa Rd to meet Highway 92. Turn left and return to Balclutha past the Telford Farm Training Institute (see above).*

### OTHER ENVIRONS

△**Kaitangata:** A former coaltown with an appetising name. *12 km SE.*

**Chicory kiln** (1881): The stone kiln on "The Inch" supplied the country with chicory until about 1950, when it proved cheaper to import. The firm would give the necessary seed to local farmers to grow the blue-flowered plant whose taproot was dried and ground to make chicory — used with or in place of coffee. *9 km. At the NW tip of Inchclutha, at the extreme end of Centre Rd.*

**Benhar:** Potteries here produce the only sanitary ware in the South Island. *7 km. McSkimming Industries. Tel. 82-215 Balclutha to arrange a visit. Allow 1 hr.*

**Lovells Flat Sod Cottage\*\*:** Once with an upstairs attic, the old sod cottage has been restored and furnished in period as a single-roomed colonial home. *12.1 km N on Highway 1.*

**Tuapeka Mouth** is a pleasant run up the left bank of the Clutha, through carefully manicured countryside. At Tuapeka the sole survivor of a number of punts across the Clutha is moved across the river by the current. This was as far upriver as the river steamers could ply, and this place saw feverish activity during goldrush times. A typically rumbustious goldtown mushroomed at the mouth of the Tuapeka River soon after Gabriel Read had made his spectacular discoveries at Lawrence. For a time the town seemed to have a future as a riverport, but the vagaries of the river at Port Molyneux and her perilous sandbanks ended what hopes there were, but not before steamers on the river had become a familiar sight. The tiny settlement was very much isolated until 1924, when a road to Balclutha was completed and the Clutha bridged at Clydevale. *36 km. The punt is generally free but there is a small charge for after-hours service.*

*Having crossed the river one may turn downstream to return to Balclutha by way of Clydevale.*

### TOURING NOTES

**Routes to** △**Invercargill:** A slower but recommended route to Invercargill is by way of △Owaka on the route described under △Invercargill-Balclutha Coastal Road.

Points of interest on Highway 1 south from Balclutha include △Clinton, △Gore, △Mataura and △Edendale.

**North to** △**Dunedin:** Almost immediately one passes Lovells Flat Sod Cottage (*see above*) before reaching in turn △Milton, △Lake Waihola, and △Mosgiel. At Lake Waihola one may leave Highway 1 to cross to Taieri Mouth and from there drive to Dunedin along the coast, by way of Brighton.

**BALCLUTHA-INVERCARGILL COAST ROAD\*\*\*** *See entry* △*Invercargill-Balclutha Coast Road.*

In 1948, Otago Centennial Historical Publications produced a series of regional histories, among them *Port Chalmers: Gateway to Otago* by H. O. Bowman; *Beyond the Blue Mountains* (West Otago) by F. W. G. Miller; *Northern Approaches* (Waitati, Waikouaiti, Palmerston, Dunback etc.) by C. W. S. Moore; *Run, Estate and Farm* (Kakanui and Waiareka Valleys) by W. H. Scotter; *The Taieri Plain* by M. S. Stewart and E. D. Farrant; *Faith and Toil* (Tokomairiro) by M. S. Shaw and E. D. Farrant and *Pioneering in South Otago* by Fred Waite.

*The Old Whaling Days* (Whitcombe and Tombs) and *Murihiku and the Southern Islands* (Wilson & Horton), both by Robert McNab, remain landmarks seventy years after publication.

## BANKS PENINSULA***     Canterbury.    Map 5.

CAPTAIN JAMES COOK made two glaring errors when he circumnavigated and mapped New Zealand — he linked Stewart Island to the South Island mainland to the exclusion of Foveaux Strait, and he showed Banks Peninsula as an island. His error in respect of the peninsula was only in time, for the massive twin volcanic craters that meld to form the peninsula were once encircled by water. Only in recent geological times has the dome come to be tied to the mainland by the shelf of mountain-washed shingle that imperceptibly crept out from the feet of the Southern Alps. Deep and narrow valleys gash the greatly eroded old basaltic cones, radiating out to the coast.

The two craters nurse the two principal harbours — Lyttelton and Akaroa, the earliest landing places for Canterbury settlers. As the South Island's only noticeably volcanic district, the peninsula is invested with distinctive character. Both geologically and geographically it is set apart from the rest of Canterbury. Spectacular views are gained from the crater walls, of which the Port Hills form part, both into the harbours and down to an unforgettable coastline. Some of the northern beaches are the finest to be found.

### SOME HISTORY

**The Kai huanga feud:** The peninsula was early favoured by the Maori as an area easily defended and with a plentiful food supply. For generations after they had over-whelmed the Ngatimamoe, the Ngaitahu grew in both numbers and wealth. Each year expeditions would cross to the West Coast for greenstone which, when pro-cessed, was traded far and wide for cloaks, potted muttonbirds and other needed items. The development of trade with the increasing number of visiting *Pakeha* promised a continuance of peace and prosperity, but instead there erupted the *Kai huanga* (eat relation) feud that not only dislocated the entire social system but nearly annihi-lated the Maori population of the district.

Undoubtedly other causes were also at work, but the immediate reason for the quarrel was the wearing by Murihaka, wife of Potahi, of a *kuriawarua* (dogskin cape) that belonged to the chief Te Maiharanui. Such an invasion of *tapu* demanded *utu* which was exacted on a slave belonging to one of Murihaka's relations. Her relations in turn took revenge, but on relatives of those who had killed the slave. So the skirmishes took place on an ever-widening basis; increasing numbers of battles were fought, and by the time Te Rauparaha judged it propitious to invade from the north (an action that inevitably forced the dislocated Ngaitahu to reunite) the tribe was depleted to the point of having little chance of successfully defending itself. (*See* △ *Kaiapoi*).

**From island to peninsula:** Cook named the peninsula Banks's Island, after the naturalist Sir Joseph Banks, who accompanied him on his first voyage. The error was detected in 1809, when Captain Chase attempted to sail the *Pegasus* between "island" and shore, but the name continued to be used uncorrected until 1813.

As whalers and traders for flax and timber became more frequent visitors, more particular names were given — in 1829 Captain Wiseman, agent for the Sydney traders Messrs Cooper & Levy, named the two harbours on the northern shoreline after his employers (Port Cooper is now Lyttelton; the latter name remains). Eight years later George Hempleman established a shore-whaling station on the southern perimeter, at Peraki, and increasing numbers of whalers were attracted to make their headquarters on the peninsula's "capacious and beautiful bays and inlets". One of these was Captain Jean Langlois, whose provisional purchase of land in 1838 led to the founding two years later by his fellow Frenchmen of the colony at △ Akaroa.

In the last few years before the assumption of British sovereignty a number of squatters arrived to take up land either leased or purchased from the Maoris, among them the Rhodes brothers (*see index*). The little bay-heads were, until the construc-tion of roads, isolated from each other and totally dependent on coastal shipping. Podocarp forest once covered the valleys, dwindling to beech and scrub on the high points. A valuable source of timber, the whole of the forest had by 1900 been virtually cleared in a riot of ruthless cutting. In the wake of the timber men, English grasses were sown. For many years cocksfoot seed, locally harvested by hand, was much sought after by North Island areas where previously-forested districts were being broken in.

### PLACES OF INTEREST ON THE PENINSULA

*Listed in clockwise order from Lyttelton.*

△**Lyttelton***: Landing place for the Pilgrims and still Canterbury's sea-door. **Governors Bay, Diamond Harbour** and **Purau** are all described under △ Lyttel-ton.

**Port Levy:** About 6 km long and over 1 km wide, the harbour is sailed by small craft. There are boating facilities on the harbour's eastern coast and on the south-eastern shore at Puari, near the pine-treed wedge of Horomanga Island (island of treacherous rock). Road access is steep, narrow and slow, but the inhospitable harbour's quality of isolation is best savoured out of season.

**Pigeon Bay,** favoured by boatowners, has limited swimming, at high tide near the camping area. Two km towards the Summit Road is the Hay Scenic Reserve, which not only nurtures an area of native bush but also perpetuates the family name of the

# BANKS PENINSULA

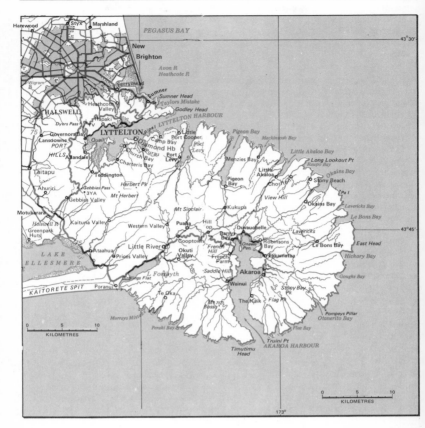

bay's first settlers. The unpretentious Knox Presbyterian Church (1898) also remembers the Hay family. As Anglicans now outnumber Presbyterians hereabouts, the building has been modified for their use. (*Near the store*). The Scot, Ebenezer Hay (1814–63) arrived on the *Bengal Merchant* in 1840, three years later establishing himself in the bay. He was among the first on the peninsula to introduce cocksfoot grass, which became an important local industry. Of historical as well as architectural interest is the attractive Brookshaw homestead (1876) (*turn right just beyond the store*) that possibly incorporates an even older, pre-fabricated structure.

**Little Akaloa**\*\* (pop. 42): Yet another haven for small craft. As the beach shelves steeply to provide an excellent anchorage, swimmers generally prefer the more gently sloping sands of nearby Okains Bay. On a knoll above the cove, set in trees, stands St Luke's Anglican Church (1906). Its predecessor was near the beach, and when estimates for its replacement proved prohibitive, J. H. Menzies (of Menzies Bay) designed a new church and organised a community effort to build it. He also gave the building distinctive character by liberally embellishing it with Maori-styled motifs, carved in both wood and stone.

**Okains Bay**\*\*\*: Fertile Okains Bay remains an inviting and unspoiled spot. At the broad, sandy, safe and gently shelving beach are traces of a wharf, demolished several years ago, on which early guidebooks noted "Visitors may have to be landed per the coal bucket." There are also a number of caves in the volcanic rock, at least one of them large enough to camp in.

The bay's timber was cut out at a prodigious rate by an early sawmiller, J. E. Thacker, whose descendants still live there. One branch of the family has established a Maori and Colonial Museum which includes restored buildings such as a slab cottage (1879), a local stable (1871) complete with gig, a smithy, and a saddlery housing material from the estate of C. E. Truscott whose family were saddlers in Christchurch for a century. The old dairy factory, as well as displaying cheese- and butter-making implements, contains a collection of early forms of transport used in the bay. Complementing the colonial collection is a Maori Antiquities Hall housing an extensive display of artefacts (including a *patu* used in the defence of Onawe pa) and a restored war canoe in its own shelter building. A rare sight in the South Island is the fully carved meeting house standing before the marae. *Open daily 10 am–5 pm. Closed Christmas Day.*

A short distance farther away from the shore stands the Church of St John the Evangelist (1863), built of local stone at the instigation of the Rev. Henry Torlesse. Opposite is the minute building (1861) that served as the local library. Most of the settlement's buildings date from Victorian times; most of its families, too, have been in the bay for a century. Like many other bays, Okains was named through a trifling incident. Captain Hamilton, who traded round the Peninsula, was sailing past the bay on one occasion when he happened to be reading a book by the Irish naturalist, Okain.

**Le Bon's Bay\*\*\*** (pop. 55): A scattering of baches back Le Bon's safe, sheltered beach and its poplar-encircled sports ground. The western arm is tipped by contorted sea-sculpted rock. Along the foot of the eastern arm run the remnants of the quay from which for a century jutted the wharf that provided the bay with its only communication. There are two fine old homesteads, and a new church, the Church of St Andrew (1959) in memory of Henry and Jane Barnett, early settlers of Le Bons Bay, who are buried beside it.

The inlet was covered in dense bush when the first European settlers arrived in 1857, to mill the heavy timber and ship it out to Christchurch. Perhaps its most momentous year was 1868, when the tidal wave that so shook the confidence of the peninsula's settlers swept ashore to lift a house and carry it bodily up the flat before depositing it on the tops of the trees. Soon afterwards a piece of gold-impregnated quartz was discovered. Supposing this to have been washed up by the tidal wave, the millhands were gripped by gold fever until lack of success brought the realisation that a practical joke had been perpetrated.

Explanations for the bay's name vary. Some say that early whalers would try out whales in the bay, which became known as Bone Bay as the beach was littered with whale skeletons. Others aver that a French vessel mistook the inlet for the entrance to Akaroa harbour and that one of the crew of the boat that landed here was named Le Bon.

△**Akaroa\*\*\*:** An enchanting Victorian village that began as the country's only French settlement. There was a bridle track out to Akaroa for the many years that passed before the road was put in. It was so well worn by honeymooners that it was known as the "bridal path".

**Peraki:** The Prussian, George Hempleman (1799–1880) came to New Zealand in 1835 and established the Peninsula's first shore-whaling station here two years later under the protection of the Ngaitahu chief, Taiaroa. His base was periodically plundered by visiting chiefs from other *hapu* of Ngaitahu and his harsh treatment of local Maoris attracted the concerned attention of Captain Stanley of HMS *Britomart*. Hempleman claimed to have purchased much of the peninsula in 1839; he was awarded an area of about 1,000 ha, but this he rejected as too small. For years he pressed for more favourable treatment but when he died in 1880 at the age of eighty-one he did so a poor man and without what he considered to be his just entitlement.

About 400 m off the east head of Peraki is a low reef. Once, in the dim light of a winter's morning, over-eager French whalers harpooned the rock by mistake, and ever since it has been called "the Frenchman's whale".

**Little River** (pop. 171) is the peninsula's largest settlement after Lyttelton and Akaroa. St Andrew's Anglican Church (1879) stands on a site given by W. Watson, a settler prominent in the early establishment of cocksfoot grass on the peninsula. Inside the Mountfort-designed building is a stone formally dedicated in 1939 as the foundation stone "for the new church". (*Off Western Valley Rd.*) On the exit towards Akaroa, past the domain (where there are two old trypots) and beside the Maori hall is a statue of Tangatahara (?1772–1847), the chief who slew Te Rauparaha's uncle Te Pehi at Kaiapohia and who led the unsuccessful defence of Onawe. The lengthy inscription in Maori recounts how Tangatahara escaped the massacre at Onawe, later to take part in subsequent Ngaitahu *taua* to the Wairau in search of *utu*. An account is given of the battles between Ngaitahu and the invaders from the north.

### ORGANISED EXCURSIONS

**Peninsula Tours:** One-day circular tours of the peninsula run daily from Christchurch on demand, departing at 9.15 am. *C.J.O. Travel Ltd, 94 Worcester St, Christchurch: tel. 69-999 or 792-869.*

## BLENHEIM    Marlborough.    Maps 6, 20 & 22.    Pop. 17,500.

*29 km S of Picton; 132 km ENE of Kaikoura; 117 km ESE of Nelson. Public Relations Office, Market St: tel. 4480.*

THE "SUNSHINE CAPITAL" of Blenheim stands on the wide open Wairau plain whose grazing potential drew to their deaths the leaders of the pioneer settlement at Nelson. Today the prospect is one of spacious riverflat, vibrant with colour except in summer, when the heat of the country's sunniest district tans the landscape to a uniform brown. For a long time simply a sheepraising centre on a riverlanding, Blenheim has since 1945 trebled in population, with improved transport attracting a variety of light industry. It centres on Market Place and the quaint band rotunda that has come to epitomise the town.

# BLENHEIM AND DISTRICT

## 6

Blenheim's earlier name, The Beaver, was bestowed by the first survey party in the area, who were caught in a flood and forced to roost in their bunks "like a lot of beavers in a dam". It was renamed when the new province of Marlborough was created, honouring John Churchill, first Duke of Marlborough, and his most famous victory, over the French at Blenheim in 1704. At the same time Picton was named in honour of Sir Thomas Picton, one of the Duke of Wellington's hard-swearing generals and a casualty at Waterloo.

The country's most extensive vineyards are being established nearby.

## SOME HISTORY

**A system of canals?** When the *Pakeha* came to the Wairau, the future site of Blenheim was by a safe ford and a good landing-place on the Opawa River, but on marshy ground so damp as to deter settlement there.

To the north-east is an area in the lee of a boulder bank to the east of the Wairau rivermouth. Covered by lagoons in the lee of the boulder bank, the area sank appreciably in the 1848 earthquake, greatly increasing the size of the lagoons and obliterating evidence which might have established that the early Maoris dug a network of canals there to assist them to snare eels and wildfowl. Certainly some depressions were made or small creeks were used in this way, but the theory that a great series of canals was developed remains unsubstantiated. Some traces of the supposed system still remain, but the pattern is now further confused by the present cooperative drains, sewerage schemes and the remnants of tank traps dug as a Second World War defensive measure. Extensive archaeological finds have been made on the boulder bank of the Wairau Bar (*see index*) itself.

**Blenkinsopp's purchase:** The Wairau Affray has its genesis in the purchase by Col. William Wakefield of a deed which apparently entitled Capt. John Blenkinsopp to some 26,500 ha of Maori land on the Wairau plain. Wakefield purchased what he thought was the deed for the New Zealand Company from Blenkinsopp's widow, at Hokianga in 1839.

Blenkinsopp, captain of the schooner *Caroline*, had for some years been whaling out of Cloudy Bay (*off the coast near Blenheim*) and had married a relative of the chief Te Rauparaha. This gave him a degree of influence which he used to induce Te Rauparaha and his nephew, Te Rangihaeata, to sell him the right to procure wood and water from Cloudy Bay in exchange for a ship's cannon. However the deed which Blenkinsopp drew up expressed the terms of a totally different bargain and in all sincerity the illiterate chiefs endorsed it with their *moko* as their signatures. Even the cannon, it seems, was not Blenkinsopp's to trade but had already been given to

Te Rauparaha's elder brother, Nohurua, by John Guard in exchange for the right to operate a whaling station at Kakapo Bay on Port Underwood.

The tale does not conclude with Blenkinsopp's double-ended fraud; for he then took the deed to Sydney and mortgaged it to one Unwin, a solicitor, for £200. Shortly afterwards Blenkinsopp was drowned and Unwin, as mortgagee, claimed title to the Wairau. Blenkinsopp's widow at Hokianga had sold Wakefield not the deed itself but a copy, and for a handsome £300. It was to prove to be the death-warrant for his brother Arthur.

Te Rauparaha, when he learned of Blenkinsopp's duplicity, angrily tore up his copy of the deed and swore that the contract was at an end. Indeed, it would have been surprising had he done otherwise.

When the time came for the New Zealand Company to attempt to enforce its "purchase", the outcome was inevitable.

**The Wairau Affray** looms disproportionately large in Marlborough's history, for its significance is generally overemphasised. Certainly it was no more than an episode as far as the Maoris were concerned.

In the face of repeated warnings from Ngati Toa chiefs, the land-hungry Nelson settlers proceeded with a plan to survey the Wairau for settlement. Surveyors were sent in and established camps up the river; they had all but finished their work when Te Rauparaha and Te Rangihaeata arrived. The chiefs had asked the Land Commissioner, William Spain, to settle the Wairau question at once (Wakefield also claimed to have purchased the block directly from Te Rauparaha) but the over-worked Spain had refused to adjudicate immediately.

Nor would Spain stop the surveys, so the two Ngati Toa chiefs did. Being careful to harm neither the surveyors nor their property, the pair and about two dozen followers destroyed everything they regarded as rightfully being the tribe's property as the products of the land — rods and survey pegs of *manuka*, and *whare* (huts) of *raupo* and *toetoe*. The Nelson settlers rashly elected to charge the pair with arson, as a *whare* built by a chief surveyor had been burned down. They hastily assembled a group to arrest the chiefs and set off in June 1843 with an assortment of arms and ammunition to "make a show". Thinking that the threat of force would suffice, little consideration had been given to the fighting ability of the ragtail rank-and-file, who "had nothing to fight for", had never before handled firearms and certainly had no wish to risk their lives for the company they felt had let them down. Even so, the Ngati Toa were to be at a considerable disadvantage in terms of firepower.

At the Tuamarina Stream the party encountered a Maori encampment (which included women, children and old people) and paused while the magistrates went ahead. They crossed the stream by walking over a canoe placed there as a bridge and informed Te Rauparaha that he was being arrested. As the two groups argued, excitement mounted and, either by design or accident, one of the Nelson settlers fired a shot. Believing death to be imminent, Te Rauparaha stretched his arms heavenward and cried: "Farewell, O Sun, farewell thou World of Light; come, O Night, come on, O Death!" The dramatic cry was an irresistible appeal for support. There was a flurry of gunfire. Some of the settlers fell, some fled and others sur-rendered, among them Captain Arthur Wakefield, leader of the Nelson settlement.

A second debate took place as the Ngati Toa argued among themselves about what should be done with the prisoners. It ended when Te Rangihaeata, a late arrival, demanded *utu* (satisfaction) for the death of his wife Te Rongo, a relative of Te Rauparaha who had been killed in the shooting. His appeal could not be ignored and the band of a dozen unarmed prisoners were tomahawked to death with Te Rangi-haeata as the principal (and perhaps the sole) executioner.

In all twenty-two *Pakeha* died and twenty-seven escaped, five of them wounded. The Maori casualties were about six dead and eight wounded. With the grudging consent of the Ngati Toa chiefs ("Better leave them to the wild pigs"), the *Pakeha* dead were buried by the Cloudy Bay missionary, the Rev. Samuel Ironside, whose considerable work in the area had been ruined in a single day.

News of the Wairau "massacre" (as it was known for over a century) shocked Nelson to a standstill. All had lost friends and relatives, as well as their able leader who died for his one serious error of judgment. In the gloom, a number of colonists left, and most demanded stern action from the Governor. But the Acting-Governor, Willoughby Shortland, in a judgment confirmed by his successor, Governor FitzRoy, elected to treat the Nelson leaders as having been in the wrong and as having been dealt with according to Maori custom. If his judgment was by European standards fair and sympathetic (in any event he lacked the forces to fight the war that was the only other alternative), it was received by the Maoris, both locally and beyond, only as a sign of weakness. Ngati Toa, who at the very least expected the Governor to take the Wairau forcibly as *utu*, evacuated the area. They considered the Governor "as soft as a pumpkin" (*he paukena te Pakeha*) when he failed to do so.

*The scene of the affray is marked by a memorial on Highway 1 at 9.5 km N. The titoki tree to which the canoe was tethered that was used as a bridge, still stands on the opposite bank. The common grave of the executed prisoners is in the hilltop cemetery, marked by a pyramid-shaped headstone. The infamous little cannon is in Blenheim on the corner of High and Seymour Sts.*

**The Wairau purchase:** To the outrage of the Nelson settlers, who eventually had to foot the bill, Governor Grey in 1847 elected to negotiate a fresh Wairau purchase with Ngati Toa, paying £3,000 for a block that extended as far south as Kaiapoi. Had he not done so, further bloodshed might well have occurred, as adventurous squatters had moved into the area to run their sheep on the tempting "no-man's-land".

European settlement on the Boulder Bank began with a combined store and accommodation house opened by James Wynen in 1847 in an area soon noted for its excesses; it was "the resort of all the disorderly characters and contributed to give the Wairau the bad and disgraceful reputation it bore". To facilitate trade with the Wairau Valley, Wynen built a *raupc* store, the Beaver Station, on the banks of the Opawa (*at the foot of High Street; marked by a memorial*) and the first building for the future town of Blenheim. He was soon joined by James Sinclair, the "King of the Beaver", a talented trader whose wife preferred the dampness of The Beaver to the excesses of the Boulder Bank.

Lack of transport hindered settlement, The *Nelson Examiner* in 1852 described the "track" from Nelson to the Wairau as having a "beautiful network of roots [with] the one advantage of preventing both men and beasts from making any long slip in the mire, which prevails to an average depth of about 12 inches". The land was opened up by a mosquito fleet of little riverboats, a service provided by a number of whalers who turned to coastal shipping as their catches dwindled. The shipping trade centred on The Beaver, with horsedrawn boats and punts carrying wool to schooners waiting at the Boulder Bank — until the 1855 earthquake so deepened the Opawa that schooners could sail right up to The Beaver. The earthquake demolished nearly every *whare* on the Wairau. The sinking of a large area of the plain by almost two metres forced some to leave the coastal area, but the possibility of direct shipping to and from The Beaver gave impetus to further settlement.

Also growing nearby was the settlement of Waitohi, preferred by the pastoralists for its deep water and because they would sooner have seen settlements grow away from the plains they wanted for their sheep. The Beaver watched developments at Waitohi with a fierce jealousy, particularly as the Provincial Government foresaw Waitohi as becoming the region's principal port — which, as Picton, it was soon to do.

**The battle for the capital:** The rivalry between the two townships dominated Marlborough's era as a self-governing province, leading to a series of shenanigans that entertained the rest of the country. Waitohi residents were justly suspicious when those at The Beaver were ready to proclaim Waitohi as Marlborough's port and capital as the price of gaining provincial independence from Nelson. The Nelson Provincial Council had virtually ignored the claims of the Wairau in planning expenditure on public works.

No sooner was separation a fact in 1859 than Blenheim (as The Beaver had by that Act become) turned on its rival of Picton (as Waitohi had become) once more. Absorbed in the struggle, the populace lost sight of the main issue, the land question, and a land policy was obscured that hindered rather than encouraged development. Within five years land revenue was exhausted, and most were already in favour of the abolition of the provincial system in favour of central government.

Before the battle for the capital was finally won by Blenheim, Picton had been awarded a railway whose cost of £60,000 was obviously far beyond the resources of a province which comprised only 163 electors. Picton, which then had not even a road to serve it, would undoubtedly have been confirmed as capital had the railway gone ahead. As it was, the Governor vetoed the necessary Loan Bill.

There were scenes of turmoil in the Marlborough Provincial Council in 1862 when the pro-Blenheim faction achieved power. The Superintendent, Captain Baillie, in a last ditch attempt to forestall them, simply suspended the Council by declaring it prorogued. The Council, however, chose to laugh, and elected instead a second superintendent, William Eyes. Both superintendents attempted to exercise power — Baillie, with the provincial seal, in Picton; Eyes in Blenheim, without it. The banks, with traditional caution, would advance money to neither. Provincial works ground to a halt and provincial officers received no pay. The Governor was petitioned to resolve the impasse, and only after the Supreme Court had decided the case by leaving it wide open (i.e. that Baillie was lawfully entitled to prorogue the Council but had transgressed the spirit of the law in doing so) was the Council dissolved and new elections held.

While Marlborough's comic-opera politics entertained the nation, its own electors had a change of heart and returned the Picton party.

Three years later the opposition Blenheim party again succeeded in carrying a motion that adjourned proceedings to Blenheim, but the Superintendent flatly refused to move. The embittered Blenheimites, whose leader, Eyes, swore to "make Picton a deserted village" by depriving it of Government money and a railway, proceeded to meet in Blenheim. There, for the second time, they elected a rival superintendent, while the governing party continued to sit at Picton.

A scandalised Governor once more dissolved the Council in the hope that fresh elections would restore sanity. This time the pro-Blenheim party achieved a clear majority and, having moved the adjournment to Blenheim, took to the bush with the Provincial goods and documents, fearing an attempt to retain them in Picton by force. The victory was a hollow one, for Marlborough had an escalating debt whose interest alone was by 1868 beyond its resources. Picton, Pelorus and Kaikoura all moved to separate, and Marlborough's only consolation was found in the bankruptcy of her fellow province of Southland.

The province limped on until, on the day abolition became effective, the Government buildings and half of Blenheim went up in smoke — a dramatic end to an institution whose existence had been both fractious and frivolous.

## THINGS TO SEE AND DO

**Some parks and gardens:** A cannon, said to be the one with which Blenkinsopp "purchased" the Wairau, is mounted by the formal gardens of **Seymour Square,** with the monument and coloured fountain that form the town's war memorial. (*The cannon is on the corner of High and Seymour Sts*). **Riverside Park** backs on to the banks of the Taylor River just above its confluence with the Opawa (*corner High and Main Sts*). **Pollard Park** incorporates the tranquil setting of the Waterlea Gardens. Beyond the tennis courts is the town's Centennial Rose Garden (*Parker St*).

**Craft Market:** The former St Andrew's Presbyterian Church serves as an indoor market. *Open Fridays, and some additional days during school holidays. Cnr Henry and Alfred Sts.*

---

Help keep this guide up to date by writing to the authors
c/- A. H. & A. W. Reed, Private Bag, Te Aro, Wellington.

---

## ENVIRONS

**Tuamarina\*:** The scene of the Wairau Affray is marked by the roadside. A signpost indicates the point where the settlers crossed the river. In the cemetery on the hill above the road is a solid white monument designed by Felix Wakefield, youngest of the five Wakefield brothers, in memory of his brother Arthur and of those who died with him. *9.5 km N on Highway 1. To reach the monument, cross the railway line just south of the signpost and turn left to follow Campbells Lane up the hillside. Detour 1.6 km return.*

**Riverlands cob cottage** (*c.* 1859)\*\*: A cobblestone path leads to a cob cottage which has served variously as farm cottage, school, stud-sheep shelter and hayshed. Now restored and preserved as a museum, it is furnished in the style of its period. *4.3 km E on Highway 1 to Kaikoura. Open daily.*

**Brayshaw Museum Park\*:** To an impressive display of old farm implements and agricultural machinery has been added a re-creation of the sort of shopping area Blenheim had last century, with shops, a bank and smithy, all containing appropriate goods and furnishings. Elsewhere in the 5.7 ha park are a model boating pond, flying circle and miniature railway. *Open daily during daylight hours.* Demonstration days are held periodically. *New Renwick Rd, by Taylor River Bridge.*

**Taylor dam:** One may swim in the dam, which is being developed as a recreation area. *Towards Taylor Pass. 5 km.*

**Woodbourne** (pop. 926): The RNZAF station here is both a maintenance base and a training centre. Secret research conducted at the base from 1963–73 by the United States was periodically the subject of controversy. It was from here that on 13 October 1928 the Australian aviator Charles Kingsford Smith and his crew took off in their *Southern Cross* to land at Sydney 22 hours later, so completing the first-ever east-west air crossing of the Tasman Sea. *8 km W on Highway 6.*

**Renwick** (pop. 883): A museum recalls John Godfrey (1823?–91) whose Wairau Hotel (the "Sheepskin Tavern") at Renwick was a frequent rendezvous for political gatherings. Serving on the Marlborough Provincial Council, Godfrey played a leading part in the political crises. At the most memorable of the Renwick meetings, a prominent local politician and runholder, Joseph Ward, argued for secession from the Nelson Province. As a member of the Nelson Provincial Council he declared: "We demand our right! We shall secure our rights by constitutional means, if possible; but if we can't succeed by constitutional means what is due to us — and *more* than due to us, by God! — we'll take up our rifles and fight for it!" The collection includes the medicine chest of Dr Thomas Renwick (1818–79), who gave his name to the town. A Nelson doctor with a wide practice, he was conspicuous in Nelson political life and was at his death a member of the Legislative Council. (*By the Post Office. Open daily.*) Trips on old gigs and wagons may be arranged (*tel. Renwick 895 or 874*). *12 km SW on Highway 6.*

Nearby, in New Renwick Road (the "back" route to Blenheim), is a cog-wheel memorial to Henry Godfrey (1825–68), in his lifetime considered the region's leading systematic agriculturalist. The memorial comprises part of Godfrey's first commercial flourmill.

**Wairau Bar:** One may picnic on the bar and drive to the collapsed old wharf on its tip. A memorial records the "pioneer settlers who from 1832 entered this river bar" and that a shipping service continued until 1965. The boulder bank on the opposite side of the rivermouth was the scene of archaeological discoveries of major significance. *18 km. At Spring Creek, north on Highway 1, turn right and continue to the end of Wairau Bar Rd.*

△**Picton\*\***: A bustling seaside town preoccupied with the scenic attractions of the Marlborough Sounds and the business of the Cook Strait rail ferries. *29 km N.* A satisfying round trip is to drive to Picton on Highway 1 and return by way of Port Underwood (*see* △*Picton, "Suggested Drives"*).

△**Lake Grassmere:** Tall pyramids of salt rise beside the evaporating ponds of the country's only solar salt works. *35.3 km SE.*

**Molesworth:** See △*Hanmer Springs.*

## SUGGESTED DRIVES

Two circular drives may be made from Blenheim. One passes through Tuamarina and Picton and returns by way of Port Underwood. The other passes through Picton before swinging west to follow Queen Charlotte Drive to △Havelock, and returns to Blenheim by way of Renwick. *Both described under* △*Picton, "Suggested Drives".*

## ORGANISED EXCURSIONS

**Scenic flights** range over the chequered Wairau plain, the Lake Grassmere solar salt works, the forests and the intricate labyrinth of the Marlborough Sounds. *MAC Air Travel, Omaka Aerodrome. Tel. 4018.*

## TOURING NOTES

**Kaikoura coast road (Highway 1):** Highway 1 from Blenheim to △Waipara is described under △Kaikoura.

**Highway 1 to** △**Picton** passes the Tuamarina monument to those killed in the Wairau Affray (*at 9.5 km; see above*), the tiny timbered Anglican Church of St John in the Wilderness (1871) (*at 19.4 km*) and the Collins Deer Park (*at 20.7 km*).

**Port Underwood route to Picton:** A leisurely alternative to the direct 29 km highway is to branch east at Spring Creek or Tuamarina and follow the shoreline of Port Underwood. Picton is finally approached by way of Waikawa. *61 km. See* △*Picton, "Suggested Drives".*

**Highway 6 to** △**Nelson:** Highway 6 passes through Woodbourne, Renwick (*for both, see above*) and △Havelock (*which see for points of interest from there on.*)

> Look here, Steward, if this is coffee, I want tea ; but if this is tea, then I wish for coffee. — Punch.

**BLUFF\*** **Southland. Maps 18 & 31. Pop. 3,016.**

*27 km S of Invercargill.*

THE PORT OF BLUFF is first and last a seafaring town. Round its sheltered waters rise storage tanks and coolstores. Across the water shine the silver buildings of the Comalco smelter, with their lengthy jetty reaching far out to gain deep water for the ships that bring in aluminium oxide from Queensland and ship out aluminium to the world. In the centre lies an artificial island, home of unique all-weather package loaders which, when not in use, bow their necks like mechanical giants. About the shore lie the rusting, rotting hulks of ships beached as no longer useful.

The port handles an expanding export trade and is the base of a fishing fleet, among them boats that dredge Foveaux Strait for its succulent oysters. From here, too, are ferried out to the Muttonbird Islands those Maoris of Rakiura descent who are entitled to harvest the birds. The total value of fish and shellfish landed at Bluff is greater than at any other port.

Within the town houses climb the lower slopes of the Old Man Bluff, the hillside from which the town takes its name. The peninsula is secured to the mainland by the narrow neck of Ocean Beach, site of one of Southland's several massive freezing-works.

A regular shipping service links Bluff with Oban on △Stewart Island.

**The port of Bluff:** Bluff, a natural harbour, has a narrow entrance protected from westerly winds and kept well-scoured by tidal flow. With no rivers flowing into the harbour, little dredging is needed.

Between the Ocean Beach and the West Channels was a low sandbank, probably formed by the ancient courses of the Oreti and Mataura Rivers before their routes altered. This sandbank has been transformed into a unique island of 34 ha to give added berthage. The project was completed in 1960 by a consortium of four French companies.

A spectacular increase in the volume of frozen meat exports through Bluff gave rise to the provision of the all-weather meat-loading berth, using covered-in conveyors to increase the hourly loading rate but use of the loaders decreased with the introduction of containerisation.

## SOME HISTORY

**Old Man's Bluff Point:** The establishment of a *kainga* at Bluff proper seems to have come late in time. There was none here in 1813 when Captain Murray hesitated to sail his brig *Perseverance* into the harbour. Instead he led a party of two boats who became the first recorded Europeans to enter the harbour. A Maori they met near the harbour entrance took them to a village some distance away on the seaward side of the bluff, whose inhabitants they found "very civil and obliging".

The expedition had been despatched by a firm of Sydney merchants hopeful of founding a flaxmilling industry in the Foveaux Strait area that would enable it to meet the unsatisfied demand for cordage that existed in Sydney, brought about by the influx of shipping into the South Pacific. One Robert Jones was aboard, seemingly one of the investing capitalists, and it was he who named the harbour Port Macquarie, out of respect to Col. Lachlan Macquarie, then Governor of New South Wales. The name was retained on maps up to 1841. Opinions varied as to the prospects for the area, but the negative view of Jones prevailed and nothing came of the scheme.

The next recorded visit was nine years later, when the 39-ton cutter *Snapper* under Captain Edwardson became the first known ship to enter the harbour, casting anchor in 3½ fathoms. It was Edwardson, as he approached, who apparently for the first time named the harbour's distinctive feature Old Man's Bluff Point. By then there was a *kainga* by the harbour entrance, but this was found to be deserted. The *Snapper*'s task, like that of the *Perseverance* before her, was to judge the prospects for a flax industry and to collect samples for assessment in Sydney. Though an abundance of flax was found near the coast, the absence of wood (needed as fuel if fibre was to be prepared) ruled out the possibility of an industry being established here.

**Jimmy the Strong:** Later ships came simply to trade for flax, and with whalers active in the area the sailor James Spencer in 1824 decided to establish a trading post at Bluff, round which formed the nucleus of today's settlement. Spencer (1790–1846), who professed to have fought at the Battle of Waterloo, also laid claim to having grown the first wheat and raised the first cattle in Southland. Tall and powerful, he earned his Maori name of Timi Katoa (Jimmy the Strong). With the coming of British sovereignty Spencer applied for some 3,240 ha round Bluff but was awarded only 162 ha together with the harbour island that bears his name. On the island Spencer and his Maori wife grew potatoes to trade to the early residents of Bluff. It is said that on one occasion the authorities tried to take possession of the island for use as a quarantine station. Workmen arrived to face the wrath of both Spencer and, more particularly, that of his wife, who chased them off with an axe and so alarmed them with her fury that they abandoned their gear, leaving their tents to blow to pieces in the wind. None returned. Spencer died at sea in 1846.

**Whaling stations:** Historians date the town from the establishment of whaling stations here by Johnny Jones (*see index*) in about 1836, that were at one time (probably inaccurately) described as "the best-managed and most successful whaling establishments on the coast". The town could otherwise claim to be the oldest European settlement in Otago and Southland.

In time Old Man's Bluff Point was contracted to The Bluff. For a time the township was renamed Campbelltown to honour the wife of Governor Gore Brown, a name that failed to displace Bluff, to which in 1917 its name was finally officially changed.

**Southland's sole port:** With settlement came the growth both of Bluff and of the importance of its harbour, which steadily overhauled rivals at New River (Invercargill) and Riverton to emerge as Southland's sole port. Bluff was declared a port of entry, less out of a desire by the Dunedin-based Provincial Council to promote the settlement of Southland than from a need to collect the revenue that was being lost to the province by the absence of customs officers south of the Otago Peninsula. But once Southland was established as a separate province Dunedin could no longer prohibit the arrival at Bluff of migrant ships direct from Britain, or maintain her monopoly on the steamer service with Australia.

An ill-starred railway linked Bluff with Invercargill in 1867, so over-extending the finances of the infant province of Southland that the firm of McKenzie & Co, who had erected piers at Bluff, distrained against the Government's offices and records to the point of trying to auction off the railway rolling stock to meet the debt (*see △ Invercargill*). An early visitor from Melbourne described the journey from Bluff to Invercargill by rail: the train "leaped away at two miles per hour, gathering a little more speed as the journey progressed".

For many years the port, as the nearest to Australia, was on the "horseshoe run" that ran from Sydney to Wellington, Lyttelton, Dunedin and Bluff, and then to Hobart and Melbourne. It returned from Melbourne to Sydney by the same round-about route. A direct Melbourne-Bluff "ferry" service was a feature until the outbreak of war in 1939.

**Man of Bluff:** "Bluff has been the keynote of his life. He started out in life at the Bluff; he built up his business on bluff." So sneered a pamphleteeer when Joseph Ward's (1856–1930) business failed so spectacularly as to topple the Colonial Bank, and the man who had been mayor of Bluff at the age of twenty-five and was then Colonial Treasurer was in 1897 reduced to filing in bankruptcy. Not that the disaster overwhelmed the Melbourne-born politician, who despite "a trail scattered with curious balance sheets, interwoven overdrafts and missing crop securities", went uncensured and wound up not only with a baronetcy but also as a prime minister — he succeeded Seddon and served from 1906–11, and held the post again 1928–30.

If financial disaster marred his private life (as it also did that of Seddon), as a politician he proved an able minister, reorganising railway accounting systems, engineering critically-needed finance for the Bank of New Zealand (later to be nationalised, in 1947) and, in 1901, introducing penny postage. Somewhat ironically he was at his best as a minister of finance — being Colonial Treasurer when only thirty-seven — but is generally considered to have been an uninspiring prime minister.

Ward lies buried in his home town (*in the old cemetery, at the end of Lagan St, off Shannon St, to the right of the path over the crest of the hill*). His statue stands at the approach to the town and his name still adorns the waterfront warehouse of J. G. Ward & Co., a subsidiary of NMA. Until fairly recently, when railhead operations switched to the artificial island, Bluff had a spacious railway station whose grandiose appearance and overgenerous dimensions are said to have reflected a departmental desire to please Joseph Ward, who was once briefly employed by the railways here.

## OYSTERS

The succulent Stewart Island oyster (*Ostrea angasi*), *tio para* to the Maori, is found unattached on the seabed throughout New Zealand from shallow mudflats to water as deep as 27 m. Nowhere are they found in such quantities and in such size as in Foveaux Strait, whence they are harvested each year. From March onwards and for a limited season dredges operate from Bluff while the country waits expectantly. The Stewart Island oyster lacks the customary deep violet edging and its white shell distinguishes it from other species.

## TIWAI ALUMINIUM SMELTER

The country's only aluminium smelter, on Tiwai Point, is owned by Comalco Limited of Australia (50%), Showa Denko K.K. of Japan (25%) and the Sumitomo Aluminium Smelting Co., Ltd., of Japan (25%). The smelter's development dates from an invitation by the New Zealand Government following the discovery in 1955 of extensive deposits of bauxite at Weipa, Queensland. Appropriately the discovery was made by a New Zealand West Coaster, geologist Harry Evans. Small red pebbles of bauxite are shipped in large bulk carriers to Gladstone on the central Queensland coast. There they are refined to a fine white powder — alumina, which is pure aluminium oxide. The Tiwai smelter imports more than 300,000 tonnes of alumina a year.

At Tiwai, electricity is used to rip the aluminium and oxygen atoms apart. Aluminium forms at the bottom of the smelting furnace, called a pot, and oxygen forms at the positive electrode, or anode, at the top. The half tonne carbon anode blocks burn out and must be replaced regularly. Australian pitch and American petroleum coke are crushed, mixed and pressed into the anode blocks, which are then baked at temperatures up to 1,150°C before being sent to the potrooms.

The smelter has 408 pots, shallow oblong steel tubs lined with carbon and containing a red hot 970°C molten liquid called cryolite. The pots are about 5m wide and 10m long. Alumina, fed in from a hopper, is dissolved in the cryolite and with a high electrical current flowing through the pot, the aluminium and oxygen atoms are separated. Aluminium is siphoned off daily and cast in a number of shapes. The oxygen reacts with the carbon anode ᴄ ᴄk to form carbon dioxide, which is disbursed through the 137m high chimney.

The smelting of one tonne of aluminium requires two tonnes of alumina, half a tonne of carbon anode and 16,000kWh of electricity — the amount an average household uses about every two years. The △ Manapouri power scheme, a major power source, unlikely to have been tapped without a major industrial user nearby, was developed for the smelter. The Japanese must export their 50% of the aluminium. Comalco exports what New Zealand cannot absorb. Comalco has interests in semi-fabricating plants in Auckland.

The Tiwai smelter accounts for almost half the Southland Harbour's total tonnage. The 194m wharf is capable of accommodating bulk carriers with capacities in excess of 45,000 tonnes. Raw materials are discharged by vacuum unloader and taken 2.3km by covered conveyor to storage buildings. The finished product is trucked back to the wharf for export or railed north from Invercargill for the New Zealand market.

In world terms, the Tiwai smelter is of moderate size, producing about 1% of the world's total aluminium. It employs more than 1,100 people. With employee's wives and children taken into account, more than 7% of Invercargill's population is directly dependent on the smelter.

*To ensure a mutually agreeable time, intending visitors should write to the Community Relations Officer, New Zealand Aluminium Smelters Limited, Private Bag, Invercargill, (tel. 85-999) for reservations and particulars of clothing to be worn. Cameras are not permitted. Watches must not be worn.*

## OTHER THINGS TO SEE AND DO

**View from Bluff Hill\*\*\*:** From the top of Bluff Hill one may enjoy a dramatic view that has attracted visitors for more than a century. As if on a map, one sees beyond the smelter on Tiwai Point, the Awarua Lagoon spreading east towards the entrance to Foveaux Strait, where only hundreds of hectares of sand dunes separate the wetlands reserve from the sea of Toetoes Bay. Below lies the town and the quaintly-pointed artificial island. To the north the New River Estuary curls towards Invercargill and behind the city sprawl the Southland plains. Offshore lies tiny Dog Island (*see below*), the long, low form of △Ruapuke Island, and △Stewart Island rising in the south-west to the tip of Mt Anglem (*980 m*).

The Harbour Board established a signal station here in 1861, a move that required the felling of an area of scrub so that the harbourmaster at Stirling Point could see the flags. The port was a fashionable picnic spot. Trains brought many visitors to Bluff on regatta days, when several hundred would make the walk to the hilltop. *Turn up Brandon St, by the Post Office, and follow the road to the summit.*

**Stirling Point Lookout** has the distinction of being at the very end of the line but is neither the most southerly point of the South Island (Slope Point, to the east, extends some 5 km further south) nor even of the Bluff Peninsula itself. The view is principally of the zebra-towered Dog Island and the expanse of historic △Ruapuke. The sheer-sloped bluff to the south obscures most of Stewart Island. Nearby is the shipping signal station. *Follow Highway 1 to its end.* A walking track extends from the end of the highway.

**Dog Island:** The miniscule island is notable only for its distinctive lighthouse tower, some 36 m high, the tallest in the country. It was also one of the earliest to be built, in 1865, from stone quarried on the island. The manned light, electrified in 1954, flashes three times each 30 seconds and is visible for 29 km. Its tower is striped to make it stand out to ships by day as well as by night. *5 km SE.*

**△Ruapuke Island:** Home of the fabled "Bloody Jack", Hone Tuhawaiki. *20 km SE.*

**Hulk of whale-chaser:** Lying as an old hulk on Tikore (Spencer) Island are the remains of *Star 2*, an industrious whale-chaser once used by a Norwegian company in the Ross Sea. The *Taratahi*, as she later became, was built in Seattle and had traded in the sealing industry round the Alaskan seaboard before she came to Bluff in about 1923. She was later used to ship fresh oysters to Wellington in saltwater tanks, a venture that proved uneconomic and resulted in the ship being laid up here in Rotten Row. *On the western shore of Tikore Island, seen from the road as one approaches Bluff.*

**Awarua Radio:** See △*Invercargill, "Environs". 15.7 km N.*

---

## BULLER RIVER\*\*    West Coast.    Maps 24 & 38.

THE PRINCIPAL RIVER on the West Coast flows swift and broad from Lake Rotoiti (in △Nelson Lakes National Park) westward through uplifted mountain blocks to reach the sea at △Westport. For most of its 169 km the river is contained within gorges, steep-sided and well-bushed, engendering much remarkable scenery particularly in the Lower Buller Gorge. Between them Highways 6 and 63 follow the river for most of its length.

The river is named after Charles Buller, a director of the New Zealand Company. It has been suggested that the title was chosen in London, at a board meeting, but research has shown that the explorers Brunner, Heaphy and Fox seriously debated the merits of several names before deciding to honour the brilliant young British parliamentarian. There are several versions of the Maori name, usually given as Kawatiri or Kawatere and freely translated as "water flowing swiftly through a rocky gorge". The river is a potential source of hydro-electric power.

### POINTS OF INTEREST ON THE RIVER

*(Note: Particularly on the lower reaches it is both pleasant and possible to walk up any of a number of the creeks that enter the river valley.)*

**Lake Rotoiti:** Wherein the river rises. See △*Nelson Lakes National Park.*

**△Murchison:** A farming centre and junction town once devastated by earthquake.

**Lyell** is the site of a since-vanished town on a goldfield that opened in 1862. Fabulous finds of alluvial gold led to the supposition that there were gold reefs nearby and by the end of the decade important quartz-mining was in full swing here. Reports of 17-, 30- and 52-ounce nuggets heightened early interest and it is even said that a 108-ounce nugget shaped like a dumb-bell was found in Irishman's Creek by a group of Irish miners who smuggled it out to Australia. If true, the find would outrank the Honourable Roddy nugget of Ross.

**△Inangahua:** Once a landing on the river before the road from Westport was built.

**Hawks Crag** (*15 km from Inangahua; 33 km from Westport*): Shorn back but still a remarkable sight is the crag that juts out to roof a roadway hewn out of conglomerate rock. The name has been attributed to the nesting of hawks in such places but an old goldminer, Robert Hawks, who dug in the locality, in later years claimed that it was named after himself. Just south of the crag one may walk up Hawks Crag Creek and follow a section of the old pack track up on to the top of the Crag.

**Berlins** (*13.5 km from Mangahua; 32.7 km from Westport*): Long known as the Old Diggings, the locality got its name from the fact that the hotel by that name here, also the local post office, was conducted by one John Berlin. A Swede, he arrived in Nelson in 1867 and for some years followed the diggings as a miner before setting up his accommodation house in 1874.

△**Westport:** A coal port on the river's mouth.

---

**BURKES PASS**      South Canterbury.      Maps 34 & 35.      Height: 670.9 m.

*18 km SE of Tekapo; 25.5 km W of Fairlie.*

THE TRANSFORMATION IN LANDSCAPE as one crosses Burkes Pass from △Fairlie to enter the Mackenzie country is total. A wooded verdant aspect abruptly gives way to vast shimmering plains of red-brown tussock that end in massive blue mountains.

The pass, known to the Maoris as Te Kopi Opihi, takes its European name from John Michael Burke (commemorated in a roadside tablet). He entered it in 1855 after the trial of James McKenzie for sheepstealing had focussed interest on the vast inland plain.

**Burkes Pass settlement:** A miniscule hamlet (pop. 79) 4.5 km to the east of the pass itself was once the most important settlement of the Mackenzie. It lost the role to Fairlie when the branch rail line from Timaru in 1884 stopped short at what is now the seat of the Mackenzie Country. But this was not planned, and opposite the hotel still stands the old stone **County Chambers** (1876), built to last but never used.

The **hotel,** too, has links with the past. The basic building of 1861, with its twin dormer windows (now flanked by wings and with its verandah built-in) still serves passersby. It was this hotel that was granted the first hotel licence in Canterbury, conditional upon there being maintained four beds for travellers and yards for cattle and sheep. Its holder, James Noonan, was drowned in the Te Ngawai River only a fortnight before his licence was to take effect.

About 150 m up from the hotel is the minute **Presbyterian Church** (1872), until 1918 the joint property of Presbyterians and Anglicans in a convenient act of union. Rupture came when a legacy was left to repair "the Presbyterian Church at Burke's Pass", and the Presbyterian Church itself found that before it could collect the money it had to buy out the financial interest of the Church of England.

---

The Automobile Association has offices throughout the country and offers members a wide range of services, from a breakdown service and legal advice to maps and details of road conditions. Its annual handbooks, listing details of hotels, motels and camping grounds, are the most comprehensive available and are issued free to members.

Reciprocal membership is generally extended to overseas visitors who are members of kindred organisations in other countries.

---

**BURNHAM***      Canterbury.      Map 7.      Pop. 1,904.

*30.5 km SW of Christchurch; 87 km NE of Ashburton.*

BURNHAM MILITARY CAMP sits on a billiard-flat plain broken only by clumps of trees. In dry nor'westers the scene is cooled by the well-grassed lawns about the camp headquarters. A young private with a farming background helped lay the lawns at the beginning of the 1939–45 war. His objection that he should be at weapons training was dismissed — the war could wait, the grass could not. When he finally reached the Middle East, Charles Upham passed into military history by twice winning the Victoria Cross, the Commonwealth's highest award for valour — one of only three in the world ever to have done so. The name Burnham was adapted by the pioneer runholder Richard Bethell from his birthplace of Burnham Beeches in Buckinghamshire, UK.

**Charles Hazlitt Upham** (b. 1908): New Zealand's most highly decorated soldier enlisted on the outbreak of the Second World War and had risen to the rank of captain when he was taken prisoner in 1942. On Crete the previous year he had destroyed four machine-gun posts, rescued a wounded man under heavy fire and then penetrated enemy-held territory to lead out an isolated company. Three times wounded in the next two days, he killed twenty-two of an enemy party advancing on Force HQ before the remainder fled in panic. In July 1942 he won a bar to his Victoria Cross by destroying an entire truckload of German soldiers, their machine guns and a tank, all with grenades. Again severely wounded, he was taken prisoner only when totally disabled.

On his return to Canterbury at the war's end he shunned publicity. Offered a fund raised by public subscription to enable him to buy a farm, he quietly declined and the money was used instead to establish a scholarship for the sons of servicemen. He farms Lansdown Station at Conway Flat, Hundalee, North Canterbury. His biography has been written by Kenneth Sandford in *Mark of the Lion* (Hutchinson).

## SOME HISTORY

**The borstal and Lee:** An industrial school was opened on the camp's site in 1874, a borstal-type institution at first for children of both sexes. In 1900 the girls were moved to Burwood. Its fame lies in the internment and escape of John A. Lee (b. 1891), a forthright and outspoken Labour parliamentarian and controversialist who denounced the school in his books *The Hunted* and *Delinquent Days*. Lee rose to be under-secretary first to the Labour prime minister Michael Savage and then to the minister of finance until, in 1939, he circulated the "Lee Letter" in which he condemned the caution and orthodoxy of his superior, Walter Nash. The Governor-General was asked to revoke Lee's ministerial appointment, but more was to follow. That same year he wrote an article, "Psychopathology in Politics", arguing (perhaps correctly) that the grievously-ill Savage was incapable of carrying on as prime minister. Those who knew Savage was fighting terminal cancer united against Lee. Savage's death just before the annual Labour Party conference sealed his fate and Lee was expelled from the Party. He could have played safe, but such was not his style. Indeed as "a perpetual thorn in the tougher regions of society's hide" he has since probably made a greater contribution than he could have as a politician. His memoirs include *Simple on a Soapbox* (1963) (Collins).

In 1918 the industrial school closed and the Defence Department took over the complex. Basically the present layout dates from 1939, when a rapid building programme established the South Island's only major military camp.

## POINTS OF INTEREST AT THE CAMP

*Note: The camp is not open to the public at large. Before visiting any of the following, permission must be obtained from the camp headquarters.*

**All Saints Garrison Church** (1864)** originally stood some 4.5 km on the way to Springston. The boys of the industrial school would walk or travel by wagon to the church each Sunday until in 1901 it was moved to the school grounds and enlarged by the boys themselves as a chapel. When the school closed the church continued to serve the small community of local civilians and eventually the camp as well. Bishop Harper's son, the Rev. H. Harper, who opened the church, recorded: "I have succeeded in collecting enough money to build the first church on the plains, south of Christchurch, at Burnham; a simple wooden structure, with open high-pitched roof, shingled outside, and with a tiny apse for sanctuary; the design was mine." Today the church is non-denominational.

Within, a plaque and bell recall Richard Bethell, son and grandson of clergymen, who arrived in the area in 1861 and gave the original site for the church. An energetic individual, Bethell is reputed to have walked about 30 km to Christchurch to do business on Fridays, to have dined at the Christchurch Club, purchased steak from a Sydenham butcher and then to have walked home again — all in the one day. Military significance is given by the several regimental flags laid up here. *Near the camp headquarters. The church is generally locked and is opened on application to the padre's office.*

**Venus plaque:** A tablet in the grounds records the sighting of the Transit of Venus on 7 December 1882 by a party of British scientists. Burnham was one of several points in the world from which observations were made so that the distance between the sun and the earth could be calculated.

**Industrial School:** Buildings that survive from the Industrial School include what is now the camp post office (then the primary school building) and several distinctive brick structures — now the gymnasium, squash courts and part of the firestation complex, and an MOWD stone building.

**Museum collection:** The camp holds the Royal New Zealand Medical Corps' Museum. *It may be visited by those with a special interest. Make prior arrangements with camp headquarters. Tel. 478-011 Rolleston.*

## ENVIRONS

**Burnham Grange** (1871): The deteriorating and now-deserted two-storeyed sod house still stands (1978). It was built by William Peter Cross, one of the earliest settlers in the district. *2.7 km NW. Drive up Aylesbury Rd. Turn left along Burnham-Charing Cross Rd. The sod house is in trees to the left about 400 m back from the road.*

## CAVE*     South Canterbury.     Maps 3, 34 & 35.     Pop. 148.

*35 km NW of Timaru; 27 km SSE of Fairlie.*

THERE IS NOW no cave at Cave. However there once was a cave where limestone is now quarried and it may have been a combination of this recess and the Rhodes family's connection with Cave, in Yorkshire, that led to the locality at first being named The Cave. The settlement grew up round an outstation on the Levels run of the Rhodes brothers (*see index*) and today the cluster of buildings serves surrounding farmers and the many visitors drawn to the nearby memorial church.

### THINGS TO SEE AND DO

**St David's Presbyterian Pioneer Memorial Church\*\*\***: On a hillside just within Mackenzie County though some distance from the Mackenzie country, stands the Norman-styled Church of St David. It was built of glacial boulders, some from the site, others from the Tasman Valley, as a memorial primarily to Andrew and Catherine Burnett (*see index*) and also to all the pioneers of the Mackenzie country in particular and of South Canterbury in general.

In the porch is an inscribed slab of alpine greywacke, used by Andrew Burnett as a table at a mustering camp in the Jollie Gorge. The porch light is a mast lantern from an early visitor to the Timaru roadstead. Within, the roof is supported by hand-adzed wood-pegged jarrah rafters; the solid, chunky pews are of rough-adzed red beech; the flooring of inlaid *totara*. All complement the rough, thrown-plaster finish of the interior walls, similar to that of a cob cottage.

The pulpit, also of boulders, is comprised of hearthstones from the Tasman Valley V-hut that was the Burnetts' first home. Its rim is of *totara*, from logs found near Mount Cook station. Behind the pulpit the window of Ruth symbolises the loyalty of the pioneer women of the Mackenzie country, and all three windows reflect South Canterbury's dependence on wool and grain. The font is an ancient mortar for grinding grain, used in Scotland by Highland ancestors of Catherine Burnett. It rests on a hub taken from a bullock dray used by the first Burnetts at Mount Cook station and this in turn rests on a squat unhewn boulder reputed to have been carried for over 100 m by Andrew Burnett when helping to build a musterer's hut. (*Burnetts Road. 2 km from Cave. Signposted. The key is available locally.*)

On the hilltop opposite the church a monument marks a Burnett family private cemetery. Just before the turnoff to the church is reached is a war memorial, engraved at length with a stirring message which was written by T. D. Burnett (*see index*), who was responsible for organising the building of St David's and for the erection of a number of memorials in a variety of settings. A memorial to T. D. Burnett himself, whose enthusiasm was largely instrumental in bringing to fruition the Downlands Water Supply scheme, appropriately takes the form of a stone water-trough (*On Highway 8, on the left, 2.2 km towards Pleasant Point.*)

**Maori rock drawings\***: There are early rock drawings in two shelters on the lower side of Dog Rock, the massive solitary slab of limestone that juts from the hillside not far from the township. The drawings, of mythical subjects, have been heavily retouched, an action which draws condemnation from archaeologists. (*The drawings are on Rock Farm, 0.9 km east of Cave on Highway 8. Ask at the homestead for permission and directions, as it is usually possible to drive the 0.7 km up to the rock itself.*) There is a pleasant view from here, down to Cave in a setting of exotic trees.

> The traveller sees what he sees; the tripper sees what he has come to see. —G. K. Chesterton.

## CHEVIOT     North Canterbury region.     Map 20.     Pop. 547.

*74 km SW of Kaikoura; 58 km NE of Waipara.*

CHEVIOT TUCKS COMFORTABLY into a corner of river flat beside State Highway 1. Politically in Nelson Province (the town is north of the Hurunui River), it belongs geographically to North Canterbury, typifying the rolling hills and lush riverflats of the region.

Cheviot is named after the run Cheviot Hills, which John Scott Caverhill called after the Scottish Border country whence he came. Some 5 km south is Nonoti. Not, as it may appear, a Maori name but one said to have been coined after a politician had been invited to name the locality when the railway was being put through. "No not I", he modestly declined.

There are trout and salmon in the Waiau River and good fishing also in the Hurunui.

### SOME HISTORY

**"Ready-Money" Robinson**: John Scott Caverhill, a "pre-Adamite" who had settled in Canterbury before the arrival of the Pilgrims, took out a pasturage licence in 1851 for the land lying between the Waiau and Hurunui Rivers and between the

Lowry Hills range and the sea. He was grazing 28,000 ha when William Robinson (1814–89) arrived from across the Tasman five years later. Impressed by the quality of Caverhill's run, he made a series of purchases from the Government, gradually acquiring all the well-watered blocks and best valley bottoms and forcing out Caverhill who thereupon purchased another property, "Hawkeswood", from two early surveyors, Lee and Jollie.

Robinson went on to purchase several other runs. According to folklore he once tendered a cheque for £10,000 to the Nelson Land Office and when the clerk expressed doubts about its size toured the local banks to collect the necessary cash, returning to the Land Office with a wheelbarrow full of notes.

After his death the Government acquired his property but not the stock. In a vast clearing sale 500 bidders congregated to vie for flocks and herds of the finest blood as some 108,000 sheep and a large number of cattle passed under the hammer.

**The Cheviot Estate:** The Cheviot Estate, about 16 km square of fine pastoral country, was ripe for closer settlement when the trustees of Robinson's estate challenged the Government's land-tax valuation of £305,000 as against their own assessment of £260,000. The Government had either to accept the lower assessment or buy the estate out at the higher price. To the surprise of the trustees and in a dramatic move which heralded a fresh and aggressive approach to land settlement, the Minister of Lands, Sir John McKenzie (*see index*) elected to buy. This he did in 1892, though the sum involved was considerable for the times. To put the small man on the land, perpetual leases of farms of from 40 to 200 ha were balloted off and the remaining land was leased for set periods. McKenzie Township (as Cheviot was first called), an estate that had previously supported eighty people, a year after subdivision had a population of 650.

McKenzie's philosophy was summed up in the couplet he quoted in Parliament before a crucial division on the Lands for Settlement Bill of 1894:

> *Yet millions of hands want acres,*
> *And millions of acres want hands.*

*A lampstand memorial to McKenzie stands opp. the Post Office. A less impressive stone to his prime minister, Seddon, is at the start of the road to Gore Bay.*

## POINTS OF INTEREST

**Cheviot Hills Domain\*\*:** The homestead block is now a scenic reserve crowded with a profusion of massive exotic trees. An ideal picnic place is by the pavilion, which doubles as a picnic shelter, and which is built on part of the ruins of the extensive forty-roomed mansion Robinson built here. (Photographs of Robinson, his mansion, and the slipway at Port Robinson are in the pavilion.) *Signposted off Highway 1 just south of Cheviot. Access also at 1.5 km on the road towards Gore Bay.*

Other relics of Robinson's ready money are the impressive homestead built as a manager's cottage (*by the northern entrance to the domain*), part of the sheep station's wool-shed, age-weary and under threat (*by Highway 1, opp. the Cheviot Hotel*) and the community hall, built from part of the woolshed for the influx of settlers (*by the Post Office*). Near Leamington (*west of Cheviot*) is a portion of an old boundary fence, built of special strength to ensure that scab-infested flocks were kept safely at bay (*enquire locally*).

**Cheviot Historical Records Society:** An unusual museum collection in that it emphasises documents, mainly relating to a state experiment in closer land settlement (see **The Cheviot Estate** above) may be seen in the premises of the Society, which also arranges lectures and tours of the district. (*Enquire of the secretary, tel. 547*).

## ENVIRONS

**Gore Bay** (pop. 57): A swimming beach, sandy in parts and with modest fishing from the point. In a mixture of buildings old and new, the two-storeyed cottage (1867) Robinson built for his wife still stands. It was to this that his shy spouse would retire while he entertained in the grand manner at his expansive mansion. *8 km SSE.* A kilometre beyond the cottage is the "Cathedral", a gully of tall, fluted cliffs (*by the roadside; stop by a short white fence on the right*). Unlike the Southland town of Gore, which honours an early Governor, the bay was named by Captain Cook after one of his lieutenants.

Beyond Gore Bay the road (not suitable for caravans) runs on to pass the "Cathedral" (*at 1 km*) and the farm of Port Robinson (*3.5 km beyond Gore Bay*), where a side road leads towards the coast. From its end a short walk leads down to the cove that housed the slipway of Port Robinson. This was used from 1879–1907, before there was any adequate roading to the region. One may continue on to rejoin Highway 1 some 7 km south of Cheviot.

△**Motunau Beach\*:** A sandy bay, a holiday settlement, and a prized ground for fossil-hunters. *47 km SW. Turnoff signposted 32.5 km S on Highway 1.*

---

A Glossary of Maori Words appears on page 343.

# CHRISTCHURCH AND ENVIRONS

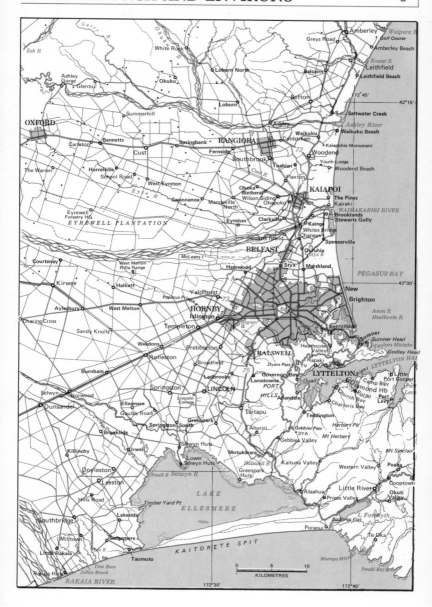

*366 km NNE of Dunedin; 350 km SSW of Picton; 254 km SE of Greymouth. Public Relations Office, cnr Worcester St and Oxford Tce., tel. 799-629.*

THE GARDEN CITY of Christchurch lies on the level plains that attracted the tightly knit Church of England settlement and then the great runholders. To the south-east the Port Hills bar the way to the port of △Lyttelton; to the west, broad alluvial fans are bounded by the seemingly abrupt Southern Alps, source of the river-shingle which built up to form the plains and the foundation for the future city's prosperity.

    The largest of the South Island centres, Christchurch yet retains something of the essentially English nature of its origins: a willow- and oak-lined Avon River meanders through its heart; a lofty neo-Gothic cathedral presides over a square; clustered stone buildings are not merely old but have a mediaeval air. Socially too, the city is perhaps less egalitarian than some, pivoting on such institutions as Christ's College (whose uniform still includes the straw boater) and the gentlemanly precincts of the Christchurch Club. More than any other, the city has a penchant for statues, the towering figures of its past enshrined in parks where the change of season is as marked as in its spiritual Motherland.

**The nor'west arch:** Edward Shortland, as he took a census of South Island Maoris, commented on the nor'wester as early as in 1844: "The NW wind all along this coast is strangely hot, dry, and oppressive, which I have never known to be the case in the North Island . . . Its peculiar dry character on reaching the east coast may, perhaps," he surmised, "be explained by the supposition that, in passing over the snow mountains, its moisture is condensed and falls on them as warm rain." Though the air is cooled as it rises over the Main Divide (at the rate of $1\,°C$ per 100 m rise at the dry adiabatic lapse rate), the latent heat of condensation is added to the air so that when the flow of air descends on the Canterbury side of the Alps its temperature rises to greater levels than before as air pressure increases. (The principle is analagous with the heating up of a bicycle pump.)

The enervating wind can blow for days at a time, when a curious arch of cloud forms to the north-west, whose changing pattern can be read by the weatherwise. It is generally followed by an abrupt change to the south-west.

**Bridle Path commemorative walk:** Each year on the Sunday nearest 16 December an organised commemorative walk takes place over the Bridle Path. Buses run from Cathedral Square to the start of the track at Ferrymead Historic Park (by the road tunnel portal). The walk to Lyttelton takes about 2 hours, following in reverse the route taken by the Canterbury Pilgrims, and is commonly made at all times of year, particularly by those descended from the pioneers. (*At other times of year start from the administration building at the Christchurch portal to the Lyttelton road tunnel. Public transport back from Lyttelton is available. One may also begin the walk from Heathcote station.*)

On Anniversary Day a Cathedral service is held by the Canterbury Pilgrims' and Early Settlers' Association, after which a chaplet of laurel leaves is placed at the foot of the statue in the Square of John Robert Godley, whose title of "The Founder of Canterbury" should in fairness be shared with Edward Gibbon Wakefield.

---

A metric conversion chart appears at the end of the book.

---

## SOME HISTORY

**Twice a bridesmaid:** It was the arrival of the French at △Akaroa in 1840 that first attracted the interest of the British. Colonel William Wakefield in 1841 asked that the New Zealand Company's Nelson settlement be established here, but paradoxically it was the presence of the French that stopped it. Governor Hobson ruled that there were too many undecided land claims on Banks Peninsula to have the uncertain position further confused.

The following year the pioneer Wellington settler William Deans elected to transfer his interests to the Canterbury Plains, becoming in 1843 the first to occupy the area effectively. William was joined by his brother John (who brought with him cattle, horses, pigs and the first sheep in Canterbury), and later by Ebenezer Hay and Captain Sinclair (both of whom had accompanied William Deans on an earlier visit and both of whom settled on Banks Peninsula, at Pigeon Bay). The Greenwood brothers were established at Purau early in 1844.

Port Cooper (Lyttelton) was again prospected in 1844, as Frederick Tuckett selected a site for the proposed settlement of New Edinburgh (Dunedin). From the Port Hills he exclaimed: "Looking down on the great plain I was at first sight delighted and astonished to behold an extent of level land so unwonted, but much wanted, in New Zealand, but the predominance of a russet tint far and near lowered my expectations, indicating too truly the extent of raupo swamp already struck by frost. It was," he declared, "deficient of almost every quality which was essential to the prosperity of a settlement, and particularly of one subdivided into . . . small properties." Though the New Zealand Company had already decided in favour of the Peninsula, Tuckett protested the pre-selection and his reports took the Scottish settlement to Dunedin. For the second time Port Cooper was passed over.

Despite their knowledge of the area, otherwise enterprising Wellington and Nelson settlers surprisingly failed to emulate the four families who had migrated to squat here, and not for seven years were new farmers or graziers attracted to the district. The enterprise of the little group was harshly rewarded. No fewer than three lost their lives at sea — Sinclair (1846) when taking a new schooner to Wellington; Joseph Greenwood (1848) while crossing by open boat from Port Levy to Motunau; and William Deans (1851) in the wreck of the *Maria* at Wellington heads.

**"Kemp's Deed":** The bungling conduct of the Government in its negotiations to purchase the Canterbury district from the Maori created a century of discontent, and it was not until as recently as 1944 that the grievances of Ngaitahu were finally laid to rest.

In 1847 the Government professed to purchase the area north of the Ashley River from Te Rauparaha's Ngati Toa, who claimed to own the land by virtue of their conquests in 1828–32. The transaction ignored the claims of the defeated Ngaitahu, who had by then resumed occupation of their ancestral lands. In laying the bogey of the Wairau Affray (*see index*), the Deed merely shifted the source of disaffection south.

The following year Ngaitahu told Governor Grey that they were prepared to sell the land south of the Ashley if adequate reserves were set aside. Grey authorised £2,000 for the 8 million ha which, he felt, in view of the small Maori population, was "as large an amount as they could profitably spend or as was likely to be of any real benefit to them".

But when H. Tacy Kemp, as Assistant Protector of Aborigines, came to negotiate the final terms of the purchase, he left the Deed blandly guaranteeing to the Maoris reserves that were neither defined nor indicated. Mantell was sent to tidy up these loose ends but he, like Kemp, made vague promises of schools and medical care to the by-then impoverished Ngaitahu — but omitted to mention them in the Deeds. Not only were these promises ignored, but the further protests of Ngaitahu concerning the purported sale by Te Rauparaha of land north of the Ashley River also fell on deaf ears. The Native Land Court in 1868 expressed doubts even as to the very basic validity of "Kemp's Deed".

Over the years further compensation was made to Ngaitahu yet it was not until 1920 that there was a full-scale investigation, which recommended that £354,000 be paid in full compensation. A further two decades were to pass before the Ngaitahu Claim Settlement Act became law, providing for the annual payment to a Trust Board of £10,000 for a period of thirty years. Thus the final payment for the Canterbury purchases was scheduled for 1974. (In 1973 the annual payment was extended in perpetuity). The Board is empowered to promote the health, social and economic welfare, the education and the vocational training of the Ngaitahu, so dealing with a grievance "created in the first instance out of misconception, prolonged through misunderstanding, and magnified by neglect".

**A Canterbury Settlement:** If "New Edinburgh" (Dunedin) had been originally destined for the Canterbury Plains, in turn "Canterbury" was expected to be sited in the Wairarapa, convenient to Wellington. Negotiations with the Ngati Kahungunu of the Wairarapa fell through, though Captain Joseph Thomas, sent from England to select, survey and prepare the site, had probably already opted in favour of Port Cooper (Lyttelton). "It is Port Cooper or nothing," he is said to have opined, for he had read the reports that, but for Governor Hobson's intransigence, would have brought the Nelson settlement here.

Both Governor Grey and Bishop Selwyn gave their guarded approval to his choice for the Church of England settlement, and Thomas set about his survey. Instructed to site the chief town of "Christchurch" on 400 ha, preferably at a seaport, he found difficulty in complying because of Lyttelton's steep hills. Initially he envisaged that the head of the harbour would be reclaimed, and "Christchurch" would have its Botanic Gardens at Charteris Bay and its Government domain near Governors Bay. However within a few days he decided that the cost of reclamation would be prohibitive, and elected to site Christchurch on the plains. His warning that the district "is and will be for many years to come principally pastoral" was ignored by his employers in London, whose view was fixed finally on an English model of intensive agricultural farming — totally inappropriate though it was for the colonists' lot.

Workmen began to level the foreshore at Lyttelton and to prepare a jetty; others began to construct a track round the coast to Sumner. The last of the country's major organised settlements was beginning to take shape.

When John Robert Godley arrived, eight months before the Pilgrims, he exclaimed: "I was perfectly astounded at what I saw. One might have supposed that the country had been colonized for years, so settled and busy was the look of its port."

**The Canterbury Association:** The Canterbury Association emerged in London as a result of a partnership between Edward Gibbon Wakefield (*see index*) and a young Tory, John Robert Godley (1814–61). Godley feared "an age of equality" and believed that his role was not to repulse it altogether but to "*retard* its progress and *modify* its effects", preparing the way for "a safe democracy". He also foresaw the destruction of Church and society in the northern hemisphere and hoped both Church and civilisation might regenerate in the newer societies of the Antipodes.

The fortunes of the New Zealand Company improved in 1846 when the Whigs regained office (the Company's directors were virtually all either Whigs or Radicals) and Lord Grey, the incoming Colonial Secretary, waived the Crown's right of pre-emption over Maori lands in the "southern province of New Zealand" and added a loan of £136,000. The Otago scheme revived to fruition, but Wakefield's prime interest was in an Anglican settlement for the country which he had foreseen as "the most Church of England country in the world".

The Canterbury Association was originally formed of fifty-three members, among them two archbishops, seven bishops, fourteen peers, four baronets and sixteen Members of Parliament. With such influence it could hardly fail, but for its enthusiasm it leant heavily on its co-founders. The Association's planned block of a million acres (405,000 ha) was to be sold for £3 per acre, with the proceeds being divided between the New Zealand Company, survey costs, an immigration fund, and a trust for the religious and educational needs of the settlement. The migrants themselves were to include "all the elements, including the very highest, of a good and right state of society".

To hasten progress, Wakefield induced the ailing Godley to journey out — gambling that Godley's friends on the Association, having despatched him to the far side of the earth, would feel obliged to support him in his task. After a rough passage on the *Lady Nugent*, Godley and his family landed first at Port Chalmers ("a very drunken set") and then at Port Cooper (Lyttelton) where the immigration barracks struck his wife as too comfortable, for they might "tempt the emigrants to remain in them longer than is necessary".

Looking out over the plains from the crest of the Port Hills "The view was really fine, on . . . the one side the harbour as smooth as a lake and quite encircled with high hills, and down below, on the other, the vast plains, as level as water, and nearly as innocent of anything like cultivation or habitation." After admiring progress, Godley at once clashed with Thomas (who lacked "a good manner with gentlemen"), arbitrarily suspending works and going to Wellington ("really a vortex of dissipation").

In London, Wakefield's gamble had failed; he noted that far from acquiring fresh vigour and enthusiasm "the affair lost its soul and body when it lost Godley, who both thought and acted for everybody". Yet the enterprise did progress, if more slowly than before, because a small group of Godley's friends felt it would have been a breach of faith for them to have allowed it to lapse completely. Advance land sales were slow. In terms of the deal with the New Zealand Company, unless the Canterbury Association sold £100,000 worth of land by 30 April 1850 the Canterbury block would revert to the Company. Some ingeniously handled land sales, plus last-minute negotiations backed by personal guarantees from Lord Lyttelton, Wakefield and two others saved the day. The Association then announced that land applications would soon close and the first colonists would be dispatched in September.

**The First Four Ships:** It is generally assumed that care was taken in selecting the assisted migrants. As for the land-purchasing "colonists", Wakefield noted that "the plan somehow repels desperate and bad people, such as commonly form a large proportion of the materials of a new settlement. Those whom it attracts are circumspect, cautious and slow to decide . . . I am not acquainted with a single emigrant who goes out as a money-grabbing speculator [rather they go] to cultivate the earth, breed horses and cattle, and grow wool."

The assisted migrant had to be under forty, and have a certificate from the minister of his parish "that the applicant is sober, industrious and honest, and that he and all his family are amongst the most respectable of their class in the parish". An interesting omission was a certificate as to his membership of the Church of England. The Colonial Office had declined to grant a charter for an exclusively Anglican settlement.

In Wellington, Godley knew little of how matters were proceeding in London, and learned of the sailing plans only when he read of them in a Sydney newspaper. Plainly he would have to restart work at Lyttelton without waiting for the financial advice he had asked for. He pledged his own credit to obtain funds and left for Canterbury on HMS *Acheron* on 28 November. Only eighteen days later, on the morning of 16 December 1850, the three-masted *Charlotte Jane* entered the port; Godley rushed to the jetty to encounter James Edward FitzGerald, jubilant at his success in being the first of the Pilgrims to land. "So overcome that he did not know whether to laugh or cry, [Godley] ended by doing both." That afternoon the *Randolph* dropped anchor, and the next day, the *Sir George Seymour*. The *Cressy*, which had sprung her fore-topmast, did not arrive until 27 December.

Governor Grey was on hand to meet the migrants, creating a favourable impression by waiving customs duty on their personal effects (a duty the astonished first migrants found inflicted on them). On hand, too, was a group of Maoris who performed *haka* to the delight of some and trepidation of others. "A strange sight they are," wrote a later observer, "with their red blankets and wild tattooed faces, here and there mixed with specimens of half European attire, a coat, trousers, hat or cap."

By the year's end a full 782 passengers had been landed at the port. The Canterbury Pilgrims had arrived.

---

The Canterbury Museum Library holds lists of passengers on early migrant ships and an extensive collection of biographies, compiled by G. R. Macdonald, which extends from pre-Canterbury Association times to about 1875.

These are made available to those seeking details of family links with early Canterbury.

---

**Bishoprics and sandbars:** Thomas's surveyors began to lay out Christchurch at the end of 1849, completing their work by March. Then, according to tradition, the surveyor Edward Jollie took his map to Thomas, "who, putting on his gold spectacles and opening his *Peerage*, would read out a name to hear if it sounded well; and if Jollie agreed that it did so, the name was put on one of the streets requiring baptism. Lyttelton, being the first town born, got the best names for its streets; Sumner, being the next, got the next best; and Christchurch, being the youngest, had to be content with what names were left, and that remainder included more than a sprinkling of Irish and Colonial bishoprics . . . Whilst Sumner died, it died too late for the names there to be used again for Christchurch."

Thomas insisted on two alterations to the street plan; he condemned little orna-
mentations such as crescents as being "gingerbread", and he would not agree to some
of the streets being wider than a chain (20 m). Jollie argued that this would enable
trees to be planted and to help limit the spread of any large fires. However he was
allowed to leave good wide streets on either side of the Avon, today a meandering
swathe of grass and trees breaking up the otherwise rectangular city.

Among the settlers transport was a dividing issue. Heavy shipments from Britain
were normally landed at Lyttelton, while schooners and ketches shipped smaller
loads round by Sumner and up the Heathcote River to some fourteen different
wharves. From 1851 there was a succession of wrecks at Sumner, until the sands were
"rich in prizes". When construction of the Lyttelton-Sumner road was suspended
for a time those who approved the road pointed to the number of shipwrecks (though
these are generally exaggerated); those who supported shipping drew attention to the
cost of the road — Captain Thomas had spent £20,000 on it even before the Pilgrims
arrived, much to Godley's anger.

Access between the town and its port continued to split the settlement into two
factions, one headed by William Moorhouse favouring a tunnel through the Port
Hills, the other headed by FitzGerald not only arguing for the Sumner road but also
strenuously opposing the tunnel Moorhouse wanted. Moorhouse finally carried the
day, and as early as December 1860 work began on the tunnel, the first passenger-
train passing through on 9 December 1867.

**Runs and regulations:** The Canterbury settlement was visualised as a closely-knit
community concerned with agriculture and not pastoral farming. A new and better
England was hoped for, not a widely scattered populace in which the control of the
Church and the traditional barriers of class and education would all break down.
Men of capital were to form a landed gentry; industrious workers were to be able, in
time, to buy small parcels of land, so forming a peasantry.

The first cracks showed in the Association's policy when land was slow to sell.
Then, to the ocean of waste country that surrounded the island of settled land, came
the "Australian prophets" — driven by the drought of 1850–51 to cross the Tasman
to try their luck as squatters. With them came considerable capital which Godley
was anxious to attract to the infant settlement. The "Founder of Canterbury" was
thus induced to alter the land regulations in anticipation of approval from London.
Instead of enforcing purchase at the minimum prices set by the Association he gave
out "form letters", promising to give the holders a lease as soon as the Association's
regulations permitted it, and effectively reducing the minimum rental of 20 shillings
per 100 acres per annum by requiring payment for less than the area actually taken up.

The device worked, so that by the end of 1855 all the plains and foothills had been
leased, and during the next ten years every area worth stocking (and much that was
not) had been taken up as part of a run, right back to the Main Divide. The pre-
Adamites (those in Canterbury before the migrants of the First Four Ships) got new
licences for their Maori leases; the Australian prophets (the "shagroons") hurried
to take up much of the accessible country; and the Pilgrims themselves, after holding
off for a time, also succumbed to the fever.

Wakefield roundly condemned Godley for giving over the Canterbury settlement
to "squatting and barbarism", yet the move into pastoralism actually rescued the
gentry among the Pilgrims from economic extinction. Godley had seen that large
agricultural estates would inevitably lose money; the limited local market could
easily be supplied by small landholders with no labour costs, and many of those with
capital lacked the experience necessary for the arduous and uncertain business of
raising crops on a strange soil. On the other hand the spartan life of a sheeprun was
devoid of "the drudgery of tillage, and the technique could be learned in a few
months, even by the city-bred." FitzGerald, whose knowledge of life had been
gained at Cambridge University and the British Museum, was making a living from
his run within three years of his arrival in Canterbury. Samuel Butler, an even more
unlikely farmer, made enough from his Mesopotamia run in four years to support
him for the rest of his life, and yet found leisure enough to write the first few chapters
of *Erewhon* for the Christchurch *Press*. For the young man with moderate capital,
"the Canterbury Settlement in its first few years presented opportunities unsurpassed
in the whole history of British colonisation."

**The Church crumbles:** The new settlement's religious institutions started badly.
First, as many as seven clergymen arrived, a greater number than the community
could hope to support; then Bishop Selwyn damned the settlement's priorities:
"Here I find neither church nor school nor parsonage in existence. Money enough
has been spent, but . . . not one sixpence of expenditure in any form for the glory of
God." Then there arrived the Rev. T. Jackson as bishop-designate. He had been
chosen for the post only after a series of bitter disappointments at the failure of better
qualified men to undertake the task and he impressed Godley as unreliable and
unbusinesslike. It seems that the Archbishop of Canterbury may have prevailed on
Jackson to withdraw his claim. In any case he returned to Britain.

William Fox wrote to Godley in 1858: "As regards its ecclesiastical aspect, I think
[the Canterbury Association] has failed altogether to realise the aspirations of its
founders . . . Complaints were not few of the hardship of having to pay twice over for
Church ministrations, once in the price of the land and now in voluntary subscrip-

tions . . . The individual clergy also with one or two exceptions are perhaps not considered very bright and shining examples of the efficacy of aspostolic descent to qualify for the ecclesiastical leadership of the model Church Colony of the nineteenth century."

Fox was a harsh critic in this matter and the majority of the settlers seem to have accepted the difficulties of the church in early Canterbury as unavoidable. It is nevertheless true that in spite of Godley's vision of an envigorated Anglicanism in a New World, of the British precedent for an established Church in a special relationship with the state, and of Canterbury's origin as a Church of England settlement, when in 1853 FitzGerald as Superintendent made his maiden address to the Provincial Council he described the Church and State as "co-existent but wholly independent" and the State as maintaining an attitude of "absolute indifference" in its dealings with the various denominations.

By 1855 the Association had gone out of existence. If it had failed to fulfil its aspirations in the religious field it had arranged for 3,549 migrants, most carefully chosen, to travel halfway round the world; it had looked after its migrants better than any other similar body had done before; the colonists had prospered, and when they took over the Association's affairs they acquired assets and not, as in the case of the New Zealand Company's settlements, considerable debts.

**More English than the English?** Christchurch is frequently referred to as being "more English than the English" and "the most English city outside England", setting store by descent from the First Four Ships with a determination that puts that quartet of vessels in the same category as that enjoyed in *maoritanga* by the canoes of the legendary "Great Migration". In the city's heart — laid out between four broad avenues as "the square mile" of the City of London — the alleged Englishness of Christchurch has visual substance in the trees and the stone and style of the older buildings.

The determined Pilgrims, too, brought cricket bats with their communion vessels (Godley himself scored 24 in the first match of the Christchurch Cricket Club) and the city has ever since served as the country's headquarters for that most English of pastimes. A rowing club was active by 1864 and archery, which attracted women competitors, was established in 1873. Lawn tennis, too, was swiftly embraced after its birth in England, courts being established in Cranmer Square in 1881. Just twenty years later there emerged Anthony Wilding (1883–1915), who in 1901 at the age of seventeen won the Canterbury championship and went on to win numerous Wimbledon titles, the Davis Cup four times (for Australasia, partnered by the Australian, Norman Brookes), and a bronze medal for tennis at the 1912 Stockholm Olympic Games. (*Wilding Park, the city's tennis headquarters, is named after him*).

**"Students of Truth":** The city's generally placid demeanour was rudely shaken by the arrival in 1890 of one Arthur Bently Worthington (?–1917), LlD, MA, preacher of "The Truth". He quickly attracted an enthusiastic congregation of about 2,000, who set about erecting a Temple of Truth, one of the finest buildings in the city, with an impressive Classical façade and a seating capacity of about 1,600. (Later renamed Choral, then Latimer Hall, it was demolished in 1966.) Revelation that Worthington (probably really Samuel Oakley) was a notorious confidence man and had been bigamously married no fewer than eight times, failed to shake the faith of his followers. However, hostility was aroused when he bought the sect's assets from trustees for less than half their original cost. As scandal followed scandal, the Government pleaded with the United States to extradite the rogue. Instead, Worthington fled to Tasmania, having first "married" yet again, a Christchurch girl. His temerity exceeded all bounds when he reappeared in Christchurch in 1897 and advertised a public lecture. Word of his return had already spread, so that he was greeted by a hostile crowd of several thousand. The entire Christchurch police force concentrated outside the hall where he was due to speak, a magistrate (for the only time in Christchurch history) formally read the Riot Act, and mounted constables with swinging batons moved in to clear Lichfield Street sufficiently to allow a police escort to lead Worthington away. But "The Truth" was not to be denied, as Worthington promptly left for Melbourne where, after again founding a congregation,

A metric conversion chart appears at the end of the book.

The Automobile Association has offices throughout the country and offers members a wide range of services, from a breakdown service and legal advice to maps and details of road conditions. Its annual handbooks, listing details of hotels, motels and camping grounds, are the most comprehensive available and are issued free to members.

he was sentenced to seven years' imprisonment for swindling a widow by pretending to be the reincarnation of the god Osiris. He ended life in New York, in prison for fraud.

**Operation Deep Freeze:** Nonstop flights from Christchurch International Airport span the 3,500 km between Christchurch and McMurdo, the main US base in Antarctica and one whose population ranges from about 200 in winter to perhaps 1,000 in summer. McMurdo, centre of considerable scientific activity, is on a continent which holds such unenviable "firsts" as the stormiest (winds of 307 km/hr near the coast), the driest (its precipitation scarcely exceeds that of the Sahara or the Gobi deserts) and the coldest (an official low temperature of –88.3 °C was recorded at the Soviet Vostok station). Antarctica contains about 95 per cent of the world's permanent ice, in places up to 4 km thick and which, if melted, would raise the level of the world's oceans by perhaps 60 m. In terms of the Antarctic Treaty (1959) the entire continent is conserved for peaceful research and exploration. Weapon tests are banned and radioactive waste from McMurdo's nuclear power station is shipped back to the United States for disposal. (The international treaty (1966) governing the moon and the exploration of outer space is modelled on the Antarctic Treaty.) New Zealand exercises control over the Ross Dependency of Antarctica (between 160 °E and 150 °W) though by the treaty no country "owns" any section. Scott Base, New Zealand's annual permanent establishment, is about thirty minutes walk from McMurdo. As elsewhere, it was the ubiquitous Captain Cook who carried out the first reconnaissance work in Antarctica.

As well as its contemporary link, Christchurch has historical Antarctic connections, having hosted a long line of Antarctic explorers. The city (as, indeed, did the whole country) identified closely with the British explorer Robert Falcon Scott, whose party of five reached the South Pole in 1912 only to discover that the Norwegian, Roald Amundsen, had preceded them by a matter of weeks. Dismayed, they turned for home only to lose their lives on a return journey at least as heroic as it was tragic. *Scott's statue stands by the Avon. The Canterbury Museum holds extensive material on Antarctica.*

## OUTDOOR SPORTS

The city's surrounding area covers a broad spectrum of sporting activity — pleasant beaches, rivers for canoeing and jetboating, Lyttelton Harbour and Banks Peninsula for sailing. Local gliders have set world records, and fishing ranges from the trout of river and lake to the salmon of the Rakaia and other large rivers. Visitors are welcome to join walks and tramps organised by the Christchurch Tramping Club and the Peninsula Tramping Club (*contact telephone numbers from the Public Relations Office*).

Lake Ida, near Lake Coleridge, draws ice-skaters in winter, and the peaks of Arthur's Pass National Park are early training grounds for many rock climbers and mountaineers.

Pre-eminent is the large number of skifields which can be visited from Christchurch including: Mt Hutt (*Mt Hutt Ski & Alpine Tourist Co Ltd, Box 446, Christchurch; 108 km via Hororata and Rakaia Gorge Rd*), Craigieburn Valley (*Craigieburn Valley Ski Club, Box 1472, Christchurch; 122 km via Porters Pass*), Broken River Basin (*North Canterbury Ski Club, Box 2718, Christchurch; 121 km via Porters Pass*), Mt Cheeseman (*Canterbury Winter Sports Club, Box 1893, Christchurch; 113 km via Porters Pass*), Porter Heights (*Commercial; 97 km via Porters Pass*), Temple Basin (*University Ski Club; also Christchurch Ski Club, Box 2493, Christchurch; 163 km via Porters Pass*), Mt Olympus (*Windwhistle Winter Sports Club, Box 25055, Christchurch; 132 km via Lake Ida*), Mt St Patrick (*Amuri Ski Club, tel. 517-563; 150 km via Hanmer*), Fox's Peak (*Tasman Ski Club, Box 368, Timaru; 153 km via Geraldine*) and △ Erewhon (*Commercial; 177 km via Mount Somers*). More distant are Tekapo (*Commercial; 264 km via Fairlie*), Lake Ohau (*Commercial; 335 km via Fairlie*) and Mt Cook (*402 km via Fairlie*).

*For full details of facilities, for booking forms, and to hire equipment contact Snowline Sport Centre, 250 Oxford Tce (tel. 67-351) or Cromb & Merritt Ltd, 110 Cashel St (tel. 60-419). Most of the fields are administered by clubs, but these in the main welcome visitors and in some cases can provide accommodation for non-members on or near the fields.*

Some books on Canterbury, its history and environs include *Early South Canterbury Runs* by Robert Pinney, *The Mountains of Erewhon* by T. Beckett and *The Port Hills of Christchurch* by Gordon Ogilvie.

Stories for younger readers set in the region include *Mary-Lou — The Story of a High Country Lamb* and *Old Duke — The Story of a Hard Case Horse* both by local author Mona Anderson. Published by A.H. & A.W. Reed.

## A WALK AROUND THE CITY

*Allow upwards of 2 hours (not including time to see over the Town Hall complex, the Museum, the Art Gallery, the Arts Centre or the Provincial Council Chambers). Light meals are available at the Museum. Park in the parking building on the corner of Gloucester and Manchester Sts. Cross Manchester St and walk along Gloucester St, passing on the right:*

**New Regent Street:** On the site of the "Colosseum" (an enormous early hall) the street has a distinctively Spanish styling.

**Theatre Royal** (1908), which now houses South Pacific Television, stands just beyond New Regent St and looks across to the wooden facade of its predecessor (1874). Beside the original theatre is the building that was the Palace Hotel (1877), whose theatrical proprietor owned the adjacent Theatre Royal and was the father of May and Maude Beatty, internationally successful actresses of the 1900s. Theatrical masks still adorn the windows of the former hotel. *Turn right up Colombo St to walk away from Cathedral Square, and bear left into:*

**Victoria Square*****: Behind the imposing statue of Captain James Cook ("Circumnavigator – Ocean Investigator Acerrimus") stands the Bowker Fountain; beyond, the jets of the Town Hall fountain fan into the Avon outside the elevated Limes Room and the restaurant of the splendid Town Hall complex (*see "Some other notable buildings", below*). To the left, the portly bronze statue of Queen Victoria inevitably presides over the square named after her. The Bowker Fountain (1931), claimed as the first coloured fountain built in Australasia, nightly plays its varied water-and-light patterns. The square was originally set aside to form the town's market place, its name being changed from Market Square in 1903 with the unveiling of the statue. *Walk to the Avon (named by the Scottish Deans brothers after a river in their native Ayrshire). The river is at times flanked by numerous willows, reputedly the descendants of slips brought by French settlers to Akaroa from the St Helena grave of Napoleon. Follow the river upstream. Between the first two bridges, on the far side of the river, is the Law Court complex. Just over the second bridge may be seen the pole-topped reddish stone tower and timber wings of the:*

**Canterbury Provincial Government Buildings*****(*described below*): *Cross the bridge and, keeping to the riverbank, walk upstream between the stone buildings and the Avon. The renowned Provincial Council chamber is the last building in the group, on the right (open daily from 10 am–4 pm; guided tours on Sundays from 2–4 pm). On reaching the road again, turn left to recross the Avon by the Gloucester St bridge. Cross the road and continue along the riverbank to reach the red brick of the:*

**Chamber of Commerce building** (1887): Standing on the site of the original Land Office, the first building erected by the Canterbury Association in Christchurch (January 1851), the present building at first served as municipal chambers. A quaint mixture of architectural styles, it has above its entrance two heraldic beasts holding shields emblazoned "Britons Hold Your Own". Between them a City Council motif shows a steam engine emerging from the Lyttelton Tunnel, a sheep, a cow, a sheaf of wheat and a plough. From the first floor, statues of Industry and Concord overlook the river. The building now houses the Chamber of Commerce and the Public Relations Office. *Crossing Worcester St as you continue to follow the Avon, to the left is a vista closed by the bronze statue of Godley in front of the Cathedral. Across the street is the:*

**Robert Falcon Scott statue** (1917): Sculpted by the widow of the Antarctic explorer, the statue underscores the link between the city and the frozen continent. Scott's widow, Kathleen Lady Kennett, was one of the few outstanding women sculptors of her day. Inscribed on the pedestal are the words scribbled with difficulty by Scott as his little group lay dying in a blizzard. *Over the Avon is the low blue-painted Canterbury Club (1872). Pass the Hereford St bridge (across which is the Gothic brick Public Library (1875) scheduled for demolition). The next bridge reached, in Cashel St is the:*

**Bridge of Remembrance** (1923): The memorial bridge was built here to replace the bridge over which many soldiers of World War I marched as they made their way from the King Edward Barracks to the railway station on the first leg of their journey to the battlefields of Asia and Europe. Just down Cashel St, to the right, stands the huge barnlike barracks (1905), built in the space of just four weeks, and for years occasionally used as an outsize concert hall. *Continue along the riverbank. A short distance farther on is:*

**St Michael and All Angels Anglican Church** (1872)***: The mother church of the Diocese of Canterbury is the successor to a modest V hut, built here within days of the arrival of the Pilgrims. It was from here that a procession of ecclesiastical and civic leaders left in 1864 to march through the streets to lay the foundation stone for the cathedral. Memorials within include a window dedicated to George Dobson (*see index*). Older than the church is the campanile (1860), designed by Benjamin

He travels the fastest who travels alone. — Rudyard Kipling (*The Winners*).

# CHRISTCHURCH CITY

8

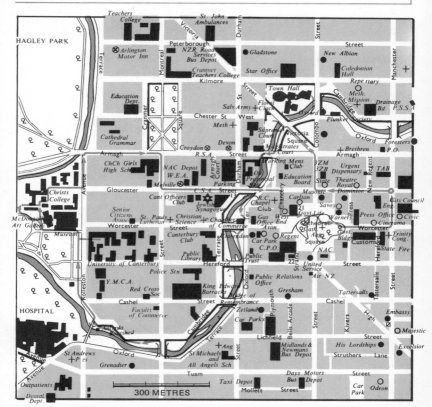

Mountfort, with a bell that came out on one of the First Four Ships. *Continue upstream and cross the Montreal St bridge. Walk by the river beneath the shade of the trees of Cambridge Tce and pass the pontoons of the:*

**Antigua boatsheds** (1882): Originally built for the Christchurch Boating Club — of entirely male membership — the sheds now cater for a very different clientele but still provide canoes for them to paddle on the timeless river. This was the farthest upstream of perhaps half a dozen such sheds. *Veer right to enter Rolleston Ave and pass the:*

**James Edward FitzGerald statue:** Topper in hand, Canterbury's first superintendent (1853–57) looks down Cashel St and over the Bridge of Remembrance. Impulsive, witty and winning in manner, FitzGerald (1818–96) came as a colonist from the cloistered retreat of the British Museum. He edited the first newspaper (the *Lyttelton Times*) launched the *Press* (1861 and still appearing), and was a logical candidate for the post of superintendent when Godley decided to return home before the elections. He never departed from his lofty ideals, which included full representation in Parliament for the Maori — his motion in the General Assembly was only lost by a narrow margin. He was instrumental in founding Christ's College, naming it after his old Cambridge college, and later (though unqualified to do so) designing the schoolroom. His idealism was generally too unremitting for him to make much impact, and he was never notable for his ability as an administrator. For the latter reason it was perhaps as well that as a national politician he declined an offer to form a ministry with himself as premier. *On the left is the entrance to the Botanic Gardens where, seated and looking down Hereford St, is the:*

**William Sefton Moorhouse statue** (1885): Moorhouse (1825–81) was everything FitzGerald was not — a graduate of the Merchant Navy and the goldfields and, though qualified as a lawyer, better known for his skill with his fists than for his forensic gifts. The lofty, urbane FitzGerald thought him so dangerous that he founded the *Press* to oppose him. Always a man of action (he undoubtedly would have prospered had he directed his energies towards his own affairs), Moorhouse formulated the railway-and-tunnel plan to link the town with Lyttelton — a scheme that at first appalled the "wealth and intelligence" of the province, but one that he saw through to success. Erratic, he was nonetheless popular, Samuel Butler remembering him as "perhaps the greatest man all round that I have ever known". His career remains an enigma, for he resigned from office almost whenever his political future seemed assured. He served as superintendent from 1857–63 and from 1866–68. *On the opposite side of Rolleston Ave is the exuberant Gothic of the:*

**Old Canterbury University Buildings** (started 1876): Now the Arts Centre (*see* "*Some Museums and Art Galleries*") the complex includes two quadrangles and a dividing library block and arcade, all in the style of functional Gothic. The den in which Lord Rutherford (*see index*) carried out his early experiments is in the western corner of the main quadrangle, marked by a plaque whose quotation (adapted from Horace) means "He created a monument more lasting than bronze." *Farther on, looking down Worcester St to Godley and the cathedral is the:*

**William Rolleston statue** (1905): Intelligent, methodical, industrious, Rolleston (1831–1903) was the supreme administrator who served as superintendent almost without opposition from 1868 until the abolition of the provincial system in 1876. Starting out as a runholder, but examining at Christ's College to keep his Latin and Greek from getting rusty (he had an honours degree in classics from Cambridge), he drifted into political life but was stranded by the abolition of provincial rule. As the model superintendent of a model province, some saw him as a future premier, but he lacked the determination to seize his chances and the resolve to hold on to them. He confessed after his final election defeat (by a single vote) to having "a greater love for the practical and administrative side of Public Life than for the political". He was, however, completely at home in the educated atmosphere of the infant Canterbury settlement.

Of Canterbury's four superintendents, only a statue of the lacklustre figure of the mild-mannered Samuel Bealey (1821–1909) is missing. Elected unopposed as a compromise between the warring factions of FitzGerald and Moorhouse, Bealey, when his term came to an end, laid down his duties as cheerfully as he had taken them up.

All four superintendents' names are commemorated by the avenues that form the original city boundary of the settlement. Sir John Hall remarked of Canterbury's showing as a self-governing province: "If the work of the other provinces had been as well done as that of Canterbury, provincial institutions might have remained in existence to the present day." *Behind Rolleston is the:*

**Canterbury Museum** (1870)***: In many ways a memorial to its first director, the geologist-explorer Sir Julius von Haast. (*See* "*Some Museums and Art Galleries*", *below*). *Walk to the left of the museum building, through the Botanic Gardens, bearing right to pass the McDougall Art Gallery (see below). About 50 m past the entrance to the Gallery is a small gate leading into the grounds of Christ's College. (Note: The headmaster has kindly agreed to allow those making this walk to come through the grounds. Visitors are asked to respect this concession and to avoid any interruption of school activities.) In the event of the gate being locked, return to Rolleston Ave and turn left to walk on past the front entrance to Christ's College. Otherwise pass through the gate and bear right through the complex of buildings old and new, skirt the quadrangle and regain Rolleston Ave.*

**Christ's College:** Founded in the first decade of settlement, this boys' secondary school holds fast to an English public-school tradition, retaining a formal uniform that still includes the straw boater. Its first headmaster, the Rev. H. Jacobs, was chaplain on the *Sir George Seymour*, one of the First Four Ships, who first opened a school at Lyttelton in 1851, using part of the immigration barracks. Visualised by the Canterbury Association as emulating "one of the great grammar schools of England both as to instruction and discipline", the first of the buildings on the present site was in use in 1857. The Dining Hall (by the road), the Hare Library (with the quaint clock) and Jacobs House are all the work of Cecil Wood, Canterbury's leading architect of the 1920s and 1930s. The Big School (1863), with a highpitched roof and designed by the unqualified FitzGerald, is to the left of the Hare Library. Farther to the left are the "new classrooms" (1886), by Benjamin Mountfort. *Turn left to continue along Rolleston Ave. On rejoining the Avon and looking out over Hagley Park, turn right into Armagh St. On the corner, on the left, is the headmaster's house for Christ's College, formerly home of Sir Henry Wigram. Walk down Armagh St to:*

**Cranmer Square:** A large open square across the length of which may be seen the iron tip of the Jubilee clock-tower (1860; re-erected here 1897), richly laced with decorative ironwork. The tower was designed by Benjamin Mountfort and intended for the Provincial Council buildings. On the far side of the square is the Normal School (1873–76), which served as a school and more recently as part of the Teachers' Training College. Somewhat grim and grey in appearance, and ill-lit internally, it appears to have been designed more for English than for Christchurch conditions, though there is no foundation for the tale that it was planned in Britain to face south — where the sun would have been had it been built in the northern hemisphere. *Turn right by the Gothic brick of the old (1880) Christchurch Girls' High School building and then turn left up Gloucester St to pass the CSA Gallery (the modern gallery and exhibition centre of the Canterbury Society of Arts) and the weathered stone façade of the Jewish Synagogue (1881). Continue on to cross the Avon (by the Provincial Council Chambers) and, after crossing Oxford Tce and continuing a little further along Gloucester St, turn right down narrow Chancery Lane to emerge in:*

**Cathedral Square:** Once little more than a tramway shunting yard, the Square is now a "peoples' place" where pedestrians stroll amid trees, tubs of flowers and shrubs and fruit and flower barrows, or gather at lunchtime about "Speakers' Corner". Of particular interest, near the Post office, is Four Ships Court, on whose marble slabs are engraved the names of the Pilgrims who arrived on the First Four Ships. Older buildings of note round the perimeter are the elegant old Post Office (1877–79), the *Press* building (1900), and the United Services Hotel (1884). *Cross to the centre of the Square, passing the statue of John Robert Godley, "the Founder of Canterbury", and enter:*

**Christchurch Cathedral\*\*\*:** Enter and climb the steep steps up through the inverted bells to the observation balconies on the tower (*open 9–4 daily; small admission charge*) for an elevated panorama of city, Port Hills, plains and distant mountains. The bellringers' vestry is hung with plaques commemorating such marathon feats as "a peal of 5,040 grandsire doubles" in three hours and "a peal of Bob Triples". (*For details of the Cathedral, see below*). *Leave the Square down the continuation of Worcester St, passing between the poetical* Press *building and the humane-if-official-looking Government Department Buildings (1911). At the corner of Worcester St and Manchester St, turn left along Manchester St. After passing the Civic Administration complex the walk ends at the parking building where it began.*

## SOME MUSEUMS AND ART GALLERIES

**Canterbury Museum\*\*\*:** Housed in one of Benjamin Mountfort's buildings (1870), the Museum lends itself to early colonial settings, with galleries depicting a pioneer Christchurch street (complete with the last of the city's hansom cabs) and a full-sized reconstruction of FitzGerald's cabin on the *Charlotte Jane*. Well-planned displays cover ethnology from Somalia to Brazil, and every aspect of New Zealand's history. The 100th Anniversary Wing includes a Hall af Antarctic Studies, antarctic library and a rooftop planetarium.

Its first director was the Austrian geologist-explorer Sir Julius von Haast (1822–87), who covered much of the South Island on journeys as valuable as they were extensive, in the course of which he discovered △Haast Pass. He used his large collection of *moa* bones as a means of exchange with overseas museums and so built up one of the country's finest museum holdings. The Museum's tradition of fieldwork has been continued by Dr Roger Duff, the present director and an authority on the Moa-hunter period.

A genealogical service assists those anxious to establish a personal link with the Canterbury Pilgrims.

*Rolleston Ave. Open daily from 10 am–4.30 pm (Sunday 2–4.30 pm). Allow upwards of half a day. Light meals are available.*

**Ferrymead Historic Park\*\*\*:** An ambitious museum project is growing on two adjacent sites, combining the activities and enthusiasm of such disparate groups as Tramway and Railway Societies, the Fire Services Historical Society, Vintage Phonographic Society, Harness Club, Aeronautical Society, and Museums of Science, Industry and Road Transport. Steam locomotives and early trams carry visitors on tracks at the Bridle Path Rd site, where the Fire Services Museum displays early equipment. An old-style bakery operates on Sundays. A nineteenth-century village is being re-created on the Truscotts Rd site, together with transport and science display buildings. The Ferrymead locale is itself of historic import, as it was from here to Christchurch that the country's first steam railway ran, serving vessels that docked in the estuary from 1863 until the line fell into disuse with the opening of the tunnel through to Lyttelton in 1867. *Bridle Path Rd, off road to Sumner. Open daily 10 am–5 pm. Guided tours 10.30 am and 2.30 pm on weekdays. Tel. 841-970.*

**Yaldhurst Transport Museum\*:** A variety of horsedrawn and mechanised forms of transport through the ages is displayed. Occasionally rides are given in early wagons. *Yaldhurst (opp. Yaldhurst Hotel). 11 km. Open weekends and holidays; tel. 427-914.*

**Canterbury Society of Arts\*\*:** Continuously on display are works by contemporary New Zealand artists, for viewing as well as for sale. *66 Gloucester St. Open Mon.–Fri. 10 am–4.30 pm, weekends 2–4.30 pm.* An earlier building once belonging to the society (1890), and presently used by the Justice Department, is opposite the main entrance to the Provincial Council buildings in Amagh St.

**McDougall Art Gallery\*\*:** As with the Town Hall, the siting of the city's Art Gallery (a building given by a successful businessman) was the subject of civic controversy before a final choice was made. A special Act of Parliament was required to permit the use of the Botanic Gardens as a site. The collection is based round the Society of Art's holdings, donated before the Society again went its independent way. Displayed are early and contemporary British and New Zealand works, pottery and sculpture (including two Rodin). *Rolleston Ave. Enter from the Botanic Gardens, behind the Museum. Open daily from 10 am–4.30 pm (Sunday 2–4.30 pm).*

**Arts Centre of Christchurch:** The former Canterbury University buildings are occupied by the Technical Institute and by forty societies and individuals who perform, teach or administer the arts. Here the professional Court Theatre performs (in an intimate theatre created from a one-time engineering lecture room), the Christchurch School for Instrumental Music weekly teaches over 1,000 children and the Southern Ballet rehearses. Light opera, pottery, painting, weaving and yoga are among other activities. *Rolleston Ave. Visitors welcome.*

## SOME OTHER NOTABLE BUILDINGS

**Provincial Council buildings** (1859–65)\*\*\*: Perhaps the finest complex of Gothic buildings in the country, and certainly the most intriguing, spreads out round a heavy red-stone tower. The vertical-timbered section, surrounding a courtyard, was built in stages — that facing Durham St in 1859, the wings flanking the stone tower in 1861. "Bellamy's" (or the "Coffee Rooms") was added at the rear in 1865 to all but completely enclose the courtyard. For some reason the recessed door from Bellamy's to the lawn was called Traitors' Gate, perhaps because, like that of the Tower of London, it can be approached from the river. The Court offices nearer the river were built in 1924.

The timbered section is worthy of a close look, though court sittings often prevent the original council chamber (1859) being seen. The crowning glory of the complex is the colourful Council Chamber of 1865, built of stone and with a massive and finely-decorated barrel ceiling, mosaic walls and stained-glass windows carrying assorted texts and homilies. Balconies accommodated both public and press. The elaborate stonework is by William Brassington, the master-mason who included touches of humour and his own likeness among the many flourishes and masks in the stonework. Others depicted include Queen Victoria, Prince Albert, Florence Nightingale, General Gordon, David Livingstone, and the artist J. S. St Quentin (who worked on the ceiling for fully two years). Behind the Speaker's dais is the Superintendent's Room, used when the Superintendent came to address the Council. A massive clock tower planned for the complex proved too heavy for the wooden tower built to carry it; it now stands on the corner of Victoria and Montreal Streets.

The architect for the complex was Benjamin Mountfort, who in time recovered from the collapse of his first building (Holy Trinity, at Lyttelton) to design most of the province's early public buildings of importance. The complex overlooks the Avon in an attractive parklike setting. *Cnr Armagh and Durham Sts. The complex is open on weekdays, generally from 9 am–4 pm. Conducted tours on Sunday afternoons (details from the Public Relations Office).*

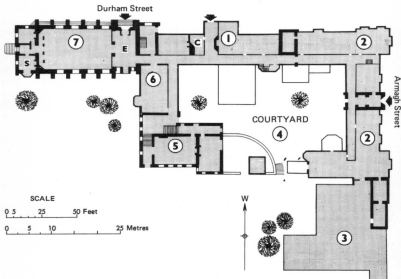

KEY:
1. First timber block 1859
2. Second timber block 1861
3. Magistrate's Court Offices 1924
4. Courtyard
5. Bellamy's 1865
6. Original timber Council Chamber 1859
7. Stone Council Chamber 1865
E. Entrance Vestibule
S. Superintendent's Room
C. Custodian's Room

*Groundfloor plan of Provincial Council Chambers, courtesy of the Department of Lands and Survey.*

**Christchurch Cathedral** (1864)\*\*\*: The tall copper-sheathed spire of the early-English Gothic cathedral rises 65.5 m above the Square, pinpointing the spiritual centre of an essentially Anglican community. (The spire has thrice been damaged in earthquakes). Planning for the cathedral had begun within nine years of the arrival of the First Four Ships, but though building began in 1864 construction was overtaken by economic depression and eight years later Anthony Trollope curtly noted that "The idea of building the Cathedral is now abandoned." However in 1881 the nave was at last ready for use. The transept and chancel were consecrated in 1904.

Without is the statue of John Robert Godley, "the Founder of Canterbury". Within, the diocese recalls its history. Tablets in the west porch record the origins of the province. Panels on the pulpit (a memorial to Bishop Selwyn, the first and only Bishop of New Zealand) portray him preaching to the Maoris; welcoming Bishop Harper as the first bishop of Christchurch; dismissing the synod that settled the constitution for the New Zealand Church; and, with Abraham and Hobhouse, consecrating Bishop Patteson (*see North Island index*). Bishop Harper himself is commemorated by a lectern and a reclining effigy, the work of the private sculptor to Queen Victoria. The two bishops also appear on the massive high altar, whose *kauri* reredos portrays (*from top left down*), the Rev. Samuel Marsden and Archdeacon Henry Williams (pioneer missionaries; *for both see North Island index*) and Tamihana Te Rauparaha (the warrior chief's missionary son); (*from top right down*) Bishop Selwyn, Bishop Harper and Bishop Patteson. The font, designed by Benjamin Mountfort, who also supervised the construction of the cathedral, was the gift of Dean Stanley, of Westminster, whose brother took the *Britomart* to Akaroa in 1840 to forestall the French. (Note: The inscription is historically inaccurate as British sovereignty over the South Island had already been proclaimed at Port Underwood.) Windows remember Joseph Hawdon (a large landholder), Sir Thomas Tancred (Speaker of the Provincial Council and first Chancellor of the University of New Zealand), Robert Heaton Rhodes (*see index*), Bishop Harper's wife Emily, and James and Joseph Greenwood (pioneer settlers on the Peninsula). Also remembered are John Studholme (*see index*), J. E. FitzGerald, Archdeacon Dudley (who arrived on the *Cressy*), John Watts-Russell (the first sheepfarmer in Canterbury, who also introduced its rabbits) and Sir John Cracroft Wilson ("the Nabob", who caused a sensation by migrating to Christchurch from India with a Noah's Ark of Indian animals and an assortment of Indian servants.

*One may climb the progressively steeper steps that lead up the tower. Cathedral Square.*

**Christchurch Town Hall complex**\*\*\*: The much-admired buildings opened in 1972 as a monument to the city's patience as well as to its artistry and skill, for it had waited fully 122 years before its first town hall was completed (the newer of the two earlier "town halls" — really only privately owned assembly rooms — had burned down almost a century before). During that time a number of Town Hall committees had debated possible sites and proposed plans until at last a group of citizens in 1957 took matters into their own hands and launched a fundraising scheme. This served to divide the city between possible sites (the history of Christchurch is marked by fierce divisions on virtually every topic since Godley objected to the cost of the Lyttelton-Sumner road). To resolve the impasse, Professor Gordon Stephenson of Perth was invited to advise, and the city surprised itself with the unanimity with which it accepted his recommendation of The Limes site (by the Avon and overlooking Victoria Square) — a site which a few months earlier only 19 per cent of the *Star* newspaper readers had favoured.

The design itself was the subject of a nationwide competition and was awarded to the Christchurch firm of Warren & Mahoney, a decision again greeted with overwhelming approval. Construction, at a cost of about $5 million, took four years, and Christchurch at last had its town hall, though as one writer has noted "its citizens experienced disbelief" that it should exist at all. The main auditorium seats 2,662 on two levels, a concert chamber (the James Hay Theatre) accommodates 1,008, and sundry other facilities include meeting rooms, a banquet room and a restaurant. A municipal administration block is to be built beside it. The complex gives Christchurch the finest conference facilities in the country. *Victoria Square. Main entrance is in Kilmore St. When the complex is not in use conducted tours of it are run half-hourly. (No morning tours at weekends). Tel. 68-899 for details. Meals available in the restaurant.*

**Roman Catholic Basilica (Cathedral of the Blessed Sacrament)**\*\*\* (1901–05): Regarded as the country's most successful High Renaissance building, the huge domed edifice is the crowning achievement of F. W. Petre ("Lord Concrete"). The dome is placed above the crossing to give the scholarly interior an even more spacious air. Anglicans are said to have preened when George Bernard Shaw admired the "splendid cathedral", but their pride turned to anguish when he went on to refer to the Basilica and its proximity to the gasworks. *Barbadoes St.*

**Riccarton House (Deans Bush)**\*\*: Deans Bush, preserving a fragment of the forest that was originally found near the city's site, was given by the Deans family as a public reserve. Riccarton House (1856–1900) was for ninety years the Deans family homestead (now used for receptions). By the homestead is the little Deans Cottage (1843), preserved as a minute museum. The second house to be built on the plains, the cottage was lived in by William and John Deans, who prudently protected the *kahikatea* forest from the wind by planting a belt of exotics.

A direct descendant, Bob Deans, has his own niche in history as the player who "scored" the disputed try for the All Blacks against Wales in 1905. None who knew him could discount his claim to have fairly grounded the ball, but the try was disallowed and the New Zealanders suffered the only loss of a lengthy tour. The try-that-never-was remains a bone of contention between the two rugby-playing countries. *Kahu Rd, Riccarton. Grounds open to the public.*

**Sign of the Takahe\*\*:** The Tudoresque stone building stands as a memorial to Henry George Ell (1862–1934), the politician and ardent beautifier who battled to provide the Summit Road and preserve the Port Hills from further development. The most ornate of his planned series of roadhouses, the hall was incomplete when Ell died and lay unused and unfinished until it was completed by the City Council in 1949. Surprisingly, Ell never saw at first hand the mediaeval architecture he sought to emulate. Within the building, in use as tearooms, are shields and coats of arms of English families with and without Canterbury connections. *Hackthorne Rd, towards Dyers Pass.* A short distance beyond is Victoria Park, enjoying a splendid view.

**Te Whatu Manawa Maoritanga Orehua:** The South Island's only carved Maori meeting house (1906) apart from museum buildings, stands in the grounds of Rehua Hostel for Apprentice Maori Boys. *79 Springfield Rd, off Bealey Ave. Park outside grounds.*

**Some other interesting buildings** include the new University campus (*Ilam Rd; details of conducted tours from tel. 488-489*); Rangi Ruru School (*Hewitts Rd*); St Peters Anglican Church (1858) (*corner Riccarton and Yaldhurst Rds*) and Cracroft House (*Cashmere Rd, near Worsley Rd intersection*; built by the "nabob", Sir John Cracroft Wilson).

## SOME PARKS AND GARDENS

**Mona Vale:** Built in 1905 by Mrs Annie Townend, daughter of George Moore (*see index*) and one of the country's wealthiest women, the imposing home is set in trim, tree-lined gardens through which, predictably, meanders the ubiquitous Avon. An inviting picnic place. The house is used for receptions, art exhibitions, etc. *Enter from Fendalton Rd.*

**Hagley Park\*\*:** "The land is flat as a pancake — treeless, featureless — except for the little river," wrote C. W. Richmond of the Canterbury plains when he viewed them from the Bridle Path in 1857. As early as 1859, a horticulturist, Enoch Barker, was engaged to make good the lack of trees, and the lofty trees of Hagley Park are the most outstanding result. There is a horse track and playing-fields for a variety of sports.

Relics round the park include the first coaching milestone (*Riccarton Rd, near the hospital*); a stone which marks the place where the Pilgrims farewelled Godley at a formal public breakfast on Christmas Day, 1852 (*Riccarton Rd, by entrance to Botanic Gardens*); and a garish American-Indian totem pole, floodlit at night, a legacy of Operation Deep Freeze, which attracts a mixed reaction from Cantuarians (*Harper Ave*).

**Botanic Gardens\*\*\*:** Within Hagley Park and bordered by a loop of the gentle Avon River are colourful formal gardens, with conservatories as well as rose and bulb beds spread among its English lawns and woodland. A kiosk serves light meals. *Access from Rolleston Ave or Riccarton Rd. Open daily.*

**Millbrook Reserve\*\*:** A delightful small reserve on the northern boundary of Hagley Park, renowned for its azaleas and rhododendrons. *Access from Carlton Mill Rd or across the Avon from Harper Ave.*

**Queen Elizabeth II Park:** Built for the 1974 Commonwealth Games at a cost of $5 million, this park contains unique back-to-back athletics and swimming stadia under a 1 ha roof. The main stadium is used for soccer, greyhound racing and rock concerts besides athletics and golf, swimming, squash and a restaurant are available for visitors. *New Brighton. Guided tours every half hour.*

**Orana Park:** A wildlife reserve established with the idea of providing more natural conditions than are found in the old-style zoos, Orana Park covers 16 hectares and is to be expanded to 80. Visitors with cars may drive through the African lion reserve. *Harewood Rd West extension. Tel. 597-109.*

## OTHER POINTS OF INTEREST

**Beaches:** Numerous beaches have their own attraction. Near at hand are those at Sumner (*12 km; see below*), Taylors Mistake\*\* (*16 km*) and New Brighton (*9 km; see below*). Farther out are Camp Bay, on Lyttelton Harbour (*42 km*), and Okains Bay (*87 km*) and Le Bons Bay (*93 km*), both on Banks Peninsula. To the north, on Pegasus Bay, are Kairaki (*24 km*), The Pines (*24 km*) and Woodend (*27 km*), all near △Kaiapoi; and Leithfield (*42 km*) and Amberley Beach (*52 km*), near △Amberley.

**New Brighton\*\*** (pop. 2,250): The seaside settlement, as well as a good beach, boasts Queen Elizabeth II Park, principal venue for the 1974 Commonwealth Games. Nearby is a small zoo and aquarium (*135 Beach Rd; open 10 am–5 pm.*)

The area takes its name from its first hotel, "New Brighton" (now a tavern) to which patrons were ferried by paddlesteamer in a grandiose scheme that saw its first proprietor, Joseph Hopkins, soon sold up. Hopkins had sought to create a new Brighton-type seaside resort, and others were to follow. In 1894 an entertainment pier opened — over 210 m long and 6 m wide and sprinkled with slot machines. For years it was a great attraction. Steamers ran excursions at weekends from Lyttelton, and crowded trams ran to and from the city. Sturdily built, the pier survived until 1965. The clock tower, close to where the pier once stood, was given by Richard Edward Green "to perpetuate the name of his father", who was brought out to install the country's first telegraph system, between Lyttelton and Christchurch, and ended up suing the Provincial Council. As Green had already donated a similar clock of like expense to Sumner, his family doubted his sanity, and only after a court hearing did the gift proceed. At its foot is a drinking fountain commemorating the coronation of Edward VII (1902). Behind, the old pier tearooms have become a seaside country club.

Each Shrove Tuesday local women compete in pancake races. The custom dates from an old English practice, when parishioners would confess their sins to their priests on the day before Lent began and then dine on pancakes in scenes of hilarity. *9 km NE.*

**Taitapu** (pop. 501): A settlement near the foot of the Port Hills, Taitapu (whose name may mean sacred stream) has a pretty stone church built by Sir Robert Heaton Rhodes to his wife's memory. St Paul's Anglican Church (1930), designed by Cecil Wood, includes both local and Australian stone. Lady Rhodes' Australian origins also gave rise to the emu and kangaroo carved in the porch above the main entrance. The font from an earlier church (1876) is still in its original place, serving as base for a sundial. (*By roadside. Key held locally.*)

Sir Robert's Otahuna property is nearby where, from the road, his imposing homestead (1895) may be seen. In spring the grounds have spectacular showings of daffodils. Rhodes (1861–1956) was a member of the House of Representatives for Ellesmere (1899–1926), holding ministerial rank, and later served on the Legislative Council. (*From the church on Highway 75 turn up Old Taitapu Rd and, opp. the domain, turn right along Rhodes Rd. The homestead block is on the right.*) *16 km SE on Highway 75 towards Akaroa.*

**Lake Ellesmere:** To the Maoris the stretch of water they called Waihora (wide waters) was of considerable value as a source of food and flax, and as providing easy transportation and good sites for *pa*. In legend the bed of the lake, in common with other South Island lakes, was dug out by Rakaihautu with his fabulous *ko* (digging stick). The lake's present name is for Lord Ellesmere, a promoter of the Canterbury Association.

Though its 278 sq km makes it one of the largest lakes in New Zealand, it has a maximum depth of barely 2 m. Essentially a coastal lagoon, it is separated from the sea by a long spit formed of gravels borne north by the longshore drift. The lake has no permanent outlet and periodically a cut is made to avert flooding, an action similar to that taken by Maoris in pre-European times. Eels and flounder abound in the brackish waters, home to large numbers of black swan and Canadian geese.

**Sumner** (pop. 2,857): Across the entrance to the estuary from the long bar of South New Brighton, the settlement was originally planned to be of considerable size and importance. The beach (with its unique Cave Rock) attracts family groups (*Described under "Summit Road Drive", below*). The stone clock tower, like that at New Brighton, remembers the man brought out to install the country's first telegraph. From the end of the beach the road climbs precipitously over a sheer bluff, affording splendid views, and reaches the delightful cove of Taylors Mistake. (*Those who wish may walk up the bluff along tracks starting in Heberden Ave*). *12 km SE.*

**Wigram:** The principal ground and training base for the Royal New Zealand Air Force is named for Sir Henry Wigram (1857–1934). "The Father of Aviation in New Zealand", Wigram as a successful merchant and Member of Parliament, was quick to see the almost limitless possibilities of aircraft for defence and transport. Unable to impress officialdom, in 1914 he established a private flying school to train pilots for the war and to promote aviation generally. Eventually the Government was sufficiently impressed to take the school over, but not before Wigram had personally spent £29,000 of his own money on the venture. In 1923 the airport, previously known as Sockburn, was renamed in his honour.

It was at Wigram that Sir Charles Kingsford Smith landed in 1928 after completing the first successful flight across the Tasman. The west-east passage took 14 hrs 25 mins and the return journey, 22 hrs 51 mins. Jets have since made the trip in about two hours. The airfield is used each January for the Lady Wigram Trophy race, one of the events of the Tasman motor-racing series. Commercial aircraft now use Christchurch International Airport, farther north. *9 km S on Highway 1.*

**Lincoln College:** As early as in 1850 there were plans to have agriculture taught at university level and when Canterbury College was founded in 1873 the proposed School of Agriculture was endowed with over 40,000 ha. The earliest buildings at Lincoln College date from 1880, when it was opened as one of the world's earliest schools of agriculture, also the first to establish three- and four-year degree courses. The original roll of 13 has increased to about 2,000. The Church of St Stephen here opened in 1877. *Lincoln. 21 km SSW.*

**Lake Forsyth,** separated from the sea by a shingle bank that periodically requires bulldozing to provide an outlet, was long regarded by the Maori as a source of food. The shingle bank at Birdlings Flat is a favoured source of gemstones. *S.*

## SUMMIT ROAD DRIVE

*70 km.* The half-day drive along the crest of the Port Hills, the northern rim of the volcanic crater that forms Lyttelton Harbour, ranks with the country's finest. It forms an essential part of the itinerary for any visit to Christchurch. The suggested route climbs from Sumner and curls along the Port Hills as far as Gebbies Pass. As the road climbs, one's first view is of Sumner, houses huddled beside a void of ocean; then down into Lyttelton Harbour; then over the estuary and the northwards sweep of Pegasus Bay. As the views alternate the aspect changes dramatically until at last one suddenly sees the silver sprawl of Lake Ellesmere and the gentle arc of the Canterbury Bight. *Several of the points of interest are described under △Lyttelton or elsewhere under Christchurch. Drive towards Sumner. Cross the Heathcote River by the estuary, where the described route begins at Ferrymead, by the foot of Bridle Path Rd. Follow the shore to pass:*

**Sod Cottage** (*c.* 1863) (*0.2 km*): Built by a worker on the country's first railway, from Ferrymead to Christchurch, the cottage has been restored and furnished and is now maintained by the city, looking much as it did when sailing vessels unloaded in the estuary. The diamond-shaped glass windows are reputedly from Godley's cottage at Lyttelton.

**Moa Bone Point Cave, Redcliffs:** In 1872 major discoveries were made here during excavations by Julius von Haast, successive layers yielding remains of European occupation; then bones of native dogs, seals and birds; thirdly, a layer which contained *moa* bones, the remains of birds, fish, and shellfish, cooking-ovens and implements. Near the middle of the cave were the ruins of a canoe shelter, built to protect a double-canoe from falling rock. At a depth of several metres the skeleton of a man was found, buried in the sitting (or pre-natal) position. The cave, one of the most important archaeological sites in the country and now thoroughly excavated, is no longer sealed off. It was occupied intermittently for more than 600 years. *The curiosity of Shag Rock is passed (4.2 km) before one enters the seaside settlement of Sumner (see above) (named after Dr Sumner, Archbishop of Canterbury in 1850).*

**Cave Rock\*** (*4.8 km*): Topped with the flagmast that signalled the state of the bar to ships approaching the estuary, is a large deposit of volcanic lava forming a spacious sea-cave. In legend the rock was a whale cast up on the shore as the result of the *makutu* (magic) of Te Ake, attempting to avenge the death of his daughter. She had died as the result of the *makutu* of the *tohunga* (priest) Turaki-po, angered after she had rejected him. Of all the people who lived here, the *tohunga* was the only one who saw something unusual in the unexpected gift from the sea, and declined to take part in a feast of whalemeat. Wisely so, as the rest of his kinfolk died of food poisoning. But Te Ake was not to be denied his *utu*, for he tracked down and killed the *tohunga*. Some say that the rock is a petrified *taniwha* (water monster), formed of the ashes of the body of Te Ake's daughter. *Follow Wakefield Ave. Enter Evans Pass Rd and climb through bare, sheep-cropped hills. At 8.6 km turn right along Summit Road. The road winds along the crest of the hills with alternating views over Christchurch and the plains, and abruptly down to Lyttelton Harbour.*

**Bridle Path** (*15.2 km*): Here, above the Lyttelton road-tunnel, the hallowed Bridle Path crosses the road (*marked by a memorial shelter*). The Port Hills formed the initial obstacle to be overcome by the Canterbury Pilgrims. To the left may be seen the venerable signal station, overlooking Lyttelton Harbour. Farther left, across the harbour, is the tiny fortified island of Ripa (*see index*). *Continue along the ridge for further splendid views. At 13.3 km one may detour briefly towards the television transmitter and from the car park enjoy a superb panorama of the Alps as far distant as Mt Cook.*

**Sign of the Kiwi** (*24.3 km*): One of Harry Ell's planned series of stone roadhouses dispenses light refreshments. (*See "Sign of the Takahe", above*). *Continue along the Summit Road. Lake Ellesmere (see above) comes into distant view at 27.8 km. At 28.8 km, to the right and below the road, is the:*

**Sign of the Bellbird:** Another of Ell's roadhouses, it fell into disrepair and has been rebuilt as a picnic shelter.

*At Gebbies Pass (33.6 km) turn left to reach Teddington and Governors Bay (see index). Either return to Christchurch over Dyers Pass (at 48.5 km turn left; 13 km), passing the Sign of the Takahe, or continue on to △Lyttelton (57.3 km) and regain the city either through the tunnel or by way of Evans Pass.*

## SOME OTHER SUGGESTED DRIVES

**THE GORGES.** The 156 km all-day drive takes in two spectacular yet completely different river gorges. *Leave Christchurch north on Highway 1, passing △***Kaiapoi.** *Branch inland on Highway 12 to reach △***Rangiora.** *At Rangiora cross the railway line and immediately turn right to follow the signposted route to Ashley Gorge, crossing the river and proceeding by way of the orcharding district of Loburn. After a pleasant run the road lifts on to the lowest lip of the foothills to afford sweeping views over the plains. A small plantation of poplars is passed before the Ashley River is recrossed at:*

**Ashley Gorge\*\*\*** (*64 km*): On the south bank a large area of level ground is shaded by poplars and is in season thick with campers and day-trippers come to picnic and to swim. In total contrast, the well-bushed north bank lifts sheer from the river's waters. A century ago the area near here was briefly the scene of a thriving flax industry. Two swaggers were engaged to plant hundreds of poplar trees to check the spread of shingle over the flax swamp. Most of these trees have perished, but a grove still survives about 800 m east of the riverbridge. *The road bears south to pass through* △Oxford *and reach the:*

**Waimakariri Gorge\*\*\*** (*86 km*): If not as totally hospitable as the Ashley, the gorge here is much more grand. Upstream the river's waters are constricted between perpendicular bare rock walls, downstream the Waimakariri's character changes completely as it fans out over a broad spread of shingle. Here, too, are swimming, canoeing and a number of picnic spots. Jetboat trips run through the gorge (*see "Organised Excursions", below*). *Cross the river and join Highway 73 near Sheffield. Turn left and pass through Darfield and:*

**Kirwee** (*110 km*): Over the irrigation channel is a curious dome, erected to Colonel De Renzie James Brett (*see index*). *Continue on to return to Christchurch.*

*Many pleasant centres are within easy reach of Christchurch. These include:*

△**Banks Peninsula\*\*\*:** The craggy volcanic craters where Canterbury's history began are in total contrast with the level, unending plains. The drive out to the picturesque settlement of △Akaroa\*\*\* should not be missed, though the French-founded village merits a stay rather than a fleeting visit.

△**Hanmer Springs\*\*\*:** The trees, hot springs and salubrious atmosphere of Hanmer make it a pleasant spot for a day trip at any time of year. Skiing in winter. *136 km N.*

△**Arthur's Pass Road\*\*\*:** A full day may be spent driving into the Main Divide, perhaps to lunch at the informal licensed restaurant at Arthur's Pass township, the alpine village headquarters of △Arthur's Pass National Park. There is spectacular alpine scenery, walks through native forest, fishing, and skiing in season. *154 km to Arthur's Pass township.*

△**Lake Coleridge\*\*** fills a glacier valley in a remote and wild setting. There is ice-skating at Lake Ida in season. En route, Hororata (*see index*) may be visited. *103 km to powerhouse.*

## OTHER ENVIRONS

△**Akaroa\*\*\*:** The Gallic-flavoured Victorian settlement was the scene of the only French attempt to colonise the country. *82 km SE.*

△**Lyttelton\*\*:** The gateway to the province may be reached in a variety of ways, even on foot along the revered Bridle Path. *13 km S via tunnel.*

△**Kaiapoi** derives its name from an historic *pa*, the scene of a series of major encounters between Ngaitahu and Te Rauparaha's Ngati Toa. *20.6 km N.*

## ORGANISED EXCURSIONS

**Sightseeing buses** leave Victoria Square daily to tour the city and the Northern Summit Road. *Midland Coachlines Ltd; tel. 799-120. Christchurch Transport Board; tel. 794-260. C.J.O. Travel; tel. 69-999 and 792-869.*

**Peninsula Scenic Tours:** All-day tours circumnavigate historic △Banks Peninsula, lunching at △Akaroa. *Peninsula Tours; tel. 69-999.*

**Waimakariri River tours** are run in jetboats and on rafts. *Canterbury and Alpine Travel Ltd; tel. 65-022. C.J.O. Travel; tel. 69-999 and 792-869.*

**Hanmer Springs/Molesworth Station:** One-day scenic tours pass through vast Molesworth station (*see index*), inland from Kaikoura. *Alpine Safari Tours Ltd., 94B Worcester St; tel. 69-999.*

*Details of longer tours are available from the Public Relations Office, which also holds details of factories who welcome visitors.*

## TOURING NOTES

**Highway 1 north to** △**Picton:** The road from Waipara to Blenheim along the Kaikoura coast is described under △Kaikoura.

**Highway 1 south to** △**Timaru** passes through Wigram (*see above*), △Burnham, △Rakaia, △Ashburton and △Temuka.

**Road to** △**Akaroa (Highway 75):** The road passes through Taitapu (*16 km; see above*). *For notes on alternative routes, see* △Akaroa.

**Arthur's Pass route to** △**Greymouth (Highway 73):** The road is described under △Arthur's Pass Road.

**Lewis Pass route to Westport and Nelson (Highway 7):** Described under △Lewis Pass Road.

**Christchurch bypass:** The through traveller on Highway 1 may bypass the city by an inland signposted route between Belfast (*to the north*) and Templeton (*to the south-west*).

**CLIFDEN     Southland.   Maps 12 & 18.   Pop. 135 (locality).**

*13 km N of Tuatapere; 95 km S of Te Anau (via Blackmount Rd). Fiordland National Park ranger station has information concerning the Park.*

THE LOCALITY of Clifden lies by the Waiau River in interesting limestone country. To the east are the Takitimu Mountains, named after one of the fabled ancestral canoes that came from Hawaiki. In local tradition the canoe found its final resting place here in times when the ocean flowed across the plains of Southland to wash the foot of the range. An unlikely *Pakeha* version tells of the settler whose improbable boast was that he could "tak' a team o' " bullocks across the range.

The district was presumably named because of the limestone cliffs in the area, which are threaded with extensive cave systems. A rock shelter on a nearby farm contains early Maori rock drawings, though indistinct and virtually indecipherable, they are noteworthy as the southern-most yet discovered. (*Of archaeological rather than general interest, the drawings are on a farm 600 m N along the Blackmount Rd.*) The road through the Lilburn Valley to beautiful △Lake Hauroko leaves Highway 96 here, as does the alternative route to △Te Anau.

### POINTS OF INTEREST

**Limestone Caves\*:** Opposite a limestone quarry one may enter a lengthy cave system. *Signposted on Clifden Gorge Rd. A powerful torch is essential.*

**Maori Girl Leap:** A remarkable rock thrusts above the river a short distance below the Waiau river bridge. In legend, rival tribes camped on either side of the river, and when those on the east bank found that one of their girls was having an affair with a young chief on the west bank, they threatened to kill her should she attempt to communicate with him again. The girl climbed to the top of the rock to signal to her lover and when her people came to punish her she leaped into the rushing river in an attempt to swim across. The legend is silent as to her fate. *Seen downstream from the bridge.*

The old bridge itself was opened in 1899 replacing the former punt. The remains of an accommodation house, hall and post office that predate the structure are by the east end of the old bridge.

> There are tourists incapable of looking at a masterpiece for its own sake. They bow into a camera, snap experiences never had, then rush home and develop these celluloid events so as to see where they've been. —Ned Rorem.

**CLINTON     South Otago.   Maps 4 & 14.   Pop. 410.**

*31 km WNW of Balclutha; 44 km ESE of Gore.*

THE FARMING CENTRE of Clinton is presided over by Popotunoa Hill, a well-wooded hill where once stood "a post set upright" (*poupou-tu-noa* — the name was misspelt by early surveyors). The post marked a boundary between lands held by Ngaitahu and those of the Ngatimamoe. The boundary did not last, however, and Ngaitahu eventually conquered the remaining Ngatimamoe territory. North of Clinton, on Burning Plain Rd, a pit of lignite continues to smoulder that has been burning since well before the arrival of the *Pakeha*. Known to the Maori as Tapu-whenua (sacred ground) when the area was taken over by the State, a water race was diverted on to the burning area, but this proved only partially successful.

Some fine fishing rivers are nearby — the Pomahaka, the Waipahi and the Waiwera. For forty-three years there was a fish hatchery in The Fishponds on Marshalls Creek, in its time the largest hatchery in the country.

**"Town of Clinton Bill 1862":** The naming of Invercargill in 1856 was a constant irritation to Southlanders, enshrining as it did the name of the leader of the unpopular Otago Provincial Council. So it was an enthusiastic Southland that welcomed the introduction by one of its Members of Parliament of a Bill to change the name of Invercargill to Clinton — "a name," he delicately suggested, "shorter and more euphonious."

Clinton was a popular choice in Southland as it was the family name of the Duke of Newcastle who, as Secretary of State for the Colonies, had sanctioned the New Provinces Act of 1858, the Act that made it possible for Southland to secede from Otago. The Bill failed. The name Clinton "wandered round looking for a home" and finally settled here, when in 1873 Popotunoa became Clinton.

### TOURING NOTE

**Old gold route to △Mataura:** Shorter in distance if longer in time is the road that follows a section of the old route to the Wakatipu diggings by way of Otaraia and Ferndale.

**CLYDE\*\*      Central Otago.    Map 1.    Pop. 585.**

*10 km NW of Alexandra; 21 km SE of Cromwell.*

A STROLL THROUGH the streets of Clyde leads past timeless cottages from an era when, as the gold town of Dunstan, Clyde dominated the district. A more aggressive △Alexandra has long since usurped Clyde's administrative functions, so helping to sustain her oldworld charm.

Hard by the left bank of the restless Clutha the village marks the southern approach to the Cromwell Gorge, an impressive canyon whose early roadworks yielded much of the stone for Clyde's buildings. In common with other towns on the Clutha, Clyde has its share of orchards, whose roadside stalls tempt travellers with freshly-picked fruit. A number of herbs, notably thyme, grow wild hereabouts and are picked and processed for commercial markets.

Clyde shares its name with the river (Clutha is the Highland equivalent of the Scottish Clyde). It may have been named after Lord Clyde, better remembered as Sir Colin Campbell, famous for his relief of Lucknow. John Turnbull Thomson named several centres after figures in and battles of the Indian Mutiny.

## SOME HISTORY

**The trials of Earnscleugh:** Earnscleugh station, taking in much of the Old Man Range, is among the oldest of the runs of Central Otago. A Dunedin magistrate, Alfred Cheetham Strode (born Alfred Cheetham he took the additional surname to collect a considerable inheritance), acquired the run in 1860 and went into partnership with a young Scot, William Fraser. When the rushes came, Fraser himself did not go after gold. In his own words he was "too busy doing other things"; instead, while he supplied the miners, he continued with improvements to the run.

The Rev. C. S. Ross described Fraser as "a thoughtful reader of books and a shrewd observer of passing events". But Fraser, who had married Strode's daughter, in a moment less than shrewd introduced rabbits to Earnscleugh. These ate out feed, and when the snowfalls of 1895 cost Fraser half his stock, the bankrupt run reverted to the State.

Carrying 100 rabbits to the acre, leaving scarcely any feed for sheep, Earnscleugh was taken up in 1901 and restocked with sheep from Morven Hills station (*see index*). Spain also bought an old brewery and began canning rabbits for export. It was he who built the present Earnscleugh homestead, "Spain's Folly", a grandiose mansion patterned on a hacienda he had seen in South America. The Government took back part of the run after the 1914–18 war to settle servicemen as orchardists and the run was still in poor shape when it was acquired by M. F. Mulvena. With stock numbers pegged and a vigorous policy to stamp out rabbits, Mulvena brought profitability back to the largest run in Central. Outbuildings on the 29,920-ha run mirror the style of the castellated brick homestead. (*The homestead is almost concealed by trees when viewed from Earnscleugh Rd, and may best be seen by turning down Laing Rd. 4.4 km S on the far side of the river. Signposted on Earnscleugh Rd.*)

**Hartley and Reilly's bags of gold:** Pioneer pastoralists opened up the hinterland but it was for goldminers to establish the first towns in Central. Just as gold was becoming progressively more difficult to win, and the miners correspondingly more discouraged, the American Horatio Hartley and the Irishman Christopher Reilly found fortune in the Clutha. Working quietly through the winter of 1862 and supplied from Earnscleugh station, they contrived to keep their success even from William Fraser, so that when they departed for Dunedin the pair pretended to have abandoned the area.

Consternation reigned in the Otago capital when the two arrived at the Treasury with bags of gold weighing 87 pounds. The alert Gold Receiver deduced from the worn and scaly appearance of the gold flakes that they had come from near Lake Wanaka, and when confronted with this the pair, who had hoped to keep their secret for longer, agreed to reveal their source. After some hard bargaining the Provincial Council offered a reward of £2,000 on condition that the two men return to the scene to point out their discoveries, and that no less than 16,000 ounces be produced from the field within three months. (The reward was not to cost the Council a penny as it would be covered by revenue from the gold.) Fortune-seekers flocked out of Dunedin. Ill-equipped, ill-prepared and knowing little of the rigours before them, they hurried inland. William Fraser, in Dunedin when the news broke, rode furiously towards Earnscleugh, expecting to be well ahead of the rush, but as he rested on the verandah at Galloway he saw to his astonishment a large group fording the Manuherikia near Moutere.

Of the two prospectors, Hartley alone returned to their scene of triumph, there to find the impatient diggers suspicious and resentful. Here were no shafts or paddocks; no trace that a considerable amount of gold had ever been won. Moreover the river was running high and Hartley, unable to get any gold out, needed police protection from the increasingly hostile crowd. The next morning the river was lower and Hartley was able to wade in and by blind stabbing with a shovel into a shoal bar, swiftly prove that gold was in the river in great quantities. Hartley, with other Californian miners, showed the diggers how to work unfamiliar river claims with a technique that involved the jabbing of long-handled shovels to scoop up river wash.

**The town blows down:** Hartley and Reilly were soon assured of their reward as the riches unfolded. Within three months some 30,000 ounces had been deposited at the Treasury at Dunedin; by the year's end, 70,000.

The first camp was at Muttontown, where the bush-ranger-to-be, Philip Levy (*see index*), had the first store. Muttontown was so called as William Fraser brought his sheep there to slaughter them for the diggers (the name persists to the east of Clyde).

The runholders were surprisingly patient with the diggers who traipsed over their holdings, disturbing stock and occasionally helping themselves. Watson Shennan recalled that the price of mutton did not exceed a shilling a pound. "One reason I may give for the moderate price was that the squatters' sheep were looked upon as common property and disappeared in a marvellous way and at a much faster rate than it was possible for their legs to carry them." Timber, too, was scarce, and one digger, in need of wood to build a gold cradle, helped himself to a privy door. An outraged runholder stormed into Clyde, but could find no trace of the door as it had already been put to use on the river.

Canvas towns concentrated on the sites of Clyde and Alexandra. With January of 1863 came a violent summer storm; dust and gravel funnelled through the Cromwell Gorge with such fury that even Clyde's courthouse was wrecked. The miners turned to more permanent materials to replace their tents, and a number of Clyde's stone and wooden buildings date from the spate of substantial building that followed this visitation.

With more comfortable buildings came a lessening in the privations endured by the thirty to forty thousand diggers who toiled along the Clutha. The early gold was running out by 1864 so groups were formed to provide the capital needed to exploit payable ground, to construct water-races and to purchase sluicing gear. In turn, ground sluicing, hydraulic sluicing and dredging were all carried on with considerable success.

**The great Clyde gold robbery:** As the frantic first rushes passed, the pattern of life settled down and steady returns were won. Twice a month the Northern Escort would collect gold from banks at Queenstown, Arrowtown and Cromwell and deposit it overnight in the lockup at Clyde. From there the main gold escort would collect it for carriage to Dunedin. Remarkably, the gold escorts, with armed police "riding shotgun" and rifle-toting troopers as outriders, were never ambushed, despite the lure they presented. Instead, one night in 1870, £13,000 in gold and banknotes simply vanished from the Clyde gaol. The town was in an uproar.

Shown a poster promising a £1,500 reward and "a free pardon in the event of the person giving such information being an accomplice in the robbery", a shoemaker, George Rennie, promptly confessed, naming Constable Malcolm McLennan of the Clyde police camp as the mastermind.

The two had emigrated from Scotland together on the *Edward P. Bouverie* the year before. McLennan had obtained a duplicate key to the outside door and loosened the screws to the inside door. The way was clear for Rennie to slip into the unguarded gaol and decamp with the shipment. But the robbery was too successful, and Rennie's horse could not cope with the load. The haul was to be buried in the local cemetery, where freshly-dug ground would provoke no comment, but Rennie did not know his way there in the dark. Instead, he set off in the opposite direction and was soon forced to hide gold bags in the rocks to relieve his overburdened mount. Then, in a moment of panic, he lit a fire to burn his false beard, moleskin trousers and bridle. Miners investigated the blaze and Rennie was soon in custody.

Miraculously, Malcolm McLennan escaped conviction, for though Rennie's evidence was corroborated in several respects, the jury reflected popular opinion that Rennie had breached "mateship" by informing on his friend. The hapless Rennie received not a pardon but a six-year gaol term — the pardon was for "accomplices", not principals in the robbery. McLennan went free, but in time the injustice of the situation was mollified by a reduction in Rennie's prison term. In 1930 a local resident, while out hunting, stumbled on gold nuggets in a perished bag which were taken as being Rennie's first plant.

Violence, murder and mayhem, the Central goldfields knew them all, yet by comparison with goldfields in Australia and California they must be rated as relatively law-abiding. There, armed holdup men robbed and killed at times with impunity; here, the greatest of all robberies was accomplished with a complete absence of violence.

**Vincent County and Vincent Pyke:** Dictatorial, of comic appearance and with a talent for sustained invective, Vincent Pyke (1827–94) made his mark both in Victoria and in Otago. He enjoyed such a degree of popularity that an opponent's ironical suggestion was taken seriously and the body of which he was first chairman was named Vincent County.

After time on the Victorian diggings of Bendigo he entered politics there to hold a variety of posts as an elected representative in the Legislative Council of Victoria. For health reasons he visited Otago in 1862 while still a councillor, and he was induced to accept the post of Secretary of the Otago goldfields. Profiting from his Australian experience (he was author of a Victorian Mining Companies Act) he drafted regulations to assist the orderly development of the goldfields and travelled widely to lecture to the miners.

Elected to parliament, he advanced the cause of Central with such passion that he was suspended by the Speaker; he pleaded for a railway, for the completion of the Haast Pass Road, and attacked the manner in which leasehold properties were auctioned, one that often enabled the original large runholder to obtain the freehold. If he was once hanged in effigy at △Cromwell for giving his casting vote (and so the county seat) to Clyde, in later years he was regularly plied with presentations by satisfied supporters.

Pyke, a lifelong journalist, edited several newspapers and wrote as well as popular novels a definitive *History of the Early Gold Discoveries in Otago* (1887).

**"Feraud the Fraud":** The change from harnessing water to sluice away topsoil to using it to feed the parched countryside marks the turning point in the development of Central Otago. Credit for being the first to irrigate is generally given to the Frenchman, Jean Désiré Feraud (*fl.* 1870), or Old Fraud as he was locally known. In about 1864 he used water from a mining race to irrigate his parched Monte Christo holding on the outskirts of Clyde. Elected mayor of Clyde in 1866, he was intent on seeing that both miners and farmers were provided with sufficient water, but his popularity slumped when he discovered that the town's water right itself was invalid. (A municipality was then not empowered to hold water rights under the Goldfields Act). With an eye to the main chance Feraud promptly resigned and claimed the Clyde water right for himself.

Previously a prosperous miner (Frenchmans Point near Alexandra is named after him), Feraud proved as successful as an orchardist, growing grapes, peaches and apricots and selling wines and cordials as far away as Dunedin to the astonishment of those who considered Central's soil dry and useless. (Two of his invariably blue winebottles are in the local museum.)

As miners found gold progressively more elusive they turned increasingly to fruit-growing. No sooner were water-races abandoned for mining purposes than the rights were taken over by prospective orchardists.

## THINGS TO SEE AND DO

**Vincent County and Dunstan Goldfields Museum**\*\* occupies the stone courthouse of 1864 with a collection of considerable interest that includes a poster listing the numbers of banknotes stolen in the Great Clyde Robbery, items from the old gaol from which the gold was stolen (which stood next door), a photograph of "Feraud the Fraud" and two of his winebottles. Sundry other exhibits relate to local goldmining activity. *Blyth St. Open Jan. and Feb. every day 10 am–12 noon; Mar. to Dec. Tues.-Sun. from 2–4.30 pm. Other times by arrangement.* A recent extension to the museum houses herb processing machinery, horse vehicles, wool and dairy displays. *Fraser St. Open 5.30–7 pm; 6.30–9 pm in summer. Parties conducted by arrangement. Tel. 832.*

**Clyde Domain:** A spacious camping ground contains facilities for picnicking, swimming, golf, bowling, croquet, tennis and other sports.

**A short walk round the village:** *1.5 km. Allow 30 mins (or 1 hr if also visiting the museum).* Park by the pick and shovel goldminers' monument at the northern end of the township. From there walk south along the main street, Sunderland St, to pass side by side, the Athenaeum (1874) and the Town Hall (1868–69). Opposite is the former Hartleys Arms Hotel (*c.* 1865), two doors from Dunstan House (1900), now a combined guesthouse and antique shop. To the right of the Hartleys Arms Hotel building is a goldminer's cottage dating from the late 1860s. A short detour left up Naylor St leads to old stone stables.

On the corner of Matau St stands the Dunstan Hotel (1903) (note the old Studebaker Service plaque on the corner). In 1862–63 the Buckingham family had their scantling-and-calico hotel on the site. They were joined here by "Bully" Hayes (*see index*), and together moved on to Arrowtown when miners rushed the new field there. Next to the Dunstan Hotel lounge bar is a cottage on a "tent section", a minute area designed to accommodate no more than a tent in times when Clyde was laid out as a primitive canvas town. Those who could afford to would buy two or more adjoining "tent" sections to accommodate a conventional house with two front rooms. Only a tiny cottage could be built on a single tent section such as this, with one room behind the other.

Turn right down Matau St to pass the old stone post office and St Michael's Anglican Church (1877). Under this locality a coalmine was worked from the riverbank until in 1885 the river flooded and the shaft caved in (Clyde sits on a bed of lignite). Close by is the museum (*see above*). Turn left up Fraser St (named for William Fraser of Earnscleugh) and by St Dunstan's Catholic Church (1906) turn left again into Sunderland St. Opposite is St Mungo's Union Church (1894). Now walk down the main street, Sunderland St (on the right, in a garden with two tall Lombardy poplars is the former Chinese interpreter's house), and return to the goldminer's monument. From there, if time allows, it is pleasant to stroll beside the Clutha along Miners' Lane.

## ENVIRONS

**Lookout**\*\*: A signposted route leads from Sunderland St. across the Clutha to wind steeply up the toe of the Cairnmuir Mountains. The view extends into the Cromwell Gorge and down to Clyde. Orchards stretch towards Alexandra, whose bridge and distinctive hillside clock may also be seen. *3.5 km. Signposted.* About 3 km beyond the lookout is Banker's Rock, a pretty spot where in 1863 a local bank manager was robbed of £1,000. Though two men were convicted of the crime and the people of the district combed the locality many times over the years, the money was never recovered.

**Fraser Domain:** A pleasant camping and picnicking area named after William Fraser, beside a stream from which runs a water race. *4.4 km. Signposted. Across the river.*

### TOURING NOTE

**Highway 8 to △Cromwell:** The route through the Cromwell Gorge is described under △Cromwell.

---

**MOBIL NEW ZEALAND TRAVEL GUIDE
NORTH ISLAND**
The companion volume to this Guide is available from bookshops everywhere.

---

**COLERIDGE (Lake)\*\*     Canterbury.   Map 2.**

*103 km W of Christchurch; 79 km NNW of Ashburton.*

LAKE COLERIDGE is typical of the Canterbury lakes, filling the long trough of a departed glacier, backed by mountain ranges and banked by open tussocklands. The region has much in common with the Mackenzie country, to the point of having sheep-stations dependent on fickle river crossings for communication with the outside world. The story of one such station, Mount Algidus, is told in *A River Rules My Life* by Mona Anderson (Reed), and its sequels. The river concerned is the Wilberforce.

Many come to Coleridge to fish, particularly at the Harper River end of the lake, and to see the first of the large hydro-electric power schemes to be undertaken by the State. The lake is named after the Rev. Edward Coleridge, a member of the Committee of Management of the Canterbury Association.

**Lake Ida:** In winter the tiny lake is the most popular of Canterbury's ice-skating venues. *35 km from the powerhouse.* There is skiing on Mt Olympus, organised by the Windwhistle Winter Sports Club (*PO Box 25055, Christchurch*).

### LAKE COLERIDGE POWER STATION

Water which would otherwise have flowed out into the Harper River is led from the lake by two tunnels, passed through nine generators with a total capacity of 34,500 kW and discharged into the Rakaia. Construction began in 1911, the station becoming operative in 1914. Over the years the transmission network throughout almost the entire South Island has evolved round the basic lines from Coleridge to Christchurch. Three 66,000-volt lines feed into the South Island system at Hororata, and two similar lines cross the Alps by way of Arthur's Pass to carry power to the West Coast. *Both the powerhouse, in a well-planted setting good for picnics, and the intake of the lake 5 km away may be visited.*

### TOURING NOTE

**Hororata** (pop. 267): The road from Christchurch at 58 km passes through Hororata (*horo* = landslip; *rata* = native tree), a farming settlement near Terrace Station, the run acquired by Sir John Hall (1824–1907) in 1852. He had wanted to take up land south of the Rakaia, but was deterred after once crossing the river. Almost immediately the diffident runholder embarked on a political career that saw him become a member of the Canterbury Provincial Council virtually from its inception to its abolition, first mayor of Christchurch (1863) and (with two interruptions) either a member of the House of Representatives or the Legislative Council from 1855 to 1893. An efficient administrator, he introduced sound business methods to the several departments for which he was in turn responsible. In 1879 he was induced to accept the premiership, but only by making a deal with four Auckland members (the "Auckland rats" who crossed the floor to support him) was he confirmed in office. After two years ill health forced his retirement from the premiership, but during that time his Government passed the Triennial Parliaments Act and an Electoral Act which embraced universal manhood suffrage. He chose to resolve the Maori question by a show of force in the infamous Parihaka Affair (*see index to North Island volume*), an unfortunate decision that now tends to overshadow his other achievements. In 1893 he helped through the House the Bill that gave women the vote, a measure he had introduced on several previous occasions and in respect of which he had tabled petitions with ever-increasing numbers of signatures.

An immensely successful farmer (in 1883 his Hororata property was valued at over £90,000), he left money to build a church in memory of his wife. St John's Church (1910), it represents her wish that "the building set apart for the worship of God should have a beauty and dignity worthy of its sacred purpose". Opposite stands its simple, timber predecessor (1875), now used as a hall, at whose consecration Bishop Harper recalled times when there was neither house nor tree between Christchurch and the settlement here. A sod cottage at Hororata is to be preserved and opened as a museum. *Hidden from view, Sir John Hall's homestead (c. 1853) is still lived in by his descendants as they farm the remaining portion of the estate.*

**COLLINGWOOD**    Nelson.    **Maps 26 & 32.    Pop. 178.**

*136 km NW of Nelson; 28 km NW of Takaka.*

THE GOLD OF COLLINGWOOD provides a gilt basis for the change in name of the wide bay on which it stands. From the Murderers' Bay (later Massacre Bay) of Abel Tasman the sweep of coast has come to be known by the more euphonious title of Golden Bay. The township, on the mouth of the Aorere River, was a shipbuilding centre as early as 1842. But though coalmines and later goldrushes promised an expansive future, Collingwood remains a quiet service town tucked inside the lazy curve of Farewell Spit. Its isolation may end if a road is put through to link the district with Karamea and the West Coast. The town is named after Admiral Collingwood, Nelson's second-in-command at the Battle of Trafalgar.

There is good fishing locally, both coastal and freshwater.

**St Cuthbert's Anglican Church, Collingwood** (1877): The quaint, vertically boarded church was designed by the explorer Thomas Brunner. Its bell (1872) was the first bell to be cast at a foundry in Nelson.

## MAORI LEGEND

**The Taniwha of Parapara:** In legend there lived in the Parapara Inlet a *taniwha* (water monster), Te Kai-whakaruaki, so large and so voracious that none could travel west from Whakatu (Nelson), Takaka or Motupipi without falling victim. It would eat as many as two hundred travellers at a time. Five tribes joined to exterminate the monster. The Ngaitahu contributed a warrior famed for his ability to slay seals with his bare hands — "Show me the *taniwha* and I will kill it with one blow of my fist," he declared. Alas, the slayer of seals was no match for Te Kai-whakaruaki and followed the path of other victims to its belly. Some of the warriors who had grouped with weapons shaped from the only *pohutukawa* tree in the district then lured the monster out of the water, enabling their fellows to ambush and kill it as it passed. The bones of many victims and a large number of treasured objects of wood and greenstone were recovered from the dismembered body, but whether the seal-hunter escaped alive from his entombment in the belly of Te Kai-whakaruaki, the legend does not relate. (*Note:* Elsdon Best has shown that the legend derives from the Society Islands. The small islands that enter the story as told there correspond with the Maori names of Motueka and Takaka). *A painting of the legend is in the hotel at Takaka.*

## SOME HISTORY

**Pighunters find gold:** The presence of gold in the region had long been suspected before there was a rush of any magnitude. Indeed, the country's first recorded discovery was made in Golden Bay, and in 1843 a New Zealand Company surveyor had found a nugget the size of a French bean in the Aorere River. Interest grew only with the rushes to California and Australia.

Prospectors were at work on a tributary of the Aorere River when in October 1856 some pighunters paused to quench their thirst. While drinking from the stream they saw gold in its bed. Further finds were made, and within a year £10,000 worth of gold had been sold in Nelson and about 2,000 ounces sent to Sydney for sale there. Enthused one Nelsonian, "Not only does a workable field exist, but it yields a better average return than the boosted fields of Australia; being more easily obtained, more generally diffused and with much less expense. There are now about 2,000 persons employed on the diggings including cooks, storekeepers, bullock-drivers, visitors."

Gold was also found in the Anatoki and Takaka Rivers, and Rocky River became famous for its nuggets, with finds of up to about 9 ounces. Yet by 1859 the miners of the Aorere fields had become disheartened. Communications were poor, and the prospects were not bright as the gold appeared to be patchy and mainly on the surface. Numbers dwindled rapidly.

In the 1860s most of the remaining miners left for Central Otago or the West Coast, though interest in some localities persisted — such as at the Pupu Springs area. The fields revived with the move into sluicing. Reefs, too, were worked — the Taitapu Gold Estate beyond Whanganui Inlet and Big River yielding nearly £125,000 before the supply of stone ran out in 1913.

Later attempts to reopen gold workings have met with scant success. The old goldmining areas are today marked only by the occasional venerable fruit tree, flowers gone wild, and scraps of privet hedge.

**A town is born:** With the goldrush came people and trade, and at the rivermouth the pioneer settler William Gibbs laid out his settlement of Gibbstown. His sections found a ready market, and inside twelve months the rivermouth grew from a pair of tents to a town with seven hotels. The Provincial Government promptly moved to lay out a town of its own, Collingwood, on the terraces of *pakihi* (*see index*) above the present town. Sections sold rapidly, but by the time the roads and drains were built the rush was on the wane. The Government's town never materialised and instead the name Collingwood simply moved to replace that of Gibbstown. (*Survey pegs and traces of the roads and drains may still be seen on the scrub-covered flat; the only section used was the 6-ha cemetery where gravestones record early and often violent deaths.*)

For many years coastal shipping provided the only reliable link with the outside world, with steamers such as the *Lady Barkly* plying across to Nelson. Stories abound of the steamer days. One tells of the captain swinging sharply to avoid what he thought was a snag, only to find it was a Mr Davidson on his way home from a party at Pakawau; another relates how a party of girls, their ball-dresses tied in neat bundles and to the tops of their heads, swam their horses across the steamer channel on their way to a dance.

> Nothing makes a man or woman look so saintly as seasickness. —Samuel Butler.

## FAREWELL SPIT

Farewell Spit, a slender sandbar of some 35 km, curves gently eastward to partially enclose the waters of Golden Bay and shelter them from the wild Tasman Sea. It comprises sand eroded from the South Island's west coast and borne northward by coastal drift until checked at Cook Strait. In its lee, Golden Bay is imperceptibly filling up with sand, becoming progressively more shallow and less extensive.

Both Cape Farewell (named by Cook as he sailed from New Zealand in 1770) and the spit were seen by Abel Tasman in 1642. The Dutch explorer turned into Golden Bay after seeing smoke rising here, the first indication that the land he had found was inhabited. Tasman named the spit Visscher's Sand-dune Hoeck.

Cape Farewell is the northernmost point of the South Island, being some little distance north of Levin on the North Island's west coast.

The spit, soon recognised as a shipping hazard, has claimed at least eleven vessels. Construction of a lighthouse began in 1869. Built literally at sea level, its tower had to be some 30.4 m high, considerably taller than most. The light, first used in June 1870 and electrified in 1954, gives one flash every 60 seconds and is visible for 24 km. In 1897 the tower was rebuilt to a height of 26.8 m. Last century, when the sea covered most of the spit at high tide, a keeper decided that a grove of tall trees would serve as a good landmark to mariners by day. As the spit was infertile, each time he went to Nelson for stores he returned with saddlebags of topsoil, eventually planting *macrocarpa* trees, a grove of which can be seen today.

There is excellent fishing from the spit, which is also a sanctuary for innumerable wading birds.

**Access to the spit:** Though four-wheel-drive vehicles can negotiate the spit at low tide, it is extremely unwise for visiting motorists to attempt the drive, notorious for its changing channels and the treacherous nature of the sand. *Collingwood Motors Ltd (tel. Collingwood 15S) operate service trips to the lighthouse (usually Wednesday) leaving Collingwood 3 hrs after high tide. Trips are run daily over the Christmas period. It is essential to book and to confirm the time of departure.*

> To make the most of your travels you should carry with you the book of Mobil road maps.

## OTHER ENVIRONS

**Te Anaroa caves\*\*:** In limestone caves near Rockville stalactite and stalagmite formations form weird groupings. *8 km SW. Signposted. Hours vary.* About 400 m beyond the caves are the Devil's Boots, where one may picnic amidst curious rock formations resembling gigantic upturned boots (*signposted*). At Rockville there is a private museum with birds, shells, minerals and Maori artefacts. Beyond Rockville lies **Bainham** (pop. 103), starting point for the △ Heaphy Track and a small farming settlement whose title combines the family names of two early settlers, Bain and Graham.

**Pillar Light on Cape Farewell\*\*:** Named by Captain Cook as he left New Zealand for the Australian coast at the end of his first visit, the cape affords magnificent views, particularly of Farewell Spit. *Start of walk signposted at 26 km from Collingwood on the road to Wharariki Beach. Allow 1 hr for the walk.* The road passes through Pakawau where there is a good beach, and the coalmining locality of Puponga, the piles of whose jetty jut forlornly from the tide. The South Island's most northerly settlement is presided over by a high rocky bluff behind Cape Farewell, whose famous feature of Old Man Rock (*signposted*) looks down on the locality.

**Westhaven or Whanganui Inlet\*\*:** The drive round the indentations of Westhaven Inlet should be timed to coincide with high tide. The road from Pakawau leads over causeways and through bush to the timber and former coalmining settlement of Mangarakau, where it swings to meet the West Coast by the mouth of the Patarau River (*excellent for whitebaiting*), *38 km return. A detour may be made en route to Kaihoka twin lakes (below). The road continues past Patarau Beach through farmland for another 10 km or so.*

**Kaihoka twin lakes\*,** dressed with native bush, form twin oases in open farmland. *24 km. On the road to Westhaven Inlet the road branches right. Signposted. The track* *to the second lake leads from the old roadmen's hut through the second gate. A pleasant picnic place.*

**Beaches:** Good beaches in the vicinity include Pakawau* (*14 km N*), Patarau (*43 km W*) and Wharariki Beach (*29 km N; road ends at a farm across which a 20-minute walk leads to the beach; signposted. There is a seal colony in the rocks to the east of the beach*).

△**Heaphy Track*****: A 5-day tramp leads from Bainham through to △Karamea on the West Coast. The concluding coastal section is particularly memorable.

## EXCURSIONS

Collingwood Motors Ltd (*tel. 15S Collingwood*) run tours to a variety of destinations which cannot be reached by private car, including the hair-raising run to the summit of Mt Burnett (*639.2 m*).

**Farewell Spit*****(*see above*): *The 4½ hr trip runs each Wednesday (starting time dependent on tides) and at other times by arrangement if parties contain six or more and book in advance.*

---

Books on New Zealand art include *Two Hundred Years of New Zealand Painting* by Gil Docking, and Wattie Award winner *Van der Velden* by T. Rodney-Wilson. Books on Maori legends include *A Treasury of Maori Folklore* and *Wonder Book of Maori Legends* both by A.W. Reed. Maori culture is described in *The World of the Maori* by Eric Schwimmer. All the above are published by A.H. & A.W. Reed.

---

**CROMWELL*****     Central Otago.    Maps 1, 29 & 36.    Pop. 1,179.**

*30.5 km NW of Alexandra; 63 km E of Queenstown; 57 km S of Wanaka.*

TO APPROACH CROMWELL by Highway 8 from Alexandra is to pass through the hostile Cromwell Gorge and emerge to encounter suddenly a tightly-knit town in one of the country's most arresting settings. As if on the prow of some landlocked ship, it perches above the junction of two swift rivers, the Kawarau and the mighty Clutha. In the distance rise ranges in winter trimmed with snow.

Born of the Clutha (the town mushroomed as a goldmining settlement) for a time it seemed that Cromwell might die by the Clutha. Revised plans to harness the rivers' power potential will still destroy much of Cromwell's endearing personality, both by flooding part of the town and by attracting a large influx of hydro workers. Orchards, numerous historic sites and the grandeur of the gorges are all imperilled.

The names of Cromwell, Naseby and Hampden reflect a sympathy and a somewhat tenuous connection between nineteenth-century radicalism and the Civil War of the seventeenth century. It is also said that the surveyor's party clashed here with Irish miners and so named the locality "to put the curse of Cromwell on them." (As an English general, Cromwell laid waste to much of Ireland).

### SOME HISTORY

**The rise of Cromwell:** The settlement grew up as The Junction on the confluence of the Kawarau and Clutha Rivers at the northern end of the Cromwell Gorge. From here the Kawarau stretches back through its own wild gorge to Lake Wakatipu, and the Clutha extends north to its source in Lake Wanaka. Both rivers were auriferous but Cromwell suffered from difficulties of access until the Australian Henry Hill in 1864 built a toll bridge over the Clutha some 200 m upstream from the junction. Hill did well for a time from government contracts, but better when he absconded to South America with money the Government had advanced to him, leaving behind a trail of debts and unpaid workmen.

An even greater barrier was a total lack of timber, so that sod huts and calico tents comprised the township until timber began to be milled on Lake Wanaka and rafted as sawn lengths down the river to Cromwell and neighbouring △Clyde, an undertaking as hazardous as it was profitable.

As Clyde and Cromwell each assumed substance, there grew an intense rivalry that saw Clyde take one side of a conflict between central and provincial governments over goldfields' administration, only to reverse its stand when it learned that Cromwell was of the same opinion. When Vincent Pyke (*see index*) resigned as warden of the Dunstan area and chairman of the county named after him, both towns laid claim to the site of the Vincent County capital. Pyke, who supported Clyde, was not only hanged in effigy at Cromwell, but his image was then thrown into the river from the Cromwell bridge. An energetic interest in local politics was nothing new, as witnessed the exploits of Cromwell's first mayor, Captain Jackson Barry.

**An autocratic egoist:** If only half the tales recounted in his memoirs are true, Captain Jackson Barry (1819–1907) was indeed a remarkable man. After exploits as a drover in New South Wales, a trader in the Malay Straits, a whaler in the Pacific, a miner in California and a coach driver in Victoria, Barry arrived in Cromwell in 1863 where he started the Victoria & Sydney Butchery to break a monopoly enjoyed by the town's sole butcher. Barry became something of a local hero as he reduced the price of meat to sixpence per pound, a gold watch and chain being presented to him by the grateful community.

Gratitude was carried to extremes when Barry was elected as Cromwell's first mayor. He recalled that he was returned "by an overwhelming majority . . . I believe the whole town, and a considerable crowd from the outlying diggings, got outrageously drunk." Autocratic to the extreme, he was in Dunedin when a vote of censure was passed against him. Hurrying back to Cromwell, he called a council meeting, locked the door and amid scenes of uproar knocked down the councillor who had proposed the offending motion. Barry then demanded to know who had seconded the motion. Having viewed the fate of the proposer, the remaining councillors disclaimed responsibility (it seems the culprit had, in any event, prudently jumped out of the window). Thereupon the mayor ruled that the motion had lapsed, and imperiously struck it from the minutes. Barry was charged with assault and fined, but remained unrepentant: "Considering the turbulent times and the unruly people one had to deal with, I still think I took the proper course, if a forcible one, of putting my councillors straight."

The mayor who regarded himself as captain and his councillors as cabin-boys was returned on no fewer than three occasions. He moved on to open auction rooms in Queenstown and Arrowtown as well as in Cromwell, and spent his later years touring as a public lecturer both in Australia and throughout New Zealand. Always entertaining, he was generally assured of an audience prepared to overlook inaccuracies as he wallowed in unlikely triumphs. His extraordinary autobiographies include *Up and Down; or Fifty Years' Colonial Experience in Australia, California, New Zealand, India, China, and the South Pacific; Being the Life History of Captain W. J. Barry. Written by himself. 1878.*

## THINGS TO SEE AND DO

**View from the reservoir\*\*\*:** The classic and much-photographed view of Cromwell is from the reservoir, perched on the slopes of the Dunstan Mountains some 100 m above the town. The view, spectacular at all times, is at its most dazzling in late autumn when snow drapes the distant Pisa Range and the riverbanks are ablaze with exotic trees. *South of the town on Highway 8 turn left at 1.4 km and drive or walk up the steep track.*

**Cromwell Borough Museum\*:** Photographs and old newspaper clippings depict the area's development. Among the wide-ranging display are items of goldmining equipment and relics of the considerable Chinese occupation. *Signposted off main st. Open 10.30 am–12.30 pm and 1.30–4.30 pm daily during holidays. Parties admitted other times by arrangement. Enquire at Borough Council Office.*

**Old Cemetery\*:** Here lie graves of those who came from other lands to seek fortune. They fell victim to rivers, to earth-falls and to riding mishaps, their fate often recorded on headstones erected by grieving widows or simply "a few friends". Two Chinese graves lie in its lowest corner (Chinese dead were generally shipped back to China for burial). *Erris St. Signposted off main st.*

**Walk along the Kawarau:** In summer the walk along the tree-shaded Kawarau riverbank, starting from the Memorial Gardens by the riverbridge, is particularly refreshing. Opposite the Memorial Gardens, above the bridge, is the old stone granary of the Cobb & Co coach line.

**Herringbone stone lines\*\*\*:** Carefully placed and replaced by Chinese miners as they meticulously worked the riverbank are several hectares of boulders, neatly stacked in the pattern of a herringbone. *Foot of Neplusultra St, off Alpha St by the Clutha.* Neplusultra Street was named by an early surveyor, whose gloomy prediction proved well astray.

> The New Zealand Forest Service has offices throughout the country which issue permits for hunting in State Forests and in Forest Parks.
> Local sports shops issue fishing licences, advise on local conditions and restrictions, and often hire out equipment.

## SOME OLD GOLD TOWNS

**BENDIGO:** A visit to Bendigo takes in three deserted gold towns, replete with ruined cottages and rambling fruit trees. *Allow ½ day. Leave Cromwell towards Tarras to reach Lowburn Ferry (at 2.5 km) and the:*

**Welcome Home Hotel** (1869): Originally built to slake the thirsts of travellers waiting to be ferried across the Clutha, the present building is the third on the site, each being built between the same metre-thick walls. Stories abound about the hotel, which refreshed ferry customers until in 1938 "the longest bridge in the world" was built to span the Clutha (as it is sharply humped, one cannot see the end of it). In the 1870s Captain Jackson Barry won a horse race along the riverbank in a £10-a-side contest that finished outside the hotel's front door. He was promptly taken to task by the *Cromwell Argus*, which fumed that the affair was a "violation of the laws of God and public decency". Where, it asked, was the local police sergeant while the Sabbath day was being so desecrated? It seems that he, too, was enjoying the races, but he prosecuted the riders just the same.

The flood of 1878 saw the Clutha invade the hotel and a rowing boat being manoeuvred through the front door and up to the bar. An even less likely customer was the goat who for years lined up for a drink. When he died he was buried on the hillside behind the hotel. The picket fence that marked the grave has since disappeared, but some locals still talk of the goat as if he died only yesterday. *Turn right across the Clutha and follow Highway 8 north along the river. The near bank has been well sluiced and the far bank is piled high with dredge tailings, now softened with willows. Pass at 10.9 km:*

**Picnic area:** A sheltered, shaded spot beside the Clutha where a rare chance to bathe safely in the river is occasionally afforded. Perhaps the coolest spot near Cromwell on a Central summer's day. *At 18.9 km leave the highway by turning right along Bendigo Rd to reach, at 22.2 km:*

**Bendigo town site** (1862): Marked by a cottage, a roofless stone bakery, a solitary chimney and an immense mullock heap. *Turn right and climb steeply to reach, at 25.1 km the site of:*

**Logantown:** Several crumbling stone cottages and some old fruit trees grace the site of the ghost town. The road leads on a further 750 m to the site of **Welshtown**, passing a number of slagheaps beside gaping mineshafts. One of the largest is a short distance along a track beside the sign "Danger. Mine holes. Deepest 159 m". In several places the gold seam in the quartz reef has been followed from the surface before plunging underground. Extreme care is necessary when exploring the field as the holes are open, deep, narrow-necked and unmarked. From both Logantown and Welshtown are magnificent views of the Lindis and Clutha river valleys which by themselves make the trip worthwhile.

*On returning to the junction on the flat at Bendigo a detour may be made by turning hard right to follow the road for 2.4 km to reach the ruins of a spacious stone hotel. The hotel and its outbuildings (possibly a store and stables) cluster by the well-worked bed of the Bendigo Creek. Return to Highway 8 by continuing along the loop road. Turn left and return to Cromwell.*

**CARRICKTOWN:** A visit to the bleak Carrick Range is very much more demanding than one to Bendigo. High on the range are scattered the occasional stone hut, traces of workings and a venerable overshot waterwheel, reached only after an energetic walk. *Leave Cromwell by Highway 6 towards Queenstown, turning off almost at once (at 0.8 km) towards Bannockburn. Cross the:*

**Kawarau River** (*5.2 km):* The modern bridge high above the river is flanked downstream by the four towering pillars that supported the original bridge. *Continue on to reach:*

**Bannockburn** (*at 5.9 km):* A stone church, post office and a scattering of houses are all that is now left of the town of perhaps 2,000 who lived here in 1867. Good alluvial gold was found on the flats, today still heavily scarred by the sluicing. *At 6.9 km turn right up Schoolhouse Rd, right again into Quartzville Rd and park (at 8.8 km) by the sign that marks the start of the stiff climb some 4 km up to the area of:*

**Carricktown:** The Carrick Range was known to the alluvial miners at Bannockburn well before the wave of quartz-reef prospecting began that led to some forty or more mines being sunk and the erection of several stamper batteries in the 1870s. The fever passed and in the realism of the morrow it was accepted that the field had belied its promise. By 1886 the area had been abandoned. There are a number of old stone huts whose ruins are camouflaged by rock outcrops, and numerous mine holes readily recognised by the inevitable accompanying mullock heap. *Allow 2 hrs. This walk should be omitted if the walk in to the overshot waterwheel is to be made. Return to the Bannockburn road and turn right to pass at 14.6 km:*

**Kawarau station:** The cob homestead, hidden in the trees, dates from 1858, as does the stone woolshed near it, which can be seen from the road. The station provided the lifeblood of Bannockburn, supplying the diggers with mutton and bread. A short distance beyond is a second woolshed, hard by the road, built from massive stones used as brakestones by waggoners descending the Nevis road, and discarded by them once they had reached the foot of the hill.

**Nevis Road:** The steep, narrow and unsealed Nevis road climbs to 1,264.9 m and is adversely affected by wet and wintry weather. When in doubt enquire locally before setting out.

One of the country's highest roads, it affords from among scattered outcrops a splendid outlook over Cromwell township and the Clutha valley. (The more intrepid may cross the range to the depleted Nevis Valley, from which even the farmers have moved. Some stone relics from goldmining times remain. Well into the present century, packhorses were used to carry in wintertime mails). *The suggested drive does not go beyond the summit, for shortly after crossing a water-race (at 22.9 km) one should stop where a track leads off to the right (at 24.2 km). Some maps show a vehicle track as running down to Bannockburn but it is impassable for anything but a four-wheel-drive vehicle, and there are no turning places. Keep bearing right as you walk down the steep formed track to see (at about 5 km) the:*

**Overshot waterwheel:** In a gully to the right, the symmetry of the rusting wheel looks quite out of place. In the 1890s it powered the stamp-battery for the Young Australia mine. *Ample time and a degree of physical fitness are essential.*

## ORGANISED EXCURSIONS

**Jetboat trips:** In an exhilarating trip, jetboats sweep along the Clutha under the branches of overhanging trees, and occasionally down through the rapids to the confluence with the Kawarau. Fishing trips are run, experienced enthusiasts can water-ski the Clutha, and families may be ferried to the river islands for picnics and barbecues. *Book at the Welcome Home Hotel, Lowburn, or the Lowburn Camping Ground.*

## TOURING NOTES

**Cromwell Gorge — Highway 8 to △ Clyde:** The first road through the inhospitable Cromwell Gorge to link Cromwell with Clyde (then called Dunstan) was built by the Provincial Council on the west side of the Clutha at a cost of £9,000. Almost as soon as it was finished, half the road was washed away in a terrific cloudburst. Engineers remade the road on the eastern bank, where it now runs. Parts of the old road can still be seen across the river. The occasional orchard relieves the hostility of an otherwise barren landscape.

The **memorial** to Hartley and Reilly (*see △Clyde*) is passed at 1.9 km, just before the gorge is entered. The beach below, Hartley Beach, was where the American successfully demonstrated the richness of the find. At 5.3 km, on the opposite bank, if one looks very carefully an overhang may be seen that has been walled in to make a small dwelling with doorway and window-opening.

**Kawarau Gorge — Highway 6 to △ Queenstown:** The route lies through the arid Kawarau Gorge, perhaps even more hostile than the Cromwell.

For some time the preferred route from Cromwell to the Arrow diggings was by way of Wanaka and the Cardrona Valley. In September 1863 it was possible, with danger and difficulty, to take a cart through the gorge, but the track was so bad that in wet weather it could take weeks to get through. In August 1863, during a great snowstorm, the escort waggon tried to cross Roaring Meg with the result that a handcuffed prisoner was washed into the stream and drowned. The gorge was wild in more ways than one: several bodies were found in the river, and travellers were waylaid, beaten and robbed in crimes popularly attributed to Philip Levy (later to hang at Nelson for the Maungatapu murders). For a time he lived in a hut on the gorge road.

At the **Kawarau claim** (*9.3 km*) visitors may pan for gold and see gold sluicing in operation. (*Occasionally closed in midwinter*).

**Roaring Meg** (*at 15.4 km*) is now marked by a small powerstation and an attractive picnic spot. The origin of the stream's name is obscure. Romantics suggest a red-headed barmaid with a raucous voice to match, but the name also occurs elsewhere, including a stream in Queensland that was apparently so called as "she roars when in flood".

Not far above Roaring Meg may be seen in the river the remains of the **"natural bridge"** where the Kawarau River curls and tightens to its narrowest point. This served early Maoris and later goldseekers as a river-crossing before access was provided by ferries and a bridge on the lower reaches of the river. In the 1860s the "bridge" saw the macabre finale to a tragedy that began when a Chinese miner returned to his claim to find his companion murdered. Suspecting a stranger who had taken up a claim nearby and who had by then disappeared, the Chinese alerted the neighbourhood. In heavy fog the stranger was seen carefully making his way across the bridge. Challenged, he refused to stop, and when a shot was fired he began to run, only to trip and pitch headfirst into the swirling waters below. About three weeks later his swag was recovered from the river. In it was found the small bag of gold that had been taken from the murdered miner.

Today the "bridge" has deteriorated into a jumble of rocks, but there is no tradition of it ever having been complete. Even the earliest visitors had to jump across a gap.

---

I never travel without my diary. One should always have something sensational to read in the train. — Oscar Wilde (*Gwendolen Fairfax*).

---

**CULVERDEN**   North Canterbury.   Maps 20 & 21.   Pop. 382

*40 km NNE of Waipara; 37 km S of Hanmer Springs.*

THE SEAT OF Amuri County and the centre of a prosperous sheepraising district, Culverden is bisected by Highway 7, which points north towards the more westerly of twin mountains, Mt Tinline (*1,738 m*). Some 3 km north, at the Red Post the road changes slightly in direction, to point towards the second twin, Mt Terako (*1,741.2 m*).

The town was named by Henry Young, a retired judge from India, who was the first settler here. He acquired his run after Sir Edwin Dashwood had failed to stock his 122,000 ha in time and offered it to Young and George Duppa. The pair agreed to split the holding, the first choice going to whichever was the first to get sheep on to it. Young, having the stronger sheep, arrived first and chose the western half, naming it Culverden after a property he had once owned near Tunbridge Wells, Kent.

### POINTS OF INTEREST

**Balmoral Forest:** In an extensive area of State forest to the south of the settlement a camping and picnic area has been developed on the banks of the Hurunui River. *12.1 km S.*

**The Red Post:** A successor to the original red post still stands jauntily if frustratedly at the intersection of Highways 7 and 70. It featured prominently on survey maps of the 1880s, when transport problems in the South Island were being studied by the government. Though scheme after scheme was prepared, none advanced beyond the planning stage so that a Red Post has since *c.* 1873 stood to mark the proposed junction of two railroads — one to Waiau, through Jollies Pass and thence to Nelson by way of Tophouse; the other to the Hanmer Plains, over the Amuri Pass and on to Greymouth. *3.1 km N.*

**Leslie Hills homestead** (1900): The imposing forty-room homestead, with many gables and an elegant central tower, may be seen from Leslie Hills Road, on land which has since 1859 been farmed by the Rutherford family. *At 13 km N on Highway 7 turn down Leslie Hills Road. The homestead is on the left at 3 km.*

**Glens of Tekoa cottage** (1857)**: This low-slung wattle-and-daub home was built by William McRae, who landed at Nelson in 1850. It contains a collection of items connected with the McRae family and their more than a century-and-a-quarter residence in the district. The property is the only one in the area which is still farmed by descendants of the original runholder. *30.6 km. Leave Culverden on Highway 7 south and turn right along Long Plantation Road to Balmoral and Balmoral Forest. At 15.4 km turn right along Shortcut Rd and follow signposts towards Island Hills. Pass the forest plantations and proceed through a gorge of the Mandanus River near its entry to the Hurunui River, then rise in the foothills to reach Glens of Tekoa. The cottage is situated behind the present brick homestead. Tel. 163M before visiting. Balmoral homestead (c. 1900) is passed on the way, at 13.6 km.*

The drive in to the foothills is particularly refreshing on a hot summer's day.

### TOURING NOTES

△**Lewis Pass Road:** Points of interest on Highway 7 both north and south of Culverden are given under this entry.

> Public Relations Offices in larger centres will generally assist with accommodation, maps and travellers' problems.
> If in doubt about road conditions, contact the nearest Automobile Association office. In holiday periods, listen for the Mobil Holiday Bulletins which are broadcast regularly from most commercial radio stations.

**DANSEY PASS**   North Otago/Central Otago.   Height: 940.5 m.
                                                    Maps 1, 25 & 28.

*Duntroon to Naseby via Dansey Pass 68 km.*

DANSEY PASS leads through the northern end of the Kakanuis, from Kyeburn Diggings (near △Naseby) over the range to △Duntroon and the △Waitaki Valley.

The pass is named after the Otekaike runholder William Heywood Dansey, lessee from 1857 until he sold out to Hon. Robert Campbell fourteen years later. Dansey, with three others, explored through into the Maniototo in about 1855 taking with them a mule and a donkey. The donkey they lost in the pass and it was not recovered until the Kyeburn run was taken up some several years later. Dansey's home still stands on the Otekaike Special School property (*see* △*Duntroon*).

Narrow in places and not sealed, the road through the pass is occasionally closed by winter snow.

*Note:* On the Central side, at the foot of the pass, are the Kyeburn Diggings and an historic hotel (*see* △*Naseby*).

**DUNEDIN***     Otago.     Maps 9, 10 & 11.     Pop. 113,300 (urban area).**

*366 km SSW of Christchurch; 202 km SSW of Timaru; 220 km NE of Invercargill.*
*Public Relations Office, 119 Princes St. Tel. 76-765.*

THE TRAVELLER from the North comes suddenly upon the "Edinburgh of the South". Highway 1 lifts gently over the hem of Mt Cargill and abruptly reveals the city below, clinging to the walls of the natural amphitheatre that enclose the Upper Harbour. Spreading over the arms of the Lower Harbour are farms, generally dairying, to complete a felicitous blend of city, sea and countryside. In its centre, Dunedin assumes the character of a city of spires — of towers, gables, of roofs bristling with turrets — and of solid, gracious, generally stone buildings that earn for Dunedin the title of Victorian City of New Zealand.

If the Scottish influence of the first settlers has been diluted over a century, Dunedin yet has the country's only kilt shop, it produces the country's only whisky, and if Presbyterians are now well outnumbered they at least give the semblance of being in the majority. The province, with Southland, has its own trace of dialect; with a distinctive burr if not an actual roll of the "r" and a choice of language occasionally more Gaelic than Sassenach. In the city's centre is a massive statue of the Scottish poet, Robert Burns, but Dunedin has its bard in Thomas Bracken. The composer of *God Defend New Zealand* and *God's Own Country* (1890) knew no reticence when extolling the city's virtues:

> *"Go, trav'ler, unto others boast of Venice and of Rome,*
> *Of saintly Mark's majestic pile, and Peter's lofty dome;*
> *Of Naples and her trellised bowers, of Rhineland far away*
> *These may be grand, but give to me Dunedin from the Bay."*

## SOME HISTORY

**Sanguine scenes:** Towards the end of the eighteenth century the Otago Peninsula was the scene of a lengthy feud between three related Ngaitahu chiefs. Strife erupted after the son of the chief Moki II had died. A second chief, Te Wera, was accused of killing him with *makutu* (wizardry) and fled to Purakanui. Attacked there, Te Wera escaped to seek *utu* (revenge) and before long the area was in a general state of conflict. Te Wera killed one of Moki II's chiefs, Kapo, who had led the warparty against him at Purakanui, and perhaps also dispatched Moki II himself. The disembowelled Kapo was eaten at Papanui Inlet, on the island for a time named after him.

Both Ngaitahu and Ngatimamoe occupied the district and were slow to feel bound by the allegiance forged at Kaiapoi when Te Raki-ihia, paramount chief of Ngatimamoe, married Hine Hakari, sister of Te Hau Tapunui, the leading chief of Ngaitahu. Jealous of the fishing successes of Ngatimamoe, local Ngaitahu spoiled the Ngatimamoe fishing grounds and damaged their canoes. In no position to strike back, the subservient Ngatimamoe bided their time before requiring retribution, carrying off a Ngaitahu chief Tarewai and slicing his flesh with cutting stones while he was still alive. His captors were distracted for only a moment, but this was long enough for Tarewai to escape and later to exact personal *utu* for the way in which he had been treated.

Years later the bones of Te Raki-ihia, the Ngatimamoe chief who had arranged the Kaiapoi alliance, were used by Ngaitahu as fish hooks — a singularly insulting act of desecration. This led Ngatimamoe, under the late chief's son, to slay Ngaitahu as they collected firewood on Te Rauone Beach (near Otakou). The incident led to even greater slaughter as revenge was claimed in full measure.

Enormous though the toll in life had been, it was eclipsed by that exacted by measles, influenza and other diseases that came with the sealers and whalers. These so reduced the number of Maoris that in 1848 the once-considerable population of Otakou stood at a meagre 110.

**Slaughter at Murdering Beach:** Captain Cook sailed past the harbour entrance in the late afternoon of 24 February 1770. Fading light and haze blurred the coastline, and the explorer was too short of time to conduct a closer inspection. It was left for Daniel Cooper in 1809, as captain of the sealer *Unity*, to anchor within or near the harbour, which was for some time thereafter known as Port Daniel. Four years later the brig *Matilda* sought refuge in the port and a boatload of her crew vanished. For a time they were believed drowned, but it later transpired that the crew had been killed and eaten by local Maoris, justly enraged by the cruelty of sealers round the coast.

More sanguine was the conflict in 1817 at what is still called Murdering Beach, when Captain James Kelly, a sealer notorious for his barbarity, was attacked while he sought to trade iron for potatoes. One of his party had been recognised as a person who had traded in preserved heads. Three of the party were lost, including the luckless trader, but Kelly and the rest of his men made it back to their brig *Sophia* where they found a group of Maoris in all innocence trying to trade. These Kelly and his crew attacked with sealing knives, and before the savage scenario was played out the ruthless Kelly and his men had killed some seventy Maoris, smashed a number of canoes, and reduced to ashes the *kainga* they contemptuously designated the "City of Otago". A measure of Kelly's singlemindedness shows in that the loss of his men

# DUNEDIN AND ENVIRONS

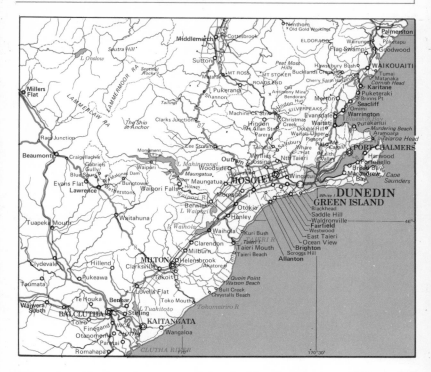

did not deter him from the purpose of the trip. He collected 3,000 sealskins before he returned to Hobart.

**"An ornamental and commodious site":** Recorded visits to the harbour were few and far between until 1832, the year in which a whaling station was established at Otakou village by Weller Bros. of Sydney. In spite of the harbour's evil reputation, it was the one safe anchorage on the Otago coast and so was favoured by deep-sea whalers who in increasing numbers were wintering over in New Zealand. The whalers grew potatoes in the off-season and, encouraged by drought conditions in New South Wales which ruined crops there, the Wellers planned to develop an agricultural settlement on the peninsula to supply the Sydney market. Their plans had come to naught when in 1840 the French navigator Dumont d'Urville visited the harbour, and was unimpressed.

Not so Frederick Tuckett, a survivor of the Wairau Affray (*see index*), who had been entrusted with the selection of the site for a Scottish settlement on the east coast of the South Island. If he was to see and dismiss the site of △Invercargill under the most dismal of conditions, the auguries were excellent when he visited the Otago Peninsula. Both Tuckett and his companion David Monro were unstinted in their praise of the sight that lay before them: "An ornamental and commodious site for a town, most suitable in every respect save the distance from the deep water of the lower harbour." Tuckett's superior, William Wakefield, endorsed the recommendation. Some inhabitants would later demur, but the choice was made.

**The New Edinburgh settlement:** The settlement had its genesis in Edward Gibbon Wakefield's theory of colonisation and was undertaken in conjunction with the New Zealand Company (*see index*) he founded. His concept was embraced by many Scots as in 1840 about a quarter of the working population of Scotland was unemployed, and those with jobs were toiling sixteen hours a day in an endeavour to keep body and soul together. In that year negotiations were in train with the New Zealand Company for it to cede a portion of its land for a Scottish colony, but these foundered as the Company's title to its lands was, at best, dubious.

The originator of the New Edinburgh scheme was George Rennie MP (1802–60), a skilful agriculturalist and sculptor who, among other achievements, was instrumental in obtaining for the British public free admission to St Paul's Cathedral, the British Museum and the National Gallery. The plan he proposed in 1842 ran into criticism because the New Zealand Company's settlements at Nelson, New Plymouth, Wellington and Wanganui were by no means overpopulated, and the land price Rennie suggested would undercut those prevailing elsewhere. The obstacles were considerable and Rennie eventually wearied of the project so that it fell to Captain William Cargill and the Rev. Thomas Burns to assume leadership and to give the movement its special character of a class settlement.

All three tapped impetus from the Disruption of 1843, the year which saw a decade of religious turmoil in Scotland finally boil over, and the Free Church of Scotland formed to cater for those Presbyterians who believed that the pulpits of their churches should be filled by ministers of their own choosing, not as a consequence of patronage that too often ignored a nominee's lack of fitness for the task. On 18 May 1843 the celebrated Dr Chalmers (after whom Port Chalmers is named) marched out of the Established Kirk of Scotland, splitting the congregation almost equally and taking with him more than 400 ministers, Thomas Burns among them. They established the Free Church of Scotland, which was quick to endorse the proposed scheme of colonisation, now to be a special class settlement of Scottish Presbyterians — of Scots who had previously proved too wary to be wooed to New Zealand by the New Zealand Company's propaganda.

In 1844, on the eve of the departure of the Otago Association's preliminary expedition, some 200 souls in all, came the news of the Wairau Affray. On top of this, fresh doubt was cast on the New Zealand Company's land titles — the site for "New Edinburgh" had not been selected, a task delegated to Col. William Wakefield. In the resulting confusion the expedition did not sail and the humbled Rennie withdrew from the enterprise.

**Otago Block purchase:** Despite Rennie's frustration, the land question was soon and simply solved. Col. Wakefield induced Governor FitzRoy to waive the Crown's right of pre-emption reserved by the Treaty of Waitangi, so enabling the New Zealand Company in this case to deal directly with the Maoris. It was Wakefield who entrusted the selection of the site to Tuckett, who at first refused the task when it was understood that the settlement was to be located where Lyttelton is today and only accepted it when he was given an unfettered discretion to select from an area extending from Banks Peninsula to Milford Sound.

The site chosen, terms of sale were negotiated. The Otakou chief Taiaroa asked £1,200 for his share, Karetai for £2,000. Tuhawaiki modestly mentioned a million. Finally Tucket persuaded the three principal chiefs to sell 162,000 ha for £2,400 and on 31 July 1844 a group mustered on the site of Port Chalmers to discuss, consent to, and sign the deed. The sum paid worked out at about a penny an acre. Payment took not the common form of blankets, pipes and axes, but of banknotes, gold and silver. Wakefield himself moved among the bustle, freely distributing halfcrowns, shillings and even sixpences to women and the children.

Surveying had just begun when news came of a crisis in London, and Wakefield was ordered to stop expenditure on the New Edinburgh settlement. The following year saw the famous three-days' debate in the British House of Commons on the state of New Zealand and the New Zealand Company, a debate that almost brought the British Government down. So strongly did Charles Buller MP attack the "misrule, opposition and obstinacy exhibited by the Colonial Office" in its dealings with the colony and the Company that only a vote on party lines saw the Administration survive. A chastened British Government entered into further dealings with the New Zealand Company, at least for a time, in a new spirit of cooperation.

**Slow beginnings:** Work on the New Edinburgh settlement was resumed and the survey completed. Two thousand properties were to be sold — to individuals, to local municipal government, to trustees for religious and educational uses, and to the New Zealand Company. The proceeds, expected to exceed £289,000, were to be divided between emigration, public works, and religious and educational purposes. The New Zealand Company was to receive a quarter of the proceeds "on account of its capital and risk".

Success depended on an ability to attract investors, but the Otago Association's cheerful optimism that all sections would be sold in five years proved well astray. By the end of 1847, when the first two migrant ships set sail, the *John Wickliffe* and the *Philip Laing*, only 72 of the 2,000 properties had been sold. Of the 344 passengers, only about fifteen held their own land orders. Already the exclusively Free Church nature of the plan was being eroded, as about half the properties sold had been bought by those with Irish or English addresses, many of them absentee speculators.

Once at Dunedin the migrants crowded into barracks, land ballots were held, sites selected, and homes of wattle and daub put together wherever level land could be found. By the year's end the *Blundell* and the *Bernicia* had added another 200 to the settlement, and in 1849 a further 500 arrived.

Development was slow as the all-too-few migrants grappled on a difficult site to carve out for themselves a town worthy of the name. A Balclutha settler described it as "pitched upon a mass of hills, having such deep gullies between them that nothing save an earthquake coming to level them could ever make it suitable for the site of a town".

The town's inhabitants were principally Scottish, with two thirds of its population Presbyterian. From the outset the outnumbered Little Enemy (as the Presbyterians were wont to describe the Anglicans) made much of the economic running so that job advertisements not uncommonly stipulated that "English need not apply".

The settlement had as its leader Capt. William Cargill, whose Scottish forebear Donald Cargill had been martyred by the English for his ideal of religious and political freedom. Capt. Cargill ordered the Methodist missionary, the Rev. Charles Creed, to keep out of Otago, and later even directed an Englishman to remove himself to Canterbury, "where he belonged". His associate and religious leader of the settlement, the Rev. Thomas Burns, provocatively dug his garden on Christmas Day to demonstrate his utter rejection of the English observance of the festival.

For all their fervour, after two years the Scottish were in the minority, yet such was their drive that they stamped their character on the growing town. Their unity split over the question of squatting. The Otago Association saw squatting as a "rankling wrong" that would bring a "demoralised class of settler" who would perpetrate "irreligion and ignorance" because they would live without churches or schools. The squatters, however, saw natural pasture for a million sheep and the *Otago Witness* argued that "sheep are the pioneers of civilisation". By 1855 public opinion supported the squatters and provincial land regulations were drawn up which allowed, if they also regulated, the woolly empires the squatters were already founding.

**Gold! Gold!** Nothing so galvanised the town and the province of which it was capital than the discovery of gold. After a false rush to the △ Lindis came Gabriel Read's auriferous eureka that in 1861 gave birth to △ Lawrence; only months later Hartley and Reilly electrified the town with their eighty-seven-pound bags of gold from what soon became the Dunstan diggings (*see* △ *Clyde*); then came the Shotover, "the richest river in the world" (*see* △ *Queenstown*), and finally, when the game of "hunting the fox" was played out, William Fox and his group were discovered extracting fortunes from the Arrow River (*see* △ *Arrowtown*). Once the town recovered from the stampede to the diggings of most of its ablebodied men, the Dunedin economy boomed as never before, and as never again since.

It was gold that gave the town and the country its strong economic base; that spawned the noble buildings that make Dunedin truly the Victorian city of New Zealand; that earned for the centre the title of Commercial Capital of New Zealand. Those traditional Scottish skills, banking and engineering, were present in full measure to the greater glory of the city.

**Taming the hills:** The hills that rise so sharply from the waterfront were in time conquered by the first cable tramway to operate outside the United States. Suggested in 1879 by a twenty-seven-year-old engineer, George Smith Duncan, the pioneer line was built by a company he founded. The line ran up Rattray St and curved to the left at St Joseph's Cathedral, the curve being overcome by a "pull curve" — a number of small wheels that eased the wire rope round the curve but still allowed the cablecar to grip. The innovation was later adopted by major cable systems throughout the world.

A continuously-running endless cable ran beneath the roadway and was gripped by a projecting arm when the passenger car was to move. Each car had a brakeman who could grip the cable at will and who also had a variety of brakes to hold the car still when it was not engaged to the cable. The cablecar system, based on the design of the world's first (San Francisco, 1873) became a landmark. By the turn of the century three private companies were operating services to Roslyn, Mornington, Maryhill and Kaikorai. Duncan later crossed the Tasman to design a cable-tramway for Melbourne; this was later reputed to be the best laid out in the world.

The cars trundled up and down the hills of Dunedin for three-quarters of a century. One by one the lines closed, and finally the Mornington cars made their last journeys in 1957. The decision to abandon the system evoked much opposition, as the city was hard to imagine without the quaint cars — in rush hours so jammed that some had even taken to riding on their roofs. (*A cablecar from the Maryhill line is in the Early Settlers' Museum.*)

> *Princes Street by Gaslight* by Hardwicke Knight (McIndoe), with photographs by Daniel Louis Mundy, records life in Dunedin's main street more than a century ago. *Dunedin Then* by Hardwicke Knight (McIndoe) provides an overall commentary on Dunedin life and history.

## A WALK FROM THE OCTAGON

*The suggested walk begins and ends at the Octagon. Allow from 1½ hrs to half a day, as the walk can take in the Early Settlers' Museum. Start at the Octagon:*

**The Octagon:** The eight-sided garden area, its form magnified by concentric Moray Place, was chosen for the city's centre in 1846 by Charles Kettle, Chief Surveyor for the New Zealand Company. Kettle died in Dunedin in 1862, victim of a typhoid epidemic caused by the town's lack of adequate sanitation following the sudden expansion that came with the goldrush era. *In the Octagon stands the:*

**Robert Burns statue** (1887): The Scottish bard is linked with the early settlers by blood as well as by nationality. The Rev. Thomas Burns, the religious leader of the initial group, was his nephew. The imposing statue of Burns with pen poised presides over the city's heart "with his back to the kirk and his face to the pub". The Anglican Cathedral remains behind him, but the Oban Hotel he once faced is now no more. The statue was unveiled by a great-great-niece of the poet in the presence of Sir George Grey. *Behind Burns rises:*

**St Paul's Anglican Cathedral** (1915)**: The cathedral of Oamaru stone rises on a site given by Johnny Jones (*see index*) in 1853, at a time when there were 1,317 Presbyterians and only 285 Anglicans, and when the latter were obliged to hold services in either the courthouse or the gaol. Behind the cathedral is a separate, "temporary" wooden belfry (1910) which is still in use. On the front façade are three bishops, Selwyn (first and only Bishop of New Zealand), Harper (first Bishop of Christchurch, whose diocese included Otago and Southland) and Nevill (first Bishop of Dunedin and holding a model of the Cathedral as it was originally planned).

In design a free interpretation of Gothic and Early English, the building has a remarkable vaulted ceiling some 20 m above the nave. Noteworthy among its fittings are the pulpit, enriched with alabaster carvings, and the font, a locally-carved replica of a font in Linton, near Nottingham. The architects were Sedding & Wheatley, of London.

The cathedral has had a chequered career. In the first place a beneficent (and, of course, Anglican) governor generously offered the Octagon itself to the Church of England for its cathedral site, an act that so outraged the vociferous and more numerous members of the Free Church of Scotland that the offer was withdrawn. Then the first permanent St Pauls (1862–63), whose bell is in the "temporary" belfry, was built of soft Caversham stone and was soon condemned. In 1877 a Cathedral Commission reported "with the exception of the Bishop, who dissented, they are all of the opinion that the present site of St Paul's would be the most suitable place in which to erect a cathedral; but in consequence of the Bishop's dissent, they have thought it inadvisable to take, for the present, any further steps in the matter." The Bishop was anxious to have St Matthews' (an elegant church in Stafford St) simply adopted as the cathedral for the diocese. The move for a new cathedral was bogged down in vestry politics until in 1900 one Mr William Harrop died, leaving over £35,000 for the purpose.

The complete design includes a chancel (in 1971 added in a sympathetic modern adaptation), two transepts and a tower above the crossing. *Beside the Cathedral are the:*

**Municipal Chambers** (1878–80): The most interesting room in the since-expanded complex is the Council Chamber itself, on the second floor. The impressive setting is heightened by the slowly curving councillors' tables, the portraits of distinguished city fathers and the mayoral seat, formerly that of the Speaker of the Otago Provincial Council. Portraits include those of George Rennie, initiator of what became the New Edinburgh Settlement, and Sir William Chambers, who succeeded in urging upon the promoters that the name of Dunedin be adopted—in a letter to the *New Zealand Journal* he complained of the suggested New Edinburgh nomenclature: "The 'news' in North America are an utter abomination . . . It will be a matter for regret if the New Zealand Company help to carry the nuisance to the territories with which it is concerned."

The original portion of the classical building was designed by R. A. Lawson. The tower was truncated in 1964, to the dismay of many residents. *In front of the Burns statue is the:*

**"Star" fountain:** An unusual musical fountain was the gift of the city's evening newspaper to mark its centenary. *It plays each evening at 9.30 and 9.45 pm during daylight saving time and at 9.00 and 9.15 pm during winter. Now walk down Stuart St which affords a vista closed by the Railway Station and framed by three towers. At the corner, pause at the:*

**Law Courts** (1900–02)**: A severe if modestly embellished stone building of Port Chalmers breccia, replete with battlements. Above the side entrance stands the figure of Justice, scales in one hand, sword in the other and noticeably not blindfolded. The wellknown representation at London's Old Bailey (erected as recently as 1907) is widely understood to be blindfolded, a misconception created by the low helmet she is shown there as wearing. Within, only the Supreme Courtroom retains its original *élan*, with a Gothic canopy rising above the Bench and with steps disappearing from the dock to the cells beneath. The walls have not been enhanced by the application of acoustic material. Above the external front entrance is the royal coat-of-arms. The design was by the Government Architect, John Campbell. *Cross Anzac Avenue to reach the:*

**Railway Station** (1904)***: Dominated by a massive copper-capped tower that is cornered with heraldic lions and edged with royal coats-of-arms, the bluestone railway station stands as impressive testimony to the faith and pride of the railway builders. It was a jubilant day when Sir Joseph Ward laid the foundation stone for the building, in the presence of a large crowd and under a banner that proclaimed "Advance New Zealand Railways". In the concourse, exaltation is everywhere to be seen; the NZR cypher is engraved on scores of windowpanes, woven into ornate scrolls above the ticket windows and incorporated in matching stained-glass windows, each portraying a locomotive approaching at full steam. Sixteen ceramic nymphets look down approvingly at a majestic mosaic floor, whose tiles repeatedly mirror the cypher between panels of varying railway motifs. The lions rampant recur both in the windows and on the plastered ceilings. The building earned for its architect, George Troup, the sobriquet of Gingerbread George. Built of Kokonga basalt, the building is faced with Oamaru stone. *On the opposite side of the road is the:*

# DUNEDIN CITY

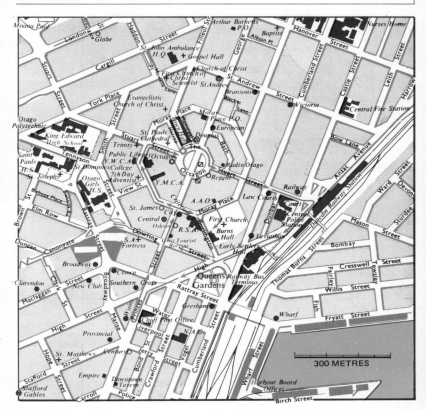

## 10

**Police Station** (1895): Like the neighbouring Law Courts, the brick police station was the work of John Campbell, whose design was heavily influenced by the English architect Norman Shaw, responsible for London's New Scotland Yard. Totally symmetrical, with hanging towers on each front corner, the building is a functional symbol of reaction against the excesses of Victorian stylism. It lost its chimneys in 1973 and now appears a trifle lightheaded. The complex, on the site of the city's first gaol, until recently incorporated the women's gaol, as well as the police station. *On the same side of the road as the police station is:*

**Otago Daily Times building:** Present home of one of the country's oldest daily newspapers, which began publication in 1861. *Continue along what has become Lower High St to pass the:*

**Early Settlers' Museum***: *Described under "Some Museums and Art Galleries",* see below. From here there is an interesting aspect of First Church. *Cross to:*

**Queen's Gardens*:** A shaded grassed area in the city's commercial heart where rise Dunedin's war memorial and statues of Queen Victoria (1901) and of the seated Donald MacNaughton Stuart (1819–94), Minister of Knox Church from 1860–94, stick in hand and the plaid he always wore about him. His disrespectful posture in the presence of his monarch is explained by his statue being erected some three years earlier than that of Victoria. *Here a brief detour may be made by turning up Dowling St for some 60 m to the:*

**Old Garrison Hall (1878):** Now occupied by TV One, the building for many years served as concert hall in addition to its martial purpose. *Turn up High St, noting the impressive buildings on the left. At the intersection is the:*

**Cargill Monument** (1863)***: Opinions differ about this High Gothic monument, modelled on the Walter Scott monument in Edinburgh. Eulogised when erected as "one of the most beautiful specimens of Gothic architecture in the power of man to design", the plinth of snarling monkeys and winged beasts has also been described as "a collection of upended stone shish-kebabs". The monument for a time fell into disfavour, when a men's lavatory stood beside it. At one stage it even wore a notice inviting passersby to refrain from expectorating.

A brass plaque in ornate script records the addition of a drinking fountain no longer "for the use of citizens", and a more modest plate, set inconspicuously at pavement level, records that it was here in 1883 that the Salvation Army began its work in New Zealand. Its officers had come at the behest of the daughter of a wealthy Otago pioneer, who wrote to William Booth in London urging him to send "officers" to New Zealand. As in Britain, the advent of the Army was not welcomed and the arrival at Port Chalmers of two officers to found the movement in New Zealand was ridiculed in the press — Britain had sent thistles, sparrows and rabbits; this further scourge was not needed. The Salvation Army held its first public meeting here to "open fire" in its campaign and quickly flourished despite the imprisonment of members during a series of Court battles over the legality of their holding meetings in public places. The Army, born of times of depression, poverty and social upheaval, is a permanent feature of the country's voluntary welfare organisations. It is still characterised by open-air evangelism. *Across Princes St on the corner of High St is the:*

**Southern Cross Hotel** (1883): The corner portion of the building incorporates the flamboyant old Grand Hotel. The public rooms on the first floor may be visited where particularly ornate ceilings remain in original form. *Turn left along Princess St to reach the:*

**Central Post Office:** If time allows one may take the lift to the seventh floor and walk round the building to obtain from each of the four corners a different aspect of the city.

Beside the Post Office is a modern building, John Wickliffe House. On reclaimed land, it occupies the site of the landing of the earliest immigrant ship from Scotland. Behind the Post Office and across Bond St stands **Edinburgh House (1866)**, of unplastered red brick and occupying a complete city block. *Almost opposite the Post Office in Princes St is:*

**Wain's Hotel** (1878): Its interior has been completely renovated but the building's exuberant façade lends considerable character to the street. Note the grotesque representations beneath the bay windows. *Turn round and walk back towards the Octagon, passing the:*

**Bank of New Zealand** (1883): In a fanciful medallion above the entrance a massive *kiwi* pecks beneath a tree-fern while a war canoe paddles past. *Continue along Princess St and on reaching Moray Place turn right to pass, on the intersection with Burlington St:*

---

A key to area maps appears on page 2.

---

**Victoria Cross Corner:** Outside the Returned Servicemen's clubrooms is set a tablet listing the country's holders of the Victoria Cross beside a relief cast of the medal they won. *Cross Burlington St and pass the plaque to the Rev. Thomas Burns and an Historic Places Trust tablet to enter:*

**First Church** (1868–73)***: "The glorious spire is indeed a psalm in stone," enthused one admirer of the Norman-Gothic building, perhaps the finest in the country. Constructed of unreinforced Oamaru stone, the building stands where once rose Bell Hill, the site of the second divine service ever celebrated in Dunedin. The first temporary church, built elsewhere, had a bell given by Johnny Jones which had been a ship's bell on a convict ship and later on the *Magnet* as it conveyed the first settlers to △Waikouaiti (*now in the Early Settlers' Museum*). A second bell was received in 1851 from friends of Thomas Burns in Scotland, but the Session decided this was too grand for "the queer looking fabric of a church" and elected to install it instead on Church Hill as a time bell. Before long the site had become known as Bell Hill and the church found some claiming that it owned neither the site nor the bell — assertions the inscription on the bell helped refute and so resolve the controversy in favour of the church. (*The old bell now stands on a plinth in the church grounds and the church has twelve new ones, installed in 1975*).

Once the hill was cut down the building of Thomas Burns's "monument to Presbyterianism at the Antipodes" could begin, to the prize-winning design of the youthful architect R. A. Lawson. Burns laid the foundation stone (precisely *which* stone is uncertain) but did not live to see the church and its piercing, uplifting spire completed. For seven years he had been the only Presbyterian minister in the province, and he continued to be the Minister of First Church until his death in 1871 at the age of seventy-six. Lawson (1833–1902) trained as an architect in Scotland before going to Australia. He found so little work in Melbourne that he turned to goldmining and journalism. He returned to his profession in 1861 and the following year won a competition for the design of this church. The judges' choice brought the young architect to Dunedin, where he stamped his harmonious designs on a variety of public buildings. He was also an Elder of the First Church Congregation.

The interior is enhanced by deep yet delicate stone carving. The capitals on the pillars flanking the pulpit depict, to the right, a bird feeding its young (symbolic of Life) and to the left, a bird about to kill a butterfly (symbolic of Death). The gallery motifs combine thistle, rose and shamrock.

To gain a better appreciation of this remarkable building one should walk right round it. The hall annexed to the church, Moray Hall, contains memorial windows moved here when the Moray Place Congregational Church building was sold to the Seventh-Day Adventists. *To the right of First Church stands:*

**Burns Hall** (1907): A simple memorial not to the poet but to the Rev. Thomas Burns. *Retrace your steps up Moray Place to cross Princes St and continue on to pass the:*

**Seventh-Day Adventist Church** (1864): The city's oldest church, designed by David Ross, was built as the Congregational Church, and was spared possible demolition when it was acquired by the Seventh-Day Adventists. *Almost opposite is the:*

**Dunedin Public Library:** The library houses the extensive Robert McNab Collection, one founded by an eminent historian and politician of the turn of the century. The Alfred and Isabel Reed Collection of early bibles and manuscripts is probably the largest in the Hemisphere. *Open daily.* The collection will be moved to a new library, to be built beside the Town Hall as part of the Civic Centre. *Continue up Moray Place to reach, on the corner with Upper Stuart St:*

**Fortune Theatre (1869):** The former Trinity Methodist Church, designed by Lawson and having an interesting stair tower, now houses a theatre-company which is currently (1978) adapting the building to fulfil its new function. *Turn right to pass the Anglican Cathedral and return to the Octagon.*

## SOME MUSEUMS AND ART GALLERIES

**Otago Museum\*\*\*:** Housed in a building (1876–7) designed by David Ross that itself ranks with the city's finest, the collection is notable by domestic standards for its art and sculpture — of Classical Greece and of Rome and the ancient civilisations of the Middle East. These reflect to a degree the wealth and beneficence of the business community at the turn of the century.

Displayed too, are early maps and paintings which depict the evolution of the city site, artefacts from Murdering Beach (once the scene of the largest Maori greenstone "factory" in Otago), and *mere* (clubs) charged with the *mana* of local Maori families deposited here only for safe keeping. A Collier flintlock rifle once belonged to Tuhawaiki, the renowned "Bloody Jack" (*see index*). Included in the Maori section are several carvings, among them a decorated sternpost and carved prow, both grafted on to a much-renovated war canoe. Clearly Ngatiawa in style, the pair must either have been captured from Te Rauparaha or have been gifts from him once peace was finally made.

An extensive collection of artefacts of Murihiku — pendants, adzes, *patu*, textiles, fish hooks and woodware — includes rock drawings removed from shelters at Duntroon, Hazelburn and Maerewhenua River. A section on *moko* (tattooing) includes two preserved heads, recalling a once-grisly trade.

The Mataatua meeting house (1872–75), in common with most of the larger carvings, comes from the North Island. The lack of large carvings in the South Island reflects the itinerant way of life of the South Island Maoris who were constantly moving to gather food, unlike their more agriculturally minded counterparts in the North. Built at Whakatane, the meeting house was presented to Sir Donald McLean as a gift to Queen Victoria. It was exhibited in Sydney and London but returned to New Zealand much damaged and has since been completely restored. The ornately-carved house is unusual for its *amo* (front uprights), each of which portrays two figures in place of the usual one. In each case the pair represents twins; those to the left are Tarakiuta and Tarakitai, holding the spinning tops that were used to lure them to their deaths — smothered in a *rua* (*kumara* pit) when they climbed in to retrieve them. Their murderer, Tupurupuru, who had acted to advance the chances of chieftainship for his own son, Rakai-tehikuroa, was traced by the flying of kites, and both he and his son were put to death as *utu* was exacted. The twins to the right, too, met a premature end; they clasp the *patu* (clubs) they used in battle before they fell in the 1823 invasion of the Bay of Plenty by Ngapuhi from Northland.

Within, the carved figures represent individual Whakatane ancestors, among them (at the base of the central *poutahu* on the rear wall), the ancestor of a number of Bay of Plenty tribes, Toi Kairakau (Toi the Wood-eater). After the Maori section, the comprehensive displays of Melanesian art and culture assume an added interest.

*Great King St. Open Mon.–Fri. from 10 am–5 pm; Sat. from 1–5 pm; Sun. from 2–5 pm. Allow upwards of ½ day.*

In a separate wing is the **Hocken Library,** one of the major resources for research into New Zealand history. It was established by Dr Thomas Moreland Hocken (1836–1910), who gave the public the extensive collection of books, maps, paintings and manuscripts compiled in pursuit of his "fascinating folly"; it has since been greatly enlarged. The library will be rehoused in the new Arts Block when completed. Hocken's Maori ethnology collection forms the foundation of the museum's ethnology sections.

**Early Settlers' Association Museum and Portrait Gallery\*\*\*:** A stern assembly of pre-1869 settlers frowns down from the high walls that enclose a wide variety of exhibits from the city's past. Outside stands the sole survivor of the fifty-three kerosene streetlamps that illuminated the city's main streets in 1863. Dunedin was the first in New Zealand and among the first in the world to use kerosene street lighting. Its engineer, John Millar, was so proud of his lampstand design, cast in Melbourne, that he had his name embossed boldly on each, together with the motto *Secundo curo.* Few knew just what the motto meant and, attributing it to Millar, translated it freely as "I am poor and cannot pay my debts." In fact it was the motto of the Dunedin Town Board and means: "I will prosper and I am cautious." An old iron hitching post (pre-1870) is beside the lampstand. Set into the building, behind glass, is Ja 1274 *Josephine*, a Class E locomotive, the first to be used on the Dunedin-Port Chalmers line and also used to haul the first through express from Christchurch to Dunedin (1878). *Lower High St. Open Mon.-Sat. 9 am-8.30 pm and Sun. from 2-4.30 pm. Allow 2 hrs.*

**Olveston**\*\*\* is a Jacobean-styled home, built in 1904–06 to the design of Sir Ernest George, a leading English domestic architect of the day. It is named after a village near Bristol where its first owner, David Edward Theomin, was born in 1852. Theomin came to Dunedin in 1879, founded a number of businesses and was closely associated with the arts. He built up a handsome collection of antiques and furnished his house in the best of contemporary taste. When Theomin's daughter died in 1966 the house was bequeathed to the people of Dunedin in accordance with her father's wishes. Overflowing with valuable antiques and early New Zealand paintings, Olveston yet remains the home of a prosperous and culturally alert Edwardian family.

In no real sense does the building belong either to the city or to the country, deriving almost entirely from Britain, even to much of its imported joinery. The influence of *art nouveau* is seen in window leadlights that portray various European writers and artists. *42 Royal Tce. Tours take 1 hour and commence Mon.-Sat. at 9.30 and 10.45 am, 1.30 and 2.45 pm, Sun. at 1.30, 2.45 and 4.00 pm.*

**Otago Art Society**\*\*: The Society uses as its gallery the former Dunedin North Post Office building. *Great King St.*

**Dunedin Public Art Gallery**\*\*\* has a wide collection of both European and of early and contemporary New Zealand art that includes one of the largest single holdings there is of paintings by Frances Hodgkins (1870–1947). Generally considered to be the finest painter the country has produced, and whose father helped establish the Gallery, Frances Hodgkins was born in Dunedin and grew up in a cultural atmosphere generated by the wealth of the goldfields. She lived most of her later life in Britain, where she was "discovered" at the age of over sixty. Her agent wrote of expecting to meet a young man, having judged by the dynamic and *avant-garde* pictures he had seen, and of being startled to meet an elderly woman. A special room is devoted to a number of works by minor old masters. Also displayed are ceramics and antique furniture. *Logan Park at end of Anzac Ave. Open Mon.–Fri. 10 am-4.30 pm; weekends and holidays 2–5 pm. Allow upwards of 1 hour.*

**Ocean Beach railway:** A working museum of steam-railway rolling stock operates at weekends and on public holidays. The line is planned to link St Kilda and St Clair beaches. *Kettle Park, St Kilda.*

## SOME OTHER NOTABLE BUILDINGS

*First Church, St Paul's Anglican Cathedral, Municipal Chambers, the Law Courts, Railway Station, Police Station and both the Seventh Day Adventist Church and the Trinity Methodist Church are all described under "A Walk From the Octagon" (above).*

**University of Otago**\*\*\*: The country's first university retains its 1878 complex of slate-roofed bluestone buildings in a soothing setting beside the Leith Stream. The design, by Maxwell Bury, derives from Sir George Gilbert Scott's Glasgow University (1870). Considered particularly fine is the clock tower building which has been rated by the Historic Places Trust as a building whose preservation is of national importance. The university's rapid expansion in recent years is evidenced by the number of impressive modern buildings in the area. As an institution, Dunedin's university dates from 1869, when it was energetically promoted by the leaders of the New Edinburgh settlement, who had a keen interest in furthering education. The Rev. Thomas Burns was the first Chancellor. *Castle St. To appreciate the finer details of the buildings, walk through the cloistered entrance from Union St to thread through the buildings and emerge in Leith St, observing the clock tower building on the right after crossing the river. Turn left at Leith St to be outside Maxwell Bury's interesting Professors' Houses (1878) at the St David's St corner.*

**All Saints' Anglican Church** (1865–75)\*: The brick church, with a polychrome decorated façade, had its foundation stone laid on clay "nigh unto a bog in which a horse disappeared". Unstable foundations predictably almost caused the building to collapse, a problem overcome now that stressed cables tie the walls to each other. The church, among the oldest in the city, has considerable charm. Of its windows, that in the west wall commemorates J. M. Ritchie, co-founder of the stock and station firm that became National Mortgage (NMA); in the south transept the founder of the *Evening Star*, George Bell, is remembered. On the north wall a window depicts a variety of native birds. *Cumberland St.* The church faces across the North Ground. Through the trees, in Great King Street, may be seen an appealing series of Victorian terrace houses.

**Cable House**\*: A picturesque pair of cottages has been rebuilt by the New Zealand Historic Places Trust to preserve an historic piece of streetscape while providing modern living conditions indoors. The originals were built by the Cable family in 1861 and owned by them for 112 years. *829 Cumberland St. Private property.*

**Knox Church** (1876)\*\*: If not as remarkable as First Church, Lawson's Knox Church is nevertheless of fine design and boasts a worthy spire. In the gallery the doors on the boxed pews belong to an era when pew space was rented by parishioners.

Outside the church, heavy with whiskers, is a bust of Dr D. M. Stuart, the church's first minister and only the second to arrive in Dunedin. *George St.*

**Otago Boys' High School** (1884)***: An outstanding example of R. A. Lawson's work, the bluestone complex incorporates a variety of forms. *Arthur St.*

**St Joseph's Roman Catholic Cathedral** (1886)***, is the work of Francis William Petre (1847–1918), an English-trained architect whose fondness for simple geometric forms is evidenced by the neighbouring **St Dom:nic's Priory** (1877)**. A building in in an economical Gothic style, the concrete priory and Petre's relationship to a wellknown Catholic peer helped earn for the architect the title of "Lord Concrete".

The elegant and sophisticated Cathedral shows why Petre ranks with Lawson as the finest of the country's Victorian architects. It was originally planned as a cruciform, with a tower rising over the crossing. Only the nave has been built so far, but this plainly establishes the excellence of Petre's concept. The interior contains stained glass from Munich, much fine stonework and two delightful rose windows. Other outstanding basilicas designed by Petre are in Oamaru, Timaru, Invercargill, Christchurch and Wellington. *Rattray St.*

**St Matthew's Anglican Church** (1874)**: The church that Bishop Nevill wanted as his cathedral would have eminently served as such. An unpretentious, simple structure, now hemmed in by too-near neighbours, it is within as simple as it is without. *Cnr Stafford and Hope Sts.*

**Larnach's Castle**\*\*\*: This exuberant baronial hall was the creation of the Hon. William Larnach as he sought to house himself and his family in the grand manner. *14.5 km (Described under "A Drive on Otago Peninsula", below).*

## SOME VIEWPOINTS

**Mt Cargill Lookout**\*\*\* *(676.5 m):* From the foot of the television transmission mast is a panorama without peer — of the harbour, the city, the whole of the Otago Peninsula, down the coast as far as the Nuggets and north as far as the hills behind Palmerston. If the height of the mountain gives Dunedin its most spectacular viewpoint, it also chills the prevailing northerly breeze. Provided arrangements are made in advance, viewing may be combined with a visit to Television One's transmission building. *8 km. At the end of George St turn left to follow Pine Hill Rd to its end. Then turn right and follow Cowan St to the summit.*

**Signal Hill (Centennial Lookout)**\*\*\* *(393 m):* A superlative viewpoint from which the aspect is predominantly to the south — of the Upper Harbour, the city and the sea on both sides of the neck of land that at St Kilda ties the Otago Peninsula to the mainland. On the podium is a piece from the rock on which stands Edinburgh Castle, a centennial gift from one Scottish city to another. Bronze statues represent the past, a closed book, and the future, a ball of yet-to-be-unwound twine. The centenary in 1940 marked 100 years of British sovereignty in New Zealand. *From Opoho Rd follow Signal Hill Rd 3 km to its end.*

*Below the Centennial Lookout is:*

**Northern Cemetery and Bracken's Lookout**\*: Approached by Lovelock Avenue (named after an Olympic goldmedallist and one-mile world recordholder), the cemetery comes into sight, dominated by the pinnacle of a Gothic mausoleum. Modelled on First Church and embellished with his family motto, it contains the remains of W. J. M. Larnach, as ostentatious in death as in life. Passing the old sexton's cottage and bearing right through the gates, the path winds through an attractive old graveyard to pass the grave of Thomas Bracken (1843–98), emblazoned with verses from one of his better-known poems, "Not Understood" (*to the right, about 60 m beyond the large macrocarpa tree*). About half way to Bracken's grave, on the left, is that of Vincent Pyke (*see index*), a dominating figure on the Central Otago goldfields. On the cemetery's southern perimeter is **Bracken's Lookout,** named after the poet, journalist and Member of Parliament who extolled the virtues of the views of his home town in "Dunedin From the Bay" quoted here. Some of the more prominent buildings are identified on a plane table. *Lovelock Ave, off Dundas St. One may continue up Lovelock Ave, past the cemetery, to reach Signal Hill (above).*

**Southern Cemetery** enjoys a low view, to the north, over the city's heart. The cemetery is one of the city's oldest and is divided into separate areas for Presbyterians, Anglicans, Catholics, Jews and Chinese. Within the Presbyterian sector lie the religious leaders, the Rev. Thomas Burns (*by roundabout*) and the Rev. D. M. Stuart. Captain William Cargill (1784–1860), also buried here, was born in Edinburgh and was in turn soldier, wine merchant and banker. As leader of the settlement he was the New Zealand Company's Otago agent and contributed to the infant township's turbulence by banning its newspaper, feuding with Governor Grey, and quarrelling with the Anglican minority that he dubbed the Little Enemy. He became the province's first Superintendent in 1853, but his retirement six years later came as a relief to those he professed to serve but whom he alienated by his inflexibility, his tactlessness and his desire above all else to preserve the exclusively Scottish character of the settlement. For all his shortcomings he must be ranked as an outstanding leader of the infant community. The Catholic section is presided over by a jaded neo-Gothic mausoleum built for Bishop Patrick Moran (1823–95), first Roman Catholic Bishop of Dunedin, and of Bishop Michael Verdon, his successor (*by South St*). Bishop Moran was an implacable opponent of State education without religious instruction. To combat secularism he founded the *New Zealand Tablet*, a Catholic weekly which has appeared regularly ever since. In 1883 he even stood for Parliament against Larnach in the hope that he might there continue to press for compulsory religion in schools, but the electors did not give the Bishop the opportunity. Johnny Jones (*see index*) is buried in the Anglican sector. *Bounded by South and Eglinton Rds.*

**Unity Park Lookout**\*\*: From here, within the Town Belt, the view is over the city and down the Upper Harbour to Macandrew Bay. A bust of the American explorer, Richard Evelyn Byrd (1888–1957), who pioneered aviation in the Antarctic, stands here as a memorial to his sailing from Dunedin in 1928 with the first expedition to explore Antarctica by air. *Eglinton Rd, off South Rd.*

## OTHER THINGS TO SEE AND DO

**Botanic Gardens**\*\* range from formal flowerbeds to stands of native bush. As one enters from Great King St a number of trees, massive with age, shade the formal areas that enclose the display houses. Between late July and early November there is a magnificent display of rhododendrons and azaelias in the Rhododendron Glen. Statues of Peter Pan and Wendy, a playground and an aviary hold appeal for children and a kiosk by the winter gardens serves lunches and light refreshments. *Great King St. Open daily during daylight hours.*

**Globe Theatre**\*\*: Added to an early home is a small, intimate theatre where new productions are staged regularly. Preference is given to works by New Zealand writers. *104 London St, tel. 88-274.*

**Moana Swimming Pool:** A modern indoor tepid swimming pool has a restaurant with views of the city. The pool has helped to establish Dunedin as a leading centre for competitive swimming. *Stuart St. Open daily.*

**Beverley-Begg Observatory** is open by arrangement. *Robin Hood Ground, Queen's Drive. To visit tel. 77-683 evenings only.*

**St Kilda and St Clair**\*\*: The pick of the ocean beaches border the city's southern suburbs, lying along what was once a bleak, windswept sandbar that built up to link the Otago Peninsula, once an island, to the mainland.

St Clair lies in the western curl, with a heated saltwater pool carved from the rock of the bluff. Second Beach is a 5-minute walk away.

Particularly at St Kilda a variety of sports clubs have built their facilities. Forbury Park here stages night trotting. At Kettle Park the Otago Branch of the New Zealand Railway and Locomotive Society has its Ocean Beach railway where steam trains operate at weekends and on public holidays. The track is planned to extend from St Kilda to St Clair, to link the two popular swimming beaches. From St Kilda an ocean drive extends along the shore, between surging surf and a golf links, to a lookout where a plane table identifies points of interest. Beyond the lookout lies Tomahawk Beach, its name apparently a distortion of Tomahaka (*toma*=burial place; *haka*= dance). At Memorial Park the first stage has been completed in the erection of the country's largest indoor sports stadium.

**Golden Arrow Drive** leads past many of the points of interest listed above and winds through the city's extensive Town Belt, a feature of New Zealand Company settlements long before they became an established feature of good town planning. Dunedin's Town Belt spreads round the slopes above the city, offering pleasant walks and a drive that alternates between thick stands of trees and wide harbour views. *The drive starts from the Chief Post Office, Princes St, leading away from the Octagon. 12 km. An explanatory brochure is available from the Public Relations Office and from the Automobile Association (Otago).*

## A DRIVE ON OTAGO PENINSULA

*The suggested route is for a full day, but even then may have to be shortened by omitting the detours to the Pyramids, Cape Saunders and to Lovers' Leap and The Chasm. The Royal Albatross Colony at Taiaroa Head can be visited only by prior arrangement (see below). There are few places at which one can buy lunch, but many good picnic places.*

The peninsula has abundant wildlife: its albatross colony is world-renowned and there are many yellow-eyed penguins (so named because of their golden heads), bar-tailed godwits, shags, and wading birds, the oystercatcher among them. The farmland is given individuality by century-old dry stone walls, often tinted with lichen, and by post-and-rail fences. The Otago Peninsula Trust promotes interest in the area at the same time as working to conserve its character (*membership enquiries to PO Box 620, Dunedin*). *Leave central Dunedin by Highway 1 south, turning left towards Andersons Bay and left again into Portobello Road to follow the waterfront to:*

# OTAGO PENINSULA AND DUNEDIN 11

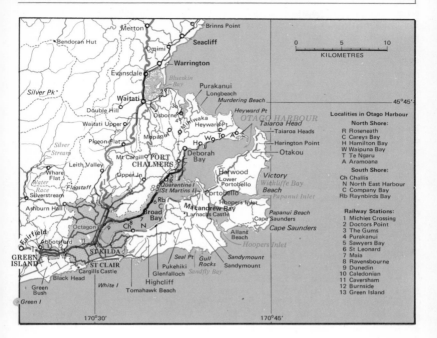

**Glenfalloch Woodland Gardens**\*\* (*10 km*)*:* The gardens, administered by the Trust, are particularly attractive from mid-September to mid-October, when many flowering plants are at their best, but at all times of year the setting is one of great appeal. The gardens have their origin in commercial gardens run for a time from 1873 by one George Grey Russell. When he returned to Britain they were handed over to a caretaker. For twenty years trees and shrubs gathered from the world over grew unchecked until at the turn of the century the Baring family put the "horticultural League of Nations" into order. Doves flutter in the trees, peacocks roam free, and tea may be taken in the most pleasant of surroundings. The original homestead (1871) still stands. *Open daily during daylight hours. Continue on to skirt:*

**Macandrew Bay** (*11.2 km*)*:* The road here was constructed in the 1860s with prison labour, convicts being housed in the *Success,* a hulk that was slowly dragged along the sea front to keep pace with the progress of the work. The prisoners also built the neat stone walls between the road and the sea. *The route continues along the foreshore (Larnach's Castle is visited on the return journey) and slowly sweeps round:*

**Broad Bay** (*16 km*)*:* At the far end of the bay is Yellow Head, a point that bears the imprint of once being a fortified Maori *pa.* It is now a cemetery reserve. *Beyond is a view of:*

**"Quarantine Island":** The camel-humped island, with twin pylons carrying power across the harbour, was first used in 1863 when the clipper *Victory* called with a smallpox case among its steerage passengers. The 400 hapless immigrants were quarantined on the island for five weeks and carpenters among them built a sixteen-bed hospital. The present two-storeyed hospital building seen on the island was used during the 1914–18 war. A boat that once plied the harbour as a ferry lies beached on the shore below it. The island held the eighty dogs for Byrd's 1928 Antarctic expedition. While here they fell ill and seemed certain to die, thus frustrating the mission. A new formula of dog biscuit was devised and manufactured locally to save all but four of the dogs and to see the expedition safely on its way. Now named St Martin Island, the 16-ha island attracts regular visitors and is leased to an inter-denominational religious organisation. *The coast road passes the inverted basin of Pudding Island before reaching Portobello, where a 2 km detour leads along the point to:*

**Portobello Marine Laboratory and Aquarium**\*\*: The tanks in the small aquarium occasionally contain not only familiar fish but also colourful sponges, sea squirts, anemones, sea slugs and octopi. All those displayed are New Zealand saltwater specimens. The sea life on show is constantly changing. The laboratory is maintained by the University of Otago. *Open daily 9 am–5 pm. An explanatory booklet is available.* On the way to the aquarium there is a good view of the hospital building and the beached ferry on St Martin Island. On the return the volcanic symmetry of Harbour Cone is seen sweeping above and behind Portobello. The cone was once the scene of an abortive goldmining venture. *Return to the coast road and turn left to continue to Otakou, where at 26 km turn right along Tamatea to reach:*

**Otakou Maori Church** (1940): From a distance the oil-painted gateway, the church and the meeting-house Tamatea appear to be carved. They are in fact of cast concrete. Built in 1940, the church is dedicated to the Rev. James Watkin who, a century before, "established in these parts the first Christian mission". To the rear is a small **museum** with a collection of Maori relics. (*Keys to both church and museum are held locally. Contact Mrs M. Taiaroa, tel. 29-343 after 3 pm.*

In the little **cemetery** behind the church lie three great chiefs, but none greater than the *rangatira* Te Matenga Taiaroa (*c.* 1783–1863). The Maori inscription on his headstone is translated on the obverse and observes: "His direction of his people was eminently good and his attachment to the Queen's rule was great." Taiaroa, of the Ruahikihiki *hapu* (subtribe) of Ngaitahu and the Ngatimoki *hapu* of Ngatimamoe, a lesser chief to Tuhawaiki, was one of the most able fighting chiefs. In 1831 he led a strong relieving force into Kaiapohia *pa* (*see* △*Kaiapoi*) during the siege by Te Rauparaha, and later took part in audacious excursions against the Ngati Toa as far north as Picton. He was also at Tuturau (*see* △*Mataura*) when Te Puoho's *taua* (war party) was slaughtered. It was Taiaroa who sold land to Johnny Jones. He signed the Treaty of Waitangi at Ruapuke Island and after the Wairau Affray visited the North Island to make peace with Te Rauparaha, thus giving rise to fear that the two might combine forces against the *Pakeha*. Taiaroa, however, was party to the sale of the Otago Block and later sold the remainder of his land claims to the Government. He did not impress the Europeans who met him, who described him as repulsive, tyrannous and avaricious — judgments doubtless influenced by his known antipathy to the *Pakeha*.

Beside Taiaroa lies Ngatata, a chief of Ngatiawa "who welcomed the *Pakeha* to Cook Strait". Ngatata I Te Rangi (d. 1854) died while visiting Otago Heads from the Wellington area. He saw much fierce fighting in the Taranaki against the better-armed tribes of the Waikato. He too signed the Treaty of Waitangi, and his son Wi Tako is remembered in Wellington as a friend of the Europeans there.

Nearby is the grave of Karetai (1781–1860), chief of both Ngaitahu and Ngati-mamoe; "under the shelter of the authority of Queen Victoria his conduct to the people of the Maori and European races was kind and liberal." "Jacky White" to the whalers, the nearest they could get to his name, was a cousin of Taiaroa. He spent some time in Sydney with the Rev. Samuel Marsden but while there he contracted measles. He brought the infection back to Otakou, where many of his people died in the resulting epidemic. He too took part in campaigns against Te Rauparaha, and walked with a limp after being wounded in the knee during a skirmish at Port Underwood. With Taiaroa and Tuhawaiki he journeyed to Sydney to sign the △Waikouaiti sale to Johnny Jones. During their stay there the trio were induced to sign away the entire South Island, a transaction which failed to impress the Land Commissioners. In later years Karetai came under the influence of the missionaries Watkin and Creed, who induced him to abandon cannibalism. Canon Stack recorded a meeting with the ageing chief at Otakou, finding him a good conversationalist and having a face so thoroughly tattooed as to be completely bluish-black. *Return to the coast road and turn right to pass almost immediately the:*

**Pompallier Memorial** (*26.4 km*): An Historic Places Trust plinth marks the site where Bishop Pompallier conducted the first divine service in Otago Harbour, on 22 November 1840. The Weller Bros. whaling station where he preached is itself recalled by a plaque on the small rock promontory some 70 m beyond the memorial. The plaque denotes the point where the whales were landed. Two iron bars used to anchor them still jut from the rock. *The route continues, to skirt:*

**Te Rauone Beach:** Backed by lupins, the beach was the scene of slaughter when local Ngatimamoe avenged desecration by Ngaitahu, who some time earlier had used the bones of a revered Ngatimamoe ancestor as fish-hooks. The unsuspecting Ngaitahu, on the beach to gather driftwood, were taken by surprise and decimated. (*See "Some History", above*). *The road now rises to afford views across to Aramoana and the lengthy mole that protects the harbour entrance. It descends to pass:*

**Pilots Beach** (*29 km*): A sheltered cove and good picnic spot where in 1823, on one of the earliest recorded visits to the harbour, the *Mermaid* dropped anchor. With Captain Kent on the vessel was the *Pakeha*-chief James Caddell (*see index*) to help Kent conduct a survey for the New South Wales Government into the prospects of developing a permanent flax trade. *The road ends at:*

**Taiaroa Head** (*30 km*): The tip of the peninsula, once a fortified *pa*, is a closed reserve, but from the road's end may be seen the signal mast and lighthouse. The signal mast, no longer used, until 1970 gave a visual signal to approaching shipping, showing one ball for ebb tide and two for flood tide. A lighthouse was proposed for the head at an early stage, but in 1854 it was considered that a light was not essential as it was "not desirable for strange vessels to enter Otago harbour at night". In 1862 the decision was reversed and in 1865, the day after the Tiri Tiri light was first established, the light began to operate. The 12 m tower stands 60 m above sea level. Flashing twice in 18 seconds, the light is visible for 32 km.

Out of sight are more modern fortifications — a massive Armstrong 150-mm "disappearing" gun, installed at the height of the Russian Scare, in about 1886. The gun, hidden in the bowels of the peninsula, rises above ground level only to fire a shot — something it has done in anger but once. During the 1939–45 war a fishing boat was signalled to stop after it had failed to observe correct procedures on approaching the harbour. *In the reserve is the:*

**Royal Albatross Colony (Taiaroa Head)\*\*\*:** Occasionally, generally only in high winds, the giant birds may be seen from the road as they wheel in and out from their nesting grounds, the only grounds in the world so close to human habitation.

The Royal Albatross (*Diomedea epomophora*), a type of petrel, is one of the world's largest birds, with a wing span of up to 3 m. Normally they breed in the remote islands of Antarctica, but an unusual sub-species breeds both here and in the Chatham Islands. It is not until an albatross is about seven years old that it can start to breed, and then only in alternate years. A single egg is laid in about November, and the parents share the eleven-week hatching period, taking turns to find food. Chicks are fed fish and squid, regurgitated by their parents and literally forced down their throats. In late September the fully-fledged chicks fly off, and may return about eight years later to start a new breeding cycle. The adult birds range out perhaps 2,500 km towards Tahiti in search of squid. It is not known whether they come down to the sea to rest or whether they sleep on the wing.

In 1919 the first egg was found at Taiaroa Head. The discovery led to the eventual protection of the area and, in 1938, the first Taiaroa-reared chick flew. Since then the number of mated pairs in the colony has slowly increased to about twelve. As they mate in alternate years this means about twenty-four pairs now breed here. Normally albatrosses mate only on remote stormbound islands where they have little to fear from man or beast, but here it is necessary for a fulltime officer to guard the colony. *Access to the colony is strictly controlled. Bookings must be made in advance through the Government Tourist Bureau, Princes St, tel. 40-349. Visiting times are strictly limited and an entrance fee is charged. Visits are completely suspended at critical mating periods and also when visitors are unlikely to see any birds there. Turn back along the coast road for 9.5 km, where turn left up Weir Rd to reach:*

**Papanui Inlet** (*41 km*): On the island here named after him, the Ngaitahu chief Kapo was disembowelled and eaten by his relatives in the feud that for some years embroiled the peninsula (*See "Some History", above*). *Here one may turn left on reaching the water to follow Dick Rd to its end and walk on to:*

**The Pyramids:** Two distinct rock pyramids, 40 m and 85 m high. The odd rock stacks were severed from the nearby marine cliffs at a time when the area was washed by the sea. (*Private property. Ask permission.*) *If not making the detour, on reaching the water turn right, passing the turnoff where a detour may be made to:*

**Cape Saunders Lighthouse:** Together with Taiaroa Head, the light marks the approach to Otago Harbour. It was installed in 1878 when it was found that ships were running past the harbour entrance. Five years later two children of the first keeper died in a fatal fire and were buried near the light. In 1954 a new tower and beacon were erected and the old kerosene light dismantled. The new tower is 6.1 m high and stands 59.5 above sea level. The light flashes once each 60 seconds and is visible for 32 km. There is good sea fishing from the rocks below the light, a neighbouring **blowhole** performs spectacularly in heavy easterly conditions, and seals and sealions are frequently seen in the area. *If not making the detour continue on to:*

**Hoopers Inlet:** The prospect lies over wide tidal flats. Harbour Cone, its south face as symmetrical as its north, comes back into view here. *At 47.8 km one may detour left for 3 km along Sandymount Rd to see:*

**The Chasm and Lovers' Leap\*\*,** examples of the frighteningly precipitous cliffs that are a feature of the peninsula's southern coast. The walk to them across tussocked farmland affords wide views of the peninsula and down to Allans Beach. At Lovers' Leap the cliffs drop a sheer 200 m to the point to which the sea has tunnelled its way inland, creating a blowhole spanned by a natural rock bridge. At The Chasm the drop is nearly 130 m. Both show how the peninsula was built up by successive ash and lava flows. *Allow 45 mins for the walk. If not making the detour left, turn right up Sandymount Rd to pass the:*

**Sandymount lime kilns\*** (*49.1 km*): The Pukehiki area seemed destined to become an important centre when its deposits of limestone were being worked in the 1870s. The lime was quarried and burnt here before being taken to Dunedin for use in cement, mortar and limewash. One of the kilns is close by the road on the left; the second is almost opposite, below the road to the right. *After passing the kilns bear left at Highcliff Rd to curl round Peggys Hill (named not after a wife but after a favoured cow) before turning right down Camp Rd to reach:*

**Larnach's Castle\*\*\*** (*53.2 km*): Built in 1871 at a reputed cost of about £150,000 by William Larnach, the castle shows the extremes to which the earlier settlers could go to enjoy their "breath of the Old World in an infant land". Larnach had the means to indulge his taste in housing on a truly magnificent scale.

Though the extravagant building was designed in Scotland, it reflects the architecture so much a feature of Dunedin, and its construction was supervised by R. A. Lawson. More accurately a baronial hall rather than a castle, it includes a ballroom of 250.8 m², a Georgian hanging staircase that relies for support on complex curves, and a spiral staircase leading to battlements which give a wide view of the district. The outstanding features are elaborately decorated ceilings, some carved by an English workman brought here to spend twelve years at his craft, and others moulded by two Italian plasterers, also specially imported for the task. Set into the ceramic tile floor of the impressive entrance hall is Larnach's crest and the self-effacing title he gave his grandiose home — The Camp.

Much of the wood, tiles, bricks, glass and marble was brought from Europe, a final extravagance being Italian marble fireplaces throughout and a massive solid marble bath. Some of the original furniture is still in the castle.

A walk in the grounds round the building is rewarding and leads past greenhouses, stables and the dungeons used by Larnach for storing firewood. Visitors may picnic in the grounds or eat at a small restaurant.

William James Mudie Larnach (1833–98) was born at Castle Forbes, Hunter River, New South Wales, the son of a wealthy station owner. He rose to be Geelong manager of the Bank of New South Wales, coming to Dunedin in 1867 to be chief manager of the Bank of Otago. Elected to Parliament eight years later, he was only two years in the House before he succeeded in unseating the Atkinson ministry and in turn became Colonial Treasurer, Minister of Public Works, and Minister of Mines. Overwhelmed by a series of financial disasters that culminated in the collapse of the Colonial Bank in which he had invested heavily, Larnach shocked the country by committing suicide in a committee room in Wellington's Parliament Buildings. His private misfortunes tend to obscure the very real ability he demonstrated in public life. On his death The Camp faced an uncertain future; the farm around it was sold off in small lots and the Crown acquired the homestead block of about 14 ha to use the castle as a mental hospital. Later used as cabaret and tourist resort, it was auctioned in 1940 for a meagre £1,250. Presently the subject of steady restoration after generations of neglect, the castle is reasserting its original bold concept, first conceived when the Otago settlement was little more than twenty years old. *Open daily 9 am to dusk. Allow upwards of 1 hr. Return up Camp Rd to Highcliff Rd, turning right to pass the:*

**Springfield homestead** (*signposted at 55.8 km*): The buildings date from *c.* 1865. Six years later saw the emergence here of the country's first cooperative cheese factory, a development now a feature of the country's dairy industry. For some years the Otago Peninsula Cooperative flourished, and with its name changed to Peninsula Pioneer Cheese Co. and a new factory at Pukehiki, it began to export at first to Britain and then to Adelaide — though its first shipment to South Australia sank with the SS *Tararua* in 1881. Of the four dairy factories once on the peninsula, only the buildings of this, the oldest, have survived. *At 59.6 km turn left down Centre Rd to pass the old Alexander Mathieson stone farmstead and barn of Everton (built during the 1870s) and the Tomahawk Lagoon before returning to the city by way of St Kilda. Alternatively continue along Highcliff Rd to pass the Rotary Lookout and descend to the city below.*

## PORT CHALMERS — PURAKANUI ROUND TRIP

*48 km. The half-day trip can be expanded to take in Aramoana and includes several beaches suitable for picnicking. Numerous splendid views of the harbour and the northern sea coast are a feature of the drive. Leave Dunedin by Highway 88 to reach:*

△**Port Chalmers**** (*12 km*): A delightful old seafaring town. From here one may detour by continuing on to Aramoana (*see* △*Port Chalmers*). *Turn back towards Dunedin and then right (signposted "Waitati") to climb past the:*

**Scott Memorial** (*13.8 km*): From the base of the anchor-capped column is a superb view of Port Chalmers and the Lower Harbour. Offshore, St Martin Island (Quarantine Island) points across to the Portobello Peninsula, all but dividing the harbour in two. Port Chalmers was Scott's last port of call on his ill-fated Antarctic expedition of 1910. *Continue up the hill and bear right towards Long Beach at 5.3 km. Continue past the Long Beach turnoff along Heyward Point Rd. Turn off (signposted) to descend to:*

**Murdering Beach*** (*12.4 km*): A lonely isolated beach with a very steep approach. The beach is so named as it was the scene of James Kelly's attack on the Maori "City of Otago" (*see* "Some History", *above*). The beach supported a Maori settlement of considerable importance. Over the years many artefacts have been taken from the sandhills, which were apparently a major greenstone "factory". Also found here was one of the medals handed out by Captain Cook in the course of his visit of 1772, one of only six to have been found in the country (*displayed in the Otago Museum*). A Classic Maori population of 2,000 has been claimed for the bay but this is generally considered to be an exaggeration. *Return to Heyward Point Rd and turn left to look down on the beach to the east of Murdering Beach, called:*

**Kaikai Beach:** Named by early European visitors as Kaikai's Beach after the chief who lived here, the beach, near the northern heads of Otago Harbour, is one of the country's older known occupation sites. *At the road's end turn round and return 4.8 km to the Long Beach intersection where bear right to reach:*

**Purakanui** (*23.7 km*): The road drops sharply to reach the fishing retreat on the western bank of the river estuary. Across the estuary, on the coast, may be seen the jutting prominence that housed the Mapoutahi *pa*.

During the inter-*hapu* squabbles of Ngaitahu that gave rise to the siege of Huriawa peninsula (*see* △*Karitane*), Moki II sent a surprise warparty to the *kainga* at Purakanui, where the buildings were surrounded and most of the inhabitants slain. Te Wera and his brother-in-law Te Rehu made a miraculous escape. After the unsuccessful siege at Huriawa, Moki II's cousin Taoka turned his attention to Mapoutahi, a superb *pa* tied to the mainland only by the narrowest of necks. A frontal attack was impossible as the entrance to the isthmus was both easily and well guarded; to attempt to scale the precipitous coastal cliffs would have been folly. However Taoka arrived in midwinter and camped near the *pa* until on one exceptionally wild night the defenders withdrew their shivering sentries and put dummies in their place. The ruse deceived Taoka's scouts and would have worked had Taoka not decided to check the position for himself. Mapoutahi *pa* was stormed and the few defenders that survived did so by descending the cliffs on vine ladders that had been used for birdnesting. *Return 6.5 km to turn right towards Waitati and to look down to the township and the tidal inlet of the Waitati River:*

**Waitati:** Combat took place here after Tutakahikura, a Ngaitahu chief from Canterbury, abducted the wives of the Ngatimamoe chief Tutemakeho, who was on a visit to Southland. Tutemakeho returned to his *kainga*, found his wives gone and pursued the party as far north as this spot, where the two groups met. It was decided to settle the matter by having the two chiefs fight in singlehanded combat. Tutemakaho won back his wives and a leaderless group of Ngaitahu returned to Canterbury. Blueskin Bay, over which the town looks, was named after Te Hikututu, a Maori so well tattooed as to warrant the nickname of Blueskin. *Turn left up Green Rd to fall in with the old main road to Dunedin, skirting Mt Cargill and enjoying magnificent views of Dunedin and Otago Harbour. Alternatively drive on to Waitati and return to Dunedin by the motorway.*

## OTHER SUGGESTED DRIVES

**Taieri Plain-Taieri Mouth Round Trip:** *88 km. The points of interest are described under the entries for* △ *Mosgiel and* △ *Lake Waihola.* The suggested route follows Highway 1 south, turning off to Mosgiel (after visiting Saddle Hill Lookout) to see the woollen mills and East Taieri church before continuing to Outram where there is a riverside picnic area. From Outram drive by way of Woodside (there is another, particularly delightful picnic place here) and Berwick to rejoin Highway 1 opposite the century-old hotel at Henley. Proceed south to Lake Waihola (a favoured boating area) where turn east to reach Taieri Mouth. Turn north to return to Dunedin along the coast.

**Waikouaiti-Karitane Round Trip:** *89 km. Most of the points of interest are described under the entries for* △ *Waikouaiti and* △ *Karitane.* Leave Dunedin north on Highway 1 to reach Waikouaiti, one of the South Island's oldest settlements. Here turn south again, turning east where signposted to the seaside settlement of Karitane where lived Sir Truby King. From Karitane return to Dunedin by way of Seacliff and the coast as far as Waitati (*described above*). At Waitati one may return to Dunedin by Highway 1 or by way of the Mount Cargill Road, the old main road which affords splendid views of the city and harbour.

△**Lake Mahinerangi Round Trip:** *127 km.* Drive south on Highway 1, turning right at Henley to Berwick and follow the at-times spectacular Waipori River upstream to artificial Lake Mahinerangi, a lake that floods an old goldtown and affords both fishing and swimming. Cross the lake to return to Dunedin by way of Outram and △ Mosgiel.

△**Lawrence**\*\*:** *184 km return.* A goldmining town of considerable character on the brink of Central Otago. The route lies through △ Lake Waihola and △ Milton.

**Some picnic places:** There are numerous inviting picnic spots round the coast, particularly on Otago Peninsula and near △ Karitane. Inland and to the north are Trotters Gorge (*68.5 km; near* △ *Palmerston*) and Bucklands Crossing (*49 km*). To the south lie Woodside (*32 km*) and Outram Glen (*27 km; both near* △ *Mosgiel*) and Whare Flat (*13 km*) where an old school has been converted into a pottery.

## ORGANISED EXCURSIONS

**Sightseeing Tours:** Coach trips through the city and round the Otago Peninsula depart from outside the Public Relations Office. *Newtons Coachways (tel. 54-878).*

**Firms and factories** that welcome visitors are listed by the Public Relations Office. These include Cadbury, Schweppes Hudson (*tel. 79-320 — 2.40 pm except Fri.*), Roslyn Mills, Kaikoura Valley (*tel. 36-009 — afternoons except Fri.*), Railways Hillside Workshops (*tel. 40-799 ext. 8487 — 10.15 am and 1.15 pm except Thurs. and Fri. mornings*), Milk Treatment Station, Logan Point (*tel. 88-517*), H. E. Shacklock (*tel. 79-590*), *Evening Star* newspaper (*tel. 40-049 — usually 2 pm*). In all cases one should make arrangements before visiting by telephoning, preferably several days in advance.

## TOURING NOTES

**Highway 1 north:** An attractive variation to the route north to Palmerston is to turn off north of Waitati, at Evansdale, to follow the northern coast of Blueskin Bay and pass through Warrington, Seacliff and Karitane (*for all, see* △Karitane) before rejoining the main road a little south of △Waikouaiti. The variation does not add significantly to the overall distance and affords unequalled views of the ocean shoreline of the northern peninsula that shelters Otago Harbour, and subsequently of Karitane and Waikouaiti Bay. Shortly after turning off at Evansdale is an interesting aspect across the bay of the Mapoutahi *pa* site (*see index*), a superb fortress taken one wild and stormy night.

**Highway 1 to Oamaru:** Points of interest on the way north are described under the entries for △Karitane, △Waikouaiti, △Palmerston, △Moeraki, △Hampden and △Oamaru.

**Highway 1 to Balclutha:** Points of interest on the way are described under △Lake Waihola, △Milton and △Balclutha.

**Central Otago via Palmerston and The Pigroot:** The road inland from △Palmerston is described under △The Pigroot.

**Central Otago via the Old Dunstan Road:** In summer it can be possible for the more adventurous with high-clearance vehicles to traverse part of the historic Old Dunstan Road, the route to the Central goldfields before The Pigroot opened. Drive by way of Mosgiel and Highway 87 to Clark's Junction, where turn left to climb steeply over the Lammerlaw Range and the Rock and Pillar to reach Styx, on the Maniototo Plain. At the Deepstream crossing are the remains of the Oasis Hotel. On reaching Styx one may join Highway 85 at △Ranfurly or carry on along the Old Dunstan Road to zigzag over Rough Ridge and descend to Moa Creek whence it is a straightforward run to △Alexandra.

It is essential to make inquiries locally before attempting either leg of this route, which is extremely slow and involves the opening and closing of innumerable gates. The track is impassable in winter, and frequently so after rain at other times of year. Contact the Automobile Association (Otago) before leaving to obtain up-to-date details of track conditions.

---

**DUNTROON**    North Otago.    Maps 25, 28 & 35.    Pop. 184.

*43.5 km NW of Oamaru; 75.5 km SE of Omarama.*

THE FARMING CENTRE of Duntroon, overlooking wide riverflats, stands on the south side of the △Waitaki Valley where it is joined by the Maerewhenua River. The district's potential for intensive farming is being expanded by more extensive irrigation.

Limestone bluffs in the area were used for shelter by itinerant Moa-hunters, and a number of rock drawings have been located. To the east of Duntroon the △Dansey Pass route to Central Otago leaves Highway 83.

Duntroon is not named for its counterpart near Canberra, Australia. Both are in localities once owned by branches of the Campbell family and each takes its name from a stronghold in mid-Argyllshire, long a seat of the Campbell clan.

### SOME HISTORY

**Seven routes to Central:** Duntroon grew up round an accommodation house opened on the town site in 1864 by James Little. Four years later gold was found at the Maerewhenua but it proved to be fine and well-dispersed, rendering the diggings a "poor-man's field". Greater excitement came with the discovery of a quartz reef between the Maerewhenua and the Otekaieke Rivers. A company was formed in Oamaru and money poured in to cut a race, build a road and install machinery. Crushing began in May 1871 but within two months the venture had crashed so completely that the claim and assets were sold up by Court bailiffs.

The interest in gold focussed attention on the Dansey Pass route and raised hopes that it might be chosen as the route for the Central Otago railway, so capturing the inland trade for Oamaru. A survey was made, but of the seven suggested routes the Dansey Pass line was rated last. It would open up no new farmland, and in any event the claims of Dunedin were certain to prevail.

### POINTS OF INTEREST

**Takiroa Rock Drawings\*\*:** Under a massive limestone bluff on a bend in the main road are pre-European Maori rock drawings of an unknown date executed in charcoal and red ochre. The earliest recorded discovery of such art, the "rude figures" were found by the Land Purchase Commissioner W. B. D. Mantell in 1852. Excavation of the shelter yielded bone, shell and artefacts showing that it was used as a campsite in Moa-hunter times. There are many other drawings in the locality but none as notable or as accessible as these. Some of the drawings were removed in 1916 to museums in Dunedin, Wanganui and Auckland. *2.4 km W on Highway 83. Signposted. A stile leads over the fence.*

**St Martin's Anglican Church** (1901): A distinctive stone church, like that at △Kurow it was built largely through a legacy from the estate of Robert Campbell's widow.

## EDENDALE   Southland.   Maps 14, 18 & 19.   Pop. 570.

*38.5 km NE of Invercargill; 26.5 km SSW of Gore.*

THE PLEASING PROSPECT of Edendale spreads over the Mataura Plains, centering on the tall chimney of its lactose factory.

**The first dairy factory:** Edendale features prominently in the transition of New Zealand's economy from dependence on gold to the grasslands pattern of the present day. For here the country's first significant dairy factory was built, from which the first exports of cheese were made to Britain. Previously small amounts of butter and cheese had been shipped across the Tasman, kept cool in brine and sawdust, methods that could never have coped with the temperatures in the tropics.

The Edendale run, 50,454 ha and the largest freehold estate in the country, was owned by the New Zealand and Australian Land Company. At a time when the company was transferring its operations to Australia and when its Southland holdings were proving difficult to sell, the New Zealand manager, Thomas Brydone (*see index*) in 1881 suggested that dairying might supplement its activities. Three hundred cows were purchased, plans were obtained from Canada, and the first dairy factory was built on the Edendale estate in 1882. The factory cost £1,200, but £500 was immediately recouped when the company won a Government award for the first export of cheese.

Brydone and William Davidson, the company's general manager, then successfully dispatched the first shipment of frozen meat to Britain, and with it went some butter from Edendale to render the event as historic from a dairying point of view as it was for the meat trade. The enterprising Davidson later decided that large-scale butter-making was feasible. He visited Denmark in 1890, and despite the strictures of a prominent Scandinavian who warned his countrymen that New Zealand would become a major rival in the dairy trade, was allowed to inspect factories, interview experts, and secure the services of a first-rate butter-maker, whom he sent out to Edendale. Export butter-making had hitherto been minimal, but Davidson's initiative was quickly parallelled in other parts of the country and the value of butter exports rose steeply to assume their major role in the country's trading pattern. Brydone also pioneered the use of artificial fertilisers, and of his success with Edendale it was said: "He redeemed it with lime, and turned a waste into a garden." The Government subsequently took the run over and split it up for closer settlement. *One may visit the factory to see the manufacture of cheese. Tel. 199. Best time to visit is from 9–11 am.*

**McKenzie's treasure:** According to local folklore the legendary sheep drover James McKenzie (*see index*) concealed his savings near Edendale in a patch of bush known by him to be *tapu* to local Maoris. McKenzie, convicted of sheepstealing and supposedly pardoned on condition that he leave the country for ever, was unable to reclaim his cache, which some say still awaits a fortunate finder.

### ENVIRONS

**Morton Mains:** The locality gave its name to a cattle ailment, Morton Mains disease, the symptom of which was starvation in the midst of long, lush grass. It was countered by an Edendale researcher, Sandys Wunsch, who was among the first to diagnose cobalt deficiency in soil. *12 km.*

## EREWHON (Sheep Station)***   Mid-Canterbury.   Maps 3 & 35.

*90 km NW of Ashburton; 102 km NNW of Geraldine.*

THE WELL-CROPPED, chequered plains of the coast tell only half the story of Ashburton County, for behind the foothills lies another world, where treeless seas of grey-brown tussock lap the shingled slopes of icebound peaks. The sheeprun at the road's end shares its history with △Mesopotamia, just across the treacherous Rangitata, as both areas were owned by the novelist Samuel Butler (*see index*). The run has adopted the title of Butler's best-known book, *Erewhon, or Over the Range,* to displace its original name of Stronechrubie. Its 25,100 ha carry about 10,000 Merino sheep and 300 cattle, its Merinos having won wide fame. At Erewhon ("nowhere" spelt backwards) one has the sensation of being far from anywhere.

**Erewhon Park** has been developed for the visitor with sporting interests. There is hunting for red deer, tahr and chamois, fishing for quinnat salmon (in the Rangitata) and for trout (in innumerable smaller creeks and rivers). There is climbing and horse-riding, and scenic flights can be arranged. Winter brings ice-skaters and skiers to the commercial slopes of Powder Snow Valley on Mt Potts (*2,191.7 m*). Equipment may be hired and tuition obtained. A variety of inexpensive accommodation is available. The complex is based on the former Mount Potts homestead and woolshed.

### ROAD TO EREWHON

The road to Erewhon lies through Mount Somers (*see index*). After Blowing Point and Ashburton Gorge a series of lakes is seen, each an isolated pool surrounded by rolling downs sparsely covered with tussock. A walking track leads to **Lakes Round-**

## EREWHON (Sheep Station)—concluded

**about** and **Emma,** and a detour may be made to Lake Heron (*see index*). The road passes both **Lakes Camp** (a popular venue for powerboats) and **Clearwater** (from which they are barred), each stocked with trout and in season affording good fishing.

To skirt Harpers Knob the road rises and gives a magnificent view of the head-waters of the Rangitata River — a broad valley of shingle intermingled with tussock, and with an island formed of debris left behind in a glacial retreat. From **Erewhon Park** may be seen on the far bank the rare clump of trees that shelters the homestead of △Mesopotamia.

Ten km farther on the road ends at **Erewhon** itself and its appealing, century-old homestead whose original two cob huts are now sheathed in iron and joined into a single building by a section of vertical boarding. Sheltering the homestead are the curious Jumped Up Downs, glacial deposits covered by windblown debris now mantled with silver tussock. Here game and native birds may be seen in small enclosures. Farming activity includes stud Merino sheep, Hereford cattle and deer farming for venison. Local folklore tells of a fossilised giant lizard as once being found embedded in Lizard Valley but, curiously, none now can locate the spot.

---

**FAIRLIE**     South Canterbury.     **Maps 3, 34 & 35.     Pop. 890.**

*62 km NW of Timaru; 46 km W of Geraldine; 43.5 km SE of Tekapo.*

THE SEAT OF THE Mackenzie County, set about with well-treed rolling downs, lies in a situation altogether alien from the wilderness of tussock- and mountain-lands it administers. Indeed the contrast as one enters the Mackenzie country by way of △Burkes Pass can be quite startling.

The mature trees that shade the town's main street are part of an Avenue of Peace, planted as a 1914–18 war memorial from Cricklewood to Tekapo. Most of those planted in the Mackenzie country could not withstand the extremes of climate, but those round Fairlie remain — even if, as of the peace, time has taken its toll.

In 1968 the town lost the railway that gave rise to its importance when the branch-line from Timaru, haunt of the *Fairlie Flyer,* closed after eighty-four years of service. However the loss caused little local concern to a town with a secure base as a servicing and administrative centre.

The usual explanation for the name of the town is that the area reminded a certain David Hamilton of the Scottish town of Fairlie in Ayrshire, yet those who have visited both see little in common. A lesser-known alternative is that the name may come from James Fairlie, a boundary-keeper who lived in a cob hut just to the west of the town's site. Until confusion with the Waikato centre caused it to be renamed, the town was known as Hamilton.

### THINGS TO SEE AND DO

**Domain:** A riverside domain near the centre of the town affords a picnicking and camping area.

**Fairlie Historical Museum:** A collection of relics is housed in a century-old hipped-roof cottage, furnished in the period. Photographs illustrate the development of the district. The cottage was built for a blacksmith, and a forge is to be recreated on the property. *Mt Cook Rd, on Burkes Pass exit from town. Open weekdays noon–2 pm; weekends 2–4 pm. Also open by arrangement.*

**Mackenzie Carnival Society Transport Museum:** An annual event at New Year is the Mackenzie Country Carnival, from which has grown an ever-increasing collection of restored wagons, gigs and coaches. *Mt Cook Rd (by historical museum). Open similar hours.*

### ENVIRONS

△**Burkes Pass:** Gateway to the Mackenzie country. *26 km W.*

**Fox's Peak Skifields:** The Tasman Ski Club is based at Fox's Peak in the Two Thumb Range. Some accommodation may be arranged. *Access via Clayton Rd (route not recommended for private vehicles). Casual skiing by arrangement with Tasman Ski Club, Box 368, Timaru.*

**Clayton:** The Clayton run of 15,390 ha and bounded in part by the famous runs of Mesopotamia, Mount Peel and Orari Gorge (*for all, see index*), was taken up in 1861 by the partnership of Kennaway, Lee and Acton — hence its name of KLA-ton. Severe snows in 1862 saw the run sold. In 1881 an Australian squatter, Hugh Hamilton, and his sons acquired the holding. They promptly declared war on the rabbits and put in miles of fencing. The run remained in the family until 1919, when the Government took much of its best land for closer settlement and halved the run's carrying capacity.

The homestead, its additions reflecting the times of wool booms, includes a portion of the original (*c.* 1876). Of stone, its original thatched roof having given way to an upper storey, it is sheltered by a verandah at the front of the house. (Like the wood, painted white, it is not immediately obvious from the road). *22 km E of Fairlie turn off Highway 79 and follow Clayton Rd. Private property.*

**Pioneer Park\*:** An amalgam of exotic-shaded picnic area and large tract of native bush. *Described under △Pleasant Point. 20 km SE.*

# FIORDLAND NATIONAL PARK

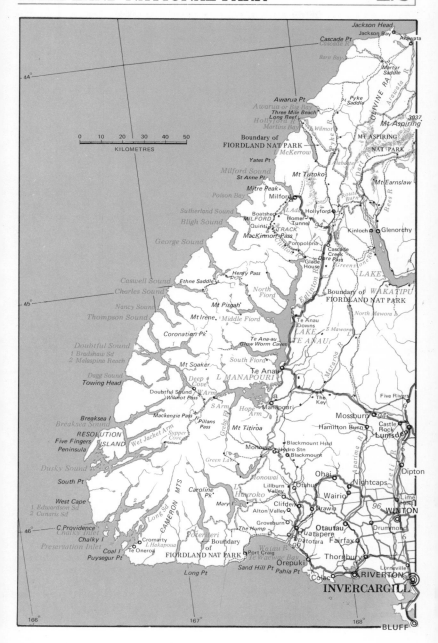

**Strathaven Clydesdale Horse Stud\*\***: Working teams of Clydesdales, horse-drawn farm implements and rides in horse-drawn vehicles give some idea of pioneer farming life. *5 km N on Geraldine Rd. Tel. 158. Open daily. 10 am–4 pm.*

**FIORDLAND NATIONAL PARK\*\*\*** **Fiordland.** **Map 12.**

**Area: 1,212,000 ha.**

*The Park Headquarters at Te Anau (PO Box 29; tel. 819) provides details on walks, tramps, and things to see and do. There is also a ranger station at △Clifden (tel. 84X Tuatapere). The* Fiordland National Park Handbook *is recommended.*

THE LARGEST OF THE COUNTRY's national parks spreads over its most rugged and most remote region, the south-west corner of the South Island. Round the coast long-fingered fiords reach into the ranges, among them majestic Milford (also the most accessible). From the coast Captain Cook in 1770 speculated that beyond "the ridge of Mountains which are of a prodigious height" there might be "Lakes Ponds &c as is very common in such like places". Proving his eye for landforms are the inland

121

counterparts of the coastal fiords, the large Fiordland lakes of △Te Anau, △Mana-pouri, △Monowai, △Hauroko and Poteriteri — as well as myriad lakelets whose multiplicity cannot but amaze those who fly over the park. The region was the retreat of the fabled Lost Tribe of Fiordland (*see* △*Invercargill*).

## THE FIORDS

Paradoxically, there is no place in New Zealand today as remote as the fiords of the south-west coast, inhabited only by lighthouse keepers and itinerant fishermen, for there was a time when, as the best charted anchorage in the country, the fiords were frequented by vessels from a variety of countries come to rest their crews and re-plenish with wood and water, and later by gangs of sealers intent on plundering the now-protected seals.

The seals were first noted (and first killed) by Captain Cook in 1773, who at Dusky Sound found "great numbers, about the bay, on the small rocks and isles near the coast". Nineteen years after he had called, a party of sealers in ten prolific months secured and skinned 4,500 seals for the China market. Sealing spread round the coast, to the islands in Foveaux Strait and to Stewart Island.

The hazardous lives of the sealers have been well recorded. Left on bleak and isolated shores they were occasionally forgotten and not infrequently left abandoned by accident — one group survived seven long years marooned on the Snares Islands. For all their hardships, too, the real profits went not to the men on the spot but to the merchants in Sydney.

The order of the fiords, from south to north, is given in the ditty:

> *Preserve your Chalk, its Dusky in Breaksea*
> *And Dagg says its Doubtful if Thompson went round.*
> *But Nancy and Charles go to Caswell for marble,*
> *And George and Bligh to grand Milford Sound.*

**Preservation Inlet:** Puysegur Point Lighthouse stands on the most south-western point of the South Island mainland in a bleak, galeswept spot. The keepers, the most isolated of all, are serviced by amphibian aircraft. Sealers operated round the area, as witnesses the historic stone slab in the Invercargill Museum, on which in 1823 the caution was scratched: "Beware of the Natives — plentey at Preservation."

A short distance inside the inlet, opposite Weka Island, are faint traces of the goldmining township of Cromarty, on Kisbee Bay, that at the turn of the century served outlying miners' camps. In pre-European times there was strife here between Ngaitahu and Ngatimamoe. Visiting Ngaitahu came in apparent friendship but local Ngatimamoe, who had fled here from the Otago Peninsula, suspected their intentions and summarily despatched them. The news reached Ngaitahu at Otakou, and they retaliated by sending a large double-canoe. It arrived by night at Preservation, where its crew hid first the canoe and then themselves. At dawn Maru, a chief of Ngai Kuri and an ally of Ngaitahu, "played the seal". Dressed in a mat he splashed in the surf to entice the unsuspecting Ngatimamoe out of their *pa* to secure the unexpected prize. Maru leapt to his feet, *patu* in hand. The other Ngaitahu and Ngai Kuri sprang from their hiding places, and the unarmed Ngatimamoe had no chance of survival. The story does not end with the taking of the *pa*, for a party of Ngatimamoe was away on a fishing expedition. As they returned homeward, they caught sight of the Ngaitahu canoe hidden in the bush, which they launched and took with them. When they found Ngaitahu in possession of their *pa* they simply sailed on to Dusky Sound. It is said that, with their canoe gone, none of the invading war-party managed to return to Otakou. Instead, they hounded the Ngatimamoe into Dusky Sound, there to annihilate them.

Varying accounts describe the discovery in 1877 in the caves of Cavern Head on the inlet's northern shoreline, of a "fossilised" man. The *Rosa*, under Walter Traill, was collecting guano from the caves when the celebrated "fossil" skeleton was found of a large man with his legs stretched out and his arms tucked up as if for burial. Traill estimated that it would have taken over a century for drips from the roof to have "petrified" the body. Later Traill returned to extract the relic, but found it smashed and much of it removed. Some say that Maoris, anxious to prevent disturbance of the corpse, removed the skeleton, but the crew of the whaler *Splendid*, anchored nearby when Traill made his find, was probably responsible for the vandalism.

**Dusky Sound:** A plaque on Astronomers Point records the visit of Captain Cook on the bark *Resolution* on his second voyage, from 27 March to 28 April 1773 after "117 Days at Sea . . . without once having sight of land". Cook had friendly contact with the few Maoris he found here — one is believed to have been Maru, the Ngai Kuri chief who had some years earlier "played the seal" at Preservation — and he released geese brought from the Cape of Good Hope: "I make no doubt but what they will breed and may in time spread over the whole Country, which will answer the intent of the founder." Acclimatisation dates back to Cook. He experimented here, too, with the brewing of beer (the first to be made in New Zealand of what was to become the national drink) — "with a decoction of the leaves of the spruce tree [*rimu*] mixed with it an equal quantity of the Tea plant [*manuka*] which partly distroyed the Astringency of the other and made the Beer exceeding Palatable and esteemed by every one on board". Which was as well, as its consumption as a means of combating scurvy was compulsory. Cook even gives his recipe in detail, explaining: "It is the business of Voyagers to pass over nothing that may be usefull to posterity."

To establish his exact position Cook had an area cleared on Astronomers Point. Visitors since 1791 onwards have been impressed by the durability of the tree stumps left by Cook's men. These can still be seen today in an area of unique botanical interest as here, and here alone, can bush be studied that has regenerated undisturbed over a period of two centuries. His men rested and restored, and his bark replenished, Cook sailed from Dusky to rendezvous with the *Adventure* at Queen Charlotte Sound.

Other vessels followed Cook to the harbour he had charted so well, among them one, by odd coincidence named *Endeavour,* which was New Zealand's first recorded shipwreck. In calm weather she can be seen on the seabed, about 7 m below the surface, where she has lain since 1795. Having abandoned the vessel the crew built the *Providence,* in which they sailed back to Sydney. There was not room for all on board, some thirty-five being left behind to be rescued in 1797. A track leads from Lake Hauroko to Supper Cove at the head of the Sound. Cook named the sound "Duskey Bay" in 1770, on his first voyage, when evening gloom prevented his entering.

**Doubtful Sound** is flanked by high vertical walls rising sheer from the sea. So steeply do they rise that the wharf at Deep Cove does not rest on piles but is canti-levered out from the shore. A hydro road links Deep Cove, at the head of the Sound, with Lake Manapouri. Regular bus trips are run over the road in conjunction with visits to the △ Manapouri hydro-electric power scheme. Launch trips on the Sound are run regularly by Fiordland Travel (*tel. 859 Te Anau*).

Cook named the Sound "Doubtfull Harbour" in 1770, but to the exasperation of the naturalists on board did not attempt to enter: "It certainly would have been highly imprudent in me to have put into a place where we could not have got out but with a wind that we have lately found does not blow one day in a month."

Just out of sight from the shore at Deep Cove are Browne Falls (*836.3 m*), nearly half as tall again as Sutherland Falls. These however have been designated a cataract — a steep stream and not an unabated fall.

**George Sound:** A tramping track leads to the Sound from the north-west arm of Lake Te Anau's Middle Fiord.

△ **Milford Sound***\*\*\*:** The most accessible and perhaps the most splendid of all the Sounds.

## THE LAKES

As the coastal fiords to the west were gouged by massive glaciers, so too was the series of elongated lakes to the east of the Main Divide. Of these, Lakes Te Anau, Mana-pouri, Hauroko and Monowai are described separately. The lakes all afford fine fishing, and majestic scenery in all seasons.

## SOME TRAMPING

*Details of track conditions and huts are available from the Park Headquarters at Te Anau and the ranger at Clifden. Please complete the Intentions Book before starting on a tramp of any duration. Moir's Guide Book (Southern Section) is an indispensable companion on any tramp in the region. More remote regions can be reached by float plane from Te Anau (arrange through Mount Cook Airlines).*

△ **Milford Track***\*\*\*:** "The finest walk in the world", from Lake Te Anau to Milford Sound, can be made independently as well as with organised parties. *See* △ *Milford Track.*

**Lower Hollyford Valley to Martins Bay***\*\*\*:** A four-to-five-day tramp leads down the Hollyford and along the eastern shoreline of Lake McKerrow, 20 km of limpid water set in a green trough with snowcapped walls. On the coast, Martins Bay was the scene of an unsuccessful settlement, of which an old homestead survives. Days can be spent on the bay, as fish are plentiful in river, lagoon and sea. In the late 1870s a party of unsuspecting English migrants was deposited here. After a cramped voyage, they had gone ashore to stretch their legs only to have the captain coolly inform them that this was their destination and that he was unable to let any of them to come on board again. Their meagre belongings were ferried to them and the schooner sailed, leaving an ill-equipped, inexperienced and bewildered band to struggle for survival. Slowly the bush was pushed back, and on the rare occasions that they visited Queens-town they were a source of humour, walking as they did one behind the other, so used had they become to traversing bush tracks. Two strokes of luck lightened their gloom. First, small amounts of alluvial gold were discovered, and then a ship carrying redundant rolling stock from Bluff to Melbourne was wrecked at Big Bay and its cargo plundered by the needy group. Carriages that once sedately chugged to and from Bluff still lie in the sea at Big Bay. The settlement slowly but surely withered away.

△ **Routeburn Track***\*\*\*:** The three-day tramp leaves the Milford–Te Anau road to traverse the Harris Saddle (*1,279.6 m*) and reach Lake Wakatipu at Kinloch. The track in part follows one cut to link Queenstown with the ill fated pioneers of Martins Bay. The bus to Milford leaves Te Anau at 8.15 am and stops to set down trampers at the start of the track that winds through both Fiordland and Mount Aspiring National Parks. *Further information from the respective park headquarters.* A conducted four-day walk is organised by the Routeburn Walk Ltd, who have their own huts and so minimise the gear trampers need to carry (*Box 271 Queenstown, tel. 100M Nov.-April*). The tramp complements rather than competes with the Milford Track. Some, having walked the Milford Track, then walk by the Routeburn to Lake Wakatipu and so reach Queenstown.

## SOME ORGANISED EXCURSIONS

**Park headquarters** at Te Anau in holiday periods conduct nature walks by day and lectures in the evenings.

**Scenic Flights*** over the area leave both Te Anau and Milford. *Mount Cook Airlines.*

**Manapouri-West Arm-Doubtful Sound***: A full day trip crosses Lake Manapouri, winds down into the bowels of the mountains to the powerhouse, and finally traverses the Main Divide to visit a fascinating fiord. *Described under* △ *Manapouri* (*Lake*). A shorter trip simply visits the powerhouse.

△**Milford Track***: "The finest walk in the world."

**Routeburn Track***: *See above.*

---

### CAUTION
Weather conditions in this area can deteriorate rapidly and rivers and creeks can become impassable in a very short time. RISK OF EXPOSURE IS GREAT. Proper equipment and previous experience is necessary before this track is undertaken.

---

### WARNING
Be prepared for all kinds of weather at all times of year.

---

## FOX GLACIER***  Westland.  Maps 13, 16, 34 & 37.

*172 km SW of Hokitika; 273 km NW of Tekapo. Westland National Park Information Office gives details of walks and tramps, answers queries of all descriptions, issues hunting permits and can help with accommodation problems. The* Westland National Park Handbook *is recommended.*

FEW SIGHTS CAN EQUAL the spectacle of the giant thrusting tongues of ice that are the Fox and Franz Josef Glaciers. Framed by valley sides of rich green bush, they protrude down valleys backed by mountains that rise precipitously to the two most massive peaks of the Main Divide, Mt Tasman and Mt Cook. Julius von Haast, the first European to explore the glaciers named them Albert (the Fox of today — a higher glacier he called Victoria) and Franz Josef after the emperor of his native Austria. The geologist enjoyed the sight of the peaks at sunset, still the highlight of any visit: "New changes were every moment effected, the shades grew longer and darker, and whilst the lower portion already lay in the deep purple shade, the summits were still shining with an intense rosy hue."

The glaciers no longer enter the bush, though a well-angled camera can create such an illusion, but are nonetheless in a setting of magnificent native rainforest. The beech is oddly absent, perhaps as a consequence of too-recent glaciations. The glacial valleys tell of the slow process of regeneration in the wake of glacial retreats, from mosses and lichens through to strapping young forests.

The glacier was renamed Fox after Sir William Fox had visited the area as Premier. Albert is retained for the upper reaches of the glacier.

**When to visit:** Both here and at Franz Josef 25 km away the pattern in spells of fine weather is for clear skies in the early morning with cloud coming down to obscure the peaks about mid-day; the peaks clear towards late afternoon, often reflecting the setting sun.

There is no "best" time to visit the glaciers, set as they are in rainforest that attracts an annual rainfall of about 4,780 mm. The general rule is for rain to predominate in spring, often to continue on into early and mid-summer. The winters are generally comparatively (but only *comparatively*) fine. An added advantage of a winter visit is that the general pattern of mid-day cloud is then less pronounced and for days at a time the snow-heavy peaks can be sublimely clear.

**Where to stay:** In holiday times there is an acute lack of accommodation, both at the township of Fox Glacier (pop. 528) and in the more scattered area of Franz Josef (pop. 431). The Westland National Park offices hold details of available accommodation and can help those in need to the extent of arranging bed and board in private homes. Over the summer period it is prudent to book well in advance.

# FOX GLACIER

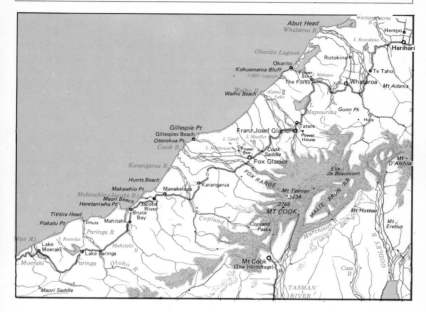

## SOME NOTES ON GLACIERS

**Glacier formation:** A glacier is fed solely by snow which, under great pressure high on the névé, is converted into clear ice. Fresh snow traps air but, as they are buried, the snow crystals are forced progressively closer together until, after many snowfalls, at a depth of about 20 m the crystals fuse into a solid mass of clear ice. This by itself is insufficient to create a glacier. Further pressure of snow and ice — perhaps as deep as 45 m — is needed to force the ice to flow. Major glaciers are also fed by high-altitude glaciers — Fox by the Albert, Jewel, Abel Jansen and the Explorer; Franz Josef by the Blumenthal, the Melchior and the Agassiz.

Observations at Fox and Franz Josef suggest that a large snowfall can have a beneficial effect on the glaciers about three years later. As far as the daily rate of movement is concerned, parts of an aeroplane that crashed on the Franz Josef in 1943, some 3.6 km from the glacier face, reached the terminal about six years and four months later, indicating an average daily rate of movement of about 150 cms.

As ice moves down a valley it begins to waste by melting, naturally faster in summer than in winter, and more quickly at lower, warmer altitudes. The melt is characteristically charged with rock flour, ground by the ice movement and giving the rivers their milky appearance. Like a river of water, a glacier moves more quickly at its centre than at its sides — where it tends to undermine valley walls and erode the valley floor, collecting rock debris termed morainic material. It is the uneven movement of the ice that gives rise to the stresses that create crevasses on the surface. These are, however, not as deep as many imagine, being confined to the upper layers of the glacial ice where the pressures are insufficient to force the ice to flow as a viscous fluid.

The névés of the twin major glaciers here are by far the largest on the western side of the Southern Alps and are fed by the prevailing westerly winds with a combined snow- and rainfall in excess of 7,700 mm. The result is the production of two glaciers which reach low altitudes (300 m) unusual outside the arctic regions.

**Advance or retreat?** A glacier would remain of a constant length only in periods when climatic conditions remained unchanged; when both the feed of snow to its névé and air temperatures stayed more or less constant. Variations in snowfall here have given rise to periodic advances, most recently in the period 1965–67 after a steady decline in both length and thickness of ice from 1951–65. But these advances have constituted local and shortlived exceptions to the general, worldwide pattern of decline.

Evidence of shortlived advances can be quickly obliterated as glacier melt sweeps away the telltale piles of gravel and moraine such as the near-vanished terminal moraine left in 1950 when Franz Josef began a retreat after a three-year advance. Evidence of glacial movement is nonetheless carved plainly into the valleys. Changes of vegetation on valley walls mark the upper limits reached by the ice over the past several centuries, and to the botanist the valley floors illustrate the re-establishment of plant life. On the valley floor, too, are *roches moutonées* (literally "sheep rocks"), massive blocks of hard rock polished into humps not by the ice itself but by the abrasive débris it collects on its way down the valley. Curious, too, are "kettle" lakes which form when blocks of ice, hitherto left deeply buried beneath morainic gravels as the glaciers have retreated, lose their insulation and melt. Small examples of these are to be seen in the valley immediately below the Fox terminal, but more outstanding examples are the lakes Matheson, Mapourika, Wahapo and Gault. The geological and botanical features of the last truly major advance, which about 14,000 years ago took the glaciers down to today's coastline, are being obliterated by the farming activities being carried out in the lower valleys.

The glaciers, presently in retreat, should not be thought of as disappearing with any degree of permanency. One need look back only about 800 years to a time when, after being reduced to mere pockets of ice on their névés, the pair, with the deterioration of the mild climate, began to advance, thrusting down the valleys and smashing into the great forests that had formed on the valley floors.

Some climatologists suggest that we are now about halfway through a warm, or inter-glacial, period and so can expect to enter a further cold (or glacial) period in about 25,000 years' time. However, man's activities have drastically interrupted the natural sequence. The "greenhouse" theory avers that in the past century man has poured millions of tons of débris and gas into the atmosphere (most notably carbon dioxide), which are serving to trap incoming heat that would otherwise be reflected away. The pollutants trap the heat in much the same way as a greenhouse, gradually warming the atmosphere and leading to reduced snowfalls and glacial recession. A contrary theory — which may also be correct, as the two forces may be temporarily self-balancing — suggests that a thin belt of stratospheric pollution, caused in the main by high-flying aircraft, is having the effect of deflecting heat away before it can be trapped by the massive lower layers, so cooling the atmosphere. One can view the glaciers as a form of barometer that will show by their movement whichever view is correct.

**The glaciers compared:** Of the two principal glaciers, Fox is the longer (13.6 km against Franz Josef's 12 km) and has a more gradual slope. Both have their névés at about 2,600 m and their terminal at about 300 m above sea level.

## SOME GEOLOGY

The geology of the area is dominated by the Alpine Fault, a phenomenon of magnitude on a world scale and the greatest geological break in the earth's crust to be found in New Zealand. This provides the startling contrast between gentle undulating coastal lowland and the steeply ascending mountains, and renders the Southern Alps a classic example of a young, fault-bounded mountain range. The period of major mountain building along the fault began about five million years ago and is a process that has continued down to the present time.

The rocks to the west of the Main Divide are predominantly schists, formed when ancient sedimentary rocks were altered (or metamorphosed) by heat and pressure. In order of increasing alteration, the three grades of schist found are mica schist, chlorite schist (a distinctive shade of green) and garnet schist (often studded with red garnets but not of gem quality). These rocks, formed deep within the earth's crust, are probably between 200 and 300 million years old, the metamorphism dating from about 150 million years.

## GLACIAL TERMINAL***

The northern approach road leads through bush and across the valley floor towards the glacier's terminal face. Points reached in previous advances are indicated and "kettle" lakes are usually seen. The access road actually passes over blocks of buried "dead" ice whose melting causes its periodic realignment. *Note: It is inadvisable to walk on the glacier without a guide. Many have found it simple enough to climb up on to the ice but quite another to climb down again. Escorted parties leave the Fox Glacier Hotel daily at 1.30 pm; boots, socks and any necessary equipment are provided. 5.3 km. Turnoff signposted "Glacier" on Highway 6, south of the township.* The road is occasionally put right through to the terminal, but this is not always possible owing to river flooding.

## SOME WALKS AT FOX GLACIER***

*Each of the walks mentioned here is the subject of an explanatory leaflet available from the park information offices at Fox and Franz Josef. They are essential to the maximum enjoyment of the walks.*

**Lake Matheson***** is renowned for its mirror images of Mts Tasman and Cook. In summer these are more usually enjoyed in the very early morning (i.e. before breakfast) when the snowclad peaks are reflected in dark water tinted by humus and algae.

The lake originated as a massive slab of "dead" ice left behind about 14,000 years ago by Fox Glacier, then in rapid retreat. Insulated by a deep layer of morainic gravels, the ice took some considerable time to melt and so collapse the gravels to form the lake. A track through the native bush that surrounds the lake has been developed as an easy nature walk and is one of the finest in the park. *Allow 1 hr return for the walk from the carpark to the raft — a pontoon which affords a good vantage point. The prime viewpoint at the extreme end of the lake, the "View of Views", is a 2 hr return walk. The walk right round the lake also takes 2 hrs but boots are essential beyond the "View of Views".*

From Lake Matheson a track branches off through the forest to **Lake Gault,** which mirrors 16 km of mountain range. (*Allow 3½ hrs. Boots essential*).

**Minnehaha Track:** Even the most transitory visitor should pause for the pleasant walk beside a tiny stream, through forests predominantly of *kamahi* and dense with fern. The odd form of the *kamahi* is a consequence of its aerial rooting. It begins as an epiphyte (perching plant), sending roots down to the ground to envelope its host tree-fern into its trunk. Many of the plants are identified. *Allow 20 mins. Start just south of the township.*

Branching off is the **Ngai Tahu Walk** (*1¼ hrs*) to a small circular swamp. Once a lakelet, the depression has filled with swamp vegetation displacing most of the water and forming a dense mat of sphagnum moss.

**Chalet Lookout:** A panoramic view of the lower glacier and the area below the terminal is obtained at a spot just beyond the ruins of the Fox Chalet, a shelter used by the earliest parties visiting the glacier. When it was in use access onto the glacier was just below the present lookout. Now the valley floor is hundreds of metres below, the glacier having receded more than a kilometre up the valley. *Start signposted at the end of the glacier view road. Allow 1 hr.*

A signposted side track branching off the Chalet Lookout route leads to the top of **Cone Rock** and the most impressive of the glacier views. *Suitable only for the fairly fit person, wearing boots. Allow 1 hr.*

The **High Valley Walk,** a loop off the Chalet track, crosses a "staircase" of some seven recessional lateral moraines.

**Moraine Walk:** A bush walk crosses both a lobe of the AD 1600 moraine and the AD 1750 moraine ridge, and passes through areas of forest both young and old. *Start signposted on Glacier View Rd. Allow 20 mins.*

**Mt Fox** (*1,021.2 m*): An old surveyors' route leads to the trig, from which a direct fix could be taken on the Okarito trig. The tramp, a steady haul from 150 m, shows changes in vegetation from zone to zone, from subtropical forest to alpine plant communities. The views can be particularly splendid, but those making the walk must be prepared even on a fine day to find that by the time they have reached the trig the mist has descended to obscure the mountains and the glacier. *Allow 1 day. Advise the park office of your departure and return.*

**Copland Valley:** A 5½ hr tramp leads in to Welcome Flat where there is a hut, and hot springs in which one can soak in a forest and alpine setting. This is the first stage of the traverse of the Main Divide by the Copland Pass (*see index*). The pass has its dangers and should not be attempted without a guide by any but the experienced. The more usual way to make the crossing is from the eastern side where a guide can be arranged at The Hermitage.

## OTHER THINGS TO SEE AND DO

**Westland National Park Visitors' Centre:** Comprehensive displays illustrate the natural history of the glacier, the surrounding forestlands and the wildlife. Information on walks, tracks, huts and queries generally is available. Evening programmes are arranged (nightly over the Christmas period), illustrated with slides and films. Over Christmas conducted nature walks are arranged in the mornings. *Highway 6. Open daily.*

**Peak Indicator\*\*\*:** A roadside peak indicator enjoys a peerless alpine panorama. A number of peaks exceed 3,000 m and the Fox Glacier is seen curling from its névé down the valley, its lower reaches framed in deep green bush. The indicator is a grand viewpoint from which to watch both sunrise and sunset. In either instance one should be in position with some time in hand, as the extraordinary light effects on the Alps last seconds rather than minutes. *8.8 km on road towards Gillespies Beach.*

**Gillespies Beach\*\*:** A wild stretch of coastline is strewn with riverborne rocks in which schists and quartz predominate. The area was extensively worked for gold, and beach workings can still be carried on with a measure of profit. Legacies of times when the near-vanished beach settlement supported a considerable population are the miners' cemetery (*signposted; 150 m walk from the road*), mountains of overgrown tailings, and the disintegrating remnants of the **gold dredge** that turned the tailings over. From here one may walk along the beach north past the dredge remains (*½ hr one way*) and **Gillespies Point** (*50 mins one way*) to a seal colony (*1½ hrs one way; the beach route can be used only near low tide*). Alternatively, a footbridge crosses the lagoon, and a track follows the historic horse track from Okarito, the port to which dredge materials were shipped to be carried to Gillespies beach. The route leads up to a tunnel through the ridge then drops back down to the beach. (*Walking time the same as for other route*). Walking south one passes **Otorokua Point** (*40 mins one way*) and **Cook Lagoon** (*50 mins one way*) before reaching the mouth of the **Cook River** (*1½ hrs one way*). Even if neither walk is made, the drive is recommended both for the bush it passes and, on the return journey, for the continuing and changing aspect of the Alps and the Glacier, particularly from the Clearwater locality. *20 km. Signposted.*

**Glow-worms** are found in a grotto just a few metres from the highway. Commonly found in deep bush and caves where the air is still, the glow-worm suspends a sticky silken thread and glows to attract tiny insects to the trap. Like a fishing-line, the thread is hauled up to the hollow nest where lives the little black caterpillar that will

## ORGANISED EXCURSIONS

emerge as an adult fly to mate and die. *Signposted immediately S of the settlement. Visit by night and take a torch to study the phenomenon.*

**Skiing:** Owing to varying snow conditions it is not possible to ski the glaciers in the manner of the Tasman from The Hermitage, just across the Divide.

**Guided glacier trips** on to the ice leave at 9.30 am and 2 pm daily. *Boots, socks and any necessary equipment are provided.* Full day trips taking in the Fox Glacier and Victoria Falls are available, weather permitting, November to May. Four-day basic mountaineering courses are also held in summer. *Alpine Guides (Westland) Ltd, tel. 825 or 828 Fox Glacier.*

**Scenic flights** by ski plane are the high point of a visit to Westland National Park, skimming as they do the two main glaciers and skirting the slopes of Mts Tasman and Cook. When conditions allow, a ski landing is made for a brief stop on the snow. A longer trip crosses the Main Divide to view as well the Tasman Glacier, the Hochstetter Icefall, The Hermitage and the Hooker Valley. Weather conditions render all routes subject to variation. *Mount Cook Airlines, tel. 812. Bookings also taken at Fox Glacier Hotel, tel. 839.*

**National Park Visitors' Centre** runs evening programmes to meet demand. At Christmas a conducted nature walk is usually given each morning. *Inquire at the Visitors' Office.*

**Helicopter sightseeing:** Particularly favoured on days when low cloud keeps the ski planes grounded is a 10-minute helicopter trip, whisking low over the ice of Fox Glacier. Hunting and tramping parties are also lifted in to otherwise inaccessible areas. *Winged Hunters Ltd, tel. 803 Fox Glacier.*

---

**FRANZ JOSEF GLACIER\*\*\*      Westland.   Maps 13, 34 & 37.**

*147 km SW of Hokitika; 25 km NE of Fox Glacier; 143 km NE of Haast Junction. Westland National Park headquarters gives information on walks, tramps and features of the park. Details of available accommodation is also held. The* Westland National Park Handbook *is recommended.*

AT FIRST SIGHT the pale green ice of Franz Josef Glacier as it thrusts towards lush, luxuriant rainforest, seems identical to that of its nearby "twin" of Fox. However each of the extraordinary rivers of ice has its own distinct if subtle characteristics.

The glacier was named by the geologist Julius von Haast to honour the emperor of his native Austria. Over the years the name has been spelt in various ways. *For a description of the area generally and glaciers in particular see the preceding entry.*

**A glacier in detail:** Of all the country's glaciers, Franz Josef has been the subject of the most study, with many photographs and reports being prepared over the last century. Until after 1893 there was a steady retreat but, in 1907, in a marked advance, the tourist track was wrecked and in 1909 advances of up to 50 m were recorded in thirteen months. The glacier then turned in retreat, shrinking in ice volume, and a 1921 report noted "a marked retreat of the ice since 1914, and still more since 1909". During the 1920s the glacier recovered about half the ground it had lost in the previous thirty years, but then retreated in spectacular fashion so that by 1946 it was over a kilometre shorter then than it had been seventy-five years before. A three-year advance was followed by the 1951–65 retreat that was broken in June 1965. Within four months the terminal face had been pushed 115 m down the valley and by August 1967, when the advance ended, the glacier had increased in length by 375 m but only slightly in volume. The overall pattern is plain: temporary advances are only minor interruptions in a steady retreat up the valley, a retreat that only climatic variations can halt.

**The Waiho River** that leads away the glacier melt in fact rises far up the valley beneath the Franz Josef and is kept in flood by frequent rain for the greater part of the year. The river carves out large caverns between the glacier ice and the valley floor, occasionally causing collapses and, when trapped water bursts free, periodic washouts of ice and scree.

The river's name (smoking water) comes not from its warm, if tiny, hot springs nor, apparently, from the river being milky with "rock flour", suspended particles of rock ground to dust by the movement of the ice. Rather it derives from the thin layer of fog that commonly forms hereabouts when warm moist air is abruptly chilled on contact with the ice-cold rivers.

### THE GLACIER TERMINAL

The approach road leads up the south bank of the Waiho River to pass the start of the 5-minute walk to **Peter's Pool** (*at 3.6 km*). The pool, a "kettle" lake which can have vivid reflections, formed in a subsidence created by the melting of underlying ice.

At the **historic viewpoint** (*at 3.7 km*) a copy of the first photograph ever taken of the glacier is displayed. A little farther on, to the left, (*at 4.3 km*) another 5-minute walk leads up **Sentinel Rock**, the largest of a group of schist *roches moutonnées* in the Waiho Valley. The rock emerged from the ice a little over a century ago and an interesting feature is the vegetation that has recolonised it. From the summit most of the *roches moutonnees* group is seen, forming a barrier across the valley. Note how lichens and mosses are steadily establishing themselves on the remaining outcrops of bare rock.

The carpark is reached at 6.4 km from which a track leads over polished rocks to the ice of the terminal face. (*Note: It is unwise for the inexperienced to venture on the ice except with a guided party. Parties leave the Franz Josef Hotel regularly. Boots, socks and any necessary equipment are provided.*)

## SOME WALKS AT FRANZ JOSEF***

*Each of the walks listed is the subject of an explanatory leaflet available from the park headquarters. They are essential to the maximum enjoyment of the walks.*

**Roberts Point:** An easy day's walk of about 5 hrs return takes in the most spectacular scenery in the Waiho Valley, following riverflats and glacial pavement, and crossing young forest and lateral moraine before concluding in a steady climb to the point itself. From a prominence that in AD 1750 was buried in ice one looks down at the main icefall. A feature of the walk is the clearly defined trim-line that records the height of the glacier ice two centuries ago, the lighter-coloured and smaller trees below it having developed as the glacier receded. *Stout shoes essential. Drive up the glacier access road and walk down Douglas Track. Cross the Waiho by the swing bridge and then turn upriver along the Roberts Point track. Those without transport can start by the Callery Gorge track to cross the Callery and follow the right bank of the Waiho.*

**Callery/Warm Springs Track:** Even to the hostile Callery Gorge the gold prospectors came in search of precious metal. Their extensive workings have largely been destroyed by floods; and races and huge heaps of tailings have been repeopled by tenacious flora to present a picture in marked contrast to the "abomination of desolation" that greeted a visitor in 1906 who lamented that "a world of loveliness lay destroyed at our feet". Where the Callery and Waiho Rivers meet may be seen an intriguing blend of the murky grey Waiho's "glacial milk" and the clear blue waters of the Callery. The Warm Springs, once developed as a bath-house, are little more than a footbath.

*The track's historical connotations render the walk unique among national parks. Allow up to 1 hr. Start just south of the park headquarters.*

**Canavans Knob:** A short walk gradually scales a *roche moutonnée*, a solitary knob of granite on the outwash plain of the Waiho. Several vantage points are passed, facing seaward, until a panorama unfolds of the Franz Josef glacier and the peaks of the Main Divide. The development of vegetation on the rock, covering a very much longer period, forms an interesting comparison with that of Sentinel Rock. *Allow ¾ hr. Start signposted 2.3 km S on the road to Fox Glacier.*

**Lake Wombat:** A feature of the easy climb to the bush-fringed lakelet is the park's prolific birdlife, including the rare crested grebe (or dab-chick). In favourable conditions the lake's dark waters mirror their surroundings. *Allow up to 2 hrs return. Signposted from the Glacier Approach Rd. Follow Alex Knob track for about 2 km before branching right.*

**Alex Knob** (*1,306.4 m*): An all-day (*7 hrs return*) walk climbs through varied rainforest. Christmas Outlook, at some 900 m, gives a fine view of the glacier framed by subalpine vegetation. At about 1,200 m the subalpine belt ceases and in season there are many alpine flowers to be seen. The gradual climb ends with a remarkable view of the entire length of the glacier, of a panorama of peaks and of the coastline from Greymouth in the north to Knights Point in the south. *Start signposted on Glacier Approach Rd.*

**Loop Track:** A track links Peter's Pool (*see above*) with the start of the Douglas Track, making an interesting round trip over the AD 1750 terminal moraine. *Allow ½ hr.*

## OTHER THINGS TO SEE AND DO

**Park headquarters\*:** Displays are mounted of the glaciers and the park's flora and fauna. The headquarters advises on what there is to see and do in the park, issues hunting permits and can help those in search of accommodation. Explanatory leaflets are provided for most of the walks. Illustrated evening programmes are conducted by Rangers to coincide with holiday periods throughout the year and from late December through January there are also Summer Nature Programmes which include both daily nature walks and evening programmes. *By Highway 6.*

**St James Anglican Church** (1931)***: The Tudor-styled church is well known for the alpine view through its east window, which forms a unique backdrop to the altar. The best view is obtained when kneeling at the sanctuary rail. From the exterior the reflection of the same scene may be photographed.

The church is named in part for the vicar, the Rev. James Young, who proposed that it be built in times when the view included the ice of the glacier, a famous scene recorded on the 1946 Peace Stamp. The receding ice disappeared from view in 1953. *By Highway 6 just south of the park headquarters.*

## ENVIRONS

*Note: Places of interest to the north and south are described under △West Coast Road.*

△**Fox Glacier\*\*\*:** Franz Josef's twin river of ice. *25 km SSW.*

**Lake Mapourika\*\*\*** in Westland National Park, its waters reflecting a bush-fringed shoreline, has boating facilities and is stocked with trout and salmon. There are picnic areas by the lake and bathing at a small beach. Birds seen here include the crested grebe, the white-throated shag and occasionally the white heron. *9 km N on Highway 6.*

**Okarito** (pop. 24): A scattering of iron holiday cottages perpetuates a locality which in the 1870s had 31 hotels, three banks, a courthouse and a population of several thousand. Its port was complete with customs house. About £6 million in gold is said to have been won from the local goldfields. The vicinity is reputed to be the area where Abel Tasman made his New Zealand landfall in 1642 (a reputation enhanced by a memorial). From the road's end a half-hour walk up to the Okarito trig is rewarded by perhaps the finest of all views of the Southern Alps — a sight denied Tasman by low cloud.

The lagoon here is often frequented by majestic *kotuku* (white heron) from the rigidly-protected breeding ground a little farther north. A rarity in New Zealand, the white heron (*Egretta alba*) is widely distributed throughout the world, often in considerable numbers. This is the only known breeding station in New Zealand, one from which the birds annually disperse to as far north as Parengarenga Harbour and as far south as Stewart Island. Brilliant white in colour, about a metre high, and with a long, sinuous neck, long legs and a long beak, the graceful heron patiently stalks its prey, be it fish, insect or small bird. The heron features in Maori legend as exemplifying rarity, grace and beauty. *28 km. Turnoff signposted at 17.3 km N on Highway 6.*

## ORGANISED EXCURSIONS

**Guided glacier trips** are run regularly (usually twice daily, at 9.30 am and 1.30 pm). Boots, socks and any necessary equipment are provided. *Enquire at the Franz Josef Hotel or the camping ground.*

**Ski plane flights** are the high point of a visit to Westland National Park, skimming the twin glaciers and skirting the slopes of Mts Cook and Tasman. When conditions allow, a ski landing is made for a brief stop on the snow. A longer trip crosses the Main Divide to view as well the Tasman Glacier, the Hochstetter Icefall, The Hermitage and the Hooker Valley. Weather conditions render all routes subject to variation. *Mount Cook Airlines. Book at the hotel, camping ground or the Airlines agency office (tel. 765 Franz Josef Glacier) in advance of holiday periods.*

**Park outings:** Over the Christmas period conducted walks are arranged by the park headquarters.

---

**GERALDINE\*\***     **South Canterbury.**     **Maps 3 & 35.**     **Pop. 2,060.**

*38.6 km N of Timaru; 138 km SW of Christchurch.*

GENTLE GERALDINE lies on the lip of the rolling Geraldine Downs, pleasantly elevated and backed by a curve of distant mountains. Studded with trees by the early Canterbury settlers in their dream of quite literally transplanting England to the Antipodes, the town is the centre of a small and prospering farming region.

For the visitor Geraldine is a convenient distance from the historic runs of Orari, Orari Gorge, Mount Peel and Mesopotamia, is near the rich native bush of Peel Forest Park and close to a number of picturesque picnic places.

Much honey is produced in a locality that also boasts the country's only linen flax factory. The town is also the headquarters of the neighbouring Kakahu State Forest. In the late summer months good bags of large quinnat salmon are taken from the Rangitata and Opihi Rivers.

The town was named to honour J. E. FitzGerald (*see index*), Superintendent of Canterbury Province, Geraldine being a family name. The link with FitzGerald is carried forward in the town's crest, which is topped by a chained monkey and is appropriate only as belonging to the arms of the FitzGerald family.

## SOME HISTORY

**The Bark Hut:** The story of Geraldine begins with the arrival of Alfred Cox, who had come across "a gentleman so well informed upon grazing matters in Canterbury [that he] finished up by offering to sell me a run not yet stocked, for which he demanded the sum of £100. I paid him the price demanded, and put into my pocket the 'licence to occupy', with the transfer of his right, title and interest therein." Cox, as it happens, was not taken down on the deal, for in 1854, on taking up his newly-acquired Raukapuka station on the eastern bank of the Waihi River, he considered it "equal in quality to the very best natural grass country that was to be seen in South Canterbury".

That same year the surveyor Samuel Hewlings arrived, with instructions to survey the country at Talbot Forest (as the area was then known, a name perpetuated by a Geraldine bush reserve) and to "get up" a small hut "on what may probably be the future site of a town". Hewlings obediently "got up" his small hut, of *totara* slab walls and rush-thatched roof, and around the "Bark Hut" the township grew as sawmillers came to level Talbot Forest to the ground.

The hut, the first in Geraldine, later served as Road Board offices and then as the town's first school. A *totara* tree still flourishes that was planted by Hewlings beside his hut to mark the birth of his daughter, the first child of European descent to be born in the Geraldine district. (*The tree and a commemorative plaque stand in Talbot St opposite the police station.*) As the bush was cut out the timber workers turned to farming, and as the vast outlying leasehold runs were slowly fragmented by the Government, Geraldine changed in character from a bush settlement to a servicing centre for local farms.

## THINGS TO SEE AND DO

**Church of the Immaculate Conception** (1934): A somewhat austere exterior of weathered Oamaru stone surrounds an ornate altar, with a frieze of the Last Supper and Stations of the Cross all carved from the same milk-white stone. *Peel St, off Talbot St.*

**Vintage Car Museum:** The collection includes a rare 1927 Morris Oxford "Empire Model" and other vintage and veteran vehicles dating back to 1906. *Talbot St. Open by request to Morrisons Garage, upper Talbot St, tel. 312.*

**Vintage Machinery Museum:** Adjoining the Vintage Car Museum is a collection of early farm machines and other items, including a horse-drawn fire engine. *Open by request to W. J. Skinner, tel. 1232.*

**Cottage Art Gallery** *opens daily 10 am–8 pm. Gresham St.*

**Waitui homestead** (1861): A year older than the homestead at Mount Peel and designed by the same architect, Waitui has marked similarities to its better-known counterpart. Built by the pioneer runholder Angus Macdonald, the old brick homestead and its additions date from times when the three Macdonald brothers held all the country from the Rangitata to the Orari and inland for 22.5 km. The house looks out over soft rolling downs to Mt Peel and the four concordant summits of Four Peaks. The original 1854 cottage is still standing behind Waitui and is used as a store. *2.7 km. Follow Waihi Tce to its end. Park at the last turning place and walk on to the gate.*

**Linen Flax Factory:** The plant now operated by Linen Textiles Ltd. at Geraldine was established during the 1939–45 war to help replace supplies of linen flax from France and Belgium, badly needed for fabric coverings for wartime aircraft. In all seventeen plants were established in New Zealand and twenty-six in Australia, of which only this remains. Straw-like linen flax (not to be confused with native flax) is grown by contracting farmers, harvested from January to March, and processed to yield such byproducts as stockfeed, linseed for paint manufacture, birdseed, and tow for pipe jointing and taxidermy; the stringy main product is presently used in Auckland for twine production. With synthetics supplanting linen flax for cordage, the factory's future may lie in the milling of the fibre to produce a lightweight hard-wearing textile of about 70 per cent wool and 30 per cent flax, suitable for summer clothing.

The flax is sown in spring and is harvested by being pulled out of the ground to preserve maximum fibre length. It is dried in stooks before being trucked to the factory where the straw is de-seeded, excess tissue is removed, and is dried outside until ready for scutching — a process that separates the woody core from the fine fibre.

The factory was formerly run by a Government-owned corporation from which the present owners took over in 1977. *3.2 km S on Highway 72 towards Winchester. Visitors should tel. 235S Geraldine to arrange to be shown over the plant. Allow 1 hour. There is less to see in the harvesting season, when the factory is generally not operating.*

**The Downs:** Even the most fleeting visit should allow for a drive on the Downs to enjoy an unequalled panorama of mountains and tree-broken plain. To the west lie the Four Peaks range and Mt Peel; to the north Mt Somers and Mt Hutt; and to the south and east lie the Hunters Hills, Timaru and the coast. On a clear day the view extends to the Port Hills of Christchurch. *Leave by Huffey or Totara St and gradually describe a circle. 7.8 km.*

**Barker's Wines** are the country's only makers of elderberry wines. The elderberry, a deciduous wild fruit-tree from Western Europe was introduced to Canterbury by early settlers both as a hedgeplant and for wine making. It ran wild and is now regarded as a weed.

Pre-dating the grape as a source of wine, for two thousand years the elderberry has

I travel; as light,
That is, as a man can travel who will
Still carry his body around because
Of its sentimental value.—Christopher Fry
(*The Lady's Not for Burning*).

been used in Europe for medicinal purposes, often served hot as a remedy for neuralgia, nervous complaints, colds and influenza. A full range of pure fruit wines is available. *8 km. Turnoff signposted at 4.5 km W on Highway 79 towards Fairlie. Open daily (not Sun.). Allow ¾ hr to see over the cellars.*

**Kakahu lime kiln** (c1880)\*: For all the world like a Norman tower, the clay-and-grey coloured kiln was one of several in the area built to burn lime for building works in Christchurch, Timaru and Dunedin. The kiln was prepared by laying a pile of *manuka* at the bottom, then trucking barrow loads of lime rock and coal across a now-vanished wooden deck from the hillside to the kiln's top. More layers were dumped in until the kiln was full, when the load would be fired from the arched doorway below, through which also the lime was extracted. The kiln was built by two stonemasons from a variety of stone types, among them limestone and marble, the interior being lined with bricks fired locally. The kiln has been restored by the Historic Places Trust and capped to protect it from dampness. *17.9 km. Turn left off Highway 79 to Fairlie at 15.1 km. The kiln is by the roadside on the right.*

**St Anne's Anglican Church**\*\*, Pleasant Valley (1862) is the oldest church in South Canterbury still on its original site and still used for its original purpose. Its pitsawn timber walls lined with cob give the tiny church a simple rustic charm. *Matai*, *totara* and *kahikatea* were felled from bush behind the minute building and both rafters and pews bear the marks of pitsaw and adze. In the small yard behind the church is the remarkable headstone of Cotsford Matthews Burdon, surrounded by kneeling angels. The east window in St Thomas's, Woodbury, is also dedicated to Burdon. *6.9 km. Turn right up Pleasant Valley Rd at 3.9 km on Highway 79 towards Fairlie.* Shortly after leaving Highway 79 an old stone cheese factory is passed, presently used as a piggery.

**St Thomas's Anglican Church, Woodbury** (1938): A Norman-styled slate-roofed building of local boulders, designed by Cecil Wood and built by members of the Tripp family, the church reflects a style of architecture prevalent in Devon, whence came Charles George Tripp (1820–97) in 1855. The massive squat tower is built to his memory, and the nave was given as a memorial to his children, Charles Howard and Eleanor Howard Tripp. Oak for the carved furniture and for memorial tablets is from the Tripp homestead at Orari Gorge, and the east window is dedicated to Cotsford Matthews Burdon, whose ornate grave is at St Anne's. *Woodbury. 8.5 km N on the way to Waihi Gorge.*

**Some picnic places:** For the through traveller the **gardens** in Cox St in the heart of the town offer settings of tall trees in which to picnic.

Farther out is **Waihi Gorge**\*, with independent camping and a wide grassed area contrasting with a bushed river face and a river that affords modest swimming (*13.6 km; signposted from Highway 79 north of the town*). On the Sundrum property, near the reserve, is an unusual "weeping" *totara*, which is an orthodox *totara* in all respects save the droop that gives it its "weep". (*Returning to Geraldine take the first turn left, and then turn right up the drive of the Sundrum holding. Private property. The tree is marked and is near the barn.*) The route lies through Woodbury, with its remarkable church (*see above*).

The **Te Moana Gorge,** on the Hae Hae Te Moana River has a number of attractive picnic and camping places but lacks swimming holes. (*19.2 km*). The route lies past historic St Anne's Church (*see above*).

**Pioneer Park** is an amalgam of exotic-shaded picnic area and large tract of native bush. *Described under △Pleasant Point. 39 km W.*

**△Peel Forest Park**\*\*\*: The mixed podocarp stands of the park contrast with the pine shelterbelts of the plains. A short distance beyond stand the historic buildings of Mount Peel station, and the road ends at △Mesopotamia, a run immortalised by its pioneer holder, Samuel Butler. *23 km to Peel Forest Park. 69 km to Mesopotamia.*

> I shall be telling this with a sigh
> Somewhere ages and ages hence:
> Two roads diverged in a wood, and I —
> I took the one less travelled by,
> And that has made all the difference. —
> Robert Frost (*The Road Not Taken*).

> Wouldn't it be better to stay peacefully at home, and not roam about the world seeking better bread than is made of wheat, never considering that many go for wool and come back shorn? — Miguel Cervantes (*Don Quixote*).

# GORE AND DISTRICT

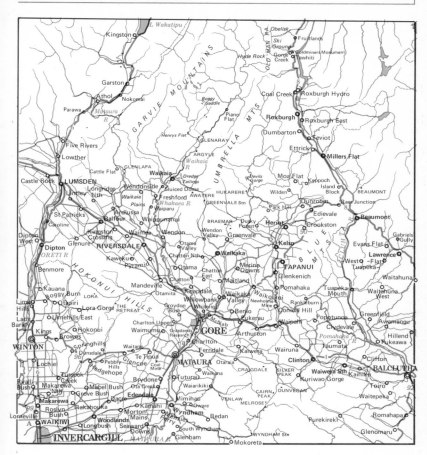

GORE**     Southland.     Maps 14 & 18.     Pop. 9,170.

*65 km NE of Invercargill; 75 km WNW of Balclutha; 59.5 km SE of Lumsden; 38 km SW of Tapanui.*

BLEAK, TREELESS AND WINDSWEPT, Gore may once have been, but its swamps have been drained, its tussocklands converted into lush rolling pasture and today Gore prospers as the solid settled hub of eastern Southland. The province's second largest town is remarkable for its total integration of town and country interests, a measure of which is the generous support forthcoming from farmers for projects in the town. Gore has the highest retail turnover per head of population of any area in New Zealand, more than twice that of Wellington and almost three times that of Auckland.

Though predominantly a sheep farming district — Gore's stud ram fairs have set many price records — considerable areas are in wheat and oats to feed the town's large mill, and the broad band of lignite that runs through eastern Southland is worked at several points. The district is prone to flooding. Indeed the Maori name for the locality was Maruawai (valley of water) after a massive flood had covered the valley from the foothills in the east to the pointed Hokonuis in the west in one vast unbroken sheet of water.

The town is strategically placed as a base from which to fish upwards of forty excellent streams, among them the Mataura, Waipahi, Waimea, Otamita, Waikaia and Pomahaka.

## SOME HISTORY

**Good advice:** If the area impressed the early settler as bleak and treeless, that such was not always the case is shown by the district's large deposits of lignite (brown coal showing traces of wood structure) and by the many stumps that have been hauled from swamps. Further, charred logs have been found east of Gore, on the Otakaramu Hills, perhaps a legacy of the "Great Fire of Tamatea" which in Maori tradition swept over much of Otago and Southland some centuries ago. Local Maoris never more than camped on the inhospitable site as they travelled to and from their permanent village at Tuturau (*near* △*Mataura*).

Several notable European travellers passed through the area in the early 1850s, but it may have been the legendary sheepman James McKenzie (*see index*) who first saw the town site through European eyes. He lived in the district for a time and tradition has it that it was he who recommended to Alexander McNab (1809–90) that he take up land near the Hokonui Hills and towards the Mataura River, advice McNab followed with profit. McNab and the McKellar brothers David and Peter had come from Australia in 1855, and while in Christchurch McNab visited the gaoled McKenzie, whom he had known on the other side of the Tasman. The pair conversed in Gaelic and so alarmed a warder suspicious of yet another escape attempt by his most notorious prisoner, that he incarcerated the indignant McNab until a Christchurch wool firm intervened on his behalf.

The following year McNab brought sheep from Australia to his Knapdale and Croydon (or Hokonui) runs. The McKellars however were delayed when their 3,000 ewes began to lamb as they were driven north from Bluff, so that it took the brothers a full year to move their flock to their Longridge run near Lumsden. So it was that in 1856 McNab came to build the first house in the district. McNab's Knapdale woolshed (1868) still stands (*10.7 km; cross the river, turn left immediately and follow signposts to Knapdale. The iron-roofed shed is on the right 500 m before the Knapdale School*).

**The Long Ford:** It was a long ford that gave rise to the township — "a high shingle bank between two deep channels [about 500 m in length which] went such a distance down stream. . . . It was easily crossed from east to west, but was a difficult and dangerous ford from west to east if the water was over [a metre] deep as the current was very swift, and the horse had to wade with breast full up against it up stream." A number of travellers nearly came to grief in the ford and it deserved its considerable reputation. (*The ford was 1 km S of the road bridge but was rendered both unreliable and unrecognisable when gravel loosened by goldmining on the Waikaia and Nokomai Rivers was washed downstream.*)

As was so often the case with riverside towns, an accommodation house, Long Ford House, with stables and "bush" liquor licence, was the first building to be erected (1862). It was burned down in the Christmas festivities of 1865 and for the next six years the stables served as an inn. (*The site is marked in River Rd, near the Mataura River bridge.*) The rail link from Invercargill opened in 1875 with the Mataura being bridged for the first time. To the consternation of the locals, the township they had for a generation cheerfully called Long Ford was described on the new railway station as Gore.

**What's in a name?** Gore was named after Sir Thomas Gore Browne (1807–87), who succeeded Sir George Grey as governor (1855–61). Though assured by one newspaper that he need do nothing but smoke his pipe and keep a good cook, he quickly experienced a worsening in race relations which he fed with his determination to acquire Maori-owned land for settlement. He tried for a time to avoid war, but is chiefly remembered as the architect of the notorious Waitara Land Deal which plunged much of the North Island into warfare during the 1860s. Sir Thomas was later an undistinguished governor of Tasmania. Not surprisingly, some have at times questioned both the sanguinary nature of the town's appellation and the doubtful honour accorded the town by its being named after a governor of dubious distinction.

Goldfields at Waikaia, Nokomai and Wakatipu generated considerable traffic through Long Ford (as the locality was known), a township all of 2.6 hectares that had been laid out in 1862 by the Southland Provincial Council, presumably at McNab's urging as he was a member. By 1875 it comprised a bare "four buildings and two gum trees". However it was soon to blossom.

**The "Big Land Sale":** In four hectic years no fewer than 200 new farms were carved out of the neighbouring runs, culminating in the "Big Land Sale" of 1877 when, in the dissolution of McNab's holdings, 97 blocks of rural land and a number of town sections in East Gore were put up for sale. Commented one observer: "The town was besieged! There was hardly standing room for them at night in the hotels . . . sections were sought at high prices amidst great excitement, and to the great disgust of the former occupier [McNab], who had held this land for a number of years from the Crown at a nominal rent." The influx of new farmers generated business as they set about improving their holdings, and the pattern was soon set for today's prospering farming centre — even if there is no successor to the combined businesses of one J. Thormahlen, who claimed expertise as "painter, paperhanger, house-decorator, hair-cutter and shaving-artist".

**Competing settlements:** For a time East Gore bade fair to outstrip Gore in size. In 1882 the former was proclaimed a town district under the name of Gordon, and Gore, on the opposite bank of the Mataura, followed less than a fortnight later. The name of Gordon honoured the first Lord Stanmore (1829–1912) who, as Sir Arthur Gordon, was governor of New Zealand from 1880–82 and as a paternal Liberal had earned the settlers' displeasure by stoutly opposing the Government's Maori policy of the time and by sympathising with the Maoris over the question of land confiscations. The choice disgusted the inhabitants, who considered Gordon a governor "of malodorous fame". The rivals amalgamated in 1890.

Local no-licence was carried in 1903, which persisted through to 1954, while the stills in the hills of the Hokonuis passed into the nation's folklore as they fed illicit whisky to a wide market.

**Stills in the hills:** The name Hokonui is throughout the country synonymous with illicit whisky, even to many unaware of the location or even the existence of the Hokonui Hills. With other facets of their Highland heritage, the Scottish settlers of Otago and Southland brought with them some knowledge of the craft of whisky distilling. Though they were otherwise of upright, virtuous and of law-abiding temperament, the prohibition against the distillation of whisky was one they could in conscience treat as inapplicable to their situation. The original Hokonui is said to have been brewed in the hills by those of Highland descent and to have been of the highest quality — something that could rarely be said of the later distillers' crude grain spirit.

As an industry the distillation of Hokonui seems to have flourished up to the time of the 1939–45 war. The height of the "moonshine hunting", when Customs men stalked distillers through the bush, was during the depression years, 1928–35. No effort was spared to conceal the stills. These were heated by burning *manuka,* and to hide the telltale columns of smoke literally kilometres of underground piping led through the bush. When the source of a suspicious puff of smoke was traced, as often as not it would prove to have emanated from the hollow of a tree, or simply from a hole in the ground. Aeroplanes were used to locate stills as early as 1924 in an attempt to overcome the sophisticated lookout systems used by most distillers which enabled them to escape, often in the nick of time, and in some cases leaving still-warm beds to be found by the police.

Periodically rumours revive the fancy that moonshining persists in the hills, but there has not been a conviction for some considerable time. An old Hokonui still is now in Invercargill's Southland museum. Police claims that it was needed at the Police Training School near Wellington were overruled, and what the *Mataura Ensign* called "this noble symbol testifying to the initiative and enterprise of our forefathers . . . with implications of freedom and good cheer" was returned to Southland in 1970.

## THINGS TO SEE AND DO

**The Remarkable Gap:** Looking north along Gore's meandering main street, which reflects the erratic course followed by wagoners as they passed between the goldfields and the port of Bluff, one sees the Remarkable Gap silhouetted against the sky. To the Maori this was Omatua, named after a chief who traversed the range some six or more centuries ago.

**Creamoata Mills\*:** At the country's only significant breakfast cereal mill, the town's largest industry, Fleming & Co processes a variety of breakfast foods from oats grown in Southland and West Otago. The oats are precooked or toasted before the husk is removed and the oat grain is ready for the roller mills. Visitors may see the entire process from the arrival of oats to their final packaging, and also enjoy a view of Gore and its surrounds from the top of the town's most substantial building. *Mersey St. To visit tel. 5199. Allow 1 hr.*

**Church of the Blessed Sacrament** (1913)\*: An imposing Lombardy-styled brick church whose discreet use of contrasting bricks and pointing creates a pleasing mosaic effect. *Faces down Ashton St to Main St.*

**Deer Park:** Several species of deer may be seen near the centre of town. *Signposted from Main St (Highway 94).*

**Gardens:** The gardens of the Gore racecourse (*3 km S on Highway 1*), like those of the aviary in Fairfield St, attract year-round attention.

## ENVIRONS

**Hokonui Hills\*\*:** Gore is fortunate in possessing, as well as its gardens, over 930 ha of native bush on the slopes of the Hokonui Hills. This is accessible at several points, the most notable being **Dolamore Park\*\*,** a well-developed bush-encircled picnic area complete with trim lawns and gardens, play areas and a tea kiosk (*11.7 km. Signposted from town's southern exit.*)

Less sophisticated is **Grants Bush\*,** an undeveloped picnic area in the fringes of the bush with a low view over Gore and the Mataura River valley (*7.2 km. Leave Gore by way of Reaby Rd*). A plough memorial, shortly before one reaches the reserve, marks the site of Alexander McNab's (and the district's) first house.

**Waikaka** (pop. 170): Waikaka had its genesis in the discovery of gold in about 1867. It was proclaimed a goldfield two years later and a series of small rushes followed, with as many as 800 miners working the area in 1873, the majority of them Chinese. A major water-race, about 15 km long and with seven flumes, to bring water from the Waikaka River was completed in 1870. The miners drifted away through the 1870s, but at the turn of the century renewed interest saw no fewer than thirty dredges working the Waikaka to win over £1 million in gold from that river alone between 1897 and 1926, turning over hundreds of hectares as they did so. During the 1930s the field entered its final phase when Robert Stewart floated a sluicing company. Then it was found how thorough the Chinese had been. No one had ever been prepared any record of the myriad of shafts they dug, and everywhere Stewart went he found the hardy Chinese had been there before him. Some gold was won but not enough to cover costs.

The shareholders' principal consolation was that for some years they had contributed to the reduction of unemployment in the area.

Without the extremes of hardship suffered by those on the diggings in Central Otago, the township has nonetheless its chronicles of riches won and fortunes lost. Today Waikaka is a quiet farming centre with scant trace of the former goldmining industry beyond occasional heaps of scrub-covered tailings and the odd dredge bucket abandoned in a paddock. Waikaka means water where shellfish may be found. *25.5 km.*

△**Mataura:** A mini-metropolis which saw the historic final encounter between local Ngaitahu and the *taua* Te Puoho had led down the West Coast and across Haast Pass. *12 km S.*

△**Waikaia:** A gold-town turned farming centre. *52.5 km NW.*

## TOURING NOTES

**Road to** △**Lumsden (Highway 94):** The road to Lumsden runs along the rich and level Waimea Plains to pass first through Mandeville (*16.7 km from Gore*), whose Railway Hotel enjoyed a large trade when it preserved its licence after Gore had gone "dry". The brewery then at Gore, the oldest in Southland, managed to survive for half a century as an oasis in a licensing desert by trucking kegs for sale from depots here and elsewhere, just beyond the bounds of temperance.

The splendid stone homestead (1885) of Wantwood House was built by George Meredith Bell after he acquired the run from the New Zealand Agricultural Company. (*At Mandeville turn towards Dolamore Park and then right along Nine Mile Rd. 3.6 km from Mandeville.*)

The New Zealand Agricultural Company was formed in 1878 to amalgamate several stations between Gore and Lumsden. It was organised by a group of well-connected politicians who also financed the railway from Gore to Lumsden. The company was from the outset enmeshed in controversy, and Sir George Grey as premier was driven to demand that Sir Julius Vogel (then Agent-General in London) sever all connections with it. The depression of the 1880s and 1890s combined with the rabbit invasion to ensure that the venture was not very successful. The old cookhouse (*c.* 1878) from the Waimea estate still stands (*6.8 km N of Riversdale, off to the right at the foot of a small hill*). The ruins of a massive twentytwo-room homestead (*c.* 1866), originally built by David McKellar and later the residence of the company's general manager, now overgrown in wild fruit trees and rampant hedge-plants, is another relic of the company's operations (*7.8 km N of Riversdale, back from the road on private property*). The now-ruined homestead once had a high wooden tower nearby from which, with binoculars, the farm manager could inspect the industry of his employees as they toiled on the wide plains below. In its heyday the block saw mock battles when the Gore and Riversdale Rifles were on manoeuvres, and the Garrison Band frequently played in the homestead's then beautiful garden.

△**Winton via the Hokonui Hills:** As an alternative to driving to Winton by way of Mataura and Highway 96, one may leave Gore by Highway 94 to turn left at Mandeville and follow the Retreat–Mandeville Rd and Matthews Rd through the Hokonui Hills to Otapiri Gorge Rd. The route then lies through the picturesque Otapiri Gorge and Otapiri before linking with Highway 6 just north of Limehills and Winton.

Another attractive variation of the route to Winton is to drive by way of Highway 94 as far as Balfour. There turn left to follow the Glenure summit road through to Highway 6. There are fine views of the Mataura Valley en route.

---

Good books on botany include *Trees and Shrubs of New Zealand* by A.L. Poole and N.M. Adams (Govt Printer); *New Zealand Flowers and Plants in Colour* by J.T. Salmon (Reed) and *New Zealand Alpine Plants* by Alan Mark and Nancy Adams (Reed).

---

**GRASSMERE (Lake)**\*\* Marlborough. Maps 6 & 20.
*33.5 km SSE of Blenheim; 98.5 km NE of Kaikoura.*

ARRESTING PYRAMIDS of salt and the pink-and-white terraces of crystallising ponds mark the site of Lake Grassmere. Here salt is recovered by evaporating seawater, a process developed by the Romans some 2,000 years ago. The importance of salt to man is reflected in both the origin of the word "salary" (from the Latin *salarium* = payment made to a legionary for the purchase of salt) and in the predominantly coastal *pa* of the Maori. Unlike the Hawaiians, the Maori did not win salt from seawater but obtained what they needed from a diet of fish.

Skellerup Industries, Cerebos Foods and the Government are now partners in the enterprise.

Nearby Cape Campbell is the most easterly point of the South Island.

## SOLAR SALT WORKS

Seawater is pumped into a 688 ha main lake where it increases in strength due to the evaporation caused by the sun and the restless wind. Still days here are rare, as is shown by the locality's Maori name of Kaparatehau (waters ruffled by wind). From the lake the water is pumped to a series of concentrating ponds where further evaporation takes place until the strengthened brine reaches saturation point (i.e. salt crystals start forming). The saturated brine is then pumped directly into the crystallizers. Spent brine is removed before the crystallizing ponds are drained for harvesting.

The harvesting begins by mid-March and lasts for about five weeks during which the salt crust is lifted from the bottom of the ponds by machinery and washed in brine in two washing plants before being stacked into 18 m high piles. These are floodlit at night to provide light for operators loading salt into the refining and bagging plant nearby.

Annual production averaging 55,000 tonnes is treated by combinations of rewashing, crushing and screening processes before being packed, or railed in bulk to customers.

In addition, a vacuum refinery produces high purity fine salt for butter, cheese and animal casings processing.

While the biggest part of the refinery's output is used by the New Zealand freezing industry for treatment of hides and skins, the adjacent packing plant supplies New Zealand's total requirement for packaged table salt.

*The works may be visited by turning off Highway 1; a short distance north of the signposted turnoff a hilltop memorial may be seen, erected to the memory of George Skellerup, whose vision and determination established the salt industry in New Zealand in 1943, initially to supply the rubber manufacturing group he had founded.*

**Why pink?** The pinkish-red tinge of the saturated brine (an effect after which the Red Sea is named) is caused by a minute form of marine life invisible to the naked eye. The organism is normally transparent in seawater, but changes colour when subjected to water with a high saline content. The brine shrimp (*Artemio saleno*), however, can be seen as a tiny graceful creature who thrives in water so saturated with salt as to prove fatal to virtually every other form of marine life. Many thousands of the shrimps congregate in corners of the salt ponds to lay their brownish-coloured eggs.

## SOME HISTORY

**Te Rauparaha's narrow escape:** In 1833 a *taua* of southern Ngaitahu journeyed here in quest of Te Rauparaha to avenge the sacking of *pa* at Kaikoura, Kaiapohia and Onawe peninsula. In an ambush on the beach the war-party surprised a group that included the Ngati Toa chief himself, who had come to catch paradise duck. It was Tuhawaiki (*see index*), the redoubtable "Bloody Jack", who all but secured Te Rauparaha. As the northerners fled, he overtook the chief and managed to grasp his cloak, but the Ngati Toa leader wriggled out of the garment and plunged into the sea. Swimming under water, Te Rauparaha managed to elude the determined Tuhawaiki. He reached a Ngati Toa canoe offshore, where one of the crew was bundled overboard to make room for him before it paddled furiously northwards.

---

△ indicates a place with its own entry.

---

### GREYMOUTH**      Westland.    Maps 2, 15 & 37.    Pop. 8,282.

*105 km SSW of Westport; 40 km NE of Hokitika; 256 km NW of Christchurch. Public Relations Office, 66 Mawhera Quay, tel. 5101.*

BESIDE THE CLEAVAGE torn through limestone hills by the Grey River stands the chief commercial centre of the West Coast. Like Westport, the town is a river port where a stone breakwater has been built to direct the scouring action of tide and river on to the river bar. As at Westport, too, one of its first settlers was the store keeper, Reuben Waite.

Greymouth grew on the later site of Mawhera *pa,* on a reserve much of which remains in Maori ownership. The *pa,* as the town does today, supported the largest population on the West Coast. Founded on gold, continued on coal, Greymouth now maintains a large timber trade that eclipses the combined activities of sheep- and cattle-raising and dairying. It stands to gain immensely from further development of the West Coast timber industry. The town (locally known as "Grey") takes its name from the river which is named after Sir George Grey, twice governor and once Prime Minister of New Zealand.

**"The Barber":** Greymouth has an infamous wind, unique within New Zealand. Technically a katabatic wind — caused by the movement of cold air down a steep slope — the current is marked by a white mist as it streams down from the upper Grey Valley to be funnelled through "The Gap" the river has cut through the limestone hills. What begins as a relatively minor, down-valley wind emerges at the town's heart as "the Barber", a wind that feels like the cold steel of a barber's razor, and is just as cutting.

**Fishing:** The extensive Grey River system contains some of the district's best fishing waters — the Little and Big Grey Rivers, the Ahaura, Arnold and Haupiri Rivers, Rough River, Nelson Creek and Red Jacks Creek as well as Lakes Brunner, Haupiri and Poerua. The trout of Poerua have a rich, orange-coloured flesh from their diet of *koura* (freshwater crayfish) and bullies.

## SOME HISTORY

**Mawhera pa:** For all that the West Coast was the first part of New Zealand to be seen by the *Pakeha*, it was in all probability one of the last areas to be settled by the Maori. The principal *pa* of the West Coast Maoris stood on the south (or left) bank of the Grey when the first European explorers visited it. However in earlier times it had been on the opposite bank until that site was destroyed by Ngaitahu raiders from Kaikoura, so rendering the site *tapu* by bloodshed. The defenders journeyed south, gathered reinforcements and returned to overtake and overwhelm their East Coast visitors at the junction of the Grey and Ahaura Rivers.

On the original site the Maoris had lived at the foot of The Gap in caves which were destroyed during the 1939–45 war as a defence measure. Re-established on the south bank, the *pa* was ultimately peopled by Ngaitahu after the northern tribe had acquired the West Coast by right of conquest. It was to the *pa* here that James Mackay came in his quest to purchase the West Coast for the Government.

**The purchase of Westland:** The central figure in the purchase by the Government of the West Coast was the young Scot, James Mackay (1831–1912) (here pronounced Mackie) who held a run at Cape Farewell while he explored the West Coast. His skill in the bush coupled with his mastery of the Maori language led to his appointment as assistant native secretary for the South Island in 1858. The following year he negotiated the purchase of the Kaikoura Block, then crossed to the West Coast to settle the terms of the West Coast purchase. But the Poutini Ngaitahu proved difficult to deal with as they were understandably reluctant to part with the country from which they derived their greenstone (*see index*).

After inconclusive discussions Mackay travelled to Auckland where Governor Gore Browne authorised him to pay up to £400 and empowered him to settle the question of reserves. Armed with a leather despatch box that held the 400 gold sovereigns, Mackay returned to the Coast, his party arriving at Greymouth's Mawhera *pa* in bad shape. Mackay himself had poisoned his right knee on speargrass so badly that he had to lance the sore with his razor. Here they encountered both Julius von Haast and the pioneer farmer Samuel Mackley, who were waiting for the *Gypsy* to arrive from Nelson with stores. All were weak from hunger by the time the schooner arrived, and there was much jubilation when she hove into sight.

A lengthy *korero* (meeting) at Mawhera proved inconclusive. Both Mackay's party and the inhabitants of the *pa* set off south down the coast some 250 km to Okarito. As they went, more Maoris joined them and there were further *korero* both at Okarito and at Bruce Bay. To clinch negotiations which he felt sure would otherwise collapse, the canny Mackay agreed to native reserves totalling 40,500 ha but managed to induce Poutini Ngaitahu to accept a price of only £300.

All returned to Mawhera *pa*, where after speeches and feasting the deed of sale was signed "under the shining sun of this day" on 21 May 1860. Mackay set off for home, nearly drowning in the Grey River as he went. Battered and triumphant he arrived back at Nelson with the £100 he had saved the Government. The only thanks he received for the successful purchase of land that within a decade was to yield over £12 million in gold came in a hostile departmental letter that berated him for allowing the deed to become water-stained and cautioned him to take better care in the future. (*An Historic Places marker indicates the place where the deed was signed; opp. the south end of the Grey river bridge. Close by is buried the chief Werita Tainui, one of the Maori signatories.*)

**The Coast's first farmer:** A witness to the sale was Samuel Meggitt Mackley (1829–1911), who made a number of early visits to the West Coast, finding gold on the beach at Okarito. In 1861 he took up a run on the Waipuna Plains, up the Grey River, being the first European to settle on the Coast. The following year he wrote to the *Lyttelton Times* predicting that the West Coast would prove to be a goldfield. (*The locality of his farm, still locally known as Mackleys, is through Waipuna—turn off up the Grey River just south of Ikamatua.*)

**A town is born:** European settlement at Mawhera (Greymouth) dates from 1863, when a Government depot was established near the *pa* to facilitate the survey of Westland. The Resident Agent staked prospectors in rations as they toiled in the bush in search of gold. Just when the Provincial Government was on the point of closing the depot and abandoning the survey came a letter from Albert Hunt.

**Gold at Greenstone:** "I can get the colour at any place. The prospects are from a half-pennyweight to three pennyweights to one dish. I have got about 38 ounces of gold. A party of four might make £150 a week here." So wrote Albert Hunt on 15 July 1864 to the Superintendent of Canterbury, claiming the £1,000 reward offered for the discovery of a payable goldfield in Canterbury (which then included Westland). Others had claimed the reward before Hunt, but all had failed as the goldfields did not

# GREYMOUTH AND DISTRICT

meet the requirement of being "reasonably accessible" to Christchurch — those who framed the conditions dreamt of a goldfield on the handy plains, not on the other side of the Alps.

If Hunt is generally accepted as the one who first found payable gold in Westland, it was not his letter but a report from another prospector, William Smart, that heightened the interest of Reuben Waite (after whom a main street is named). He chartered the *Nelson* to bring the first party of diggers to the scene and to establish the first store at what was to become Greymouth. Strikes at Waimea and Hokitika soon followed. In March 1865 Julius von Haast described the scene as diggers flocked from Canterbury across Arthur's Pass: "An endless train of gold-diggers with pack horses, packers driving horses before them, diggers with handcarts and even women walking slowly along the side of their husbands and often leading pack horses, all going to the new Eldorado."

In a little-publicised move the Provincial Government had actually withdrawn the reward in 1861, simply promising to "treat liberally" anyone who revealed a goldfield. However applications for the reward were showering in as late as 1865. A Goldfields Discovery Rewards Committee was set up which recommended that Hunt's claim for a reward be considered, but after much haggling the reward of £1,000 was reduced to a gratuity of £200 — and then made only to recognise Hunt's services "in exploring and developing the resources of [the Province's] western portion". Hunt felt badly about his treatment — though perhaps those whose claims went completely without recompense had greater cause for sorrow — and his resentment is often said to have triggered his bizarre duffer rush (*see* index).

**Reuben Waite** (?1823–85) is a good example of a goldfields operator who sought no gold himself but rather to prosper on the more certain if still hazardous business of supplying stores to diggers. When he was at Nelson and Collingwood, West Coast Maoris bought goods from him, paying in gold, an incident that led to his settling first /\Westport and then Greymouth. London-born, Waite was a graduate of the Victorian goldfields and did not hesitate to charge outrageous prices for often mouldy flour and water-damaged stocks. He prospered, even though resentful diggers deliberately "put him through" by running up bills for the express purpose of moving on without paying. Though he later acquired a run of about 240 ha near Inangahua, on which the gold-rich diggings of Waite's Pakihi were discovered, he died at Nelson a pauper having unsuccessfully petitioned Parliament to reward his services in pioneering the Coast.

## THINGS TO SEE AND DO

**South tip:** From the signal station on the breakwater at the mouth of the Grey River, a chain of snowtipped mountains may be seen south across the surf, seemingly sweeping seaward to culminate in Mts Tasman and Cook. Towards the town is a curl of wharf and, to the north, the ridge of the Twelve Apostles leaning towards the abrupt Gap. *The route lies through the suburb of Blaketown, whose geography is confused by lagoons. At the seaward end of Mackay St turn left along Boundary Rd. Turn right to cross the tidal lagoon. Turn right again, and at the end of Packers Quay turn left to follow the riverbank to the signal station, where there is a plane table.*

**War Souvenir Museum:** Propaganda, medals, weapons, plaques, badges, cartoons etc. are displayed in the foyer of the RSA clubrooms. *187 Tainui St.*

**Dixon Park:** A glade by the main road with gardens, trees, meandering stream and vintage band rotunda. *Corner Tainui and Brunner Sts.*

**Plywood factory** may be visited. *Fletcher Wood Panels, Paroa. Tuesdays at 1.30 pm, other times by arrangement. Tel. 26-759 to confirm.*

**Some walks:** A bush walk through **King Domain** up the hillside near The Gap affords a variety of views, the more sweeping as altitude increases. (*Park in Smith St opp. railway station. Walk up Mount St for 150 m to enter the bush by steps on the left.*)

A leisurely walk may be made to the **South Spit** (*see above*) and the Signal station to see the view of the Alps.

## ENVIRONS

**Shantytown (Rutherglen)\*\*\*:** No trip to the Coast is complete without a visit to Shantytown, the reconstruction of a typical old gold-town complete with furnished goldbuying office and bank, hotel, printing shop, store, stables, station, gaol and assorted craftsmen. The church (1866) came from the oddly-named goldtown of No Town — reputedly named by a surveyor who remarked that the settlement looked impressive on paper but was really "no town". The short railway takes visitors through the bush to the Chinese workings. Gold may be panned and ground sluicing is demonstrated. *12.7 km. At Paroa, 8 km S on Highway 6, turn left. Signposted. Open daily.*

**Wildlife Park\*\*:** An assortment of wild game is held, including chamois, tahr, red deer, goats, wild pigs and large eels. Trophy heads are also displayed. *8.7 km. At Paroa, 8 km S, turn left. Signposted. (Near Shantytown.)*

**Lake Brunner\*,** like the lakes to the south, fills a glaciated hollow dammed by moraine. A pleasant swimming and boating lake with excellent trout-fishing, its shoreline offers a number of attractive picnic places in the vicinity of the fishing lodge at **Mitchells.** There is a settlement of some size at **Moana** (pop. 70).

The lake, whose Maori name is Moana Kotuku (lake frequented by the *kotuku*) was named by John Rochfort to honour Thomas Brunner who, in 1848, was the first European to explore the lake. Brunner's diaries tell of hardships and all manner of privations in the course of his epic 550-day trek through the forests of the Coast, during which he was forced to eat his dog to survive (explorers, living off the land, would take dogs with them to help in the capture of game). Back at Motueka, Brunner could well sigh: "So, thank God, I am once more among civilised men." The saga, simply recounted in his journal, impressed the people of Nelson far more than did the West Coast.

There was a spectacular duffer rush to nearby Kangaroo Lake in 1865 when as many as 800 men set off in pursuit of the "Kangaroo" party who had taken out a claim there. Curiously there was a boat waiting to ferry the diggers (for fifteen shillings a head) across the lake, but it was extending coincidence beyond credence that a well-stocked store should be ready for them on the ground. There was no gold to be had. The prospectors bolted, and the irate mob tore the store to shreds, plundered its provisions and showed mercy only in giving its proprietor time to flee. The duffer rush ended in near tragedy when on the return to Greymouth 200 of the men were marooned in swampy ground. They had to climb trees, there to cling for their lives until a flood abated. This duffer is ocassionally incorectly attributed to Albert Hunt. *32 km. A round trip of 88 km can be made by driving to △Kumara and thence through close bush to Mitchells, where the lake is at its most picturesque. The road leaves the lake for a time before rejoining it at Moana.*

**Runanga** (pop. 1,465): The coal town of Runanga rests at the feet of the Paparoas, one peak of which will support no growth and is known affectionately as Old Baldy. *An easy 1½ hr (return) walk leads to Coal Creek Falls and favoured swimming holes (start at*

> Most of
> The beauties of travel are due to
> The strange hours we keep to see them. —
> William Carlos Williams.

end of Ballance St or Seddon St South). *7.6 km NE on Highway 6.* Just 1 km south of the town is a roadside monument erected by the district to two mine payclerks "who met a tragic end at this spot" in 1917. Their lone murderer was later hanged in the Lyttelton gaol.

**Rapahoe Beach (Seven Mile Beach):** A safe stretch of swimming be    are on an otherwise wild coastline. *11 km N on Highway 6.*

## SUGGESTED DRIVES

**MARSDEN—SHANTYTOWN ROUND TRIP:** *34 km.* The duration of the trip depends on the time spent at Shantytown and the Wildlife Park. Leave Greymouth by Marsden Rd to pass through **Boddytown** (*4 km*) and enter the exquisite bush that at times meets overhead. At the intersection (*15.1 km*) one may detour left to reach the few houses that today comprise the locality of **Marsden** (*15.8 km*), an area still pitted with mineshafts and once the scene of intensive goldmining. Turn right and proceed to **Shantytown**\*\*\* (*20.8 km; see above*). After visiting, continue on through the former goldtown of **Rutherglen** (*22.2 km*), turning right (*at 24.5 km*) to reach Wildlife Park\*\* (*25 km; see above*). Return to the Rutherglen road to join almost immediately Highway 6 at **Paroa.** Turn right and return to Greymouth.

**GREY VALLEY ROUND TRIP:** *100 km (excluding detours). In summer the drive through the old coalmining valley, now given over to pastoral pursuits, can be made an all-day trip by pausing to picnic, swim and pan for gold in the Moonlight Creek. Leave Greymouth on Highway 6 to cross the river by the Cobden bridge. Bear right to pass through Taylorville, detouring briefly at 22.1 km to reach:*

**Blackball** (pop. 384) (*detour 2 km*): Nestling on a lip of river terrace at the foot of the Paparoas is an old coaltown, still home to miners as well as forestry workers. Just through the township are the dilapidated remains of the outbuildings of the Blackball mine. *Return to the Blackball turnoff. Turn left to pass dredge tailings (at 24 km) and cross the:*

**Moonlight Creek**\* (*at 30.5 km*): Upstream from the bridge, beyond heaps of tailings, may be seen the skeleton of the *Atarau* gold dredge, a rare sight as virtually all the old dredges have completely disintegrated. *Detour left at 31.3 km to wind along a timber road up the Moonlight Valley, through the Paparoa Forest to reach the:*

**Bailey bridge**\*\* (*detour 5.8 km*): A delightful bushed picnic and swimming spot where those with pans can often find colour. The region was pioneered by the ubiquitous Captain George Moonlight (*see index*) and is reputed to have had, in the late 1860s, the hemisphere's first stamp battery. Several horses were killed while transporting its heavy parts. The valley revived during the 1930s, when many of the unemployed turned diggers with some success. One party lingered on until 1939, finally exhausting the rich pocket it had found. *Continue up the Grey Valley to cross both the Otututu and Mawheraiti Rivers before joining Highway 7 at:*

**Ikamatua** (*50.6 km*): A rail and timber centre. *Turn right down Highway 7 to cross the Grey River. Immediately off to the left, through Waipuna, lies the West Coast's first farmland, settled by Mackley. Follow broad riverflats to pass through the old goldtown of Ahaura and reach:*

**Ngahere** (*at 76.6 km*): A timber township that also serves up-valley farmers. **Lake Hochstetter** (*28 km*) may be reached from here via Nelson Creek, an unspoiled, bush-girt lake the setting for picnics, boating and fishing. *Continue on towards Greymouth, passing through:*

**Stillwater** (*86.9 km*): Home of a major timbermill. In the small Stillwater cemetery (*detour 300 m; signposted*) is the mass grave of thirty-three of the miners who died in the country's worst-ever mining tragedy, in the Brunner mine in 1896. Others buried nearby shared their fate. In all sixty-seven died in the explosion that ripped through the shafts. Rescue work, in air so foul that men could not work in it for more than ten minutes at a time, was personally supervised by the premier, Richard Seddon. *The bridge across the river to Taylorville is passed, close by the tall chimney of a vanished brick kiln (across the bridge and slightly upriver are the old Brunner coke ovens). Conspicuous on an island in the river is the:*

**Brunner Memorial** (*seen at 90.8 km*): A monument to a pioneer explorer of Westland. It was on the opposite bank that Thomas Brunner (*see above*) discovered the coal deposits. On both sides of the road hereabouts are the interesting remains of the Brunner Mine, first worked in 1864 and for many years one of the most productive mines in New Zealand. There are plans to create an historic reserve and generally enhance the area.

> A man travels the world over in search of what he needs and returns home to find it. — George Moore (*The Brook Kerith*).

**Dobson** (pop. 423) (*91.4 km*): An early coaltown named after George Dobson (1840–66), the son of Edward Dobson, Surveyor for Canterbury Province, who with his brothers Arthur and Edward was a pioneer surveyor of Canterbury, Nelson and Westland. It was George who confirmed that his brother Arthur's pass (*see index*) was the best crossing from Canterbury to Westland. While working on road construction here in 1866, George was mistaken by the Sullivan gang (*see index*) for a young goldbuyer, Edward Fox; he was strangled by the transported convicts, and buried in a shallow grave in the bush. The infamous gang's exploits ended after the murders of five men at Maungatapu. One member, Sullivan, told the police where Dobson's body had been buried, and boasted of "twenty or thirty people" who had been "put away" between Hokitika and Greymouth. The murder profoundly shocked the Coast, who named the township in George's memory. The monument marks the place where the murder occurred (*presently obscured by scrub, across the railway line*). *Continue to follow the Grey River seaward. The road slithers round the bluff, passes through The Gap and re-enters Greymouth.*

## ORGANISED EXCURSIONS

**Gold panning** is conducted under expert guidance at Shantytown. The more independent may purchase gold pans from local hardware stores and wash in localities of their own choosing or those suggested by the Public Relations Office.

**Coalmines:** State coalmines may be visited, principally the Strongman mine (near Runanga and Dunollie) where visitors are conducted over the installations and taken underground. (*Preferably arrange visits at least a day ahead by telephoning the mine manager concerned; for Strongman tel. 27-860 Greymouth. Children under thirteen are not taken underground. Visits may also be arranged through the Public Relations Office.*)

Those with time to spare may catch the Rewanui miners' train to spend a day up in the Paparoas at the present Liverpool mine. A visit to the former mine here included a trip in a hoist from railhead to mine entrance, an experience unfortunately no longer either necessary or possible. *1.50 pm Mon–Fri. Special timetables Xmas holiday period. Details from Public Relations Office.*

## TOURING NOTES

**Route to Hokitika via the 1865 trail:** At Kumara Junction (*18 km S on Highway 6*) turn off to pass through △Kumara, turning right at 27.3 km to follow the old 1865 gold trail as it winds through diggings largely overgrown by bush. The Wheel of Fortune claim at now-vanished Goldsborough is passed before reaching the locality of **Stafford.** Here (*at 40.3 km*) one may detour briefly to visit an evocative goldtown cemetery where, in a bush setting, lie two of Richard Seddon's infant children, buried beside his uncle, Nathan. The route continues along the 1865 trail to pass the junction with Awatuna Rd (*at 41.7 km*). Some 30 m down Awatuna Rd a short track leads into the scrub from which in a lakelet may be seen the near-submerged and burnt-out remnants of the *Stafford* gold dredge. Do not turn down Awatuna Rd but continue straight ahead to rejoin Highway 6 (*at 45 km*). The highway south crosses the Arahura River, revered by both ancient Maori and present-day Coaster as a prime source of greenstone, before reaching △Hokitika (*at 54.2 km*). *The route adds 14 km to the through journey.*

△**West Coast Road (Highway 6):** Points of interest north and south of Greymouth are described under this entry. The coastal route to △Westport is strongly recommended as it passes the curious Punakaiki rocks (*see index*) with their booming blowholes.

---

**HAAST PASS ROAD\*\*\* North-West Otago/South Westland. Map 16.**
*146.5 km from Wanaka to Haast Rivermouth Bridge.*

THE HAAST PASS ROAD, connecting Lake Wanaka with South Westland, is the most historic and most recently opened of the transalpine routes, following an ancient greenstone trail. Although the road, much of it unsealed, traverses some of the Island's most rugged country, it presents little difficulty to the motorist. The region's rainfall is among the country's highest and can prove vexing to visitors, who are not infrequently obliged to drive through the pass while cloud obscures much of its magnificent surroundings. There are numerous picnicking and camping places on the way. The road, which is continually being upgraded, is seldom closed by snow.

## SOME HISTORY

**Early travellers:** At 563.9 m the lowest pass on the Main Divide, Haast marks the boundary between Otago and Westland. The route was regularly used by Maori parties visiting Westland for greenstone, but its most notable travellers were the members of a *taua* (war-party) in 1836. Te Puoho, relative and lieutenant of Te

# HAAST PASS ROAD

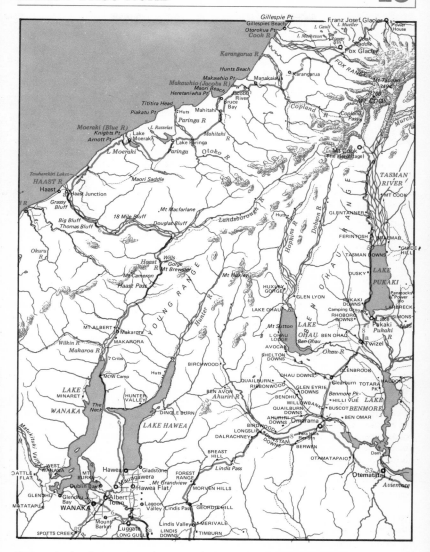

Rauparaha (*see index*), elected to take the Otago Ngaitahu by surprise by journeying down the West Coast and crossing through the Haast Pass. The arduous journey took almost a year before Te Puoho crossed the pass with a war-party of about 100. At Makarora (at the head of Lake Wanaka) a *kainga* was attacked, but one of the villagers contrived to escape and warn his kinsmen at Lake Hawea.

The *taua* travelled on to traverse the Crown Range and continue as far south as Tuturau (*near △Mataura*). There it was Te Puoho's turn to be caught off guard, few of his men surviving the slaughter. During the celebrations that marked the last of the South Island's tribal confrontations "round and round went the staked head of the dreaded Te Puoho, while children spat and women reviled".

The first *Pakeha* to find the pass was Charles Cameron, in January 1863. A gold prospector, he left Dunedin determined to get to the West Coast by the most direct route, noting that "travelling in this part is very dangerous, on account of the glaciers giving way on the mountains with a loud thundering noise". Hard on his heels was Julius von Haast, who was careful to name the pass after himself and do all he could to discount Cameron's claim to have preceded him. He could not, however, overcome the fact that Cameron had buried his powder flask to the west of the pass on the summit of Mt Cameron, to be found there in 1881. Vincent Pyke followed and, after a tortuous return journey, glibly noted that a road "could be made at a trifling expense".

**Roadbuilding:** For all Vincent Pyke's protestations, by 1880 the Haast route had been developed only as a packhorse trail. Roadbuilding was not to begin until 1929 — and then only as an unemployment relief project. Lake Hawea and Makarora were linked in 1931. In the next nine years the road was pushed through to the Gates of Haast and a wharf built at Jackson Bay to handle shipments of equipment.

Work was interrupted by the war and did not resume until 1956. Four years later Haast township was linked to Wanaka, ending a century of isolation for farmers on the coast. Many bridges were built and substantial engineering problems overcome before the difficult 56 km of the Paringa-Haast section was completed, in November 1965, a century after Pyke had travelled the pass. His "trifling expense" totalled $11 million.

The Haast Pass Road has had a dramatic effect on South Island tourism, opening up the West Coast to the motorist in a way that enables much of the Island to be encompassed by a circular route.

## POINTS OF INTEREST ON THE ROAD

*In geographical order starting from △ Wanaka. The road cuts through the north-east corner of the △ Mount Aspiring National Park.*

**The Neck** (*43 km from Wanaka; 103 km from Haast Rivermouth bridge*): The narrow strip of land dividing Lakes Wanaka and Hawea was where a branch of the ancient Hawea Glacier joined the Wanaka Glacier as together they gouged out the lake beds. At this time the ice extended as much as 1,000 m above the level of the lakes.

**Makarora** (*65 km from Wanaka; 82 km from Haast Rivermouth bridge*): The area was once densely forested with *kahikatea*, *matai* and silver beech. From the 1860s timber was felled here, pitsawn, tied into rafts, floated the length of Lake Wanaka and down the Clutha River to the embryo goldtowns of △ Cromwell and △ Clyde. There is excellent fly-fishing for brown and rainbow trout in the locality. A jetboat service operates here (*Haast Pass Tourist Service*) and a ranger station is maintained by the Mount Aspiring National Park.

**Davis Flat** (*80 km from Wanaka; 66 km from Haast Rivermouth bridge*): Here a track leads to Stewarts Creek Falls (*about 800 m; allow ½ hr return*).

**Haast Pass** (*82 km from Wanaka; 64 km from Haast Rivermouth bridge*): A plaque records the first explorers to traverse the pass. At this point the old bridle track used by cattle drovers and other early travellers runs to the east of the highway.

**Fantail Creek Falls** (*86 km from Wanaka; 60 km from Haast Rivermouth bridge*): Perhaps the most photographed and certainly the most publicised sight on the journey. Readily seen from the road.

**Gates of Haast** (*92 km from Wanaka; 54 km from Haast Rivermouth bridge*): Here the Haast River, after flowing along a level valley, drops through a gorge. The schist of the mountains is evident in the huge river boulders and the vertical walls near the bridge. Above the bridge are the remains of an earlier structure destroyed by floods in December 1957. A walk here leads upstream along the old bridle path to the Wills River, which meets the Haast in the gorge. (*About 800 m; allow ⅓ hr.*)

**Thunder Creek Falls** (*94 km from Wanaka; 52 km from Haast Rivermouth bridge*): The falls, reached through about 100 m of silver beech, drop nearly 30 m from the level of the glacier ice when, 10,000 years ago, a glacier was scooping out what was to become the bed of the Haast River. There is good fishing for brown trout between the falls and Clarke Bluff.

**Pleasant Flat** (*98 km from Wanaka; 48 km from Haast Rivermouth bridge*) and **Clarke Bluff** (*105 km and 41 km respectively*): Picturesque localities for photographer and picnicker.

**Haast Rivermouth bridge** (*146 km from Wanaka*): The 732.4 m bridge was completed in 1962 at a cost of $552,000. It comprises three 219.4 m continuous sections of Callander-Hamilton steel truss, linked by two 36.6 m two-lane passing-bay spans. The bridge, designed for a flood flow of 11,330 m$^3$/s (400,000 cusecs), stands some 3 m above the highest known flood level. Nearby **Haast township** (pop. 208) was formed as a Ministry of Works camp and has persisted as a timber town and small servicing centre though never planned as a permanent settlement.

*The coastal route north and south of this point is described under △ West Coast Road.*

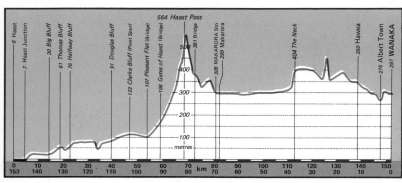

*Profile of the Haast Pass Road*

## HAMPDEN   North Otago.   Map 28.   Pop. 319.

*25 km NNE of Palmerston; 34.5 km SSW of Oamaru.*

A SEASIDE VILLAGE on Highway 1, Hampden for generations had an old fashioned common — the subject of frequently-revised bylaws which at first allowed ratepayers to graze "three head of great cattle" and gave residents the right to cut firewood. The common was sold in 1951 to raise money for a public hall. Hampden derives its name from the settlers' interest in the Civil War. Hampden was one of the Roundhead leaders.

A good beach and motor-camp attract summer holiday makers.

### SOME HISTORY

**A Keystone Cops Chase:** Hampden, once one of the country's smallest boroughs, was for a time expected to develop as a commercial centre for the port at △Moeraki, but harbour developments were ultimately won by △Oamaru. Hampden grew quickly and by 1862 had two hotels, the Hampden and the Clyde — even though today it has only the Hampden Tavern.

It was the Clyde that witnessed in 1865 the start of an at-times ludicrous episode when two ex-convicts, Alfred Davis and John Evereste, stole from the hotel a revolver, ammunition and two horses. They set off for the Waitaki, plundering as they went. At Duntroon a shot was fired when they robbed a publican, and such were the numbers of their victims that before long not one but two posses set out to capture the bushrangers. In a scene that belongs to the silent movies one posse chased the other up to Omarama — the second group in full pursuit of their quarry, the first fleeing for their lives. Once identities had been sorted out the groups returned to Otematata where they found first Evereste, exhausted and asleep, and then Davis, hiding under a bed. Davis drew a sixteen-year gaol term on a charge of attempted murder. Evereste, less culpable, received six years.

### POINTS OF INTEREST

**Hampden Museum:** A small collection includes the now-redundant mayoral chain of office (1878–1967) and a plaque from an 1878 stagecoach which was involved in a fatal crash on its last run, the day before the Dunedin–Oamaru railway line opened. *Open by arrangement.*

**Moeraki Boulders***: Unusual septarian boulders are found at Moeraki Beach (*3.4 km S*) and at Katiki Beach (*10 km S*). *Described under* △Moeraki.

### TOURING NOTES

**Coastal route north to** △**Oamaru:** By the restored stone flourmill (1879 — now a licensed restaurant and motel) just north of Waianakarua one may turn right to leave Highway 1 and follow an attractive stretch of coastline past All Day Bay and through Kakanui to Oamaru. *Described under* △Oamaru.

**Alternative route to** △**Palmerston:** One may turn off Highway 1 at 7 km south of Hampden to pass through Trotters Gorge (an enchanting picnic place) and cross the Horse Range to reach Palmerston. This provides a pleasant alternative to the main road but bypasses an interesting section of Highway 1.

## HANMER SPRINGS***   North Canterbury.   Maps 20 & 21.   Pop. 832.

*136 km N of Christchurch; 141 km SE of Reefton.*

THE MASSIVE TREES and comfortable accommodation of Hanmer Springs are a far cry from the bare tussock in which the thermal springs were first found; pools where for a number of years the only amenity was a flagpole on which was hoisted an article of apparel appropriate to the sex of those bathing there. Hanmer subsequently blossomed as a fashionable spa, where thousands came to "take the cure". With the passing of that era it has become a mellow holiday town with a firm base in forestry. Its name, deriving from Thomas Hanmer, an early settler, is commonly misspelt by transposing the middle consonants — an error extending back for over a century.

**Fishing:** There is excellent fishing in the Waiau (trout and salmon), the Clarence and also the Acheron, Boyle, Hope and Lake Tennyson.

### A MAORI LEGEND

**The fire of Tamatea:** The hot springs were known to the Maori, who in local legend linked them with the sending of fire from Hawaiki to warm the fabled Ngatoroirangi as he lay freezing on the summit of Ngauruhoe in the central North Island. After the fire had erupted from Ngauruhoe's volcanic ridge it rolled down the surface of the land to burn out the channel of the Wanganui River. Reaching the sea, the fire rose into the air, making for Banks Peninsula. A piece of the fire dropped from the sky at Hanmer to form the origin of the hot springs here. Another piece ploughed a black mark along a ridge at the head of Lyttelton Harbour that was known to the Maori as Te Whaka-takanga-o-te-ngarehu-o-te-ahi-a-Tamatea (the falling of the embers of the fire of Tamatea).

## SOME HISTORY

**"Taking the cure":** William Jones, manager of a run near Culverden, is generally regarded as the *Pakeha* discoverer of the springs. In April 1859 he investigated what at first seemed to be "a remarkable fog". He aroused interest in the area, but twenty years later there was only a crude dressing shed here. Local tradition has it that a pair of trousers hoisted on a pole indicated "men only". A skirt denoted the opposite.

As the springs grew in popularity, facilities improved with a sanatorium opening in 1914, whose manager was officially instructed that "Old and Decrepit Guests May Have Their Meals In Bed". The "cure" comprised early nights, regular walks to enjoy the invigorating air (Hanmer is 366 m above sea level), daily bathing and regular drinking of the waters. A massage department offered vigorous treatment, with rubbing and pummelling for those anxious to restrict their girths. The sanatorium burnt to the ground in 1914 and in its stead was built Queen Mary Hospital (1916) as a convalescent hospital for the wounded and invalid of the 1914–18 war.

Queen Mary Hospital continued with hydrotherapy and the treatment of functional nervous disorders until 1971, since when it has concentrated on the treatment of alcoholics. *A New Zealand Historic Places Trust plaque near the bath house records the discovery of the springs for Europeans by William Jones.*

**Full House:** A second Historic Places Trust noticeboard (*a short distance along Jollies Pass Road*) records that Edward James Lee and Edward Jollie in March 1852 reached the pass with 1,800 sheep, the first flock to be driven south from the Wairau by the inland route explored by Lee the previous December. A large proportion of the flocks that stocked the Canterbury runs came this way.

The Nelson Provincial Government in 1862 established a small cob accommodation house at the foot of Jollies Pass. It was destroyed by fire in 1927. Tradition records that in its licensee's eyes the house was never full — if the top of the billiard table was booked there remained available the floor beneath.

**Champagne Flat:** The bridge over the Waiau by which Hanmer is approached dates from 1886, built to replace an earlier bridge (1864–74) that perished in a particularly blustery nor'wester. The contractors marked the opening of the bridge in 1887 with hospitality on such a lavish scale that the name Champagne Flat is still given to the site of the refreshment marquee. The Ferry Accommodation House (1875) still stands near the river. (Known as Lochiel, it serves as a farmstead.)

## THINGS TO SEE AND DO

**Thermal pools** within the grounds of Queen Mary Hospital are open to the public daily. These are to be replaced by a modern complex financed by local fund-raising efforts and a Government grant. The soft blend of fairly saline water contains a little alkaline carbonate and some lithium. Principal ingredients are sodium chloride and sodium borate. Methane gas from the springs has been tapped for heating. Prolonged immersion was considered beneficial for chronic arthritic diseases and certain skin ailments. *Enter from Jacks Pass Road, diagonally opposite the post office.*

**Conical Hill\*\*\*:** A short walk zigzags to the summit for the view over the varied shades of Hanmer Forest, particularly colourful in autumn. In the distance the Waiau River curls across the Waiau Plain. A plaque records the contribution to Hanmer's development made by Duncan Rutherford of Leslie Hills. *Start from end of Conical Rd. Road access available with a permit from the forest headquarters.*

**Hanmer Forest\*\*** dates from 1902 when for the first of many years convict labour was used to establish plantations. As in other early forestry areas, a wide variety of species was planted on a trial-and-error basis by European foresters uncertain of the district's potential. Unlike some other areas, at Hanmer many of these species flourished with the result that today Hanmer boasts the largest number of different exotic species in the country — a statistic lent colour and vibrance in autumn. Over the years the forest area has grown steadily. Later plantings have been predominantly of *radiata* pine and Douglas fir. Annual production exceeds 28,000 m3 of sawn logs, principally for the Christchurch market, and about 6,300 m3 of poles and fencing materials. Selected areas of the forest are open to the public. Two forest walks begin from Jollies Pass Road and lead through widely varied stands of exotics. The No. 1 walk in part follows the old coach road to Jollies Pass. (*No permit needed; pamphlets are available at the Forest headquarters. Both walks are signposted.*)

A 13-km drive through the centre of the forest has also been opened (*a permit is required, issued from the Forest headquarters, 2.1 km on Jollies Pass Rd. The drive is generally open daily but may be closed on winter weekends and in exceptional conditions.*)

Hunting blocks are open to shooters. (*Details from Forest headquarters.*)

**Some other viewpoints:** More elevated but less wide views than those from Conical Hill are obtained from both Jacks Pass Rd and Jollies Pass Rd. An unparalleled vantage point is the fire lookout on a hill halfway to the summit of Jollies Pass (*a short walk from the road — the road itself can be in very poor condition. Enquire locally*). A much longer walk follows a recently opened subalpine track on Mt. Isobel from the summit of which magnificent views are obtained. Information should be obtained from Forest headquarters, particularly in winter when the higher reaches may be under snow or fog.

## ENVIRONS

**Old Accommodation House, Acheron River:** The drive over Jacks Pass enters the tussocklands of Molesworth station and follows the bare-banked Clarence downriver before crossing to the single-storeyed cob accommodation house. The drive ends at the locked gate which leads on through Molesworth. *A round trip can be made by returning by way of Jollies Pass, but this route is at present not recommended for the average vehicle. Jollies Pass may be closed in favour of Jacks Pass. 27 km to the accommodation house.*

**Molesworth station:** The 182,000 ha of the Molesworth station comprise the country's largest single holding. From 1852 successive runholders grazed huge numbers of sheep on the vast property until the combined effects of over-grazing, burning, snow losses, and particularly rabbits, saw the giant run abandoned to the Crown in 1938. A determined assault on the rabbits, coupled with a switch to cattle, brought profitability to Molesworth by 1961. *Access usually from Blenheim via Seddon. Unrestricted access to some 32,380 ha; remainder usually closed to the public except for organised tours in summer.*

**Lake Tennyson:** A slow but interesting drive leads over Jacks Pass to follow the Clarence upriver to its source at Lake Tennyson, a favoured fishing and picnicking place. *40 km. 1½ hrs one way.*

**Some picnic places:** There are many picnic places round Hanmer, including areas on the forest walks and forest drive. There is safe swimming for children in the Hanmer River, though deeper holes are found in the Clarence on the way to Lake Tennyson.

**Amuri Ski Club** operates a skifield with two rope tows on Mt St Patrick (*1,649.5 m*), *19.2 km from Hanmer. Enquire locally.*

## ORGANISED EXCURSIONS

**Horse treks** lead through Hanmer Forest and the surrounding country; trekking holidays and riding lessons are also available. *Hanmer Trekking Centre, Jacks Pass Rd, tel. 7097. Open Aug.-May.*

**Scenic flights** over the Alps and the North Canterbury plains operate out of Hanmer airport by arrangement with the Canterbury Aero Club. *Tel 588-234 Christchurch.*

## TOURING NOTES

**Route to Christchurch:** The route to Christchurch as far as △Waipara is described under the entry for △Lewis Pass Road.

**Rainbow route to Tophouse:** Rather than cross the △Lewis Pass and travel through △Murchison, an alternative if rugged route to Tophouse (and so to △Nelson Lakes National Park, Nelson or Blenheim) follows for some 50 km the western boundary of the vast Molesworth station. The road runs up the Clarence River valley, which provides summer grazing for Molesworth stock. Lake Tennyson is passed, where fishing, boating and swimming can be enjoyed, and some 16 km farther on fishermen can leave their cars to walk about 2 km in to the small Tarndale lakes. Highway 63 is joined at 11.5 km east of St Arnaud and 83 km south-west of Blenheim. *Leave Hanmer by Jacks Pass. The route crosses private land, passes through numerous gates and crosses several fords. It is suitable only in dry weather. The road is maintained by the Electricity Department to a standard only sufficient to meet its own requirements. Permission should be obtained from the owner of Rainbow station, through which the road also passes (tel. 402X Wakefield). The occasional locked gate is generally opened on request. 103 km. 3½ hrs driving time to Tophouse.*

## HAUROKO (Lake)**     Fiordland.   Map 12.

*98.5 km NW of Invercargill; 31 km W of Clifden. Hunting permits and track advice from the ranger station, Fiordland National Park, Clifden.*

THOUGH LAKE HAUROKO is not very well known, it lies in a beautifully wild setting between bush clad slopes that become more precipitous as one travels up the lake. Its name (sounding wind) is apt, as the lake is open to winds from both north and south. Care must be exercised by boat users, as there is little shelter. Red deer are found throughout the area, pigs to the south and south-east. There is a camping area about 6 km from the lake by the boundary of △Fiordland National Park.

**Mary Island:** On Mary Island in 1967 a fine example of a Maori cave burial was discovered. The remains, supported in an upright position by *manuka* stakes, are those of a Maori woman of high rank who died in about 1660. A steel grille preserves the *tapu* of the burial ground.

## SOME WALKS AND TRAMPS

**Bush walk:** A 20-minute bush walk leads from the picnic shelter to the road's end.

**Lookout Bluff:** The track follows the lake's edge before climbing steeply to a bluff about halfway up Oblong Hill. *2½ hrs return.*

**Boundary Track:** To reach a secluded beach, follow the lake's shore south to the start of a track that leads over a small peninsula. *4 hrs return.*

**Dusky Sound:** The three-day tramp to Supper Cove on Dusky Sound starts at the Hauroko Burn, at the head of the lake. *Refer to* Moir's Guide (Southern Section). *Further details from the Park Headquarters at* △ *Te Anau and from the ranger at* △*Clifden.*

---

**HAVELOCK**\*\*    Marlborough.    Maps 6, 22 & 26.    Pop. 290.

*76 km E of Nelson; 70 km W of Picton (via Blenheim); 41 km NW of Blenheim.*

HAVELOCK WEARS a peaceful, time-honoured air as she sits at the head of Pelorus Sound contemplating her expansive past. Ideally sited to become a busy centre serving the delightful cruising arms of Pelorus, Mahau, Kenepuru and Tennyson Inlet, Havelock has so far escaped the boom which has so altered Picton. Pelorus Sound boasts excellent sea-fishing, and the Rai and Pelorus Rivers offer freshwater sport for the angler. The local fishing fleet lands succulent scallops.

**Camping:** Arrangements can be made with local launch proprietors for campers as well as day-picnickers to be landed on and collected from reserves round the Marlborough Sounds and to be supplied with provisions at regular intervals during their stay. *Details of reserves and camping permits from the Department of Lands and Survey, Box 97, Blenheim (see also △Marlborough Sounds).*

### SOME HISTORY

**No flash in the pan:** Negotiations for the purchase of the Pelorus district opened in 1851, Governor Grey noting that the area "is regarded by the inhabitants of Nelson as essential to the prosperity of their settlement." Once completed, Commissioner McLean reported that "the Ngatikaua . . . now reduced in numbers to about 50 souls were, after making provision for reserves and cultivation, paid £100 for the extinction of their remaining title, with which sum they appeared well satisfied, it being the first time since their conquest by Te Rauparaha that their claim had in any way been recognised."

The town sparked to life in 1864 on the site of a Maori *kainga* with the discovery of gold at Wakamarina. Unlike many goldtowns its virile birth was matched by growth, for though the gold proved shortlived, the local timber did not. There was a bridle track from here, over the Maungatapu Mountain to Nelson, to whose natural dangers of river crossings was added in 1866 the grisly recollection of the Maungatapu murders (*see* △Nelson).

### LAUNCH TRIPS\*\*\*

Launches leave regularly on day-long trips delivering mail and stores round the reaches of the sound to farmers, bach-owners, and campers. Most popular are the trips to Tennyson Inlet and to Titirangi. Before campers are ferried to camping places they may be asked to produce evidence of the consent of either a farmer or of the Department of Lands and Survey. *Book with J. W. Jones, 42A Wither Rd, Blenheim, tel. 7412. A launch leaves on one of the routes on most weekday mornings.* Fishing and picnic parties are taken out by arrangement.

### OTHER THINGS TO SEE AND DO

**Havelock Museum**\*: Housed in the former St John's Methodist Church, the displays feature the district's interest in gold, timber and illicit liquor (by the "bush still" is a letter of caution from the Customs Department). Honour-roll plaques from the local school trace Lord Rutherford's scholastic career. Outside is an old Saddleback bush engine (1894) which hauled many logs down the Pelorus Valley. *Main St. Open daily.*

**Town walk:** A short walk up the hill behind the township leads through native bush to the local waterworks, whence there is an excellent view of the town and the sounds. A little distance above the dam, the track runs into the creek where at night the opposite cliff-face can be spangled with glow-worms. *Start behind the Garden Motels.*

**Rutherford Youth Hostel:** The old Havelock school has been converted into a large youth hostel and named after the school's most famous pupil, Baron Rutherford of Nelson (*see index*). Another distinguished former pupil is Dr William Pickering, a leading scientist in space exploration in the United States. *Cnr Main St and Lawrence St.*

**Post Office** (1875): The quaint gabled post office has an ecclesiastical appearance which appears to be the only foundation for the tradition that it was originally designed as a church. *Main St.*

## ENVIRONS

**Canvastown** (pop. 132-locality): Credit for the first discovery of gold in the Waka-marina River is given to one Elizabeth Pope, who is said to have found the precious metal accidentally in 1860 while rinsing her sawmiller husband's shirts in the river. The locality was rushed four years later when reports of payable gold being found by Rutlands, Harris and Wilson at Mountain Camp Creek (*marked by a memorial*) led to scenes described in the *Nelson Examiner*: "As I returned to Nelson yesterday from the Pelorus the 32 miles of road teemed with parties rushing for gold. Some, who were old hands, were well equipped. Others, green as the foliage around them, toiled under loads which in their ordinary transactions they would not have attempted to carry along a level road." In a single day a thousand people arrived at the locality of which the *Examiner* wrote: "A number of canvas houses . . . some are bell shaped but many have wooden frames and are of no inconsiderable size." People poured in; gold poured out. But within a month the field was on the wane. Floods washed diggers out of their claims and so disheartened many that they left the field entirely. The rush was over by the end of 1865, but gold continued to be won for many years, though a great deal of work was done for little return. Attempts to work the mines continued well into the present century.

It was gold from the Wakamarina diggings that led to the deaths of four men in the Maungatapu murders, one of the worst recorded incidents on a New Zealand goldfields (*see page 228*).

A roadside memorial incorporates miscellaneous pieces of mining equipment. The predecessor of St Paul's Anglican Church (1910) was built for use by the more persistent of the diggers. *10 km W of Havelock on Highway 6.*

**Cullens Point Lookout:** A spectacular view of the lower Pelorous Sound, Havelock and the Kaituna Valley extends on clear days to the prominent peaks of the Inland Kaikoura Range. *Take Linkwater turnoff 0.85 km S on main highway. Signposted.*

△**Marlborough Sounds*****: The general area is described under this entry.

## TOURING NOTES

**Road to** △**Nelson:** Highway 6 passes Canvastown (*at 10 km*), the attractive bush reserve at Pelorus Bridge (*19 km*) and the settlement of Rai Valley (*at 27 km*).

At Rai Valley cheese may be bought from the dairy factory and bread from a bakery with a national reputation for the tasty and the unusual. Detours may be made to a pioneer cottage and to historic French Pass (*see index*) the scene of Dumont d'Urville's epic passage in 1827. From Rai Valley the road winds through bush over the Rai Saddle and the Whangamoa Saddle before descending to Nelson.

**Road to** △**Picton:** Though a map would seem to suggest otherwise, Highway 6 to △Blenheim provides the quickest route to Picton (*for details, see* △*Blenheim, "Touring Notes"*). The picturesque coastal Queen Charlotte Drive to Picton (*37 km*) is described under Picton, "Suggested Drives".

---

**HEAPHY TRACK*****        Map 32.

*Between Bainham and Karamea. Detailed map and hut particulars are published by the Department of Lands and Survey. Start 16 km from Karamea or 14 km from Bainham. No permit is needed except for firearms. Trampers should notify their itineraries to the nearest New Zealand Forest Service ranger, who can advise on track conditions; also, report back to him immediately on completing the journey. Though the walk over easy grades rising to about 900 m can be made in light footwear, boots are strongly recommended.*

ONE OF THE FINEST walks there is links Golden Bay with the West Coast. Between four and six days are usually allowed for the tramp, the longest section of which is the 7-hour stretch of some 24 km between Brown Hut and Goulands Downs Hut. The best time to make the walk is in February and March.

From the north-east the route winds through magnificent stands of native forest, an expansive area of red tussock country (the Gouland Downs) and further bush before reaching the coast. There luxuriant ferns and groves of *nikau* palms impart a tropical air. An abundance of birdlife may be seen, including the South Island *kiwi* and the blue mountain duck. Deer are scarce.

The track is named after Charles Heaphy VC, draughtsman to the New Zealand Company from 1840, who though he made a number of exploratory trips in the district, never in fact made this traverse. Instead, with Thomas Brunner in 1846 he took the longer passage round the coast. The first to follow the route was James Mackay (*see index*) in 1860, returning from land purchase negotiations with Maoris at △Greymouth. It was developed as a pack track for prospectors. For the long term, a controversial road has been proposed to link Karamea with Golden Bay, which would follow the exquisite coastal section and part of the inland route.

*Note: In all seasons trampers should be prepared for all weathers. There have been floods and even snowstorms over the Christmas period.*

**HOKITIKA\*\*     Westland.    Maps 2, 15, 17 & 37.    Pop. 3,530.**

*45.6 km SW of Greymouth; 290 km NE of Haast Junction. Westland Public Relations Office, Weld St, tel. 1115 (after hours 1232).*

THE "CAPITAL OF THE GOLDFIELDS" now has an economy based on the trees of Westland's vast forests, on the grass of neighbouring alluvial flats, and on the processing of minerals (including greenstone). Symbol of the affectionately named "Hoki" is the Romanesque tower of its St Mary's Catholic Church, rising to dominate the townscape and to embody the predominantly Irish nature of the goldfields. Inland rises the endless chain of mountains that isolated the West Coast to a degree that only the discovery of gold could overcome. As a former capital in times of provincial government (Westland enjoyed a brief period of independence from Canterbury before the provincial system was abolished), Hokitika retains a number of the governmental offices that administer the Westland region, though it is now only half the size of Greymouth.

Lying at the mouth of the Hokitika River, the town had one of the country's foremost ports, remembered now only by a long disused lighthouse on the cliff at Seaview and by disintegrating timberwork at the rivermouth. So obscure was the area before the goldrushes of 1864–65 that even the river's name was uncertain. Hokitika, Okitiki and Otatika were all in common use until the Post Office standardised the spelling. The meaning of Hokitika (*hoki* = to return; *tika* = in a straight line) has been interpreted in a variety of ways.

## GREENSTONE

**The legend of greenstone:** In local tradition there lived in Hawaiki the chief Ngahue, a daring navigator who was driven from his homeland by a woman, Hine-tu-a-hoanga, who invoked the aid of a great green *taniwha* (water monster), Poutini (literally, a star) to capture him. The monster hotly pursued the chief's sailing canoe until at last Ngahue saw the stupendous mountain of Aorangi (Mt Cook) beckoning to him and commanding him to sail north. Arriving at the mouth of the Arahura River (*about 6.4 km N of Hokitika*), Ngahue watched as the sun hid her face, to cover the land in shadow save only for the gleaming icefields of Tara-o-Tama at the river's source.

With the *taniwha* close behind, the navigator read the omen as a sign to make his way inland. The watermonster pursued him up the river until he reached a deep rock pool at the foot of fearful rapids. There the *taniwha* was injured, and sank to the bottom to be transformed into greenstone. The thankful Ngahue, attracted by the beauty and hardness of other greenstone in the pool, selected a block and carried it back to his canoe at the rivermouth. To the north the sky was bright, to the south and west it was dark and forbidding. By this Ngahue knew it was then safe for him to return home.

Arriving back at Hawaiki with his precious greenstone, he found his people at war, people to whom he described the riches of the uninhabited land he had visited. His kinsfolk, tired of strife, fashioned two sharp axes from the greenstone. With these they felled seven huge trees from which were hewn the canoes *Arawa, Tainui, Mataatua, Takitimu, Kurahaupo, Tokomaru* and *Matuwhaorua*. (*The legend is not consistent with other accounts of Ngahue and it is likely that at least the ending, which would support the long-debated "fleet" theory of Polynesian migration, is an embellishment dating only from European times. The legends of other tribes have Ngahue accompanying Kupe.*)

**Tamatea and his wives:** Other accounts relate differing origins of greenstone, perhaps the best known of which, the legend of Tamatea, explains the reason why differing types of greenstone are found in different parts of the South Island.

Tamatea (or Tamatea-pokai-whenua) was either deserted by his three wives or they were abducted by Poutini. One he found at Anita Bay (at Milford Sound), turned into greenstone. As he wept, his tears entered the stone to give it the characteristic flecks as well as the name of *tangiwai* (water of weeping). Her children had clambered over the ranges inland, so explaining the presence of greenstone near Lake Wakatipu.

Travelling north, Tamatea heard voices from the Arahura River valley, attracting him inland. Near the Kaniere Mountains he stopped to cook some birds, but when his servant Tumuaki burnt his fingers and put them in his mouth to ease the pain, he was breaching *tapu*. So Tamatea was not to find his other wives who, like Hine-tangiwai, had been turned into greenstone, of the types *auhanga* and *pounamu*. Some of the most revered greenstone contains flaws, known as *tutae-koka* (*tutae* = excrement; *koka* = seabird of the type that Tumuaki was cooking).

**Some notes on greenstone:** The term greenstone is applied in New Zealand to both nephrite (jade) and bowenite. The stone, which took the place of hard metals in the Maoris' stone culture, was used for making adzes and chisels as well as the famed fighting axe, the *patu pounamu*. Ornaments included ear pendants and the renowned *hei-tiki*.

Nephrite is found in the Taramakau-Arahura region as river boulders washed down from parent rock deposits some 1,200 m up on the Griffin and Tera Ranges. Some is also found in the Wakatipu region. Bowenite (lighter in colour and by the Maori termed *tangiwai*) is found at Anita Bay in Milford Sound.

# HOKITIKA AND DISTRICT

## 17

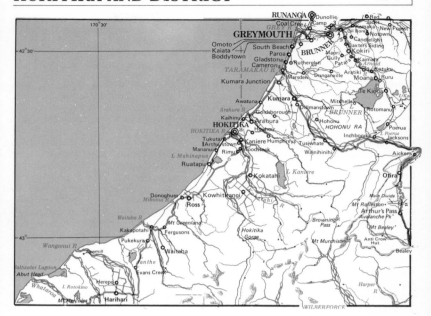

Three Hokitika firms process local greenstone into jewellery, bringing blocks in by helicopter from mineral claims in the exceptionally rugged mountains, or quarrying the stone in old river terraces. The stone is so hard that diamond saws are used to cut it. A profitable local hobby is to scavenge for greenstone at weekends, particularly after floods and sudden freshes, for a good boulder can be worth as much as $22 per kilo. The stone is not, however, readily recognisable in its raw state by those unfamiliar with it. For example, the famed Nicholson boulder, which reputedly weighed as much as 3,720 kilos, had for some time been used in ignorance for river catchment work.

To protect the greenstone deposits, the export of raw, unworked stone is prohibited by law. *One may see the working of greenstone from raw block to highly-polished finished article at the Westland Greenstone Co. (near museum in Tancred St, Hokitika, tel. 713), at the Hokitika Jade Co. (110 Revell St, tel. 363) and Howe Holdings Ltd. (Revell St.)*

### SOME HISTORY

**The greenstone country:** Ancient Maori trails to the greenstone country converged on Hokitika from the south via △Haast Pass, and from the east by way of the Browning and Whitcombe Passes.

Prized though greenstone was — the South Island itself was known as Te Wahi Pounamu (the place of greenstone) — the area's permanent Maori occupation seems never to have been large. Indeed, the many parties that set out in search of the precious stone raided the *pa* at the mouth of the Arahura River, in the heart of the greenstone district, time and time again. In 1857 James Mackay noted a meagre eighty-seven Maoris on the Coast, "taking all the pahs from [Little] Wanganui to Foveaux Straits". Small though their numbers were, the Poutini Ngaitahu were careful to exclude the areas they considered most important from their sale of Westland, negotiated with Mackay. Some 1,215 ha comprised the largest of the reserves, covering the lower course of the Arahura, their principal source of greenstone.

In tradition the Ngati Wairangi tribe had migrated here, to live in peace and isolation as they tapped the virtues of the stone. Then came the fateful day when the demented Raureka wandered up the Hokitika River and crossed into the Mackenzie country by Browning Pass, there to ridicule the tools the recently-arrived Ngaitahu were using to build a canoe. She introduced them to greenstone, whose superiority they were quick to acknowledge. For a time Ngaitahu were content to trade for supplies of the stone, but at length war flared, Ngati Wairangi were crushed, and for the first of many times the Arahura *pa* was looted. Ultimately Ngati Wairangi ceased to exist as a separate tribe and were absorbed into Ngaitahu, or Poutini Ngaitahu as the *hapu* here became known.

The point has been made that the story of Raureka has been widely misunderstood. Archaeology establishes the widespread use of greenstone long before the time of this incident, and it seems that the significance of the story lies not in the discovery of greenstone by Ngaitahu but in the finding by Ngati Wairangi of a new and easy route into Canterbury.

Te Rauparaha (*see index*) sent a war party south in 1828 under Niho, in the belief that there was a great store of greenstone at the Arahura *pa*. Though they took the *pa*, they found no stone. The *taua* returned north, not empty handed but with the chief Tuhuru (father of Werita Tainui who was later to sell the West Coast to the *Pakeha*) and ransomed him for the fabled *mere* Kai-kanohi. The district had not seen the last of Te Atiawa and Ngati Toa, for eight years later another war party, under Te Puoho, followed the coast down from Golden Bay as far as Haast, killing and destroying as they went only to be annihilated at △ Mataura when they had crossed into Southland.

**European discoverers:** Abel Tasman sailed up the coast in 1642, noting "a great land uplifted high", and an unimpressed Cook described Westland as "an inhospitable shore, unworthy of observation, except for its ridge of naked and barren rocks covered with snow. As far as the eye could reach the prospect was wild, craggy and desolate."

Cook's gloomy description was borne out by the explorers, among them Charles Heaphy, who described a visit in 1846 to the small *pa* at Taramakau: "We found here six men and about fifteen women, with a large proportion of children," he noted. "The inmates of each house were busily engaged in making [*mere*] pounamu and ear pendants of that material, for 'trade' or presents to the northward. They saw the slab with a piece of mica slate, wet, and afterwards polish it with a fine sandy limestone [a calcareous sandstone that overlays the Brunner coal seams] which they obtain in the vicinity. The hole is drilled with a stick pointed with a piece of Pahutani flint. The process does not appear so tedious as has been supposed; a month sufficing, apparently, for the completion of a [*mere*] out of the rough but appropriately shapen slab. . . . A native will get up at night to have a polish at a favourite [*mere*], or take one down to the beach and work away by the surf. A piece of greenstone and some slate will be carried when travelling, and at every halt a rub will be taken at it."

Wrote Henry Harper in 1861 of the near impenetrable forest that was Westland: "I doubt if such a wilderness will ever be colonised except through the discovery of gold."

**"The most rising place on earth":** Within two years of Harper's musings a little gold had been found in the Taramakau district, and surveys begun. By the following year the Canterbury provincial government was considering abandoning the West Coast surveys when William Revell (after whom the town's main street is named), the government's agent on the Coast, told of his conviction of the presence of payable gold.

In July came the rush to the Greenstone Creek after two Mawhera (Greymouth) Maoris had stumbled on gold while searching for greenstone. The *Pakeha* they told soon confirmed the richness of the field and the town of △ Greymouth began to take shape. By the end of the year further fields were found to the south and Hokitika was rapidly emerging on a bleak sandspit on the rivermouth.

The storekeepers John Hudson and James Price erected the first makeshift store in October 1864 (*the site is marked in Gibson Quay*). They were soon joined by others, but the cost of transporting provisions down the beach from Greymouth was high and the diggers — who could measure the worth of the field only against the cost of provisions — tended to drift north again. The first ship to brave the rivermouth, the SS *Nelson* in December 1864, was thus a local heroine as by doing so she more than halved the freight rate and triggered a demand for allotments in the town.

Then came the big rushes to the fabulous fields of Waimea, Kaniere and △ Ross. Miners poured into the area both by sea and by land. About 6,000 arrived in March 1865 alone — most from the Otago diggings — and early in April came the start of the "Australian invasion" with an influx of diggers from Victoria. That same month Julius von Haast visited to report: "When we at last entered that city of yesterday, we could not conceal our astonishment that, in so short a time of only a few months, such a large place could have sprung up — the principal street, half a mile long, consisted already of a large number of shops, hotels, banks and dwelling-houses, and appeared as a scene of almost indescribable bustle and activity."

Estimates of the town's early population fluctuate wildly. Some suggest numbers that run into tens of thousands, but Philip Ross May, in his definitive work on *The West Coast Gold Rushes* (Pegasus) accepts as reasonably accurate the census figures of 4,866 for Hokitika in 1867 and an estimate of 6,000 for its resident population at the peak of the previous year (the figures would not reflect the great numbers on the surrounding diggings). The West Coast's European population was put at over 25,884, almost 12 per cent of the country's total.

The boom waned as suddenly as it began. The last real rush on the Coast was in May 1867, to Addisons Flat near Westport, and even at that time the alluvial deposits were showing signs of exhaustion. Many independent prospectors moved off to the newly-proclaimed fields on the Coromandel Peninsula, leaving it for the adventure to become an industry as larger groups and combines constructed water-races to sluice payable ground. As sluicing returns too, declined, came the boom in dredging. In 1903 there were some sixty-three gold dredges on the Coast. The last of the local dredges, the *Kaniere* (built in 1938), was latterly working at △ Kumara.

In the years 1865–67 alone, over 1.3 million ounces of gold were exported from the Coast, then worth in excess of £5.2 million. Until 1895 the West Coast remained the country's chief gold-producing region.

**Running the blockade:** "A stranger visiting Hokitika for the first time would be struck with astonishment at the multitude of wrecks and remains of wrecks with which the beach is covered." So editorialised the *West Coast Times* in 1865 at a time when it was common for Hokitika to have a dozen vessels stranded ashore at any one time and when the newspaper, in addition to the usual shipping notices, had a special and oft-filled column captioned "Vessels Ashore". The volume of shipping was heavy; the waterfront was crowded four deep, vessels were turned round inside two days, and within minutes of a departure an empty berth was reallocated. In one five-day period no fewer than forty-two vessels crossed the bar, and on one momentous spring day nineteen sailing vessels either entered or left the port, most of them bound for overseas. These were heady days indeed. In 1864 the Hokitika River had been no more than an uncertain name on a map, yet in three hectic years its unpredictable rivermouth had blossomed into the country's busiest port.

But the casualties were many. Ships had to enter through a narrow, S-shaped channel at so sharp an angle that unless there was a good breeze, a sailing vessel could not preserve sufficient steerage way through the rollers to round the corner of the spit. A ship would often "drop bodily off before the sea, and two or three tremendous seas lift her broadside on to the beach, there to be pounded to pieces by the following tides". Little wonder, then, that crowds would watch as the vessels "ran the blockade", often betting among themselves on the chances of a ship going ashore. Auctioneers and beachcombers abounded, and there was as well a thriving trade in refloating the beached boats — raising them with screwjacks and running them down greased inclines into the river for as much as £1,000 a time. As wreck followed wreck, Melbourne insurance companies steadily increased premiums until they reached five times the rate charged for vessels trading between Melbourne and Brisbane — a longer voyage. Finally risks were absolutely declined and the trade with Australian ports was greatly reduced. Eventually a towing service was provided which, coupled with the lessons of the past, saw the port achieve a measure of dependability, and by 1867 the 1865 Dunedin freight rate of £12 a ton had dropped to £2 10s.

Not only shipping suffered, for the capricious river with its floods and heavy freshes ate into the sand of the North Spit where many merchants had built, and before steps were taken to check the river's encroachment £10,000 worth of stores and shanties had toppled into the water. Today only traces of the wharf piles and breastwork remain, towards the end of once-busy Gibson Quay. Similar signs of protection works on the tip of the south spit also survive.

The port closed in 1954.

**An underworked gold escort:** Anxious to see all it could of the precious metal, Christchurch agitated for the establishment of an overland gold escort to discourage the shipping of gold north to Nelson. Hokitika warned that the banks would never trust an escort forced to cross such wild country but, lashed by Christchurch newspapers, the Provincial Council hurriedly got together a string of stations across the Arthur's Pass route, and furnished them with men, changes of horses, weapons and twelve splendid gold boxes. In December 1865 the gold escort set out from Christchurch in triumph, to arrive at Hokitika 4½ days later "jaded and mud-splattered". Their departure for their return to Christchurch contrasted with the fanfares accorded them on the east coast, for it was marked by only laughter and derision. The escort was carrying a pitiful 15 pennyweight of gold — less than a single ounce — perhaps the most expensive gold ever carried anywhere. A full £12,014 15s 5d had been spent in setting up the escort, which was disbanded after its solitary trip.

As a chastened Christchurch reflected on the cost, it was obvious that whatever the risks involved, sea passage was infinitely less expensive than the costly coaches. The forging of the Arthur's Pass road could be seen as a luxury for the stock that were driven along it, for no great flow of merchandise rolled to and from Christchurch. The Coast's gold continued to leave by sea and its supplies to come inward by the same route. Bemoaned the Christchurch *Press:* "Fortune has seldom been in a more perverse and freakish mood than when she bestowed upon Canterbury the exceedingly equivocal blessing of the West Coast goldfields."

Moves were soon afoot that led to the emergence of Westland as a separate self-governing province, moves motivated by Hokitika's opposition to goldfields revenue being spent on a road it never really wanted, and moves that the disappointed Christchurch was not inclined to oppose. As gold output declined the district diversified into timbermilling, farming and coalmining. The mushroom cities with their numerous saloons and stores settled down into homely townships.

**Kokatahi Band:** The Kokatahi Band sprang from goldrush nostalgia in about 1910. It comprises an unlikely collection of farmers and timberworkers with not a miner among them, dressed in red shirts, black bandanas and white moleskin trousers and playing an improbable collection of instruments from the bones to the "lagerphone". Their cheerful cacophony has taken them throughout the country and beyond, all the while a folklore building up about the band's capacity for beer. The band, it is said, can be diverted from an engagement by any publican anxious to drum up trade; once, after playing at Kumara (about 35 km away) some members are reputed to have taken a full week to make the journey home.

(A fondness for copious quantities of alcohol is deeply entrenched in the Coast's mythology if entirely lacking any basis in reality.)

## THINGS TO SEE AND DO

**West Coast Historical Museum**\*\*: A comprehensive collection of gold-mining equipment provides the predominant theme for a town founded on the discovery of alluvial gold. Scale models portray methods of gold recovery, ranging from the deep shaft of the Ross United Gold Mining Co. to a working bucket dredge. Maori working of greenstone, sketches by the explorer C. A. Douglas and a large photograph collection illustrate events on the West Coast over the centuries, a prison cell reflecting the era when Hokitika had a vigorous male population and over 100 hotels. A Victoria Cross, won by Samuel Mitchell at the battle of Gate Pa, Tauranga, in 1864, and a piece of "red cloth" given to a Tongan chief by Captain Cook and subsequently presented to Premier R. J. Seddon are prize exhibits. *Open Mon.–Fri. from 9.30 am–4.30 pm, Sat., Sun. and statutory holidays from 2–4 pm. Extended hours during holiday seasons.*

**Gibson Quay** runs to the sea along the northern bank of the Hokitika River, once the scene of intense shipping activity. An Historic Places marker (*at the junction with Revell St*) records the site of Hudson & Price's first store. At the quay's end may be seen surf breaking on the bar and the rotting remains of the harbour's wharves and timberwork. This is a good spot from which to savour the grandeur of the mountains at sunset.

**Statues:** The former provincial capital has three white marble statues; of an old goldminer making an indeterminate gesture (*on Highway 6*); of Richard Seddon (*see index*) for twenty-seven years the district's Member of Parliament, here looking less flamboyant than his portrayal in Wellington's Parliament grounds (*in front of the Government Buildings, Sewell St*); and of the Scottish poet, Robert Burns (*Cass Sq.*). Burns, who here in a predominantly Irish community has lost his nose, has no fewer than three statues in New Zealand, all in the South Island.

**St Mary's Catholic Church** (1914)\*: Of Romanesque design and dominating the Hokitika townscape is the most substantial church building on the West Coast. The interior includes a marble altar, pulpit, communion rail and fonts. The Stations of the Cross are all in oils. The church stands on the site of the former St Mary's, built in 1865 as the second Catholic church to be established on the Coast. *Sewell St.*

**Seaview**\*: At the entrance to Seaview Hospital stands the *kauri* base of a **lighthouse** (1879) that held a dioptric light fuelled by gas from the town supply. The light was closed in 1925. Close by, where from the lip of terrace there is an excellent view, rises a tall **obelisk** to commemorate four early casualties on the Coast — Charles Townsend, the government agent drowned at Greymouth in 1863; George Dobson (*see index*) in 1866 a victim of the infamous Sullivan gang; Charlton Howitt, an explorer who drowned in Lake Brunner in 1863; and Henry Whitcombe (*see index*) who in the same year drowned in the Taramakau River shortly after crossing from Canterbury by the pass that now bears his name. Beside the obelisk is a **cemetery,** whose early headstones, like the plinth, record the toll exacted from the diggers and their families. *Seaview Hospital. Signposted N on Highway 6.*

**Plane table**\* identifies a number of the features visible from the viewpoint, Mts Cook and Tasman, Whitcombe Pass and Clarkes Pass among them. *1 km. On road to airport. Signposted from Highway 6.* This is another good place from which to view the play of the setting sun on the snow tipped ranges.

**Some factories:** Greenstone processing factories may be visited (*see above*). A glass-blowing factory also welcomes visitors. (*Lower Revell St, tel. 1261*).

**Glow-worm dell**\*\*: An evening visit to a well-bushed bank reveals in the utter blackness thousands of pricks of light used by the worms to attract tiny insects to the sticky lines they drape down to snare their food. *Signposted N on Highway 6. A torch is useful.*

---

The West Coast is portrayed with paintings and sketches in *Westland* by Brent Trolle, and *Gold Trails of the West Coast*, by Tony Nolan, explores the unique history and character of the region.

Irvine Roxburgh illustrates the development of a typical coastal area in *Jackson's Bay — A Centennial History*. All are published by A.H. & A.W. Reed.

---

## LAKE KANIERE ROUND TRIP

*58 km. The drive can be drawn out to fill a day by picnicking at the lake and detouring to Hokitika Gorge (an added 35 km) on the return. Leave Hokitika on Highway 6 south, to fork left at:*

**Kaniere** (pop. 310) (*4.5 km*): Huge heaps of tailings to the left result from the dredge that was later moved to Kumara. Over 175,000 ounces were won here. *Bear left again at 5.3 km. At 12 km wooden fluming leads water from the lake over the Kaniere River shortly before the road enters the Kaniere Scenic Reserve. The bush, with conspicuous totara, closes in to frame vistas of forested mountains until the view opens at:*

**Lake Kaniere*** (*18.1 km*):* Bathed in glorious light the lake's placid waters frequently mirror the well-wooded hills that surround it and the snow-capped Alps that rise behind them to the south and east. In summer the lake draws boatowners, waterskiers, swimmers and picnickers. There is modest fishing. A short detour right to **Sunny Bight** leads past baches tucked away in the trees to a good picnic and beach area where a track leads into the bush. *Turn left to cross the head of the Kaniere River and the water-race that feeds a small power station. Pass Hans Bay and Hans Is and occasional camping spots. At 20.8 km a track leads up Mt Tuhua. Beyond are:*

**Dorothy Falls** (*63.1 m*) (*at 24.9 km*): A slender column curls through a cleft in the rock face. *Seen from the roadside. To the right flat-topped Mt Pilot may be seen rising steeply from the water's edge. After crossing the Styx River the road leads through some of the Coast's most fertile farmland back to Kaniere and so to Hokitika. After passing through Kokatahi (42.7 km) (birthplace of the wellknown band; see above) one may turn left for Kowhitirangi and then follow the signposted route to the Hokitika River Gorge*** (see below).*

## OTHER ENVIRONS

**Hokitika River Gorge***:** In an incomparable bush setting the limpid river's azure waters for most of the year lie deep and clear in a narrow rock chasm. *32.9 km. Leave Highway 6 at Kaniere to travel by way of Kokatahi (15.4 km) and Kowhitirangi (22.5 km). At the road's end a short track leads down to a suspension bridge across the chasm.*

The track leads on to cross the Whitcombe Pass and so reach the headwaters of the Rakaia River. The first Europeans to use the pass were John Baker and the novelist Samuel Butler, who in 1861 crossed into Westland only to turn back when they found the Coast so heavily wooded. Butler had undertaken "to verify the [dismal] reports of others with my own eyes, but I have little faith in the success of the undertaking and should go more as a traveller and an explorer than as a person intending to make money by the expedition". It was following Butler's Pass that Whitcombe and Lauper came, with little food, no gun and no tent, hoping to meet up with prospecting parties. Famished, weak and weary, they tried to cross the Taramakau River, where Whitcombe was drowned. Their expedition did no more than prove that the pass was unsuitable for a road line.

The route to the Hokitika Gorge passes through the locality of **Kowhitirangi** (*at 22.4 km*), the scene of the most tragic of New Zealand's manhunts. When a local farmer, Eric Stanley Graham, patently suffering from a deep-seated persecution complex, took to threatening his neighbours with firearms in 1941, local police decided to intervene. Arriving to remove his considerable arsenal, all four of the Hokitika police contingent were shot. Three were killed outright, and the fourth was later to die from his wounds. Over the next twelve days home guardsmen, volunteers, police from other areas and troops armed with machineguns hunted for the deranged farmer — a superb shot who could shoot a stag between the eyes at 500 paces. As terror gripped the area and residents huddled together in public halls for safety, the 200-strong army of searchers was augmented by a spotter plane and a bomber carrying live bombs. Three more were to die before a police sergeant finally stalked the fugitive Graham and shot him from a range of about 25 m. Within hours Graham died from his wounds in hospital to end the strangest manhunt in the country's history. News of the state of siege even reached Japan, then at war with New Zealand, where Tokyo Rose broadcast a message to Graham, exhorting him to hold the South Island while a second man was sent to take the North. The incident, charged with the pathos of the situation of a "man alone", forms the basis for Jack McClenaghan's successful novel *Moving Target* (Reed). To erase the memory of the tragedy Graham's house, scene of most of the deaths, was burned down (*it stood almost opposite the Kowhitirangi School*) and even the name of the locality was changed (from Koiterangi). However a memorial on the Kaniere Hall records the district's debt to those who died in the hunt.

**Blue Spur goldmine***:** A gold-sluicing claim, set in about 10 ha of bush, is where sluicing may be seen and explained. A number of mineshafts are safe to enter, in some cases forming intricate series as they followed the thin black line that marks the gold-rich sand. Some have vertical shafts through which from deep in the hillside the sky may be seen. Others have shafts back-filled as miners saved extracting mullock by simply dumping it in abandoned side tunnels. Visitors may pan for gold and are taught something of the skills involved. The old river terrace above the claim is liberally pitted with vertical shafts, many of them marked by clumps of gorse. *5.8 km. Turn off signposted 1.5 km S on Highway 6. Allow upwards of 1 hr. Usually open on weekdays from 10–12 noon; 1.30–5 pm. For weekend hours check at the tourist centre. Extended hours at holiday periods.*

**Shantytown***:** A growing replica of an old goldtown complete with a sluicing claim. *37.5 km. Turn right at Paroa, north on Highway 6. Described under △Grey-mouth.*

**Lake Mahinapua***:** The lake is approached through a tunnel of bush roofed with fern. Shallow and barely above sea-level, the lake is favoured by yachtsmen. When the tide is right one can go by small boat from here down the Mahinapua Creek and so reach Hokitika, a route used in the days of river steamers. A good picnic place. The rare crested grebe is occasionally seen here. *10.9 km S. Leave Hokitika by way of the* combined road-rail bridge on Gibson Quay (*locally known as "the longest xylophone in the world"*). *The lake may also be reached by a track through the bush that leaves Highway 6 at 13.2 km S of Hokitika.*

## ORGANISED EXCURSIONS

**Conducted tours:** Hokitika Tour & Charter Service run short trips out to the Blue Spur goldmine, to Shantytown, and halfday tours round Lake Kaniere (taking in Blue Spur) and over the 1865 trail to △Kumara. An all-day tour to △Franz Josef Glacier includes a stop at △Ross. An evening tour takes in Blue Spur, the glow-worms, the museum and a greenstone factory. *Details from the tourist centre, 29 Weld St.*

## TOURING NOTES

△**West Coast Road:** Points of interest along Highway 6 north and south of Hokitika are listed under this entry.

**Alternative route to △Greymouth via the 1865 trail:** Immediately north of the town Highway 6 crosses the Arahura River, a source of prized greenstone. Thereafter (*at 9.2 km*) one may turn off inland to pass (*at 12.5 km*) the intersection with Awatuna Road, 30 m down which a short track leaves the road to run into a lakelet and the near-submerged and burnt out remnants of the *Stafford* gold dredge. The route continues along the 1865 trail through the all but vanished goldtown of **Stafford** where a brief detour (*at 14 km*) leads to an evocative old cemetery where two of Richard John Seddon's infant children lie buried. The road winds through diggings claimed back by the bush, passing the Wheel of Fortune workings (*at 17.3 km*) at vanished **Goldsborough** before reaching △**Kumara** (*at 29.7 km*). From this point it becomes no longer practicable to follow the 1865 gold trail, which continued over the river and up the Greenstone Valley before swinging north to cross to **Rutherglen.** Highway 6 is rejoined at 36.4 km. *The alternative route adds 10 km to the direct route.*

---

**HYDE**      Central Otago.   Maps 1 & 25.    Pop. 121 (locality).

*29 km NNE of Middlemarch; 37 km SE of Ranfurly.*

THE HANDFUL OF old buildings that comprise the Hyde of today huddle above the Taieri River on the foothills of the forbidding Rock and Pillar range. To both north and south, but more noticeably to the north, splashes of colour mark places where flumes have tortured the soil to win alluvial gold.

The settlement, at first called Eight Mile as it was that distance from the Hamilton diggings across the Rock and Pillar, is named after John Hyde Harris, Superintendent of Otago 1862–65. It lies at the apex of the large triangle of Strath Taieri, a plain some 40 km long with △Middlemarch near its base. Over the Taieri ridge, on the eastern side of the plain, lies a flat "best described by its name, Moonlight, bleak, cold and cheerless".

The district is subjected to strong nor'westerly winds whose arrival is usually heralded by a long cloud that appears over the valley, known locally as the "Taieri pet".

## SOME HISTORY

**Wheelbarrow Jack:** The first Europeans in the area took up Taieri Lake station, a run linked with Johnny Jones and the Studholme brothers — *for all see index* — and Deep Dell station, also once part of Johnny Jones's expansive estate. It was probably an early shepherd who found the first gold in 1862, so precipitating a rush notable more for its leisureliness and want of mad stampede. For all the lack of frenzy, a township grew to accommodate perhaps as many as 2,000 diggers on the Hyde and neighbouring fields.

Among those who trudged to Hyde was Johnny Hallwertson, who trundled his belongings from Dunedin in a wheelbarrow. Month after month he tunnelled into the hillside until he was as deep in the hill as he was in debt. Still he persisted. Just when all regarded him as completely insane and the storekeeper had refused him further supplies, "Wheelbarrow Jack" struck paydirt. Within a matter of days he had recovered £2,000 worth of gold.

## POINTS OF INTEREST

**Bold proposals:** An ambitious scheme was to bring the waters of the Shag River to Hyde, but after some years of work and the expenditure of many thousands of pounds a mistake was found in the levels and the water would not flow. The whole project ended ruinously for all concerned. Another plan was to divert the Taieri on a V bend along a tunnel through which the river still runs. The scheme succeeded in re-routing the river but failed to reap any riches. (*The tunnel may be seen by walking down between the railway viaduct and the rail tunnel, seen from the main road 3.2 km N of Hyde. It is occasionally possible to walk through the tunnel when the river is low. Enquire locally.*)

A second group of prospectors set out to "turn" the river by means of a stone wall, so hoping to make accessible riches they expected to be in the riverbed. One hundred Chinese were engaged, who skilfully constructed the necessary wall, so turning the river into its new channel. But money ran short, troubles brewed between the partners, the Chinese left and the Hyde miner in charge of the work found himself alone to meet the debts. Curiously, there was apparently no attempt to work the river course, about 800 m of which still lies high and dry. (*The wall may be seen on the river about 7 km S of Hyde. Ask directions locally*.)

Another unprofitable venture was the Star of Otago, at the time regarded as the country's largest mining tunnel. Three years were spent in tunnelling to the foot of a deep shaft which had apparently been sunk on to good gold but which proved barren. The tunnel was continued to other shafts with the same heartbreaking results until it was found that the holes had only been "salted" with gold from Naseby to enable the claim to be sold at a handsome price — a form of dishonesty rare on the New Zealand goldfields.

For all the heartbreak, many did well. On one occasion the fortnightly gold escort to Dunedin carried out more than 1,300 ounces from the Hyde diggings alone. The *Otago Witness* observed that Hyde was "remarkably lively, in a state of excitement and gaiety — horse racing, balls and suppers every night".

**Taieri Lake Station,** an early Taieri run, lies to the south of Hyde. The century-old homestead may be seen to the west of the road (*at 13 km S*). The woolshed (*c.* 1860s) is about 400 m away, complete with the turret that accommodated a back breaking screw woolpress. The stone ruins of an early boundary rider's cottage are about 2 km to the west of the township (*not seen from the road; ask directions locally*).

A Glossary of Maori Words appears on page 343.

# INANGAHUA    Buller.    Maps 21, 24, 37 & 38.    Pop. 122.

*47 km ESE of Westport; 113 km NE of Greymouth; 54 km W of Murchison.*

THE SMALL JUNCTION and farming settlement of Inangahua was the focus of national attention in 1968 when a major earthquake damaged buildings so severely that for a time the entire population was evacuated. The earthquake affected other centres from Karamea to Hokitika.

Before the road was built that follows the flow of the Buller through a spectacular gorge, the only route inland from Westport was by river. At this time Inangahua, as "The Landing", saw the first machinery for crushing quartz being taken from Westport to △Reefton. At the height of the goldrushes there were over a thousand diggers at work in the tributaries of the Inangahua. Freight by the Buller was £75 a ton, and life was hard: "There is nothing here but only the bare flour, and tea without sugar . . . the quality [of the grog] is so reduced that it would take some chemical man to know whether it was brandy or water."

In pre-European times the Inangahua River teemed with the whitebait from which its name derives (*inanga* = whitebait; *hua* = abundant).

There are some splendid limestone caves in the vicinity, favoured by speleologists, including one system over 5 km long that extends right through a hill.

A key to area maps appears on page 2.

# INVERCARGILL**    Southland.    Map 18.    Pop. 53,900 (urban area).

*221 km SW of Dunedin. Information from the Southland Progress League, Crawford House, Don St, tel. 84-538.*

THE COUNTRY'S SOUTHERNMOST city, the "capital" of Murihiku (the tail-end of the land), stretches over open plains beside the New River estuary. While its level setting inhibits a ready appreciation of the city's geography, it makes possible broad main streets and many fine public gardens. More than this, it gives rise to the views over rooftops of the slender square tower of First Church and of the massive dome of St Mary's Basilica, each so much a feature of the townscape. Long summer twilights are recompense for a climate that has been compared unfavourably with that of more northern regions.

Invercargill, many of whose streets are named after Scottish Rivers, shares Dunedin's origin as an essentially Scottish city. Dunedin rose to prosperity on gold, and if Southland was largely denied the glitter of the goldfields, the province has found a more enduring asset in its grass. For it is on Southland's grasslands and an evenly-spread rainfall ensuring year-round growth that Invercargill's substance and prosperity rest. The city is ringed with massive freezing works, with a combined annual kill of nearly 7 million. Its port at △Bluff ranks high among the nation's leading export outlets. The city's debt to its pastures is acknowledged in the Blade of Grass, a revolving statue of polished steel outside the Civic Administration Buildings (*Esk St*).

## SOME NOTES ON SOUTHLAND

To the northerner, only Stewart Island stands between Southland and the Antarctic, and certainly the coastal district holds some unenviable national records — the lowest mean average temperature, the lowest annual average of bright sunshine hours, and the highest number of rain days. But the spread of its annual rainfall of 1087 mm is such that pastures do not dry out in summer, and the resultant productivity of Southland's farms, even for a country where high productivity is often the norm, is astonishing.

To add to the prolific developed areas, much undeveloped land is being brought into production, principally between Lakes Te Anau and Manapouri, and the district's beech forests under proper management should provide a base for industries of national importance.

There are large reserves of limestone and sub-bituminous coal, and reports of various mineral deposits over a wide area suggest that there are minerals to be won in substantial quantities, the main question being where, rather than if, these will be found.

There is the unparalleled magnificence of △Fiordland National Park, and of Lakes Te Anau, Manapouri and Hauroko; and some splendid beaches where townships such as △Riverton and △Orepuki hold fast to haunting histories. In contrast with the beech forests is the fossil forest at Curio Bay. For the fisherman there are fish, for the hunter, game; and for all is the lure of △Stewart Island, viewed invitingly across Foveaux Strait.

## SOME HISTORY

**The Lost Tribe of Fiordland:** As was often the case, the traditions of one Maori tribe were erased in their defeat by another, and so Southland tradition extends back not far beyond the conquest of the region by Ngatimamoe. The Waitaha tribe had settled the northern reaches of the South Island and had gradually filtered south as their numbers grew in what they called "the food-abounding island". Generations of peace ended with the invasion by Ngatimamoe, who quickly asserted superiority and absorbed the Waitaha only in turn to suffer a similar fate at the hands of Ngaitahu.

For Southland's sub-tribes of Ngatimamoe, a dream provoked their final downfall. Kana Tepu, a Ngatimamoe chief on Stewart Island, dreamed one night of catching a white crane and interpreted this as an omen that he should slay a Ngaitahu chief. To this end he led a war-party north to the Otago Heads. But there Kana Tepu was himself slain, and in the series of clashes that followed, local Ngatimamoe were gradually conquered as one by one their *pa* fell and their *hapu* were slaughtered.

It was in Southland that the Ngatimamoe made their final stand. Rakiura (Stewart Island) had already fallen to Ngaitahu. Beyond lay a stormy and desolate sea. For a time an uneasy peace lingered, but land problems revived the spirit of *utu*.

Some historians say that the Ngatimamoe were driven up the Aparima River, and that not far from the site of △Lumsden a desperate battle was fought. For a time the Ngatimamoe seemed in the ascendancy; Kaweriri, chief of Ngaitahu was mortally wounded. But Ngaitahu rallied. As the Ngatimamoe retreated they made a last stand at Teihoka but were again overwhelmed. The Ngatimamoe withdrew to the north-west until they reached Lake Te Anau. It was some years later, by the lake, that the final battle was fought and the fate of Ngatimamoe was sealed. The few survivors fled, and some scattered remnants of the tribe sought refuge in the wild depths of the forests to give rise to the legend of the "Lost Tribe of Fiordland". As the final clash was towards the end of the eighteenth century it may have been members of the "Lost Tribe" who were seen by Captain Cook in the course of his visit to Fiordland and this would explain their reluctance to make contact with him. From time to time some further evidence of occupation was seen, and as late as 1842 a sealing party in one of the fiords saw smoke and found a number of artefacts which may have belonged to descendants of the Ngatimamoe who escaped at Te Anau. Speculation about the chances of their being rediscovered persisted into the twentieth century.

**"Mere bog":** The surveyor Frederick Tuckett was sent to the South Island in 1844 to recommend to the New Zealand Company a site suitable for the New Edinburgh settlement of Dunedin. It is popularly believed that Tuckett rejected the site of Invercargill, reporting that it was "a mere bog, utterly unfit for human habitation". The origin of this oft-quoted phrase has hitherto eluded historians, but the comment may well have been made.

For the theory runs that local whalers were far from enthusiastic at the prospect of organised settlement in their area, so when Tuckett called he was carefully escorted not to the Mataura Valley, the Waihopai Plains, the New River Valley or to the rich western districts, but to the forbidding forest and swamp at the head of the Waihopai estuary. And when he moved on to Bluff he was just as carefully shown the Awarua bog, then euphemistically named Seaward Moss. Little wonder then that Tuckett favoured the Otago Peninsula.

Today reclamation has radically altered the aspect. Forest has vanished, swamp has been drained, and the airport stands on what was once a rushclad mudflat submerged at high water. Much of the reclamation was carried out by prison labour, the Government acquiring the site of its borstal farm in return. Flying out of Invercargill's airport one sees drainage ditches extending long and deep across the seaward plains.

# INVERCARGILL AND ENVIRONS

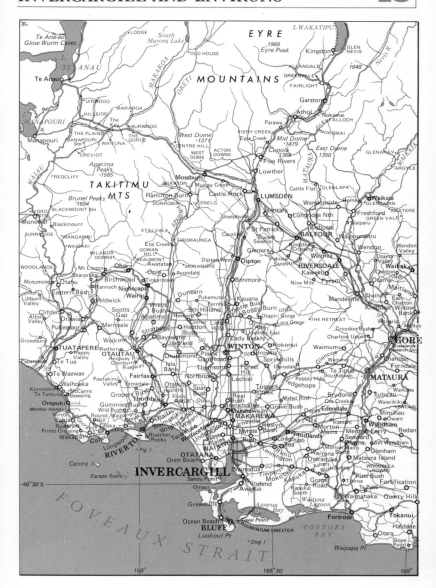

**Murihiku purchase:** Walter Baldock Durrant Mantell (1820–95), son of a noted English geologist, arrived at Wellington on the *Oriental* in 1840. He held a number of official posts until, in 1848, Sir George Grey appointed him Commissioner for "extinguishing native land claims in the Middle Island". Under the Treaty of Waitangi the Maori could sell land only to the Crown. It was for Mantell to negotiate terms with South Island Maori owners, though his duties were principally to set aside Maori reserves and to reconcile Ngaitahu to purchases largely effected by H. Tacy Kemp.

Mantell became Commissioner for Crown Lands for Otago in 1851, and it was in that capacity that, on his own initiative and to prevent illegal squatting, he negotiated the purchase of the Murihiku Block of some 2.8 million ha. The block, which extended south from a line from Milford Sound to Waiwera and to Nugget Point, and which included the offshore islands in Foveaux Strait excepting only Stewart Island and the Ruapuke group, was agreed to be sold for £2,000. However the Government (one historian has said it "did what it has done ever since and probably will in the future") ignored the plight of Southland, it sent no money, and as weeks dragged into months the Maori owners spoke of increasing their price to £9,000. To carry the matter through, Mantell mortgaged his own home personally to raise the first deposit. After a delay of seventeen months, in August 1853 the deal was concluded — an extra £600 being paid to the owners for their "expenses".

The Government now had control over "the tail end of the land" and could regulate land occupation. Mantell, who had placed his career and not a little of his own money

159

in jeopardy, was congratulated by the Governor for his "very great service to the public" and was reimbursed both the amount of his house mortgage and his expenses.

**A port of entry:** Pastoral runholders, many of them former Australian squatters, took up most of Southland's readily usable land, which they held under licences that could be cancelled by the Government when the land was needed for closer settlement. Once the land was taken up in this way, made possible only by lack of official interest in the area, the runholders' agitation for development was echoed in Dunedin. There Johnny Jones (*see index*) as chairman of the Dunedin Town Board, in January 1856 publicly exhorted the visiting governor, Col. Gore Browne, to establish "a port of entry at the southern extremity of the Province [which] would be of vast moment to importers of stock into that extensive and important district . . . shortening the sea voyage, and obviating the expense and hazard of being compelled to come round to Otago Harbour to report." Jones probably had the interests of Southland less close to his heart than the loss of revenue, as he went on to add: "There is a remnant of an old whaling-station at the south, whose consumption of imported articles is entirely lost to the revenues of the Province."

Before he left Dunedin, the Governor announced plans for a new town in the vicinity of the Bluff which he proposed to call Invercargill to honour Captain Cargill (*see index*), the Superintendent of Otago — but strictly speaking, Inver, a Gaelic prefix meaning at the mouth of, is misused when coupled with a man's name instead of with the name of the river concerned. Repaying the compliment, Captain Cargill renamed the Bluff, Campbell Town, after the Governor's wife, who was a Campbell. When Dr J. A. R. Menzies (1821–88) heard of the compliment paid to Cargill, the man who was to become the first superintendent of Southland Province condemned it as undeserved, because Cargill had opposed rather than aided the Southland settlers in having the port proclaimed.

**Kelly of Inverkelly:** By March 1856 John Kelly (*c.* 1800–57), a seaman-turned-settler of Irish extraction who had spent many years on Ruapuke Island, moored his boat in the Otepuni, a tributary of the Waihopai estuary, and put up a *whare*, the town's first building and the home for his wife and assorted children. Of strong religious temperament, Kelly had taken his children from Ruapuke to Otago Heads to have them baptised by Bishop Pompallier, but comparatively little else is known of him. He acted as boatman for the rush of intending settlers that followed Gore Browne's announcement. Kelly acted unwittingly in establishing himself on the future site of the city and in applying for 40 ha. He received a belligerent reply to his request from officialdom, which gave no indication that John Turnbull Thomson (1821–84), Otago's competent chief surveyor, had selected the site for the new town.

To Thomson it was an obvious choice. Here traffic could centre at a point easily reached by coastal shipping. To the north the site was in forest, and this would supply essential timber, and if the south was partly swamp it could be easily drained. (In fact, the swampy ground which surrounded the town was to pose endless problems for the early roadbuilders.) Thomson's name is commemorated in Thomsons Bush (now also known as Waihopai Reserve) and Turnbull Thomson Park. St John's Anglican Church has an imposing east window in his memory. Kelly's name is remembered in Kellys Point, Kellys Rock (south of Ruapuke Island) and Kellys Beach (at Port Adventure on Stewart Island).

**The port at New River:** John Kelly lived long enough to establish the beginnings of a port which was to expand rapidly. At Kellys Point he built a stockyard by his *whare* and turned the Otepuni into a harbour and its bank into a wharf. In 1860 a jetty was built that within three years had been extended and doubled in width.

Invercargill cherished ambitions for her estuary port and fought any suggestion that Bluff offered a superior harbour site, notwithstanding the at-times treacherous New River bar, criticism of which in the Dunedin press would provoke "a storm of indignation rivalling the breakers on the bar for violence". Before Bluff became virtually the sole port, New River was busy enough from 1856 to about 1864, and though Bluff gradually eclipsed Invercargill, coasters used New River regularly for over forty years, a trickle of trade continuing until it closed in 1962. (*The old wharf area may be seen by the Waihopai bridge on the city's western exit.*)

**A taste of honey:** Governed by the Otago Provincial Council from Dunedin, a remote centre in times when the principal form of communication was a hazardous sea voyage of up to a fortnight, the small number of settlers in Southland felt their interests were being overlooked, particularly in matters of land settlement. Dissatisfaction at neglect gave rise to agitation for self-government, and as soon as Southland achieved the minimum European population of 1,000 the necessary steps were taken to have it proclaimed a separate province. They were almost thwarted: Dunedin, in a last desperate bid to block secession, came within a single vote of having the country's New Provinces Act suspended.

The break from Otago could not have come at a less propitious moment. Within weeks of provincial independence came news of Gabriel Read's gold finds (*near △ Lawrence*), and the rush to Central Otago was on. While the coffers of the Otago Provincial Council were swollen with revenue from the diggings, Southland searched in vain for comparable goldfields within its own boundaries. To Southland's added chagrin, many of its younger men departed for the diggings across the new border.

Certainly Southland soon benefited to a degree. Invercargill, as the nearest centre to the goldfields that opened at Wakatipu saw a building boom in 1863. Demand soared for meat, for food of all kinds and for working bullocks. By the year's end both Invercargill's and the province's populations had more than trebled.

Gold fever was contagious. Unfortunately members of the Southland Provincial Council itself were not immune to the virus and in a moment of delirium embarked on the construction of a wooden railway to △Winton to facilitate transport north to the goldfields. A conventional railway from Invercargill to Bluff was also started. The wooden railway proved a disaster, the gold boom faded, and the Council found itself hopelessly and irretrievably in debt. Indeed, so parlous had the province's affairs become that one enterprising creditor obtained a court judgment for over £15,000 and proceeded to seize not only the Bluff-Invercargill railway complete with rolling-stock, but even governmental offices, furniture and the records of the Land Office. In scenes of uproar the sheriff had auctioned £20,000 worth of government property for a meagre £438 before the whole proceedings were ruled out of order.

In 1869 a visitor from Melbourne recorded that "a general air of decay hung over the whole town . . . This once, we were told, was a scene of unwonted bustle, now silent, deserted and undone . . . The only excitement was caused when a dog rushed out to snap at the heels of the horses." Nine heady years of enterprise and independence had culminated in financial disaster. In 1870 a penitent Southland was reunited with Otago. Southland was far from finished, but the lesson was learned that the region's future lay not in quickly-won riches but in her solid if less spectacular assets of farmland, timber and coal. *The old Provincial Council chambers (1864) still stand as an anonymous, single-storeyed building next to Calder Mackay's in Kelvin St.*

**Licensing trust control:** The concept of licensing trust control originated in Invercargill which, in 1943, "went wet" after thirty-seven years of local no-licence. Inspired by a successfully run municipally-owned hotel at Renmark in South Australia, the suggestion was made that the Invercargill City Council operate the new local liquor licences. The Labour Government of the day was receptive to the principle and constituted the Invercargill Licensing Trust, with members appointed by the Government, the City Council and the now defunct South Invercargill Borough Council. Subsequently the trust was made elective and the Invercargill Trust, with this variation became the model on which district trusts have been established throughout the country. In its three decades of operation the Invercargill Trust has accumulated assets worth over $25 million and distributed tax-paid profits of over $575,000 to local cultural, sporting and welfare bodies. As a result, in other areas throughout the country, trust control has been generally preferred in referenda to the alternative of brewery ownership.

Consult the Index when looking for a name in this Guide.

## THINGS TO SEE AND DO

**Southland Centennial Museum and Art Gallery\*\*\*:** The carefully displayed collection centres on the province, its history, fauna and natural resources. Displays of stone tools incorporate the reconstruction of an adze-making site discovered at Bluff. Early European relics include a copper spike and other material from the *Endeavour* (not Cook's bark but the country's first recorded shipwreck, in 1795 at Facile Harbour, Dusky Sound). A curious stone bears the caution "Beware of the Natives Plentey at Preservation", scratched by sealers in 1832 and found near Cape Providence. A cannon is reputed to have been part of the price paid when Peter Williams in 1832 purchased land between Preservation Inlet and Dusky Sound, and was later used at Tiwai Point to guard the entrance to Bluff Harbour during the Russian scare of the 1880s.

Other displays of nautical interest include whaling relics, the octant used by Captain Elles on the *Philip Laing*'s migrant voyage to Dunedin in 1848, the flamboyant figurehead from the barque *England's Glory* lost near the entrance to Bluff Harbour in 1881, and a float devised by seamen shipwrecked on the Auckland Islands in 1866 that carried a message of their plight to Stewart Island. The museum also contains an observatory (*open Wed. from 7–9 pm April–Oct.*) and a tuatarium. The latter is the only place in New Zealand where *tuataras* can be seen in a closely simulated native environment which even includes whistling frogs. *Gala St by main entrance to Queen's Park. Open Mon-Fri. 10 am–4.30 pm; Sat. 1–5 pm; Sun. and public holidays 2–5 pm. Allow upwards of 1 hr.*

In front of the museum is a section of fossilised forest dating from the Jurassic era of about 160 million years ago. The specimens were moved here from the fossil forest area at Curio Bay (*see index*).

**Queens Park\*\*\*** is the venue of many and varied sporting activities. Its 81 ha include formal gardens, an aviary, a duckpond, deerpark, and a play area where bronze statues of large animals encircle an enchanting children's fountain. *Enter from Queen's Drive. The spacious Winter Gardens are open Mon.-Fri. 10 am–4.30 pm; weekends and public holidays 1.30–4.30 pm.* Along the park's northern perimeter stretch the Tudor-styled brick buildings of the Southland Boys' High School.

**Some churches**\*\*: The city's principal churches, all of brick but otherwise of contrasting styles, are within a few blocks of each other. **St John's Anglican Church** (1887), a spacious building, has an ornate east window, a memorial to the surveyor John Turnbull Thomson (*Tay St*). A short distance away, viewed over the heads of *ti* trees, is Byzantine-styled **First Church** (1915) whose perfectly proportioned square campanile wears a slender look for all its 32 m. The façade of one of the most successful churches of its style is composed of variously-coloured bricks to achieve a mosaic effect in keeping with the building's appearance. In the portico of the remodelled interior is a wood-carved representation of da Vinci's Last Supper, purchased in Venice in 1870 by the Rev. T. S. Forsaith. Forsaith (1814–98), trader, politician and pastor, acquired a reputation for dealing fairly with Maori landowners and was a valued advisor to early governors and officials. It is occasionally suggested that he was the country's second, and shortest-lived, premier when on 31 August 1854 he was invited to select three colleagues and join the Executive Council. His "ministry's" views were set out in the Governor's address to the second session of Parliament but were rejected by the House, and after fully four days of power Forsaith and his colleagues resigned. Constitutionally, however, Henry Sewell must be regarded both as the country's first prime minister, and as its shortest serving (14 days). *Tay St. The church is locked when not in use. Key available from Presbyterian Social Services office next door.*

Two blocks away, best viewed from the gardens that flank the Otepuni Stream, rises the copper dome of **St Mary's Basilica** (1894–1905), the work of F. W. Petre. Its brick exterior contrasts with the interior lining of milk-white Oamaru stone. Petre is responsible for a number of notable ecclesiastical buildings. *Tyne St. Best viewed from Forth St.*

**City Art Gallery**\*: The city's art collection ranges from a Lindauer Maori group and early views of Bluff to the work of contemporary New Zealand artists. It is housed in the former home of Sir Robert Anderson (1866–1942), whose family created Anderson Park when they gave to the city the homestead and its 23.9 ha of surrounding garden, lawn and native bush. Sir Robert, born in Queenstown, was a self-made man who began his career as a thirteen-year-old office boy and rose to join with Sir Joseph Ward in establishing the concern of J. G. Ward & Co., now an NMA subsidiary. In later years he held directorships in a number of national concerns. *6.9 km. Leave the city north by Dee St. Turn right at 5.2 km and follow signposts to Anderson Park. The gallery is open from 2–4.30 pm daily (not Mon. or Fri. unless also a public holiday).* The house incorporates tearooms and one may picnic in the extensive grounds.

**Bank Corner:** On the intersection of Dee and Tay Streets no fewer than four bank buildings compete for custom. The Bank of New Zealand boasts a plaque recording the site where John Kelly landed stores for the district's first settlers in 1856. Some 40 m down Dee St can be seen the low iron balustrades that mark the Otepuni Stream, now a trickle, but navigable in Kelly's day. Almost opposite, the ANZ Bank also remembers Kelly: "In the bush three chains [60 m] to the north, the first settlers in Invercargill, John Kelly and his wife and family, built their home in March 1856 and here he died on May 17, 1857."

In the centre of the intersection, neatly sited on a rise from the Otepuni Stream, a uniformed trooper tops the clocktower memorial (1907) to the Boer War. Behind him Clyde St (as Dee St becomes) closes on a vista of distant Bluff Hill. *Dee and Tay Sts.*

John Kelly lies buried in the **Eastern Cemetery** in a plot that for generations was marked only "Niven" — his second wife's name by her previous marriage. The omission of an appropriate headstone has now been made good. (*3.5 km up Tay St on the city boundary. The grave is about 40 m from the entrance. On entering, turn left. The plot is the third on the right at the drive's end.*)

## ENVIRONS

**Oreti Beach**\*\* extends for several kilometres north from the mouth of the Oreti River. Sandy, generally lacking in shade, and backed by vast areas of lupin-covered sand dunes, the beach is patrolled at busy periods and offers safe bathing. The sand dune area includes the Teretonga Park motor racing circuit (which annually stages one of the Tasman series), as well as golf links, and stock car, go-kart and motor cycle tracks.

The succulent *toheroa* is taken from the beach in season (*generally a few weeks in winter; details of restrictions are posted locally*). A type of clam and not unlike a large *pipi*, the *toheroa* (*Amphidesma ventricosum*) grows up to 15 cm in length, and burrows deep into sandy beaches that are backed by sand dunes. These trap fresh water in lagoons whose seepage promotes the growth of the plankton on which the *toheroa* feeds. When being chased the *toheroa* can move through the sand with astonishing speed. *Toheroa* are eaten raw, baked in the shell, minced for fritters or made into the wellknown soup. *9.7 km. In Clyde St turn right at the roundabout below the Troopers' Memorial.* At 6.7 km the route crosses the Oreti River estuary, used for yachting, powerboating, water-skiing and sculling, particularly in the vicinity of the well-wooded domain by the river bridge.

**Awarua Radio:** Owing to its geographical position, Awarua Radio is one of the best receiving stations in the world, being opposite the main transmitting stations in Britain and not being screened by mountain ranges. Historically the station has been connected with many notable events such as various Antarctic expeditions and pioneering trans-Tasman flights. The station was built for the New Zealand Government by German radio experts, opening in 1913 with only one transmitter, a long-wave spark type. Its mast was supported at the base by glass insulators. When any of these became cracked it was necessary to use jacks to raise the 124.9 m mast while a new insulator was being installed. Today Awarua Radio has sixteen transmitters ranging in power from 60 to 5,000 watts and eleven communications receivers with from six to sixteen valves covering low, medium and high frequency bands. A network of masts ranging from 12.2 m to 45.7 m was erected when the station was rebuilt during 1938–39.

Meteorological reports are relayed, a radiotelephone service operated for coastal ships and a radio-communication service established with lighthouses as distant as Milford and Doubtful Sounds. A continuous link with long-distance shipping is maintained to any part of the world. Arrangements are made for emergency medical services for ships which do not carry doctors. A call has even been received from a ship off the Chinese mainland. Awarua was the only station to answer the call, and when the operator learned that a fireman had been badly burned following a blowback from a furnace, he referred the case to the Southland Hospital. In a very short time information on appropriate treatment was forwarded to the ship. Three days later a message was received from the vessel to say that the fireman was well on the way to recovery.

The station covers an area of 283.5 ha. Until about 1940 the riggers who maintained the aerials had to wear thigh boots, so swampy was the ground. *The station lies by Highway 1, 11.4 km towards Bluff. It is closed to the public as some messages are confidential.*

△ **Bluff\*:** The province's busy port faces across to the aluminium smelter of Tiwai Point. *27 km S.*

△ **Stewart Island\*\*\*** is served by a regular ferry from Bluff which usually allows day visitors about four hours on the island, time for a minibus tour of its 20 km of road. Stewart Island Air Services Ltd operate scheduled services from Invercargill airport. *Ferry details from Ministry of Transport, tel. 8119 BLF; Stewart Island Air Services Ltd office is at the airport, tel. 82-168.*

△ **Riverton\*\*:** A charming oldworld seaside settlement. *39 km W.*

△ **Lake Hauroko\*\*:** A forested lake in Fiordland National Park. Its unpredictable waters require care from boatowners. *133 km NW.*

△ **Fiordland National Park\*\*\*:** Floatplane charters can be arranged by trampers and hunters wishing to be flown in or out of the remote fiords that snake in to the forests of the Park. *Mount Cook Airlines, Invercargill, tel. 82-168.*

## SUGGESTED DRIVES

**Tuatapere round trip:** An all-day drive along the coast of Foveaux Strait to the brink of Fiordland returns by way of the Ohai-Nightcaps coalmining region. Leave Invercargill by Highway 6 to turn left along Highway 99 to pass through △ Riverton, △ Orepuki, △ Tuatapere and △ Clifden. Continue on what has become Highway 96 to reach △ Ohai, △ Nightcaps and △ Winton before returning to Invercargill by way of Highway 6. *210 km.*

**Curio Bay:** A pleasant halfday or full day may be spent driving out to Curio Bay and Waikawa along the route described under △ Invercargill-Balclutha Coastal Road. Return by driving beyond Waikawa to link with Highway 92, where turn left back to Invercargill. *79 km return.*

## ORGANISED EXCURSIONS

**Tiwai Aluminium Smelter:** Groups are regularly shown over the smelter but, because of requirements concerning the need for proper clothing and footwear, visits are restricted to parties who make prior arrangements. *Contact Community Relations Officer, N.Z. Aluminium Smelters Ltd, Private Bag, Invercargill; tel. 85-999. For details of the plant see Bluff.*

**Coach Tours:** To meet demand at holiday times day tours are run both through the Chasland and Catlin districts to △ Owaka, and to △ Milford Sound and △ Queenstown. *H & H Travel Lines.*

## TOURING NOTE

**Roads to Balclutha:** For points of interest on Highway 1, see the entries for △ Edendale, △ Mataura, △ Gore and △ Clinton.

For those who would rather be off the macadamised main highway the coastal route is recommended, see △ Invercargill-Balclutha Coast Road, below.

## INVERCARGILL-BALCLUTHA COAST ROAD***     Highway 92.
##        Map 19.

TWO ROUTES LINK Invercargill with Balclutha—State Highway 1, a slick, macadam-ised 140 km run of under two hours; and the slow, winding, and partly unsealed 169.5 km of Highway 92. The former whisks the traveller through miles of fertile plain and neat, folding farmland. The latter, the coastal road, threads through large reserves of native bush which spill down to the water's edge with only steep cave-pitted cliffs or sheltered, golden beaches to separate trees from sea. Along the coastal route new farmland is still being won from the forests. In patches bleached skeletons of dead trees litter hillsides oversown in grass, and elsewhere stumps protrude from land long since broken in. Both the primeval forest and the newly-won land bear the imprint of frontier New Zealand. In the bush is a wide variety of birdlife; the coast abounds with marine life, including colonies of penguins and the occasional sea leopard.

### SOME HISTORY

**A slow line:** Much of the area's Maori tradition has been lost, but legend tells of giant *Maeroero* in the hills who kept the relatively few Maoris who inhabited the district, close to the shore. Sealers, whaling ships and bay whaling stations (at Fortrose, Waikawa, Tautuku and Port Molyneux) all operated along the coastline, and later gold was dredged from the beaches at Waikawa. The era of early European contact is overshadowed by two remarkable men, the Ngaitahu chief Tuhawaiki (Bloody Jack) (*see index*) who dominated the area in which he was born, and Tommy Chaseland, half European half-Aboriginal, a gentle giant of a man who, like Tuha-waiki, attracted his own fund of folklore.

Timbermilling began in earnest in the 1860s to supply the Dunedin market, and the almost impenetrable forests were slowly opened up by the Catlins railway, a line only 68.4 km long but not completed until 1915, thirty-three years after work first began.

> For my part, I travel not to go anywhere, but to go. I travel for travel's sake. The great affair is to move. —Robert Louis Stevenson.

### POINTS OF INTEREST ON THE WAY

*In geographical order from Invercargill. The suggested route in the main lies along Highway 92. Running distances are exclusive of detours.*

△**Invercargill**\*\*: Southland's principal centre and the country's southern-most city. *The route lies due east before swinging south to cross the Mataura River and reach:*

**Fortrose** (*pop. 111 locality*) (*45 km from Invercargill; 124.5 km from Balclutha*): A faded, jaded settlement on the shores of tidal Toetoes Harbour, the estuary of the Mataura River. It was the site of an early whaling station managed by Tommy Chaseland, which enjoyed a first flush of success when there was an astonishing take of no fewer than eleven whales in seventeen days. But this was far beyond the capacity of the available casks, so much of the catch went to waste and within two years the station was closed as whales never returned to the locality. The inlet was named by the whalers as there was a chief Toitoi here, and from "Toetoe's place" it became Toetoes Harbour. Offshore lies the long low form of △Ruapuke Island, with Green Island to the east. *Beyond Fortrose bear right to leave Highway 92 and follow the Fortrose-Otara Road passing through undulating mixed-farmland. Just after the Otara School is the turnoff to:*

**Waipapa Point** (*detour 4.2 km*): The low-lying point, with hidden reefs extending well out to sea, marks the eastern entrance to Foveaux Strait and is difficult for mariners to see in thick weather. The point acquired its 14-m wooden-towered light-house after it had claimed the SS *Tararua* in 1881 in the country's second-worst shipping disaster. The 828-ton screw steamer, rigged as a three-masted schooner, had sailed from Port Chalmers for Bluff en route to Melbourne when in thick misty rain she struck Otara Reef, about a kilometre off shore. Instead of making for the open sea, the lifeboats headed for the shore, only to be dashed on the rocks; those who remained with the vessel clung to the wreck in pounding seas for almost twenty-two hours before her masts snapped and, with men and women still clinging to them, toppled into the sea. As if to complete the tragedy the hull turned over to drown those still aboard. In the final count, of the 151 aboard only 20 survived. The captain, blamed by the Court of Inquiry for grave navigational errors and for failing to post a proper lookout, perished with his ship. The bodies of sixty-five of the victims lie buried in the Tararua Acre (*signposted*), and the vessel's boiler may occasionally be seen on the rocks below. The light was ordered immediately and was first shown in January 1884. The tower stands only 21.4 m above sea level and is visible for 22.5 km, the light flashing once each 10 seconds. *The light may be inspected by arrangement with the principal keeper. Return to the turnoff and turn right to follow the Otara-Haldane Road, passing the turnoff to:*

# INVERCARGILL-BALCLUTHA COAST ROAD `19`

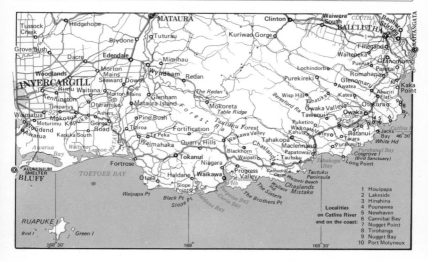

**Slope Point** (*detour 16 km*): Contrary to general belief, this point reaches some 5 km further south than does Stirling Point at Bluff, rendering Slope Point the southern-most portion of the South Island mainland. *The road does not extend to the end of the point but turns westward to reach the coast. The route continues to skirt the flax-backed mudflats of the Haldane Estuary before cutting across to reach:*

**Porpoise Bay**\*\* (*72.3 km from Invercargill; 97.2 km from Balclutha*): A wide stretch of golden sand and safe sheltered water that arcs north from South Head to the entrance of Waikawa Harbour. *On reaching the bay turn right for 1.4 km to pause at the:*

**Curio Bay Fossil Forest**\*\*: The sea-washed rock terrace here is the original floor of a Jurassic forest, dating back some 160 million years. The subtropical forest of *kauri* and lesser trees such as cyclads and conifers flourished at a time when grasses and flowering plants had not evolved. It was overwhelmed in a massive volcanic eruption that buried the forest in a flood of ash. The land, which extended south from here with a coastline across what is now northern Southland, subsequently disappeared beneath the sea and when the present landmass re-emerged, sea action cut back the sandstone formed by the volcanic ash to reveal petrified broken logs lying on the ancient forest's floor, and stumps still in their original positions of growth. Fossil forests of this age are rare throughout the world, and this one is absolutely protected. *Signposted. Walk down the track at low tide and across the shelf, the old forest floor, to the right. The forest remnants, low stumps and fallen logs, are not immediately apparent but are readily recognisable once one becomes accustomed to the formations. Return along the length of Porpoise Bay and follow the road along the western bank of Waikawa Harbour to:*

**Waikawa** (pop. 76) (*77.3 km from Invercargill; 92.2 km from Balclutha*): The hamlet here, "the town the boom passed by", is the successor to a whaling base, originally just inside North Head and in the 1840s known as Success River after Edward Cattlin's whaling ship. Some shipbuilding was carried on here — the 96-ton *Jane Anderson* was launched with a bottle of champagne, and in 1860 Captain C. Dwight built a schooner of 56 tons he named *Oamaru Lass*. Some years later he loaded her with timber and took her to the town after which she was named. There in a storm the ship returned the compliment by being driven high and dry on the beach. When the storm abated the ship was refloated — and renamed *Noah*.

The settlement moved here across the bay as first timber and then wool began to be shipped out from as far inland as Wyndham. From 1874–84 the township was ministered to by an egocentric but otherwise unremarkable pastor, the Rev. James Henry, who died in Sydney in 1919. Determined that his name be not forgotten he endowed no fewer than three separate memorials to himself — in his Aberdeen birthplace, in Waikawa and in Sydney. His black granite monument (*above the road, opposite the cemetery*) records that he founded "the Henry scholarships" — a reference to an allowance (so far as is known unclaimed) for the first child with the surname Henry to be born here. For a time gold was won from the beaches here.

Waikawa means bitter water and is also the name of a shrub. Unless the name relates to the salty estuary, the region is most likely named after the shrub rather than the water, which is here pure and pleasant. *4 km north of Waikawa turn down Progress Valley Rd for 150 m, where, upstream from the Waikawa River bridge, are the:*

**Niagara Falls:** The locality was named Niagara, it is said, by a wit who claimed to have seen both the world's tallest and the world's smallest falls at Niagara. The "falls" here, barely a ripple on the riverbed, are of insufficient magnitude to be perceptible at high tide. *Continue north to rejoin Highway 92, turning right to wind through reserves of predominantly beech forest and:*

**Chaslands** (*95.5 km from Invercargill; 74 km from Balclutha*): A school and an occasional house comprise the locality of Chaslands, a former milling centre, which takes its name from a promontory to the south, quaintly named Chaslands Mistake.

Tommy Chaseland (1801?–69), a legendary figure from the coast's whaling era, managed the whaling station at Fortrose established in 1834 and was later briefly associated with another station at Taieri Mouth. He was an expert whaler and boat-man and reputedly could sight land when a full fifty kilometres away from it. Once, legend has it, he called from the lookout that he could see a whale. The captain with his glass could see nothing, but Chaseland persisted that he could see a whale, that it was dead, and that it had a harpoon stuck upright in its back with several fathoms of line attached. The ship diverted to find the whale in exactly the circumstances he had described. The precise nature of his "mistake" is unresolved; some say that one foggy day while Chaseland was piloting an American whaler to Otakou Harbour (Port Chalmers) he mistook the headland for Cape Saunders, but realised his error in time to avert tragedy. However such a mistake seems unlikely for the man who knew "every yard of the coast and every rip of the tide", and it is probable that Chaseland's error is being confused with the wreck of the *Otago*, lost off the headland in 1876.

Others say that he induced Sydney owners to fit out a brig to plunder the seals once plentiful on the headland; that the crew, ill-disciplined and over-eager to slay the seals, ignored his advice to wait; that they attacked the herd as it came ashore with the result that the seals stampeded to the safety of deep water, never to return. The brig returned to Sydney emptyhanded, and the abortive venture was Chaseland's mistake. He, however, gave his own explanation. He landed a sealing party one evening when the headland was heavy with seals, but instead of killing them then and there, he elected to wait until the next morning — by which time the herd had disappeared. Like that of his fellow Australian, Cattlin, Chaseland's name has passed misspelt into the region's geography. *The road winds on through steep, rough country to pass the turnoff to:*

**Cathedral Caves**\*\*\* (*99 km from Invercargill; 70.5 km from Balclutha*): *Described under △ Owaka, "Environs". The caves are accessible only from one hour before low tide to one hour after. A 20-minute walk down a steep face to Waipati Beach is involved and a powerful torch is essential for those intending to venture any appreciable distance into the caves. The road runs on through stands of native bush to pass the start of the track to:*

**Lake Wilkie**\*\*: A short, 100 m track leads through bush to the shore of a forest-fringed lakelet, known to botanists for the unique forms of plantlife it maintains. *Signposted. A short distance beyond is the access to:*

**Tautuku Bay**\*\*\* (*107 km from Invercargill; 62.5 km from Balclutha*): An enchanting stretch of sand. *Described under △ Owaka, "Environs". The road then climbs Florence Hill for a splendid view back to Tautuku Bay, drops to cross the Maclennan River, and winds on to pass the turnoff down Purakanui Road, to:*

**Purakanui Falls**\*\*\*: *Described under △ Owaka, "Environs". Signposted. Proceed straight on from the falls to reach Lakeside Rd and Catlins Lake. Cross the bridge over the lake to reach:*

△**Owaka**\*\* (*138 km from Invercargill; 31.5 km from Balclutha*): A quiet farming town, the centre of the Catlins district.

*Between Owaka and Balclutha detours are possible to* **Cannibal Bay**\*\*\* (*described under △ Owaka, "Environs"*) (*turn off 4 km after Owaka; 27.5 km from Balclutha*) *and to* **Kaka Point**\*\*\* *and* **The Nuggets** (*both described under △ Balclutha*) (*turn off 7 km after Owaka; 24.5 km from Balclutha*). *Both are loop detours, but the routes converge on Highway 92 at 25.1 km from Owaka; 6.4 km from Balclutha at the:*

**Telford Farm Training Institute:** *Described under △ Balclutha. The route then follows the south arm of the Clutha River to end at:*

△**Balclutha** (*169.5 km from Invercargill*).

## KAIAPOI\*    North Canterbury.    Map 7.    Pop. 4,746.

*20.6 km N of Christchurch.*

KAIAPOI WAS FOR a century been a household name for the excellence of its woollen mills. After fighting a losing battle to keep its river port open for coastal shipping services the town has come into its own as a satellite centre for burgeoning Christ-church — though Henry Sewell (later prime minister) was somewhat premature when he asserted in 1853 that Christchurch had already reached its peak — "New-comers will not settle there. Witness the *Minerva* people, they are all off to Kaiapoi." The town grew up in the 1850s as timber was cut for Christchurch and Lyttelton, and ferries were established on the Waimakariri River. The river port was the shipping centre for North Canterbury until in 1872 the railway opened to no great local enthusiasm. In the present century the port has revived periodically and is still used by pleasure craft.

**Jetboat trips** up the Waimakariri Gorge are run by Canterbury and Alpine Travel Ltd, (*tel. 65-022 Christchurch; book at least one day in advance*).

## SOME HISTORY

**Kaiapohia pa:** The site of the *pa*, one of the first established by the Ngaitahu after their migration from the North Island, was very different in pre-European times. It was then a peninsula of about 2 ha jutting out into one of many lagoons. Well protected with deep ditches, high earthwalls and stout palisades, it seemed impregnable. The population of about a thousand made Kaiapohia one of the largest and most important of the Ngaitahu settlements, and the permanent home of the tribe's leading chiefs.

After the *kai huanga* (*see index*) feud had set relative against relative and disrupted the usual Maori form of kinship alliances between *kainga*, *hapu* and *iwi*, Te Rauparaha (*see index*) finally moved from the north to devastate *pa* at Kaikoura and Omihi. At Kaiapohia in about 1828 he posed as a friend interested only in trading for greenstone. The Ngaitahu took the initiative, luring in to their *pa* with hospitality eight of the Ngati Toa's closest companions, suddenly to strike them down. The dead included Te Pehi, Te Rauparaha's uncle, a noted warrior who in 1824 had emulated Hongi Hika in voyaging to Britain to obtain European weapons. Te Rauparaha withdrew but returned to exact a terrible vengeance. First he moved to kidnap the Ngaitahu chief, Te Maiharanui (*see* △*Akaroa*), and two years later attacked Kaiapohia. The invading Ngati Toa were fortunate in arriving at a time when many Ngaitahu warriors were away. During a siege of about three months the absent Ngaitahu were able to return across the lagoon, but they could not prevent the Ngati Toa from constructing a trench along the neck of the peninsula which zigzagged up to the *pa*'s palisades, where they piled scrub in preparation for setting the *pa* alight. The Ngaitahu were alive to the danger. Each night they removed as much as they could but were still not able to stop a huge pile accumulating. When all was in readiness and the Ngati Toa were waiting only for a favourable wind, the defenders took the initiative once more and fired the pyre themselves. The strong nor'wester (which should have carried the flames away from the *pa*) was, as it almost invariably is, followed by a sudden southerly change, which came just as the fire had taken hold, to fan the flames back into the *pa* and to kindle the century-old fortifications. Before the stunned Ngaitahu could redeploy their defences, Ngati Toa poured through the smoke to complete the destruction. Inevitably a cannibal feast followed (*on a sandhill near the present main road*). To seal his triumph, Te Rauparaha sailed his canoes from the mouth of the Ashley River across to △Akaroa, where he successfully attacked the remaining Ngaitahu stronghold of Onawe.

Kaiapohia was left in ruins. When the coming of Christianity liberated many captives, returning Ngaitahu chose to settle in other areas. The Canterbury pilgrims found barely ten Maoris living in the Kaiapohia district. So great had been the slaughter that, twenty years later, before the Rev. James Stack could start work on his section (which adjoined the *pa*) he had to cart off by the drayload human bones left from the feast.

With the draining of swamps and lagoons, the *pa* surroundings have changed beyond recognition. Traces of the earthworks remain. A circular column, crowned by a well-tattooed squatting figure, commemorates the site. The inscription makes no mention of the tragedy. *600 m along Preeces Rd; turn off Highway 1 at 9 km north of Kaiapoi.*

**A generous gesture:** When in 1868 the district was proclaimed a borough the Town Council met to choose Kaiapoi's first mayor. Two candidates were nominated, Matthew Hall and Dr Charles Dudley. The voting was tied, so Matthew Hall as chairman gallantly rose to exercise his casting vote — in favour of himself. (Norman Kirk, later (1972) to become prime minister, was Kaiapoi's youngest-ever mayor in 1953, at the age of 30.)

The first few years were devoted almost entirely to formulating schemes to protect the township from flooding, but the Council did not limit to its boundaries the scope of its vision. During the Boer War it formally noted its "indignation at the gross, vile and baseless libels on the British troops by the German Press and its entire confidence in the Imperial Government". A footbridge providing access over the Kaiapoi River which was constructed at the turn of the century still bears the name of Mafeking Bridge.

## POINTS OF INTEREST

**St Bartholomew's Church** (*c.* 1861)** originally stood on a sandhill, above the flood level but without allowance for the boisterous nor'wester. In a gale most of the sandhill disappeared, leaving the curious little building, an "inverted V", perched up in the air. The structure (1855) was removed in sections and rebuilt here to an enlarged design by Mountfort and Luck. *Cass St.*

**Kaiapoi Mini Museum** contains material related to the district and has as its oldest exhibit a travelling trunk carved in 1769. *High St, above public library. Open Thurs. from 2–4 pm, other times by arrangement; tel. 8622.*

**M.V. Tuhoe** which formerly traded out of Kaiapoi to Wellington, Napier and Gisborne has been preserved and is permanently moored at the port. It serves as a novel gallery for art exhibitions.*Visits by arrangement with C. T. Williams, tel. 7134KI.*

## ENVIRONS

**Morwenstow Stud and Museum:** An unusual feature of the Morwenstow stud is a museum collection which includes saddles from 1906 onwards and a variety of shoes, stirrup irons, spurs, bits and bridles. The largest exhibit is the weighing scales used by the Canterbury Jockey Club in 1867. Also held is a collection of early turf registers, issues of racing rules and other early books on aspects of racing and bloodstock. The stud, where some five stallions stand and where there are upwards of 200 horses at any one time, covers 200 ha of prime grassland. *Telephone Kaiapoi 7030 to arrange a visit. 2.5 km from Kaiapoi. Turn left down Pa Rd and at its end turn left into Revells Rd.*

**Belfast** (*9 km S*) originated as a market garden settlement (1901), a hamlet with allotments of one or two acres where workmen could establish a part-time interest on the land. A freezing works followed (1915). Earlier an hotel had been built at the Seven Mile Peg here, to this day known simply as The Peg. There are pleasant riverside picnicking facilities on the bypass towards Harewood.

**SOME BEACHES:** The long stretch of rather exposed sand that forms the sweeping curve of Pegasus Bay is accessible at several nearby points.

**Waikuku Beach** (*13 km N*), on the south bank of the Ashley rivermouth, combines the shelter of river swimming (and, in season, whitebaiting) with ocean surf and the shade of pinetrees. **Woodend Beach** (*8 km NE*), not as popular with campers as Waikuku, is perhaps the more appealing though it lacks a river. **The Pines** and **Kairaki** (*4 km E*) are reached by a straight 2 km-long avenue of Lombardy poplars. A variety of facilities is available at Pines Beach (camping ground; mini-golf, etc.). The road ends at the Waimakariri rivermouth, another good whitebaiting spot, where surf is seen breaking on the bar.

**Maori Church of St Stephen, Tuahiwi** (1865): Built as part of the Maori mission established by the Rev. James Stack, the little wooden church has a foundation stone that was laid by Sir George Grey. *6 km. Tuahiwi.*

---

## KAIKOURA*** Marlborough. Map 20. Pop. 1,949.

*191 km NE of Christchurch; 132 km SSW of Blenheim; 74 km NE of Cheviot.*

THE ROCK-GIRT HOOK of the Kaikoura Peninsula juts out from the shadow of the Seaward Kaikoura Range, scattered with holiday homes and permanent residences. An incomparable sight is the snowclad mountains viewed across the bay as they tower to heights of over 2,600 m.

Kaikoura means to eat crayfish (*kai* = food; *koura* = crayfish), a name bestowed in mythology by the chief Tamatea-Pokai-Whenua (*see index*) as he paused to eat here while pursuing the runaway wives who were ultimately transformed into greenstone in Westland. Today, as in the past, crayfish looms large in the peninsula's fishing economy. But Kaikoura is also a farming centre, basically dairying, for there is a deceptively large area of level land between the peninsula and the mountains. There are grazing runs on the hill country.

There is excellent surfcasting from the shore and the rocks hereabouts, for a wide variety of fish.

**Crayfish:** Two species of saltwater crayfish (or crawfish) are found in New Zealand, each being a variety distinct from those found elsewhere in the world. The common spiny crayfish (*Jasus edwardsii*) has reddish purple and orange markings that change to a uniform red on being boiled. Males may reach a length of 50 cm but females seldom exceed half that size. Similar to lobsters (but lacking the lobster's powerful pinchers) they live in rocky areas, in the shelter of seaweed, and at times half-buried in sandy gravel. The smooth-tailed green, or "packhorse", crayfish (*Jasus verreauxi*) is much larger than the spiny crayfish. Found most abundantly in the North Island areas of Coromandel and the Bay of Plenty (and not at Kaikoura), it frequently exceeds 60 cm in length. Both varieties are sought for export markets, where high prices are paid for the delicately-flavoured flesh of their tails.

## SOME GEOLOGY

Like Banks Peninsula, the Kaikoura peninsula originated as an island. It has been "tied" to the mainland by a gradual accumulation of silt, sand, stones and mud. Captain Cook, when he first viewed it, aptly described the peninsula as "some low land that made like an Island". Unlike Banks Peninsula it is predominantly of limestone and is not volcanic in origin.

# KAIKOURA COAST ROAD

## 20

## MAORI LEGEND

**An oarsman's seat:** In one version of the Maui myth of the creation of New Zealand, the North Island was the fish (Te Ika a Maui), the South Island the canoe (Te Waka a Maui) and the Kaikoura peninsula the thwart, or oarsman's bench (Te Taumanu o te Waka a Maui) against which the demigod braced himself as he drew the fish to the surface. This has been interpreted as suggesting that Maui may have made landfall on the South Island and climbed the Kaikoura Peninsula, whence he first sighted the North Island.

## SOME HISTORY

**A plentiful food supply:** The peninsula, easy to defend and with plentiful resources of food, must have had considerable appeal to the earliest occupants of New Zealand. The first discovery of a Moa-hunter grave was made near the present-day site of the Old Wharf, in 1857.

It seems that the tribe of Waitaha occupied the district until about AD 1500, when they were conquered and absorbed by Ngatimamoe migrating from the North Island. They in turn a century later were overwhelmed by Ngaitahu after a series of battles along the coast and a fluctuation of fortunes. On the peninsula was the largest of the Ngaitahu *pa* when, in 1828, Te Rauparaha invaded from the North Island in the series of battles known as Niho Manga (the battles of the barracouda tooth) (*described in "Introduction"*).

The peninsula was for centuries prized territory, as witnessed by the etching of *pa* sites on virtually every defensible promontory. Each in the chain of *pa* was visible to others, so that a unified defence could be presented to aggressors.

**Captain Cook and the Lookers On:** In local tradition Cook is said to have named the Seaward Kaikouras the Lookers On. Hawkesworth's chart applied the name to the range, but in fact Cook gave the name to the Kaikoura Peninsula itself. In February 1770, as he sailed *Endeavour* south after making the momentous discovery of Cook Strait that forever dispelled the long-cherished concept of *Terra Australis Incognita* (Unknown Southern Continent), Cook recorded that "in the PM Four double Canoes wherein were 57 Men Came off to the Ship, they kept at the distance of about a Stones throw from us and would not be prevail'd upon to put along side . . . from this we concluded that they never had heard anything of our being upon the coast. After looking at [us] for some time [they] pull'd in for the land like an Island . . . on which account I call'd it *Lookers on*."

It is clear from Cook's journal that the name was originally intended for the peninsula and not for the mountains.

Sealers doubtless near-exterminated the herds of the peninsula long before the first of many whaling stations was established in 1843, by Robert Fyffe who, with his nephew George, later pioneered the region's sheep country.

---

The country's birdlife is studied in *Birds and Birdsongs of New Zealand* by G. Williams and K. & J. Bigwood, the *Fiat Book of Common Birds in New Zealand*, Volumes I & II, and the *Fiat Book of Uncommon Birds in New Zealand*, all by J. Marshall, F. Kinsky and C. Robertson, and published by A.H. & A.W. Reed.

---

## A DRIVE ALONG THE PENINSULA***

*The short drive to the northern tip of the peninsula offers fine views across the sea to the towering Seaward Kaikouras. Even the most transitory visitor should make this detour. Leave Highway 1 to drive along the northern foreshore (West End becomes the Esplanade) passing:*

**The Garden of Memories** (*0.8 km*): A small garden shaded by Norfolk pines and arched with a number of whalebones. On the hillside above are traces of the fortifications of Takahanga *pa*.

**Edward Percival Marine Laboratory** (*2.5 km*): A marine research laboratory maintained by the Zoology Department of the University of Canterbury. (*Not open to the public.*)

**New Wharf** (1906) (*3 km*): A major fishing fleet operates out of Kaikoura. Much of the country's crayfish exports is packed here.

**Old Wharf** (1882) (*3.7 km*): Built before there was any road link with the outside world. A house built by the whaler George Fyffe in about 1860 stands opposite the wharf. Blubber was rendered down in trypots here and a handful of whalers had huts in the vicinity. Various whaling stations operated from points round the peninsula, the last (at South Bay) closing in 1922. Just beyond the Old Wharf is Jimmy Harmer's Beach, a safe bathing place for children. *The road ends at 5 km at a rock reef, below the lighthouse, on which lives a:*

**Seal colony:** From here at low tide seals may be seen in the distance, basking on the rocks. Seals by the hundred are found right round the tip of the peninsula. This may be reached by walking from South Bay (*see below*). *Return along the Esplanade. Turn left up Yarmouth St and then half right to climb the hill. Then turn left along Scarborough Tce to pause at:*

**Nga Niho pa site**\*\* (*11 km*): A spectacular site on the lip of a precipice above the town, believed to have been fortified as a second line of defence and never occupied. Some of the defence earthworks remain and an illustration identifies the peaks within view. *Continue along Scarborough Tce to the:*

**Lookout point*** (*at 11.4 km detour to the right*): A splendid vantage point atop the water reservoir, with views of both sides of the peninsula. *Return along Scarborough Tce. Bear half right along the highway (being careful not to make a hard right turn). Take the next turning to the right, Takahanga Tce (beside the hospital), at the end of which is:*

**Takahanga pa****: Traces of the fortifications remain. From the little Maori cemetery (many abandoned *pa* sites were later used as burial grounds) is a superb view over the township to the Seaward Kaikouras. The *pa* fell to Te Rauparaha in 1828 but the southern branches of the defeated tribe subsequently reclaimed the *mana* of the area by defeating the northern invaders.

## OTHER THINGS TO SEE AND DO IN THE AREA

**Kaikoura Historical Society's Museum:** A growing collection has its emphasis on items of local significance, among them Maori artefacts found in the region, and the activities of the area's whalers. *Open weekends 2–4 pm. Parties admitted at other times by arrangement. Ludstone Rd.*

**Seal Colony:** The seals on the tip of the peninsula may be reached from the recreation area at the end of South Bay, starting about ½ hr before low tide. The walk out takes 30 min. Return as the tide begins to turn. Keep to the inland side of any particular seal, leaving his passage to the sea open.

**Mt Fyffe Road**:** An attractive view extends over the poplared Kaikoura hinterland to the coast both north and south of the peninsula. *Turn down Hawthorne Rd from the main north exit from the town. Turn right at its end to follow the road more or less straight up the lower slopes of Mt Fyffe. 7.7 km.*

**Maori Leap Caves**:** The limestone caves, hollowed out by underground streams, contain delicate butter-coloured formations tinted with iron oxide. Their name has no basis in Maori tradition. *By Highway 1 at 3 km S. The caves are at present (1978) closed as unsafe. Enquire locally about resumption of conducted tours.*

**Mangamaunu Beach:** A wild open beach which attracts surfers. *17.5 km N.*

**Two drives:** A pleasant inland drive up the Puhi Puhi Valley through bush and with views of river provides contrast with the seascapes of the coast. *Turn inland from Highway 1 at Hapuku, 12.6 km N of Kaikoura. A second inland drive through bush is up Blue Duck Valley. Turn inland at 19 km N.*

## COAST ROAD

The coast road for the 99 kilometres from the Waima River to Oaro follows the indentations of a wild coastline, affording constantly-changing seascapes as it skirts an exposed, rock-strewn shore at the foot of the Seaward Kaikouras. There are usually a number of opportunities to eat crayfish, either from roadside stalls or at Kaikoura's Cray Pot restaurant in the centre of the town. *Places are listed in geographical order from north to south.*

△**Blenheim** (*264 km from Waipara*): The principal centre of Marlborough, whose wide Wairau plains enjoy an unequalled quota of sunshine.

**Riverland Cob Cottage**** (*4.3 km from Blenheim; 259.7 km from Waipara*): A pioneer cottage museum. *Open continuously. From the Wairau Valley the road lifts over Welds Pass (196 m) and Dashwood Pass (163 m) to the Awatere Valley. A view of Tapuaenuku (2884.3 m), highest peak of the Kaikoura Ranges, is signposted.*

**Seddon** (pop. 587) (*24.5 km from Blenheim; 239.5 km from Waipara*): Previously known as Starborough, the locality was renamed to honour Richard John Seddon (*see index*) who was active as prime minister in breaking up the larger estates for closer settlement. The township is approached by a curious double-decker bridge on which road traffic uses the lower deck and rail the upper. In the cutting opposite the school (*imm. S of the township*) fragments of *moa* shell are frequently found, a phenomenon which occurs over a wide area wherever the subsoil is cut into. There was conspicuously a considerable population of *moa* here as long ago as several million years. Inland, up the Awatere River, are the historic sheepruns of Welds Hill and Molesworth.

△**Lake Grassmere salt works*** (*detour 1.8 km at 33.5 km from Blenheim; 230.5 km from Waipara*): The country's only solar salt works, where seawater is evaporated from wide shallow ponds.

**Ward** (pop. 153) (*44.8 km from Blenheim; 219.2 km from Waipara*): A small farming centre named after Sir Joseph Ward, who was in office when the Flaxbourne estate was broken up into smaller holdings. On the road to Wards Beach a noticeboard records the locality's place in history as comprising part of the original Flaxbourne run. The first great South Island sheep run, it was established in 1847 by Charles Clifford and Frederick Weld (*see index*) on Ngati Toa land leased from Te Puaha. Some 3,000 sheep were shipped from Sydney to Port Underwood in 1847, and at its peak the run covered about 26,600 ha and carried 70,000 sheep. *The road soon meets the coast and turns south to follow the shoreline, virtually uninterrupted, for 99 km.*

**St Oswalds Anglican Church, Wharanui** (*57.2 km from Blenheim; 206.8 km from Waipara*): Built by the Murray family in memory of a son who died in early adulthood, the stone church (1927) contains several memorial windows. In the grounds are a number of family graves. *A short distance beyond the church, looking north one may see the lighthouse on Cape Campbell, the most easterly point of the South Island mainland.*

**Kekerengu** (*67.8 km from Blenheim; 196.2 km from Waipara*): A number of victims from the wreck of the SS *Taiaroa* are buried here. The locality is named after a handsome young Ngati-Ira warrior whose beautiful mother was captured by Te Rauparaha and became Te Rangihaeata's wife. Because of this the warrior was spared, but when he himself became involved with another of Te Rangihaeata's wives, both mother and son were forced to flee from Kapiti Island. Wherever they sought shelter with relations, reprisals were exacted in full measure by the outraged Te Rangihaeata — slaughter which led the chiefs at Kaiapohia (*see index*) to kill Te Rauparaha's uncle, Te Pehi, and so provoke further bloodshed.

Kekerengu's ultimate fate is uncertain, though he escaped the clutches of those who first sought him. He is said to have later visited Kaikoura. On finding only three people there, he killed and ate two of them and took the third, a young girl, for a wife. Ngaitahu are said then to have pursued him to the Clarence and to have killed and eaten his party there.

**Clarence River** (*89 km from Blenheim; 175 km from Waipara*): To the Maori Waiau-toa (rapid water), the river in legend is the male spirit of the lofty inland mountains and Waiau-uha (now simply the Waiau River) is the female. Moving from the Spenser Mountains the waters become separated. As Waiau-uha laments the parting, her tears fell as warm rain to melt the alpine snows, swelling both rivers to massive proportions.

In a grove of gumtrees a little distance behind the new church, on the Woodbank property, is the common grave of some of those who died in the wreck of the *Taiaroa*, lost off the rivermouth in 1886. Local folklore tells of the vessel having on board an opera company and relates that the captain was in his cabin familiarising himself with the prima donna when the ship struck the rocks. He then deserted the singer in favour of the cook, and with the latter disappeared up the Clarence having cached the ship's valuables and the crew's pay near the rivermouth, where the hoard still awaits a fortunate finder. The captain did in fact reappear at the Court of Inquiry, which suspended his master's certificate for two years for failing to take cross-bearings. The inquiry was told that after three times having turned back to collect late-arriving passengers (on one occasion a warp snapped, narrowly missing several bystanders) the steamer had finally left Wellington for Lyttelton with forty-eight aboard. With such omens it was almost inevitable that the 438-ton steamer should run on to the rocks at the mouth of the Clarence, becoming a total loss and drowning thirty-four of those on board. (The captain's cabin from the *Taiaroa* is at the Kaikoura Museum.)

Some 2 km north of the riverbridge, puzzling traces of Maori cultivations may be seen in the faint lines of stones extending down the lower slopes of the hillside. Stones collected were placed in rows as ground was prepared for the planting of *kumara*. Extensive *kumara* gardens here once supported a large population.

*From here south are several attractive picnic areas by the ragged rocks that characterise the region. Occasional cottages sell cooked crayfish.*

△**Kaikoura***** (*127.2 km from Blenheim; 136.8 km from Waipara*): Even the most fleeting traveller should pause to detour briefly out along the peninsula and look back at the snow-draped Seaward Kaikouras.

**Maori Leap Caves**** (*130 km from Blenheim; 136.8 km from Waipara*). *See entry on previous page.*

**Waiau turnoff** (*at 132.4 km from Blenheim; 131.6 km from Waipara*): A slow and largely unsealed alternative route south via the Conway Hills, △Waiau and △Culverden, particularly attractive in its early stages, leaves Highway 1 at this point. South of the turnoff the coast road passes through two curious tunnels rough-hewn from the rocks.

**Parnassus** (*194 km from Blenheim; 70 km from Waipara*): A sheepraising locality whose classical name comes from a run taken up by Edward Lee, a keen classical scholar who saw in a hill a likeness to Mt Parnassus in Greece.

△**Cheviot** (*208 km from Blenheim; 56 km from Waipara*): The township planted by Sir John McKenzie and his fellow Liberals on the expansive estate accumulated by the prospering William "Ready-Money" Robinson. The domain, with the ruins of Robinson's mansion, makes an appealing picnic place.

**Motunau** (*241 km from Blenheim; 23 km from Waipara*): The turnoff here leads to appealing △Motunau Beach.

△**Waipara** (*264 km from Blenheim*): Some 3.3 km north of the junction with Highway 7 is St Paul's Anglican Church, a memorial to the remarkable George Moore.

Recommended reading is *Kaikoura; A History of the District*, by J. M. Sherrard (Kaikoura County Council).

**KAITANGATA**     South Otago.     Maps 4 & 9.     Pop. 31 (vicinity).

*12 km SE of Balclutha.*

THE HILLS THAT rise steeply behind Kaitangata are still seamed with the coal that generated the town. As the mines closed the settlement switched roles from coaltown to a suburb of nearby △Balclutha. One may drive up the road between the Post Office and the venerable Presbyterian Church (1877) for a pleasant view over the "Inch".

**A bloody name:** The origin of the town's name (literally *kai* = food, *tangata* = man) is uncertain. Polynesian mythology tells of the demigod Rupe who forced his way through the heavens to reach the dreaded abode of Rehua, Lord of the Tenth Heaven. There he set about cleaning and beautifying Rehua's dwelling-houses, to which he began to add a new building. His son, Kaitangata, was fixing a heavy beam when it sprang back suddenly, crushing him on the ground. As Rupe picked up his dying son, Kaitangata's blood poured over the several heavens, staining them a deep red so that whenever the sky had a ruddy tinge, succeeding generations of Polynesians would exclaim "Kaitangata stains the heavens with his blood once more!"

There seems to be no particular reason why this locality should be named after Rehua's son. A more likely explanation is that a fight took place here between Ngaitahu and Ngatimamoe in about 1765 in which the latter were defeated, and which was followed by the customary form of feasting. (*Kaitangata* = human food, sometimes euphemistically called long pig). It is also said that nearby Lake Tuakitoto was more correctly called Rangitoto (or Rakitoto, its southern equivalent), meaning day of blood, after a murderous battle had taken place on its shores. A third explanation is that Kaitangata, a skilled painter and one of the crew of the wrecked *Araiteuru* canoe (*see index*), found a supply of *maukoroa* (red clay paint) in the hills here.

### SOME HISTORY

**Epitaph to a coaltown:** There was a river-landing settlement here when, in 1869, the discovery of good-quality coal saw the Kaitangata Coal Company formed to transform the sparsely-settled rural area into a compact coaltown. For nearly a century the centre prospered, broken only by a mining disaster in 1879 and by a temporary hiatus in 1926 when the shale company at △Orepuki crashed, causing difficulties for the company working here which had invested heavily in the Orepuki project. Annual production exceeded 120,000 tons, but gradually dwindled until, under State management, the last of the mines of any consequence closed in 1970. There is still much readily accessible coal, but this tends to be soft and sulphurous. The remaining large reserves of high-quality coal are too deep to be worked economically.

**The Kaitangata disaster:** The events leading up to the 1879 underground explosion in the Kaitangata Coal & Railway Co.'s mine shocked the nation. Not only did thirty-four men lose their lives, but an inquiry revealed defective ventilation, the use of naked lights underground, and a refusal by the manager ("confessedly unskilled") to rectify the company's hazardous methods. Public indignation provoked legislation that provided for strict control over the working of all coalmines.

### ENVIRONS

**Wangaloa Domain:** A picnic area and a track to a sandy swimming beach are beside the golf links. *6.4 km.*

There is safer bathing farther up the coast, in Wangaloa Creek at Measley Beach. It was here that a Maori war party organised by Tuhawaiki to fight Te Rauparaha fell ill. When measles and influenza had taken their toll there were not enough men to man one canoe. Previously there had been nine. The warriors, confused by the *Pakeha* ailments, lay in the surf expecting the cold water to cure their fever. This only helped to kill them. *14.6 km.*

**Lake Tuakitoto:** The low-lying shallow lake is a wildlife sanctuary favoured by a variety of wading birds. *6.3 km N on Lakeside Rd.*

**KARAMEA\***     Buller.     Maps 32 & 38.     Pop. 187.

*98 km NE of Westport.*

THE DAIRYING CENTRE of Karamea lies on a predominantly rich apron of coastal plain, trapped between sea and rugged ranges. This remote West Coast village, at the end of Highway 67, enjoys a micro-climate that earns for it the accolade of "winterless" Karamea. Inland, its bushed slopes streaked with earthquake scars, lie range upon range of steep, forbidding country. The scars show how vulnerable is the slender thread of road south that provides the only access to the district's small population. A second, controversial road has been proposed that would in part follow the Heaphy Track north-east to Collingwood and Golden Bay. There is trout fishing and surf-casting, deer in the hills and good river swimming. Pleasant camping spots abound.

Karamea is probably a shortened form of Kakara-taramea (*kakara* = scent; *taramea* = speargrass), as Maoris would journey long distances to come here to gather speargrass for its scent.

## SOME HISTORY

**A special settlement:** Karamea has been conscious of its isolation since its inception in 1874 as a special settlement organised by the Nelson Provincial Council. Its past is a tale of sorrow, hardship and endurance with few parallels in the country's history. Unsuspecting settlers, lured by land grants, were put ashore to find their promised allotments buried in dense bush. Some literally walked out; others without money to travel from Westport to Nelson, had to stay. For nearly three years the bush was felled and homes constructed before it was found that the land being cleared was useless *pakihi* (barren land) whose shallow cementlike subsoil trapped surface water and would not allow it to drain. The initial years of fruitless endeavour are written on the barren wastes of the south terrace.

The luckless settlers moved their activities upriver to Arapito. There the soil was excellent, but in 1877 a flood destroyed their hard work, leaving them on the brink of starvation. The tenacious settlement recovered once more, for the land was, in the main, rich indeed.

An added discomfort was the erratic steamer service, which caused food scarcity even when the initially-impoverished settlers had money enough to buy it. The road through to Westport did not open until 1915. The township's port on the Karamea River was ruined in the 1929 Murchison earthquake.

## THINGS TO SEE AND DO

**Limestone arch\*:** A remarkable limestone arch bridges the Oparara River. *9 km N on Highway 67 turn right to follow a logging road through the bush to the river. Ask permission at the mill. Inadvisable at times when logging trucks are working.*

**Limestone caves:** There are interesting limestone caves above the Oparara River, some with stalactite and stalagmite formations. *Inquire locally for directions.*

△**Heaphy Track\*\*\*:** The township is the first hint of civilisation at the southern end of the five-day tramp. Those who are not inclined to walk the track in full may do well to drive to the Kohaihai River (where the road north ends) and to walk the first two or three km of the magnificent coastal section.

**Wangapeka Track:** A less well-used track leads up the Little Wanganui River and over the Wangapeka Saddle to emerge on Highway 61. *Described under* △*Nelson.*

> The use of travelling is to regulate imagination by reality, and instead of thinking how things may be, to see them as they are. —Samuel Johnson.

## KARITANE\*\*     East Otago.   Map 9.   Pop. 346.

*34.5 km NNE of Dunedin; 21 km SSW of Palmerston.*

THE DELIGHTFUL SEASIDE village of Karitane looks across a curve in the Waikouaiti estuary to the Huriawa Peninsula. At low water boats lie in disarray across the riverbed but at high tide the sheltered waters deepen and spread to reflect the surrounding landscape. In the trees near the flagstaff that for years signalled the local fishing fleet is the two-storeyed twin-gabled homestead of King's Cliff where Sir Truby King founded the Plunket Society, whose Karitane nurses are a national institution. The peninsula, jagged, ragged and at odds with an otherwise lazy landscape, was the scene of a famous siege and was an island before the river changed its course, a situation Sir Truby King at times feared would recur. Fishing, boating, sandy beaches and a choice between river and ocean swimming have for generations made Karitane the haunt of Dunedin families.

Opinions vary as to the meaning of Karitane (literally: *kari* = to dig; *tane* = men) but one legend tells of a local girl, Wairaka, who desired as a husband one of a visiting group. That night she crept into the visitors' communal hut and scratched his face as he lay sleeping to identify him in the morning as her betrothed. But another among the visitors, who had seen the looks Wairaka had given her intended and who desired the girl for himself, changed places with him and so Wairaka had scratched the face of the wrong man. The incident gave rise to a proverb: "What a terrible mistake Wairaka made in the dark."

## SOME HISTORY

**Huriawa Peninsula:** The peninsula was a superb natural *pa* site. Volcanic in origin, it rises sheer from the sea and had the twin blessings of a reliable spring and a small cove on its northern side where canoes could be safely beached. It was selected for this purpose in *c.* 1730 to serve Ngaitahu under Te Wera, but had in all probability previously been used by Ngatimamoe.

Te Wera had only just been chosen as chief by his Te Ruahikihiki *hapu* when they became embroiled in continual strife with his belligerent cousins, Taoka and Moki II. Trouble began when Te Wera was accused of practising *makutu* (wizardry) on his kinsfolk and of killing them. First he sought sanctuary at Purakaunui (*see index*) where Te Rehu, his brother-in-law, held sway. Attacked there, the pair made a miraculous escape and arrived at Huriawa to find that a *tangi* (mourning ceremony) for them had already begun. Together they exacted vengeance, and in turn Taoka arrived at Huriawa and proceeded to lay siege. For six months the siege continued, as the *pa* had its own water supply and fishing parties could put out at night to supplement food stored on the wellnigh impregnable promontory. An anxious moment came when one of Taoka's scouts crept in by way of the blowholes and stole the image of Te Wera's protecting deity. Despair swept through the *pa* when Taoka was seen across the river waving it triumphantly above his head, but Te Wera's *tohunga* (priest) Hautu restored it to the *pa*, some say simply through the air, by means of a powerful *karakia* (incantation). Finally Taoka was forced to withdraw for want of food, as the defenders had denuded the area of vegetables before his *taua* (war-party) arrived. Later Taoka turned his attention to Mapoutahi *pa* (*see index*) to telling effect. Te Wera survived ultimately to die as an old man at Stewart Island.

The blowholes on the peninsula are attributed to a romance. A couple eloped and eventually returned, expecting forgiveness. Instead their irate families took them to the peninsula and hurled them from the cliffs. The young girl, heavier than her husband, is said to have caused the larger blowhole, that nearest Puketeraki Beach. There are in reality not two but three blowholes, but surviving mythology does not explain the third.

**The reluctant missionary:** A whaling station opened at Karitane in 1837 and it was here in 1840 rather than at what is now △Waikouaiti that the Rev. James Watkin (1805–86) elected to live, despite the fact that he had come from Sydney at the instigation and at the expense of Johnny Jones (*see index*). The Methodist missionary, who had been praying for a return to Britain, did not relish the experience; he chose for the text of the first Christian sermon preached in Otago, "This is a fearful saying", and when his successor, the Rev. Charles Creed, arrived in 1844 Watkin greeted him with the words, "Welcome, Brother Creed, welcome to Purgatory."

Certainly there was little for Watkin to enthuse over. The settlement was a hotbed of drunkenness, immorality and violence, from which the Maoris mainly suffered, and the two-roomed native *whare* Jones provided for him was hardly suitable for one with a wife and five children. Certainly the nauseated Watkin tried, taking a firm stand against the vices of the *Pakeha* and the "savage customs" of the Maori. To a degree he succeeded; mission schools were established, converts made and an elementary Maori reader prepared and published. But Watkin was never reconciled to his position and was intensely relieved to sail for Wellington, leaving his degenerate parishioners behind. Tortured by ill health, he continually doubted his own considerable ability and lamented his lack of support and the depravity of those around him. A rare moment of elation came when one of his converts at △Moeraki refused to give the census-taker Shortland any information because it was the Sabbath. Of Bishop Selwyn he conceded: "I think he is a good man, as far as his church prejudices will allow."

**Sir Truby King** (1858–1938): In later years the settlement blossomed as a seaside resort and owes its geographical form partly to Sir Truby King, who had no sooner built his home on the peninsula than he became fearful that the river might cut through the slender isthmus that ties it to the mainland. He would not hesitate to rouse residents on stormy nights and direct them as they slaved to carry sand and build up the *manuka* sandbreaks he had placed on the narrow neck. Eventually the breaks were built up to such a degree that the danger passed. King was also the moving force behind the planting of the various gums and hardy deciduous trees.

King is perhaps the best known of New Zealand's medical reformers. Son of one of the first settlers at New Plymouth, he attended university at Glasgow and returned to become superintendent, first of Wellington Hospital and then of the Seacliff Mental Hospital. A reformer in many fields he is best remembered for his founding of the Plunket Society (named after Lord Plunket, then Governor-General) which in his lifetime saw infant mortality drop by two-thirds, from 88.8 to 30.9 per 1,000 births. It was at his Karitane home that the first Plunket baby was reared. The Royal New Zealand Society for the Health of Women and Children (to give it its full title) remains an integral part not only of the country's public health services, with Plunket Rooms throughout New Zealand staffed with Plunket nurses trained to educate mothers in child care, but of New Zealand society itself. Its success led to an invitation to King to establish a similar organisation in Britain. On his return in 1921 he became first Director of Child Welfare and then, until his retirement in 1927, Inspector-General of Mental Hospitals. Karitane nurses, trained in baby care, help mothers with their children.

The phenomenal success of the Plunket Society and the worldwide acclamation that followed have overshadowed other important aspects of his work. Truby King made major contributions in many fields — nutrition, plant acclimatisation, control of coastal erosion, alcoholism, psychological medicine and medical jurisprudence. His many achievements in the field of psychiatric medicine include dietary innovations, the establishment at Seacliff in 1898 of the country's first "open" ward, the early development of the villa-hospital concept, and a study of the influence of dental disease on the physical and mental wellbeing of psychiatric patients. Change was not easily brought about and Truby King was frequently the centre of controversy, but invariably the soundness of his forcefully expressed views prevailed.

## THINGS TO SEE AND DO

**Waikouaiti Maori Foreshore Reserve:** A picnic reserve runs along the riverbank near the new wharf, whence a short track leads up to a terrace where stands the Watkin Memorial. Shaped like a lectern so that it may be used as such at future memorial services, the cairn marks the place where Watkin conducted the first Christian service in Otago, on 17 May 1840. The cairn stands on the fringe of an old Maori cemetery and affords a delightful prospect across the river and foreshore to Waikouaiti and to Matanaka, where Johnny Jones had his homestead. In the river beyond the new wharf is a swimming hole still locally known as King's Hole. *Signposted.*

**Blowholes:** Ask directions locally to the blowholes of the myth. These are seen to best advantage at high tide.

## ENVIRONS

△ **Waikouaiti:** The town that began as Otago's earliest organised settlement is now called by the name that once applied to Karitane. *6.5 km.*

**Seacliff** (pop. 137): Sir Truby King, a man of many parts, was for some thirty-one years superintendent of the mental hospital at the village of Seacliff. The setting was superb, but the enterprise got off to the worst possible start. A magnificent-looking series of stone buildings was designed by R. A. Lawson, whose commission was at the time the largest ever paid in the Colony. In Scottish Baronial style, the three-storeyed Oamaru-stone buildings were modelled on the Norwich County Asylum in England, with a 50 m tower. Criticism was not limited to the design — dayrooms received little sun, bedroom windows were too high to see the view, and for the 1,273 doors there was an embarrassing diversity of keys. The very foundations proved woefully inadequate for the notoriously unstable site. Not long after the £78,000 contract had been completed, a royal commission was set up which criticised both architect and builder. For all the outcries through the years over the unsafe nature of the buildings, it was not until 1972, nearly a century later, that the last of the patients were finally evacuated to Cherry Farm and the last of the complex demolished.

King transformed into a hospital a place the public had hitherto regarded as a gaol. After he became Superintendent in 1888, patients were given outside work, greater liberty and more exercise. The use of violence by warders was banned. The Seacliff farm flourished, and King's careful attention to livestock and seed selection drew the resentment of neighbouring farmers who envied his success at A & P shows. Poultry was raised and in 1903 the patients began a fishing enterprise that fed the asylum twice a week and supplied other institutions throughout the South Island. Ever attentive to staff, Truby King emulated Johnny Jones in buying land and helping them to finance their own homes. It was while King was at Seacliff that he recognised the importance of nutrition both for mental patients and, as an adjunct to his rearing of cattle, for children.

The asylum's most notable inmate was Lionel Terry (1874?–1952), an Englishman educated at Eton and Oxford who tramped the country in 1901 lecturing on the perils of New Zealand being taken over by the Chinese. In his book of poetry, *The Shadow*, he extolled the virtues of "pure . . . unpolluted northern blood" and saw in the quiet industry of the Chinese a subtle attempt to conquer the country by weakening the Anglo-Saxons with "luxury and idleness". His book did not sell well. On learning this he made his point more dramatically by walking the streets of Wellington to find and shoot an elderly Chinese, who, he reasoned, was too old to care much about living anyway. He promptly confessed and wrote to the Governor complaining of "alien invaders". Terry tapped an extensive well of anti-Chinese resentment and his trial caused a sensation. Sentenced to death, his sentence was commuted to one of life imprisonment and he was removed here after setting fire to the gaol at Lyttelton. He escaped on numerous occasions, to be fed, clothed and concealed by his many admirers, some 50,000 of whom signed a petition for his release. Finally King offered Terry a degree of liberty conditional on his not escaping again, terms he accepted for the rest of his life. At the time of his death here in 1952 he wore long flowing robes and long flowing hair, and was convinced he was the second Messiah. (Some of Terry's poems are in the museum at Waikouaiti.) *Seacliff. 5.9 km SW.*

**St Barnabas's Anglican Church, Warrington\*:** This delightful church nestles under tall trees on a site that slopes gently seaward. Bishop Nevill (1837–1921) came here to consecrate the church in 1873 and one can appreciate why the man who went on to become Primate of New Zealand chose to be buried here. Within, the sombre interior is characterised by rich inscriptions and by a remarkable series of seven lights. These, in comprising the west window, spangle virtually the entire wall with coloured light. *10.3 km SW.*

A metric conversion chart appears at the end of the book.

## TOURING NOTE

**Coastal route to Dunedin:** The coastal route south to Waitati is superior to Highway 1. It affords magnificent panoramas, first north over Karitane and Waikouaiti Bay (*3 km*) and in the latter stages south across to the ocean beaches that lie along the northern arm of Otago Harbour. Seacliff and St Barnabas's Anglican Church, Warrington are also passed (*for both see above*).

---

△ indicates a place with its own entry.

---

### KUMARA* Westland. Maps 2, 15, 17 & 37. Pop. 304.

*28 km NE of Hokitika; 24 km S of Greymouth.*

SEVERAL TOWNSHIPS on the West Coast boast Seddon Street as their principal thoroughfare, but it was Kumara, a little distance from the Taramakau River, that witnessed the political birth of the immortal prime minister. Born a booming goldtown, Kumara was for some time the scene of the country's last working gold dredge.

Kumara means sweet potato but the town may have been named after a flower (either of the convolvulus or the bush-lawyer variety). It may also originally have been *kohimara*.

## SOME HISTORY

**An unlikely strike:** The rush to the Kumara diggings is said to have begun after a wandering prospector had come across a party of sly-groggers. While digging out the foundations for the tubs of their illicit whisky-still on the banks of the Taramakau, they had struck payable ground and switched their activities from making wash (illicit spirit) to washing gold. The account is unlikely, as an official reward of £200 for the discovery was made to a prospector, James Robinson, though it is possible that the real circumstances of the find may not have been spelt out in detail to the inquiry. The stampede to Kumara that marked the grand finale to the saga of the West Coast began in June 1876. Among the first of the arrivals was a storekeeper-publican from Big Dam, near Goldsborough, one Richard John Seddon.

**"King Dick":** Anecdotes are legion concerning Richard John Seddon (1845-1906), the Kumara publican who survived bankruptcy to become New Zealand's most dominating political figure. Though the son of Lancashire school-teachers, Seddon left school at the age of fourteen and, after serving an apprenticeship in an engineering shop, migrated to Melbourne in 1863. From the Victorian goldfields and the Melbourne railway workshop he moved to Hokitika, where he turned his Australian experience to good account, investing the proceeds in goldfield stores. On the diggings he gained renown as much for his strength and his ability with his fists as for his astonishing natural aptitude for legal work. His services as a lay-advocate in the Warden's Court were so much in demand that it was only appropriate that the self-taught expert in mining law should in later life be the recipient of an honorary doctorate of laws from Cambridge University. However his earnings in the Warden's Court could not offset his losses elsewhere, and he was forced in 1878 to file in bankruptcy.

The year before, his dabbling in local politics had seen him become the first mayor of Kumara, and in the following year Seddon was elected to Parliament as a determined follower of the Liberal leader, Sir George Grey. He condemned large landholdings and Chinese immigration alike, while proposing that North Island Maoris be pacified by the building of railways through their land. From this unlikely beginning he blossomed into a master of parliamentary procedures and was the first to realise the implications of the rise of the Labour party, advocating that the Liberals support the just demands of the workers:

On the death of John Ballance, Seddon assumed both party leadership and the office of premier. For thirteen years he held unquestioned sway. Rugged, ruthless, and a forceful speaker on the platform as well as in the House, Seddon dominated the political scene to an extent never seen before or since. King Dick he was called by friend and foe alike, albeit for differing reasons.

Under his leadership the Liberal Party set the pattern for today's welfare state. The country became the first in the world to extend the vote to women (a measure Seddon agreed to only with reluctance), the world's first Old Age Pensions Bill was forced through a determined "stonewall" erected by the Opposition, and the world's first industrial legislation incorporating a form of compulsory arbitration was passed. Other enlightened measures, and Seddon's personal imperialism, saw him win election after election, each more decisively than the one before, until in 1905 his party held a full sixty-five of the eighty seats and faced an impoverished Opposition that numbered all of fifteen. Yet his election wins did not reflect any growing competence: Seddon's overbearing nature brooked no contradiction, and the reforms ran out as the talented ministers he had inherited from Ballance passed from the scene. Finally the cabinet comprised comparative nonentities, chosen by Seddon for their acquiescence to his will. On the left the Political Labour League defected and in what should have been the party's finest hour the seeds of its destruction were already apparent.

But the man to whom power was everything would neither let go nor let up. "Diversion," recalled William Pember Reeves (the Minister of Labour who gave the country the world's most complete labour code), "he appeared neither to have nor want. I cannot recall hearing him talk of any non-political subject for ten minutes." A biographer has noted, too: "His political morality was not immaculate; his patriotism unduly blatant; the principles of democracy that he advocated so zealously found no place in his cabinet, his party, or in any institution over which he exercised control; yet the autocratic power he acquired was seldom abused in the larger sphere of government, and his statesmanship was always guided and governed by a genuine love of humanity."

He died suddenly, of a coronary attack, as he ended a hectic tour of Australia and shortly after telegraphing the Victorian State premier: "Just returning to God's own country" — a telegram that gives rise to the legend that it was he who first coined the phrase now sometimes abbreviated to Godzone. *The site of Seddon's home, neighbouring his likewise vanished Queen's Hotel, is marked by an Historic Places Trust plaque and has become a picnic site. At the eastern extremity of the main street (Seddon St), 100 m past the Mitchell turnoff and on the opposite side of the road.*

**Kanieri Dredge,** the last of the country's big dredges, has for a number of years been both seen and heard working on the Taramakau River near the township. Built in 1938 on Lake Kaniere, the dredge scooped up about two tons of spoil at a time. Large rocks were rejected immediately and the remainder was sprayed with water while it underwent a mechanised form of goldpanning — pulsators washing the dirt away and the heavier gold remaining. About 10,000 ounces of gold were won each year.

## POINTS OF INTEREST

**Mineshafts:** A series of short shafts burrow beneath the river terrace. *Behind the Hotel Theatre Royal (Seddon St).* The hotel was originally a vaudeville house, featuring travelling shows.

**Londonderry Rock\*:** A huge monolith, sluiced round and slightly undermined, stands in a sea of tailings. *Drive 1.6 km down the track by the Kumara School. A 5-min track leads over heaps of tailings to the rock.*

## ENVIRONS

**Kumara cemetery:** Here lie natives from many lands (one "native of Canterbury NZ" is almost incongruous). Some were killed in mining accidents. *Turn up opp. the Empire Hotel for 2.7 km.*

**First Westland Goldfield:** The first payable goldfield in Westland was found by Albert Hunt in 1864, near Kumara. Behind the plaque recording the discovery may be seen part of an old tailrace. *9.3 km on the road to Mitchells.*

---

**KUROW     North Otago.     Maps 28 & 35.     Pop. 470.**

*66 km NW of Oamaru; 53 km SE of Omarama.*

THE RIVERSIDE FARMING centre of Kurow lies beneath the St Mary's Range at the end of the branch line from Pukeuri. The township has an ephemeral transport role for the Upper Waitaki power scheme which has kept the rail line open for longer than might otherwise have been the case. Here, too, the Waitaki is bridged, to serve the Hakataramea Valley of South Canterbury. The town, with streets named after New Zealand governors, was laid out in 1880 when work began on the line, then planned to extend up the Hakataramea.

Kurow is a corruption of Te Kohurau (many mists, or a hundred mists) the Maori name for Mt Bitterness (*1900.8 m*), which is frequently covered with fog. A legend tells of a chief, pursued up the range by his enemies, who conjured up a heavy fog with an effective *karakia* (chant) that enabled him to escape. Te Kohurau was also the name of the burial cave of Uenuku, a fabled chief in Hawaiki.

In winter there is skiing on the Awakino grounds behind the township (*contact the Waitaki Ski Club, PO Box 191, Oamaru*).

**Fishing:** Kurow is a natural centre for fishing the Hakataramea and Waitaki Rivers, and the hydro lakes. Trout and salmon draw fishermen throughout the season.

## SOME HISTORY

**Campbell of Otekaieke:** Pre-eminent among early runholders was the Hon. Robert Campbell (1843–89), whose greatuncle founded the celebrated Australian family who owned the land that became the Federal Capital Territory. (Some even claim that Canberra was the nearest an Australian Aboriginal could get to pronouncing the name Campbell.)

He held a share in three Benmore runs as well as in Lake Ohau, controlling some 84,840 ha. In the course of acquiring extensive properties in Southland and Central

Otago as well as in the North Island, his firm bought Otekaieke where, in the Scottish-styled Baronial mansion that still stands, the Eton-educated doyen of the sheep-kings took up residence. His holding of the lease provoked strong local feeling, one correspondent to the *North Otago Times* objecting that "The true progress of the district, with the welfare of hundreds involved in it, is made to give way to the covetousness of one rich man."

Extremely active in local affairs, Campbell was almost silent in Parliament and as a Member of the Legislative Council, where virtually his only contribution was roundly to condemn attempts to make a better class of land available for closer settlement, as this would deprive large runholders of the most fertile areas of their leases. In 1885 he was questioned by a Parliamentary committee, where it was established that his company had deliberately evaded provisions restricting land aggregation. From then on he took little part in public life.

## THINGS TO SEE AND DO

**Kurow Museum** displays a small collection in which photographs illustrate the importance of the valley as a route to Central Otago by way of the △Lindis Pass. Early farm implements are also displayed. *Main St. Open 2-3 pm daily and by arrangement with Mr B. Appleby, tel. 865 (working hours) or 679.* There were three accommodation houses here, one of which survives as a home (*by the highway 2.5 km E of the town*).

**The Chapel** (1896)*: The Hon. Robert Campbell's wealth is epitomised by the grandiose stone vicarage to which the Anglican church is simply an appendage. Together with stables, they were built largely with a legacy from Campbell's widow. *By Highway 83 — to S of the town.*

**Jetboat:** A service for fishing, shooting and picnic parties as well as water-skiing and pleasure runs is operated by Mr A. B. Main, Te Kohurau Milk Bar. *Main St, opposite Post Office. Tel. 625.*

## ENVIRONS

**Waitaki hydro-electric power station** (*6.4 km N*): *Described under* △*Waitaki Valley.*

**Aviemore hydro-electric power station** (*14 km N*): *Described under* △*Waitaki Valley.*

**Hakataramea Valley*:** There are some excellent swimming and fishing spots on a most picturesque route to the Mackenzie country. (*Note:* The Hakataramea Pass is negotiable only in dry summer weather. Enquire locally before attempting the through route to Tekapo.)

**Otekaieke Special School for Boys:** Robert Campbell's homestead block has since 1908 been held by the Department of Education as a residential school for children of below average ability. Fruit and vegetables are grown and forestry provides older boys with useful training as they work at a number of jobs to find the occupation that best suits them. The school's counterpart for girls is at Nelson. Of historical interest is the evolution of dwellings that still remain on the property, all within a few metres of each other — the cave wherein J. P. Taylor, the original runholder, lived from 1855; Dansey's little stone cottage (*c.* 1857); and finally the sumptuous mansion (1877) and splendid stone stables built by the Hon. Robert Campbell. Otekaieke is a corruption whose origin is uncertain. *Owing to the nature of the school casual visitors are not admitted to the grounds other than by prior arrangement with the principal. The partly-obscured homestead may be seen from the road. Turn up the side road signposted "Otekaieke" 12.7 km S of Kurow. 15 km.*

## TOURING NOTE

**Highway 82 to** △**Waimate:** At Kurow one may cross the Waitaki and follow Highway 82 to Waimate.

To make the most of your travels you should carry with you the book of Mobil road maps. A table of distances between major centres appears on page 363.

**LAWRENCE*** **Central Otago. Maps 4, 9 & 14. Pop. 585.**
*92.5 km W of Dunedin; 37 km NW of Milton; 58 km SE of Roxburgh.*

LINES OF POPLARS give way to an avenue of silver birch trees as Lawrence is approached from the south. The town, on the fringe of Central Otago and tilted towards the golden gully that brought it into existence, is characterised by its Victorian architecture, reflecting every style and embodying every material. In its buildings its story is plainly written; one of burgeoning growth followed by gentle decline. Lawrence is now a farming centre with some of its quaint cottages serving as cribs for Dunedin owners.

**Tuapeka Domain:** Rising steeply above the town is the tree-shaded reserve where in 1911 no fewer than 300 old goldminers congregated to dedicate a cairn to commemorate Gabriel Read's fabulous find of half a century before.

## SOME HISTORY

**"Gold, Gold, Gold!"** The people of Otago had become accustomed over a period of ten years to reports of fabulous gold discoveries that invariably faded to insignificance, yet they were thoroughly aroused when a letter appeared in the *Otago Witness* in July 1861 addressed to the Superintendent of Otago, Major Richardson: "Had I made anything like an exhibition of my gold, the Plain would have been deserted by all the adult inhabitants the next day, and the farmers would have suffered seriously from a neglect of agricultural operations at this season of the year. Although the being able to work secretly for a time would greatly benefit me, I feel it my duty to impart these facts."

The news seemed too good to be true, but the letter-writer, Gabriel Read, was known to have had Californian and Australian experience, and his assertions were quickly confirmed — gold was found in every hole that was sunk over an area 56 km long by 8 km broad.

The stampede to Gabriel's Gully was on. Reported one observer from the fields, "Men whom I had never met before save with a smile on their countenance, and a joke on their lips, I met there, grave and solemn, as if the cares of a nation were centred on them — they could not even appreciate a joke." By the end of July there were 11,472 persons in the district, twice as many as in the Otago capital.

There in Dunedin, "Gold, gold, gold is the universal subject of conversation . . . The number of persons leaving town each morning is quite surprising. The fever is running at such a height that, if it continues, there will scarcely be a man left in town . . . The Tokomairiro plain is positively deserted . . . if the fever continues, there will be little crop to reap . . . On the last Sunday the congregation at church consisted of the minister and precentor." As Vincent Pyke was to write, "society was temporarily unhinged".

Other discoveries quickly followed. A shepherd's wife found payable gold in Munro's Gully, then Gabriel Read discovered a further field at Waitahuna. More finds confirmed the permanence of the Otago goldfields and in October the Superintendent could assure the Provincial Council that "Whatever may be the character, extent, richness, and remunerative nature of our Goldfield, I have no doubt that for many a day to come it will yield to industry a fair return for labour, and to capital a fair return of profit."

**Gabriel Read:** There is no more fascinating figure on the Otago goldfields than their discoverer, the Tasmanian, Thomas Gabriel Read (1824–94), who sailed to the Californian goldfields and later was caught up in the Victorian rushes. The violence and excesses of the fields there disgusted him and he was back in Tasmania when he heard rumours of finds in Southland. Read arrived in Dunedin and, against the advice of many, made his way to the Tuapeka area, prospecting as he went. Hearing of a find by one Black Peter — a half-caste East Indian from Bombay — he set off for the area, and to the accompaniment of good-natured derision disappeared into the hills and gullies. On 23 May 1861 he struck gold in what was to be known as Gabriel's Gully. In his own words "At a place where a kind of road crossed on a shallow bar I shovelled away about 2½ ft of gravel, arrived at a beautiful soft slate and saw the gold shining like the stars in Orion on a dark frosty night." Once satisfied that the deposit was rich indeed, he wrote his remarkable letter, giving location and prospects, holding back nothing.

The public-spirited Read was prepared to take his chance with the others with pick and shovel, relying on collecting the £500 reward offered by the Provincial Council. Soon he was off again, fossicking far and wide as a paid prospector for the Provincial Government, but his tastes had changed: he collected the reward, which the grateful Council actually doubled, and after a wide tour of the country he returned to Hobart.

Upright and altruistic almost to a fault, Read did all he could to preserve a form of order on the goldfield he had found. Frequently he adjudicated in disputes and at all times displayed the greatest concern for the welfare of the community, even to the extent of paying £50 to bring the first religious services to the field. When he suspected that the banks were underpaying the diggers, Read sent gold to Sydney for independent assay. Though the results increased the return to the miners, it was for the uncomplaining Read to bear the cost of the exercise.

Widespread lawlessness had been predicted by the *Otago Witness*, but Read played a part in seeing that such fears were not realised. His action in immediately making public his find is in direct contrast with the deceit and subterfuge that surrounded the other and later notable discoveries — of Hartley and Reilly on the Clutha and even more so of William Fox and his associates on the Arrow.

**Black Peter:** The luckless Edward Peters (?–1893), known as Black Peter — whose modest success as a prospector had led Read to the goldfield — also applied for the reward. His claim was ignored by the Provincial Government, but eventually (and some twenty-seven years after the event) Parliament agreed to grant him a modest £50 conditional on the public finding a like sum. This it did, and so, belatedly and inadequately, Black Peter finally received a measure of the recognition that was his due.

**Sister townships:** Two town sites were surveyed in 1862, Lawrence (where the Wetherstons and Gabriels Gully streams met), and Havelock (now Waitahuna) where the Waitahuna River was usually forded. The sister townships were given related names, honouring both Sir Henry Lawrence (the heroic defender of Lucknow during the Indian Mutiny of 1857) and Sir Henry Havelock (who led the first relief column to that beleaguered Indian city only to find himself besieged until the arrival of Sir Colin Campbell). The name Havelock, however, never gained currency and eventually was changed to Waitahuna to bring officialdom into line with local usage.

Pressure from the goldfield brought government officials to Lawrence well before there was any proper accommodation. When court sittings were held in a tent "the presiding Magistrate occasionally suffered the indignity of having his papers whirled in his face by some passing gust of wind. The Clerk of the Bench might be seen laying violent hands on depositions that would not remain in their proper places, or else endeavouring by the exercise of considerable ingenuity to find some spot where they might be safe from the streams of water that poured in on rainy days."

For all this the town developed rapidly, though its borough council enjoyed a rough passage. Meetings were lively, opinions forthrightly expressed, and the sight of petulant councillors storming out of meetings to resign in protest became so commonplace, and the expense of by-elections so great, that a fine of £10 was occasionally imposed on the departing member to recover at least some of the cost of the resulting by-election.

With the town sited on the junction of two important goldbearing streams, silting caused by mining operations resulted in flooding. Gabriels Gully Creek was diverted to join Wetherstons some short distance below the town's centre, and a sludge channel was built for town drainage parallel to the Wetherstons Creek.

The peak of the gold boom was reached in 1862, when nearly 200,000 ounces were taken out by the gold escort. Within four years the yield had slumped to 28,000 ounces and slowly further declined until, by the late 1930s, production finally ended.

## GABRIELS GULLY ROUND TRIP**

*8.4 km. A short round trip leads through old gold workings and returns along a ridge which affords wide views of the town and surrounding countryside. The trip can be extended to be one of 14 km by turning off at Jacobs Ladder to visit Victoria Dam and return by Monros Gully. From the town turn down the road signposted "Gabriels Gully" to cross the sludge channel and Wetherstons Creek and pass the:*

**Lawrence flourmill site** (*0.1 km*): For a time much grain was grown in the region and supplied to mills at Evans Point and at Lawrence. *Cross Gabriels Gully Creek bridge and continue up Gabriels Gully itself, now deep with broom-covered tailings, to reach the:*

**Blue Spur Treasure House** (*0.9 km*): A collection of relics of the departed Blue Spur township, a settlement sufficiently substantial to have produced three Judges. *Open by arrangement with the occupants of the house behind. Continue on up the valley to pass the:*

**Pick and Shovel Monument** (*3.3 km*): The monument records Read's finding of gold in the gully in 1861. There is a picnic area opposite. *Continue up the valley, bearing left up the steep zigzag of:*

**Jacobs Ladder** (*3.5 km*): A biblical allusion, the name was regularly given to steep rises. (*Near the top of Jacobs Ladder one may turn right to descend to Victoria Dam* (*5.2 km: one of the last of the sluicing dams) and return to Lawrence through the workings of Monros Gully). On the ridge at the top of Jacobs Ladder lies the:*

**Blue Spur town site** (*4.1 km*): The since-departed township was once down in the Gully but was moved here to make way for the tailings that now fill the Gully to a depth of nearly 20 m.

*From here the road undulates along a ridge that affords lovely views of Lawrence set in rolling countryside. When the road dips into Gabriels Gully turn right and return to Lawrence.*

## ENVIRONS

**Wetherston:** Adjacent to Gabriels Gully is the site of another rush, provoked in 1861 when the Weatherston brothers combined prospecting with pighunting. Within hours miners were pouring over the hill from Gabriels Gully and by the year's end there were over 5,000 on the most populous field of the time.

The rush to Wetherston saw the two local banks, the Bank of New South Wales and the Union Bank, run out of banknotes. Falconer Larkworthy, manager of the Bank of New Zealand at Dunedin, saw the chance to establish his bank in the area. He printed his own notes and exchanged them for about 4,000 ounces of gold. Uproar followed when the Union Bank questioned the notes' legality and accepted them only after enraged miners had threatened to take the law into their own hands. For the Bank of New Zealand the publicity won could not have been bought, and the grateful directors rewarded the enterprising Larkworthy by appointing him managing director in London.

The once-feverish scene is today almost deserted, but the brick remains of the Black Horse Brewery may be seen at the road's end, beside which a track leads up the valley to the Phoenix Dam, a sluicing dam good for fishing and today used for the Lawrence water-supply. A second track leads over to Gabriels Gully. The brewery, founded in 1866, closed in 1923 after being taken over by New Zealand Breweries. It had served a wide and appreciative public, but none so lacking in discrimination as those who drank the day a spoiled brew was run off down Brewery Creek. Hens, ducks, geese and even pigs were all supposedly seen lying on their backs with their feet in the air. In spring the area is renowned for its array of daffodils. *2.8 km off the road towards Waipori.*

**Waitahuna** (pop. 160): Originally named Havelock, the official name never displaced the local title of Waitahuna and it is said that for this reason a post office intended for Waitahuna was in fact built in Havelock, on the Marlborough Sounds. The town was busy enough during the 1870s, but was on the wane by the time a post office was finally built, in 1879, for only two years later it was removed for want of patronage.

After the dredging era passed, Waitahuna gradually declined as Lawrence assumed the role of service centre to the surrounding rural area. It had in any event developed more slowly than its sister settlement, the goldbearing Waitahuna Gully some little distance away attracting the greater attention. Today the last building of the Waitahuna Gully settlement, the solid **Athenaeum** (1870) serves as a woolshed and as testimony to the miners' misplaced conviction that the gold would last. In the midst of the old workings a **cairn** marks the place where Baldwin and Gabriel Read discovered the Waitahuna gold in July 1861. *At 10.9 km S of Lawrence on Highway 8 turn left to Waitahuna Gully. The Athenaeum is at 14.3 km and the monument at 15.9 km. One may continue through Waitahuna Gully to rejoin Highway 8 some 8 km south of Waitahuna.*

---

The New Zealand Forest Service has offices throughout the country which issue permits for hunting in State Forests and in Forest Parks. They also advise as to the best hunting areas.

---

## LEWIS PASS ROAD*   Map 21.   Height: 863.7 m.

A ROUTE FOR Canterbury Ngaitahu as they journeyed to Westland for greenstone, yet neglected in goldrush times, the Lewis Pass was not roaded until as late as 1937. It marks the point on the Main Divide that separates the Waiau from the Maruia watershed. European explorers of the area, from 1860, were Lewis, Maling, Stuart, Travers and Rochfort.

### SOME HISTORY

**Routes to the greenstone:** The Ngaitahu of Canterbury used a number of routes across the ranges to the greenstone (*see index*) country, among them the Lewis Pass, Arthur's Pass, Whitcombe and Browning Passes, Harper Pass (beyond Lake Sumner) and the Amuri Pass. To prevent their feet from being torn on broken rock and by the barbs of *matagouri*, they wore sandals of plaited flax. For food they carried fern-root, *kauru* (a sweet substance extracted from the roots of the *ti* tree) and *kumara*, but also relied on the eels, *weka* and pigeons they could catch on the way. For the return journey there was *kai tangata* (human flesh), carried by slaves who themselves were destined for the ovens when their usefulness was over.

### POINTS OF INTEREST

*Listed in order from west to east on Highway 7, from Reefton to Waipara.*

△**Reefton*** (*199 km from Waipara*): The Town of Reefs, "Quartzopolis", where relics of goldmining days lie in the surrounding bush. Immediately after leaving the town, Highway 7 in turn passes Blacks Point (where there is a museum and a rebuilt quartz battery) and Crushington (where the remains of the Wealth of Nations battery are by the roadside) as it follows the ever-shrinking Inangahua River.

**Rahu Saddle** (*676.4 m*) (*37 km from Reefton; 162 km from Waipara*): Here the road leaves the Inangahua River to fall in with the Rahu, a tributary of the Maruia. Hereabouts the road passes through stands of attractive native bush.

**Springs Junction** (pop. 53) (*45 km from Reefton; 162 km from Waipara*): Here Highway 65 from △Murchison joins Highway 7. Soon the road enters the dense beech forest of the Lewis Pass Scenic Reserve. This is the most splendid section of the route, with mountains towering above the forest, and alpine vistas at every turn.

**Maruia Hot Springs** (*61 km from Reefton; 138 km from Waipara*): A solitary hotel in the bush has pools where one may enjoy the luxury of a hot swim in an alpine setting. Maruia, a valley deep in the mountains, means sheltered, or shady. The valley was disputed by the ancient Maori, not only as a route to the greenstone country but also for its *weka* and for the eels found at the sources of the rivers.

# LEWIS PASS ROAD

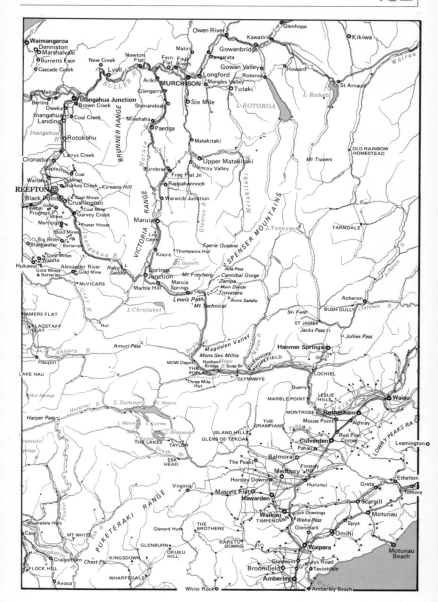

## 21

**Lewis Pass** (*863.7 m*) (*66 km from Reefton; 133 km from Waipara*): Shortly before reaching the summit the road follows a perilous lip high above the Maruia River. A little beyond the summit, at the mouth of Cannibal Gorge, a plaque records the early European explorers of the area. Ngaitahu visiting the West Coast for greenstone would take prisoners to carry the precious stone back to Canterbury. On reaching this point, and with food running low, the slaves would be despatched. To the Maori the Gorge was Kapai-o-kai-tangata (good feed of human flesh).

The road begins its descent, in turn following the courses of the Lewis, Boyle and Hope Rivers. The pass was not named until Julius von Haast honoured the surveyor whose daughter was his relation by marriage.

**Magdalene Valley** (*83 km from Reefton; 116 km from Waipara*): Tradition persists that there was once in Magdalene Valley a French colony now marked by cypress groves, grapevines and crumbling monastery walls. Its only factual basis lies in the presence here in 1860 of two French aristocrats, Gerard Gustavus Ducarel, Count de la Pasture, and his brother, Henri Philippe Ducarel de la Pasture, who together farmed Glynn Wye. The Count lived in Christchurch but would frequently visit his estate. On one occasion his buggy was upset, the Countess falling out to lend her title unceremoniously to Countess Creek.

**Glynn Wye deer farm** (*105 km from Reefton; 94 km from Waipara*): A deer farm here is generally open to the public. The Lewis Pass road owes its construction to

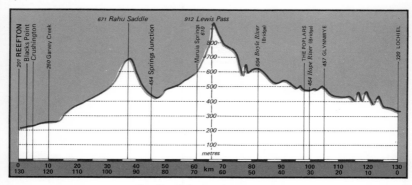

*Profile of the Lewis Pass Road*

E. P. H. Burbury, who took over Glynn Wye in 1923. His persistent mustering of support in Westland, Canterbury and Nelson saw "Burbury's" road opened in 1937. A short distance further on is **Horseshoe Lake,** one of many appealing wayside picnic places.

△**Hanmer Springs**\*\*\* (*detour 10 km at 131 km from Reefton; 68 km from Waipara*): A well-wooded village with thermal springs and miles of forest walks.

**Marble Point** (*141 km from Reefton; 58 km from Waipara*): Pink Hanmer marble has been quarried here for some time.

**Mouse Point** (*152 km from Reefton; 47 km from Waipara*): Said to have been named after a plague of mice, though others suggest a likeness in its silhouette.

**Red Post Junction** (*155 km from Reefton; 44 km from Waipara*): The red post on the junction of Highways 7 and 70 is a replacement for the original red post placed here in *c.* 1886 (*see* △*Culverden*).

△**Culverden** (*158 km from Reefton; 41 km from Waipara*): A small farming service centre. To the south lies the Balmoral State Forest, which is closed to the public, but an extensive rest area has been formed on the north bank of the Hurunui River.

**Hurunui Hotel**\* (*172 km from Reefton; 27 km from Waipara*): The picturesque hotel may date from 1860 when one John Hastie was granted a conditional licence for the "Hurunui Accommodation House". Conditions included "that he keep eight beds in four bedrooms; shelter for six horses; provide a stock yards for yoking up cattle; provide horses for travellers to ford the river; and also direct strangers to a safe fording place." Beside the two-storeyed hotel, built of pitsawn timber and limestone blocks possibly hewn from Weka Pass, are the similarly styled stables that now serve as a haybarn. The hotel's garden is lent atmosphere by old farming equipment. Hurunui means flowing hair. The relevance of the name is uncertain.

△**Waikari** (*184 km from Reefton; 15 km from Waipara*): A village famed for large-scale excavations of *moa* bones made in nearby Pyramid Valley after World War II.

**Weka Pass** (*193 km from Reefton; 6 km from Waipara*): The impressive outcrops of weathered limestone that line the pass contain a number of shelters in which Maori rock drawings have been found. The famed Timpendean shelter may be visited. *Enquire at the second farmhouse on the right, south from Waikari. See also* △*Waikari.*

△**Waipara** (*199 km from Reefton*): Here Highway 7 ends as it merges with Highway 1. Nearby Glenmark is wellknown for the excavations of *moa* swamp. From this junction the highway to Christchurch passes through △Amberley and △Kaiapoi.

A Glossary of Maori Words appears on page 343.

**LINDIS PASS**     North Otago.     Maps 1 & 36.     Height: 970.4 m.

*Between Omarama and Tarras.*

THE LINDIS PASS links the Waitaki basin with Central Otago, following a Maori trail well used by Ngaitahu, who would come up the Waitaki River each summer and follow the route to Lakes Wanaka and Hawea. When Te Puoho (*see index*) surprised the small settlement at Hawea in 1836, some made good their escape to the coast along this path. The first European to discover the pass was John Turnbull Thomson (*see index*) in the course of his 1857 survey of the Otago hinterland.

### SOME HISTORY

**McLean of Morven Hills:** Hearing of a vast tract of unclaimed land, in 1858 young John McLean set off from Canterbury to be guided over the Lindis pass by the chief Te Huruhuru. As he stood on the summit of Mt Grandview (near Hawea), McLean saw a boundless plain covered with snowgrass growing to waist level and stretching out towards Wanaka. He immediately took out a licence for over 200,000 ha, a standard condition being that he adequately stock the run within a year — a near impossible task in the circumstances. He bought what sheep he could afford and prudently laid in a goodly supply of whisky.

McLean's day of reckoning came when the stock inspector called to check that the run had been sufficiently stocked. The young runholder was waiting, with his scotch if not with his flock. The pair spent many genial hours broaching the whisky between inspections of the run, while the sheep were furiously driven from block to block so that the inspector, benumbed and befuddled by boundless Highland hospitality, reported that the stocking condition had been fulfilled.

In time Morven Hills was indeed well stocked and boasted both a massive stone woolshed and a stone-and-mud homestead. Both are still used on the homestead block of the since subdivided property. The run, named by McLean after the range that faces the Isle of Man, was carrying at least 160,000 sheep, though estimates run as high as 250,000.

A group of buildings near the roadside dates back over a century. John McLean's homestead (*c.* 1868), still lived in, is partially obscured by the old stables. Two huts (both *c.* 1868), one originally a school the other a smithy then a store, are to the right, and in the distance is the long cookhouse (*c.* 1870), with chimneys at either end. The massive stone woolshed (*c.* 1880), which holds 1500 sheep and once had thirty-four stands, is out of sight on the plateau to the left of the buildings, behind the new homestead. *15 km W of the summit.* A boundary rider's hut on Morven Hills is now incorporated in the homestead on Northburn station, *8.7 km from Cromwell.*

**Otago's first goldfield:** Traces of gold in the Lindis River were noticed by Thomson when he visited the pass. Under a provincial ordinance runholders could receive a subsidy for building dray roads along routes that were likely to be those of future main roads. This encouraged pastoralists in the Lindis region to combine to improve the track up the Central Otago side of the Lindis Pass. It was while he was working on the road that a labourer, Samuel McIntyre, struck gold, in April 1861. Within a week the roadmen had washed four pounds weight of gold and by the end of the month there were about 400 diggers on the field. The paddlesteamer *Geelong* was packed on every trip she made up the coast from Dunedin to Oamaru.

But few diggers won sufficient gold even to cover expenses and it soon became apparent that there were no fortunes to be made. Forty diggers testified that McIntyre was entitled to the reward offered by the Provincial Government for the discovery of the first payable goldfield. But before the roadman's claim could be considered, his find was totally eclipsed, for not two months later came Read's dramatic find at Gabriel's Gully. The diggers deserted the Lindis, some for the Tuapeka diggings, others, doubtless chastened by the experience, for home. By December the area was deserted and the Lindis had returned to its pastoral loneliness.

**Deer:** The first red deer to be liberated in Otago were freed in the Lindis region in 1871. Presented to the Otago Acclimatisation Society by the Earl of Dalhousie, they were shipped from Scotland to Port Chalmers on the *City of Dunedin* and the *Warrior Queen*. By paddle-steamer the seven deer were brought up the coast to Oamaru, to end their journey to freedom by bullock-wagon. From the Lindis the deer gradually spread south through Otago and Westland to form the basis of today's world-renowned herd. A **monument** near the summit marks the centenary of the liberation.

For travel in the North Island of New Zealand use the *Mobil New Zealand Travel Guide: North Island* (Reed).

---

**LUMSDEN**      Southland.   Maps 14 & 18.   Pop. 591.

*77 km SE of Te Anau; 106 km SSW of Queenstown; 81 km N of Invercargill; 59.5 km NW of Gore.*

"THERE IS NOT a great deal of Lumsden, nor is it a particularly wide-awake centre," observed a journalist some sixty years ago. "At the present rate of progress Lumsden will have a thousand inhabitants in 1950, and may then achieve the dignity of a municipal borough."

There is still not a great deal of Lumsden, but the district has not stood still. Wide, flat, well-farmed plains extend south and west, and towards Te Anau large areas of previously marginal land are being brought into production by the Department of Lands and Survey.

Lumsden combines the activities of farming centre with junction town. Main highways reach to Queenstown, Invercargill, Te Anau and Gore. To the traveller, Lumsden's importance lies in the *Kingston Flyer*, a veteran train which in summer months steams to and from Kingston, on Lake Wakatipu.

The Oreti River is well stocked with trout.

# SOME HISTORY

**A fortuitous mist:** A celebrated conflict took place at Waitaramea, on the Five Rivers Plain, in about 1725 when Ngatimamoe and Ngaitahu clashed. For some time both lines held firm, but as Ngatimamoe began to give way their chief Makohu, mistaken for a common warrior by the Ngaitahu chief Kaweriri, succeeded in slaying his opposite number. Then a marked man, Makohu retreated to the rear with speed but was pursued by a much younger man, anxious to avenge his leader's fall. Makohu headed for the West Dome mountain but, as the pair climbed, was quickly over-hauled. Turning, he called out, asking the name of his pursuer and learned that it was none other than Temai-werohia, a distant relation of his. The young man, finding he was chasing a relative, gave up the chase but saw another in hot pursuit so pretended to be having trouble with his *paraerae* (footwear). The third man, Parakiore, con-tinued the chase alone and, as the gap closed, Makohu repeated *karakia*, imploring the gods to give him fleetness of foot. Still his pursuer continued to gain on him. Again Makohu repeated his *karakia*. The gap was visibly lessening when Makohu realised that Parakiore was using the same *karakia*, so Makohu changed his prayer, pleading for mist. Soon the fog descended to envelop the pair high on the mountain. Parakiore shouted that Kaweriri was not dead, to which Makohu replied "Yes, he is. I felt him heavy on my arm when I thrust. If he is not dead now he will be by the time you return." The mist cleared from around Makohu but remained dense and swirling about Parakiore, so that the Ngatimamoe chief was able to make good his escape. *A plaque set in a boulder at Lowther 9.5 km on the road to Queenstown marks the area of the battle.*

**Which Elbow?** The first land in the district was taken up in 1861 and before long the Elbow Hotel had opened on the eastern side of the Oreti river. The site was a poor one. The building was moved across the river where, as The Elbow (to distinguish it from bare Elbow opposite) a tiny settlement grew up on the route to the Wakatipu diggings. The title of Elbow had been given to the locality by the surveyor J. T. Thomson, as here the Oreti River, after flowing in an easterly direction for many miles, suddenly swings south.

Both Elbows were considered for the railway in 1874, the western side being renamed Holmsdale after the Hon. Matthew Holmes (1817–1901), a prominent local runholder who as a progressive agriculturalist further enhanced the small fortune he had made in Geelong, Victoria, by shipping wool and supplying the diggings. The eastern side was renamed Lumsden as a compliment to the Hon. George Lumsden (1815–1904), like Holmes a Scot, a local politician and a former trader, if not as successful. It was Holmsdale that continued to attract the waggoners on their way to the diggings, but as the railway line approached, Holmsdale faded away and the hitherto deserted site of Lumsden began to assume the dimensions of a township.

The district's progress, steady and unspectacular, was set back by the exceptional snowfall of 1878 which first drove the sheep from the hill tops into the gullies and then buried them in deep drifts. The snowfall of "terrible '78" scattered devastation throughout Otago and Southland, its one redeeming feature being that thousands of rabbits, in their burrows safe from the snow, were drowned in the succeeding floods.

**Chewings fescue:** The region is famous for the production of Chewings fescue, a strain of grass now known the world over. It emerged in a haphazard manner and bestowed immortality somewhat accidentally on George Chewings, an Australian who in 1887 was far from pleased by a section of hard, wiry grass on his newly ac-quired run. His instinct was to get rid of the grass, but his manager assured him that its seed was saleable — it had after all been sown some years earlier from hard fescue seed originally imported from Britain. Within weeks Chewings had harvested his first fescue and, after a holiday in the North Island spent proclaiming the value of his grass to the owners of Rotorua pumicelands, was receiving orders by telegram. To save expense the "Mr" was omitted. Orders simply asked for "Chewings fescue". Trade blossomed. Before long large areas of Chewings fescue were being harvested in the district for marketing in Britain, the United States and South Africa.

Today Chewings fescue is little used as a pasture grass, as it thrives on unimproved land and with farm development has been phased out. Some is still harvested, as its hardwearing qualities make it ideal for the grassing of sports areas.

# THE KINGSTON FLYER

From late December to April the age of steam is relived on the 61 km of railway line between Lumsden and the terminus of Kingston, on Lake Wakatipu. Brought out of retirement and carefully restored are vintage rolling stock — a refreshment car, a combined car and guard's van, two ordinary cars and a gallery car (commonly called a birdcage). The elegant train is hauled by the last of the Ab class of coal-fired locomotives, the last two survivors of 152 which were designed by NZR engineers and introduced in 1915. The sobriquet *Kingston Flyer* was at the end of the century affectionately bestowed on the passenger trains which had a reputation for making good time between Gore, Lumsden and Kingston.

One can at times leave the *Kingston Flyer* at Kingston and continue on by bus or by launch to Queenstown. Alternatively, the return train trip may be made, either directly or later in the day after picnicking by Lake Wakatipu. *The return fare is only slightly more than the basic fare. Details of connecting services are available from the railway booking offices. The train leaves Lumsden twice daily for the 4-hour return trip, at about 8 am and 1 pm.*

## ENVIRONS

**West Dome Deer Ranch (Mossburn)\*\*:** Stags, hinds and fawns browse in a natural habitat of tussock, *manuka* and grassland through which one may drive to see and photograph the deer at close quarters. Occasionally mobs of a hundred or more are seen trotting across the grasslands, but unequalled is the spectacle of the stags as they clash during the roar in autumn. A commercial deerfarm, the ranch carries up to 2,000 deer, the largest park herd of red deer in the country. *23.8 km. Turn off at 19.2 km at Mossburn. and follow signs. Open daily during daylight hours. Occasionally closed in winter. Tel. 24D.*

**Mavora Lakes:** The attractive Mavora Lakes area is becoming increasingly popular for boating, swimming, tramping and climbing. The lakes were named by David McKellar (*see index*) after his horse, Mavora (a Gaelic term of endearment). *The access road branches from the Lumsden-Te Anau road at Centre Hill (33 km). 72 km.*

## TOURING NOTES

**Road to △Te Anau:** On Castle Rock station, just after crossing the Oreti River on the Te Anau exit from the township, tree plantations (thinned with age) once commemorated the dispersal of troops during the Battle of Waterloo — the work of Thomas Barnhill, an early runholder with an interest in history. At 53 km the road passes through the locality of The Key. There was an hotel here until about 1919 when local runholders, to temper the drinking habits of their employees, purchased the licence and allowed it to lapse. Predictably the ploy failed, for the labourers simply went further to slake their thirsts, and would linger at Mossburn for up to a month at a time.

**Road to △Queenstown:** On the route north two roadside memorials are passed. The first, a boulder at **Lowther,** marks the site of the Battle of Waitaramea (*9.5 km*) (*see above*). The second, a cairn on **Dome Pass** (*at 19 km*), marks the site of the Jolly Wagoners Hotel, an accommodation house which fully earned its name. The four "unknown pioneers" remembered by the memorial as "somebody's loved ones" would probably include Margaret Smith (drowned in 1866 when a coach was upset in Fryer's Creek), a cook who died of wounds, a miner from the Nokomai diggings, and James Cannon, who declared *tutu* berries as being fit to eat, ate them to illustrate their harmlessness — and died of poisoning.

**Road to △Gore (Highway 94):** *For points of interest near Riversdale and Mandeville see "Touring Notes" under △Gore. The turnoff to the former goldtown of △Waikaia is passed at Riversdale.*

---

A key to area maps appears on page 2.

---

*13 km S of Christchurch.*

THE SEA-DOOR to Canterbury wears a wellworn air as it clings to the side of the ancient volcanic crater that cradles its sheltered waters. Lack of level land ruled out its becoming the provincial capital. For some years larger than Christchurch, in recent times Lyttelton has suffered from the proximity of that city, as many of those who man its wharves now commute through the tunnels between port and city.

The port is named after Lord Lyttelton, a leading member of the Canterbury Association without whose active support the scheme for a Church of England colony might well have failed. Hagley Park in Christchurch is named after Lord Lyttelton's family seat.

**Annual Bridle Path Walk:** On the nearest Sunday to 16 December, hundreds make an annual pilgrimage over the Bridle Path to mark the anniversary of the berthing of the first of the First Four Ships. Convenience overcomes nostalgia in that the descendants walk over from Heathcote and bus back from Lyttelton. On 16 December itself, the old stone signal station at Lyttelton simulates the arrival of the *Charlotte Jane*, posting in order flags to indicate the sighting of a ship, its identification, and finally berthing directions. *The 1½ hr walk over the Bridle Path may be made at any time of year, starting either from Heathcote or from Lyttelton. Ask directions locally.*

## SOME HISTORY

**The Pilgrims arrive:** As the Pilgrims first saw it, Lyttelton appeared as a straggle of cottages, with a wooden jetty and a steep road that petered out into a path that zigzagged through brown tussock to the summit of the Port Hills. This was upgraded to a bridle path when it became obvious that the coast road to Christchurch via

Sumner would not be finished for some time. The settlement already had a population of 300, comprising a few local Ngaitahu, about seventy European roadmen and the rest "loose elements from Wellington". The site of Christchurch was then a mosaic of swamp and tussock grassland, with rare pockets of *kahikatea, matai* and *totara* in the Papanui and Riccarton districts.

From the outset and for some years Lyttelton's population exceeded that of Christchurch, Henry Sewell in 1853 remarking of the latter that "it has already reached its zenith, and will not advance beyond the status of a village". Remarkably, within a month of the Pilgrims' arrival Lyttelton had acquired its own newspaper, the *Lyttelton Times,* edited by the astute J. E. FitzGerald. The newspaper later moved to Christchurch, flourished into a daily, and continued publication to 1935.

The extent of the reclamation since carried out is shown by the thumblike rock near the bottom of Oxford St, now encircled by railway buildings, on which a plaque records that the Pilgrims landed on 16 December 1850 "near this spot".

**Lyttelton-Christchurch Road Tunnel** (1964): The country's longest road tunnel has an elaborate ventilation system that takes up about half its size. At each end a curved section helps reduce the effect on drivers of their emerging into bright daylight. Almost 2 km in length, the tunnel and its approach roads cost a total of $7 million. It eliminates 8 km of hill climb and descent. *The toll plaza is on the Christchurch side.*

*For notes on Canterbury's history (and on the Christchurch-Lyttelton rail tunnel) see △ Christchurch. For further notes on the peninsula, see △ Banks Peninsula.*

## THINGS TO SEE AND DO

**Lyttelton Historical Museum**\*\* centres on the port and her ships. Displayed are photographs, early drawings and plans of the port, items from the migrants' ships, ammunition from harbour guns, and articles from the *Terra Nova*, the supply ship for Scott's ill-fated expedition to the Antarctic. *Lyttelton Community Centre, Hawkhurst Rd (by road tunnel entrance). Open Sunday from 2–4 pm (and by arrangement).*

**Timeball Station** (1875–76): The castle-like signal station closed in 1935, when, for the last time, the lowering of the timeball signalled the precise hour of one to enable mariners to set their chronometers. Largely built by convicts from the former Lyttelton gaol, it has been restored by the Historic Places Trust and the Lyttelton Maritime Association. *Reserve Tce. Turn off the Sumner Road immediately before the lookout and plane table. Then turn right. Open daily (except Xmas Day and Good Friday) 10.30 am–12 noon, 1–4.30 pm.*

**Three churches:** In a street with three stone churches, the Anglican **Church of the Most Holy Trinity** (1860)\*\* appeals by reason of its perfectly-proportioned interior and the historical interest of its furnishings. Four large wall tablets, together with the wrought-iron alms box, the bell and two sanctuary chairs came from England with the Pilgrims, as did the set of Communion vessels, stamped with the crest of the Canterbury Association and one of few remaining complete sets. Near the chancel hangs an elaborate corona, also dating from 1860 and originally lit by candles. Murals and wall-paintings were executed by Canon Coates, vicar from 1891–1913. The church building saw a false start. Built to a plan by Mountfort with his typically high walls, the initial portion was opened in 1853. It was built of bricks incorporated in a timber framework, but the timber shrank and for safety the building had to be first abandoned and then demolished. The present church was the first of many in the diocese to be built of stone.

On higher ground opposite Holy Trinity, stands **St Joseph's Catholic Church** (1865), its grey stone contrasting with the Anglicans' volcanic rock. Within is a painting of the barque *Boieldieu* which in 1904 struck foul weather on leaving Sydney for Falmouth with a cargo of wheat. Disabled in the storm, she drifted far to the south of New Zealand and would most certainly have perished but for first a fortuitous windchange and then, when 50 km from Lyttelton, the assistance of a passing ship. The painting is a gift from her French captain and crew as a votive offering for the response to their prayers.

Completing the street's ecclesiastical trilogy is **St John's Presbyterian Church** (1864), again of stone, whose tall shingled spire and general appearance differ markedly from those of its neighbours. *Winchester St (two blocks above the waterfront).*

Camping grounds, motels and hotels are listed in the Automobile Association handbooks.

All travelling becomes dull in exact proportion to its rapidity. —John Ruskin.

**Town clock** is dedicated to Dr Charles Hazlitt Upham (1863-1950), "the little doctor" who for over half a century was acclaimed as "the most practical Christian in New Zealand — he will take nothing from the poor but will dispense his last blanket to keep them warm". When a testimonial fund was opened, the Rev. Father Cooney, making the presentation, noted: "It is no use giving the doctor money. He only gives it away again." Charles Upham, VC and bar, (*see page 69*), is a nephew.

Below extend the foundations of Lyttelton's once-imposing gaol (1861) in whose predecessor the convicted sheepstealer James McKenzie (*see index*) was interned after the only Supreme Court trial ever held in Lyttelton. The gaol was a ready source of labour, for work on the Sumner Road (where the prisoners' red stone walls still stand), on the signal station, the Ripa Island fortress, and on so many other projects that the Borough Council objected strenuously when the gaol was finally transferred to Christchurch. Garden beds and creeper now soften the harsh lines of the buildings, and bricked-up doors bar entrance to the grim cell block. There were underground cells near the clock. *Oxford St.*

## POINTS OF INTEREST ROUND LYTTELTON HARBOUR

**Governors Bay** (pop. 411) (*10 km from Lyttelton*): Governors Bay, (where HMS *Fly* carrying Governor Sir George Grey anchored as he waited to greet the first of the Four Ships) is a pleasing orcharding locality. A jetty reaches out to deeper water in the tidal bay, where a number of boats are moored. The settlement looks across to Quail Island (*see below*), on whose beach at low tide may be seen the hulks of several ships, run aground, having first been stripped at Lyttelton. Stone from quarries here was used for the Canterbury Provincial Council building in Christchurch.

St Cuthbert's Anglican Church (1860-62), on the western exit, is faced with stone but has thick cob walls, appreciated from within. The church has a poetic approach up a tree-lined path flanked with venerable headstones. Its separate belfry, subscribed to by Anglicans over a wide area, is a memorial to the Rev. Henry Torlesse. (*If the church is locked, the key is held nearby.*) Neighbouring is the former Governors Bay vicarage, now a hostel for youth groups. The church has a set of Canterbury Association communion vessels. About 400 m beyond, on the opposite side and below the road, is Ohinetahi (1864), a three-storeyed stone homestead.

**Godley Head light** (*11 km from Lyttelton*): At the northern entrance to Lyttelton Harbour, the Godley Head light is among the country's earliest (1865). Unlike most other towers, Godley Head is built of stone quarried on the site. Standing 96.6 m above sea level, the tower is 6.1 m high and sends three quick flashes each 26 seconds which are visible for 38 km. The light was electrified in 1946.

The approach is from the summit of Evans Pass, along a road which is essentially the northern continuation of the Summit Rd, and offers views down to Sumner and Taylors Mistake as well as of plains and mountains. The point was fortified in wartime; some defence buildings remain. *Access to the light is restricted. A locked gate bars the access road before the lighthouse comes into view.*

**Diamond Harbour** (*26 km from Lyttelton*): The growing settlement of Diamond Harbour is given character by the many fine old gumtrees which still stamp the area with the imprint of its Australian pioneer, Mark Stoddart. Its sheltered harbour, at the foot of rock walls on which large trees grow wherever they can obtain a toehold, has a secluded quality that belies the unseen presence of so many houses. Paths zigzag down the rock faces, one leading to a minute bathing beach.

The settlement faces across the harbour to Lyttelton, to which it is linked by an inexpensive scheduled ferry. Above the tiny beach stands Godley House (1880), a mansion built by Henry Hawkins from profits on contracts to develop the port at Lyttelton. Now a private hotel and tearooms, it has no connection with the leader of the Canterbury settlement. Nearby is Mark Stoddart's cottage (1862), a tiny wooden building prefabricated in Australia for reassembly here (*the last driveway on the right before Godley House*). The bay was named by Stoddart "from the glitter of the suntrack on the water". *Seen from the road just beyond Diamond Harbour is:*

**Ripa Island** The tiny wall-girt island of Ripa (a contraction of Ripapa) all but touches the eastern arm of the bay on which Purau stands. For many generations there was a *pa* here, so it was an appropriate site for the construction in 1885, during the Russian scare, of Fort Jervois — built by prisoners from the Lyttelton gaol and described in the British House of Commons as "the strongest port fortress in the Empire". The fort is honeycombed with tunnels and gunpits. It was here in 1917 that the German, Count Felix von Luckner, was imprisoned after his celebrated escape from Motuihe in the Hauraki Gulf. Earlier, in 1880, Maoris taken prisoner at Parihaka in Taranaki were held here without trial. The island was then being used as a quarantine station, and it was piously hoped that no ships carrying infectious diseases would arrive during the term of their stay. The island's name (*ri* = a flax rope; *papa* = flat rock) refers to times when canoes were hauled up on to the island's tiny shelving beach. The island is now leased by the Navy League as a training ground for Sea Cadets.

**Purau** (*29 km from Lyttelton*): The small settlement on the inlet beyond Diamond Harbour has sheltered sandy beaches nearby, of which the most accessible is Camp Bay (*5 km along a narrow road; signposted*). Like its neighbour, Purau too has stately gumtrees, most conspicuously a plantation a short distance towards Port Levy. In total seclusion among the trees is Purau homestead (1853–55), "the handsomest house in New Zealand", built for Robert Rhodes (*see index*) from local red stone as convin_.ng evidence of his conviction that Canterbury held a great future. Purau means a two-barbed spear.

**Quail Island:** The largest island in the harbour was probably the last point of volcanic activity, being a small secondary cone built up on the crater that formed Lyttelton Harbour. There is no record of permanent Maori occupation. The first European, Captain Mein Smith, flushed quail in 1842 while walking about the island, a native quail now extinct. When in 1885 Ripa Island was chosen as a defence position, Quail Island assumed its role of quarantine station, where many migrants spent some time before, with the coming of steamers, a quarantine anchorage was established just inside the Heads. For the seven years to 1925, Quail Island was declared a leper station, though there were never more than nine patients at any one time. The dogs and ponies for two Antarctic expeditions were accommodated here; Shackleton's in 1907 and Scott's in 1910.

## ORGANISED EXCURSIONS

Diamond Harbour Launch Services operate a scheduled crossing between Lyttelton and Diamond Harbour. Fishing trips and harbour cruises with a full commentary are also run (dependant on patronage). *Particulars at the wharf. Tel. 8368.*

## TOURING NOTES

**Christchurch via Evans Pass and Sumner:** A roadside plane table identifies points of interest round Lyttelton Harbour.

△ **Banks Peninsula:** Refer to this entry for other details of the peninsula.

## MACRAES FLAT*       Central Otago.    Maps 25 & 28.    Pop. 58.
*19 km SE of Hyde; 32 km NW of Palmerston.*

ONLY THE VENERABLE stone of Stanley's Hotel gives substance to the old goldtown of Macraes. In a short street of otherwise decaying buildings the old hotel faces across to its trim, rockwalled holding paddock and stables and looks out across Macraes Flat, a plain broken by ponds and tailings, legacies of the search for alluvial gold. The locality is named after John Macrae, a shepherd on a Shag Valley run.

## SOME HISTORY

**Goldrushes:** Gold was found here in the winter of 1862, and a series of small rushes took place in the vicinity — to the Fillyburn and other tributaries of the Taieri, to Deepdell Creek and to Coal Creek. By September 1865 a solid settlement numbered about 300, complete with bank, store, post office and a restaurant owned by Johnny Jones. The boom came later, in 1868 and 1869, when both an upper and lower township sprang into existence. Dredging began in 1898, but stiff clay and a shortage of running water rendered the ventures unprofitable. In 1933 the Macraes Flat Gold Mining Company began operations with an electrically-driven eight-inch gravel pump. Successful for some years, the company was faced with rising costs and the depletion of staff by military duties, and was forced into liquidation.

**"While I live, I'll crow":** The rampant red rooster by the entrance to Stanley's Hotel is the symbol of a bitter feud that for decades divided the village between two protagonists, the two local publicans. Tom Stanley, who rebuilt the hotel when he acquired the licence in 1882, was short, thickset and hardy, and continued to be a wagonner until over seventy years of age. The hotel was rebuilt by one Budge, as noted for his craftsmanship as for his capacity for ale. He was paid in beer and it is said that he accounted for seventy-two hogsheads (about 17,200 litres) before his five-year task was done, and that he completed the building only to find that he owed the publican money.

Bill Griffin, whose United Kingdom Hotel has not survived, was Stanley's lifelong enemy. Those at Macraes who patronised one dared not patronise the other. Just why the two were so antagonistic is today a mystery, but Stanley apparently thought it necessary to have on hand a stockwhip, a sawn-off shotgun, knuckledusters, a cosh and a catapult. Each swore to outlive the other, each undercut the other's prices. When Stanley emblazoned his inn with his motto, Griffin retaliated with "Estd. 1864 — Still Going".

Only the swaggers were accepted by both establishments and the story is told of The Shiner, the swagger who never worked — and never paid. One day he presented himself at Stanley's bar and demanded a drink. "I can pay in stamps," he asserted. The drink pulled and the glass drained, The Shiner was asked for the stamps. "How many would you like?" he offered, and began to stamp his right foot. The furious Stanley was pacified only by the suggestion that The Shiner be sent over to the United Kingdom Hotel to take Bill Griffin down with a bottle of whisky as the prize. He accepted with alacrity and when he left Macraes, The Shiner had done himself proud — for Bill Griffin had been first to be paid in "stamps" that day and, in riling Tom Stanley, The Shiner had been taking up Bill Griffin's offer of free board and lodging should he succeed.

Stanley's Hotel is still in operation. If it has outlasted that of Griffin, Stanley himself did not — dying at the age of seventy-six. Griffin outlasted his rival by two years, living to be ninety.

When, in 1976, Stanley's Hotel came on to the market, it was bought by a company consisting largely of its patrons and the Historic Places Trust.

## ENVIRONS

**Deepdell Creek:** A small battery here is still used to crush quartz to extract schee-lite, a mineral used in the production of steel and which in time of war has been worth over $1,000 a ton. The mouths of numerous mineshafts stud the hillside with blue-grey fans of spoil to riddle a reef system that extends for some 26 km. Fortunes fluctuated, but the presence of the scheelite with the gold meant that both could be won, a conjunction that enabled several mines to show a profit. *5.8 km. Leave Macraes Flat by the exit towards Dunback, turning left up Golden Point Rd at 1.4 km.*

**Nenthorn:** The Nenthorn goldfield was late in coming into production, even though years earlier Christina and Isabella McRae had used cake-tins to wash up good samples of gold from the Nenthorn Creek. The quartz-bearing reefs remained to be discovered by a rabbiter, William McMillan, who in 1888 found loose pieces of gold-bearing quartz. He hurried to Naseby where he lodged his claim and quietly slipped out of town. Alerted by the court bailiff, a number of horsemen trailed him back through the night, and found their task made much easier by the colour of McMillan's white horse.

A town soon blossomed to boast a jockey club, post office, hotels, banks and its own newspaper, the *Nenthorn Recorder*. Reticulated water was even considered. Life was hectic. A waiter at Laverty's publichouse related: "Never in my life have I seen such drunkenness, so many brawls and fights with knives, boots, lumps of wood, etc., brought into play. I have seen Laverty's manager standing on the bar, with a short stockwhip, lashing these men like a bullock driver."

In twelve short years the town rose and fell. Today a few stone and cob walls, a single pinetree and gaping mineshafts are all that mark the Nenthorn field. Most of the gold remains. *16.8 km. Leave Macraes Flat towards Hyde, turning left towards Nenthorn at 2.7 km. Pass the intersection with Butter and Egg Road (along which walked the farmers' wives to carry produce to the miners). At 11.8 km turn left and ford a creek. Bear left at 16 km where the main track tends right to pass the lonely shell of a derelict hotel. At 16.8 km one is in the town's main street, marked by the odd chimney and the dwindling bases of sod cottages.*

## MAHINERANGI (Lake)  Otago.  Map 9.

*59 km SW of Dunedin; 30.5 km NE of Lawrence.*

AN INTRICATE SHORELINE belongs to an artificial lake created for hydroelectric power generation where a dam pens back the waters of the Waipori River and many of its tributaries. When the lake was formed it flooded the goldworkings of Waipori town-ship, an action taken only after extensive tests had proved that the area's potential for gold production was lower than even the most pessimistic of the forecasts.

The drive from the Taieri plain up to the lake is particularly impressive as the road curls through a scenic reserve and passes the power complex. At Waipori Falls settlement, where houses cling to a precipitous rock face, a waterfall may be seen as a line etched on a distant gorge wall. The road continues through pine and larch forests to reach the lake, where there is swimming and fishing in season. One may cross the bridge over the lake and proceed to △ Dunedin by way of Outram, or swing southwest to reach △ Lawrence.

The lake is named for Mahinerangi Barnett, whose father was mayor of Dunedin in 1911.

### WAIPORI FALLS DEVELOPMENT

The Waipori River, which rises in the Lammerlaw Range, once ran through a narrow rocky gorge, falling 225 m in 4 km in what was known as Waipori Falls. The area's potential as a source of hydro-electric power was realised by a miner, John Lawson, who secured water rights. Later, a private company acquired these and planned to supply power to the gold dredges working on the flat above the falls, as well as to Dunedin. After many bitter clashes the Dunedin City Council, which diametrically opposed the idea of having to buy power from private interests, bought the company out for £31,000. After the 1914–18 war extensive tests on goldbearing prospects were carried out before authority was obtained to create Lake Mahinerangi — at first by a dam 12 m high, then 18 m high and finally 33 m high.

Not until 1935 was the Dunedin city system connected to the State electricity scheme, but as Waipori power has been much cheaper than that sold by the State, the Waipori complex has been further developed since then. A total generating capacity of 60,000 kW can be maintained. The undertaking is without parallel in New Zealand as an example of municipal enterprise.

## MANAPOURI (Lake)

**MANAPOURI (Lake)***      Fiordland.    Maps 12 & 33.**

*12 km SW of Te Anau.*

THE UNSPOILT BEAUTIES of Manapouri have been praised by innumerable travellers. A soft, feminine lake, a scattering of wooded islands, banks dense with bush and an horizon bounded by the Kepler Mountains; all these contribute to the fame of this favoured corner of the △ Fiordland National Park.

Paradoxically it was a plan to raise the lake, and so destroy much of its charm, that focussed the country's attention both on Manapouri in particular and the environment in general. The largest petition ever presented to Parliament, with some 265,000 signatures was tabled in 1970. The unsympathetic response from the National Government contributed to its election defeat of 1972, and one of the first moves by the incoming Labour administration was to pledge that the lake would not be raised. To be the subject of such tribulations no lake could have been more appropriately named than Manapouri — "lake of the sorrowing heart".

The lake affords limitless possibilities for the boatowner, and for fishermen after Atlantic salmon and brown and rainbow trout. The power scheme on West Arm, massive though it is, has generated perhaps more political than electrical heat, but is an undertaking well worthy of a visit.

### SOME MYTHOLOGY

**The tears of two sisters:** The myth is recounted of the old chief who lived in Fiordland. Of his great family of sons, none had survived a series of bloody battles, and of his two daughters, one had been brought up by his brother, a great *tohunga* (priest). Only the lovely Koronae was left to him, and great was the consternation at the *kainga* (village) when she failed to return from a walk in the forest. For several days the whole *hapu* (sub-tribe) searched for her, until her sister, Moturau, dreamed of Koronae lying disabled in the forest. Her *tohunga* uncle made her a kite, painted red to protect her from the *maeroero* (wild men of the woods) and directed her to follow the kite, which would lead her to her sister. For three days Moturau followed the kite, string in hand, until it came down on a tableland between two high mountains. There she found her sister, in great pain and close to death. By this time, Moturau too was suffering from exhaustion. As the two sisters held each other they wept bitterly and long. Their tears rent the hills far apart and in this way the lake of Manapouri was formed before their spirits left their bodies to begin the long journey to Cape Reinga.

Moturau (hundred islands) was the original name for the lake, the name of Manapouri being transferred by a mistaken surveyor from one of the Mavora Lakes. Manapouri, however, is a name in keeping with the tale.

### MANAPOURI HYDRO-ELECTRIC POWER SCHEME

The potential of Lake Manapouri as a power source was recognised as early as 1904, and was seriously studied both in the 1920s (for use in the manufacture of fertilisers) and again in the 1940s. It was the discovery of vast deposits of bauxite in Queensland (as it happens, by a New Zealander) and the need for massive quantities of electricity to convert this into aluminium (*see* △ *Bluff*) that provided the necessary large-scale industrial demand without which the project could never have been viable.

The lake's waters are diverted through intakes at West Arm to plunge down vertical penstocks to turbines in a powerhouse 213 m below ground level. The water is then discharged along a 10-km tailrace tunnel, through the Main Divide and out into Deep Cove on Doubtful Sound. The last of seven generators was commissioned in 1971.

Access to the cathedral-like powerhouse, 110.9 m long by 18 m wide and 38.8 m high is by a 2.1 km tunnel that spirals down through solid rock with a gradient of 1 in 10. The tunnel's natural rock walls and the ceiling of the powerhouse are unlined, with only grouted rockbolts reinforcing the ceiling and walls.

Both Lake Manapouri and Lake Te Anau (which flows into it) provide storage for the station. A plan to raise Manapouri by about 12 m was abandoned in 1973, but it is necessary to control the levels of both lakes to extract maximum power. The control structure for Manapouri is just below the confluence of the Mararoa and the Lower Waiau Rivers, so diverting the waters of the Mararoa through the lake. A second control structure is on the Lake Te Anau outlet.

To transmit power to the Comalco smelter at Bluff and surplus power to the national grid at Invercargill, 160 km of line were installed and access roads built over 58 km of forbidding country. During construction a cantilevered wharf at Deep Cove and a road over the Wilmot Pass to West Arm were built so that supplies could be shipped in to Doubtful Sound and, where necessary, trucked over the Main Divide. The road was built to better-than-usual standards to take massive transporters and is now used by tourist buses. The passenger liner *Wanganella* was moored at Deep Cove to serve as a floating hostel for some of the 1,500 employed on the project.

The annual energy output of the country's largest power station is up to 5,200 GWh, with a peak power output of from 630 to over 700 MW (energy and power vary according to the level of the lake). The total cost of the scheme (excluding transmission lines) was over $138 million. This is being substantially recouped by an elaborate pricing formula embodied in an agreement between the Government and Comalco.

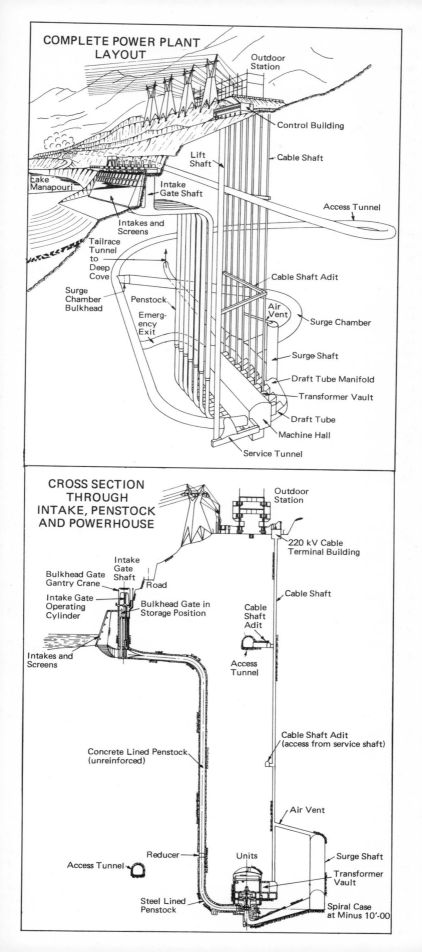

## COMPLETE POWER PLANT LAYOUT

Outdoor Station

Control Building

Cable Shaft

Lift Shaft

Access Tunnel

Lake Manapouri

Intake Gate Shaft

Intakes and Screens

Tailrace Tunnel to Deep Cove

Surge Chamber Bulkhead

Penstock

Emergency Exit

Cable Shaft Adit

Air Vent

Surge Chamber

Surge Shaft

Draft Tube Manifold

Transformer Vault

Draft Tube

Machine Hall

Service Tunnel

## CROSS SECTION THROUGH INTAKE, PENSTOCK AND POWERHOUSE

Outdoor Station

220 kV Cable Terminal Building

Intake Gate Shaft

Road

Bulkhead Gate Gantry Crane

Intake Gate Operating Cylinder

Bulkhead Gate in Storage Position

Cable Shaft

Cable Shaft Adit

Access Tunnel

Intakes and Screens

Concrete Lined Penstock (unreinforced)

Cable Shaft Adit (access from service shaft)

Air Vent

Access Tunnel

Reducer

Units

Surge Shaft

Transformer Vault

Steel Lined Penstock

Spiral Case at Minus 10'-00

MANAPOURI (Lake)—concluded

## ORGANISED EXCURSIONS

**West Arm Underground Powerhouse — Doubtful Sound\*\*\***: A trip runs across the lake to West Arm where a bus spirals visitors down to the powerhouse deep in the mountains, 213 m below. There, in a vast cavern hewn from solid gneiss, are the seven turbines, each driving a 100,000 kW generator.

The bus emerges to wind over picturesque Wilmot Pass (*670.9 m*) to reach the coast at Deep Cove on Doubtful Sound (*see index*). In a majestic setting are seen the waters of the lake hurrying from the mountainside after their 10 km journey through the tailrace tunnel. The mosses and ferns by the road show how resilient the rainforest is as it regenerates on dynamited hillsides. *Booking is essential, particularly at holiday periods. Fiordland Travel, both at △ Te Anau and at Pearl Harbour (near Manapouri settlement). Tel. 859 Te Anau, 602 Manapouri.*

An abbreviated trip simply visits the powerhouse. There is no road link between Manapouri settlement and West Arm. The powerhouse cannot be visited independently.

**Lake trips:** Other trips are run on the lake. Arrangements may be made to be dropped off on one of the innumerable beaches and to be collected later in the day. A popular trip is to **Stockyard Cove** for a leisurely walk along a nature track there. *Fiordland Travel.*

## MARLBOROUGH SOUNDS\*\*\*   Marlborough.   Map 22.

*Activities centre on △ Picton and △ Havelock. Permits to shoot on the many reserves should be obtained from the Marlborough Sounds Maritime Park Board, c/- Department of Lands and Survey, Box 97, Blenheim, which also publishes a handbook to the Sounds reserves. Details of guesthouses in isolated bays are available from good travel agents and at Picton and Havelock.*

THE MYRIAD ISLANDS and intricate coastline of the Marlborough Sounds present limitless possibilities for the boatowner and the camper. Here the sea claws with long fingers into the north-east tip of the South Island, creating innumerable sheltered coves and blissful vistas of vibrant greens and blues. The complex configurations of land and sea are the result of the area being depressed, allowing the sea to drown an elaborate network of branching river valleys. At times the land drops so steeply to the sea as to give the appearance of glacier-formed fiords. Little of the coast is accessible by road, but launch services from Picton and Havelock will land campers on the many reserves that comprise the Marlborough Sounds Maritime Park, and regularly deliver supplies and mail to them during their stay.

The area was named in 1857 after John Churchill, Duke of Marlborough, in the belief that the new province should, like Nelson and Wellington, bear the name of a great fighting hero. Blenheim was named at the same time to honour the Duke's most famous victory.

**Pelorus Jack:** For many years a dolphin met ships crossing through French Pass as they plied between Nelson and Wellington. So regularly would he accompany them across Admiralty Bay, enjoying a free ride on the invisible "pressure wave" created below the surface by a moving ship, that tourists would make the passage simply to see him cavort round their vessel. The Government's action in protecting the Risso's Dolphin by Order in Council (1904) saw his fame spread round the world. For nearly twenty-four years Pelorus Jack (probably more correctly Pelorus Jill) was at his post before he disappeared at the end of 1912. This would approximate the lifespan of a dolphin. It is thought that his unusual behaviour was caused by his being orphaned before he was fully weaned.

To the Maori the disappearance of Pelorus Jack showed that Ruru had at last been freed from his curse, for in legend there were two Maoris living on Pelorus Sound who loved the same woman. When she chose one as her husband, Ruru, the rejected suitor, flung them both from a cliff-top, uttering as he did so a *karakia* so malignant and so powerful that the incantation killed a passing dolphin. When Ruru confessed to the *tohunga* what he had done, the old priest was angry. To punish him, he forced Ruru's *wairua* into the body of the dolphin, bringing it back to life, and commanded it to meet every canoe that entered French Pass. Years went by, but the *tohunga* refused to lift the *makutu* (spell). The *tohunga* finally died, but his successor found he had not the power to release Ruru. So for centuries the dolphin continued his vigil. Perhaps it was in 1912 that the spirit of the old *tohunga* finally released Ruru's spirit from the body of the dolphin.

### MAORI LEGEND

**Kupe and the wheke:** One version of the legend that tells of Kupe's discovery of New Zealand recounts that Kupe and Ngahue, while fishing out from Hawaiki, were annoyed by a large *wheke* (octopus) which kept stealing their bait. They resolved to catch the *wheke*, but as they chased him he led them halfway across the Pacific. On the Wairarapa coast, at Castlepoint, Kupe nearly caught his quarry in a cave, but the chase finally ended in the Marlborough Sounds when, at Whekenui Bay (*whekenui* = big octopus), the octopus was finally cornered and killed. One interpretation of the

# MARLBOROUGH SOUNDS

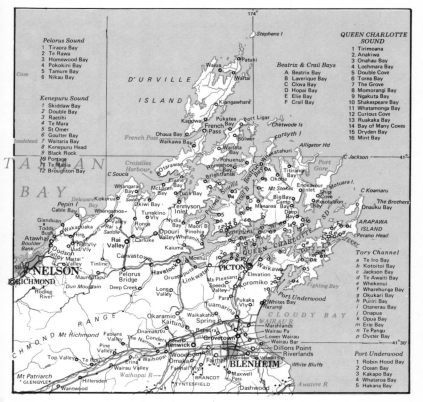

## 22

**Pelorus Sound**
1 Tiraora Bay
2 Te Rawa
3 Homewood Bay
4 Pokokini Bay
5 Tamure Bay
6 Nikau Bay

**Kenepuru Sound**
1 Skiddaw Bay
2 Double Bay
3 Raetihi
4 Te Mara
5 St Omer
6 Goulter Bay
7 Waitaria Bay
8 Kenepuru Head
9 Black Rock
10 Portage
11 Te Mahia
12 Broughton Bay

**Beatrix & Crail Bays**
A Beatrix Bay
B Laverique Bay
C Clova Bay
D Hopai Bay
E Elie Bay
F Crail Bay

**QUEEN CHARLOTTE SOUND**
1 Tirimoana
2 Anakiwa
3 Onahau Bay
4 Lochmara Bay
5 Double Cove
6 Torea Bay
7 The Grove
8 Momorangi Bay
9 Ngakuta Bay
10 Shakespeare Bay
11 Whatamonga Bay
12 Curious Cove
13 Ruakaka Bay
14 Bay of Many Coves
15 Dryden Bay
16 Mint Bay

**Tory Channel**
a Te Iro Bay
b Kotoitoi Bay
c Jackson Bay
d Te Awaiti Bay
e Whekenui
f Wharehunga Bay
g Okukari Bay
h Puriri Bay
i Otanerau Bay
j Onapua
k Opua Bay
m Erie Bay
n Te Pangu
p Oyster Bay

**Port Underwood**
1 Robin Hood Bay
2 Ocean Bay
3 Kakapo Bay
4 Whataroa Bay
5 Hakana Bay

full legend, which relates elaborate details of the chase as it progressed throughout the Sounds, is that the story provided the Maori navigator with a chart of the Cook Strait area.

## SOME HISTORY

**Cook at Ship Cove:** Like thousands after him, Captain Cook was captivated by Queen Charlotte Sound. No fewer than five times did he call at Ship Cove, there to careen his ships, replenish stores and restore the health of his crew. It was while he was here on his first visit, in 1770, that he climbed a hill on Arapawa Island and for the first time saw open sea to the east. The passage the Dutch explorer Tasman had missed in 1642 now bears the illustrious Yorkshireman's name, though apparently not from his own choice. The modest Cook does not once mention the strait as being named after him, though it so appears in a separate journal kept by Joseph Banks, the naturalist on board *Endeavour*.

From Ship Cove, too, Cook crossed to Motuara Island where "we took [the post] up to the highest part of the Island and after fixing it fast in the ground hoisted the Union flag and dignified this inlet with the name of *Queen Charlottes Sound* and took formal possession of it and the adjacent lands in the name and for the use of His Majesty, we then drank Her Majestys hilth in a Bottle of wine and gave the empty bottle to the old man [who had attended us up the hill] with which he was highly pleased." Cook claimed the land for his King, and named the Sound for his Queen. He also exceeded his instructions by making such a claim, and for generations the British Government was careful to exclude New Zealand from the published lists of its territories.

On his second voyage Cook made a rendezvous here with the *Adventure* in 1773, and within eighteen months had returned to Ship Cove twice more. Vegetable gardens were established on Motuara (a group of Russian explorers harvested cabbages from the plot in 1820), and at Ship Cove he landed the country's first sheep — a ram and a ewe from the Cape of Good Hope but inside three days they had eaten *tutu* and died of poisoning. Here, too, Cook, who until then had had doubts as to the practice among Maoris, witnessed a cannibal feast at the bay he named Cannibal Cove. On the debit side, a boat's crew of ten, sent from *Adventure* to gather scurvy grass and celery, became embroiled with a group of "natives", were killed and eaten.

Consult the Index when looking for a name in this Guide.

After the Russians came the Frenchman, Dumont d'Urville who "in order to render greater services to geography" came to New Zealand to carefully chart areas that Cook had not visited. Much of the maze of the Marlborough Sounds he had left uncharted, so it was Dumont d'Urville who gave the Sounds such names as Cape Soucis, Croisilles Harbour (after his mother's family), French Pass and D'Urville Island. Dumont d'Urville was not anxious to name the island after himself, but French Pass (or *Passe des Français*) was a name he willingly gave to commemorate an epic passage.

**The French at French Pass:** Jules Sébastian César Dumont d'Urville (1790–1842), a talented naval officer who was instrumental in procuring for France the world-famous statue of the Venus de Milo, led a three-year voyage of exploration in the course of which valuable records were compiled of New Zealand and its inhabitants. He had earlier visited it as a junior officer in 1824 under Duperrey.

After exploring Tasman Bay, where he named Astrolabe Roadstead after his vessel and Adele Island after his wife, Dumont d'Urville at first impetuously attempted to take French Pass head-on. Only after near-disaster did he anchor his vessel in slack water. Convinced it was possible to sail through the narrow channel though it seethed with a tidal rip, the explorer climbed a ridge overlooking the pass, there to contemplate the problem. He confessed to thinking that within a few minutes, and solely because of his desire to make the passage, the vessel might be hurled to destruction on the rocks: "Ten officers, a complete crew, the people of that floating city . . . might they not within a few hours be reduced to trying to find their salvation on a bare inhospitable coast; with nothing before them but to drag out a miserable existence, or perhaps to perish there without ever seeing their family or their friends again?"

The moment of weakness passed, and at slack water on 28 January 1827 the corvette set sail for the pass. At the critical moment, just as she entered the pass, the wind failed and the current bore her to port. The *Astrolabe* would respond to neither helm nor sail changes, and as she graunched on the rocks a cry of terror went up from the crew. The tide was strong enough to carry her over the reef, the wind rose again, and she entered Admiralty Bay erect and majestic — if with pieces of her false keel bobbing in her wake. To preserve the memory of the ordeal, Dumont d'Urville named the channel *Passe des Français* as it proved the severance of the island from the mainland, but his officers insisted that the island be named after their commander, and as he "did not think it right to refuse this mark of esteem on the part of his brave companions", he reluctantly named the island D'Urville.

**Invaders from the north:** Dumont d'Urville and the *Astrolabe* had just left the area when it erupted in bloodshed. Once again a northern tribe, driven from its ancestral lands, was forced to migrate southwards and to invade the South Island. But this time the northerners, the Ngati Toa and the Te Atiawa with them, had muskets. The battles were bloodier, the slaughter on a wider scale, and annihilation of the local tribes more certain. In a campaign that lasted several years, Te Rauparaha's men from Kapiti crossed Cook Strait with one of the largest fleets of canoes ever assembled, to dispossess the hapless Rangitane and Ngati Apa of the Sounds area. The invaders were in complete control by the time Colonel Wakefield arrived in 1839 to buy land for the New Zealand Company, and had been there long enough to support their claim to the land by right of conquest and subsequent occupation. Te Rauparaha's invasion, among others, was made possible by the whalers who had established themselves at Kapiti and in the Sounds. They traded the guns he needed while they slaughtered the whales which regularly migrated through the Strait and often came into the Sounds to calve.

## QUEEN CHARLOTTE SOUND

At the head of Queen Charlotte Sound lies the South Island rail terminal and port of △Picton, whence launches run to most parts of the sound. The wellknown holiday guesthouse at The Portage is on Kenepuru Sound and is accessible by road, but is most easily reached by launch from Picton. The Portage is so named as it was a point where canoes were carried across a narrow neck of land to save a much longer journey by sea.

The inter-island car-rail ferries from Wellington enter the Sound by way of Tory Channel. *Some distance north of the entrance to Tory Channel is:*

**The Brothers:** A cluster of barren rock and sizable islets in the throat of Cook Strait is the nesting place of innumerable seabirds and the home of the rigidly-protected *tuatara*, a lizard (*Sphenodon punctatus*), occasionally referred to as a "living fossil". The *tuatara* is the only survivor of the order of prehistoric reptiles which included the giant dinosaur — the remainder became extinct over 100 million years ago. The *tuatara*, with a rudimentary "third eye", grows to a length of about 60 cm and lives to an age of a century or more. It is also found on Stephens Island (off D'Urville Island).

To the Maori the rocks were Nga Whatu-kaiponu (eyeballs that stand as witness), in legend the eyeballs of the octopus slain by Kupe in Whekenui Bay. Save only for those of the highest rank, all who sailed past would cover their eyes, honouring a tradition established by Kupe himself. A dreaded *tapu* applied to the rocks, as rough and dangerous seas were often encountered here; those who breached the *tapu* risked the overturning of their canoe, and death by drowning. Tradition tells of some navigators actually blindfolding their crew members hereabouts so that they would not panic.

The rocks all but claimed Cook's *Endeavour* in February 1770, when "we narrowly escaped being dashed against the Rocks by bringing the ship to an Anchor in 75 fathoms water, with 150 fathoms of Cable out. Even this would not have saved us had not the Tide . . . by meeting with the Island changed its direction." With these few words the navigator dismissed an incident which might well have cost him both his vessel and the lives of all on board. A lighthouse serves to warn the present-day mariner.

**Tory Channel:** John Guard's schooner *Waterloo* was trading with the Maoris in 1827 when a violent storm drove it into Te Awaiti Bay. From a hill there Guard saw whales passing close to the shore and within months was back to establish the country's first bay-whaling station. Success was spectacular (in 1830 alone he made a profit of over £20,000), but triple disaster struck the transported Londoner when the *Waterloo* was wrecked, his second whaling station at Port Underwood plundered, and then his second vessel, the *Harriet*, wrecked on the Taranaki coast. After a bloody encounter in which his wife was rescued from Maoris who had killed and eaten other crew members, Guard established himself on land bought from Te Rauparaha and Te Rangihaeata at Kakapo Bay (*see index*), where his descendants still live.

When the *Tory* arrived in 1839 with the advance party from the New Zealand Company, the settlement at Te Awaiti, probably the oldest European settlement in the South Island, was also the largest. It was Guard who piloted the *Tory* through the Sounds while Colonel Wakefield inspected possible sites for settlement.

Whaling continued from the area until 1964. Buildings and tanks associated with the enterprise still stand in neighbouring Whekenui, the bay where in legend Kupe finally slew the octopus.

*The northern shore of Tory Channel comprises:*

**Arapawa Island:** Wellington Head, on the slopes facing Cook Strait and marking the entrance to Tory Channel, was where the first swimmers to conquer the chilly waters and unpredictable tides made their landings from Wellington — Barry Devenport in 1962 and Keith Hancox fifteen months later. It was from a hill on the island on 23 January 1770 that Cook first discovered the existence of Cook Strait, a discovery that banished for all time the long-cherished geographers' notion of a great southern continent. (*Now called Cook's Lookout, the hill has a suitably-inscribed memorial.*) The island's name may be more properly rendered Arapaoa, because of the *paoa* (downward stroke) with which Kupe killed the octopus.

**Ship Cove:** There are few spots as historic as the bay to which Cook came on no fewer than five occasions; the hills were then heavily bushed, the stream sparkling clear and at dawn the bellbirds, wrote Joseph Banks, "seemed to strain their throats with emulation, and made, perhaps, the most melodious wild music I have ever heard". So glowing were Cook's accounts of this, his favourite place, that for half a century Europeans thought of New Zealand in terms of Queen Charlotte Sound. It was across on Motuara Island that Cook hoisted the Union Jack; the first potatoes to be planted in New Zealand were planted here, and liberations were made of pigs and goats "so that we have reason to hope this country will, in time, be stocked with these animals". In 1820 a Russian expedition with the *Vostock* and the *Mirnyi* stayed here for nine days, exploring and studying the customs of the Maori, for Emperor Alexander I. *A memorial to Cook at Ship Cove is flanked by cannon presented by the British Admiralty. There are picnic facilities on the reserve here. Sea access only. Visited by passenger launches from Picton.*

At neighbouring Cannibal Cove, Cook's suspicions of the practice of cannibalism among the Maoris were confirmed: "There was not one of us but had the least doubt but what this people were Canabals but the finding this Bone with part of the sinews fresh upon it was a stronger proof than any we had yet met with, and in order to be fully satisfied of the truth of what they had told us, we told one of them that it was not the bone of a man but that of a Dog, but he with great fervency took hold of his fore-arm and told us again that it was that bone and to convence us that they had ate the flesh he took hold of the flesh of his own arm with his teeth and made shew of eating."

**Other reserves** in Queen Charlotte Sound include Motuara, Long, Pickersgill and Blumine Islands, and Resolution Bay, Endeavour Inlet, Big Bay, and much of the northern shoreline from Edgecombe Point (opp. Blumine Is.) to Grove Arm. Mistletoe Bay is a particularly appealing spot reached after a 10-km launch trip from Picton. Accessible by road from Picton are reserves along Queen Charlotte Drive, including the camping ground at Momorangi Bay.

## PELORUS SOUND

Pelorus Sound, which embraces Kenepuru and Mahau Sounds, is named after HMS *Pelorus*, which explored the Sound with Guard as pilot in 1838. There are numerous reserves, generally accessible only by launch from Havelock. Some are well-bushed and with good walking tracks; some are ideal for picnicking or camping.

**Tennyson Inlet Scenic Reserve** (*6240 ha*): The largest of the reserves in the Marlborough Sounds Maritime Park has stands of beech forest, with *rimu*, *nikau* and coastal bush on the lower slopes, and is inhabited by a wide variety of birdlife. Perhaps the most beautiful arm of the Sounds, it gives some idea of how the whole region must have impressed its early European visitors. *Accessible by road from Rai Valley via the Opouri Valley. 32 km from Rai Valley.*

**Crail Bay Historic Reserve:** On a small knoll here are some pits cut from soft rock in times of early Polynesian occupation. *2½ hrs by launch from Havelock, or a 79 km drive (one way) from Havelock.*

**Guesthouses:** Attractively-sited guesthouses on Kenepuru Sound, especially favoured by those on fishing holidays, are at The Portage, Te Mara, Raetihi and Hopewell. All are accessible by road and also by launch from Havelock. The Portage is also readily accessible from Picton.

## D'URVILLE ISLAND

D'Urville Island, on the east side of Tasman Bay, is severed from the mainland by the swirling waters of French Pass (*see below*). In legend Hinepoupou lived on Rangitoto (as D'Urville Island was named) with her unfaithful husband, Manini-pounamu. To rid himself of his wife, Manini-pounamu took her to Kapiti Island where he left her marooned. But Hinepoupou recited *karakia* and called upon the *atua* to give her the strength she needed as, hour after hour, she battled through the waves of Raukawa (Cook Strait). Her marathon swim ended on Nga Whatu-kaiponu (The Brothers), whence she made her way along the coast to the shores of her island home. However Hine-poupou did not return to her husband. Instead she again invoked the aid of the gods; while he was out fishing a sudden squall overturned his canoe and Manini-pounamu was drowned. (This is the only recorded legend in which a woman was successful in swimming across Cook Strait.)

## FRENCH PASS

The swirling waters of the pass which severs D'Urville Island from the mainland make Dumont d'Urville's feat as impressive today as it was in 1827 (*described above*).

In legend, Kupe as he journeyed to New Zealand had with him on his canoe a fabulous shag, Te Kawau-a-toru, whose duty was to find tidal and river currents. None of the rips the shag found were strong enough to test his strength until he reached this point. At full tide Te Kawau-a-toru swooped down to dip one wing in the rip of French Pass. But the strength of the current was too great, catching the shag's wing and dragging the fabled bird into the racing water. Had Te Kawau-a-toru won the struggle the channel would have been sealed. His loss allowed the canoes of the intrepid to paddle through the passage, and the shag himself was turned into a reef that for all time will withstand the racing waters of the pass. *60 km by road from Rai Valley; 124 km from Picton via Queen Charlotte Drive; 87 km from Havelock.*

The road passes Goat Saddle (*at 16 km from Rai Valley*), previously known as Kissing Saddle. Observed officialdom in 1958: "It is held by some that, although the kiss has gone from the name, the ancient practice is still carried on with, if anything, increasing enthusiasm, and that the restoration of the original name would be in order."

## STEPHENS ISLAND

Stephens Island, the western gatepost to Cook's turbulent strait, towers loftily above the tide-troubled waters. Like Cape Jackson it was named by Cook after a secretary of the Admiralty. Cook did not land, but had he done so he might have found the largest concentration there is of the enigmatic *tuatara* (*see index*) or the unique Stephens Island frog — one that neither dives nor swims and knows no water other than rain. Its tadpoles live in their eggshell until their metamorphosis is almost complete. The protected frog (*Liopelma hamiltoni*), the "Adam among frogs" and the ancestors of all other frog types, is found only in a small area near the island's summit. The manned lighthouse on the island is among the country's most powerful, being visible for over 50 km. *Permits are required to visit the island, a protected wildlife sanctuary administered by the Department of Internal Affairs.*

## PORT UNDERWOOD

Geologically Port Underwood is part of the Marlborough Sounds yet geographically it belongs more to Cloudy Bay. Points of interest are listed under △Picton, "Suggested Drives".

## ORGANISED EXCURSIONS

**Launch trips:** A variety of launch, fishing and mail trips run from △Picton and from △Havelock.

**Scenic flights** range over the intricate labyrinth from both Blenheim and Picton. *MAC Air Travel, tel. Blenheim 4018.*

*53 km NE of Invercargill; 12 km SW of Gore.*

FOUR TALL SMOKING industrial chimneys, a massive freezing works and the South Island's largest papermill combine to give Mataura the air of a miniature metropolis. The town, astride the Mataura River, owes its origin to once-impressive falls. These, today but a shallow weir, were a source of power rare in Southland and may even escape the notice of the traveller. To the north of the town, Cardigan Bay Road honours the birthplace of the world's first pacer to win over $1 million — the most famous of the many successful trotters bred in the district.

Numerous trout streams in the vicinity, among them the Mataura River (also a source of delectable lampreys), draw many anglers.

Mataura (reddish eddying water) refers to swamp water tinged with iron oxide that once drained into the river.

**Kanakana:** The Mataura Falls were long known to the Maori as Kanakana as they were visited annually for supplies of that succulent fish. The *kanakana* (lamprey) is a rather grotesque eel-like fish of a length of up to 45 cm, the survivor of an archaic group. A predator that rasps away the flesh of its victims simply to suck their blood and juices, it is, notwithstanding, a delicacy and is still sought after by local residents who boil them (like muttonbirds) to free them of fat before roasting or frying. The *kanakana* has a suckerlike mouth that it uses to climb the waterfall.

Local Maoris still retain fishing rights at the falls.

## SOME HISTORY

**A final, bloody encounter:** A *kainga* at nearby Tuturau, unfortified though it was, in 1836 saw a bloody encounter when followers of Te Rauparaha (*see index*) for the final time clashed with South Island Ngaitahu.

Te Puoho, a relative of the Ngati Toa chief, went south from Collingwood with a *taua* (war-party) of a hundred or so. In one of the most remarkable outflanking movements in history, the group battled down the wild West Coast and through the Haast Pass to take the Ngaitahu, and the Ngatimamoe they had absorbed, completely by surprise. Isolated *kainga* were attacked and their occupants slaughtered lest word would get south to Tuhawaiki (Bloody Jack) on Ruapuke Island. From Hawea, to Wanaka and Wakatipu the *taua* made its way, to follow the Mataura River from near Kingston to Tuturau. However, though they rushed the Tuturau *kainga* and took it completely by surprise, some Ngaitahu managed to escape, to carry the news of invaders to Tuhawaiki. As members of an eeling party they had encountered the *taua* before it moved to the attack.

Immediately a well-armed war party was assembled on Ruapuke Island, for Tuhawaiki had long been arming his followers for defence against Te Rauparaha. Canoes sped to the rivermouth and the Ngaitahu hurried inland. So it was that as Te Puoho's *taua* lay resting from their arduous trek, sated with both *kanakana* and *kai tangata* (human flesh — occasionally euphemistically termed long pig), they were overwhelmed in the dawn. Many were massacred; a handful taken prisoner; only one escaped. Te Puoho himself was shot as he woke from slumber and suffered the gross indignity of having his head (the most *tapu* part of his body) severed, to be taken back in triumph to Ruapuke for further desecration. *3.6 km. A memorial above the road marks the approximate site of the* kainga. *Cross the Mataura River and turn right along the road towards Wyndham. The* kainga *was about 400 m to the left of the column. There is no formed access to the memorial itself.*

**City of the Falls:** The development of the town is reflected in its succession of names — in turn The Falls, The Ferry, Mataura Bridge and then, finally, Mataura. Like others, the town grew on a major river ford round an accommodation house. The ford above the falls had its hazards and the *Otago Witness* headlined an occasion when Bishop Harper in 1857 had a "narrow escape of his life . . . [He] had not kept to the proper ford. His horse was washed downstream and had his Lordship not been an expert swimmer he would in all probability have been drowned." The following year a series of changes of mind on the part of the Otago Provincial Council eventually saw a wooden bridge erected, resting on a rock in the centre of the falls. About 1.6 m wide and only 1 m above the river level, the bridge was at all times showered with spray. This prompted the dynamiting of the rock face, detracting from a sight of some consequence. In 1861, shortly after a messenger had crossed the bridge carrying documents to complete the separation of Southland from the Province of Otago, the whole structure was swept downstream by floodwaters — a coincidence whose symbolism was not lost on the inhabitants of Southland.

**Father of Mataura:** The accommodation house came into the hands of James Pollock when it was the only building in Mataura, and he justly laid claim to being the father of Mataura. He bought the first section, built the first house, introduced the first blacksmith, the first shoemaker and the first saddler. He built a general store and an hotel, lobbied to obtain a post and telegraph office and then, to enliven proceedings, organised the first racemeeting. Industry followed. Papermills in 1875, a dairy factory in 1887 and meatworks in 1892. The district's lignite and coalfields remain largely untapped.

## MATAURA PAPERMILL

The papermill here is not only the oldest papermaking unit in the country, but an updated successor of the first mill ever to produce paper commercially in New Zealand. It originated in 1875 when an Invercargill syndicate obtained water rights to the falls and began producing brown paper. Within three years the original plant was swept from its foundations by floodwaters, necessitating the erection of a completely new plant.

Papermaking requires much water, and the mill daily draws from the river over 4.5 million litres. The company has its own opencast coalfields about 5 km away from which about 31,000 tons of lignite are trucked annually to fire the factory's boilers. Water from the falls is still used to generate electricity.

A unique groundwood mill (so called as wood is ground, not chipped) is the only one of its kind in the country and the only plant in the world to pulp *Pinus radiata* in this fashion. For papers requiring other types of wood, pulp is brought in from the North Island and imported from Finland.

Wood pulp is soaked and blended before it is strained and combed by refiners. Thinned with water, the pulp is fed on to a moving belt of open-mesh wire wove, through which the water drains to leave a mat of damp paper. This is dried out with presses and steamheated rollers before being ironed by steel rollers and placed on reels. The finishing department includes a number of bag machines, as bags account for nearly 10 per cent of total sales. The two paper machines produce about 15,000 tons of paper annually in a variety of grades. *Visits to the mill may be arranged by telephoning the Personnel Manager, NZ Paper Mills Ltd, preferably in advance, at Mataura 3 or 215. Allow 2 hours.* The falls themselves are best seen from the river-bridge.

---

This book is being continually revised to ensure that it remains the most comprehensive guide book to the South Island. If you have any suggestions for future editions, please write to the publishers at Private Bag, Te Aro, Wellington.

---

## MESOPOTAMIA**  South Canterbury.  Map 3.  Area: 40,500 ha.

*69 km NNW of Geraldine.*

"NEVER SHALL I FORGET the utter loneliness of the prospect — only the little far-away homestead giving sign of human handiwork, the vastness of mountain and plain, of river and sky; the marvellous atmospheric effects — sometimes black mountains against a white sky, and then again, after cold weather, white mountains against a black sky." So wrote Samuel Butler of Mesopotamia in his classic novel *Erewhon*.

At the very end of the road from △Geraldine by way of △Peel Forest, the Mesopotamia of today preserves the name of the original run in just such a setting. Though Butler has departed the scene for more than a century, by a clerical quirk a minute area of land is still in his name. Near the homestead, which is of recent vintage, are the remains of what may have been Butler's dairy.

**Samuel Butler:** With no experience of sheepfarming, but with £4,000, abundant common sense and a determination to double his capital as quickly as possible, Samuel Butler (1835–1902) arrived in New Zealand in 1860. He spent a chilly and lonely winter camped on his initial run before he concluded that it was suitable for sheep. A neighbour, John Caton, built a hut on Butler's run and, when the pair could not come to terms over it, they literally raced each other to Christchurch to buy the freehold of the disputed section. Both arrived before the Land Office was due to open, and when it did Butler found that Caton had got at the appointment book (which determined the order in which applicants would be seen) before the office had opened, so as to enter his name above that of Butler — whose name, much to Butler's astonishment and quite fortuitously, had been entered the day before by his solicitor on a matter of some quite different business. The Land Board resolved the now-famous dispute in Butler's favour, whereupon he retired to his solicitor's study and "worked off his excitement by playing Bach fugues for the next two hours".

Caton's notoriety is best illustrated by his earmark — a crop off both ears — and it was noted that "from his yards no straggler returned".

Butler bought up surrounding leases in quick succession, naming the station Mesopotamia (from the Greek *mesos* and *potamos*, "land between two rivers") where his piano (he composed music in the Handelian tradition) occupied half of his hut. He had a poor opinion of the state of culture in the colony, conversations at the Christchurch Club being "purely horsey and sheepy" and "it [did] not do to speak of John (*sic*) Sebastian Bach's 'Fugues' or pre-Raphaelite pictures". His mission was accomplished in 1864 when he cleared £8,000 on the sale of the run to William Parkerson. He promptly returned to Britain but left his money in New Zealand bearing interest of 10 per cent. He sold out with perfect timing as prices were soon to tumble.

Butler, son of a clergyman and grandson of a Bishop of Lichfield, was a classical scholar who refused to follow his forebears into the church. Indeed, it was only after stormy family scenes that he came to New Zealand. His letters home, published by his father under the title *A First Year in Canterbury Settlement* (1863), form the best account of contemporary life, even if Butler later described the book as so bad he could not bring himself to open it a second time. A series of articles written for the Christchurch *Press* formed the basis for his later classic work, *Erewhon, or Over the Range* (1873), in which he satirised both the Darwinian theory of evolution and conventional religion. He exhibited at the Royal Academy (he was a passable water-colourist) but later devoted himself almost exclusively to writing, publishing three books in a dispute with Darwin during which he embittered the anthropologist and never really satisfied himself. His other wellknown novel, *The Way of All Flesh* (1903), was published after his death.

**Dr Sinclair's grave:** Andrew Sinclair (1796–1860), a Scottish doctor, met New Zealand's Governor-designate, Robert FitzRoy, in Sydney and accompanied him across the Tasman as his Colonial Secretary. In New Zealand he inaugurated the Civil Service, and by the time he resigned twelve years later he had formed the nucleus of an efficient organisation. Sinclair then devoted his time to scientific pursuits, for he was already world-known for his gifts of shells and insects to the British Museum and his publications on botanical subjects. It was here, in the high country, on one of his extensive journeys of exploration, that he was drowned while attempting to cross a swift stream. His companion on his last journey, Julius von Haast, named a peak (*2,140.6 m*) at the head of Forest Creek in his memory. *The grave is in a small cemetery on the riverflat below the homestead.*

> The booklet *Samuel Butler at Mesopotamia,* by P. B. Maling (Government Printer) describes the novelist's sojourn here.

## METHVEN   Mid-Canterbury.   Map 3.   Pop. 918.

*95 km from Christchurch; 32 km from Ashburton.*

THE TOWN OF METHVEN stands at the old railhead from Rakaia, astride the common intersection of no fewer than six roads. A farming and distribution centre it is also assuming a winter-holiday role as the nearby Mt Hutt skifields are developed. "Old Methven" once stood at the junction of Mt Hutt and Marawhiti Roads at a convenient stopping place for coaches between Rakaia and Alford Forest. However in 1878 planning engineers found that the last few miles of the branch railway line would be uneconomic, and so sited the railhead at the road junction, where the businesses of Old Methven were quick to re-establish themselves.

A floral festival, complete with procession and sports, is held annually (*first Saturday in November*).

### POINTS OF INTEREST NEARBY

**Methven Public Library** (1883): In 1882, during a pig shoot on nearby Pudding Hill, one of the hunting party became lost. Despite the strenuous endeavours of many over a long period, no trace of the man, Hugh Anderson, was ever found. Anderson's family in England sent £100 to reward those who had searched so diligently, but the men refused to accept the gift. Instead it was offered to the township, who used the money to found the library. Anderson's portrait hangs within. *Highway 77.*

**Church of All Saints** (1879): Testimony to the ferocity of the Cantuarian nor'-wester is given by All Saints. A church was built at Methven in 1880 but was destroyed by the wind four years later. All Saints, which then stood at Sherwood, 21 km away, was picked as a replacement. In a fortnight of nor'westerly gales even three steam traction engines could make no headway against the wind, and only when it abated could the church arrive safely at Methven. Other hindrances — low telegraph wires and fragile bridges — ensured that the journey took seven weeks. *Chapman and Allington Sts.*

### ENVIRONS

**Mt Hutt skifield**\*\*\*: One of the closest skifields to Christchurch, Mt Hutt is also one of the newest. Its height and exposure to southerly winds assure the basin of sufficient snow by about early May for a season that lasts into October. Equipment is for hire and a ski school provides instruction. *26 km.*

**Highbank power station** (1945) forms part of a combined irrigation and power generation scheme. Water-races lead 66 km from the Rangitata to the Rakaia River. Originally the scheme was designed so that water could be taken from the race in summer and used to irrigate the mixed farming area between the two rivers; and in winter, when irrigation is not needed and power demand is high, the head of water could be used to generate electricity. The most remarkable feature of the scheme is that the water crosses the Hinds River, both branches of the Ashburton River and a number of streams. This is accomplished by a series of inverted siphons, by which the water is taken under the intervening riverbeds.

From the Rangitata, water flows through the diversion race at the usual rate of 28 m³ per second and, with the aid of the abrupt drop from the plains down to the level of the Rakaia River, power is generated from a gross head of 104.2 m. One large vertical-shaft generator with a capacity of 25,200 kW is driven by a 36,000 hp Francis turbine.

Coincidentally, the scheme was the second to be built on the Rakaia, and neither actually uses water from that river — the Lake Coleridge scheme diverts waters from the Harper and Acheron Rivers. *The station, in its well-wooded setting, may be visited. 12 km NE.* As the road reaches the lip of the riverbank there is a wide view down into the braided valley.

**Rakaia Gorge\*\*\***: Here the Rakaia River flows deep and swift through the gorge to emerge and completely change in character by sprawling its waters lazily over a wide shingled bed. There are pleasant camping and picnicking spots near the arched riverbridge. *17 km on Highway 72.*

In legend a *taniwha* (water monster) once lived near the gorge, where he cultivated food. When a demon personified in the form of a violent nor'westerly gale came down the Rakaia from the Main Divide and flattened the *taniwha*'s cultivations, the *taniwha* resolved to prevent future destruction. He journeyed to the mountains and brought back rocks and boulders with which he hoped to snare the demon, and with them he so narrowed the course of the Rakaia that it now flows between two rocky walls. The *taniwha* did not manage to capture the demon nor'wester, but succeeded in taming him so that the havoc the wind once wrought has been much reduced.

A table of distances between major centres appears on page 363.

## MIDDLEMARCH    Central Otago.    Maps 9 & 25.    Pop. 200.

*83 km NNW of Dunedin; 66 km NNW of Mosgiel; 66 km S of Ranfurly.*

MIDDLEMARCH LINGERS in a broad valley in the lee of the Rock and Pillar Range, a bleak mountainous chain with outcrops of large rock that give it the appearance of a well-used and much-abused saw. From the distance Middlemarch appeals as a town of poplars and pines set on the well-watered plains of the Strath Taieri, the glacial valley where now flows the Taieri River. The town, the natural centre of a large outlying district, was named not after George Eliot's novel but because near it flows a creek that formed the march (or border) between two sheepstations.

**Cottesbrook station\*\***, due east of the town, was first taken up in *c.* 1856 yet within six years was reported as having an area of 12,150 ha and carrying 3,281 "diseased sheep" rife with scab. William Gellibrand acquired the run in 1868, by which time he had aggregated over 67,960 ha in the area, with 537 cattle and 50,399 sheep.

During the 1870s the flocks increased so rapidly that there was no way of profitably disposing of surplus stock — large numbers were sold for 6d each for boiling down for the sake of tallow; others were simply driven over precipices. Gellibrand, after a visit to Cottesbrook, worried about what he should do with his surplus stock as he embarked at Port Chalmers to sail to Australia. "Kill them — kill them all off!" he muttered, to the consternation of his cabin-mate who, sure of his homicidal tendencies, reported Gellibrand to the captain — who promptly offloaded the indignant runholder at Bluff. Within a fortnight of his departure Gellibrand was back at Cottesbrook.

In 1882 the Government subdivided Cottesbrook, and Gellibrand tried to circumvent legislation designed to put the small man on the land, by employing "dummyism": anxious to retain as much as he could around the homestead block he bought land in the names of rabbiters, miners, and station hands. Suspicious for once, the Land Board withheld the licences while they investigated a situation that showed that Gellibrand had even brought Tasmanians over from Australia to sign for land and then return on the first boat home. The illegally taken-up land was declared forfeit, and once the subdivision had been properly completed a large number of old Cottesbrook employees were on the land. The shepherds had become landowners; the squatter the displaced person.

Today Cottesbrook covers 1,620 ha. Its picturesque T-shaped woolshed, with dormer windows and twenty-four shearers' stands, dates back for a century and in its heyday in a single season once produced no fewer than 999 bales of wool. The former cookhouse, with a chimney, is just beyond the station entrance, with the later slaughterhouse over towards the woolshed. The homestead, added to and painted, now lacks the considerable character of the other buildings. *2.6 km E on the road to Macraes Flat.*

**MILFORD (Road to)\*\*\*      Fiordland.    Maps 12 & 33.**

*119 km from Te Anau to Milford Sound.*

THE MOST MODEST appraisal of the road from △Te Anau to △Milford Sound must rank it as among the finest of all alpine drives. Mountains rise vertically to tower more than a kilometre sheer above the road, reducing primeval beech forest to a mere carpet of greenery. Even the Homer Tunnel, man's attempt to master the ranges, is left rough-hewn from rock. In all seasons the mountains present a dramatic spectacle, be they heavy with winter snow or festooned with the hundreds of waterfalls that come with the thaw and with the torrential downpours of summer. For the first 29 km the road skirts the lateral moraine of the glacier that gouged the bed of Lake Te Anau, then enters the forests of red, silver and mountain beech that clothe the ice-carved valleys of the Eglinton, the Hollyford and the Cleddau.

---

## SOME SUGGESTIONS

Leave Te Anau in the early morning, by 8 am at the latest.

Take insect repellent and a raincoat whatever the weather; the rainfall at Milford is phenomenal.

Take most of your photographs on the way to Milford, when the sun is at the most favourable angle.

Do not attempt to take a caravan or trailer beyond Cascade Creek.

---

### POINTS OF INTEREST ON THE WAY

*The weather is unpredictable at all times — Milford Sound has one of the country's highest rainfalls — but both the road and the fiord can be rare spectacles whatever the weather. Occasionally the road is closed for a few days by ice, snow, or the danger of spring avalanches.*

**Mirror Lakes** (*signposted at 56 km from Te Anau*): At most times the lakes reflect nearby mountains. Being small they are less susceptible to being roughened by wind.

**The Avenue of the Disappearing Mountain** (*about 56 km*): The landscape plays tricks with perspective: a giant peak visibly shrinks as one drives towards it.

**Cascade Creek** (*74 km*): There are numerous picnic places hereabouts, a restaurant and a hostel. Caravans and trailers are not permitted beyond this point.

**Lake Gunn** (*76 km*): A larger lake, Lake Gunn is less prone to mirror the mountains but is the more memorable when it does.

**The Divide** (*signposted at 82 km*) (*530.2 m*): The lowest of the passes across the Southern Alps is the point of departure for walks to **Lake Howden** (*2 hrs return*) and to **Key Summit** (*2½ hrs return*). From the latter there is an excellent view of Mt Christina, with Lake Marian nestling in the valley below and other peaks of the Darran Range rising behind. From this point, too, lead the **Routeburn** and **Greenstone** tracks through to Lake Wakatipu.

**Hollyford Camp** (*at 85 km detour right for 8 km*), a motor camp, has an interesting **museum\***. Displayed are relics from *Endeavour* (wrecked in Dusky Sound in 1795; see △*Fiordland National Park*), items from the early settlements of Martins Bay and Big Bay, and from the construction of the Homer Tunnel. *Open daily.* The road continues a further 9 km beyond the camp, down the exquisite Lower Hollyford Valley, to where a 30-minute (*return*) walk leads to a view of the **Humboldt Falls\*\***. These, in three giant leaps, crash into the Hollyford River.

From the road's present end a 4-to-5 day tramp leads to Martins Bay (*see index*). Tramps along the route are occasionally conducted by the Hollyford Tourist Co. Present conjecture is that the road may one day be pushed through to link with the Haast Pass Road.

At the turnoff a **memorial** records Davy Gunn's epic feat when in twenty hours he came 90 km through the bush from Big Bay to fetch help for the victims of an air crash in 1936.

**Homer Tunnel** (*98 km*): The unlined tunnel, rough-hewn from rock, was begun in 1935 as an unemployment project and was not completed until 1952. A short tunnel of 1,219 m, it was driven from one side only through rugged mountain country to even more severe weather. Three men were killed, and the portal and camp were several times buried by avalanches. It is named after Harry Homer, who in 1889 discovered the Homer Saddle and even at that date urged the construction of a tunnel. The museum at Hollyford Camp contains photographs of the construction as well as carbide lamps and tools used on the job.

The tunnel's floor slopes down to the Milford side, with a grade of one-in-ten. *The tunnel is open only for 25 mins past the hour for traffic to Milford, and for 25 mins past the half-hour for traffic from Milford.* Any delay passes quickly as the scenery is deserving of a lingering look. There are short nature walks signposted at each end. *Through the tunnel one emerges in the upper reaches of the breathtaking Cleddau Valley, to drop steeply down past:*

**The Chasm** *(signposted at 106 km):* A 5-minute walk leads along a well-formed track to the point where the roaring Cleddau River has carved its way through solid rock.

*Albeit winding and slow, only a short distance remains to Milford Sound — in Donald Sutherland's judgment the most beautiful region on earth.*

A key to area maps appears on page 2.

## MILFORD SOUND***     Fiordland.    Maps 12 & 33.

*119 km NNE of Te Anau; 286 km NW of Queenstown.*

THERE ARE THREE ways to Milford, a fingerlike indentation in the coast of △Fiordland National Park — by road, by plane and on foot, each giving a different and equally memorable perspective. At the end lie the deep waters of Milford Sound from which rises the sheer glaciated slab of Mitre Peak to lend the fiord its special charm. Much-photographed, the pinnacle promises to be a perfect cone, an illusion dispelled when it is seen from the sea as simply one peak in a chain. From hanging valleys where once subsidiary glaciers joined the departed main ice flow, tall falls now drop their mountain-fresh waters cleanly into the sea. The mingling of mountain, bush and fiord is broken only by a smattering of fishing boats and a scattering of buildings at the head of the sound. The region's rainfall ranks with the country's highest, a phenomenal 6,240 mm.

The Maori knew Milford Sound as Piopiotahi (the single thrush) as the fabled creator-discoverer Maui is said to have had with him a large bird brought from Hawaiki. When Maui was crushed to death between the thighs of Hine-nui-te-po, the sorrowful bird, who witnessed the tragedy, fled here to give its lonely name to the secluded sound. The origin of the *Pakeha* name is uncertain.

**Accommodation** is limited but ranges from luxury to hostel. Booking is essential. The Milford Hotel has a pleasant smorgasbord for day visitors.

### SOME GEOLOGY

A fiord is formed where the sea enters a deeply excavated glacial trough after the melting-away of the ice. One of the finest of the New Zealand fiords is Milford Sound, enclosed by walls that rise 1,200 m vertically from the sea. Its most striking geological feature is the steep-walled, flat-floored depression that occupies the middle third of the fiord. The Entrance Sill ceases at a depth of 120 m, to the west of Stirling Falls at a point where steep rock spurs narrow the sound. To the east the sound broadens but at the same time plunges steeply to a depth of 290 m, so that the water inside the fiord is very much deeper than it is at its entrance.

The phenomenon has been interpreted as a rock-basin cut from the bed of an existing glacial valley during a later phase of glacial advance. The Entrance Sill, at the seaward end of the basin, is a rock barrier and not terminal moraine from the younger glacier — a theory reinforced by the hard rock spurs to the north and south of the Sill. The thickness of the ice that excavated the basin is shown by the height of the subvertical cliffs, practically devoid of vegetation, that rise from below sea level to truncate the U-shaped profiles of older glacial valleys. These "hanging valleys" are particularly noticeable in the area. Where once smaller glaciers served as tributaries to the main iceflow, streams now run and enter the principal valley as waterfalls, e.g. the Bowen, Stirling and Sutherland Falls. Sinbad Gully is another hanging valley, but this can escape notice as its mouth is at sea level. The Jervois Glacier on Mt Elliott is the surviving fragment of the great glacier that formed both the Arthur Valley and Milford Sound.

### SOME MYTHOLOGY

**The handiwork of Tu:** In mythology the god Tu-to-Rakiwhanoa set about rendering the new land habitable when the South Island came into being as the petrified hull of a part-sunken canoe. He began his work in the south, where his inexperience with a mighty axe still shows in the broken nature of the coastline and in the scattering of islands. As he worked his way north his skill increased, so that by the time he came to carve out Milford Sound his artistry had been perfected.

Resting from his labours, he was visited in turn by the Earth Mother (who persuaded him to form the level area where the Milford Hotel now stands) and then by the Goddess of Death, Te Hine-nui-te-po, who at Sandfly Point liberated the sandflies and mosquitoes that obeyed all too well her injunction that they multiply.

Tu left his work uncompleted and it was for a lesser god to finish the task by providing a pass from Milford to the interior. At the Homer Saddle he hacked at the foot of the ridge, only to make it steeper, and at the MacKinnon Pass he forgot an important phrase in his *karakia* (incantation) so that further progress became impossible. Exhausted, he sat down to rest on Mt Elliott (Te Manini-o-Ruru, the weariness of Ruru) so forming the depression that became the névé of the Jervois Glacier. The myth, as was customary, ascribes to a number of features names appropriate to the fable.

**Deserting wives:** In legend the three wives of Tamatea-Pokai-Whenua, commander of the *Tairea* canoe, fled to the West Coast. As Tama chased desperately after them his shoulder-mat brushed the sides of Milford Sound and from the shreds grew the flax-like *kiekie* commonly seen round the coastline. It was here that Tama found one of his wives, but turned into greenstone. The tears he shed for her flecked the stone and gave it the name of *tangiwai* (water of tears). The greenstone here, found principally about Anita Bay, is inferior to the harder *pounamu* found near △ Hokitika and Greymouth. It was nonetheless a prized mineral, so that Maoris came long distances, some by way of the Milford Track, to collect the precious stone. Otherwise the region held little appeal. The cold, the wind, rough seas and difficult tracks were aggravated by rain, sandflies and mosquitoes. The Maori seldom came here except for greenstone.

## SOME HISTORY

**The hermit of Milford:** "If ever I come to anchor, it will be here!" So declared the pioneer of Milford Sound, the remarkable Scot, Donald Sutherland (1843–1919) when he visited the fiord with a sealing party. And return he did, albeit some fourteen years later. In his first two years at Milford he never so much as saw another human face as he explored the surroundings, living off the land and scheming to develop deposits of greenstone and asbestos. An old friend, John M'Kay, had joined him in his plans by the time the discovery of the Sutherland Falls (*see index*) was made, when the pair startled the world with their claim that the falls were over 1,000 m high. The Government sent a party in to confirm the find.

Tourists attracted by the falls began to come by boat and overland. Sutherland built his John o' Groats Hotel at Milford City (forerunner of today's modern complex) and the man who claimed he could "live on the smell of the north wind, and a *raupo* hut is as warm as a palace" was entertaining nobility in a region where for some years he had lived as a hermit. When visitors left, Sutherland would enter his own cryptic comments on them in his famous Visitors' Book, such as "The two meanest scunkes that ever came into this sound."

It was at this time that Sutherland married a longsuffering Dunedin widow. Together they ran the hostel, with Sutherland guiding groups to and from the falls he had found, and in the off-season working on the formation of what were to become the latter stages of the renowned △ Milford Track. *Sutherland's grave is signposted near the car park, between the hotel and the wharf.*

**Will Quill's climb:** A nonchalant entry in Sutherland's Visitors' Book reads: "On track to Sutherland waterfall from Milford Sound from Oct. 1889 to May 1890, being the first to reach the summit of Sutherland waterfall, highest in the world, on March 9, 1890." It disguises the triumph of the brave if brash William Quill who, in 3½ hours, climbed to the top of the falls. It was he who found at their head the lake that now bears his name. A contemporary wrote: "The daring feat of the adventurous Quill will never be emulated by any but those absolutely hankering to mature their insurance policies, or possessed of a morbid desire to be gathered up in a shovel."

Within a year the youthful Quill had met his end. He was lost while climbing on the Gertrude Saddle and was traced only to the edge of a precipice down which he presumably plunged to his death. His climb has only once been repeated, by a track-guide in 1950 who, after a 6-hour climb, reached the summit only to find no alternative route down but by retracing his steps in the gathering gloom.

The falls, for years thought to be the world's tallest, plummet 580.3 m down in leaps of 248.4, 228.9, and 103 m.

## TRIPS ON THE FIORD***

Both the one-hour and the two-hour cruises on Milford Sound take in Stirling Falls, where fresh water drops a sheer 146 m to the sea. The longer trip goes out to the mouth of the fiord, to the Tasman Sea and Anita Bay (a source of *tangiwai* greenstone). *In holiday periods it is essential to book in advance, through the Milford Hotel, the Mount Cook Travel Bureau at the Te Anau Hotel, or through Fiordland Travel at Te Anau. Competing services are operated. Where appropriate, lunch may be booked for the longer trip.*

A time-travel map is on page 362.

## OTHER THINGS TO SEE AND DO

**Scenic flights*** lend fresh perspective to the majestic landforms. One may fly one way and bus the other between Milford and both △ Te Anau and △ Queenstown. *Mount Cook Airlines.*

**Bowen Falls*** (*160 m*) spout from a hanging valley over a near vertical face to the sound. Generally the falls strike a rocklike basin to fan out in a frothy crescent, but after heavy rain an immense volume of water can overshoot the basin to thunder straight into the sea. Water tapped from the river here is used to generate electricity for the hotel complex. *A 10-minute walk round the point beyond the wharf leads to the foot of the falls. They are seen to greater advantage from the water.*

**The Lookout**\*\*: A 5-minute walk up a track behind the hotel brings an elevated and deeper view of the sound and of Mitre Peak.

Suggestions and directions for other walks are available from the hotel. It is not possible to walk to the Sutherland Falls as they are too far distant to be reached and return in a day, and the Fiordland National Park headquarters, who control the Milford Track, permit it to be walked only from Te Anau to Milford.

## TOURING NOTE

For points of interest on the road between Te Anau and Milford Sound, see △Milford, Road to.

---

### SANDFLIES

The ubiquitous and ever-troublesome sandfly is no new intruder to the region. On 11 May 1773 Captain James Cook, at Dusky Sound wrote: "The most mischievous animal here is the small black sandfly which are exceeding numerous and are so troublesome that they exceed everything of the kind I ever met with, wherever they light they cause a swelling and such an intolerable itching that it is not possible to refrain from scratching and at last ends in ulcers like the small Pox. The almost continual rain may be reckoned a nother ilconveniency attending this Bay."

Cook wrote in pre-Dimethylphthalate days, but the modern visitor should go well prepared with insect repellent (and raincoat).

---

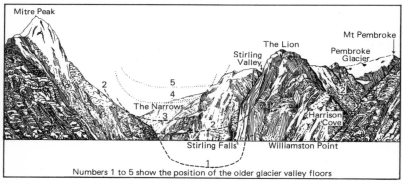

Numbers 1 to 5 show the position of the older glacier valley floors

*Milford Sound from the head of the Sound*

---

### MILFORD TRACK\*\*\*    Fiordland.   Map 23.
*From the head of Lake Te Anau to Milford Sound.*

"THE FINEST WALK IN THE WORLD" has been the undisputed description of the Milford Track for nearly a century, an opinion endorsed by thousands who have made the four-to-five day trip.

The "walk" begins by launch along Lake Te Anau to Glade House. The second day covers 16 km beside the Clinton River through beautiful native forest to Pompolona Huts (named after the Italian pancakes that were a specialty of the explorer-guide Quintin McKinnon). The third day, on the 15 km leg to Quintin Huts, more open country is encountered, culminating in a magnificent view of Mackinnon Pass, down the Clinton Canyon and north into the Arthur Valley, with towering mountains on all sides. The day concludes with a visit to the Sutherland Falls (*580.3 m*) (*see index*) — among the world's highest and as awesome as any. On the final day the walk leads an easy 21 km, down the Arthur Valley, skirting Lake Ada to reach Sandfly Point. From there walkers are collected to cover the last 3 km to Milford by launch.

**Quintin McKinnon** (1851–92), like Sutherland, a Scottish Highlander, pioneered the track from Lake Te Anau to Milford by first discovering the pass that today bears his (misspelt) name. He then accepted a contract to form a track, and to guide visitors

# MILFORD TRACK

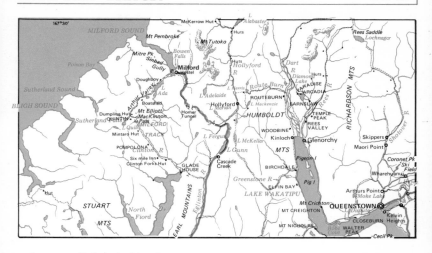

and carry mail along it. Like Sutherland, too, McKinnon fought as a mercenary (for the French in the Franco-Prussian war) before coming to New Zealand, where he quickly established himself as an outstanding athlete. He took part in one of the first inter-provincial rugby matches ever played.

Once qualified as a surveyor, McKinnon succumbed to the spell of Fiordland, making a series of notable journeys of exploration. It was on a routine trip up Lake Te Anau that he disappeared; his empty boat was found, leading to the theory that it had capsized in a sudden squall and that McKinnon had drowned. *A white rock jutting from Lake Te Anau is a memorial to McKinnon—it was discovered by a party searching for him. A cairn erected by the Gaelic Society, the Otago Rugby Football Union and the Government marks the pass McKinnon discovered.*

## CONDUCTED WALKS

Conducted trips along the Milford Track leave from Te Anau each Monday, Wednesday and Friday from about December to early April, and daily from mid-December to mid-January. Booking, through travel agents anywhere, is essential well in advance, as accommodation at the huts is limited. Advantages of the conducted walk are the company of experienced and knowledgable guides and the provision of all food and bedding, minimising the amount walkers need carry. Packs and parkas may be hired at the Te Anau Hotel. The walk can be readily made by the normally active of any age.

## INDEPENDENT WALKERS

Three Fiordland National Park huts are maintained for the so-called "Freedom Walkers", at Clinton Forks, Lake Mintaro and Diamond Creek (Dumpling Hut). Each contains a central room, bunkrooms with mattresses and a stove (no cooking utensils). Only limited numbers can be accommodated. Make the preliminary approach, giving details of tramping experience, to the Park Headquarters, PO Box 29, Te Anau. Huts must be booked and paid for in advance, and there is a small track charge.

A maximum of twenty-four will be booked into huts at any one time.

There is no overnight accommodation at Sandfly Point. Buses regularly run from Milford to Te Anau for the return journey. The track cannot be walked from Milford to Te Anau.

*Note: Camping is prohibited within 800 m of the track. In any event, conditions are generally unsuitable for camping. The independent walker should carry a good map and a copy of* Moir's Guide Book to the Great Southern Lakes and Fiords of Otago and Southland (Southern Section), *which gives a detailed description of the track and particulars of a number of possible side trips.*

---

## CAUTION
Weather conditions in this area can deteriorate rapidly and rivers and creeks can become impassable in a very short time. RISK OF EXPOSURE IS GREAT. Proper equipment and previous experience is necessary before this track is undertaken by the independent walker.

---

*55.5 km SW of Dunedin; 25 km NE of Balclutha.*

HAPPILY NAMED, MILTON still centres on its mill and the solid prosperity of surrounding farmland. The work of the mill has changed, however, from grinding flour and oats to spinning wool, and farming activities now emphasise sheep-raising and dairying as well as mixed farming. To the north of the commercial area, on the main road, is a slight kink caused where surveyors met, having miscalculated as they laid separate lines from north and from south. For the traveller, Taylor Park is a good picnic spot with an excellent swimming pool.

## SOME HISTORY

**Poet or mill?** It was late in 1857 that Peter McGill's flourmill began operations by the east branch of the Tokomairiro River. An oatmill was added and as millhands began to build homes near the mill a settlement took shape. It has been debated whether the town's name is simply a contraction of Mill Town or was bestowed in honour of the English poet, John Milton. Perhaps both explanations may be accepted for in 1886 a surveyor named Robert Gillies claimed in a letter to the *Bruce Herald* that he had christened the town when he did a survey there in 1862, stating: "I selected the name of the poet Milton because I thought that by doing so the people in the township by the mill were likely to adopt the name also and thereby avoid the nuisance of two or three names, which is so common where there are two or three proprietors." Whatever the reason, the town's streets are, appropriately named after English and Scottish poets. Not far from the town is the intriguingly-titled district of Moneymore, but the name means only broad meadows.

With the discovery of gold in 1861 at Gabriels Gully, the district assumed new importance as its situation made it a principal link between Dunedin and the diggings. Initially the area was virtually left to the charge of women, for even the local minister hurried off to the goldfield, there to preach on the second Sunday after the rush began.

**Saving Milton:** The Salvation Army's arrival in Milton was welcomed by the *Bruce Herald* as likely to have "little more lasting effect for good . . . than a travelling circus". Hostility boiled over in 1893 when the Borough Council charged members with breaching bylaws by "beating a drum, blowing a cornet, and carrying torches". The charges provoked violent repercussions throughout the country. Despite eager offers by sympathetic members of the public to pay the 5s fines imposed, local Corps members preferred to serve seven days in the Dunedin gaol, then to be welcomed back to Milton as martyrs by their supporters.

## THINGS TO SEE AND DO

**Alliance Textiles' Woollen Mills:** The mills on which the town is now centred opened in 1897, only eighteen months after a day-visitor had sparked local interest by writing a letter to the *Bruce Herald* suggesting the establishment of a woollen mill. At first elementary lines of flannels and blankets were manufactured, but today the mill's products cover a wide range. As the mill expanded it acquired the buildings of Peter McGill's flourmill, so underlining the transition of the town from one type of mill to another. Visitors are welcome to see the metamorphosis of wool into garments. *Tel. 8024 to arrange a convenient time preferably a day or more in advance. Allow 1 hr. Elderlee St* (named after the early surveyor, James Elder Brown, universally known as the "elderly Brown").

**Three churches:** The **Tokomairiro Presbyterian Church** (1889)** is a particularly splendid stone building, designed by R. A. Lawson. The original plan called for a much higher steeple but was reduced on account of expense. The church retains the Maori name for the locality (literally paddling through swamp), a reference to the marshy character of the plain as the early Maoris knew it. An earlier church (1863), now used as a hall, stands beside the present church. It was soon replaced as it had an immense square tower that proved too weak to withstand the winds. When the pew rents were being set for the wooden building the pioneers revealed a preference for back seats that has not died with them. Seats at the rear used to cost almost twice as much to rent as those at the front. *Main street (Union St).*

The **St John's Anglican Church** (1866) has been rebricked but is otherwise the same as the building that was dedicated by Bishop Selwyn who, by coincidence, was passing through the town on his way from the Otago goldfields at the time the church was completed. St John's thus has a link with the first and only Bishop of New Zealand. *Main street (Union St).*

The **Catholic Church of the Immaculate Conception** (St Mary's) (1892) was built to the design of F. W. Petre, noted for a number of fine churches. The few Catholics who arrived in the early days of the predominantly Presbyterian district of Otago experienced difficulty in forwarding the interests of their faith. Among the obstructions placed in their way is said to have been the lack of a central site for their church. Beside the church is its Gothic predecessor of Baltic timber (1869), now a hall. *Dryden St.*

**Tokomarino Historical Society:** An old cottage (*c.* 1858) and a museum contain a range of interesting exhibits, including Milton pottery fired at a time when it was hoped that Milton would become the centre of a considerable ceramics industry. *Museum, Union St, open Sun. 2–4 pm from October to June, other times by arrangement. Cottage, 12 Shakespeare St, open by arrangement.*

**Milton Nursery** covers about 36 ha producing some sixteen species of forest tree, principally *Pinus radiata*, Douglas fir and Alpine ash. Stocks held for supply to State forests in Otago and Southland exceed 9 million. As well as forest trees, poplars, ornamental trees and shrubs are supplied. *Springfield Rd, on town's NE boundary. To visit contact the Forest Ranger, NZ Forest Service, tel. 8235.*

## ENVIRONS

**SOME COASTAL PICNIC PLACES: Bull Creek** is reputedly the farthest point south that the southern *rata* is to be found in its natural state. There is shade here and sea swimming. (*19 km ESE*).

By contrast **Toko Mouth** is a more open area, where a smattering of cribs marks Milton's most popular swimming beach. (*15 km SE*.)

At **Chrystalls Beach** there is safe swimming only in the lagoon, the prime point of interest being the walk to Cooks Head Rock, a curious sugarloaf of hexagonal basalt blocks some 23.8 m high. The beach is named after the genial bachelor, Francis Chrystall, one of the district's earliest European settlers, who for many years ran a boardinghouse here. (*17 km SE*.)

**Rotary Lookout** (*316.5 m*) will afford an excellent view of the town and the district, from Toko Mouth and the Nuggets to the high country near Roxburgh. *6 km. To be signposted from main street when access road completed.*

**Lovells Flat Sod Cottage\*\*:** Once with an upstairs attic, the old sod cottage has been restored and furnished in period as a single-roomed colonial home. *11.6 km S on Highway 1. Signposted. Open continuously.*

> If in doubt about road conditions, contact the nearest Automobile Association office. In holiday periods, listen for the Mobil Holiday Bulletins which are broadcast regularly from most commercial radio stations.

## MOERAKI\*\* North Otago. Map 28. Pop. 143 (locality).

*78 km NNE of Dunedin; 38 km SSW of Oamaru.*

THE PICTURESQUE FISHING village of Moeraki lies on a rare protrusion on the North Otago coastline, a fat tongue whose northern tip curls to form a sheltered natural harbour. Though the first Europeans to settle in North Otago did so in this delightful spot, Moeraki's future as a port of substance never materialised. It remains today an attractive fishing port with a miniscule population, best known for the curious "Moeraki boulders" which litter nearby beaches.

The lack of good water in the area is explained in legend. The sea-god Tangaroa, masquerading as a whale, was insulted by a youth as he went to fetch water. Tangaroa responded by spouting seawater all over the hillside, to impregnate the springs and to render water at Moeraki brackish to this day. Moeraki means sleepy sky, or a place to sleep by day.

### SOME HISTORY

**Sectarian rivalry:** The first European settlers in North Otago were the whalers who in 1836 established a bay-whaling station on the northern side of Moeraki Point, a promontory then so bush-covered that native pigeons would land on the whalers' heads. The whalers enjoyed success for a time — 23 whales in 1837, 27 in 1838 and 25 in 1839. That their calling was a dangerous one is shown by an account of the loss of a new boat: one boat was holding fast to a large catch; another came to help "when [the whale] suddenly made a rush right in their direction, and went clean over her, turning her over by sheer weight, and in a minute or two our brand-new boat was floating about the bay in shingles".

In the reverse of the more usual pattern, a Maori settlement grew up near the whaling station, comprising Ngaitahu who had fled from Kaiapoi after being routed by Te Rauparaha.

Though Bishop Pompallier had visited the area, the Maoris were divided between the "Children of Wesley" (with Watkin working from Waikouaiti) and "the Church of Paihia" (after the northern converts Te Whiwhi and Tamihana Te Rauparaha had called in 1843 to good effect). Shortland in 1844 reported that the factions "maintained constant disputes on the subject of religion . . . In their small place there were consequently two chapels, and the rivalry of the two congregations might be noticed even in the loud and obstinate din which issued from the two iron pots, the common substitute for a belfry." The whalers, as they intermarried, stayed on despite the fall-off in the whaling trade, and turned to farming.

**"A marine bauble"**: Moeraki was more attractive to shipping interests — some speculators foresaw Moeraki as a "Port Chalmers" to Hampden — but Oamaru was better sited to serve the North Otago runs. Gradually Moeraki lost trade to Oamaru, largely because of poor access. Local agitation saw both a road to the port constructed in 1862–63 and the building of a jetty. However the jetty was soon worm-eaten and the road could not stand up to heavy traffic.

When condemned in 1871 the jetty was described as "one of the marine baubles upon which the Provincial revenue has been thoughtlessly and recklessly expended . . . 'the jetty' simply acts as a groin, and no more effectual method could have been taken to silt up the harbour."

A new jetty was built at right angles to the old. Prospects brightened with the construction of the Dunedin-Oamaru railway, as much material was landed here, so much so that the port was given a second chance to re-establish itself. A branch railway line was built along the unstable hillside to the north, but slips were frequent and so weakened the piers of the viaducts that after two short years, in 1879, the line was abandoned. *Traces of the railway's route may be seen.*

## MOERAKI BOULDERS***

The Moeraki Boulders are geological curiosities which weigh several tons, are up to 4 m in circumference and which lie on Moeraki Beach much as if a giant, weary of his play, has walked away from a game of bowls — so much so that the early whalers named them The Ninepins. The spherical, grey, septarian boulders were formed on the sea floor about 60 million years ago by the gradual accumulation of lime salts round a small centre. Their shape is thus caused by chemistry and not by wave action. The cracks in the boulders, or concretions as they are more correctly called, are typical of this type of growth and are filled with crystals of calcite. The boulders appear from the bank behind the beach as the softer mud-stone in which they rest is weathered away by the sea. Formerly plentiful, many of the concretions have been removed. Those left are generally too heavy to have been taken away. Though not unique such concretions are rare, and the area is now protected as a scientific reserve.

In Maori legend the *Araiteuru* canoe (one of the large ancestral canoes that came from Hawaiki) was wrecked on Shag Point while on its way south in search of greenstone. Foodbaskets and *kumara* on board were washed ashore. The *kumara* became irregularly shaped rocks and the circular food-baskets became the Moeraki Boulders, called by the Maori, Te Kaihinaki (the food-baskets). The reef at the mouth of the Shag River is said to be the petrified hull of the canoe, and a prominent rock nearby to be the mortal remains of its navigator, Hipo. Names of passengers are given to hills in the area. The legend is an example of how a colourful story would be woven round the physical features of the landscape to perpetuate a knowledge of geography in a culture without a written language. *A short detour from Highway 1 at 3.2 km N of the Moeraki turnoff leads to Moeraki Beach where the boulders are a 10-minute walk along the sand. Signposted.*

Smaller examples of septarian boulders, which the whalers called Vulcan's Foundry, are on Katiki Beach, a good bathing and picnicking beach (*6.5 km S of Moeraki*).

## OTHER POINTS OF INTEREST

**Kotahitanga Church** (1862) originally stood on the Maori *kaik* on the top of the hill near the Uenuku meeting hall. Like the reserve, the church was too far from both port and settlement and fell into disuse. The building was later moved, first to Centenary Park and then to its present site. Within the simple wooden structure are stained-glass windows crafted in Rome in *c.* 1861, depicting Christ, Mother and Child, and an elderly Maori leader, Matiaha Tiramorehu. *Key held locally.*

**Moeraki Lighthouse** was built in 1877 as the nearby Fish and Danger Reefs had caused many shipping fatalities. The wooden tower, 8.5 m high, has been heavily braced to withstand southerly gales. The light, 51.8 m above sea level, was electrified in 1943 and is a group-flash light with a range of 30.6 km. *Signposted. The light may be inspected by arrangement with the keeper, preferably before mid-day. 5 km.*

**Trotters Gorge*****: A grassed picnic area surrounded by native bush and flanked by huge limestone bluffs. A sheltered scene in contrast with the coast. *9.1 km. Turnoff right from Highway 1 signposted at 5.1 km S. If the second stream cannot be forded follow the track to the right to cross to the picnic area by a footbridge. This route also offers a pleasant alternative passage to Palmerston but bypasses an interesting section of Highway 1.*

> A metric conversion chart appears at the end of the book.

> Roam abroad in the world, and take thy fill of its enjoyments before the day shall come when thou must quit it for good. — Sa'di (*Gulistan*).

## MONOWAI (Lake)    Fiordland.   Map 12.

*44 km NW of Clifden; 46 km S of Manapouri.*

LAKE MONOWAI in Fiordland National Park is an object lesson to power planners. Raised in 1925, the lake half a century later still has an unsightly shoreline, even if up the lake where the banks are steeper the consequences have been less disastrous. Nearby is Boreland Lodge, owned by the Southland Youth Adventure Trust. The lake is noted for its brown trout, but the "drowned forest" makes fishing from the lake shore difficult. Tracks lead to Rodger Inlet (*3½ hrs*) and to Clark Hut on the Grebe River via Green Lake (*9 hrs*). *Further details from the park headquarters at △ Te Anau and the ranger at △Clifden.*

Monowai is a corruption of Manokiwai (fixed channel full of water), a reference to the depth of water in the long narrow lake despite the lack of any large rivers flowing into it.

### MONOWAI POWER STATION

With a capacity of 6,000 kW, the power station is by the banks of the Waiau River into which the lake flows, using water drawn from the lake by way of a canal. Built in 1926 by the Southland Electric Power Board as the first scheme for rural distribution in the country, the plant was taken over by the State in 1936 and is today the New Zealand Electricity Department's second-to-smallest installation. *Visitors welcome.*

## MOSGIEL*    East Otago.   Map 9.   Pop. 9,281.

*17 km W from Dunedin.*

MOSGIEL LIES ON the broad green swathe of the Taieri Plain, the prospering agricultural district of which it is the centre. In contrast with nearby Dunedin its streets are straight, flat and wide, but it, too, has a proliferation of churches.

The Taieri Plain, originally a series of swamps (as was the town site itself), was settled by arrivals on the *Philip Laing* and *John Wickliffe*, who slowly succeeded in draining the wide area. Much highly productive land was reclaimed where there are now sheep and dairy farms, racing stables, marketgardens and a thriving small-fruit industry. To the east lies Saddle Hill, so named for its silhouette, from where there is an exceptional view of the town and the Taieri Plain.

Mosgiel, named after a Scottish farm owned by Robert Burns, was so called by the poet's great-nephew, Arthur Burns, the son of Dunedin's Dr Thomas Burns. He founded the township in 1856 and established the woollen factory for which the town is famous. Somewhere Mosgiel has lost a letter, as the original Burns farm was Mossgiel. Its Scottish origins, however, are reflected in the presence of the country's only whisky distillery.

### MOSGIEL WOOLLEN MILLS

It was in 1868, when James Macandrew as provincial superintendent offered a £1,500 bonus to the first man in the province to produce 5,000 yards of woollen cloth, that Arthur Burns took up the challenge and proposed to establish a woollen mill on his Mossgiel farm. He travelled to Britain to raise the capital, to buy plant and to recruit labour. Plant and labour presented no problem but it was a year before sufficient money was raised. Thereafter events moved swiftly. Plant and skilled workmen left Britain in January 1871, arriving in Dunedin in May. In September the first wool was carded and by the year's end the bonus was his. At the time the *Otago Daily Times* noted the establishment of "an industry which bids fair to become an important feature of the Trade and Commerce of Otago". The province's first mill was eventually sold by Burns to the company that still operates it. The complex incorporates a brick building, originally the first flourmill on the Taieri, that was converted by Burns into the dyehouse for his new woollen mill. Previously it had supplied flour to the goldfields.

At the mill the visitor may see the conversion of raw wool into finished fabric. Scouring removes dirt and impurities, and carding arranges the fibres roughly in the one direction; the wool is then spun, woven, and given a suitable finish. The factory here produces tweed, domestic flannel, blankets, rugs, socks, knitwear and yarns. *Factory Rd. Visits may be arranged on weekdays. Tel. MSI-6199 at least a day in advance. Allow up to 2 hrs. The plant closes for maintenance work for three weeks over the Christmas period.*

### OTHER THINGS TO SEE AND DO

**Holy Cross College:** The old Mossgiel homestead (*c.* 1870) of Arthur Burns is conspicuous among the later brick buildings. It is ironical that a property selected by the Rev. Dr Burns should now be owned by the Catholic Church and train the priests whom the arch-Presbyterian so dreaded. The Church acquired the property when Bishop Verdon (to whom the new chapel is dedicated) bought the block in 1899 to make good the lack of a seminary. The former chapel, an annexe to the homestead, is hung with etchings of early Rome. *Church St. Visitors welcome by prior arrangement with the rector; tel. MSI-6990.*

**Invermay Agricultural Research Centre:** At Mosgiel the Ministry of Agriculture and Fisheries maintains two research farms plus administrative facilities and a laboratory complex. The 500 ha Invermay farm includes flat land, rolling downland and unploughable hill country. Research is carried out on farming problems of Otago and Southland with emphasis on pasture and crop agronomy, soil fertility and the breeding and raising of sheep, cattle and deer. The 925 ha Waiora Farm specialises in the farming problems and development of hill country. *Dukes Rd, Silverstream Park. Those with a special interest may visit on weekdays by appointment. Allow 2 hours. Tel. MSI-5009.*

The **Invermay homestead** (1862) was built by John Gow and remained in his family for almost a century. He had preceded Dr Burns to the area and built his home of solid concrete. Slate carried on the *Agra* as ballast, the ship Gow came out on in 1852, was used to floor the kitchen. Much of the Gow property now forms part of the Invermay Research Station but the homestead is part of the University of Otago's Animal Breeding Centre. (*2.5 km along Factory Rd.*)

**East Taieri Presbyterian Church** (1869)\*\*\*: Elevated and skilfully proportioned the brick church is another of R. A. Lawson's ecclesiastical masterpieces. It is built of double brick in Flemish style (the bricks alternate between lengthways and widthways), and is pointed with rose-tinted stone. The interior, lavish by Presbyterian standards, includes a window that depicts Christ among the pioneers with survey map, bullock dray and children. The manse behind the church dates from 1877. *Cemetery Rd off Gladstone Rd. 2.1 km.*

## TOURING NOTES

**Highway 87 to △Middlemarch:** From Mosgiel the road to Middlemarch and so to Central lies through Outram, just east of which one passes some delightful colonial homesteads. On the banks of the Taieri River is the much-frequented picnic spot of Outram Glen. The farming centre of Outram grew up as a staging post on the way to the diggings and has a certain oldworld charm.

Some 2 km west of Outram, just as Highway 87 rises to leave the Taieri Plain, is a splendid two-storeyed building (1875) that served as the manse for the West Taieri church, now demolished. The 2.4 ha of glebe land are today used for the culture of mushrooms. At Lee Stream (*23 km*) is a weary stone hotel (1858) that predates the goldrushes and only two decades ago was still open for business.

**Old Dunstan Road:** In summer it is possible for the intrepid with a high-clearance vehicle to traverse part of the historic Old Dunstan Road, the route to the Central goldfields before The Pigroot was opened. Turn off Highway 87 at Clark's Junction (*36 km*) to climb steeply over the Lammerlaws and the Rock and Pillar Range to Styx (*see index*) on the Maniototo Plain (*44 km from Clark's Junction*). At Deepstream Crossing are the remains of the Oasis Hotel. On reaching Styx one may either join Highway 85 at Ranfurly or carry on to zigzag over Rough Ridge and descend to Moa Creek, whence it is a straightforward run to Alexandra (*by this route 111 km from Clark's Junction*).

*Note:* Inquiries should be made locally before attempting either leg of this route, which is extremely slow and involves driving over a rough track as well as the opening and closing of numerous gates. The road is impassable in winter and frequently so after rain at other times of year. Contact the Automobile Association (Otago) before starting, to obtain up-to-date details of road conditions. The route is little used and there is no assistance readily available for those who strike trouble.

**MOTUEKA\*\*\*     Nelson.   Maps 26 & 32.   Pop. 4,384.**
*51 km NW of Nelson; 57 km SSE of Takaka.*

MOTUEKA IS SET APART, not so much by its rivermouth setting and the reflections in the smooth tidal reaches of Tasman Bay, but by the patchwork of tobacco and wire-hung hopfields beside big boarded kilns, and by the large tobacco factories that fringe the town. For Motueka, as well as harvesting much of the country's pip fruit, is the centre of New Zealand's only commercial plantations of hops and tobacco. These activities manifest the town's equitable climate and draw to it each summer large numbers of seasonal workers to harvest fruit, tobacco, hops and raspberries.

Motueka (more correctly Motuweka) has been translated as the crippled woodhen — one used as a lure to trap *weka*. The name (literally *motu* = clump of trees; *weka* = woodhen) comes from Hawaiki, where it may have had a different connotation.

## SOME HISTORY

**Land of plenty:** When Europeans arrived, there was a Maori *kainga* at Motueka which had already been visited by Octavius Hadfield, who had sailed across from Waikanae to bring Christianity to the area. Soon the plains were dotted with huts as the settlers, many of them retired army and naval officers, set about clearing dense bush to win today's fertile farmland. Well could Dr Greenwood's wife enthuse in 1843: "The climate is delightful. It has neither the rains of Auckland nor the winds of Port Nicholson [Wellington]. The waters abound in fish of excellent quality, and the land with birds, pigeons, quails, wild duck and parrots."

Potatoes were exported to the Australian goldfields, but communications closer to hand were also by ship. Small trading vessels plied round the coast to overcome the lack of roads and rivercrossings, and to provide the region with its solitary lifeline.

## SOME NOTES

**Orcharding:** Each of the newly-won farms had its own small orchard. Demand led to the shipping of fruit to Wellington, so that before long the original small homestead orchard had in many cases grown to become the leading feature of a farm. In 1910 the success of a trial shipment of apples to Britain, coupled with a Government-guaranteed price, saw the industry enjoy a passing boom. Since 1948, when the Apple and Pear Marketing Board was established, there has been a steady increase in orcharding areas, with the Motueka crop growing to exceed one million cases annually. Today Motueka ranks as the country's most prolific orcharding region, her apples alone being exported to more than forty countries. *The Appleby Research Orchard (tel. Richmond 5253) may be visited by prior arrangement by those with a special interest. Experiments are conducted with new varieties, nutrition, cultivation, pest control and pest diseases. Visitors are welcome at the Apple and Pear Marketing Board's cannery at Stoke (tel. 79-679 Nelson) where fruit and fruit-juices are canned and apple wine produced.*

**Tobacco:** The Maoris being quick to take up smoking, tobacco was grown widely from the time of early European settlement. Later it was grown to supply early Canterbury runholders, who would dip their sheep in a tobacco solution to counter the dreaded scab. Commercial growing at Motueka, after a shortlived attempt in 1888, really dates from 1916. While attempts in other regions failed, farms proliferated in the Motueka region, so much so that the amount now grown is done so only under licence. A corresponding minimum percentage of New Zealand leaf content has been imposed on tobacco manufacturers.

The minute seed (a small teaspoonful will produce enough seedlings to plant an acre) is raised in seedbeds and planted out in November. The plant grows rapidly to a height of about 2 m when, after about two months, the flowerhead is broken off to divert growth to the leaves. The growth of laterals is similarly checked. The leaves ripen from the bottom up, and are harvested over a period of up to eighty days. They are placed in a tobacco kiln where a temperature of 30 °C and a constant humidity are maintained for from 36 to 96 hours. Starches and chlorophyl break down and the leaves turn yellow or orange. To hold this colour, enzymatic activity is checked by raising the temperature to about 50 °C and reducing the humidity by opening the kiln's ventilators. Further drying completes the process, after which steam is introduced to prevent the tinder-dry leaves from shattering. The curing process takes from five to seven days. An average tobacco farm has about 7 ha in cultivation. Some 340 growers produce a crop to an annual value of $9 million, most combining their activities with dairying, orcharding or the growing of hops.

*The plant of W. D. & H. O. Wills (tel. 188) and Rothmans (tel. 423) may be visited by arrangement (peak time is from May to July). The New Zealand Tobacco Growers' Federation (tel. 1606) can usually arrange visits to tobacco farms. The Tobacco Research Station (tel. 501) may also be visited by arrangement, usually on Friday afternoons.*

**Hop growing:** Like tobacco, hops were introduced by early settlers who were with varying success growing them elsewhere throughout the country. In recent years production has been restricted to the Motueka region. Hops are grown for the female plant's flowers which, when ripe, contain the lupulin used by brewers. Hop gardens are on mixed farms, covering about 4 ha of flat sheltered land planted with poles which are festooned with running wires some 4 m or more above the ground. The perennial climbing plants grow from root stocks left undisturbed in the soil. In spring the stronger shoots are "strung" to train the vines, and in late January the old leaves are stripped to check the upward spread of red spider during the heat of February. The hops are mechanically harvested in late February and early March, and dried in kilns within eighteen hours of picking. The kiln, usually at one end of a two-storeyed building, has a wire-mesh floor through which hot air is drawn by a fan set in the roof. After almost ten hours in the kiln, the dried hops are baled and marketed to brewers throughout the country. The recent development of a seedless hop by the Hop Research Station at Riwaka has created considerable export possibilities. *The Hop Research Station (tel. 515D) at Riwaka may be visited by arrangement.*

## OTHER THINGS TO SEE AND DO

**Te Ahurewa Maori Church** (1897): The church, whose name means sacred place and whose interior is decorated with Maori motifs, replaced the earlier chapel of Amate which stood beside it. The guiding force behind Te Ahurewa was the Rt. Rev. Frederick Bennett (1871–1950), who was ordained the year before the church was built and went on to become in 1928 the first Bishop of Aotearoa. The gates commemorate the Bishop, who himself presented the altar in memory of his wife, whom he married here in 1899. The simple little church was roughcast and renovated in 1955. Within the grounds is an old canoe, one of the last to be used on the Motueka River. *Pah St (turn off opp. Post Office). Services on the third Sunday of the month. Key available locally.*

**Fifeshire font:** A font carved from the mast of the illfated migrant ship *Fifeshire* wrecked on Arrow Rock at Nelson in 1842 is in St Thomas's Church (1911). The original church on the site was built of rammed earth, but before the roof timbers were up a heavy storm caused the structure to slump into a muddy heap. By 1848 a wooden replacement was ready for use. *Main st.*

**Fearons Bush:** About 4 ha of bush, a remnant of that which once covered the whole of the Motueka district, now shades the town's motorcamp. *Fearon St. Signposted "Motor Camp" off main st.* Another pleasant picnic place beneath tall native trees is **Thorp's Bush.** *Signposted off main st.*

**Some beaches:** Nearby beaches include the Motueka Beach Reserve (*close to the wharf; camping ground*), Sandy Bay (*19 km*), Marahau (*23 km*) and Kaiteriteri (*14 km*).

## ENVIRONS

**Kaiteriteri\*\*\*** (pop. 232): Houses cling to green hills, the water is clear and blue and islands crowd the bay's mouth. Between rocky points sweeps the gentle arch of the finest beach imaginable. A large motorcamp takes up the level land that backs the golden sand, in summer crowded with holidaymakers.

Launch trips run along the intricate coastline of △Abel Tasman National Park to the Astrolabe Roadstead and the remarkable curiosity of Split Apple Rock (*enquire at the store*). At the northern end of the beach is Kaka Point lookout, a former Maori occupation site whence a track leads down to Breaker Bay. Below Kaka Point, at the end of the main beach, is a spring where Capt. Arthur Wakefield (*see index*) drew water while searching for a site for Nelson. He very nearly chose Kaiteriteri.

Some 4 km before Kaiteriteri is reached a millstone cairn is passed. Built of stones from an early (1844) flourmill, it commemorates Arthur Wakefield and Riwaka's pioneers. From the cairn is a good view over valley and sea. Just beyond Kaiteriteri is delightful Honeymoon Bay, past which the road winds to the locality of Marahau. *14 km N.*

**Marahau\*\*:** The beach looks across the Astrolabe Roadstead to Adele Island. Marahau (where there is a motorcamp) is an access point to △Abel Tasman National Park. A three-day tramp leads round the Park's coastline to Totaranui (*details of the track and huts from the park information offices at △Takaka and Totaranui; further details are under △Abel Tasman National Park, "Some walks".*) Arrangements may be made at Kaiteriteri to walk part of the track and be collected by launch. *23 km N of Motueka. 9 km beyond Kaiteriteri.*

**Riwaka River source\*\*\*:** In a truly delightful setting the Riwaka River emerges from a limestone cavern at the foot of a high bushclad cliff. The short walk along a well-formed path to the riverhead passes through beech forest, with some *rimu, miro, kamahi* and *hinau* underlaid with tree fern. The bush is the better enjoyed by walking the alternative, though rougher and longer, Nature Walk. A short distance from the source is the Crystal Pool, whose deep waters have remarkable clarity. The river has been explored underground for about 60 m by skindivers who found a limestone cavern some 25 m high, roofed with stalactites.

There are picnic places at the carpark, and swimming in the distinctly cool river. There are also a number of picnic spots some distance downstream, in the **Moss Reserve**. *16.4 km. Leave Motueka on Highway 60 towards Takaka, turning left where signposted shortly after passing the Kaiteriteri turnoff.*

**Riwaka** (pop. 1,000): A pleasant settlement across the river from Motueka is the centre for hop research (*see above*). In St Barnabas' Anglican Church (1912) are the quaint 1848 box pews taken from an earlier church at Motueka and, apparently successfully, deposited in the sea to counter borer. The church, too, is built in part of timber from its predecessor. *8 km N.*

△**Abel Tasman National Park\*\*\*:** A stand of native bush, indented with coves whose golden sand contrasts with the greens of the forest. *Access from Marahau (23 km), Canaan (35 km) and △Takaka (57 km).*

**Riverside Community (Lower Moutere)** is a commune that has survived since 1940 when, with New Zealand locked in war, it was founded as a Christian pacifist community by three people with a small orchard. Since then it has flourished to support about sixty people of all ages, and its assets are very substantial. Open to Christians of all denominations (also to those who are not Christians), its purpose is to build "from the ground upward" a more Christian, brotherly, peaceful and non-violent world by the renunciation of war, private ownership and private profit.

The community are not as communal as many. They eat communal meals only twice weekly and on special occasions. Each family is housed separately and is domestically independent. Each is provided with a free house, milk, eggs, fruit, vegetables, power, telephone and firewood. Medical and dental expenses are paid, meat and honey subsidised, and a cash allowance made according to the number of children.

Before anyone is accepted as a member there is a probationary period of a year. The community grew to no blueprint but developed gradually, adapting to experience.

Its substantial orchards and mixed farm are centred on an elevated village overlooking a valley of orchards and dairyfarms enclosed by hills crowned by Mt Arthur. The view from the church window, particularly when snow is on the mountain, is a favoured subject for photographers. Three of the houses are built of rammed earth (*pisé de terre*) and two of fortified earth (soil-cement). The church, engineering workshop and some other buildings are also of fortified earth. Until recently all building was done by the community itself.

Although known as Riverside there is in fact no river — for the waterway that runs by the highway here is shown on maps as the "Company's Ditch". When the New Zealand Company colonised Nelson the valley was an impassable bog. A drain was dug which gradually enlarged to the size of a river, but in long dry spells it can dry up completely. In early times, too, coaches could not get through the valley but ran along the hills. The "Old Coach Road", technically still a public thoroughfare, runs through the community property beyond the "village".

*6.4 km S on Moutere Highway. Visitors welcome. A roadside stall dispenses fruit, vegetables and literature.*

**Arthur Range:** The range holds possibilities for both tramper and rock-hunter. Old gold workings in the Baton area have an aura of mystery.

## SUGGESTED DRIVES

**Nelson round trip:** The 103 km trip takes the inland route to Nelson, returning along the coast through Ruby Bay and Tasman. *Described under △ Nelson, "Suggested Drives".*

**Kaiteriteri-Marahau:** Pass through Riwaka and turn right to drive through Kaiteriteri and on to Marahau (*for all, see above*). Return by way of Sandy Bay Road, signposted from Sandy Bay. *40 km.*

**Motueka River Valley-Brightwater round trip:** The 148 km drive follows Highway 61 along the east bank of the Motueka River through Ngatimoti (where there is an early church of pitsawn timber, consecrated in 1884) and Woodstock before joining Highway 6 at Motupiko. Turn left at Highway 6 to climb over the Spooner Range. The segments of the drive from the Spooner Range lookout to Pea Viner Corner and from Pea Viner Corner back to Motueka are described under Nelson, "Suggested Drives".

**Takaka Hill ("Marble Mountain") and Canaan:** 65 km. Follow Highway 60 towards △ Takaka, climbing up Takaka Hill for a series of spectacular views back over the Motueka Valley and across Tasman Bay to Nelson. At 20.6 km pass the entrance to Ngarua Caves (*see below*), and turn right along the slow and rough Canaan Road to wind through country with a ghostly character. Dead trees stand gaunt in a graveyard of weatherworn marble. At the road's end a 40-minute walk leads to Harwood's Hole. This remarkable chasm, considered the twelfth deepest in the world and the largest in the hemisphere, is fully 370.6 m deep. The area is favoured by potholers and there are many deep sinkholes (*tomo*) hereabouts. (*For notes on the "marble mountain", see △ Takaka*).

## ORGANISED EXCURSIONS

**Ngarua Caves\*\*:** Fascinating caves with delicate formations tunnel into the "marble mountain" of Takaka Hill. *Visits to the caves are conducted by Hickmotts Bus Lines (tel. Motueka 10). Open in summer holiday period and occasionally at other times. Allow ¾ hr for the guided tour.*

> When looking for a placename, first consult the Index at the back of the book.

**MOTUNAU BEACH\***     **North Canterbury.**    **Map 20.**    **Pop. 100.**

*47 km SW of Cheviot; 37 km E of Waipara.*

PERCHED HIGH ABOVE the sea and huddled low by the modest Motunau River are the houses of fishermen, of the retired, and the baches of holidaymakers. The river, home to a fleet of fishing boats, has to the north of its mouth an area favoured by fossilhunters. Their quarry is usually found in hard boulders eroded from lime-cemented layers in the otherwise soft, siltstone cliffs that back the beach. Many marine shellfish fossil crabs, fossilised whalebone and fossilised sharkbone have been found, but more important have been finds of the fossilised bones of seabirds dating back some 10 million years. A second beach, aptly named Sandy Bay, is good for swimming.

Motunau (*motu* = island; *nau* = scurvy grass) refers to the scurvy grass collected by Cook on his visits to New Zealand and used with success to combat vitamin deficiency among his men. It grew on the curious flat-topped island here until eaten off by stock.

## SOME HISTORY

**The *Buccaneer* and "Bully" Hayes:** Looking out to sea one morning, John Caverhill (the luckless licence-holder pre-empted from Cheviot by "Ready-Money" Robinson) saw anchored off Motunau Island the *Buccaneer*, a vessel commanded by the infamous Captain "Bully" Hayes (*see index*), a rogue who in his brief sojourn in New Zealand left a welter of folklore in his wake. Fearing that the island might become a refuge for other such nefarious characters, Caverhill applied to Governor Gore Browne for permission to exercise control over the island. His request was granted and on 10 January 1857 a deed was duly signed: "Mr J. S. Caverhill of Motunau in the Province of Canterbury, is hereby authorised in the name of Her Majesty to enter upon and take exclusive hold of Motunau Island in the Province of Canterbury, until this authority shall be revoked." It never has been.

To make the most of your travels you should carry with you the book of Mobil road maps.

**MOUNT ASPIRING NATIONAL PARK\*\*\***     **Central Otago/Westland. Map 36. Area: 287,253 ha.**

*Park Headquarters at △Wanaka provides information on walks, tramps, hunting and fishing. The* Mount Aspiring National Park Handbook *is recommended. There are also ranger stations at Glenorchy (on Lake Wakatipu) and at Makarora (on the △Haast Pass Road).*

THE ALPINE PARK of Mt Aspiring, a slice of the Southern Alps, embraces a complex of glaciated mountains, bushcovered slopes, and friendly riverflats. To the north the park extends to the Haast River, and to the south to a boundary shared with △Fiordland National Park. Though the area holds special appeal for the mountaineer the valleys offer excellent opportunities for all types of tramper. Points of access are from the △Haast Pass Road that cuts through its north-east corner, from the head of Lake Wakatipu, and from △Wanaka up the Matukituki Valley.

In the heart of the park rises its highest peak, Mt Aspiring (*3,033.6 m*), sharpened by the intersection of cirque walls to give it its classical pyramid form when viewed from the south-west.

. Chamois and red deer are lightly distributed throughout the park.

## SOME TRAMPS

*Trampers and climbers in the park should have with them* Moir's Guide Book (Northern Section), *published by the New Zealand Alpine Club.*

**Matukituki River:** The 7 km walk from Raspberry Creek to Aspiring Hut, mainly over grassy flats, takes about 2½ hrs (*one way*) and can be a good, stiff return walk for a day's outing from Wanaka. Beyond lies the Cullers Route to the Dart Valley by way of Cascade Saddle, a route for the experienced tramper and then only in good weather. A walk of only 2 km from the vehicle limit leads over river terraces to a fine view of the Rob Roy Glacier. *Note: If driving up the west branch of the river beyond Cameron Flat, discretion is essential as the track is at the mercy of both rain and river. Towing, if available, is expensive.*

**Wilkin Valley:** Accessible by jetboat from Wanaka and from Makarora or by fording the Makarora and Wilkin Rivers, the Wilkin Valley and its tributary valleys the Wonderland, Newland and the Siberia, afford some of the most satisfying tramps in the park.

**Rees and Dart Valleys** form a straightforward round trip, leaving from the Glenorchy-Paradise Road on Lake Wakatipu and taking approximately four days. The Saddle-Dart hut section requires special care.

**Routeburn Valley\*\*\*:** The 3-day tramp leaves the Kinloch Road on Lake Wakatipu to cross the Harris Saddle and reach the Te Anau-Milford Road. There buses from Milford will stop for trampers. The track traverses both Mount Aspiring and Fiordland National Parks. *Further information from the respective park headquarters and ranger stations.* A conducted 4-day walk is also possible, in both directions. (*Routeburn Walk Ltd, PO Box 271 Queenstown, or tel. 100M Nov.-April*).

△ indicates a place with its own entry.

**MOUNT COOK NATIONAL PARK*** South Canterbury. Map 34. Area: 69,958 ha.**

*Mount Cook village is 106 km NW of Tekapo; 96 km N of Omarama; 333 km W of Christchurch. Park headquarters open daily for details on walks, tramps, climbs and things to see and do. The* Mount Cook National Park Handbook *is recommended.*

SAMUEL BUTLER, first sighting the lofty peak of Mt Cook (*3,762.9 m*) from the Two Thumb Range, exclaimed "I was struck almost breathless by the wonderful mountain that burst on my sight."

The motorist comes upon the country's highest peak not as suddenly, but by the steep-walled valley of the Tasman River. Nor does the mountain stand alone but surrounded by a host of massive peaks, scores of which exceed 3,000 m and about two hundred of which rise to heights of over 2,500 m. A vast tableau of alpine scenery surrounds the settlement, where there is an inevitable conflict between the demands of visitors and the conservation objectives of the National Park. Accommodation ranges from the luxury of The Hermitage Hotel through motels and chalets to a youth hostel.

---

### CAUTION

Cars parked overnight in winter conditions should have either anti-freeze added to their radiators or their radiators drained. Anti-freeze fluid is available locally.

---

**Two navigators:** Mt Cook was named after the Yorkshire navigator in 1851 by Captain Stokes in the course of the survey carried out by HMS *Acheron.* Its companion, Mt Tasman (*3,496.1 m*), was named after the Dutch explorer eleven years later, by Julius von Haast. Paradoxically, neither discoverer seems to have seen either peak.

## SOME MYTHOLOGY

**Cloud in the sky:** A fragment of a sketchily recorded myth concerning the mountain relates that when Rangi (the Sky Father) and Papa (the Earth Mother) were united, not only did they have children but their offspring, too, had children amongst themselves. Some of the sky children came down to earth, among them Aorangi (cloud in the sky), and his younger brothers Rangi-roa, Rangi-rua and Rarangi-roa. They came together in the canoe *Te Waka-a-Aorangi* (the canoe of Aorangi). The canoe became the South Island of New Zealand, and when the four brothers were turned into mountains, Aorangi became Mt Cook, Rangi-roa became Mt Dampier, Rangi-rua is now Mt Teichelmann and Rarangi-roa became the Silberhorn.

A second fable tells of the passengers of the wrecked *Arai-te-uru* canoe (*see* △*Moeraki*) making their way north by way of the Mackenzie country when they saw the lofty peak. It was taller than others to which the names of members of the party had been given and was jokingly called Aorangi after a boy who was with them. Tired from walking, he was being carried on his grandfather's shoulders to be higher than the rest.

## THE CONQUERING OF COOK

A young Irish clergyman and member of the Alpine Club of London, William Green, was drawn to New Zealand after seeing photographs of the untamed Cook. Two Swiss joined him as guides and in 1882 they launched their assault. In fine weather they were barred by a jagged ice-seamed ridge from the south, and when they attempted the Ball Glacier route they were defeated by avalanches, ice-walls, precipices and shattered rock. Turning their energy to the northern side and using the Haast Ridge approach they were not far from the summit when the weather broke, and in a howling gale they spent a night at 3,050 m, clinging to a rock ledge that afforded some slight shelter, listening to the booms of intermittent avalanches, and struggling to keep awake and warm. At daybreak they turned back to their base camp, reaching it after an absence of sixty-two hours.

The adventures of Green's unsuccessful party received wide publicity, and stimulated interest in the sport in New Zealand, so that when in 1894 news came that an English climber, Edward Fitzgerald, and an Italian guide, Mattias Zurbriggen, were on their way to attempt the climb, three New Zealanders determined to beat them to the top. At about 3 am they launched their final assault. Of the last minutes of the climb, Tom Fyfe recalled: "I am afraid that the reckless way we romped over those last rocks was very foolhardy; but one would indeed need to be phlegmatic not to get a little excited on such an occasion. The slope of the final ice-cap was easy, and required only about a hundred steps which were quickly cut, and at 1.30 pm on Christmas Day we exultantly stepped on to the highest pinnacle of the monarch of the Southern Alps." Easier routes were found than that followed by the first climbers, so that it was sixty-one years later that their passage was repeated, on the one hundredth conquest of the peak.

The forestalled Fitzgerald was disappointed to the extent of refusing to climb Mt Cook at all, instead making the maiden ascents of Mts Sefton, Tasman and

Hardinger. His guide, however, climbed Cook, alone and by a different route, on 14 March 1895. Zurbriggen, who had begun life as a smuggler in the Italian Alps, climbed major peaks the world over, but rated his solo ascent of Cook as worthy of a chapter in his autobiography, *From the Alps to the Andes*. Since the New Zealand trio of Fyfe, Graham and Clarke first climbed Cook, climbers from the world over have matched their skills against her slopes, leaving only the hazardous Caroline Face untamed. Again, New Zealand climbers were the first to make this ascent, when in 1970 Peter Gough and John Glasgow made the climb. Among the famous names of those who conquered the mountain's various ridges is that of Sir Edmund Hillary to whom, with three others, the South Ridge fell in 1948.

## SOME GEOLOGY

Rocks to be seen in the Park include a greenish schist of chloritic variety, as well as the green, purple, and greenish-blue volcanic rocks that add variety to the otherwise uniform greywacke.

The region was under the sea about 150 million years ago, when rocks were laid down by the pressuring of clay, sand, silt and gravel to create today's greywacke and argillite. Fossils are conspicuously absent, suggesting that the area was for some reason inhospitable to marine life. A lengthy mountain-building period began about 100 million years ago, broken by a long period of erosion. Further mountain-building followed, after which glacial ice carved the landscape into its present form in four major advances, during the last of which the terminal moraine that dams the Pukaki Valley was deposited, so forming the lake. The glacial forms are seen in U-shaped valleys, the curves of cirque walls, and the sharpening of peaks, as well as in the constructed landforms of moraines and gravel plains.

The Tasman Glacier, 29 km long, is today the longest to be found in the world's temperate regions. (*See* △*Fox Glacier for general notes on glaciers.*)

## FLORA AND FAUNA

The feature of the park's flora is the mountain buttercup, the Mount Cook Lily (*Ranunculus lyallii*) of which the noted botanist, Dr Leonard Cockayne, wrote: "[Its flowers are] pure white, the petals at times so numerous that the flower looks like a semi-double, and thirty blossoms to a stalk, each nearly [8 cm] in diameter, are quite usual. It may easily be seen then, what a glorious spectacle is a hillside clothed as far as the eye can see with close colonies of this noble plant." The splendid buttercup, the snow gentian and the blossom of the mountain ribbonwood form a trio of white against a background of sombre green.

Best known of the birds is the *kea* (*Nestor notabilis*) an alpine parrot found only in the South Island; its unabashed curiosity ranges from behaviour that is entertainingly playful to acts of outright destruction. Generally olive-green in colour, with the undersides of its wings a bright vermilion and with a ferociously-curved beak, the *kea* (named because of its querulous call of *eea-aaa*) nests in rocky crevices chiefly above 600 m. Notoriety for attacks on sheep (a fairly rare occurrence) denies the *kea* outside the park the protection afforded most other native birds. Thousands have been destroyed for the sins of few.

Other native birds commonly seen in the park's forested areas are the *kereru* (native pigeon), the *ngiru-ngiru* (yellow-breasted tomtit), the tiny, seemingly-tailless *titipounamu* (rifleman) and the *riroriro* (grey warbler). The *ruru* (morepork), the native owl, is more often heard than seen.

Tahr and chamois (and to a lesser extent red deer) are found in the Park. Tahr were liberated here in 1904 after five specimens had been presented to the Government by the Duke of Bedford. They thrive in an environment similar to that of their native Himalaya. The chamois, first freed in the Hooker Valley in 1907, were obtained as the result of a great chamois drive in Austria, which took place at the personal request of the Emperor to return in kind gifts made to Austrian zoos. Both liberations are now regretted, as herd numbers have risen dramatically with consequential damage to vegetation, and soil erosion. With rabbits, hares and deer, tahr and chamois are regarded as noxious animals whose shooting is encouraged. (*Note: A permit is required to carry a rifle in any national park.*)

## SOME WALKS AND TRAMPS***

*Note: Boots and socks may be hired at The Hermitage. The tramper should make use of the pamphlets and up-to-date information available at the park headquarters and notify the ranger on duty of his intentions.*

**Bowen Track:** A 10-minute walk starts opposite the Youth Hostel and passes through dense subalpine scrub to end at a vantage point from which the view extends up the Hooker Valley to Mt Cook.

**Governors Bush:** A delightful walk leads through a precious remnant of beech forest and circles back to the highway. *Starts south of the Park headquarters. Allow 1¼ hrs.* The bush is so named as it was near here that an early governor, Sir George Bowen, camped on a visit to the mountains. He expressed the wish that nothing be allowed to destroy the beauty of the setting in which he had stayed. So enchanted was the governor that he despatched a case of champagne to his guide. *Brochure available from the park headquarters.*

**Kea Point:** A brochure identifies plants and items of natural history as the walk crosses a series of shingle fans before entering dense subalpine scrub. The easy walk ends at a point overlooking the Mueller Glacier. Views include the ice face of Mt Sefton and the three peaks of Cook. *Start in front of The Hermitage. Allow 3 hrs return. The walk can be shortened by driving beyond The Hermitage as far as Foliage Hill to join the track there.* A branch track leads to **Sealy Tarns,** long narrow lakelets on the steep Sealy Range at times warm enough to swim in (*5 hrs return*).

**Hooker Valley:** Perhaps the best of the walks branches off the Kea Point track to cross the Hooker Flats and to pass near the remains of the original Hermitage (1884–1913). The Hooker River is crossed twice to reach Sefton Stream from which, only a short walk away, is the terminal face of the Hooker Glacier. The track continues to Hooker Hut, the usual starting point for the crossing of the Copland Pass (*see below*). *Times (one way): Lower Swing Bridge, 1 hr; Upper Bridge, 1½ hrs; Sefton Stream, 2 hrs.*

**Red Tarn–Mt Sebastopol:** The track leaves the highway south of the park headquarters to zigzag steeply to three small tarns (unsuitable for swimming). There are some fine views of the Mount Cook Range. The more energetic may continue on to the summit of Mt Sebastopol (*1,468.2 m*). *4 hrs or 5½ hrs return.*

**Wakefield Track:** One can either start as for the Hooker Valley and bear right after crossing the first swing bridge or, to walk the track the other way, begin from the Ball Hut Road. The track is of interest as it was used as a walking track by the earliest mountaineers and sightseers. *Allow 2½ hrs.*

**Copland Pass** (*2,132.8 m*): The pass over the Main Divide to Fox Glacier is a true alpine crossing, subject to rapid changes in weather. As a short time is spent on ice, the traverse should not be attempted by a party lacking experience in alpine travel. The crossing is usually made from the Mount Cook side as it is a long and steady tramp down the western slopes to Welcome Flat Hut and the relaxing hot spring there. One night is usually spent at Hooker Hut before the pass is crossed, and a second at Douglas Rock Hut. A third hut is at Welcome Flat. Guides are available at the park headquarters and from Alpine Guides Ltd at The Hermitage who will give a party any necessary tuition and see them either safely over the pass to the top of the Zigzag or accompany them on down the other side.

## OTHER THINGS TO SEE AND DO

**Park headquarters:** Displayed are collections of mountaineering equipment, including that used by early and famous climbers in the region. Also shown are exhibits of flora and fauna. Specimen rocks from throughout the park illustrate its geology. Details of walks and climbs in the area are available, as well as local weather forecasts. *Open daily.*

**Glacier trip\*\*\*:** A 3-hour trip begins with a bus ride along the bumpy road to Ball Hut followed by a 1½-hour walk that includes a strenuous 100-m descent of the steep moraine wall to reach the white ice of the Tasman Glacier. Flatter and less jumbled than the ice of either the Fox or Franz Josef, the Tasman Glacier is less easy to get on to. *Trips run from The Hermitage. Fare includes bus, guide and hire of any necessary equipment.*

**Scenic flights\*\*\*** by minute skiplane are an ingredient essential to an appreciation of the Alps. Particularly recommended is the longer flight which takes in the West Coast glaciers of Fox and Franz Josef. When conditions allow, the highlight is a landing on the snow on the upper reaches of the glaciers. *Mount Cook Airlines, tel. 849.*

**Skiing the Tasman Glacier:** The advent of the skiplane has made it both possible and popular to be flown to the head of the Tasman Glacier, thence to ski a full 13 km down to Ball Hut. *Equipment for hire. Parties should be accompanied by a guide or a ski patroller (enquire at park headquarters). The ski descent is not generally possible from December to May.*

**Guided trips:** Park rangers are readily available to accompany individuals or parties on climbs and trans-alpine crossings as well as on short walks. *Enquire at the park headquarters.* Alpine Guides (Mount Cook) Ltd (*PO Box 20. Mount Cook; tel. 834*) provide a complete mountain guiding service, including trips over the Copland Pass and the Graham Saddle (*2,668.6 m*). Safe practice in mountain travel is taught to any of average fitness, and courses at a School of Mountaineering are run at set dates. Skiing instruction is given and groups are accompanied down the snow of the Tasman Glacier. (*Office in The Hermitage.*)

**Skiing:** The park saw the country's first skiing when in 1893 Marmaduke Dixon, Thomas Fyfe and Guy Mannering used blades from a reaper-and-binder as makeshift skis to cross the Grand Plateau. For over half a century skiers have come here to enjoy their sport but access has become progressively more difficult, so that although the region has one of the largest snowfields in the world's temperate regions, there is little skiing available other than alpine skiing. Those who enjoy ski touring can, in spring, travel over the snow from the Godley and the Rangitata. *Equipment for hire from Alpine Guides. There is some alpine skiing the year round.*

*63 km E of Westport; 130 km SW of Nelson.*

ENCIRCLED BY MOUNTAINS and at the junction of the Buller and Matakitaki Rivers, the town of Murchison stands on a small inland plain at odds with the rugged ranges that enclose it. Born of gold fever, cleared of bush and once devastated by earthquake, Murchison today services both surrounding farmland and the road traffic of a junction town. It has seen drilling rigs come and go, and unhurriedly awaits the boom residents feel sure oil is waiting to bestow.

The town takes its name from a nearby mountain (*1,469.8 m*) which Julius von Haast named in honour of Sir Roderick Murchison, a distinguished Scottish geologist. Originally the town was named Hampden — Liberal opinion of the 1860s had a great admiration for the Roundheads of the English Civil War — and most of the street names, Fairfax, Chalgrave, Hotham, Cromwell and Waller are named for generals or battles of that war. As there was a Hampden in North Otago, the old name (perpetuated by a local hotel) was changed to save confusion over mails.

> National Park Information Offices advise on walks, tramps, flora, fauna and accommodation. Displays illustrate the significance of each area.

## SOME HISTORY

**Fairweather by Moonlight:** Murchison began as a goldmining settlement. One of the most colourful characters was the Scot, "Captain" George Fairweather Moonlight (1832–84). Despite the legends which grew up in his lifetime, the name was real, as was his habit of travelling alone and often at night. Originally a seafarer, he left his ship to join the Californian, and later the Victorian gold rushes. In Otago he made important gold discoveries, he explored much of the Buller back country, and after prospecting successfully in the Grey Valley he settled as a store and hotel keeper first at Maruia and later at Murchison. His personality and strength made him the leader of the small community, and for some years he maintained law and order in an unconventional but effective way. Dressed in crimson shirt, knee-breeches, Wellington boots and maroon sash, he was an impressive and respected figure. But misfortune overtook him. He lost his wife, his business failed, he went back to his gold prospecting. Finally he died alone in the bush, not far from Glenhope. In the Nelson cemetery his grave and that of his wife are marked by a monument raised by public subscription. A cairn at Glenhope records the contributions of Moonlight and others to the settlement of the Hope Valley (*by Highway 6 at 6.8 km N of Kawatiri Junction*).

**"The Lost Tribe":** Last century the gold diggers working in the Glenroy and Upper Matakitaki area were often known as the "Lost Tribe", of which many tales are told — most without foundation. It seems that the name originated in the 1870s when some miners from the isolated area were registering claims at the Lyell and were asked for their address. More fanciful stories tell of a lost tribe of Maoris, or of descendants of original settlers whom no one had seen for years.

Tom May was the proprietor of the original Mammoth Hotel, which was sited a little nearer the Matakitaki River than are the present ruins at Horseshoe Terrace. He had an entirely male staff who were known by such nicknames as Brandy Mac and the Scorpion. When the ale was flowing freely, May would hold "court" and as "king" would "knight" his followers. When a number of Chinese were working in the district he learnt enough of their language to be able to help them in official business and added the title of "Emperor of the Chinese" to that of "King of the Lost Tribe". Like many other goldfield suppliers, May gave too much credit. When he met his death by drowning in 1897 he was a comparatively poor man.

**The Murchison Earthquake:** On 17 June 1929 the whole country was rocked by earthquake shocks with an epicentre not far to the west of Murchison. In force it was probably the worst New Zealand has experienced since European settlement began. The town and its surrounding countryside, a typical pastoral region, were transformed in a fortnight of tremors into a shambles of landslides, wrecked buildings, broken bridges and ruined roads. Westport and Greymouth were badly shaken, and with Nelson also suffered heavy structural losses. Subsidences and upthrusts considerably altered the topography of the area. Murchison was temporarily evacuated, but most of the residents soon returned to make good the damage and continue with their farming.

Some two years later came the Hawke's Bay earthquake, the country's greatest natural disaster, which demonstrated a measure of what would have occurred in the Murchison Earthquake had it centred on a more populous region. As it was, seventeen lives were lost.

Forty years of forest regeneration have healed the numerous scars on the mountainsides, and only the experienced eye can detect the changes so recently wrought in the landscape. For the traveller one obvious sign is the Maruia Falls (*some 21.7 km S on Highway 65*), created by a change of course of the Maruia River caused by the earthquake so that it now flows over an old upthrust.

# MURCHISON AND DISTRICT

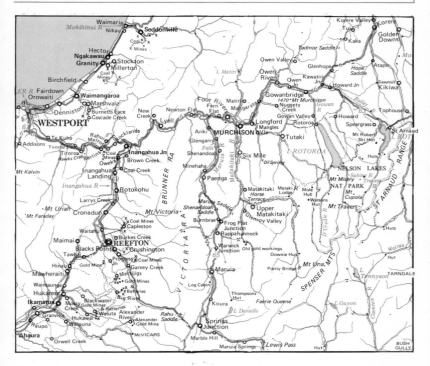

## 24

**Oil searches:** Petroleum gas bubbles from several streams near Murchison, and a natural gas vent in the Blackwater Valley has been used for cooking by trampers. The gas and traces of oil in the area have encouraged oil exploration. Over the years two wells have been sunk, but to date success has been elusive.

## THINGS TO SEE AND DO

**Murchison Museum:** A growing collection concentrates on the town's early history, the area's goldrushes, and the devastation of the 1929 earthquake. *Fairfax St, beside Murchison Motor Engineers Ltd. Open Mon. to Fri. (summer) and Mon., Wed., Fri. (winter) from 2–4 pm. Other times by arrangement.*

**Hampden Hotel:** The hotel that perpetuates the town's first name holds a rare bottle of "Hokonui" (*see index*). The Commercial, across the road, is the latter-day successor to the original "Moonlight's". *Waller St.*

**Some picnic places:** Riverside Domain, a pleasant spot by the Buller River, is a picnic place favoured by both through travellers and local residents (*signposted on the town's northern exit*). There are numerous other picnic spots along various river valleys — particularly up the Owen Valley and up the Mangles Valley, where there is swimming by the Mangles bridge and fishing along its length. A good walking track leads to Lake Matiri up the Matiri Valley (*ask permission locally*).

## TOURING NOTES

**Maruia Saddle Route:** An alternative route to Frog Flat and so to Springs Junction (one that can be combined with Highway 65 to make an 80-km round trip) is to take the Maruia Saddle route up the Matakitaki Valley (*signposted at the southern end of the town*). The road winds up the narrow valley before dropping steeply to link back with Highway 65 at Frog Flat Junction. The scenery is spectacular, and there are traces of gold workings, particularly round Horse Terrace (*at 27 km*), where prospected the "Lost Tribe". The derelict Mammoth Hotel may be seen by the roadside at 28.5 km, the successor to the house kept by Tom May.

In terms of distance the alternative route is 8 km shorter, but it is some 30 mins longer in driving time. *Recommended only in fine weather.*

Placenames on Highway 65 such as Rappahannock and Shenandoah derive from George Moonlight.

**Highway 6 to △Westport via △Inangahua:** *Described under △Buller River.*

**Lake Rotoroa via Tutaki and Braeburn Track:** A delightful bush drive to Lake Rotoroa is by way of Tutaki. Bear left where the road branches above Tutaki School and turn right where signposted to follow part of an old gold trail. There are several watercourse. *Recommended for fine weather only and not for small cars or caravans.*

**NASEBY\*\*\*     Central Otago.   Maps 25 & 28.   Pop. 124.**

*13 km NNE of Ranfurly; 93 km NE of Alexandra.*

ENDOWED WITH FINE TREES in a district generally lacking in shade, Naseby well merits its reputation for being the most picturesque of all the goldfield settlements. Quiet and unhurried, its simple Victorian atmosphere is seemingly unruffled by the demands of another age. Naseby is in summertime thronged with campers and crib owners, but even their presence is absorbed by the town's considerable charm. In winter, day visitors come to the country's centre of curling, to indulge in that Scottish pastime and to ice-skate.

The town, now a timber centre based on nearby State plantations, is probably named after an English town. In turn it was earlier known as Parkers Diggings Mount Ida, and Vincent (after Vincent Pyke).

## SOME HISTORY

**A friend for life:** Miners flocked into the area in 1863 to congregate by the Hogburn after the Parker brothers, sons of the Victorian Protector of Aborigines, had found gold in a blind gully about 1 km from the present town site. Though the field was to return no fabulous finds (it was known as a poor man's field), there were good wages for those willing to work. John Bremner, a storekeeper, saw the field on his arrival in the bitter winter of 1863 and recorded snow-covered tents and makeshift bivouacs where conditions were so pitiable that his gesture in giving an empty case to a miner desperately trying to kindle a fire made him "a friend for life".

Within a week of the discovery by the Parkers' group there were 500 men in the area, within a month 2,000. Later this figure reached 5,000, but the opening of neighbouring fields, among them Hamiltons, saw numbers dwindle. Water was scarce on the field, and for the first few months of the rush the men worked round the clock to provide it, using hurricane lamps at night until water was led in from high in the ranges by races with such exotic names as Enterprise, Hit-or-Miss, and Undaunted. Later, to break a monopoly situation, the Government constructed a race some 120 km long, from the head of the Manuherikia River. (This, and a complementary sludge channel, have since proved of benefit for irrigation purposes.) Hotels opened, such as the Ancient Briton and the Old Victorian, and a large clothing store modestly described itself as The Wonder of the World.

When the rush to the West Coast goldfields got under way the number on the field plummeted to a few hundred, and though gold production persisted into the 1930s, it has long ceased.

## A CURLING CENTRE

The town is among the main centres of skating and curling. Curling, basically a game of bowls on ice, is played with curling stones, each with a gooseneck handle, which are bowled along the ice towards a tee (a fixed object). The game gets its name from the right or left spin imparted to the stone by the player just as he releases it, so causing the stone to prescribe an arc in the appropriate direction. Each team comprises four players, led by the "skip" who dictates and designates with his straw broom where he wants each shot laid. Supporting players use their brooms to sweep frost or moisture from in front of a moving stone to help it carry further. The ice is kept scrupulously clean and before a game is started the surface is "pebbled" by sprinkling it with warm water. The "pebbles" freeze in a few minutes to form tiny ice knobs on which the stones ride and which make it possible to control them and help give the necessary "curl".

The game is probably Scottish in origin. The oldest club in existence, dating from 1795, is the Royal Caledonian Curling Club, the Mother Club of clubs in Scotland, Canada, the United States and Sweden as well as in New Zealand. Though played on ice, the players do not wear skates. It is said that the warmth of a "nip" while wintry winds blow produces the comradeship in the game that so endears it to its devotees. In other parts of the world, curling is usually played on indoor rinks.

## THINGS TO SEE AND DO

**Maniototo Early Settlers' Museum\*:** The building itself is now a museum piece, built in 1878 for the Maniototo County Council. Held here are early photographs of curling contests, old curling trophies, a complete file of the *Mount Ida Chronicle* (1868–1926), goldworking implements and mineral samples from the Naseby School of Mines. Outside is an early kerosene lampstand, a reminder that electric street lighting came as recently as 1948, and opposite is an open-air display of transport equipment, including the venerable Ranfurly horsedrawn hearse and an old chaff-cutter. *Leven St. Open 2–4 pm daily and extended hours during holidays. Closed June-July.*

**Watchmaker's Shop:** In 1868 Robert Strong opened a watchmaker's business. To-day his shop may be seen as it was then complete with show cases, workshop and jeweller's shop. *Leven St.*

**Ancient Briton** (1863)\*: Like several other buildings in the street, the older portion of the hotel is built of sundried mud bricks. It was originally set back from the road.

# NASEBY AND DISTRICT

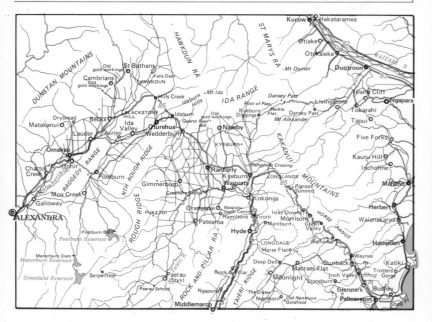

## 25

Its signboard, depicting a caveman moving a reluctant mate back to his lair, is in keeping with other aspects of the town's main street, such as the nearby watchmaker's shop (started in 1865 and closed only in recent times on the death of its founder's elderly son). No longer is there a billiards room in the hotel to serve as a makeshift surgery, and no longer is a doctor, resident at the miner's insistence and expense, there to stitch up gashes and to banish the "blue devils" that hounded those who overindulged in so-called whisky. Nor is today's visitor likely to encounter the custom that all strangers "shout" the bar. He who overlooked this duty in earlier days usually found his mount gone, but a volunteer standing by to retrieve it — albeit for a price more than sufficient to cover the overlooked round of drinks. Within are photographs and mementoes from curling contests. *Leven St.*

**Hogburn sludge channel\*\*\*:** The Hogburn sludge channel (the stream was so designated to allow miners to flush their washings into it) extends some miles northwest from the town. The fluted faces of its cliffs, sculpted by jets from the miners' sluicing monitors, create subtle light effects, particularly on sunny days. *At the top of Leven St. Turn right by the Town Hall. One can walk or drive for over 1 km and picnic in the shade of self-sown trees.*

**Athenaeum** (1865)**\*\*:** The tiny corrugated-iron building began its long life as a Union church — a building used by various denominations in an ecumenical spirit well in advance of the age. It served as church, Sunday school and dayschool until in 1872 it became an Athenaeum and as such it continues to do duty, if under the less grandiose title of Reading Room and Library. *On main approach to township.*

**St George's Anglican Church** (1875): The church has a stark simplicity and boasts that its arches are load-bearing, not, as in many, purely decorative. Its carved choir stalls and lectern were executed by its Naseby builder, W. Jacobs. The church is built of sun-dried brick as no local stone was available. Opposite the church is mounted an old sluice monitor. *Derwent St.*

**Welcome Inn walking track\*\*:** The track leads from the foot of Leven Street to the summit of the hill on which the mud-brick Welcome Inn still stands, now a home. A magnificent view extends over the sequestered village, with the tortured cliffs along the well-sluiced Hogburn stretching away to the right. *Allow 20 mins.*

**Swimming dam:** The swimming dam mirrors the tall larches that rim its banks. *Signposted. 800 m.*

**Trail rides:** Horse and donkey rides are run over the Christmas period and range from 1-hour rides for novices to campouts over the Mt Ida Range for the more experienced. *Naseby Trail Rides (W. McMillan), Box 36, Naseby, tel. 250G Ranfurly.*

Each traveller should know what he has to see, and what properly belongs to him, on a journey. — Goethe (*Conversations with Goethe*).

## ENVIRONS

**Dansey Pass Hotel\*\*\*:** The drive out towards △Dansey Pass leads through the inhospitable Kyeburn Diggings. By the Kyeburn River, cliffs have been slashed back to create fluted slopes, and high-heaped tailings litter the riverbanks. The Kyeburn Diggings cemetery is passed and at 39 km the Dansey Pass Hotel is reached, the kink in the building matching the crook in the road. Opposite, a water-race, built by Chinese, curls like a sheeptrack round the hillside.

The present Dansey Pass Hotel building, since added to, was built in the 1880s from schist by a stonemason who took payment out in beer, a pint for each stone laid. Local tradition relates that when he completed his task he went on a monumental binge and rolled homeward only to fall into an empty grave in the cemetery. Waking in the morning, benumbed and befuddled, he looked at the sky framed by the sides of the grave to declare: "This must be the Day of Judgment — and I'm the only one called!"

It was in the original hotel building here that the Parker brothers let slip their find at the Hogburn and with the inevitable rush to Naseby came discoveries on the Kyeburn. The hotel today offers accommodation in the remotest of areas and refreshment particularly welcome to those who have made the narrow and tortuous traverse of Dansey Pass itself.

**Kyeburn station:** The Kyeburn runs were taken up in 1858 by a partnership that, with its properties on the other side of the Kakanuis, controlled about 101,250 ha. The pair, Alexander McMaster and John Borton, did not visit the runs but installed a manager. As wheeled vehicles could not cope with Dansey Pass, the route from Duntroon lay by way of Shag Valley, a trip that took a week. Mackay John Scobie McKenzie (1845-1901), whose descendants still control the run, acquired the property in 1875, the year he won the hand of Adela Bell, daughter of F. Dillon Bell of Shag Valley. He had come to New Zealand five years earlier to manage a property for the New Zealand & Australian Land Company, and successfully induced two investors to put up the money that put him on the Kyeburn. Before long he had prospered sufficiently to buy his partners out.

A scholarly man, Scobie McKenzie dabbled in journalism before plunging into politics. With some reluctance he agreed to oppose the sitting member for Mt Ida and did so on the basis that his opponent had left the district and so could not really be interested in its future. Believing McKenzie had been returned, a jubilant crowd carried him in triumph through the streets of Naseby — but special votes arrived during the night which reversed the result. Three years later he succeeded, and proved a brilliant politician; a believer in temperance, he opposed prohibition; an opponent of female suffrage, he was yet at the top of the poll at the next election after it was carried; elected to support the Stout-Vogel coalition, he became one of its strongest critics.

The present Kyeburn station comprises 12,150 ha, some 10,125 ha of which are on the Hawkdun and Kakanui Ranges. The station is perhaps the last to have retained its mules. The temperamental creatures have been worked on the run since 1896.

The shearing shed (1870) still has its turret, built to accommodate a back-breaking screw-press. Shearers' assistants would be in the turret to catch fleeces thrown up to them, to fill the press and finally to trudge in an endless ox-like circle to wind the press down. There was no spring release, so once this had been accomplished and the bale sewn they would have to repeat the monotonous manoeuvre, albeit in the opposite direction.

The town of Naseby is in the middle of the old Kyeburn runs, whose holders during the goldrushes were remarkably patient with the diggers, raising no objection to them grazing their cows on run pastures. *13 km SE.*

---

The symbol △ indicates a place with its own entry in the Alphabetical Section of this Guide.

---

**NELSON\*\*\*      Nelson.   Maps 26 & 27.   Pop. 33,000.**

*135 km W of Picton; 117 km WNW of Blenheim; 130 km NE of Murchison; 425 km N of Christchurch. Public Relations Office, Trafalgar St; tel. 83-470 (closed public holidays).*

NELSON, A CITY of gardens and gorgeous sunsets, looks out over Nelson Haven and across the broad curve of Tasman Bay to the tall Tasman Mountains. The city abounds with allusions to the sea. Her streets and parks echo the exploits of the admiral after whom she was named, as well as those of ships that brought the pioneer settlers — Arrow, Whitby, Fifeshire, Brougham, Will Watch, Mary Ann. By a documentary quirk the letters-patent by which Queen Victoria created the Diocese of Nelson also proclaimed that "the said Town of Nelson shall be a City." So it was that in 1858 Nelson became the first in the country to enjoy city status, albeit with a population of less than 2,700. The names of her first bishops, too, are borne by streets — Hobhouse, Suter, Mules and Sadlier.

# NELSON AND ENVIRONS

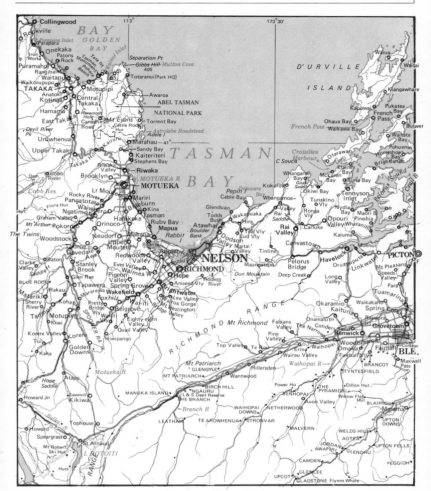

## 26

Today, forestry, fruit and fishing preoccupy the city's port; to the west lie the country's principal apple orchards, followed by tracts of tobacco plants and wire-festooned fields of hops. The city's considerable natural charm is further enhanced by many imposing old timber buildings. To the most equable climate of any New Zealand centre are added golden beaches and two national parks of widely differing character.

**Handicrafts:** Nelson is known for its vigorous interest in music and the arts, attracting a creative community which includes spinners, weavers, and silversmiths, and potters who relish the district's fine and varied clays. *The Public Relations Office holds details of local cottage industries where visitors are welcome.*

## SOME HISTORY

**Conquerors from the north:** The early occupation of the Nelson-Golden Bay area is lost in the mists of antiquity as tribe after tribe migrated from the North Island, each in turn conquering the one that had preceded it and obliterating the history and traditions of the defeated. Perhaps four centuries ago Waitaha living here sent a gift of food across Raukawa (Cook Strait) to Ngatimamoe living near Wellington. The recipients, far from being grateful, repaid this generosity by crossing the strait and seizing the land from which the food had been sent. The tribe of Ngati Tumatakokiri also came south about this time, the two tribes sharing between them land from the West Coast to Canterbury. It was Ngati Tumatakokiri who gave Abel Tasman his hostile reception in 1642.

**Abel Tasman names Murderers' Bay:** Bloodshed marked the discovery of New Zealand by Europeans, just as it was to mar their first landing over a century later. On 13 December 1642 the Dutch explorer Abel Tasman and his vessels *Heemskerck* and *Zeehaen* arrived off the west coast of the South Island. The little ships followed the coast of "a large land uplifted high" without detecting any sign of habitation until they saw smoke rising near Cape Farewell. Anchoring in Golden Bay near the Tata

Islands, just offshore from Abel Tasman National Park, the vessels were inspected by two canoes. The Maoris called out in "a rough loud voice" and blew on an instrument that sounded like a Moorish trumpet. An officer on the *Zeehaen* replied on his own trumpet, and a strange duet that was to be the only communication between the two groups continued until, with nightfall, the canoes departed.

Early on the morning of 19 December the *Zeehaen*'s cockboat rowed across to the *Heemskerck* so that the officers could confer. It was returning to the *Zeehaen* with a crew of seven men when two canoes attacked it. Four were killed, but three of the crew swam to safety and, in the face of gunfire, the attackers withdrew to the shore unscathed. Tasman elected to leave "as no friendship could be made with these people, nor water nor refreshments could be obtained". The bay, because of the "detestable deed", he named Moordenaers, or Murderers', Bay. Just as they were leaving, eleven crowded canoes put out from the shore, but were discouraged by a volley from the ships.

Tasman was intrigued by the possibility of there being a passage separating the landmasses (he noted the tide running from the south-east), but his officers, weary of the winds of the region, discounted the possibility. It was left to Cook to discover and give his name to the strait that for ever dispelled the possibility that Tasman had found the geographers' *Terra Australis Incognita*, the Unknown Southern Continent. The Dutchman sailed north on 6 January 1643 leaving via Cape Maria van Diemen. Tasman, whose lack of enterprise was to earn him an official rebuke, had not even landed on the country he had found, and his discovery aroused little interest in Europe's trading centres, for it could provide no tropical spices and the fierce inhabitants were a bar to any search for precious metals. (*A memorial to Tasman is by the road to Totaranui at 7.4 km from Takaka.*)

A few years after Tasman left, the area erupted in violence as once more a northern tribe, this time Ngaitahu, were driven south from their tribal lands. Ngaitahu held the Nelson-Golden Bay region for about a century before they in turn gave way to Ngati Toa. Coming from the Waikato, the Ngati Toa crossed the strait under Te Raupahara after the local tribes of Ngati Apa, Ngati Kuia and Rangitane had been rash enough to join an unsuccessful attack on Te Rauparaha's newly-acquired Kapiti Island stronghold in 1824. In the invasion, many tribes from Taranaki and Wellington joined with Ngati Toa so that from 1828 fleets of canoes ferried the northerners across the strait to fight a succession of battles. *Pa* were sacked (including one at Nelson itself) and their defenders ceremoniously dispatched to the ovens. By the end of 1830 the conquest of the northern half of the South Island was complete. The Nelson Province tribes had been annihilated (those who fled into the hills from Motueka and Riwaka were hunted relentlessly) and, though repeopled by the invading tribes and their allies, the Maori population was never again to reach the same density.

The whalers in the Marlborough Sounds lived through these turbulent times (John Guard's base was ransacked in 1834) and by the time Colonel William Wakefield arrived in 1839 to buy land for the New Zealand Company, he found Nelson and the Sounds with a small Maori population who in the main had been in possession for only about ten years.

**A New Zealand Company settlement:** In 1839, Col. William Wakefield as agent for the New Zealand Company, bought among others, a large block of land at the north of the South Island. He also bought at Hokianga what he thought was Blenkinsopp's deed to the Wairau (*see △ Blenheim*).

The Company was quick to establish settlements at Wellington, Wanganui and New Plymouth. A group of intending colonists then proposed that a further settlement be established — "not the rival but a helpmate", — and on a larger scale than the others. They urged the Company to sell in England 201,000 acres of land divided into 1,000 allotments, each costing £300 and each comprising a town acre, a suburban block and 150 acres of rural land. The Company embraced the scheme and within two months the ships of the preliminary expedition under William's brother, Captain Arthur Wakefield, had set sail. The *Whitby* and the *Will Watch* had seventy-seven migrants on board and the fast brig *Arrow* was soon to follow.

Despite the Company's confidence — days after the sailings a dividend of 10 per cent was declared — there were early signs that the settlement was doomed to poverty. Most of those with capital who wished to emigrate had already done so; land was slow to sell and much that did sell was taken up by speculators. Half of the allotments remained unsold, and three-quarters of the buyers (among them the philosopher and economist John Stuart Mill) had no intention of leaving England.

In September, first the *Lloyds*, and then the trio of the *Fifeshire*, *Mary Ann* and *Lord Auckland* left England, the *Lloyds* carrying the wives and children of the men of the preliminary expedition. The trio was favoured with the flag-waving pomp and ceremony of a royal sendoff and, as became a Nelsonian settlement, was reminded that "Christian England expects that every one of you will do his duty to her God as well as to her."

A key to area maps appears on page 2.

**A town without a home:** Even at that advanced stage, no one knew where Nelson was to be. The Company, originally limited by the British Government to the selection of a site within the bounds of the land it had purchased from the Maoris, argued for a free choice. Lord John Russell as Colonial Secretary would do no more than give Governor Hobson a discretion.

The Company wanted Port Cooper (Lyttelton), but Hobson told William Wakefield it could go outside the purchase limits only if Nelson were sited near Auckland. This would have seen the port and then-Government centre of Auckland quickly drain the new settlement of both population and trade, but "so transparent a device for peopling his own pet metropolis" was seen through by Col. Wakefield. He rejected the bizarre suggestion that Nelson township be on the site of present-day Warkworth, with its rural blocks over 160 km away, at Thames. Warned that he would be "perfectly irresponsible for the consequences", Col. Wakefield had no option but to choose within the limits of the blocks of land he had purchased. He opted for Tasman Bay.

**The finding of Nelson Haven:** The reluctant Col. Wakefield led the *Will Watch* and the *Whitby* to Kapiti Island, there to receive an assurance from Te Rauparaha that he was in favour of a settlement on Tasman Bay. The vessels then crossed the strait and anchored in the Astrolabe Roadstead.

Shore parties explored the coast and the interior, returning with conflicting reports, and the group was on the point of siting the settlement at Kaiteriteri when one of the local Maoris (who were obviously being secretive about the matter) let fall a hint that there was a small harbour to the south. An expedition to find it rowed the length of the Boulder Bank, in ignorance of the haven behind it. On the way back they decided to land; Captain Moore jumped from the boat, climbed on to the Bank and saw to his surprise "a sheet of water considerable in extent". On 1 November the *Arrow* sailed into the Haven, the entry of the first vesesl being celebrated by three cheers and the firing of a gun.

There was insufficient land to meet the Company's ambitious plan (drawn up half a world away and without any idea of local conditions) but because of the attitude of Hobson there was no real choice. With the finding of the Haven came the founding of Nelson. Colonel Wakefield, filled with misgivings about the selection, felt it prudent to send someone back to England to reassure the Company's directors. The glowing reports that Charles Heaphy published on his arrival there proved that no better man could have been chosen for the task.

An immediate problem was that none of the Tasman and Golden Bay chiefs had been party to the land deal with Te Rauparaha, and they were highly incensed at any suggestion that the Kapiti-based chief could alienate their land. To make *utu* (compensation), Wakefield gave each chief presents of blankets, guns, tobacco, pipes and gunpowder, and obtained their grudging recognition of the sale.

On 13 December the Company's flag was hoisted on Britannia Heights, and a month later it was joined by a nine-pound cannon, placed there as a signal gun (*the same, or a similar one, may be seen on Britannia Heights today*).

First of the migrant ships to arrive was the *Fifeshire*, on 1 February 1842 (the anniversary day of Nelson ever since). She broke her back on Arrow Rock as she sailed out on the ebb tide not four weeks later. A fortnight after the arrival of the *Fifeshire* came the long-awaited *Lloyds*, with the wives and children of the hard-working advance party. As she anchored a sorry tale began to unfold. Summarised Wakefield: "We have got the *Lloyds* at last but in a sad mess, she has lost 65 children and has been a floating bawdy house throughout the voyage, the master at the head of it." Wakefield refused to pay either the captain or the doctor, Dr Bush, declaring the latter to be a "prevaricating vaurien". The experiment with a shipload of women was never repeated.

A steady trickle of ships followed, so that by May 1842 the population of Nelson stood at about 2,000. There were, however, too few gentlemen and with too little money. In theory part of the payment for a land purchase covered the fares for eight adult migrants. As well as going out to the colony himself, the land buyer was expected to take with him sufficient capital to employ those migrants, either directly or indirectly. But many of the land buyers did not go at all, and some of those who did arrived with less than £100 capital yet were "unacquainted with agricultural pursuits and unfitted by previous habits to put their hand to the plough or spade".

The New Zealand Company had attracted working men by the prospect of guaranteed employment. By the end of 1842, a year that had begun with a spirit of optimism but had been overtaken by economic depression, capital had been depleted and many small men driven into bankruptcy. Even their leader, Captain Arthur Wakefield, saw little prospect in subsistence farming and urged his brother Felix, who was not a wealthy man, to migrate to Tasmania rather than to Nelson.

The settlement was also plagued by a shortage of easily usable land. When news came of the grassy plains of the Wairau (land the Company considered it had bought twice — once from Te Rauparaha and again from Blenkinsopp's widow) the land-hungry settlers pressed on with the surveys that provoked the deaths of their leader and some twenty-one fellow-settlers in the Wairau Affray (*see △ Blenheim*).

The suspension of the New Zealand Company's business in 1844 hit Nelson extremely hard. Three hundred engaged on public works were laid off and, though the handful of modest capitalists did what they could to create employment, there were few jobs and little cash. Trade by barter became the rule and many families survived on a diet of potato eked out with wild pig and birds. "The people . . . had neither money nor food. Money, however, was no good . . . as there was nothing to buy . . . Some gathered sow thistles and boiled them; others dug up the potatoes they had planted, and peeled them to eat, and planted the skins . . . We grew up like wild people."

Nor was the Government prepared to help except by offering work at Wellington — to men who had not got the fare to get there. Only squatting on unoccupied land saved many families from starvation.

*On the city shore, along Haven Rd (about 100 m beyond Vickerman St) a marker acknowledges the place where Captain Moore and his party landed after discovering Nelson Haven. A low stone on Rocks Rd (opp. foot of Richardson St) marks the point where Arthur Wakefield landed on 1 November 1841.*

**The German settlements:** The New Zealand Company moved early to tap the stream of 20,000 or more Germans who were emigrating each year, principally to the United States. Agents were appointed at Hamburg and elsewhere, the result being sailings on the *St Pauli* and the *Skiold*. Both arrived at Nelson, though the *Skiold* was intended for the Chatham Islands until, to forestall the plan, the British Government annexed the islands, proclaiming them a part of New Zealand and asserting that Germans settling there would be treated as aliens. The British Government allowed the migrants to settle in New Zealand only on the undertaking that they would become British subjects.

Several winedressers were in the party, planning to establish vineyards at Nelson. The grapevines of their leader, John Beit (the only capitalist among them) did not survive the voyage out on the *St Pauli*. His fellow migrants struck back at the "fat arrogant man" in the only way open to them. When at last his petty despotism exceeded all bounds, they threw salt water over his plants and so killed them.

No sooner had the Germans on the *St Pauli* landed in 1843 than the Wairau Affray threw the settlement into disorder. Colonel Wakefield, to free the Germans from the tyrannical Beit (nicknamed "the German snake" and whose son was called Mangel-wurzel as he was "an inferior kind of beet") offered them three months' rations and land on deferred terms at Moutere. This was near the Lutheran mission whose members had also come out on the *St Pauli*.

The mission failed. There were few Maoris at Nelson, none at all near its allotment, and throughout the country the Maoris were in the main already under some form of spiritual guidance. The Rev. J. F. H. Wohlers was disheartened on learning that they were expected to establish a farm as well as to preach to the heathen: "I knew the fatigue of much manual labour would exhaust energies required for learning and teaching, as well as the zeal for missionary work proper." Anxious to avoid trespassing on the spiritual domain of other denominations, Wohlers eventually found a fertile field on the remote island of △Ruapuke, near Foveaux Strait.

The Germans called their valley Schachtstal (today Upper Moutere), after Captain Schacht, commander of the *St Pauli*, and their settlement, St Paulidorf after his ship. Winter floods forced the Germans out of Upper Moutere, some moving to Waimea East and others joining the *Skiold* party, later arrivals who had settled at Ranzau (the Hope of today).

The *Skiold* settlers arrived in 1844, having set sail after the New Zealand Company had suspended operations and in the directors' (but not the migrants') sure knowledge that certain hardship awaited them. Each migrant was formally contracted to Count Ranzau in a document whose High German and legalese must have made comprehension impossible and which committed the Germans not only to work for the absentee count but to repay him the cost of their fares. They landed at Nelson the day after all labourers on public works had been summarily dismissed.

As Nelson emerged from the recession that followed, a number of the German settlers moved back to Upper Moutere. There, church services were conducted in German until 1907, the year Pastor Thiel, who had felt unable to preach effectively in English, left the parish. A stable and conscientious group of settlers, the Germans assimilated rapidly, without conflict yet without losing complete touch with their German culture. Their loyalty was unquestioned in two World Wars, and Wohlers even asked if "the German admixture may have been conducive to the political quiet of the place?" *St Paul's Lutheran Church (1905) at Upper Moutere and that at Hope both have headstones inscribed in German.*

**The Maungatapu murders:** Perhaps the most grisly killings in New Zealand's history, and certainly the most notorious, took place in 1866 on Maungatapu Mountain. There, using Murderers' Rock as a place for ambush, the Sullivan gang waylaid a party of four as they journeyed along the bridle path between Pelorus and Nelson with gold dust worth £300. So completely did the four travellers disappear that murder was immediately suspected, and a quartet of strangers in the area was detained on suspicion. Correctly so, for they were Philip Levy, Richard Burgess, Thomas Kelly and Joseph Sullivan, Londoners with unsavoury criminal reputations in England and Australia and on the Central Otago goldfields. Nothing could be done until Sullivan (in exchange for £200 and a free pardon) showed the police where the bodies had been hidden. The trial of the remaining three took a dramatic turn when

Kelly, conducting his own defence and savagely crossexamining Sullivan, asked him why he had killed a fifth man, one James Battle. The three were convicted and executed; shortly thereafter Sullivan was himself convicted of the murder of Battle but was saved from the gallows by his earlier co-operation. The gang, in a trail of wanton slayings, had previously also murdered George Dobson (*see index*) near Greymouth. *Murderers' Rock may be seen by those who walk the Maungatapu Track. The death masks of the executed convicts and other items connected with the tragedies are held by the provincial museum.*

**The cradle of rugby:** It was at Nelson in 1868 that the Nelson Football Club was formed to indulge in a hybrid pastime described as a mixture of Association football (soccer) and Australian Rules. Inevitably it was also played at Nelson College, where a picked eighteen took on the rest of the school! The two groups switched to rugby union in 1870 when Charles Monro, son of the Speaker of the House of Representatives, returned from attending school in Britain. Under his tuition the Nelson club became the country's first rugby football club, and on 14 May 1870 the first match of what was to become the country's national sport was played at the Botanical Reserve at Nelson, when the club defeated Nelson College by two goals to nil. Other games followed, culminating in an historic encounter with a side of Wellingtonians at Lower Hutt. A newspaper reporting the team's return to Nelson commented that if their talents on the playing field were on a par with their intemperance off it, "it should be worth a trifle to see them play".

Tries were then incidental, the prime object of the game being to place-kick, drop-kick or "speculate" goals direct from the field. Rules were more or less made up as the game progressed, being enforced by the captains as there were no referees. Such was the growth of rugby that the old political provincial units have split and split again, so that there are today no fewer than twenty-six "provincial unions" in the country. Their symbol of supremacy, the Ranfurly Shield, is challenged for and contested with a parochial fervour unmatched by even international fixtures. (An older club than Nelson is the Christchurch Football Club, but this did not adopt the game of rugby until five years after the Nelson Club had done so.)

**The Dun Mountain Railway:** Just as Nelson and Christchurch have disputed the claim to having the oldest rugby club, so too have they joined issue over the first railway. Nelson's claim rests on a horsedrawn tramway built to ferry to the port copper mined from deposits high on the Dun Mountain. Some 21.5 km in length, the Dun Mountain Railway opened on 3 February 1862, fourteen months before the railway was ready at Ferrymead, near Christchurch. But at Ferrymead steam locomotives were used, for though the Dun Mountain Railway was by Act of Parliament permitted to employ "locomotive engines or other motive power", it was prohibited from doing so within the boundaries of Nelson City — on the only reasonably level section of the line. Long after the remainder of the Dun Mountain line had been dismantled, the 2-km section through the city to the port continued to operate, carrying passengers at a "safe slow pace" until, with the rails in a worn condition, the line closed in 1901. Some of the rails were used to reinforce the dam that retains the city's water-supply, leading to the suggestion that the Dun Mountain Railway continues to serve Nelson. (*The occasional trace of the railway may be seen by those who walk the Dun Mountain; a commemorative plaque is in Upper Brook St*).

Paradoxically, though Nelson lays claim to having the first railway, today it has none at all. There was for some years a line from Nelson to Glenhope, but it was isolated from the rest of the South Island's railway system and had to be closed for lack of freight. To meet agitation for a line, in 1957 the National Government constituted a "notional" railway, subsidising the road transport of goods between Nelson and Blenheim down to what it would have cost had a railway actually existed. That same year Labour took the crucial Nelson seat with its promise of a real railway, but the Labour Government did not survive in office long enough to make good the promise, beyond in 1960 ceremoniously tipping the first truckload of spoil into the mudflats at the start of the proposed line.

A hindrance to Nelson's plea for a railway has been the outstanding success of Transport (Nelson) Ltd, one of the country's largest and most dynamic road transport operators. Its fleet of "Newmans" buses perpetuate a coach run started in 1879 by the brothers Tom and Harry Newman.

**Baron Rutherford of Nelson** (1871–1937): "The father of nuclear physics" was born at nearby Brightwater and educated at Foxhill (1876–81) and Havelock (1882–86) before attending Nelson College (1887–89), Canterbury University College, Christchurch (1890–95) and Cambridge University, England (1895–98).

No physicist could have embarked on his career at a more auspicious moment, as the discovery of the X-ray (1895), radioactivity (1896), and the electron (1897) had completely transformed the older scene. Rutherford, endowed to grasp and successfully exploit the possibilities, undertook a vast range of experimental work on problems at the very limits of human knowledge. In forty-two extraordinarily active years he made four outstanding discoveries in the field of atomic physics, any one of which would have assured him of immortality and which, in combination, ushered in the nuclear age. For it was Rutherford who first succeeded in "splitting" the atom. Honours were showered on him — the Nobel Prize for Chemistry (1908), the Order of Merit (1925), elevation to the peerage (1931), and no fewer than twenty-one honorary doctorates from universities round the world. Even more than over his professional abilities (he "altered the whole viewpoint of science" . . . "one of the greatest men who ever worked in science"), his contemporaries praised his personal qualities ("transparent honesty of character" . . . "a genius for friendship and good companionship" . . . "highly respected by his colleagues, admired and loved by the great host of his pupils"). He lies buried in Westminster Abbey, beside Sir Joseph Thomson, the discoverer of the electron. *Lord Rutherford is remembered in many ways. A memorial at Brightwater marks his birthplace; a hall at Foxhill and a Youth Hostel at Havelock record the places of his primary schooling. Within the city, Rutherford Street, Rutherford Park and the modern Rutherford Hotel further ensure that he is not forgotten.*

## MUSEUMS AND ART GALLERIES

**Nelson Provincial Museum\*\*\*:** The new museum is heir to the Nelson Literary and Scientific Institution, founded aboard ship before the first Nelson settlers had even arrived. Displays are changed occasionally and may include Maori artefacts of local origin, documents relating to the New Zealand Company's venture, sketches of Nelson in its formative years, and items related to the Wairau Affray, Julia Martin (*see index*), Lord Rutherford and the Maungatapu murders. *Behind Isel House, Stoke. Open Tues.–Fri. from 10 am–4 pm, weekends and public holidays from 2–4 pm. Allow 1 hr.*

By the museum stands picturesque Isel House (*c.* 1848–1905), a two-storeyed stone homestead set in impressive gardens. The house contains the Marsden family's collection of china and furniture. *The grounds are open to the public. The house itself is open from 2–4 pm on weekend afternoons (in January also open 2–4 pm on Tuesdays and Thursdays).*

**Broadgreen** (*c.* 1855)**\*\*\*:** Modelled on a Devonshire farmhouse, Broadgreen was built for one Edmond Buxton. One of Nelson's oldest houses, it is now elaborately furnished as it might have been in Buxton's time, with scullery, dairy, study and nursery in addition to more customary rooms. The earth used in the building's cob construction was excavated on the site, thereby hollowing out a cellar which remains dry despite being nearly as deep as the nearby well. Surprisingly, only two families have owned the building. *Nayland Rd, Stoke. Open at weekends from 2.30–4.30 pm (in Jan. also open on Tues. and Thurs. Not open in June and July).*

**Suter Art Gallery\*\*\*:** Displayed in a Tudoresque building adjoining the delightful Queen's Gardens is a small but stimulating collection which centres on a large number of works by John Gully, who lived locally for a time. Thirty-three of his paintings were bequeathed to the gallery by Bishop Suter. The Art Society had its genesis in a sketching club formed by the Bishop. Of paramount importance is the wellknown view of Ship Cove, executed by James Webber, the official artist on Cook's third voyage. The middle gallery dates from 1844 and was for over half a century the Matthew Campbell School. *Bridge St, by Queen's Gardens. Open daily from noon–4 pm.*

A little distance behind the Art Gallery is the old fire-engine house (1866), the last survivor of the Nelson Provincial Council buildings. Here too the victims of the Maungatapu murders were laid out. The building may be refurnished as an early fire station.

**South Street Galleries:** In a street which is itself of interest for the number of early houses which survive there, two have been converted into galleries. The red house at No. 12, a military cottage of the nineteenth century, is used for exhibitions; visitors should view the tiny garden at the back as well as the house. The brown house on the corner of Nile and South Streets contains some of the finest Nelson pottery. *Open 10 am–4 pm; during Jan. and Feb. 10 am–5.30 pm. Also 6–9 pm Friday nights. Pottery demonstrations arranged for groups on request during holiday periods. Tel. 80-097.*

**Nelson Harbour Board Museum** comprises photographs depicting a century of port development and reclamation. *Cnr Collins St and Wildman Ave. Open by arrangement. Tel. 82-099.*

**Bishop's School** (1844): From the 1840s to the 1930s schools of various names and types used this building, one, re-established in 1860 by Bishop Hobhouse, accounting for its name. Only a minor part of the building dates from 1844. There are plans to furnish it as a Victorian school when restoration is completed. *Nile St.*

## SOME PARKS AND GARDENS

**Queen's Gardens\*\*:** Providing an attractive setting for the Suter Art Gallery (*see above*) are expansive formal gardens. *Cnr Bridge and Tasman Sts.*

**Isel Park\*\*\*:** A plantation of century-old trees shades a ground-cover of rhododendrons and azaleas, creating a superb surrounding for the mansion of Isel House. Created by Thomas Marsden (1810–76), the region's largest landowner, the grounds stand tall with trees brought from all parts of the world by ships' captains commissioned, it is said, to return with exotics from the lands they visited. The stone portion of the homestead was built over the period *c.* 1880–1905. The wooden portion at the rear, the original Isel Cottage, dates from *c.* 1848. *Main Road, Stoke. The house is occasionally open to visitors in summer. Behind is the Provincial Museum (see above).* By the entrance is the Church of St Barnabas (1864), with the graves of settlers who arrived with Captain Arthur Wakefield.

**Botanical Reserve\*\*\*:** A series of paths cross and recross as they zigzag up Botanical Hill. From the summit a view is enjoyed over the city to the lone spire of Songer Tree on the Port Hills, and beyond over Tasman Bay. The Boulder Bank seems completely to encircle Nelson Haven, and away from the harbour the prospect lies up the picturesque Maitai Valley. A trig plaque here from the 1877 survey is said to mark the "centre" of New Zealand, but is in fact the point of origin for surveys of the Nelson District. The playing-fields below in 1870 saw the country's first rugby match, commemorated on a plaque just inside the main gates of the reserve. *Cnr Hardy and Milton Sts. 20 mins walk to summit.*

**Anzac Park\*\*:** Towering palms impart an exotic, tropical air. A little distance away is the illuminated Moller fountain (*Haven Rd*). Opposite, in Rutherford Park, is the **Trafalgar Centre,** a conference centre and indoor sporting arena. *Junction Haven Rd, Halifax and Rutherford Sts.*

## SOME OTHER NOTABLE BUILDINGS

**Christ Church Cathedral** (1925–67)\*\*\*: On a splendid site the cathedral rises to dominate the city and to close the vista up its main street. Surrounding gardens are a favoured summertime lunch spot for neighbouring officeworkers.

The hill, once the site of a Maori village whose history was eradicated by Te Rauparaha, in 1842 became the site of the New Zealand Company's depot. First Octavius Hadfield (the missionary from Otaki) and then Bishop Selwyn held services here, Selwyn later purchasing the crest as the "singularly beautiful" site for a church. Selwyn ministered in a "Church tent", erected on the lower eastern slopes (*the site is indicated by a plaque about 30 m from the War Memorial*). The following year came the Wairau Affray, when apprehensive settlers fortified the hill, naming it Fort Arthur to honour their lost leader (*a fragment of the earthworks remain, indicated by a plaque to the left as one leaves the cathedral's main door*).

The first church (1850) was replaced in 1886. Construction of the present building, the third, began in 1925 with the then-Governor-General, Sir Charles Fergusson, laying the foundation stone — little realising that it would be for his son, forty years later and also as Governor-General, to represent the Queen at the Cathedrals' dedication. Over the years the design of the building was radically altered, among other reasons because of the Murchison earthquake, which dictated the abandonment of the planned Gothic tower. The initial section was built of solid Takaka marble (*see index*), a material ruled out by cost for the later stages, when concrete blocks were used and veneered with a plaster made from the stone.

Within are a number of memorials: an antique alms box, along with cathedral plate presented to Bishop Hobhouse in 1858 by the Oxford parish he had served prior to his consecration (*by main entrance*); plaques recalling "those who fell at the Wairau", the pioneer explorer-surveyor Thomas Brunner (*see index*), and Captain Arthur Wakefield (who "planted the Settlement of Nelson"); a memorial window is dedicated to Thomas Renwick (*see index*).

Outside, above the ecclesiastical "west door" (though the cathedral is in fact sited south to north), are seven carved heads: from left to right, George V (reigning monarch in 1927), Bishop Selwyn, Bishop Suter (second bishop of Nelson, 1866–91), Bishop Sadlier (fourth bishop of Nelson, 1912–34), Bishop Mules (third Bishop, from 1892–1912), Bishop Hobhouse (first bishop of Nelson, 1858–65), and Archbishop Averill (primate of New Zealand in 1932 when the first portion of the cathedral was dedicated). *Open daily 8 am–4 pm and during services. From 26 Dec. to 31 Mar. guides are on hand to show visitors round the building. Trafalgar Square.*

The steps leading down to Trafalgar Square and Trafalgar Street form the traditional setting for civic welcomes to distinguished visitors.

**Bishopdale\*\*:** On land secured by Bishop Hobhouse is the Bishop of Nelson's residence (1925) and the original Chapel of the Four Evangelists (1877), built for students for the ministry then studying at Bishopdale as well as for local settlers. Maxwell Bury's design, enchanting in its simplicity, reflects his instructions: "Nothing will be expended on ornament, everything being as plain as possible." Predominantly of *kauri* and with vertical weatherboarding, the chapel's style can scarcely be denominated. Beneath the baptistry floor is an unusual immersion font:

"It is well to have one place in the diocese at least where, if desired, it can be resorted to." The giant oak trees that flank the entrance to the main driveway were planted in 1864 by Hobhouse's two small sons. *Waimea Rd (main exit towards Stoke). The chapel is open to the public.*

**Melrose** (*c.* 1880) typifies the many grandiose Italianate homes built in Nelson in the early 1880s, when there was a keen competitive spirit among the gentry. The building belongs to the city and a Melrose Society is co-ordinating restoration. *Brougham St/Trafalgar St South. Open daily 12 noon-8 pm. Tel. 87-269.*

## SOME OTHER POINTS OF INTEREST

**Nelson Haven:** Overlooked by the city, the haven is sheltered by the slim long finger of a boulder bank which stretches fully 13 km from Mackays Bluff. It was from this bluff that the hard igneous boulders of grandiorite were exposed and eroded, to be rolled by the tide in a south-westerly direction to form the curious bank. The shape of the boulders becomes progressively less angular and more rounded as one proceeds from the Bluff along the bank. The natural bank-building process is still continuing.

Off the south-west tip of the bank spreads Haulashore Island, similar in origin and separated from the bank by a cut (made in 1906 and several times extended and deepened). For a time, before the channel was made, the broad end of the bank was known as Fifeshire Island, as it was here that salvage from the *Fifeshire* was auctioned in 1842 after the migrant ship had foundered on the nearby cone of Arrow Rock. The rock, too, has at times been called after the vessel. It marked the early entrance to Nelson Haven, which required a practised pilot as tides are extremely rapid and the channel (between rock and island) very narrow.

On the bank itself still stands the country's second lighthouse (1861–62), made of iron cast in Britain and shipped out to "lead vessels down the bay". To deter them from attempting to enter by night, the beam was screened by ear-shaped shutters so that it could not be seen unless a vessel was 1.6 km offshore. Between the light and the cut are the remains of a powder magazine built in the township's first years of settlement.

In legend the haven was created by the *tohunga* Te Maia who, before leading his people across from the North Island, came here to say appropriate *karakia* that in time created the sheltered waters he named Whakatu (*waka* = canoe; *tu* = to pile up; i.e., the place where broken canoes were dumped), the Maori name for Nelson.

*The northernmost end of the arm may be reached at The Glen (13.5 km).*

**Princes Drive viewpoint (Davis Lookout)\*\*\*:** From the Port Hills a remarkable view extends down to Haulashore Island, Rabbit Island, Tahunanui and across the bay as far as Abel Head in Abel Tasman National Park. At the end of the road a short track leads to the trig and Atkinson Observatory. *Princes Drive.*

Returning to Nelson one may cross the intersection with Richardson Street and Washington Road, and drive along Britannia Heights, shortly passing on the left the **Songer Tree.** This redwood was planted in 1900 by William Songer on the spot where in 1841 Captain Arthur Wakefield hoisted the Union Jack.

**Tahunanui Beach\*\*\*:** A safe, sheltered stretch of sand serves as the city's principal beach. A variety of amusements along the foreshore includes a large pool for model boats, skating rink, tennis courts, and Natureland (*open daily*), a display of wild life. *Tahunanui; at end of Rocks Rd.*

**Rabbit Island\*\*:** About 11 km of beach, sand dunes and pine trees. *25 km W. Open daily.* Other good beaches include **Kaiteriteri\*\*\*** (*65 km*) (*see index*), **Cable Bay** (*22.5 km*) and **The Glen** (*13.5 km*).

**Wakapuaka cemetery\*:** Early tombstones of interest include those of Captain George Moonlight (*see index*) and of the victims of the Maungatapu murders. *Atawhai Drive (Highway 6).* Also from here is an attractive distant view of the city.

**Scenic drive:** A signposted 27-km circular route starts from the church steps in front of the Cathedral. It passes the Cawthron Institute and Museum, Botanical Reserve, Queen's Gardens, Nelson College, Bishopdale, Isel Park, Broadgreen, Tahunanui Beach, Princes Drive lookout, and concludes by following Wakefield Quay to return to the Cathedral. *Full details from the Public Relations Office. For descriptions of most of these points, see above.*

## SOME WALKS

**Flaxmoor Hill (The Grampians):** A rough track leads from the top of Collingwood St, but an easier way of gaining the summit's superb viewpoint is from Blick Tce, walking up the roadway to the television installations. *Allow 1½ hrs.*

**Reservoir Reserve:** From the pleasant, well-bushed picnic and camping area here, a track leads up **Fringed Hill** to the fire lookout, whence there is an excellent view (*2½ hrs return*). A longer walk is on to **Dun Mountain,** where occasional sleepers from the abandoned railway and odd traces of coppermining may be seen. The track leads on to the curious "mineral belt" that extends from Abel Tasman National Park to Tophouse (*allow a full day*). *Permits and further particulars should be obtained from* the Brook Motor Camp caretaker. *End of Brook St. 5 km.* On the way the Dun Mountain railway plaque is passed.

**Maitai Valley:** An attractive picnic and camping area. A walk from here follows the **Maungatapu Track,** the old bridlepath to Havelock on which the sensational murders took place. One may also walk to **Rushpool,** where the site of an old Maori quarry may be seen. Hard rounded stones from the Boulder Bank were brought there to shape adzes and other tools. *Details from the caretaker at the Maitai Valley Motor Camp.* The valley itself is a particularly pretty setting in autumn.

**Botanical Hill:** A short if steep zigzag to the "centre" of New Zealand. *See "Some Parks and Gardens", above.*

## SOME TRAMPS

△**Heaphy Track\*\*\*:** A superlative 5-day tramp leads from near Bainham (in Golden Bay) to △Karamea (on the West Coast). The unique coastal section south from the Heaphy River has exquisite charm.

**Wangapeka Track:** A route (for the experienced tramper only) follows a prospectors' trail that for a time promised to be roaded as a link through to the West Coast. The hope was denied by the precipitous and unproductive nature of the surrounding country. Over 25 hours of tramping link Wangapeka with Little Wanganui on the West Coast. *The route passes through State Forest and particulars of the track and its huts should be sought from the New Zealand Forest Service.*

## SOME SUGGESTED DRIVES

**MOTUEKA-KAITERITERI ROUND TRIP:** An all-day 145-km drive leads along a picturesque coastline and through plentiful orchards, and tobacco and hop-growing districts. The drive is at its prettiest in early spring, when one looks over blossom on fruit trees to snow on mountain ranges. The trip may be shortened by omitting the section beyond Motueka. *Leave Nelson by way of Highway 6, branching off at Three Brothers Corner (13 km) to follow Highway 60 through Pea Viner Corner (19 km) and pass (on the left):*

**Stafford Place** (1866) *(19.3 km):* The Redwood family's homestead is set in trees well back from the road. Two sons of Henry Redwood, an original Nelson settler, have their individual places in history. The eldest son, also Henry, was twenty when his father migrated. He had owned and ridden racehorses in England and was quick to import seven thoroughbred stallions (among them the famed sire *Sir Hercules*) and a number of brood mares. His stud and training stables won fame and a string of enviable successes throughout Australasia so that in his lifetime, and to the present day, Henry Redwood was known as "the father of the New Zealand turf".

Francis Redwood (1839–1935) left Nelson to study for the priesthood in France and Ireland before returning home to become, in 1874, the youngest Roman Catholic bishop in the world. He lived to become the oldest, founding many churches, hospitals and orphanages, and introducing a number of notable Orders to New Zealand. The Archbishop of Wellington is remembered as a man of true simplicity and a great humanitarian, though he lost no opportunity to draw attention to "the subtle poison of Socialism [which] is permeating the minds of many" and which, like prohibition, he saw as an attack on his faith. *For a closer view, detour 600 m up Redwood Rd. Continue to pass the brick Redwood stables (hard by the roadside). The route then runs through some of the orchards which produce about half the country's apple crop. At 30 km turn off to:*

**Mapua** (pop. 489) (31.4 km): A 1.6 km detour here leads to Port Mapua, with its complex of agricultural buildings, including a chemicals factory where fruit sprays are manufactured, limeworks, coolstores and bulk stores. *The route now lies along the coast, passing:*

**Ruby Bay** *(33.8 km):* A pleasant sandy beach with swimming at high water and several picnic places. *Passing the McKee Memorial Domain the road rises to pass an:*

**Observation Point** *(35.9 km):* A splendid view extends down to Ruby Bay, and across Tasman Bay to D'Urville Island and French Pass *(for both, see index).* The wedgelike depression here was caused before the road was built, when goods had to be winched up the hill from boats in the bay below. *Continue on to:*

**Tasman** (pop. 538) *(39.6 km):* Here a signposted detour may be made to Kina Beach and its domain. It was in Mamaku Pa, on a plateau just beyond the domain turnoff, that the local Maoris gathered in the last of their several unsuccessful attempts to resist Te Rauparaha's invaders. With traditional weapons matched against firearms, the fight was less than one-sided. A branch road runs along Kina Peninsula to the Domain, where there is good water-skiing, sheltered bathing, and picnic spots beneath a canopy of pines. *The route continues to:*

△**Motueka\*\*\*** *(51.7 km):* The heart of the country's hop and tobacco industries is swollen by casual workers at harvest time. *Leave Motueka by Highway 60, passing through Riwaka before taking a detour road to pass the:*

**Wakefield cairn** *(60.3 km):* Erected to the memory of Captain Arthur Wakefield and to the coming of Riwaka's first settlers. Millstones incorporated in the memorial are said to have been cut out in 1844 either by William Mickell, the district's pioneer flourmiller, or his partner. Prior to Mickell's mill becoming a local institution, some settlers had even used coffee mills to grind their corn. The view from the cairn merits a stop to savour the prospect which greeted Arthur Wakefield when first he saw the plains. *Seascapes are enjoyed from this point onwards to:*

**Kaiteriteri*** (*64.7 km*) *(described under △ Motueka):* Here golden sand shimmers in a sheltered bay. At the parking bay at the far end of the beach a low stone wall encircles the spring from which Arthur Wakefield drew water on 9 October 1841. The road climbs to Kaka Pa Point, from which a giddy view of the beach is obtained. There are now no apparent traces of the fortifications that once terraced the point. By the turnoff a track leads down to Breaker Bay. *The drive may be abbreviated at this point by returning to Motueka. Otherwise continue along a slow road to skirt:*

**Sandy Bay** (*71 km*): It was from here that Takaka marble (*see index*) was shipped out for the capital's Parliament Buildings.

**Marahau** (*73.6 km*): An area popular for its beach and its proximity to △Abel Tasman National Park. The view from the foreshore is of Adele Island, separated from the mainland by the Astrolabe Roadstead, both named by the French navigator Dumont d'Urville in 1827. Marahau means wind on a garden. (*For further details see* △ *Motueka.*) *Here the road ends. Return to Motueka, bearing right at 83.2 km where signposted to rejoin Highway 60 and so to return to Motueka. Leave Motueka by way of the inland route to Nelson (Moutere Highway) passing the:*

**Riverside Community, Moutere** (*97.6 km*): An unusual pacifist Christian settlement. (*Described under* △ *Motueka.*) *4.8 km farther on, tame eels may be fed by hand* (*Wilsons Rd, signposted*).

**Upper Moutere** (*11.1 km*): The former German community of Sarau still has a Lutheran flavour. Its name is an enlargement of *motu* (island) — there was once an island off an indentation in the coast nearby. The continued use of the name shows how the Maori would cling to a name long after the reason for it had disappeared. Quaint St Paul's Lutheran Church (1905) has headstones inscribed in German. After passing through the settlement, one may pause to look back at its enchanting setting, lent a Bavarian air by the church steeple. *Continue on Highway 60 to cross the Moutere Saddle (182.8 m) and descend towards Nelson, enjoying wide views of the Waimea Plain and of Tasman Bay.*

**THREE BRIDGES-SPOONER SADDLE:** The 97-km drive crosses rich, closely-farmed plains liberally sprinkled with some of the region's oldest churches, cob cottages and a variety of kilns. *Leave Nelson by the port along Haven Road and Rocks Road (the convict-built road is lined with spiked chains).*

**Settlers Memorial** (*opp. foot of Richardson St; 1.6 km*): A low stone set under the chaining marks the point where Captain Arthur Wakefield landed on 1 November 1841. *The road continues to pass the islet of:*

**Arrow Rock:** The small upthrust of rock on which the *Fifeshire* foundered. *In turn the route passes* Tahunanui Beach (*3.2 km*) (*see above*), *and the entrance to* Isel Park *and* St Barnabas Anglican Church, Stoke (*7 km*) (*see above*). *Leaving the suburb of Stoke the route lies past numerous orchards before entering:*

**Richmond** (*pop. 6,587*) (*9 km*): In Queen St, a short distance beyond the shopping centre, a massive gumtree marks the racecourse entrance. Over 115 years old, it was planted by one Francis Otterson, who arrived on the *Lord Auckland* in 1842 and was one of the number of pioneers who lost their lives by drowning. *Shortly before the tree is reached the main route swings left to pass, on the left, Church St, at the end of which stands:*

**Holy Trinity Church, Richmond** (1872): A striking old church incorporates windows dedicated to its architect, Charles Beatson, and to John Wallis Barnicoat (1814–1905). The latter came with Otterson on the *Lord Auckland*, survived the Wairau Affray and was the only member to serve continuously on the Nelson Provincial Council from its inception in 1853 to its abolition in 1876. For the last nineteen years he was its Speaker. *Pass straight through Three Brothers Corner (at 13.4 km) to reach:*

**Hope** (*pop. 1,009*) (*14.9 km*): The village here began as the German settlement Ranzau. An 800-m detour down Ranzau Road leads to Ranzau School and St John's Lutheran Church, whose gravestones record the settlement's German origins. *Beyond Hope the road passes a gracious two-storeyed cob house (1863) with three dormer windows set in orchards to the left. The road crosses the Wairoa River to enter:*

**Brightwater** (*pop. 731*) (*18.9 km*): *Follow the signposted route towards Wakefield and Spring Grove.* A memorial marks Lord Rutherford's birthplace. It was at Spring Grove that the brothers Tom and Harry Newman began the twice-weekly coach service to Murchison today maintained and expanded by Transport (Nelson) Ltd. (The company's story is told in *High Noon for Coaches* by J. Halket Millar (Reed)). *The route continues through:*

**Wakefield** (*pop. 833*) (*25.3 km*): Named by an early missionary after both his native village in Yorkshire and the leader of the Nelson settlers, who had recently died in the Wairau Affray. A short detour signposted Pig Valley leads to St John's Anglican Church (1846), the oldest existing church in the South Island, whose chancel bears on its roofboards the prints of a cat who, one wet day in 1846, ran over the timber as it lay ready for use. A curiosity is the grave of Dr Thomas Oldham, who bequeathed £14,000 to the diocese but whose will, for some mysterious reason, described him as being "Robert Grey Brewster, formerly of Stamford, South Ashton under Lyne in the County of Lancaster, England, surgeon, but now for many years practising as a surgeon, for family reasons, under the name of Thomas Oldham . . . ". Nestling on the hillside, the church enjoys a pleasant aspect.

In Faulkener's Bush Reserve, a stand of tall trees affords a shaded picnic place.

*Beyond Wakefield the road passes through hop-growing country, studded with hop kilns, to enter the tiny settlement of:*

**Foxhill** (pop. 78) (*31 km*): Rutherford Memorial Hall recalls that the scientist received his first five years of primary schooling here.

*Follow Highway 6 towards Murchison, climbing the saddle of Spooners Range to reach:*

**Spooners Range Lookout**\*\*\*(*40.8 km*) (*464.3 m*): The view extends over thousands of hectares of the Golden Downs Forest and across Tasman Bay to D'Urville Island. A number of peaks are identified on a plane table.

Golden Downs Forest covers over 30,000 ha, including parts of the catchments of the Motueka, Motupiko, Tadmor, Sherry and Wai-iti Rivers. Predominantly *Pinus radiata* and Douglas fir have been planted over an area which comprised beech forest before the early European settlers burnt it to clear the land for farming. They had only limited success in establishing pastures, and bracken, fern, *manuka* (and later, gorse) reoccupied the land. Local school children participate in the planting and care of trees in a small sector established in 1953 as Coronation Forest.

*Turn round and return to the foot of the range. Either retrace the direct route to Wakefield or detour by turning right to follow Wai-iti Valley Road for 7 km. Then turn left down 88 Valley and so reach Wakefield (detour adds 5 km to the through route).*

*From Wakefield continue back to Brightwater where bear left along the road to Waimea West to pass immediately:*

**St Paul's Anglican Church, Brightwater** (1857; enlarged 1896) (*64.3 km*): The porch was actually built by Nelson's first bishop, Bishop Hobhouse, in memory of his wife "whose soul was required" in 1864. Hobhouse had resigned for reasons of his own health just two months before his wife died in childbirth. He returned to England only to live on to 1904 and the age of 87. Mary Elizabeth Hobhouse lies buried in the churchyard, together with a number of relatives of Lord Rutherford, his grandparents among them. Beside the church is the reserve of Snowden's Bush, a pleasant picnic place. *Cross the Wai-iti River and pass the clean upright lines of:*

**St Michael's Anglican Church, Waimea West** (1866) (*69.7 km*): Designed by the explorer Thomas Brunner (*see index*) in memory of Francis Horniblow Blundell. In the churchyard lie Bishop Mules (Nelson's third bishop), John Kerr (who at Nelson reputedly first ploughed South Island soil), members of the Blundell family and the Hon. Constantine Dillon (yet another pioneer who died by drowning). *Continue on to turn right back towards Nelson at 74.2 km by the:*

**Catholic Church of St Peter and St Paul** (1869): The gates are dedicated to Archbishop Redwood, whose migrant parents arrived in 1842 to settle nearby. Their homestead (1866) is set well back from the main road. (*To see the homestead detour left at Pea Viner Corner and continue for 700 m. The building is on the left.*) *Turn right at Pea Viner Corner. Cross the third of the "Three Bridges" on the drive (Appleby Bridge) and pass:*

**St Alban's Anglican Church, Appleby** (1868) (*76.1 km*): The area derives its name not from neighbouring orchards but from the Westmoreland birthplace of an early settler. *Continue on to:*

**Three Brothers Corner** (*80.1 km*): There are several explanations for the corner's name, the most usual being that a settler, Richard Hyland, lost four sons in infancy, three of whom were buried here near the family home with a tree planted over each grave. The trees have gone, but the tale has a happy ending as the Hylands went on to rear fully fourteen children. *Continue the 16 km back to Nelson, pausing if time allows at Waimea Potteries (on the left).*

**CABLE BAY:** *51 km. Leave Nelson by Highway 6 towards Blenheim. At 11.2 km detour left to:*

**The Glen** (*13.5 km*): The point where the curious Boulder Bank that protects Nelson Haven adjoins the mainland is a good surfcasting spot. Eighty years ago it was considered a "pleasant afternoon's stroll" from the city to the bluff — and back. *Return to the main road, turn left and continue for 3.2 km where turn left along the signposted road to Cable Bay. On the corner here is:*

**St John's Anglican Church, Hira** (1888): A small church with a chimney where one might have expected a cross. At the time it was built St John's minister used to travel his parish on horseback and occasionally stay in the church overnight, hence the need for heating. *Continuing, the road rises to follow the side of the valley and afford a view of:*

**Delaware Bay:** Seen across a wide lagoon, severed from the sea by a slim sandbank. It was on this sandbank that local Ngati Apa gathered in 1828 in a bloody quest to resist Te Raupahara's invading and better-armed Ngati Toa. Great was the slaughter as the Ngati Apa fought valiantly but vainly in the battle which spelt the virtual end of the tribe. The dead of both sides were buried in the sandhills, and periodically the shifting sand reveals bleached and crumbling bones. Gallantry was again displayed in the bay when on 3 September 1863 the brigantine *Delaware* was caught in a northerly gale and dashed against the bay's eastern headland. Five Maoris appeared on the shore and threw themselves into the surf until eventually they managed to secure one of the lines thrown to them and drag ashore a hawser which they secured to a boulder. The crew and their sole passenger crawled along the hawser to safety. Many times the Maoris, among them the young and beautiful Huria Matenga (Julia Martin), plunged into the pounding surf to help the men ashore. Her bravery made her a legend in her lifetime and earned comparison with Grace Darling, the English lighthouse keeper's daughter who thirty years before had similarly helped her father effect a dramatic rescue in dangerous seas. The people of Nelson subscribed to present Huria with a gold watch and the others with silver watches. Huria and her husband Hemi (who also helped in the rescue) are buried in the cemetery on the tip of the peninsula. (The museum at Nelson holds items concerned with the incident; Huria's portrait by Lindauer hangs in the Suter Art Gallery). *There is no public access to Delaware Bay. The road ends at:*

**Cable Bay:** A picnic spot with safe bathing at low water. It was here that the first telegraphic cables laid across the Tasman, from La Perouse (N.S.W.) in 1876, had their terminal. The ragged ends of the three cables may be seen jutting from the beginning of the Boulder Bank which ties Pepin Island to the mainland. The bach close by encloses the last of the cable station's buildings.

*Returning to Nelson a short signposted detour into Nelson cemetery may be made to see the public memorial to the victims of the Maungatapu murders (who were "waylaid, robbed and brutally murdered") and to obtain a good view of the city's eastern aspect. The sandstone obelisk is set well back on the main ridge and is encircled by an iron railing.*

**PELORUS BRIDGE:** *114 km return. Follow the road towards Blenheim, passing the turnoff to Cable Bay (see previous drive) to climb through bush to Whangamoa Saddle (356.5 m) and descend to:*

**Rai Valley** (pop. 223) (*40 km*): A settlement known for the quality of its cheese (which may be purchased cheaply at the dairy factory) and for the excellence of its bakery, where many novel shapes and sizes have been produced to claim a variety of world "firsts". A short detour here leads to the Rai Valley Pioneer Cottage at Carluke. The cottage (1881) was built of split slabs and shingled with *totara* by its first owner, Charles Turner. It has been restored by members of the Turner family as a tribute to its first New Zealanders. (*Key may be obtained from Mr Owen Young in the white farmhouse on the left between the turnoff and the Carluke bridge*). A turnoff here leads to French Pass (*see index*).

**Pelorus Bridge** (*57 km*): A delightful scenic reserve where one may picnic in native bush, perhaps on crisp, still-warm Rai Valley bread. A 40-minute bush walk leads along the Totara Walk. A shorter track leads to a waterfall. (*Both signposted.*) From here, too, a road leads up the Maungatapu Valley from the end of which a track leads over Maungatapu and into the Maitai Valley — the original route from Nelson to Havelock and Blenheim, and the scene of the Maungatapu murders. At Pelorus Bridge there are camping facilities.

Beyond lie Canvastown (*65 km*) and △Havelock (*76 km*); *for both, see* △Havelock.

## ORGANISED EXCURSIONS

**Tours** range from a brief look at city highlights to gold adventure tours and an all-day trip to Farewell Spit or the Cobb Dam, or French Pass (*for each see index*). Those interested in seeing arts, crafts, herbs, antiques and old homesteads are also catered for. *Details from the Public Relations Office.*

**Scenic flights** to see the slim finger of Farewell Spit, the rugged hinterland and the drowned river system of the Marlborough Sounds operate from the airport at Tahunanui. *Nelson Aero Club, tel. 79-550.*

**Trail rides** of varying duration are run by OK Corral (*tel. 84-342, evenings*).

**Safaris:** Molesworth station (*see index*) may be visited in late summer on a two-day safari. An all-day trip runs from Pelorus Bridge along an old goldminers' trail up Maungatapu and passes the scene of the murders before descending to reach Nelson through the bush of the Maitai Valley. Other tours are also run. *Skyline Safaris, tel. 86-160.*

## TOURING NOTES

**Highway 6 to** △**Havelock** passes through the dairying settlement of Rai Valley and Pelorus Bridge Scenic Reserve (*for both see above*). At 64.7 km the former goldcentre of Canvastown is passed (*see* △*Havelock*) and then △Havelock is reached (*at 76 km*). From there the quicker route to Picton is the longer in distance, via Blenheim.

# NELSON LAKES NATIONAL PARK

**27**

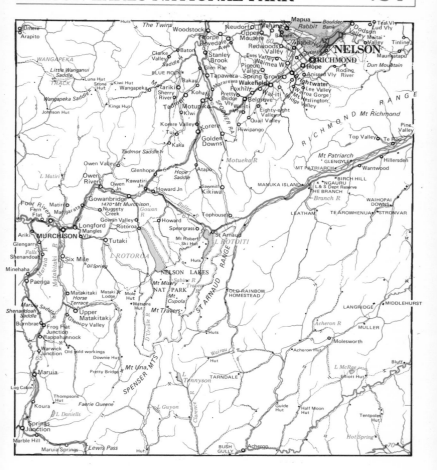

## NELSON LAKES NATIONAL PARK***   Nelson.   Map 27.
### Area: 57,470 ha.

*St Arnaud (pop. 113) is 119 km SSW of Nelson; 103 km ESE of Blenheim. Park headquarters at St Arnaud provide details of things to see and do in the area and hunting permits. The park handbook,* Nelson Lakes National Park Handbook *is recommended.*

NELSON LAKES NATIONAL PARK preserves in perpetuity the rugged, mountainous country that surrounds the slender, beech-fringed glacial lakes of Rotoiti and Rotoroa. Activities centre on St Arnaud township, by Lake Rotoiti. There a blend of shaded picnic spots and open grassed areas looks along a sliver of lake from which mountain ranges rise abruptly on either hand.

Each lake has its own claims for attention. Lake Rotoiti is the more popular, with better swimming, more open ground, a host of picnic places along its eastern shore, and comparatively fewer sandflies. If Rotoiti is favoured by numbers of powerboat owners and water-skiers, Rotoroa is preferred for their absence, as well as for its lack of development, more prolific brown trout and country less arduous for the hunter. Powerboat regattas are periodically held on Rotoiti. The twin lakes may yet be united, as a hydro-electric power scheme has proposed the raising of Rotoiti by perhaps 8 m, with a canal or tunnel to carry its waters into Rotoroa. From there a tunnel through the ranges could drop the lakes' combined waters into the Mangles River. The prospect promises to attract considerable opposition.

Today von Haast's prophecy of 1859 may be seen as fulfilled: "I had no idea that such a jewel in point of landscape existed so near Nelson, and I am sure that the time is not far distant when this spot will become the favourite abode of those whose means and leisure will permit them to admire picturesque scenery."

Recommended reading: *The Enchanted Coast* by Emily Host (McIndoe) and *Historic Gold Trails of Nelson and Marlborough* by Tony Nolan (Reed).

## MAORI LEGEND

**The digger of lakes:** In tradition, Rakaihautu, a giant among men, arrived in the *Uruao* canoe long before the coming of the ancestral canoes. Setting off southward to explore the land on foot, he reached the upper Buller Valley where he seized an enormous *ko* (digging stick) and gouged out the beds of what filled to become Lakes Rotoiti and Rotoroa. As he continued south along the line of the Southern Alps, he dug and named a whole series of lakes. His crowning achievement was the creation of Whakatipua (Lake Wakatipu), after which he journeyed north again to form Waihora (Lake Ellesmere) and Wairewa (Lake Forsyth). His work complete, he climbed a hill on Banks Peninsula (Mt Bossu) and there thrust his mighty and much-used *ko* into its summit. The fable may be simply a colourful way of describing a journey of exploration.

## SOME GEOLOGY

The region combines the influences of the Alpine Fault and of glaciers. The movement of the Alpine Fault, the major geological feature of the South Island, is illustrated by the differences in height between the mountains to the north-east of the fault line (which have been raised to heights in excess of 2,100 m) and those to the north-west (which rise only to about 1,000 m).

Both lakes fill valleys carved out by glaciers, each having the sheer, precipitous valley walls characteristic of the glacial lake. When the glacier that formed Rotoiti reached the area of St Arnaud, it forked on striking the hard rock of Black Hill, piling up moraine so that when the glacier receded (about 16,000 years ago) the lake's peninsula was left behind. The lake itself is typically restrained by a mass of terminal moraine. As the world's temperatures slowly rose, the ice retreated and the depressions it had caused filled with water. These depressions are now being filled in by gravel borne down by the rivers and streams that feed the lakes. In earlier times of glacial advance the ice of Rotoiti extended beyond the perimeter of the park, nearly to Tophouse. Geologically the lakes were in fact "dug out" as if by a *ko* in the manner of the Maori legend.

## FLORA

There is a wide variety of vegetation in the park. Lake Rotoiti is fringed by a mixture of red, silver and black beech interspersed with *kamahi*, some mountain beech, and northern *rata* which in season is a mass of bright red flowers. The gold of the flowering *kowhai*, interspersed with flax, *toetoe* and *rata*, encircles the comparatively lower fringe of Lake Rotoroa. Also found on the perimeter of Rotoroa are *matai, miro* and *rimu*. Tree trunks are often covered with moss and lichen flora, ranging in colour from greys and greens to yellow.

On the shingle slides are found highly specialised plants able to cope with conditions ranging from searing summer heat to winter snow. Generally blue-grey, they can be difficult to see, but on more stable ground the forget-me-not (*Myosotis traversii*) flourishes with its white and cream flowers.

The geologically distinct area of Black Hill and the peninsula on Rotoiti have vegetation that has been modified by fire. The forest, generally mixed beech and *kamahi*, contains abundant mosses and lichens both on tree trunks and on the forest floor, where in spring upwards of a dozen varieties of ground orchids may be seen.

## EUROPEAN EXPLORATION

With the land problems encountered by the infant New Zealand Company at Nelson, every rumour of grassy plains in the hinterland was followed up. The first European to see Lake Rotoiti was the twenty-three-year-old surveyor John Silvanus Cotterell in 1842, who, with a companion and a Maori guide, traversed in less than a fortnight more than 300 km of tangled, trackless terrain from Nelson by way of Tophouse to the Clarence River. The following January the party retraced their steps to Tophouse and continued south-east to discover Rotoiti and the Buller River. By June, Cotterell was dead. A Quaker who refused to carry a gun, he died in the Wairau Affray (*see index*).

In March 1846 William Fox, the New Zealand Company's ambitious agent at Nelson, set out with the zealous explorer Thomas Brunner and his companion Kehu. They "discovered" Lake Rotoroa (a Maori paddling a canoe across the lake is shown in Fox's painting of the scene) and Fox reported to Colonel William Wakefield: "While enjoying the delightful scenery of the lakes I could not help reflecting on their adaptation for the summer residence of invalids from India, who could find among them everything calculated to restore health, and might soon surround themselves with many of the amusements and resources of a watering place."

On this trip Brunner and Kehu formed an association which led to their embarking, with three others, on one of the country's epic journeys of exploration from Nelson to a point not far from Hokitika. By the time they returned to Nelson, after nearly two years in the field, they had been given up for dead. But as they returned they neared Rotoiti, when Brunner wrote: "I saw six sheep here, and the tracks of a large flock, which much astonished me, as there was no station when I formerly passed this way."

The Scot, George McRae, had driven 400 sheep up from Nelson and in 1848 acquired the Rotoiti run. Seven years later William Thomas Locke Travers, a Nelson solicitor, explored the region in some detail and gave many features names associated with the Crimean War — the St Arnaud Range he named after the French commander in the Crimea. He also named the Spenser Mountains and its peak, the Faerie Queene. He did not name the Travers Range, for this name was bestowed by Julius von Haast (*see index*), the Austrian geologist who in 1859 was commissioned by the Nelson Provincial Council to explore and report on the area south and west of Nelson. Von Haast also named Mt Robert (after his son in Germany, whom he had never seen), Mt McKay (after his companion, James Mackay; *see index*), and the Sabine and D'Urville Rivers.

Once gold was discovered on the West Coast, the excitement created by the finds generated the need as well as the will to upgrade the rough track from Nelson to the Coast.

---

National Park Information Offices advise on walks, tramps, flora, fauna and accommodation. Displays illustrate the significance of each area.

Local sports shops issue fishing licences, advise on local conditions and restrictions, and often hire out equipment.

---

## THINGS TO SEE AND DO IN AND AROUND THE PARK

**Park headquarters:** Visitors to the park can obtain advice on proposed trips and maps, handbooks and leaflets from the headquarters building at St Arnaud settlement, Lake Rotoiti. (*Tel. 806*). Opposite it is a gold-sluicing nozzle last used near Howard. As late as the depression of the 1930s, many were eking out a living on the nearby goldfields of Maud and Maggie Creeks and other tributaries of the Howard River and even now one meets with the occasional prospector.

A ranger station at Lake Rotoroa deals with enquiries about Rotoroa Camping grounds and local hunting permits. *Tel. 167W Murchison.*

**Buller River source:** The impressive Buller River bypasses the customary gradual accumulation of tributaries, flowing at once swift and adult from Lake Rotoiti, its impatient waters contrasting with the usually placid surface of the lake. *West Bay. 3.9 km from St Arnaud by road.*

**Mt Robert lookout** (*884 m*)*:* A narrow winding road leads to the lookout from West Bay, crossing a wooden bridge over the Buller a short distance from its source. The view is down on to West Bay, to the curve of the Buller River, and across the peninsula to Kerr Bay and St Arnaud township. From this vantage point is seen how the glacier that gouged out the lake bed fragmented against Black Hill and deposited at the fork the pile of moraine that is the peninsula. *3.4 km from Highway 63: turnoff signposted "West Bay Motor Camp"; 7.2 km from St Arnaud.*

**Walks at Lake Rotoiti:** The generally precipitous nature of the country round the two lakes removes most of the walks into the category of tramps. However two fairly level and easy walks are popular with family groups. The first, the Peninsula Walk (*allow 2 hrs*) starts at the eastern lakefront at St Arnaud and skirts the perimeter of the peninsula round to West Bay. The track branches up to Rotoiti Lodge (used by organised youth groups) and so back to the township. One may continue along the foreshore to the source of the Buller River. (*An explanatory brochure is available.*)

The second walk is the Lake Head track round the shoreline of Lake Rotoiti, a walk which can be accomplished by family groups inside a day. There are many appealing picnic and swimming spots on the way. The track begins at the eastern foreshore of Lake Rotoiti.

Somewhat more demanding is the walk up Black Hill (*2 hrs return*), starting from Highway 63 and leading to a point some 125 m above Lake Rotoiti which affords views of the lake itself, the St Arnaud Range to the east and, to the west, the Buller and Speargrass Creek Valleys.

From the Mt Robert Lookout, the Pinchgut Track zigzags through beech forest to the skifields (*3 hrs return*). An all-day walk can be made by following Paddy's Track (*start just before the Mt Robert Lookout*), to wind up over the north-east face of Mt Robert before turning west to link with the Pinchgut Track and so to return to the lookout.

**Walks from Lake Rotoroa:** A half-day walk leads from the parking area along Porika Track. Once out of the forest a view is obtained along the length of the lake, with Mt Misery at its head to close the vista.

The rather rough lakeside track leads along the eastern shoreline. It is a full days' walk out to Sabine Hut at the head of the lake. Information about shorter walks is available from park headquarters.

---

He who would travel happily must travel light. — Saint-Expurey (*Wind, Sand and Stars*).

---

**Tramping:** Easiest of access, the Travers Valley is more popular with trampers than either the Sabine or the D'Urville, and has an intricate network of tributaries and many routes to high peaks. All three valleys offer magnificent fishing for brown trout. Huts are placed at strategic points throughout the park and beyond. Details of huts and tramps are available at the park headquarters.

**Fishing:** There is good fishing for (generally brown) trout, in Lake Rotoiti and even better in Lake Rotoroa. Better still is the fishing in the headwaters of both lakes, up the Travers, D'Urville and Sabine Rivers. Both the Buller and Gowan Rivers have their sources in the park, and both merit the angler's attention. *Permits available from the National Park Board. Season usually from October 1 to April 30.*

**Skiing:** The season at Mt Robert extends from about July to September. Facilities have been established by the Nelson Ski Club (*PO Box 344, Nelson*) which include some accommodation and instruction. Access is on foot along the Pinchgut Track from the Mt Robert lookout. In season there is also skating near Black Hill on a pond off Highway 65.

**Hunting:** Red deer and chamois are found in the park — deer generally in the valleys and chamois on the open tops. Hunting permits for the Lake Rotoiti watershed are available from the park headquarters at St Arnaud, and for the Lake Rotoroa watershed from the ranger at Lake Rotoroa.

**Scenic flights** may be arranged from △Blenheim and △Picton.

## ENVIRONS

**Tophouse\*:** The cob-walled iron-chimneyed hostelry, now a private farmhouse, dates from 1887 and its licence from 1844 — only two years after Cotterell explored the route which for many years was the overland link between Nelson and Blenheim. In 1894 a lodger murdered the acting licensee and held a governess and three children hostage before finally committing suicide. The building is still pockmarked by shot from the siege. After nearly 130 years of service to wayfarers from wagoner to modern motorist, Tophouse lost its liquor licence in 1971. *Tophouse. At 3.4 km from St Arnaud turn off Highway 63 towards Nelson. At 8.6 km take the first turning right. Tophouse is on the right at 9.2 km from St Arnaud.*

**Cotterell Memorial:** A marker records Cotterell's finding of the Tophouse route from Nelson to the Wairau (Blenheim) in November 1842. Seven months later the young surveyor was dead. A Quaker, Cotterell refused to carry a gun and died in the "Wairau Affray" (*see page 62*). *By Highway 63 opp. turnoff to Nelson and Tophouse. 3.4 km from St Arnaud.*

**NIGHTCAPS     Southland.   Map 18.   Pop. 532.**

*21 km N of Otautau; 37 km NW of Winton; 8 km SE of Ohai.*

THE ODDLY NAMED oldworld township of Nightcaps unfurls along the foothills that mark the north-western perimeter of the Southland plains. The name derives from the hills that rise behind the town. Some say because early settlers saw a resemblance in the silhouettes of the Nightcaps (*343 m; due north from the town*); others that the peaks are regularly "capped" with mist or snow.

A coalfield of vast proportions extends in a broad band across northern Southland, but it was here in the 1860s that a boundary rider from Birchwood station noticed coal in a creekbed. Impromptu mining gave way to an organised assault on the deposits in 1880 with the formation of the Nightcaps Coal Company, which built its own railway and trucked out about 1½ million tons over a period of forty years before the mines were exhausted. Gradually △Ohai grew on a site nearer the mines that opened to replace the old. Much of Nightcaps workforce is committed to the mines there, and the balance to serving neighbouring farmland.

A time-travel map is inside the back cover.

**OAMARU\*\*     North Otago.   Map 28.   Pop. 13,480.**

*116 km NNE of Dunedin; 250 km SSW of Christchurch; 119 km SE of Omarama.*

OAMARU IS GIVEN the air of a white stone city by the stately buildings that border her tree-lined streets. The town lies in the crook of Cape Wanbrow, a knuckle on the North Otago coastline. Sheltered to the south by this high headland and to the west by low hills, the chief town of North Otago enjoys a warm, dry climate reflected in her luxuriant gardens.

Inland, intensive sheepfarming and cashcropping on the downs and lowlands give way to more extensive sheepraising on higher country. There is marketgardening on the coast at Kakanui. Much local limestone is worked, including creamy Oamaru stone of building quality.

# OAMARU AND DISTRICT

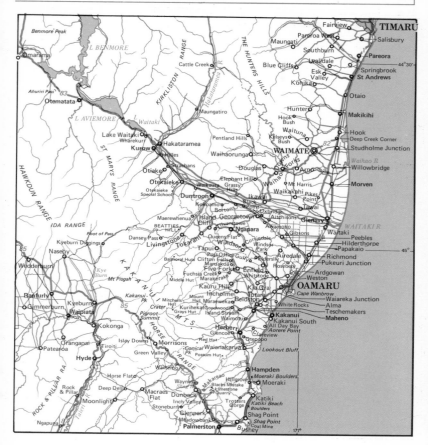

## 28

The meaning of Oamaru is obscure. It may mean place of Maru, Maru in some traditions being a sea-god, in others a celestial being personified by a glow in the sky. However, another legend tells of Tamatea's party from the *Takitimu* canoe making their way north after their vessel had foundered in Southland near the mouth of the Waiau River. The fire they carried with them is said to have been carelessly mislaid here so that it sank into the ground, causing an inferno that burned for many years (*O-ahi-maru* could mean place of sheltered fire). The limestone in the area is said to be the fire's solidified ashes.

**Oamaru stone** is a white granular limestone of Tertiary age in the same category as the Oolites of Britain and the Caen stone of France. It is found in thick horizontal beds with no vertical joints, and can be quarried simply with a circular saw as the stone is then extremely soft. It gains somewhat in hardness on exposure and is often resistant to weathering.

However some of the stone used externally in buildings has deteriorated quickly, perhaps because of the presence of small quantities of impurities such as sand and clay. Nevertheless Oamaru stone is superior in lasting qualities to similar stone from other localities but it seems that it weathers best when laid in the same plane as it occupied before it was quarried.

The stone, of considerable purity, has been used for numerous important buildings — Auckland's Town Hall, Post Office and St Matthew's Church; Wellington's Customhouse; Christchurch's Catholic cathedral; and for Dunedin's First Church, Town Hall and Anglican cathedral. The creamy stone has also been widely used in conjunction with other stones, especially for interiors where its softness, its uniformly clean appearance and its regularity of grain allow shaping to virtually any form. (*Weston, 5 km W, is the centre of the limestone industry.*)

## SOME HISTORY

**An unhappy landing:** Exceptions to the generally inhospitable coastline that stretches from Otago Peninsula to Banks Peninsula are the capes at Moeraki and Oamaru, so that the development of Oamaru largely evolved round the growth of her port to the detriment of that at △Moeraki.

The sealing trade bypassed the area, Moeraki was the site chosen for a whaling station, and Oamaru begins to emerge only with the arrival of Hugh Robison who, in 1853, took up a run that included the town site — then a deserted wilderness of brown tussock, flax and speargrass.

The original Oamaru run had been bought and sold three times before H. C. Hertslet moved here from Moeraki in 1858 to build an accommodation house. From there he operated a derrick and landing gear installed by the provincial government in recognition of the landing's increasing importance to North Otago runholders. At the same time Charles Traill (*see index*) arrived to open the first store.

The landing acquired a bad reputation, richly deserved, as witnessed by both the regularity and number of wrecks on the coast. Indeed, the story is told of how Johnny Jones (*see index*) agreed to serve the district; but his *Annie James* arrived at Oamaru only to scamper back to Moeraki fully laden, to the chagrin of the runholders who had assembled to unload her.

The town was laid out in 1858 under the direction of John Turnbull Thomson, a Northumbrian who bestowed the first street names, all of them of English and most of them of North Country rivers. The first public building of Oamaru stone, a little courthouse, was built in 1864, the year before the saga of the harbour began.

**The saga of the harbour:** As accident followed misadventure at the landing, so grew agitation for a jetty, and in 1865 a petition was presented to the central Parliament to have the provincial system of government altered. As much as £150,000 had been derived from North Otago land sales, it noted, very little of which had been spent in the district. Instead, palatial buildings had been erected in Dunedin and provincial income expended to divert to the provincial capital the goldfields trade that local opinion felt could more economically have gone to Invercargill and to Oamaru: ". . . if [our] interests are to be saved from ruin, and this valuable and important district to become prosperous, it must be by a total change of the Provincial system of Government, which centralises expenditure on the Capital, to the impoverishment of the Agricultural Districts." The petition did not succeed.

Within a month tenders had been let for the Oamaru jetty. Building commenced, but progress was slow. Shipping losses persisted. By the end of 1867 an L-shaped jetty had been completed, supported by iron piles only 12.5 cm in diameter. Further works were needed to shelter the jetty, and just a fortnight after a Government inspector had criticised its construction, the jetty was swept away in a night of terror. Three ships also perished, and there were losses by drowning both of passengers and of a group living by an inland stream. (*The jetty remains on the borough seal.*)

Argument over possible harbour developments continued until finally a breakwater, 365.6 m long, with a railway along the foot of Cape Wanbrow was begun and the nexus of today's port created. Later the happy discovery was made that the harbour bed was not of rock but of impacted shingle, and could thus be dredged to accommodate larger vessels. Extension plans were drawn up to increase the breakwater to 548.4 m, to build a rubble mole to the north, and so enclose the whole harbour.

**The New Zealand & Australian Land Company:** Though the company's interests ranged over the country as a whole — in 1878 holding over 1.2 million ha carrying 12,000 cattle and 700,000 sheep — its activities in the Oamaru district have special relevance, for it was here on the company's Totara estate that New Zealand's prolific frozen meat export trade began.

The company was formed by the amalgamation of the New Zealand holdings of various unincorporated societies in Scotland, to which it greatly added. Before the company virtually withdrew its interests in favour of Australia (where it is now domiciled as a subsidiary of Dalgetys — its New Zealand holdings have been transferred to Dalgety New Zealand Ltd), it sent two dynamic individuals out from Scotland to reorganise its activities, even though one of them, William Soltau Davidson (1846–1924) eventually urged the sale of much of the company's New Zealand undertaking.

Between them, Davidson and Thomas Brydone (1837–1904) arranged the country's first trial export of meat. They were quick to see the potential of refrigeration and the opportunity it offered to ship to Britain, for sale as mutton, carcases which would otherwise have been merely boiled down for tallow if not simply slaughtered as surplus stock. At the time sheep were raised almost solely for their wool, and Davidson could vividly recall sheep on overstocked runs being "knocked on the head and thrown down a precipice as a waste product". Even the advent of boiling-down and meat-preserving works offered only a poor return when compared to the value of a sheep as fresh meat in a market handy to centres of population.

Davidson was by then the company's general manager and Brydone its New Zealand manager. Brydone oversaw the preparation of the first carcases at the Totara estate (*just south of Oamaru*) and Davidson himself, who had made the shipping arrangements, came out from Edinburgh to join Brydone in personally stowing aboard the first few carcases. The ship used was the clipper *Dunedin* (1,300 tons), originally built to carry 400 passengers and converted to refrigeration expressly for the trial shipment. The Land Company was to pay freight of 2½d per pound and to bear the risks involved. After a false start (a breakdown saw the hatches opened and meat intended for Britain sold in Dunedin) the vessel sailed from Port Chalmers in February 1882 with a load of some 130 tons. Ninety-eight days later she arrived at London where the meat opened up in good condition and sold for 6½d per pound.

The success of the venture led to more ships being fitted out for the trade, Davidson living to see annual exports soar to 6 million carcases. The *Dunedin* was not as lucky. She made nine further voyages before she went down off Cape Horn in 1890, probably after striking an iceberg.

Brydone and Davidson are also known as the fathers of the nation's dairy industry as they engineered a switch to cows on the company's Southland estates, establishing the country's first export dairy factory at △Edendale. Also of importance was Brydone's pioneering of artificial manures, particularly lime, and Davidson's breeding of Corriedale sheep at the Levels (*near Timaru*). He was developing the strain at the same time as James Little, near Ngapara.

**Corriedale sheep:** It was on the Corriedale run in 1866 that James Little (1834–1921) began to cross long-woolled Romney and Lincoln rams with Merino ewes to produce in due course the Corriedale breed — a strain with the dual virtues of long wool and prime carcase. Today there are over 1.5 million Corriedale sheep, mostly in Canterbury, Otago and Marlborough. Corriedale flocks have also been established throughout the Americas, in Australia, Japan and South Africa. (*A roadside memorial by the Corriedale run records Little's work. 22.5 km on the road to Ngapara.*)

**Three schools:** Oamaru is an educational centre of some distinction, by odd coincidence her three best-known schools all being related by their connections with the family of Sir Henry Miller (1830–1917). Sir Henry, who was educated at Eton and rowed for Cambridge in the boat race of 1849, was a local runholder who completed half a century in the Legislative Council (the since-abolished Upper House), for twelve years as its Speaker.

The State boarding and day school, **Waitaki Boys' High School,** owes its existence not only to Sir Henry (who was dedicated to the establishment of an Eton in the Southern Seas) but also to the enthusiasm of Samuel Shrimski, a Polish Jew whose commercial premises were the first in the town to be built of stone. Shrimski is remembered by the Hebrew Script in the school crest (meaning Jehovah, the Fountain of Wisdom) and Sir Henry by the school motto he suggested, *Quanti est sapere.* The school opened in 1883 in the building to the left of the main complex; the central and southernmost blocks were added later. Behind the stately stone complex is the Hall of Memories, the school's assembly hall and a repository for historical items primarily with a naval flavour. The building symbolises the infectious patriotism of Frank Milner (1875–1944) who for thirty-eight years was revered as headmaster and known simply as "The Man". In the history of New Zealand education Milner holds a place similar to that enjoyed in England by Arnold of Rugby and Sanderson of Oundle. He was a pioneer in widening a previously narrow curriculum to provide for an all-round schooling. (*The Hall of Memories may be visited when not in use. Enquire at the headmaster's office. Waitaki Avenue off Thames St.*)

Sir Henry's daughter Fanny married the next-door neighbour, St John McLean Buckley of Redcastle, whose homestead block is now occupied by **St Kevins College** (Sir Henry's home, Fernbrook, still stands nearby). The Redcastle property, earlier held by Hugh Robison, came into the hands of John McLean of Morven Hills (*see index*) at a time when he and his family held over 200,000 ha and shore 250,000 sheep. The brick homestead and stables still stand, their newer neighbours designed to harmonise with them. Dating from the turn of the century they were built by Sir John Buckley, whose nephew inherited the property and married Sir Henry's daughter. The school was founded in 1927. (*Thames St*).

It was Sir Henry's son George who married Violet Teschemaker, the third daughter of William Henry Teschemaker (1829–88) whose homestead block was, in recent years until it closed in 1978, occupied by the **Dominican Convent (Teschemakers).** The homestead, of Oamaru stone, dates from 1863. There are also Maori rock drawings on a nearby limestone outcrop. *12.7 km.*

A readable history of the region is *White Stone Country; the Story of North Otago* by K. C. McDonald (North Otago Centennial Committee).

## A WALK AROUND THE TOWN

*The walk leads past many of the town's attractive buildings of Oamaru stone and takes in the old commercial area by the harbour. Allow 1½ hrs. Start in Thames St at the foot of Severn St by the Boer War memorial and walk south to pass, on the western side of the street, the* **Waitaki County Council Chambers** (1882) *the* **Oamaru Borough Council Chambers,** *and the* **Courthouse** (1883)*: A particularly splendid building with Corinthian columns adding to its classical air. Opposite, on the corner of Wear St, is the:*

**Brydone Hotel** (1880): Built as the Queen's Hotel, the upstairs public rooms have been restored to their original style. This Trust hotel holds a number of items connected with the pioneer of the frozen meat industry. The hotel runs trout and salmon fishing safaris in season. *Turn right down the alleyway to reach the:*

**Gaol stables** (1869): A low stone building, the stables are all that remain of a prison whose cream stone and hexagonal turret (complete with battlements and with hanging towers on each corner) fully deserved its description as "the handsomest building devoted to the punishment of crime in the colony". *Return up the alleyway and turn right to continue down Thames St to pass:*

**North Otago Museum:** Occupying a site adjacent to that where Hugh Robinson built a sod hut in 1853, the Athenaeum (1882) now houses a small district museum illustrating aspects of local geology and the settlement of the area by both Maori and Pakeha. *Open Mon.-Fri. 1–4.30 pm, weekends 1.30–4 pm. Further on rises the:*

**New Post Office** (1884)**: a handsome building of intricate detail and design. Beside it is the **Old Post Office** (1864)**, now occupied by government departments and with a simple Portuguese air. *Almost opposite, side by side, are the impressive chambers of the:*

**National Bank** (1870) and the **Bank of New South Wales** (1884)***: Both classical buildings are faced with Corinthian columns whose capitals are carved with luxuriant acanthus leaves. Both were designed by R. A. Lawson (*see index*), architect for a number of Dunedin's notable buildings.

**Thames Street Bridge:** The central portion dates from 1861. It was widened to the width of the street in 1876. *On the near corner, on the intersection with Itchen St, is the:*

**Old Bank of New Zealand** (1878): Originally built by the Colonial Bank, when that institution failed, the chambers here, along with other assets, was acquired by the Bank of New Zealand. They are now the premises of the Oamaru Operatic Society. *On the opposite corner is the:*

**Old AMP building** (1871): The building retains its frieze, unlike many others throughout the country whose statuary was removed as an earthquake risk. *On the third corner is:*

**St Luke's Anglican Church** (1865): Of Oamaru stone, the church has grown over the years, the nave being enlarged in 1876 and the chancel and tower added in 1913. *Now walk down Itchen St towards the harbour.* On the right is the former **Star and Garter Hotel** (1867–68), now used by a theatrical society. *Turn right up Tyne St, an area once variously called Wall St and Mortgage Alley, passing the old* **Union Bank building** (1878), *now converted into squash courts. Walk up Tyne St to the Wansbeck St intersection and the:*

**Northern Hotel** (1880): When the present structure was erected to replace an earlier building (1860), popular feeling was that the hostelry's name should have been changed. It refers to the hotel's position in Otago — not in the town. Farther up Tyne St, on the right at No. 40, is the former harbour flagstaff (1862). Salvaged from a wrecked vessel it served in several positions before being moved here. *Turn left down Wansbeck St. After one block turn left again to follow narrow Harbour St between rows of venerable warehouses and pass the* **Harbour Board offices** (1874). *Continue on to rejoin Itchen St. Follow Itchen St past the foot of Thomas St and on past St Lukes' Anglican Church, looking down to* **Meek's Mill:** The oldest portion of the four-storeyed building dates from 1878. *By the RSA rooms turn right down through the memorial garden to walk along Seven St, passing the entrance to the Public Gardens on the left and the swimming baths on the right.* There is an interesting aspect of the New Post Office across Takaro Park. *Continue down Severn St to pass the two-storeyed rough-hewn stone* **Police Station** (1915) *and the* **Baptist Church** (1889) *before once more reaching the Boer War memorial.* The trees along Severn St were planted as part of the town's memorial to the 1914–18 war. *Once back at the memorial one may cross Thames St and turn down Coquet St to see:*

**St Paul's Presbyterian Church** (1876)*: Presbyterian services were first held in Oamaru in a woolshed, but for about a century an elegant stone building has been the mother for Presbyterian churches throughout North Otago. It stands on the site of the first church (1865).

A map on page 2 shows the areas covered by the various sectional maps in the Alphabetical Section.

A table of distances between major centres appears on page 363.

### SOME OTHER THINGS TO SEE AND DO

**Public Gardens*:** Venerable trees and well-established garden displays reflect the maturity of the town. There is a children's statuary. *Severn St.* Some 2 km away, in a reserve in Old Mill Road (Phoenix Rd), off Chelmer St, is the huge waterwheel (1878) from the Phoenix mill.

**St Patrick's Basilica** (1893)**: A fine building of Oamaru stone, F. W. Petre's Basilica has few peers outside the main centres. The portico and outer domes were added in 1903, and the building completed in 1918 with the addition of the sanctuary and the main dome. The interior is particularly splendid, showing the original creaminess of the stone and featuring Roman arches and Corinthian columns. *Foot of Usk St, off Thames St.*

**Lookout reserve (Cape Wanbrow):** The point to the south of the port gives a wide view down over the town. *Signposted off upper Tyne St.*

**Cape Wanbrow:** The W. G. Grave Memorial Track leads round the cliffs of the lighthouse reserve to Bushy Beach. Grave, an energetic citizen who canvassed the district by bicycle to raise the money for the Boer War monument, organised the group that began to form the track but died before it was completed. *Start at Friendly Bay or at Bushy Beach. Allow 1 hr one way.*

**Scott Oak** looks down on Friendly Bay, the port in and out of which a mysterious ship furtively slipped in the darkness of the early hours of 10 February 1913. Neither the identity of the ship nor that of the two men who landed was revealed. The pair would say no more than send a cable to London that shocked the world with the news of the deaths in the Antarctic of Captain Scott and his companions. The ship transpired to be the *Terra Nova. End of Arun St off Wharfe St.*

**The Homestead** (*c.* 1864) was built by Matthew Holmes (1817–1901), a land baron who reputedly boasted that it was impossible to stand anywhere in Otago or Southland without seeing land in which he had, or in the past had had, an interest. For a time he was buyer-in-chief to the New Zealand & Australian Land Company, and later New Zealand general manager. It is even now impossible to unravel the dealings to discover how much land he bought personally and how much he held merely as nominee. He made his mark not only as a runholder but as a politician, and as an importer and breeder of pedigree stock. His stud of Clydesdale horses, of Lincoln, Romney, Leicester and Cheviot sheep and of Hereford and Shorthorn cattle were famous beyond New Zealand and contributed to the quality of flocks and herds throughout the country. The Homestead is now used for receptions. *South Belt Rd, overlooking Awamoa Park.*

## SUGGESTED ROUND TRIP SOUTH

*The 63 km round trip runs south along Highway 1 to beyond Herbert before it swings to the sea and returns to Oamaru by way of the coast and Kakanui. Leave Oamaru travelling south by Highway 1:*

**Totara Estate Memorial** (*8.2 km*): A memorial gateway marks the entrance to the killing sheds built to prepare the first carcases for the British market (*see "Some History", above*). To the left, atop Sebastopol Hill, is a castle-like cairn in Brydone's memory. To the right, in the trees, is the old Totara estate homestead (1868). *Continue on to:*

**Maheno** (pop. 203) (*13.7 km*): Here turn right to reach the Church of St Andrew (1938), a boulder church erected as a family memorial by the Nichols of Kuriheka, who came to New Zealand from Tasmania. Furnishings include wooden panelling carved with native birds, Roman currency in use at the time of Christ, and specimen stones from ancient English shrines. *From Maheno a detour may be made to:*

**Kuriheka (Goodwood):** The Kuriheka estate of 9,440 ha was acquired by Col. Joseph Cowie Nichols who had come from Tasmania as a child. Keenly interested in matters military, he obtained a variety of 1914–18 war field-guns which are mounted in paddocks surrounding the Kuriheka war memorial. The palatial farm buildings, primarily of stone, are in a tree-shaded setting. Within the woolshed brass plaques record the years of service of longtime employees. The property is still in the Nichols family, who built the Maheno memorial church. (*From Maheno follow signposted route west for 8.4 km*). *Return to Highway 1 and continue south to reach:*

**Herbert** (pop. 315) (*21.7 km*): A farming and poultry-raising hamlet. The stone Presbyterian church dates from 1866. The locality is named after Sidney Herbert, a British secretary of war. Its earlier name, Otepopo, is still applied to the church and the local school, though its meaning (rotting wood) is now inappropriate for solid buildings of Oamaru stone. To the south are the headquarters of Herbert Forest. *Continue south to reach the:*

**Old Mill House** (1879) (*26.5 km*): A stone flourmill has been restored to serve as a licensed restaurant and motel complex. The Waianakarua River here is good for swimming and for whitebaiting from September to December. The stone bridge (1874) over the river is worth inspecting from river level. *Turn left at the river to reach the coast. The route passes All Day Bay (the whalers' corruption of the Maori name for the adjacent point, Aorere) and:*

**Kakanui** (pop. 323) (*52 km*): A marketgardening district. In the early 1870s Kakanui had a busy port, shipping out canned meat for export. With the introduction of frozen meat the local canning industry collapsed. The river estuary is good for swimming, boating and fishing. *Continue north to follow the coast and the signposted route back to Oamaru.*

## OTHER ENVIRONS

△ **Waitaki River:** Its broad waters mark the provincial boundary between Canterbury and Otago. For the visitor interest lies in the hydro lakes and the river's renowned quinnat salmon. *22.5 km N.* On Highway 1, at 13.7 km N, a signboard denotes the 45° south parallel, a point equidistant between the equator and the South Pole and now the name of a domestic whisky.

**Moeraki boulders\*\*\*:** *Described under* △ *Moeraki. Signposted 34.8 km S on Highway 1.*

**Bushy Beach:** A track leads down to a beach heavy with kelp and with areas of orange-gold sand among the gravel. A nice picnic place. *2.5 km S along Bushy Beach Rd.*

> The car has become an article of dress without which we feel uncertain, unclad, and incomplete. — Marshall McLuhan (*Understanding Media*).

## OHAI    Southland.  Map 18.    Pop. 710.

*29 km N of Otautau; 45 km NW of Winton; 8 km NW of Nightcaps.*

THE COALMINING settlement of Ohai stretches along Highway 96 on the foothills that break the north-western Southland plains. Ohai State Coal, non-coking coal with a low sulphur and ash content and a high calorific value, is used extensively by Southland industries. Over 265,000 tons are produced each year.

### COALMINING AT OHAI

Coalmining in the district on a substantial scale began at neighbouring △ Nightcaps in 1880, the name of Nightcaps coal becoming a household word throughout the southern half of the South Island. The existence of sub-bituminous coal at Ohai had been known for over fifty years before any quantity was mined — during the 1914–18 war when the mines at Nightcaps began to run out. The mining centre gradually moved the 8 km from Nightcaps to Ohai, and Ohai today provides employment for much of the Nightcaps workforce.

There are several seams of coal nearby, up to 22 m thick and all suitable for mining. Winning the coal is not easy, however, as the seams are not flat but lie on quite steep grades, having been broken up by earthquake faults. Coal from all the mines hereabouts, both underground and opencast, is trucked to a conveyor that lifts it to a central screening plant by the main road. There the coal is screened to separate out slack and is sorted into the various sizes for household and industrial use before it is loaded into trucks or railway wagons. The centralised plant has cut handling costs and serves to produce a more uniform product. *During working hours one may see the opencast mining operations, and by prior arrangement it is possible for small adult groups to be conducted underground (allow ½ day). In either case contact the District Manager, State Coal Mines Office, Ohai, tel. 788. For notes on coalmining generally, see* △ *Westport.*

**Ohai Railway Board:** The railway that links the town with Nightcaps and Wairio (where it joins the New Zealand Railways network) is unique in being administered and owned by an independent board. The original private line from Wairio to Nightcaps was both built and owned by the Nightcaps Coal Company. Though there have been moves to have the Railways Department assume responsibility for the line, the Ohai Railway Board (a public body) has always been an efficient undertaking. The Mines Department, the line's biggest customer, is represented on the Board along with members of local bodies.

## OHAU (Lake)    South Canterbury.   Maps 16 & 34.

*39 km N of Omarama; 92 km SW of Tekapo; 319 km SW of Christchurch.*

LAKE OHAU LODGE stands above a charming stretch of water whose surface occasionally mirrors the surrounding mountains and, at sunset, a red-tinged Mt Cook. The lake, which marks the boundary between Canterbury and Otago, draws summertime campers, boatowners and fishermen in quest of trout. In winter the lodge assumes the role of ski resort as enthusiasts come to enjoy the slopes of the Lake Ohau skifield on Mt Sutton.

### SOME MYTHOLOGY

**Tearful brothers:** In mythology the Waitaki River (water of tears) was formed by the weeping of two brothers as they mourned their sister, who had been drowned at the rivermouth. She had been turned into a rock, and the brothers became two hills near Lake Ohau. Their tears scoured the land until they found a way to their sister.

The lake was originally Ohou (place of Hou), after a follower of Rakaihautu, the giant digger of the inland lakes. Ben Ohau was named Te Rua-taniwha (the cave of the *taniwha*), as a *taniwha* frequently raided the Rapuwai who lived at the head of the lake. The tribe piled the stream the water monster used to walk along with bundles of *manuka* so that the next time the *taniwha* came his feet were entangled in the branches. He was speared to death before he could struggle free.

Later, Ngatimamoe lived by the lake until, in a pattern familiar throughout Canterbury and Otago, they were attacked and overwhelmed by Ngaitahu.

## POINTS OF INTEREST

**Lake Ohau Lodge:** A licensed hotel, it serves as a holiday and fishing lodge in summer, and as a growing skiing centre in winter. Casual meals available.

**Lake Middleton:** A little lake, close to Lake Ohau, is very much warmer for swimming and water-skiing. A well-used camping spot.

**Walks:** Tracks at the head of the lake up the Hopkins Valley and through the Temple State Forest hold picturesque possibilities for tramper and walker alike. *Details from Lake Ohau Lodge.*

**Mt Cook view:** One can walk up the ski road for a better view of Mt Cook (*4 hours return*).

---

This book is being continually revised to ensure that it remains the most comprehensive guide book to the South Island. If you have any suggestions for future editions, please write to the publishers at Private Bag, Te Aro, Wellington.

---

## OMARAMA    North Otago.    Maps 1, 16, 28 & 34.    Pop. 382.

*119 km NW of Oamaru; 116.5 km NE of Cromwell; 87 km SW of Tekapo.*

THE VILLAGE of Omarama lies across the junction of Highway 83 from the △Waitaki Valley, and Highway 8, which comes from Central Otago through the △Lindis Pass to link with the South Canterbury lakes. It has an increasing role as a point from which to fish a wide area for trout and landlocked salmon. Omarama means the place of Marama (literally, *o* = the place of; *marama* = moon, or light).

**A gliding centre:** On the fringe of the Mackenzie country, Omarama is renowned as a gliding centre. Every Christmas pilots and their gliders converge here, and many enthusiasts have small huts near one or other of the two airstrips. The locality is ideal for gliding, being inland about as far from the coast as one can get in the South Island, away from the sea breezes that kill the essential thermals. The giant mountain-ringed basin heats up well in summer, with the cooler lakes and mountain slopes providing vital heat contrasts. Moreover, Omarama is well sited for gliders to get on to the high wave that forms over the country in prevailing north-westerly conditions. The wind strikes the far side of the mountain chain to rise sharply, so sucking air streams up the leeward slopes to form "lee waves" of rising air that can extend as high as 10,000 or 15,000 m. These are important to give the height needed for long crosscountry flights. Omarama is also handily placed to Central Otago, another excellent gliding area and one over which competition "tasks" extend. Two world records have been set here.

## SOME HISTORY

**A forced eviction:** Boundary disputes over Maori land sold to the government culminated in an upheaval at Omarama that foreshadowed the infamous invasion of Parihaka in the Taranaki. A group of Maoris living at Omarama on land they claimed still to own drew the ire of local runholders who, though they employed many of them, objected to their dogs and declared the Maoris to be trespassers when they were hunting *weka*. Certainly the settlers' suggestion that as many as 2,000 sheep had been killed by the Maoris' dogs was a gross exaggeration.

To the Maoris, their claim to occupy the land was reinforced by the fact that the government had paid only a fraction of a penny an acre under the relevant deed of sale, yet was now reselling at about £2 an acre. On 9 August 1879 the *Oamaru Mail* reported: "Twelve mounted constables, armed with carbines and revolvers, took their departure by this afternoon's train for the scene of the trouble." Despite the bitter cold (the constables' beer was frozen in the station cellar) the Maoris stayed put until the constables arrested their chief, Maiharoa, at which point they agreed to leave. A reporter noted, "They seem to be awed by the force which was brought against them and are not expected to make any resistance." Sadly the group farewelled their tribal lands for, though of Ngaitahu, Maiharoa could also trace his ancestry back to the district's Waitaha Moa-hunters. The sorrowing group made its way down the Waitaki to a small reserve near the coast.

This dispute was not finally settled until 1944, when the government agreed to pay Ngaitahu an additional £300,000 spread over thirty years.

## ENVIRONS

**Tara Hills Research Station** is a high-country tussock property of 3,340 ha, a substation of Invermay at △Mosgiel. Development by topdressing, oversowing, border-dike irrigation and the establishment of lucerne, has dramatically increased carrying capacity. Research centres on the use of improved tussock country by both sheep and cattle, pasture establishment and fertiliser requirements, sheep and cattle breeds, nutrition and management. *Signposted off Highway 8 to the SW. Visits by appointment on weekdays for those with a special interest. Tel. 830.*

## TOURING NOTES

**Clay Cliffs:** Rising above the Ahuriri River and seen some 7 km on the way to the △Lindis Pass are the fluted Clay Cliffs, a precipice weathered into massive pipelike columns. In some lights there is a remarkable range of colouring.

△**Waitaki Valley:** Details of the hydro-electric power schemes and points of interest on Highway 83 are listed under this entry.

---

A Glossary of Maori Words appears on page 343.

---

**OREPUKI     Southland.   Map 18.   Pop. 177.**

*20 km SE of Tuatapere; 68.5 km W of Invercargill.*

THE SMALL UNHURRIED farming settlement of Orepuki on the south-eastern arc of Te Waewae Bay is heir to a past that has repeatedly failed to fulfil its promise. Today the population is but a fraction of the 3,000 or so who lived here at the turn of the century; its several hotels have dwindled to one, and governmental offices have long been closed. When Orepuki's new post office opened in 1960 one newspaper was bold enough to label Orepuki a "ghost town" and drew at least one reader's indignant denial — "Orepuki is no 'ghost town'. We are proud of our new post office. Our beach is considered one of the best in Southland and Mother Nature has blessed us with the view of the most picturesque sunsets in the southern hemisphere."

Orepuki (literally crumbling cliffs) is a corruption of Aropaki (bright expanse), said to have been bestowed on the district by a group of Maoris as they emerged from the dense bush of Pahia Hill and saw Te Waewae Bay.

**Monkey Island Beach*** is a pleasant corner and one of the few safe swimming places on Te Waewae Bay. The origin of the name comes from the tiny island offshore in which some see a likeness to an ape. The naming of the island after an animal is consistent with other names in Foveaux Strait, such as Dog Island, Pig Island and Rabbit Island. *3.1 km S.*

## SOME HISTORY

**A peripatetic town:** Today's township stands on its third site. Originally Orepuki was at Monkey Island, a short distance south, where in the early 1860s prospectors were extracting very fine gold from the beach. The Commissioner of Crown Lands, Walter Pearson, visited in 1866 and described the technique, noting that the miners were concentrated towards the southern end of the beach: "The gold is obtained by stripping off the sand and shingle [to a depth increasing from 30 cm to 3 m as one nears the Waiau] to within a few inches of the bottom, which is soft sandstone. This washdirt is generally passed through sluices, the bottoms of which are covered with blanket, or, better still, plush. Great care is required, owing to the fineness of the gold dust, and the difficulty of separating it before it is swept off from the black sand with which it is mixed and which appears to be nearly as heavy. Even with a quick-silver plate at the end of the sluice some gold is lost, it being light enough to float . . . one party obtained 20 ounces in four days." As there is still gold to be washed, the visitor with time in hand may care to emulate the diggers of a century ago.

At the time of Pearson's visit the prospectors had begun to move inland to wash more profitably by ground-sluicing in Prospectors Gully. As their numbers grew the township, complete with buildings, was uprooted and moved some 6.5 km to its Garfield site. There sluicing operations came right into the town. Two enterprising prospectors even paid for the removal of the school building to the Orepuki School's present position in the expectation of washing handsome returns, and it seems the pair did indeed do well. With the arrival of the railway in 1885 came the township's final shift, to its present location by the railway station.

**The promise of shale:** Coal and shale mining began in 1879. The coal operations enjoyed scant success as the deposits proved inferior to those at △Nightcaps, but outside interests were attracted by the prospects for shale. In London the New Zealand Coal & Oil Co. was formed with a capital of £180,000, most of which was poured into Orepuki. A mine was developed and a gigantic shale works erected, with large storage tanks and tall, broad refracting chimneys designed to produce refined shale oil, paraffin wax, tar and sulphites of ammonia. The town's population soared; new houses were built; a spirit of optimism gripped the area. As soon as operations began in 1899 the omens of failure were there to be read in the thick, pungent sulphurous fumes that pervaded the town, heavily tarnishing metal — even silver coins in miners' pockets. But the local population gladly tolerated the conditions for the prosperity the industry spelt, and were shattered when, without warning, the works abruptly closed in 1902. So unexpected was the closure that rumours of an international intrigue masterminded by American oil companies quickly gained credence, but the explanations for failure were fourfold: too high a sulphur content, soaring mining costs, difficulty in working the fractured shale deposits, and the government's removal of duty on imported kerosene and paraffin.

For years the works lay idle. From time to time plans were made for their revival but none was carried through. In the 1930s most of the equipment was sold and many bricks from buildings carted away. A single large brick storage building (*a short distance inland; ask directions locally*) is all that survives intact, but from the shore to the hills there are traces of extensive excavations beneath the gorse and broom.

So the population of Orepuki slumped as it had boomed. Optimism was raised once more by an ambitious attempt to win iron and platinum from the beach's ironsands. But the smelter, too, quickly failed, and for many years, with that of the shale works, its derelict machinery stood as mute testimony to the hopes and heartbreaks of the town. As the prospectors had done before them when the gold ran scarce, those of the shale workers who did not leave the area turned to the sawmills for a living before the township settled into the comfortable role of a farming centre.

> A key to area maps appears on page 2.

## OTAUTAU    Southland.    Map 18.    Pop. 970.

*38 km NW of Invercargill.*

THE QUIET FARMING centre of Otautau, seat of Wallace County, extends along the foot of the hills that build into the Longwood Range, the western border of the Southland plains. Its pleasant setting in rich country was chosen not by planners, who sought to site the settlement on the eastern bank of the Otautau Stream, but by wagoners. They persisted in preferring the present site as a convenient place to stop after an all-day haul from Riverton as they headed for the Wakatipu diggings.

At one time the town's prosperity was based on the timber trade, when Otautau was home to five mills fed with logs from the Longwoods. This pattern is perpetuated by the present mill which processes timber trucked in from Tuatapere. Of greater importance is the servicing of surrounding farmland, particularly the late summer stock sales when tens of thousands of sheep, most from outlying stations, pass through the Otautau saleyards. There is good cropping locally. For a time an Otautau farmer held the world record for the yield of wheat per acre, a distinction now accorded a farmer in Washington, USA with a crop of 205 bushels to the acre.

Otautau means the place of Tautau (literally — *o* = the place of; *tautau* = greenstone ear-pendant with curved lower end).

**Holt Park** is set at the foot of a river terrace whose steep face serves as a natural grandstand. There are large sports meetings here each Labour Day with events as varied as Highland dancing, cycling and woodchopping. A world woodchop test has been staged here. *Signposted.*

> A metric conversion chart appears at the end of the book.

## OTEMATATA    North Otago.    Maps 1, 16 & 28.    Pop. 692.

*95 km NW of Oamaru; 24 km SE of Omarama.*

OTEMATATA, by the Waitaki River, was created in 1958 as a construction town with a peak population of over 4,000, for the Aviemore and Benmore hydro projects. Crib owners have filled much of the void left when the workers (and some of the buildings) moved on, enjoying the facilities offered by the hydro lakes for boating and fishing, and augmenting the town's permanent population of New Zealand Electricity Department maintenance staff. Otematata means place of good quartz, or flint.

**Benmore dam**\*\*\*: A short distance away is the country's largest hydro dam. A jetboat operates on the lake. *5 km. Described under* △*Waitaki Valley.*

### TOURING NOTE

An alternative route down the Waitaki Valley from here is to drive across the Benmore dam. Follow the Waitaki's Canterbury bank down river to the Aviemore dam, whose crest forms the route back to the Otago bank and Highway 83.

**OWAKA**✳✳     South Otago.   Maps 4 & 19.   Pop. 467.

*31.5 km S of Balclutha; 138 km ENE of Invercargill. The South East Otago Reserves Board provide information from their office in Catlins Forest Park building, Owaka. Tel. 8.*

THE PEACEFUL FARMING town of Owaka, the centre of the Catlins district, found its valley site when the railway pushed through the bush from △Balclutha. The settlement, previously preoccupied with the milling and shipping of timber, had perched on a hillside above the bridge that now spans Catlins Lake. The town's surrounding reserves of native bush, splendid beaches, waterfalls and sea-carved caves draw regular visitors from as far as Dunedin and Invercargill. The winning of further farmland from the forest will add to the wealth of an area favoured with an adequate rainfall spread evenly through the year.

The expanse of Catlins Lake, 8 km from the sea, is properly a broad river, both tidal and salty. At low neap tides its waters all but vanish, but at other times the lake, stocked with sea-run trout, is as much as 5 km across. It is also a popular yachting and boating area and has artificial island *maimai* that betray the interest of duck-shooters.

Owaka means place of a canoe.

## SOME HISTORY

**Cattlin's Country:** Edward Cattlin (as he spelt his name) (d. 1856) was a whaling master, operating his brig *Genii* out of Sydney. The rising tide of colonisation impelled him to indulge in a modest land venture — for £30 and an assortment of muskets and gunpowder he secured from Tuhawaiki and Karetai ("Bloody Jack" and "Jacky White") a block of 5½ million acres. As defined by Cattlin himself, the block extended for 32 km on either side of the Catlin River and inland for a depth of 90 km.

Once British sovereignty was proclaimed, Cattlin lost little time in pursuing his claim, but he found officialdom surprisingly unsympathetic. He died at Sydney in 1856, before his claim had been determined, and final irony came seventeen years later when his estate received a grant more in keeping with the price paid — 92 ha. Still, as Hocken noted, "his name and story are imposed on a widespread district, and with this he must sleep content".

**The disappearance of Dr Schmidt:** An area that hints of mystery, the Catlins hides the details that surround the disappearance of Dr G. F. R. Schmidt. Dr Schmidt, a German geologist, was engaged by the Otago Provincial Council in 1855 to explore the Fiordland and Catlins districts, looking for useful minerals, preparing botanical maps and collecting specimens for the Otago Museum. He had originally come to New Zealand to further his theory that this country had once been joined to the South American continent and, though highly regarded by many, in Dunedin he was considered as something of a charlatan.

Two labourers were assigned to accompany the scientist, a pair who found Schmidt so pompous and overbearing that they threatened to throw him in the Mataura River. Schmidt summarily sent them on to Port Molyneux to wait for him there, while two part-Maoris took their place. Some time later, when the party was overdue at Port Molyneux, search parties set out. One of the Maoris, Jimmy Nixon, was found at the old Tautuku station and he told of having deserted after Schmidt had attacked him. But of the two others no trace has ever been found. The puzzle hardens into suspicion when it is considered that Schmidt was carrying money and other valuables. Whether the original escort, the bellicose "Bill the Butcher" and his companion, waylaid Schmidt somewhere on the deserted coast, or whether he died of exposure in the bush, remains a mystery. Perhaps the valuables Schmidt had with him still lie hidden near Jacks Bay, somewhere north of Penguin Bay, the point to which the searchers traced Schmidt's path.

**Catlins River railway:** The area, one of continuous dense beech forest, was settled in the 1860s, when timbermillers moved in to cut for the Dunedin market. Gradually the bush gave way to pastures, green even in summer as rainfall is spread evenly throughout the year. Among the mills was the "big mill" of Messrs Guthrie and W. J. M. Larnach (*see index*). On the southern shores of Catlins Lake, at Hinahina, the ambitious enterprise employed several hundred men and became the centre of a thriving village from which it is said four or five schooners would often sail in a single day, laden with timber bound for Port Chalmers. Through to the 1930s the bush supported as many as thirty sawmills, of which only a handful survive.

A major factor in the region's advance was the coming of the railway, but though the contract for the first section was let in 1879 it was twenty-five years before the 35 km between Owaka and Balclutha was completed. Earlier, the region's principal transport had been by sea. In 1872 Captain Charles Hayward had been appointed harbourmaster, and the port on the Catlins River was soon shipping out more timber than any other port in the South Island. But in 1887 Hayward's port was abolished, trade had languished, the readily accessible bush had been cut out, and other means had to be found to recover the timber. Eventually, after thirty-six years, the railway was pushed as far as Tahakopa. The line closed in 1971.

## THINGS TO SEE AND DO IN THE CATLINS DISTRICT

**Catlins Historical Society Museum:** The small collection reflects the varied activities of the region, among them whaling, timbermilling, coalmining and the advent and exit of the railway. Displayed is the flag of the SS *Manuka* which in 1929 was wrecked on Long Point, a graveyard for many ships. All 204 aboard were safely rescued and many tales are told of the locals who helped themselves to the cargo as it was washed ashore. Customs officers hurried to empty rum and spirits on the sand, while other casks were cached in the bush by some, only to be discovered and reconcealed by others. One portly salvager was seen astride a draught horse, a 100 lb bag of flour in front of his saddle and yards and yards of carpet wound round the horse's nether regions.

Opposite the museum lies an anchor which may be from the *Bessie*, a vessel which ran aground in the Catlin harbour in 1887. She was salvaged by Capt. Hayward, who set off to Dunedin, intending to have the ship rigged out as a fishing boat. But two days later one of his sons struggled out of the bush with the news that his father, brother and a companion were all lost with the ship. They had been sheltering off Long Point when they dropped anchor. The anchor chain jammed before the two anchors bottomed and while the men worked furiously to free the offending link the ship drifted, struck a rock and capsized. *Waikawa Rd. Hours vary.*

**Pounawea:** Though tidal, the estuary here is preferred by swimmers, being considerably warmer than the open sea. There is excellent fishing, particularly nocturnal fishing for flounder, as well as picnic places and camping at the domain. Offshore from the domain is an old dolphin, a relic from milling times when timber ships would moor to the bollard to swing around the bend in the river. The channel has since altered. The estuary is ideal for yachting, boating and water skiing. *4 km.*

**Tautuku Beach**\*\*\* is a superb bush-backed beach along an unspoiled stretch of shore. Here the bush dips down to the sand, its trees meeting in a dense canopy over the approach road. A number of cribs nestle on Tautuku Peninsula, at the southern extremity of the beach, but access to these is only across the mouth of the Fleming River, so explaining the cheerful assortment of elderly tractors and four-wheel-drive vehicles parked at the road's end. To the left is Isa's Cave, and off the northern point is tiny Rainbow Island, named after its blowhole which, in certain conditions, performs with prismatic effect. Its Maori name is Rerekohu (flying mist). *29.7 km. Signposted south on Highway 92.* Tautuku Peninsula was the site of the whaling station "Tauchuk", established by William Palmer in 1839 for Johnny Jones (*see index*). Palmer stocked Rainbow Island with rabbits for use as food, an act that local folklore attributes to Captain Cook. Tuckett in 1844 described the whalers as living

**Jacks Bay**\*\*\*: A magnificent beach, dotted with the occasional crib. The beach is barred to the north by the imposing rock of Hayward Point, and to the south by Tuhawaiki Island, which from the beach appears as part of the mainland. From the southern end of the beach one may walk over the point to reach Jacks Bay Blowhole and continue to the indentation of Penguin Bay. *9 km.*

At 5 km on the way, after crossing Catlins Lake, one passes at Hinahina the site of Guthrie and Larnach's "big mill", marked only by a heap of stones on the edge of the estuary carried here from Britain as ballast by timber ships.

**Jacks Bay Blowhole**\*\*\* is an awesome opening in farmland far from the sea. A cleft known to the Maori as Opito (the navel), it plunges some 60 m down to the water, its perpendicular sides of solid rock fringed with fern. The sea rushes in to the bottom of the pit through a subterranean tunnel about 200 m in length. Before the bush was cleared the blowhole could be located only by the thunderous booming of its imprisoned waters, appealing to Dr Hocken as "a huge grave in the forest".

*10.5 km. Signposted. One may either drive over farmland to the blowhole or park by the farm gate and walk for some 10 mins along the track. The blowhole is to the left, fenced off for safety, partway up the hillside. It is at its most impressive in heavy weather and at high tide. A little farther on from the blowhole is Penguin Bay, where penguins come ashore in the late afternoon to nest in the forest.*

**Purakaunui Bay** is popular with campers who prefer to shun developed areas. Green pastures along the foreshore make a pleasant contrast with the native bush in an adjacent reserve. The Purakaunui River flows into the sea at the southern end of the bay and is safe for children. *15 km.*

**Purakaunui Falls**\*\*\*: An easy path through predominently beech forest leads to the head of the falls, which cascade over a series of broad terraces. Steps continue down to the foot of the falls where the best view is from a platform over the stream. These valleys were localities for wonderful stories, as Tuckett related in 1844: "They say the eels ascend the falls unitedly in a train, intertwining with each other, when the Maoris catch them in great numbers." *17 km.*

*The falls are best photographed at about 11 am on a sunny day.* A trip to the falls may be readily combined with visits to Jacks Bay and the blowhole.

**Tahakopa Bay and Old Coach Road:** A track follows the Old Coach Road to the mouth of the Tahakopa and Maclennan Rivers. At low tide one can return via the estuary shore, a haunt of wading birds. Native bush walks will be found at the nearby holiday settlement of Papatowai, in the vicinity of the camping area.

A metric conversion chart appears at the end of the book.

on the peninsula "in comfortable little cottages, and had cleared and cultivated some ten acres of land, on which were grown wheat, barley, and potatoes. They also had ducks, fowl and goats." After about seven or eight years the station was abandoned.

Nearby the Otago Youth Adventure Trust has established a youth camp, where groups of schoolchildren stay while studying the area's natural environment. The Royal Forest and Bird Protection Society also maintains a lodge here, in its own private conservation reserve. The lodge is also available to non-members of the Society (*book through Mrs F. B. Bennet, Papatowai RD, Owaka; tel. 160M*).

Dr David Monro, also here in 1844, wrote: "Behind Tautuku a visitor may explore the mountain dreaded by the Natives on account of its being the favourite residence of the Mairoero (i.e. *maeroero* — the South Island equivalent of the North Island's *patupaiarehe*). This is a wild man of the woods, strong, cunning and mischievous, and addicted to running off with young people and damsels. His body is covered with coarse and long hair, which also flows down from the back of his head nearly to his heels. To compensate for this excessive quantity behind, his forehead is said to be bald. He was vividly described to us by a Maori who had seen one long ago, when he was a little boy, and was of opinion that there is not a more fearful wild fowl than the Mairoero living." *A short distance beyond the turnoff to the beach is:*

**Lake Wilkie**\*\*, a bushgirt lakelet in a picturesque setting, known to botanists for the unique plant life it supports. *A short, signposted walk of about 100 m leads to the lake's edge.*

**Cathedral Caves**\*\*\*: The most fascinating feature of this compelling coastline is a series of remarkable interlocking sea caves, between 30 and 50 m in height, some cut back into the cliffs for over 100 m. They were named by Dr Hocken's group in 1892, "as being appropriate from their ∧-shaped roofs and their reverberating qualities". Dr Hocken recorded "full test being made by whistling, singing, and coo-eeing". Coal seams may be seen in the cave entrances. The caves can be visited only from one hour before low tide to one hour after. Care must be taken at all times, as the occasional freak wave has drenched more than one visiting group. *38 km. On Waipati Beach. Turnoff signposted at 36.2 km south-west of Owaka on Highway 92. Tide times are generally posted at the start of the access road. 20 minutes' walk down a steep track from the end of the access road. A powerful torch is essential if one is to venture any distance into the system.*

**Waipati Beach:** If the tide is not right for a visit to Cathedral Caves a walk along the beach to the Waipati estuary wilderness area is a worthwhile alternative. *The beach is deceptive in length — allow 45 mins each way.*

**Cannibal Bay**\*\*\*: Dr Hocken noted in 1892, "History discloses no reason why this pretty beach should labour under its suggestive name except for the fact that some human skulls and bones were found here by Dr Hector." But Dr Hocken, his self-contradiction escaping him, went on to note that they discovered shell in a sandbank, "evidently the remains of a Maori feast many years ago", and dug into the bank — "Our spoils are trifling — a few fish and seal bones, a human kneecap and a portion of human backbone."

A low bank of dunes extends south-west to separate False Island from the mainland. One may climb some 70 m up the island for a magnificent view of the coastline and to see the remains of a windlass used by whalers who operated out of the cove below the point. Beyond False Island lies attractive Surat Bay, named after a migrant ship which in 1874 struck a rock farther down the coast. A hundred of her passengers were landed at Jacks Bay before, with all sails set and her ensign flying upside down, her captain sailed the sinking *Surat* straight on to the beach. The captain was considered drunk and was imprisoned, but some eyewitnesses claimed that he was quite sober. The ship was a total loss and much of her timber found its way into the construction of local houses.

Tradition relates that when one of Te Rauparaha's scouting parties came south it was ambushed at Cannibal Bay by Tuhawaiki. Te Rauparaha's men returned to attack hastily constructed fortifications and to drive the defenders up on to False Island, where many of them were killed — perhaps explaining the cannibal feasts. Tuhawaiki himself is said to have survived only by diving into the surf and swimming some 10 km to Tuhawaiki Island, off Jacks Bay. *11.6 km. Turn off Highway 92 down Cannibal Bay Rd. Signposted.*

## TOURING NOTE

For points of interest both north and south of Owaka see △ Invercargill-Balclutha Coastal Road.

---

Though we travel the world over to find the beautiful, we must carry it with us or we find it not. — Ralph Waldo Emerson (*Essays*).

**OXFORD     North Canterbury.    Maps 2 & 7.    Pop. 890.**

*67 km NW of Christchurch; 32 km E of Rangiora.*

AS A SETTLEMENT Oxford is as scattered as the population it serves. The town grew as the quite separate communities of West Oxford and East Oxford until in time the two merged to become a geographical entity.

A bush camp was established here in 1852 in conjunction with sawmilling, an industry which perished in 1898 when extensive forests were burnt out. Oxford is now the centre of a large area of sheepfarming, cropping and dairying. Its name is attributed to the education at Oxford University of a number of early Canterbury settlers. The intriguing name of Cust (*14.8 km E*) was bestowed by the Canterbury Association in honour of two of its leading members, J. H. Cust MP (educated at Oxford, UK) and General Sir Edward Cust.

There is tramping in the Puketeraki ranges to the north-west of the town.

### ENVIRONS

**Waimakariri Gorge\*\*\*** presents a dramatic sight as the river, at one moment trapped in the narrow confines of the gorge abruptly broadens, fanning out over the plain. There are picnic and swimming spots, jet boating and good trout and salmon fishing. *14 km SW*.

**Ashley Gorge\*\*\*:** Level ground shaded by poplars faces north to a well-bushed rock face rising sheer above the river. A pleasant camping and picnicking place. *8 km NNE*. There was once a flaxmill near here, employing more than 100 men as a plant of sixteen strippers processed flax from a swamp a short distance to the north of the riverbridge. The poplars hereabouts were planted by two swaggers at the instigation of a runholder, to prevent shingle from hillside gullies being washed over the flax swamp.

**St Cyprian's Anglican Church, Carleton,** with its unusual chimney, was built at West Oxford as a magistrate's court in about 1870. Bought by the church in 1936, it was remodelled internally and renamed after the lawyer who became Bishop of the Church in North Africa in about AD 300. *4.3 km E on Highway 72 on the corner of Steffans Rd.*

Consult the Index when looking for a name in this Guide.

**PALMERSTON     East Otago.    Maps 9 & 25.    Pop. 892.**

*56.5 km NNE of Dunedin; 59.5 km SSW of Oamaru.*

NEAR THE COAST in the lower valley of the Shag River lies the junction town of Palmerston, where "The Pigroot" to Central Otago leaves Highway 1. Above the village sweeps the seaward hill of Puketapu (sacred hill), named after a slave who in legend survived the wreck of the *Araiteuru* canoe (*see △Moeraki*). Capping its crest is a stone monument to Sir John McKenzie.

The township grew on the route to the goldfields and was once both important and considered likely to flourish. Its name even compelled Palmerston in the North Island to qualify its title — now by contrast a city that ranks among the country's largest provincial centres. The town is named after Lord Palmerston, prime minister of Britain for terms between 1855 and 1865. "A conservative at home, a liberal abroad" he was a minister for over fifty years yet "there is no enduring achievement to his credit, but he left many bitter legacies".

**Sir John McKenzie** (1838-1901): In the 1840s most of the coastal land between Seacliff and Palmerston, and inland as far as Shag Valley, was "Johnny Jones Country". It was cleared, cropped and grassed as he directed. Some years later McKenzie, as a young man, came from Scotland to shepherd on and finally manage Jones's Shag Valley run. With him he brought a Scot's keen interest in land questions and he was quick to acquire 24.3 ha when the run was cut up in 1865.

Over the next sixteen years McKenzie was elected to every possible public body with the sole exception of the House of Representatives. In 1881 this was remedied and he held his seat for twenty years until ill health forced his retirement. In Parliament he did not allow his natural reticence to impede his opposition to land laws that allowed abuses which effectively kept the small man off the land. When the Liberal Party came to power in 1890 he became Ballance's Minister of Lands and Agriculture, passing laws against "dummyism", to facilitate the subdivision of large estates, and finally compulsorily taking large private estates to open up "land for the people". In 1901 the Duke of York's train halted at the Shag Point siding where the ailing McKenzie stepped aboard to receive a popular knighthood. Six weeks later he was dead.

When the hilltop memorial was unveiled, Ballance's successor, Richard Seddon, said that McKenzie had "swept aside difficulties and quelled opposition by the irresistible force of success. The homesteads of settlers planted on the soil by his efforts," he said "will ever be his monument." Not so the memorial. After a few years it collapsed, to be later rebuilt here on a smaller scale. *A walking track leads to the summit of Puketapu where a plaque relates McKenzie's progression from shepherd to knight. Allow 1½ hours. In the annual race to the summit and back the distance is covered in under 20 minutes. Signposted.* From here there is an outstanding view of surrounding countryside and of the coast from Moeraki Peninsula to the north to Taiaroa Head to the south.

## ENVIRONS

**Shag Point\*:** Above a shoreline seething with kelp a collection of cribs is strung along the Point, off whose tip motionless shags may be seen congregated on the rocks. For centuries there was an important stronghold of the Ngatikane *hapu* of Ngaitahu on the end of the peninsula. Coal has been mined here since 1863, for many years being shipped out from the now-defunct Shag Point Harbour, today a place to launch boats. Traces of a long-departed branch railway line may be seen by the roadside. In 1890 the mines here saw an early confrontation between capital and labour. In a trial of strength the company was forced to re-employ two union leaders when infant unions closed ranks to black the company's activities. *Turn off 8.6 km N on Highway 1. The end of the peninsula is 2.7 km from the main road.*

**Shag River Mouth:** There is a Moa-hunter campsite here from which as recently as 1941 an incomplete egg was recovered. It is reputed to have been the culminating point of regular *moa* drives down the valley. Skeletons of giant birds from here are displayed in the Otago Museum at Dunedin. Offshore a prominent reef is said to be the *waka* (hull) of the *Araiteuru* canoe, and a prominent rock the mortal remains of its navigator, Hipo (*for the legend, see △ Moeraki). 7 km. Signposted.*

**Trotters Gorge\*\*\*:** An impressive picnic spot. Also an alternative route north. *12 km. Signposted. (See △ Moeraki.)*

## TOURING NOTE

△ **The Pigroot:** The early stages of the route into Central Otago are described under its own entry.

---

To make the most of your travels you should carry with you the book of Mobil road maps. A table of distances between major centres appears on page 363.

---

*21.5 km N of Geraldine; 51 km W of Ashburton. Forest Park Headquarters (tel. 826 Arundel) at Peel Forest township (pop. 130) for details of walks and tramps (no hunting).*

THE MIXED PODOCARP stands of Peel Forest Park on the South Canterbury foothills contrast sharply with the pine shelterbelts of the plains. As a verdant oasis on dry summer days — the region is otherwise largely denuded of native bush — the forest has a host of delightful picnic spots among trees and a series of walks to waterfalls. There is excellent salmon fishing in the Rangitata, particularly in February and March, though the river is not recommended for swimming. The river at nearby Orari Gorge is quite safe. A small camping ground is run by the park headquarters, who can also arrange scenic flights over the high country. The area was named after the British prime minister, Sir Robert Peel, who died in 1850.

## FLORA AND FAUNA

Native trees in the park include *totara, matai* (black pine), *kahikatea* (white pine), *konini* (fuchsia), *kowhai* and abundant varieties of fern. Indigenous birds are seen in good numbers, among them the native pigeon, kingfisher, numerous bellbirds, kingfisher, rifleman, tomtits, waxeye, the occasional ground lark and the odd *tui* and parakeet.

The area was not spared the plunder that marked the Canterbury settlement's first fifty years, when timber was scarce. The hamlet here was a brisk and busy milling settlement until, in 1908, it proved cheaper to import timber from Australia. The delightful area of Agnes Mills Bush was spared, and remains in its virgin state with native creepers, clematis and parsonia clinging to its trees and in season spangling the forest with the freckles of their white flowers.

## SOME WALKS

*A number of signposted walking tracks have been formed through the bush. Stout footwear is advisable.*

**Big Tree Walk:** An easy walk from the Stone Bridge through the virgin forest of Agnes Mills Bush leads to a splendid *totara* over 9 m in circumference. *Start from Te Wanahu Flat. Allow 1 hour.*

**Acland Falls:** An easy track, mainly through stands of *konini* and *mahoe* leads to the 15 m drop of the Acland Falls. *Start either from opposite the camping ground (allow 40 mins) or from Te Wanahu Flat (allow 1½ hrs).*

**Fern Walk:** A pleasant walk noted for its variety of ferns threads through the bush along the lower slopes, from the Stone Bridge to Blandswood. *Start from Te Wanahu Flat. 1¼ hrs to Blandswood.*

**Rata Falls** (*17 m*): A moderately difficult track leads to falls at once the highest and the prettiest in the park. The last section follows the creekbed and involves some rock hopping. In January and February the flowering *rata* are a feature of this walk. *Start from halfway up the hill at Blandswood. Allow 1¾ hrs.* For the less energetic, an easy track to **Emily Falls** (*8 m*) starts at the same point, but veers left. (*Allow 1¼ hrs.*)

## MOUNT PEEL STATION

**"To see for yourself":** To runholders John Acland and Charles Tripp the twin barriers presented by the hazardous Rangitata River and the near-impenetrable Peel Forest were dual blessings, as they ensured the isolation of their sheep in times when there was a real risk of strays contaminating the flock with scab. They were in no hurry to pierce the bush with a road, and it was for the timbermen to open it up, forming a way for drays along the track blazed by the station employees.

John Barton Arundel Acland (1823–1904) and Charles George Tripp (1820–97), both law graduates, became interested in the Canterbury settlement and on their arrival in the colony in 1855 they found that all the rich plains and lowlands had been taken up. With their limited capital, only £2,000 each, they elected to take up country hitherto presumed fit only for pigs. In a letter written at the time, Acland recorded the attitude of the experienced squatters, one of whom "laughed at our exploring and said that the banks of the Rangitata were perpendicular; he would not attempt to take a horse down for fifty pounds, and the opposite country impassable. We replied that it was very likely, but we had a fancy for looking at it. In the Colonies you always like to see for yourself, and the worse account you hear of unoccupied country, the greater the reason for going to look at it." So confident were they, that Acland and Tripp actually applied for runs before they had even been on the country. Setting out from Christchurch, they became the first Europeans to explore the upper waters of the Rangitata, Orari and Ashburton Rivers in the spring and summer of 1855–56. Only then did they take up the runs that were to become Mount Somers, Mount Possession, Mount Peel and Orari Gorge, as well as part of Mesopotamia and Hakatere.

In 1862 the partners divided the runs between them; Mount Peel becoming Acland's, and Orari Gorge and Mount Somers that of Tripp — Mount Possession had been sold the year before.

The Government halved the Mount Peel run in 1912, reducing its carrying capacity from 45,000 to below 20,000 sheep. The run has since been further reduced. It is one of few still to be owned by descendants of the original runholder, and has lately been farmed by Sir John Acland, knighted for his services to the Wool Board. The original family encouraged employees to marry and live on the station, envisaging the growth of a considerable community, but the land was not suitable for intensive farming.

**Mount Peel homestead and church\*\*\*:** The exquisitely proportioned homestead (1865) may be seen from the roadside some 8 km beyond Peel Forest settlement. Built of pitsawn timber and bricks fired on the property, the homestead is set in a plantation of century-old trees.

Close by is the Acland family church, the Church of the Holy Innocents (1868–69), which is open to visitors. The simple structure built of Rangitata River stone and Mount Somers limestone by William Brassington (the mason responsible for much of Christchurch's Provincial Council Chambers) is furnished with an altar and pews of *totara*. The church contains memorials and stained glass dedicated to members of the Acland family, and an ornate tablet to Charles Tripp. Without, at the east end of the church, is the grave of the original Acland with, close by, that of Elizabeth Hawdon (1851–1921) "the first born child of Christchurch, Canterbury", whose father was the celebrated early Christchurch photographer, Dr Barker.

The church is named after three infant children, among them Emily Dyke Acland (1864), who are buried in the churchyard. Both Acland and Tripp were devout churchmen, studiously observing church festivals even when alone in the bush on lengthy journeys of exploration. *8 km N of Peel Forest settlement turn left up a driveway just before reaching the homestead entrance, and park by the church.*

## OTHER POINTS OF INTEREST

△**Mesopotamia\*\*:** The run renowned as once being held by Samuel Butler lies at the road's end. *47.5 km NW.*

Consult the Index when looking for a name in this Guide.

**Little Mount Peel tramp:** A shelter has been built near the summit of Little Mount Peel (*1,307.9 m*), reached by a hard 3-hour climb. This is best made in the late afternoon, when one can shelter overnight and hope to see a spectacular sunrise.

**St Stephen's Church, Peel Forest:** Included in the stained-glass window is a representation of Milford Sound's Mitre Peak, dedicated to an early climber of the glacial wedge.

> The New Zealand Forest Service has offices throughout the country which issue permits for hunting in State Forests and in Forest Parks. They also advise as to the best hunting areas.

---

**PICTON    Marlborough.    Maps 6 & 22.    Pop. 3,276.**

*29 km N of Blenheim; 37 km E of Havelock (via Queen Charlotte Sound); 146 km E of Nelson (via Blenheim).*

PICTON IS A BUSTLING TOWN, busy with little ships and those who sail in them. As the South Island terminal for the Cook Strait rail-ferry, the many passengers and cars to and from Wellington ebb and flow with timetable regularity. In an incomparable setting at the head of exquisite Queen Charlotte Sound, the town enjoys a vista of green and blue bushclad ranges dropping sheer to a sheltered lakelike sea. The view is broken by the verdant hump of Mabel Island in the harbour's throat. Landward the town is ringed with steep hills.

The rapid growth in inter-island rail freight has seen the Waitohi River channelled and the mudflats at its mouth reclaimed for marshalling yards. Activity with the rail ferry and the occasional overseas ship to the west of the harbour is balanced by a multitude of small craft in and about the marina to the east. Linking the two is a developed foreshore with massive palms and a variety of amusements.

Picton is named after one of the Duke of Wellington's generals, a casualty at Waterloo.

There are deer and pigs nearby and unparalleled fishing in the Sounds themselves.

**Marlborough Walk:** Each year on a date in early January, hundreds of all ages set out from Blenheim on the 29 km walk to Picton. Leaving any time after 6 am and finishing by 6 pm, those who complete the journey in under twelve hours are rewarded with medals.

### SOME HISTORY

**Problems with The Beaver:** Picton's development is inextricably interwoven with that of Blenheim, the continued rivalry between the two settlements dividing the province of Marlborough and for years dominating the considerations of administrators to the detriment of the district.

Whereas Blenheim evolved from an economic base as the distribution centre for the Wairau, the site of Picton was carefully chosen by Nelson settlers for purchase by the New Zealand Company so that they might receive some measure of justice from the Company in the way of land grants. The committee of settlers opted for Picton on the score of its harbour and densely wooded forests.

The initial obstacle was a reluctance to sell on the part of the local Maoris of Te Atiawa, who established an important *pa* here after Te Rauparaha had conquered the region. But once the Maori owners were satisfied in 1850 and had moved to neighbouring Waikawa, the new landowners experienced frustration at the lack of any road and the rapid rise of The Beaver (Blenheim). The tiny village of Picton, largely a resort of timberworkers, vainly petitioned the Nelson Provincial Council for action, in 1856 adding to their complaints a lack of protection: "Robberies and Burglaries are becoming of daily occurrence and we are afraid to leave our homes by night or day."

Neglect on a wider scale led to the separation of the province of Marlborough from that of Nelson. For several tumultuous years Picton was the new province's capital (*see △ Blenheim*). If it ultimately lost that role to its bitter rival, Blenheim, Picton almost landed an even bigger prize when it was seriously considered as a site for the country's capital. A quaint reminder of the time when Picton was robbed of the title of provincial capital is to be found in the grounds of Holy Trinity Anglican Church. After the clock from the provincial-council building had been removed to Blenheim, a sundial was sent for from England and was safely placed in the churchyard (1871) so that no future political powers could interfere with it.

**The Cook Strait ferry:** For over a century the turbulent waters of Cook Strait divided the country's railway system into virtually two independent and unconnected sections. In December 1862 the *Southland Times* recommended that a New Zealand

Grand Junction Railway be built from Bluff to the Bay of Islands, with "powerful steamers spanning the vexed waters of Cook's Straits". Prime Minister Richard Seddon in 1898 suggested a ferry service between Picton and Wellington, and four years later his eventual successor, Sir Joseph Ward, predicted that a steamer rail ferry was "bound to come". Several committees reported unfavourably on the proposal, and not until August 1962 was the first roll-on roll-off car-rail ferry *Aramoana* put into service on a run which represents a milestone in the development of the country's road-and-rail services.

The ferries, operated by the New Zealand Railways, take about 3 hrs 20 mins to cross the Strait, leaving Picton and Queen Charlotte Sound by way of Tory Channel and making an essentially east-west passage. Only half of this time is spent in the open sea, one hour being spent in the sounds and some forty minutes in Wellington Harbour. *For points of interest in Queen Charlotte Sound and Tory Channel, see △ Marlborough Sounds.*

**Cook Strait:** The Strait itself, crossed by four major fault lines, 23 km across at its narrowest point and of depths of up to 365 m, lies in the westerly wind belt known as the "roaring forties". Gales of up to 240 km/hr have been recorded in the vicinity of Wellington. The strait represents the only large gap in a chain of mountains extending over 1,400 km, from Puysegur Point on the south-west tip of the South Island to the North Island's East Cape. It is thus a natural channel through which airstreams approaching central New Zealand are diverted and funnelled. As well as for its winds, the Strait has a deserved notoriety for currents as treacherous as they are erratic. Notwithstanding, there are legends of Maoris managing to swim the Strait, but it was not until 1962 that the first *Pakeha* was successful, when Barrie Devenport made the crossing in 11 hrs 13 mins. Fifteen months later the feat was repeated by Keith Hancox, in 9 hrs 34 mins. Both were helped by the local knowledge of the last of the Cook Strait whalers. The first woman conqueror was 15-year-old Meda McKenzie who, in 1978, swam the Strait in both directions.

## LAUNCH TRIPS***

A proliferation of launch trips round the enchanting △Marlborough Sounds compete for the visitor's attention. One should study the full range of available excursions before making a final selection. Deservedly popular are the mail runs, which scurry in and out of many coves delivering mail and stores to various homesteads throughout the sound. Halfday cruises leave for a variety of destinations, launches are available for charter by the hour, and self-drive boats may be hired. Fishing trips run to meet demand. A fast 24-hour water-taxi service is available.

Launch operators are in a colourful cluster at the corner of London Quay and Wellington Street (near the post office and the marina). They include Red Funnel Launches (*tel. 104K*), Friendship Launch Services (*tel. 255*) Friendship Cruises Ltd (*tel. 175*), The Cream Run (*tel. 887M*).

## OTHER THINGS TO SEE AND DO

**Smith Memorial Museum**\*\* emphasises the whaling trade carried on locally for nearly 140 years. Relics include harpoons and harpoon guns and numerous implements used in the catching, killing and rendering-down of the many luckless whales who were intercepted off the open coast by whalers based in the shelter of the Sounds. Others were slaughtered when they ventured into calmer waters to calve. *On foreshore domain, London Quay. Open daily 10.30 am–3 pm, Sept.-June.*

**Victoria Domain Lookout**\*\* offers a view back towards Picton and an extensive panorama of Queen Charlotte Sound. *2.5 km. Signposted on the way to Waikawa Bay.*

**Shelly Beach and Bob's Bay:** A humped footbridge straddles the mouth of the boating marina, leading across to the eastern harbour shore and to the Shelly Beach track. From Shelly Beach the track leads on for about a kilometre to end at Bob's Bay, a sheltered cove popular with swimmers and waterskiers.

**Echo:** The scow *Echo* lies beached opposite the entrance to the marina. Built on the Wairoa River in 1905, she shipped 14,000 tons of cargo each year across Cook Strait, from Blenheim to Wellington, until she was superseded by the rail-ferries in 1965. A major American feature film, highlighting her exploits when the *Echo* saw service in the Pacific during the 1939-45 war, was entitled *The Wackiest Ship in the Navy*. The scow is fitted out to serve as shore clubroom for a boat club.

**Essons Valley Reservoir:** A 3-km walk leads through bush to the reservoir. By night glow-worms may be seen at various points about halfway along the track. *Follow Devon St to its very end, passing under the railway viaduct and parking by the locked gate.* The more energetic may tackle **Mt Freeth** (*610 m*), a fairly easy walk, whence Mt Egmont may be seen on an exceptionally clear day.

## ENVIRONS

△**Marlborough Sounds**\*\*\***:** There are numerous guesthouses in secluded bays round the sounds. It is also possible to camp on some of the multitude of reserves. Local launch proprietors will ferry picnickers and campers and regularly deliver supplies and mail during their stay. *Camping details from the Department of Lands and Survey, PO Box 97, Blenheim.*

**Waikawa Bay** (pop. 70): Its bays now flecked with yachts, Waikawa was where Maoris living at Waitohi (Picton) moved after the purchase of the Picton site for the new town. Signs of early Maori occupation may be discerned on the gorse-covered approaches to the settlement (*enquire locally*). *5 km NE*. Some 3.2 km farther on, on Karaka Point, are traces of the village Te Rae-o-Te-Karaka, which featured in fighting as successive tribes invaded from the north.

> A traveller has a right to relate and embellish his adventures as he pleases, and it is very unpolite to refuse that deference and applause they deserve. —Rudolf Erich Raspe.

## SUGGESTED DRIVES

**QUEEN CHARLOTTE DRIVE—HAVELOCK ROUND TRIP**: *105 km. Leave Picton by way of Queen Charlotte Drive. The road climbs steeply to pass:*

**Lookout\*\*\*** (*1.6 km*): The best vantage point from which to view Picton and its surrounds. *The road crests the ridge to pass the freezing works and drop to:*

**Shakespeare Bay** (*3.7 km*): Here the hulk of the *Edwin Fox* lies stranded on the shore. Built from best Burma teak to the order of the East India Company and launched at Sulkeali (Bengal) in 1853, this once fully-rigged clipper in a varied career carried convicts to Fremantle, ferried troops to counter the Indian Mutiny and served in the tea trade before in 1873 making the first of five trips bringing migrants to New Zealand. With the advent of refrigeration she was converted to a freezer, holding meat until it could be shipped out. In this role she was brought to Picton where after several years, she was converted into a coal hulk. Final ignominy came when the once-proud clipper was reduced to a breakwater. A restoration society purchased for 10 cents the remnants of a vessel which over a century ago sold for £30,000. *The road climbs to cross Wedge Point and afford the first view of the Grove Arm. At times the road runs along a bush-dressed shelf, high above the water, with intermittent views of the Arm through the trees.*

**Momorangi Bay** (*14.6 km*): A grassed area by the beach is ideal for picnicking in a spot which offers swimming, boating and fishing. Onwards from here are views across the Arm to Anakiwa.

**The Grove** (*17.3 km*): A farming settlement in an attractive seaside setting.

**Anakiwa** (*detour at 19.8 km for 4 km*): A village nationally known as the headquarters of the Cobham Outward Bound School where young people participate in outdoor activity designed to promote self-confidence and leadership. The road ends on a grassed plateau a short distance beyond the school, whence a good walking track leads through the Iwatuaroa Scenic Reserve to Davies Bay and Bottle Bay (*allow up to 2 hrs*). Viewed across the Arm from here the hamlet of the Grove adds interest to a pretty scene. *Return to the Picton-Havelock road and continue through Linkwater (the turnoff to The Portage and Crail Bay and so named as it joins the heads of two sounds) to reach:*

△**Havelock** (*37 km*): A venerable village and the centre for activity on Pelorus Sound and beyond. (*If time allows, the outward trip may be extended by continuing to the old gold settlement of Canvastown (a further 10.5 km) and beyond to picturesque Pelorus Bridge ( a further 19.4 km). Return by way of Highway 6 through* **Renwick** (*66 km*), **Woodbourne** (*69.2 km*) (*for both see* △*Blenheim,* "*Environs*") *and* △**Blenheim,** *pivot point of the Marlborough region. At Blenheim turn north up Highway 1 to pass:*

**Tuamarina** (*86.7 km*): Setting for the Wairau Affray in which twenty-two settlers and a number of Maoris lost their lives. *Described under* △*Blenheim.*

**Collins Memorial Deer Park** (*97.9 km*): A deer park with picnic area and playground.

**PORT UNDERWOOD—TUAMARINA ROUND TRIP**: *103 km.* A slow road winds round fascinating Port Underwood before linking with Highway 1 for the return to Picton. *Leave Picton by way of Waikawa Bay Road to pass:*

**Waikawa** (*4.8 km*) (*see above*) and **Karaka Point** (*8 km*): A tongue of level rock protrudes into the bay. Apparently eminently defensible, Karaka Point, as the fortified village of Te Rae-o-Te-Karaka, featured in the wars which took place as successive tribes invaded from the north, usually obliterating the defenders and their history. In *c.* 1720 resident Ngatimamoe were driven out by Ngaitahu, and in the late 1820s the *pa* was again successfully attacked when defending Ngati Apa, with little knowledge of firearms, were overwhelmed by the muskets of Te Rauparaha's Ngati Toa. Tracks lead down onto the *pa* site itself, and to the beach below. *The road then assumes the somewhat tortuous character that it retains until Rarangi. It climbs to the:*

**Summit** (*300 m*) (*15.3 km*): A magnificent birdseye view down to Port Underwood looks across to the island of Horahora-Kakahu (*see below*), reef-tied to the mainland, where British sovereignty over the South Island was finally and formally proclaimed in 1840. The sheltered harbour arm contrasts sharply with the open sea beyond. *At 19.2 km, just before Oyster Bay, detour left to reach:*

**Ngakuta Bay** (*30.8 km*): A cairn here commemorates the founding of the Cloudy Bay Methodist Mission by the Rev. Samuel and Mrs Ironside, the second mission station to be established in the South Island. The cairn is on the site of Ironside's Ebenezer Church. A talented linguist, Samuel Ironside (1814–97) was able to preach an extempore sermon in Maori within five months of his arrival in New Zealand, in 1839. Working at Hokianga, he accompanied the local chiefs to the meeting at Waitangi and is said to have persuaded Tamati Waka Nene to make the famous speech which induced others to accept the terms of the treaty. Ironside signed as a witness. On 20 December 1840 the missionary arrived here to establish a mission station. It was immensely successful, converts travelling from here to all parts of the eastern South Island; in less than three years no fewer than sixteen churches had been erected in the region. Ironside warned Captain Arthur Wakefield against proceeding with the survey of the Wairau, and buried the dead leader of the Nelson settlement after he had ignored his advice. After the Wairau Affray the mission broke up. Many of the local Maoris elected to return to the North Island rather than face the anticipated reprisals. Ironside himself moved to Wellington, where for some years he was a knowledgable advisor on Maori affairs to successive governors. He later served in Australia, and died at Hobart.

By the roadside, a capstan from the US sailer *Homewood* records both the mission and the pioneer farmer Jerome Nugent Flood (1812–87), who grazed sheep here which he had earned by driving Weld's flock from Ocean Bay to Flaxbourne (*see index*) in 1847. Flood's solitary grave lies on a low knoll about 80 m back from the memorial. *Beyond Ngakuta Bay the road to Fighting Bay is barred at 30.6 km by a locked gate. Permission to use the private road beyond may occasionally be obtained from the District Electrical Engineer, tel. Nelson 81–149.*

**Fighting Bay** (*35.4 km*) is the South Island terminal of the Cook Strait cable that feeds power generated in the South Island to the North Island grid and vice versa. The bay's name is based on the belief that Te Rauparaha was almost captured here by Tuhawaiki but the probability is that the incident occurred by △ Lake Grassmere. The name is not devoid of relevance for it has been recorded that there were here "for long years old bones and broken skulls whitened on the foreshore". *Return to the turnoff and bear left to immediately reach:*

**Oyster Bay** (*48.5 km*): Originally Te Tio (the oyster), the name is an instance of a *Pakeha* adoption of the translation of a Maori name. In 1838 HMS *Pelorus* called here for wood, water and repairs before she left with John Guard to explore the sound which now bears the sloop's name. The bay saw whaling stations and shipping for forty years from about 1840. A cottage at the northern end of the bay, still lived in, was built by John Guard's son.

**Kakapo Bay** (*53.9 km*): Named after a dark-green, flightless bird (*Strigops habroptilus*), the bay was the site of a whaling station founded by John Guard. As many as 150 whalemen would muster here in season with perhaps twenty whaling-schooners moored offshore. Hundreds of tons of amber oil were drawn each year from trypots at the head of the beach. Guard, who had earlier founded a station at Te Awaiti, preferred Kakapo Bay to Tory Channel because a ship could make Cloudy Bay in any weather, and it was easier to tow a dead whale into Port Underwood.

When Samuel Ironside and his wife landed here he found "half a hundred rude whalers, scum of every maritime nation and of the convict settlements of Australia . . . and cannibals and pagans of the Ngatitoa and Ngatiawa tribes". He noted that "of the two races, the Maoris were on the whole the more desirable neighbours".

Opposite an old farmstead, still lived in by John Guard's descendants, is a tiny cemetery where the pioneer whaler and members of his family are buried. Also buried here, about 50 m away, is the Maori wife, Kuika Rangiawa, and two children of the trader James Wynen who was murdered at the bay in 1842. Local Ngati Toa were induced by Ironside to hand the murderer, a dissolute whaler named Dick Cook, to the authorities for trial. After Cook escaped conviction on a technicality (Cook's Maori wife was not permitted to give evidence against him), the resulting bitterness lingered to underscore Maori mistrust at the time of the Wairau Affray. Cook escaped the gallows but was soon afterwards drowned at Port Underwood.

John Guard (*c.* 1796–?) has rather obscure origins but emerges as a seaman off the New Zealand coast in 1823. On one of his trips he sighted whales in Cook Strait, and about 1828 established a whaling station at Te Awaiti, on Tory Channel, possibly the first European settlement in the South Island. Later he founded a second settlement here at Kakapo Bay. The plundering by Maoris of his schooner *Waterloo*, after she had been wrecked in 1833 caused him to abandon Te Awaiti.

For a short time he resumed trading, but in 1834 his barque *Harriet* was wrecked off the Taranaki coast. His wife and children were held captive while he went for a ransom of gunpowder, but returned instead with HMS *Alligator*, whose crew forcefully rescued Guard's family before wreaking a bloody vengeance on the Maoris who had killed and eaten the crew of the *Harriet*. Two years later the family settled here, whence Guard left to pilot HMS *Pelorus* and later the *Tory* on surveys round the coast. The founder of the whaling industry in Cook Strait then fades from history, probably leaving whaling in the 1840s in favour of farming round Kakapo Bay, where his descendants still live.

**Horahora-Kakahu Island signpost** (*55.1 km*): The signpost indicates the island where on 17 June 1840 British sovereignty was finally proclaimed over the South Island. The spot where the ceremony took place is marked by a white memorial (*visible from hereabouts*), towered over by a huge *macrocarpa* tree. (*See △ Akaroa for details of "The Race for Akaroa". See Introduction for an account of the acquisition of sovereignty over the South Island.*)

**Ocean Bay** (*56 km*): John Blenkinsopp (whose fraudulent land deal precipitated the Wairau Affray) had a whaling station here. When the Sydney solicitor Unwin, as mortgagee of the land Blenkinsopp claimed to own, tried to assert title to it, his firm sent a number of men and some cattle over to occupy the land hereabouts. None of the men survived, their deaths remaining a mystery. It was here in 1847 that Weld's sheep were landed for his Flaxbourne run. The bay, near the entrance to Port Underwood and facing Cook Strait, was named by early whalers as it commands a view of the open sea.

**Robin Hood Bay** (*63.1 km*): The bay was named before 1842 (when Samuel Ironside recorded it in his baptismal register) apparently by an early settler and after Robin Hood Bay in Yorkshire. Buried anonymously here is Te Rongo, Te Rangihaeata's wife and a near-relative of Te Rauparaha. It was her death in the Wairau Affray that provoked the execution of the *Pakeha* prisoners. The grave, which was desecrated by a *Pakeha* schoolteacher, is no longer visible. *About 5 km further on quite unexpectedly the Wairau Plain unfolds, and a dramatic view extends over the Wairau Bar and the lagoons to the ranges on the southern border of the plain. Continue on to detour at 70 km to:*

**Whites Bay** (*detour 2 km*): An appealing sheltered beach offers safe bathing at all times. About 200 m out it shelves steeply into deep water. The bay is named after an American whaling captain's slave boy, who deserted ship in 1828 to live here for many years. This was also the South Island terminus of the first telegraph cable to link the North and South Islands (1866). The original cable house (1867) still stands on the foreshore. It has been restored and houses a small collection of items appropriate to its history. (*Open most days. Enquire Marlborough County Council. Tel. 3248 Picton*). *Continue on to:*

**Rarangi** (*73.1 km*): An open, somewhat exposed beach sweeps south for several kilometres, offering good surfcasting. A track at its northern end leads past a deep sea cave and round the rocks to Whites Bay. *From here follow the signposted route to Tuamarina (site of the Wairau Affray; see △ Blenheim) and return to Picton by way of Highway 1.*

## ORGANISED EXCURSIONS

**Launch trips and fishing trips:** *See above.*

**Bus tours:** A variety of sightseeing tours is offered by Marlborough Scenic Tours Ltd (*tel. 262*), including a full-day round trip to Nelson (via Havelock and returning by way of the Kaituna Valley and Rapaura) and to The Portage (incorporating a launch trip across Queen Charlotte Sound). Half-day tours run to △ Havelock, Momorangi Bay and △ Blenheim, along Queen Charlotte Sound (incorporating detours to Anakiwa for a tour of the Cobham Outward Bound School and returning via Tuamarina), and a round trip along the shores of Port Underwood. *Some of the excursions incorporate launch trips. Book through Friendship Launches (tel. 255), Red Funnel Launches (tel. 104K) or Friendship Cruises (tel. 175M).*

**Scenic flights** operate, when conditions allow, from a strip at Waikawa Bay, and at all times from Omaka aerodrome, Blenheim. Amphibious craft also operate. The geomorphology of the Sounds is only fully appreciated when viewed from the air. A selection of local routes ranges over the quilted Wairau plain, the forested Pelorus Valley, and the △ Lake Grassmere salt ponds. *Marlborough Aero Club, tel. 4018 Blenheim; Float-Air Picton Ltd, tel. 433M Picton.*

## TOURING NOTES

**Highway 1 to** △ **Blenheim** passes the Collins Memorial Deer Park (*at 7 km*), the tiny timbered Anglican Church of St John in the Wilderness, Koromiko (*1871*) (*at 8.3 km*) and the Tuamarina monument to those killed in the Wairau Affray (*at 18.2 km; see* △ *Blenheim*).

**Highways 1 and 6 to Nelson:** The quickest route from Picton to Nelson is via Highways 1 and 6. Points of interest on the way are described under △ Blenheim and △ Havelock.

**Queen Charlotte Drive route to** △ **Havelock:** A slower if shorter and more scenic drive to Havelock is the route via Blenheim that follows arms of both Queen Charlotte Sound and Pelorus Sound. *37 km.*

The definitive history of the region is *Marlborough; A Provincial History* edited by Sir Alister McIntosh (Marlborough Provincial Historical Committee).

*78 km.*

THE PIGROOT is the name loosely given to Highway 85 which leads from △Palmerston through to the Maniototo Plains. The naming of the route has led to speculation that there were wild pigs here by the thousand who rooted up the ground in search of succulent speargrass roots. Others suggest that the name was bestowed by early wagoners disgusted with the road's condition. However it seems probable that the name derives from Pigroot Hill, a prominence named in 1857 by John Turnbull Thomson. In the course of his survey of Central Otago he ventured into an area where the animals were unafraid of man — so much so that a huge inquisitive boar actually rubbed noses with his horse, an incident Thomson later sketched. The name therefore belongs to "Thomson's farmyard", together with Horseburn, Sowburn, Hogburn, Fillyburn and other such names.

The route spawned the town of Palmerston, which grew up as a campsite on the Pigroot passage to the Central Otago goldfields, a route for all its name superior to the gruelling Old Dunstan Road (*see index*). Longer than the bleak and exposed Old Dunstan Road, The Pigroot offered an easier and more sheltered passage. Coach lines abandoned the Old Dunstan route in 1864, though some hardy wagoners continued to use it for several years.

As one climbs steadily up today's fast highway to the interior, the topography slowly changes. The landscape assumes the barren, glaciated look of the Maniototo and the stone buildings so typical of Central grow progressively more frequent.

## POINTS OF INTEREST ON THE WAY

△**Palmerston** (*78 km from Ranfurly*): A farming centre and junction town on Highway 1.

**Alexandra Hotel** (*c.* 1860) (*6.9 km from Palmerston: 71.1 km from Ranfurly*): The old stone hotel and its stables, hard by the roadside, may be restored as a local museum. In wagoning times there were no fewer than five hotels between Palmerston and the Pigroot halt — Alexandra, Carriers' Arms (Inch Valley), Junction (Dunback), Green Valley and Waihemo. The last named was bought by the Bell family and promptly closed as they found it too great a distraction for their employees. The rest fell victim to the "local no-licence" option at the turn of the century.

**Dunback** (*13.5 km from Palmerston; 64.5 km from Ranfurly*): In the height of the rabbit plague, a cannery here dispatched 260,000 rabbits in six months, handling 2,000 a day. Just north of the hamlet is the turnoff to △Macraes Flat.

**Waihemo Grange** (*16 km from Palmerston; 62 km from Ranfurly*): Built in the 1860s, the handsome steep-gabled stone homestead is seen from the highway to the south, tucked away among trees. The upper storey, added later, is said to have been haunted by the ghost of Mary Ann Evans, the novelist George Eliot. The run, once held by Johnny Jones, was later acquired by Captain J. Hamilton's partnership (of Hamiltons — *see* △*Ranfurly*). One of the group, Frederick Wayne, bought his partners out and built the homestead. His flock smitten with scab, Wayne was saved from ruin by his partner in an Irish venture, Col. Kitchener (father of Field Marshal Lord Kitchener), who bought the run from him for £20,000 in 1871. Older than the homestead are a barn-turned-crib and, opposite it, a since-enlarged shepherd's hut of schist. (*Turn north along Waynes Town Road at 15.8 km from Palmerston (62.2 km from Ranfurly) for 300 m to see the barn and the hut. Both are in private ownership.*)

**Shag Valley station** (*25.7 km from Palmerston; 52.3 km from Ranfurly*): The Shag Valley run was once held by the colourful Johnny Jones of △Waikouaiti. Impressive century-old stone shearers' quarters to the left of the homestead entrance date from his time. Jones's woolshed has not survived, venerable though its successor is.

He sold the run to Sir Francis Dillon Bell (1822–98) in 1864. Sir Francis, son of a London merchant trading in France, came to New Zealand in 1843 to purchase land for the New Zealand Company. Already fluent in French he quickly mastered the Maori language. Elected to the House of Representatives he made his mark as one who advocated Maori membership of the House and as one who believed in the invalidity of the Waitara Land Deal.

In 1869 he accepted a post in Fox's ministry and travelled to England with Featherston, where the pair's "courtly and attractive manners" helped raise a loan of £2 million for Vogel's public works policies. Later, as Agent-General in London, Sir Francis raised a further £8 million in loans. He might easily have achieved high political office but never courted popularity; too good an administrator to be a successful politician, he had the added handicap of being able to see too plainly the points of view of his opponents. As a pastoralist he realised from the outset that his class should retire automatically before the advance of the agriculturalist — something many others were vainly to resist. His son, Sir Francis Henry Dillon Bell (1851–1936) also achieved a knighthood for his public services. He made his mark as a reformer both of law and of institutions and, like his father, held a variety of cabinet posts over a long period. The younger Sir Francis became the first New Zealand-born prime minister when, on the death of Massey and in a caretaker capacity, he held office for little more than a fortnight in 1925.

## PIGROOT (The)—concluded

The management of the Shag Valley run was left to Sir Francis's second son, Alfred, who is credited with the making of the country's first telephone (an earlier telephone installed at Teviot was imported). A flair for communication runs in the family, as his son Frank made history in 1924 when from here he made the first short-wave radio communication with England (*A memorial is by the gate.*) The run, much reduced in size, is still held by the Bell family.

A short distance to the west of the entrance is the site of the Waihemo Hotel, popular with coaches, as its German proprietor would treat passengers to their fill of fruit from his orchard. Some of the trees survive, most notably a massive walnut whose size is attributed to the action of a Coal Creek shepherd. When 200 Merinos died in a shearing-time snowstorm he buried them around its foot.

**Green Valley** (*30.3 km from Palmerston; 47.7 km from Ranfurly*): On the south side of the road the former Green Valley coaching inn has been converted into a farmhouse.

**Pigroot summit** (*47.6 km from Palmerston; 30.4 km from Ranfurly*): 640 m above sea level.

△**Ranfurly** (*78 km from Palmerston*): Administrative centre for the Maniototo.

---

The Automobile Association has offices throughout the country and offers members a wide range of services, from a breakdown service and legal advice to maps and details of road conditions. Its annual handbooks, listing details of hotels, motels and camping grounds, are the most comprehensive available and are issued free to members.

---

## PLEASANT POINT     South Canterbury.   Maps 3 & 35.   Pop. 1,019.

*19 km NW of Timaru; 14.5 km W of Temuka.*

A BROAD GREEN SWATHE sweeps through Pleasant Point, a township sloping gently to the sun, marking the route where once the railroad ran. The old station still stands, beside it the *Fairlie Flyer*, the two combining to form the focal point of the township and a unique railway museum. "The Point" is a junction. Here the rivers Tengawai and Opihi meet to embrace a large area of fertile land, and here also converge many roads — from Cave, Totara Valley, Opihi, Waitohi and Timaru.

### SOME HISTORY

**From outstation to village:** Sheep now graze on many of the townsites wishfully set aside throughout South Canterbury by the Canterbury Provincial Council. The Council clearly hoped that the district would support a much greater population than it does even today, and doubtless envisaged a liberal scattering of little "English" villages, providing ready labour for landowners. Ironically Pleasant Point, an example of what the Council had in mind, in fact emerged not by design but grew up round Hodsock, an outstation on the Rhodes brothers' Levels run. Its name, at first The Point, came from a feature on the river, a landmark for travellers moving inland up the Opihi. To its residents the town today remains simply, The Point.

### THINGS TO SEE AND DO

**Pleasant Point Railway and Historical Museum\*:** The museum, housed in the old station buildings, was formed to preserve the town's associations with the *Fairlie Flyer* that plied the branch line to Fairlie for eighty-four years before the line was closed in 1968. The original booking office is in the style of the 1930s, when rail travel was at its peak. A display of railway equipment extends back over nearly a century. Ab 699, the restored locomotive standing in the station, was built in Thames (NZ) in 1922 and in forty-six years of service covered over 2 million km. *Main St. Open Sun. from 1.30–4.30 pm and extended hours during summer and holiday periods; enquire at Public Relations Office, Timaru.*

### ENVIRONS

**Pioneer Park\*:** A 34-km drive past the park's memorial gates leads to an area of magnificent exotics in whose shade one may picnic before setting off for walks in native bush. The 510 ha park, established in 1958, had its genesis in a gift of land from a vocal conservationist and owner of Raincliff and Mount Torlesse stations, Percy Hawkins Johnson (1868–1955). A specialist in Black Poll Angus cattle, Johnson was a foundation member of the New Zealand Alpine Club and, with "Guy" (George Edward) Mannering and Marmaduke Dixon, came close to being the first to conquer Mt Cook. The gates also remember T. D. Burnett (*see index*). In the park, at the road's end, are the remains of a hut built *c.* 1853 by Michael John Burke (*see index*) after whom Burke Pass was named.

The park was once part of adjoining Raincliff station, which Burke took up in 1853. He held the run he knew as South Downs until 1858, when he sold the pastoral licence to about 22,500 ha together with 2,000 sheep, for £5,500. Much of the run was later freeholded, and when it was subdivided in 1901, Raincliff was carrying 30,000 sheep. The limestone homestead, the third, stands out of sight from the road in what is perhaps the most splendid of all the South Canterbury homestead plantations, and is approached by way of a driveway flanked with beeches. It was at Raincliff that Jessie Mackay (1864–1938) wrote much of her early poetry, while her father managed the run. Well known as a suffragette and prohibitionist, she used her considerable talents to promote the feminist cause. At her death she was receiving a Civil List pension. An award for verse established by the PEN Society commemorates her name, but her poetry today is not highly regarded.

The drive to Pioneer Park from Pleasant Point passes several points of interest. At 17 km, on the left, the attractive two-storeyed limestone homestead (1874) of Rockpool stands near the road, behind twin walnut trees. Built of stone quarried on the property, it relates perfectly to its setting.

**St David's Anglican Church** (1907), Raincliff, is passed at 18 km, a church built on land given by Arthur Hope, then owner of Raincliff, and containing a wall-brass in memory of the Purnells, who purchased Raincliff from Burke.

A group of Maori rock drawings are beneath a rock overhang, on the right hard by the roadside at 19.2 km. At 20.2 km one passes the entrance to Raincliff station.

**Hanging Rock Bridge\*:** A delightful picnicking and swimming spot by the Opihi River where a limestone bluff, abruptly undercut by the river, juts out over the water. At the northern end of the bridge another overhang that once sheltered Maori rock drawings has had its archaic art obliterated by vandals. *11.2 km NW. Signposted.*

---

**PORT CHALMERS\*\***     **East Otago.**    **Maps 9 & 11.**    **Pop. 3,123.**

*12 km N of Dunedin*

PORT CHALMERS, heavy with the atmosphere of a town preoccupied with ships and shipping, leans back from the sea in a crook in the Otago Harbour. On an elevated site, overlooking the solid town centre, rises the clock-towered stone spire of the Church of Iona. Opposite, on the headland and commanding the harbour, stands the splendid signalmast said to have once served as mainmast on the pirate ship *Cincinnati*.

Towards the heads, hulks lie rotting that include the *Don Juan*, reputedly a Spanish slaver. In less sinister vein the port has a place in history; it was here that the Otago Block was purchased and the first Dunedin settlers arrived; it was from here that the first trial cargo of frozen meat was shipped to Britain in 1882 (*see* △*Oamaru*) and here that three Antarctic explorers called; Scott, Shackleton and Byrd.

Today some of the shipping trade has been lost to the Dunedin waterfront, but despite dire predictions through the years the town has survived; as a suburb for Dunedin, as home to a substantial fishing fleet, and as the deep-water port of Otago, it has been revived by the advent of container shipping.

Tentatively named New Edinburgh, the port was renamed at the settlers' request after the Rev. Dr Thomas Chalmers, a leader in the Scottish Disruption of 1843 and in the resultant Free Church of Scotland.

## SOME HISTORY

**The gateway to Otago:** The town saw the beginnings of Otago settlement in several respects. It was on the foreshore here that the deed to purchase the Otago block was signed in 1844 (*see index*), and here, too, that the pioneer settlers first landed from a boat off the *John Wickliffe* on 23 March 1848 to found both the province and the port (*Plaques mark the site in Beach St, opp. the Post Office*).

For some time the port was indeed the gateway to Otago, but its prosperity was steadily if slowly eroded when the Victoria Channel was opened to bring shipping and development to the Dunedin waterfront on the Upper Harbour. The channel was systematically dredged and enlarged, to the greater detriment of Port Chalmers. The development involved substantial borrowing that saw a Bill to authorise a loan of £700,000 imperilled when in 1884 Port Chalmers' Member of Parliament, James Macandrew (a former superintendent of Otago), successfully moved that the figure "6" replace the figure "7". The Bill was in jeopardy but Vincent Pyke, the Member for Dunstan, retrieved the situation for Dunedin by moving the addition of the words "ninety-nine" to raise the total to £699,000 — it being impossible to restore the original amount once the House had given its decision. Battle was then waged by a Port Chalmers group determined to gain a greater share of loan moneys for the town's port. But as the Minister of Marine was none other than W. J. M. Larnach, it is not surprising that efforts to have the Minister investigate alleged misuse of loan money by overspending on the Upper Harbour, came to nought. The geographical handicaps of nature weighed heavily in favour of Port Chalmers, but the will of the commercial community in Dunedin prevailed, and the further development of the Victoria channel proceeded.

## THINGS TO DO AND SEE

**Port Chalmers flagstaff**\*\* occupying a commanding position on the headland, was one of a chain of three signal stations used to control shipping in the harbour, the others being at Taiaroa Head and on Signal Hill. It is supposedly built from the mainmast of the pirate ship *Cincinnati*, sailed by Captain "Bully" Hayes (*see index*) described by Robert Louis Stevenson as "a naval hero, whose exploits and deserved extinction left Europe cold". The flagstaff was restored in 1971 after a move to demolish it had been thwarted — opposing restoration one local councillor protested that it commemorates a murderer and a rapist and so should be ripped down and given to elderly pensioners for firewood. The *Cincinnati*, old and decrepit, had put into Port Chalmers, and Hayes, as was his practice, ran up debts, took on stores and attempted to put to sea without paying, but this time had his ship impounded. The ship was condemned and never sailed again. Hayes was accused of having taken passage-money from intending passengers in Sydney and of sailing without them but, before leaving for Arrowtown, he claimed they had refused to accept the accommodation he offered. *Flagstaff Lookout.* A plane table identifies points of interest.

**Iona Church**\*\*: Built in 1883 on a prime site, the former Presbyterian church, now the United Church of Port Chalmers, dominates the landscape of the little township with its stone clock-tower rising some 50 metres. The stone church was completed in times of prosperity, and the depression that followed was exacerbated by the loss of shipping (and so parishioners) to the Dunedin waterfront. It was thirty-three years before the church was free of debt. The original church on the site (1852) was the second in Otago and only the third Presbyterian church in the South Island. Its successor (1871) still stands and adjoins the later building to serve as its hall. *Church St.*

The **Anglican Church of the Holy Trinity** (1874) is built of local stone. The building's plain coloured glass projects intriguing light-patterns on to rough-textured walls. *Scotia St.*

**Original Union Steam Ship Company building** (1865?): A reminder that one of today's prominent shipping companies had its origins at Port Chalmers is this three-storeyed brick building, by the portside entrance to the rail tunnel. The company was formed in 1875 by Sir James Mills (1847–1936). He had a dazzling career in the employ of Johnny Jones, on whose death he became, at only twenty-two, manager of Jones's Harbour Steam Company. Six years later as an enterprising twenty-eight-year-old he used the Harbour Company as the basis on which to build the Union line. *Turn right by the Post Office (1877) and cross the railway line.* Now occupied by Skeggs Fisheries.

**Koputai Museum:** A small collection of local interest. *Pioneer Hall, George St. Hours vary.*

**Some hulks:** The port has been the graveyard for many ships once their usefulness ended. The remains of several can be seen, of which the more interesting include the 3,585-ton SS *Broxton*, built in Seattle in 1918 and in her time reputedly the largest wooden steamship afloat. She traded coal from Newcastle and the USA and visited Port Chalmers on her maiden voyage. Arrested for debt at Lyttelton in 1923, she was bought by the Union Steam Ship Company and converted into a hulk. She now acts as a buffer for ships entering and leaving the dock. (*Seen on the waterfront 300 m north of the Post Office.*)

Immediately north of the old slip in Careys Bay lie the remains of a floating dock (1868) built by a local syndicate as the largest marine structure in Australasia. Close by are the bones of the *Moa*, a 219-ton brig and the first vessel of substance to be built in Auckland. Her keel was laid down in 1845 and she was launched four years later to serve in the Australian trade and as a naval coal depot ship in the Land Wars.

Farther still round the shore, in Deborah Bay, lies the most romantic wreck, that of the *Don Juan*, a Spanish slaver and by repute a pirate vessel. She was purchased in 1874 by William Larnach's partner, Walter Guthrie, from Jose Antonio Garcia y Garcia, in San Francisco, as the *Rosalia*. Once brought to Port Chalmers an examination revealed that she had been the *Don Juan*, a British-owned ship registered at Liverpool. Refused a certificate of seaworthiness she was converted into a hulk and used as the local office of the Union Steam Ship Company. An old Spanish log was found that established the ship's connection with the slave trade, a situation reinforced by the wrist and ankle shackles discovered in the hold. Her decks had been pierced for guns but no further evidence has been found that she was once a pirate. (*2 km; at low tide her ribs protrude from the water close in by the shore.*)

Everything in life is somewhere else, and you get there in a car. — E. B. White (*One Man's Meat*).

**Scott Memorial**\*\*\*: From the base of the anchor-capped column that affirms the port's link with Scott of the Antarctic is a superb view over the town, spreading to left and right across the point, and of the Lower Harbour. Offshore "Quarantine Island" (*see index*) points across to the Portobello Peninsula, all but dividing the harbour in two. Port Chalmers was Scott's last port of call on his illfated expedition of 1910. *1.7 km on the road to Waitati.*

## ENVIRONS

**Aramoana:** At the northern side of the harbour entrance is an assortment of cribs by an ocean beach good for swimming and for surfcasting. On the harbour side are tidal mudflats with shellfish and a varied array of birdlife, among them godwits, pied oystercatchers, black-billed gulls and the rare Siberian wader. From the mole may be seen the Taiaroa Head Lighthouse, the occasional seal, and huge albatrosses wheeling as they circle their colony across the water. The tidal area is a possible area for reclamation for industrial use. Midway to Aramoana is a particularly attractive aspect looking back across the bays to Port Chalmers. *10 km NE.*

**Murdering Beach:** A picturesque scene of slaughter where local Maoris, in 1817, provoked beyond endurance, attacked a sealing party in one of few clashes between Maori and sealer in the area. The sealers grossly overreacted, destroying an entire village here. *11 km NE. Described under* △ *Dunedin, "Suggested Drives".* Just beyond lies Kaikai Beach, one of the country's oldest habitation sites; named by early visitors after the chief whose *hapu* lived here.

**Purakanui** (pop. 99): A tiny retreat near the prominence that housed the Mapoutahi *pa. 10.3 km N. Described under* △ *Dunedin. "Suggested Drives."*

> Public Relations Offices in larger centres will generally assist with accommodation, maps and travellers' problems.
> Their addresses and telephone numbers are given at the beginning of appropriate entries.

## PUKAKI (Lake)\*\*\*      South Canterbury.   Maps 16 & 34.

*38.5 km NNE of Omarama; 48 km SW of Tekapo.*

"THE SCENERY of this part of the Waitaki is magnificently picturesque," wrote its first surveyor, John Turnbull Thomson in 1857, "yet possessing so much dreariness, wildness, and sterility, as to be forbidding, and to the solitary traveller appalling." Thomson's description of the Waitaki is still apt, as the paradox of hostility and wild beauty remains.

The view up the glacier-formed lake to the Southern Alps as they rise abruptly to culminate in Mt Cook, a tableau occasionally perfectly mirrored in the lake's milky waters, is a spectacle for all seasons. The country's tallest peak, seen from Highway 8 at 8 km east, is best viewed from the road along the lake's east bank, leading to Mount Cook station. Pukaki village has been re-established on the lake, which is being raised to form the main storage lake of the Upper Waitaki power scheme (*see Twizel*). Here the approach road to The Hermitage and △ Mount Cook National Park leaves Highway 8.

Pukaki means head of the creek, but there is a legend that Rakaihautu (who scooped out the southern lakes) saw its bulging outlet and called it *pu* (heaped, or bunched up) *kaki* (neck).

**Two runs:** Mount Cook station, at the head of the lake, is unique in that it is the only property in the Mackenzie still to be held by descendants of the original runholders. It was taken up in 1856 by Andrew and Catherine Burnett, to whom their son, Thomas Burnett (*see index*) built the memorial church at △Cave. He was also responsible for the memorial at Burkes Pass, the inscription on which is typical of his concern for the environment. One of the first to see the dangers of denuding the countryside, Thomas Burnett was vocal to the end, his last speech in Parliament being devoted to the menace of erosion. The foundations of the first Mount Cook homestead, a one-roomed hut of black birch logs, still remain (*83 km up the lake's east bank*).

To the south of the lake lies the homestead block of the early run of The Wolds, the first of the Mackenzie runs to be taken up, in 1856 by Francis Sinclair and John McHutcheson. The latter, after living for a fortnight on rice and sugar, walked the 100 km to the nearest store — at Timaru — and set off home with a 15 kilo swag the next day. Soaked in a river crossing, he determined to reach his home that same day and made The Wolds by midnight, having walked from Timaru to Pukaki in less than fifteen hours. He confessed, "I was so thoroughly done up, that I lay in bed for 30 hours afterwards, too wearied to move a limb or wink an eye." The run was named by its next owner, Ostler, after his Yorkshire birthplace. Tennyson's couplet is as appropriate for here as it is for Yorkshire: *The long dun wolds are ribbed with snow, And loud the nor-land whirlwinds blow. (Passed at 28 km east, en route to Tekapo.)*

| QUEENSTOWN | North-West Otago. | Maps 29, 30 & 36. | Pop. 3,133. |
|---|---|---|---|

*171.5 km NE of Te Anau; 93 km NW of Alexandra; 285 km NW of Dunedin; 187 km NNE of Invercargill; 493 km SW of Christchurch (via Fairlie). A Public Relations Office (a commercial concern) helps with accommodation and books scenic trips. Queenstown Mall, tel. 540.*

THE SOUTH ISLAND'S most frequented resort slopes in a seductive setting to the waters of Lake Wakatipu, where tame trout wait idly to be fed. All around is the contrast between smooth, glacier-rounded hills and the jagged summits that reached above the ancient ice floor. Visitors from the world over congregate here in all seasons to lend the town a gay, cosmopolitan air.

Local folklore tells of gold prospectors pronouncing the town as "fit for any Queen" and then formally christening the settlement "Queenstown" on a blacksmith's anvil.

### SOME MYTHOLOGY

**The hollow of the giant:** In mythology there lived here a *tipua* (demon) named Matau who captured a beautiful girl and took her back to his mountain home. She was rescued by her lover who, while the enervating nor'wester blew, set fire to the giant as he lay sleeping on a bed of fern. The flames licked his body, causing him to draw his knees up in pain, but before he could gain consciousness he was suffocated by the smoke. The flames were fed by fat from his enormous body, and as the fire burned he sank deeper and deeper into the earth to form a vast chasm. Only his heart was not reduced to ashes. Rain began to fall and snow on the mountainsides was melted by the heat of the fire. Soon the chasm had filled with water to form a lake whose outline mirrors the outline of the giant with his knees drawn up in agony — his head at Glenorchy, his knees at Queenstown and his feet at Kingston. To this day his heart is beating to produce the eerie if slight and always rapid rise and fall in the lake's level, the reason for which remained unexplained until comparatively recently. (*There are similarities between this myth and that of the Clutha (Matau) River, see △Balclutha. However some authorities do not consider them to be of identical origin.*)

Wakatipu is a contraction of Whakatipua (*whaka*, or *whanga*=space; *tipua*, or *tupua*=demon), space of the giant.

Other legends also explain the making of the lake, one of which recounts how, with other inland lakes, it was dug out by Te Rakaihautu with a fabled *ko* (digging stick). Wakatipu was the greatest of the lakes he dug, being so long and so deep. (This legend has the added advantage of according with the geological explanation.)

### SOME HISTORY

**The water of greenstone:** The Maori would journey to Lake Wakatipu in his quest for greenstone. Deposits were found near the lake itself, though of a variety not as highly prized as that of Westland. One of the fabled greenstone routes to Westland led from the head of the lake by way of the Hollyford Valley.

The lake was deserted when young Nathaniel Chalmers (*see index*) in 1853 saw the expanse of water from the heights of the Remarkables. He did not descend to the lake itself, which his guide Reko told him was called Te Waipounamu (the water of greenstone). Instead they crossed the Kawarau River by the "natural bridge" over which generations of Maoris had preceded them and so many gold prospectors were to follow.

It was some three years later that the first Europeans visited the lake itself, when John Chubbin and his party reached Kingston. It was a common practice for explorers to burn the land as they went, for it was otherwise almost impassable, high with speargrass and choked with *matagouri*. Here fire turned on the group. John Morrison carelessly lit his pipe and the resulting blaze forced them to wade well out into the chilly lake there to stay up to their necks with their horses for about three hours, until the fire burnt itself out.

Another three years passed before the first *Pakeha* sailed on the lake. The Highlander Donald Hay, explored it by *mokihi* (flax raft) despite the bitter cold of midwinter, 1859. In the course of his visit Hay came across an exquisite little lake, today called Lake Hayes (often mistakenly attributed to the notorious blackbirder, "Bully" Hayes). After an enterprising four months Hay went to Dunedin to apply for the run he wanted, only to find that a speculator on the Land Office staff had already taken it. He refused Hay's offer, and the hard-done-by Highlander returned to Victoria.

**Enter William Rees:** "Speargrass, often more than three feet high, and masses of *matagouri* constantly impeded us, especially in the gullies. Our trousers from the thighs downwards were filled with blood and it was with the greatest difficulty that our poor horses and pack mule could be urged to move forward." So did William Gilbert Rees (1827–98) describe his historic journey from Moeraki. The going had been so tough that three of his party of five had turned back, leaving Rees to continue with only Paul Nicholai Balthasar Tunzelmann von Alderflug (1828-1900) — the son of a Russian army officer and said to have been a godson of the Czar.

Together the pair explored the lake and then — it is said, but seemingly without foundation — drew lots to determine which side of the lake each would have. The pair travelled back to Dunedin to claim the runs they wanted, burning

# QUEENSTOWN AND ENVIRONS

off as they went in anticipation of driving in sheep. Rees settled on the future site of Queenstown and von Tunzelmann (as he was more usually known) on the far side of the lake. Some placenames were bestowed: Rees gave a list that included "Shotover River, named by myself after my late partner's property near Oxford (G. Gammie); Rees River, named by my cadet, Alfred Duncan, whom I put in charge of the first sheep I sent up to the Head of the Lake; Mount Alfred, named after Alfred Duncan; River Von, named after my friend and companion, Nicholas von Tunzelmann, who took up a station on the north side of it; Cecil Peak and Walter Peak, named by surveyors after my eldest son's Christian names; Frankton, named by Sir John Richardson, then Superintendent of Otago, after my wife's Christian name, Frances; Mt Nicholas, named after Nicholas von Tunzelmann; Bob's Cove, named after my first boatman, Bob Fortune; Crown Range, named by myself from remarkable mass of rocks at highest Point; Coronet, ditto."

For two years they were undisturbed as they stocked their runs and formed minute communities in an otherwise vast loneliness. They were not to be lonely for long.

**"The richest river in the world":** Rees's days were numbered when William Fox and his party found gold in the Arrow (*see* △*Arrowtown*). Rees quietly supplied them with provisions, being concerned that there be no general rush, at least before his shearing was finished. He was as anxious as Fox to keep the strike secret. As fate would have it, no sooner had shearing begun in November 1862 than two of the shearers, Thomas Arthur and his mate Harry Redfern, had a prospect in the Shotover, taking out several poundsworth of gold simply with a pannikin and a butcher's knife. Rees could see that it was fruitless to try to contain their excitement. He paid them off, gave them provisions and watched them go. With a third man they pegged out the renowned Arthur's Point claim and within two months the trio had won £4,000.

There followed the largest rush the country has ever seen. There was gold everywhere. Rees's temporary role was to abandon farming to keep the thousands supplied with food and to ferry diggers up the lake from the site of Kingston. Though perfectly placed to profiteer, Rees was not one to capitalise on such a situation, and served the diggers both as ferryman and supplier at prices substantially lower than others in a similar situation elsewhere. The measure of this remarkable man is shown by the trust that reposed in him. Before the arrival of police and gold escorts, diggers would leave as much as 5,000 ounces of gold at a time with him, without weighing it and without asking for a receipt. His famous whaleboat took the first gold to the foot of the lake, all of 25,000 ounces and all on trust.

Rees's station homestead, which he called The Camp, quickly became a settlement and formed the nucleus of today's town. As diggers flocked into the district, Rees simply demolished his woolshed and rebuilt it as the Queen's Arms Hotel — the predecessor of today's Eichardt's. Already miners were making incredible journeys to the upper reaches of the Shotover River. On Mt Aurum, the "golden mountain", they found the quartz reefs of Bullendale; they worked alluvial drifts at Skippers and at Stoney Creek; and they made rich strikes such as the phenomenal find at Maori Point. There Dan Erihana (Ellison) and Hakaraia Haeroa went to the rescue of a dog when it was swept downriver and before nightfall had collected a full 25 lbs of gold from the surrounding rock crevices. The Shotover River, the *Otago Witness* boldly proclaimed, was "the richest river in the world".

**A disappointed Rees:** Just before the rush, Rees had applied for the freehold of about 32 ha, the homestead block that included the site of today's town. His application was now refused, Rees protesting furiously that as runholder he held the pre-emptive right of purchase. More than this, his entire lease of over 40,500 ha of pastoral land was cancelled. "Nothing I can get will compensate me for that run," Rees declared. Queenstown was surveyed, and on the first day of sales the Government recouped almost the entire £10,000 it had paid the reluctant Rees.

The embittered Welshman removed himself to Kawarau Falls (where his cottage still stands) but did not let the Government's parsimony sour his enthusiasm for the area. Particularly he is remembered for his sporting interests — he was a champion athlete and, as a talented cricketer, played for Otago against the All England team of 1864. He is said to have given his cousin, the immortal Dr W. G. Grace (with whom he shared his Christian names), his first cricket bat, though this is improbable as that greatest of all cricketers had a father and several older brothers who were also enthusiasts of the game.

Rees did not fare as well as he deserved. In 1867 he left to become manager of Galloway, near △Alexandra, and later became a stock inspector. Von Tunzelmann met with little better luck, being eventually ruined by the ravages of rabbits.

**Vogel's Vision:** Sir Julius Vogel in 1889 published *Anno Domini 2000*, a prophetic book that described New Zealand as Sir Julius thought it would appear at the end of the millennium. In it he visualised the future damming of the Kawarau River, and related how, as the river's waters receded, those watching experienced "delirious joy" as gold was taken out by the shovelful.

Dreams of gold by the ton — "Indeed, could it reasonably be measured in terms of tons?" asked the company — inspired the founding of the Kawarau Gold Mining Company in 1921, an enterprise which caught the imagination of speculators in New Zealand and throughout Australia. Consents were obtained and in 1924 work on a dam at the outlet to Lake Wakatipu was begun. Construction took two years instead of three months, and cost nearer £100,000 than the budgetted £30,000. However on 23 August 1926 thousands assembled on the Frankton Flat to witness for themselves the miracle foretold by Vogel. But though the gates were closed they all went home disappointed as the river level had not fallen at all. For days the impatient and increasingly apprehensive speculators waited. When eventually the water level did start to abate, it revealed debris of mining from earlier times, showing that at some stage the river had fallen naturally and had been worked over. A little gold was won, but the scheme was fundamentally misconceived, for the Shotover and Arrow Rivers continued to flow into the Kawarau, and their waters flooded back up the gorge to create a still lake between the river junctions and the dam. Proposals to dam the two tributaries predictably found little support amongst the disillusioned investors. In any event, too, very deep shingle was revealed that barred any substantial recovery of gold.

The gates were closed again in 1927 for two months, when experienced miners managed to win a paltry 78 ounces — a meagre return for their considerable effort. Again, during Depression years they were closed to enable the unemployed to fossick the river. But Vogel's Vision remains unfulfilled, and the dam remains as a symbol of the hopes and heartbreaks of hundreds of investors.

The project was not altogether futile. It has provided in the control structure a useful roadbridge between Frankton and Kingston, which also gives limited control over the lake's level to augment water storage for power generation at △Roxburgh.

### SKIING AT CORONET PEAK

The dry powder snows of Coronet Peak (*1,619.6 m*) offer the best skiing in Australasia. The season extends from about July to September, when enthusiasts from all round the Pacific congregate to enjoy the possibilities of the mountain's treeless slopes.

# QUEENSTOWN STREET MAP

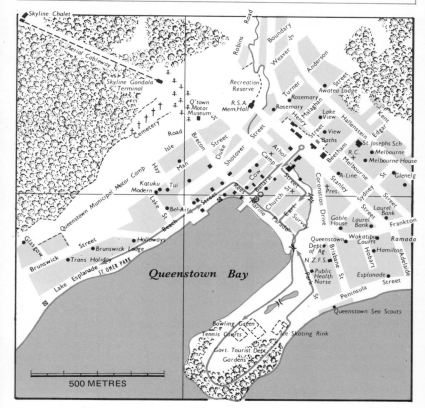

## 30

500 METRES

Buses from Queenstown each winter's morning take skiers the 18 km to the Alpine Restaurant, some 1,188 m above sea level. From there a fast Pomogalski chairlift rises vertically for almost 450 m, practically to the summit where the view alone is worth the journey — indeed, the chairlift runs in summer also to enable non-skiers to enjoy the far-reaching alpine panorama. As well as the chairlift, there are Pomos and ski-tows. Except in the August school holidays, winter accommodation is less of a problem than elsewhere, as the town is geared for a much larger influx of visitors in summer. *All necessary equipment is available for hire. Professional instructors conduct a ski school.*

## A WALK AROUND THE TOWN

*Allow 1 hr. Park by the library (cnr Ballarat and Stanley Sts).*

**Old stone library** (1876–77): was built in conjunction with the courthouse (1875–76), the two sharing a party wall. The little cluster of buildings combines with splendid trees to enshrine the atmosphere of old Queenstown. The two giant *sequoia* were planted a century ago by a town clerk who claimed that every courthouse in California had "trees of justice" in whose shade witnesses could sit while waiting to be called. *Walk down Ballarat St, cross the little humped stone bridge (c. 1863) and turn left along Camp St to pass:*

**St Peter's Anglican Church** (1932): A much photographed stone church that looks very much older than its age. *Along Camp St turn right down Earl St. At the waterfront turn left to pass the:*

**Buckhams Wakatip Cordial Factory** (est. 1862): The complex of buildings here has recently suffered from the demolition of one important feature and the survival of others is now a matter for anxiety. *Continue, and enter the:*

**Government Tourist Gardens:** Fringed with firs, the gardens afford an interesting aspect of the town and of Frankton. They contain extensive lawns and rose gardens as well as a variety of sporting greens and an open-air ice rink. The peninsula comprises glacial moraine, and on one gigantic boulder are inscribed the last words of Scott of the Antarctic. The country as a whole closely identified with the explorers, who trained in the Mt Cook area and sailed from Port Chalmers on their way to the South Pole. The boulder, an erratic deposit of greywacke, was probably borne here by the glacier from the head of the lake. *Return to the waterfront and walk towards the town to the foot of Church St. On the near corner is the venerable Lake Lodge of St Ophir (1863). Opposite is the:*

**Site of Rees's original homestead** (*c.* 1862): A chimney still stands from one of Rees's buildings, now incorporated into a more recent (if century-old) cottage. *Continue along the foreshore. On the waterfront wall just before reaching Eichardt's is:*

**Rees Memorial Plaque:** A bronze plate commemorates the founder of Queenstown. *Opposite, at the foot of Ballarat St is:*

**Eichardt's Tavern:** Part of the Spanish-styled building, to the right and identified by an engraved keystone above its lower window, dates from 1871. The former hotel, a successor to Rees' woolshed-turned-bar, was bought by Albert Eichardt from Sergeant-Major Bracken (see △ Arrowtown) with a nugget won in a controversial raffle at Arrowtown. He demolished the Queen's Arms and rebuilt the premises as Eichardt's. The room in the lakeside front corner was specifically set aside for drunks, who labelled their cooling-off chamber the Stone Jug. Eichardt, of proud Prussian military bearing, ran a renowned establishment that had to withstand competition from other houses that offered quoits matches, bellringing contests, "greasy poles" and even ratbaiting in a rat-pit for the entertainment of their patrons. For many years Eichardt's portrait looked down from the wall of the main bar, and whenever his painted countenance winked, custom had it that drinks were on the house. (The portrait recently disappeared with one of the patrons.) *Continue past the end of the jetty. Here, immediately to the right, a small brass tablet indicates the:*

**1878 flood level:** In the flood boats were rowed along Ballarat St and, it is said, the lake's waters lapped the top of the bar in Eichardt's where the barman, up to his waist in water, continued to dispense drinks. In the bay swim tame trout (protected by a ban on fishing there), who congregate round the jetty, waiting to be fed. *Continue to follow the waterfront to pass the:*

**Steamer wharf:** Home of TSS *Earnslaw*, the "Lady of the Lake". (*Excursions run in summer months.*) *Walk on along the shore to reach:*

**St Omer Park:** From here is a pleasant view over the water to the heart of the town and across to the botanic gardens. The park is named after François (Frank) St Omer (1862–1950), who is credited with the planting of the willows along the foreshore, reputedly with slips brought from Napoleon's grave on St Helena. *Now retrace your steps to the foot of Ballarat St and walk up through the mall to return to the old library. The walk may be extended by walking on up to the top of Ballarat St, from which there is an interesting view of Queenstown and the bay.*

## OTHER THINGS TO SEE AND DO

**Bob's Peak Cableway\*\*\*:** A Pomogalski gondola lift rises some 446 m over a distance of 731 m in one of the steepest lifts there is. From the restaurant at the summit is a breathtaking view over town, lake and mountains. *Brecon St. Runs continuously. The road to the summit is closed to vehicles but may be walked.*

**Queenstown Motor Museum\*\*\*** displays a splendid assembly of veteran and vintage cars. Of particular interest are a 1922 Rolls Royce Silver Ghost (originally owned by a lord mayor of London), a supercharged Mercedes 500, a 1909 Renault, a 1903 De Dion (Invercargill's first rental car), an 1885 gentlewoman's tricycle (with a differential in the rear axle) and the Austin 7 Special in which the late Bruce McLaren began his racing career. *Brecon St. By foot of cableway. Open daily. Allow upwards of ¾ hr.*

**Cemetery:** The old graves include those of Henry Homer (*see index*), marked with a slab of rock from the pass he discovered, and of von Tunzelmann, marked by a rough block of white quartz. At the top end of the cemetery a plaque from the Otago Chinese Society commemorates the Chinese goldminers. The Chinese script reads: "The Nineteenth-Century Chinese who sought gold in ice and snow — we remember them." With one exception the Chinese buried here were exhumed for repatriation to their homeland, but the ship on which the bodies were being carried was wrecked off Cape Egmont. *Brecon St. Near foot of cableway.*

---

National Park information Offices advise on walks, tramps, flora, fauna and accommodation. Displays illustrate the significance of each area.

Local sports shops issue fishing licences, advise on local conditions and restrictions, and often hire out equipment.

---

## SOME WALKS

**Queenstown Hill** (*901.2 m*): A leisurely climb affords wide views of the Queenstown-Frankton area from the cairn at the summit. *Allow 2 hours return. Track signposted from both York and Malaghan Sts.*

**Ben Lomond** (*1,752 m*): For many years it was the custom for summer visitors to set off at midnight on a clear moonlit night to reach the summit in time to see a spectacular sunrise over the Remarkables. The view by day is dramatic if not as exciting. *About 6 hrs return. Track starts from Lomond Cres. (near municipal camping ground).*

**Macetown:** A day-long walk to the site of a departed goldtown starts from △Arrowtown.

**Bullendale:** From the end of the giddy Skippers Road one may walk on to old gold workings. *Ask for detailed directions in Queenstown.*

## SOME TRAMPS

*Those on a tramp of any duration should have with them the appropriate volume of* Moir's Guide Book (*published by the NZ Alpine Club*).

**Routeburn Valley:** A 3–4 day tramp leads from Kinloch over the Harris Saddle to the Te Anau-Milford Road, where buses from Milford stop for trampers. *Details under △Fiordland National Park.* A conducted walk is organised by Routeburn Walk Ltd (*Box 271 or Tel. 100M during Nov.-April*).

**Dart and Rees Valleys:** A number of excellent tramps can be made in the area, full details of which are in *Moir's Guide Book (Northern Section).*

**Rere Lake:** A walk of about ¾ hour from Elfin Bay along the start of the Greenstone Valley track leads to the lake.

**Greenstone Valley:** The 40-km tramp from Elfin Bay to Lake Howden, taking about 11 hours, is usually spread over two easy days. Being for the most part downhill, the return trip is easier travelling and usually accomplished in a day. A good round trip is the walk up the Routeburn to Lake Howden, returning down the Greenstone Valley.

**Ascent of the Remarkables** (*2,342.3 m*): The more energetic will not be content with merely admiring the Remarkables from a distance. Numerous routes lead to the top, from the difficult direct approach up the Wakatipu face to the straightforward ascent described in *Moir. A full day. Allow ample time for the very tiring descent.*

## LAKE WAKATIPU

The ancient glacier valley in which lies the Z-shaped lake shows a remarkable consistency in depth, 377.5 m at its deepest point out from Halfway Bay and only 12 m shallower some 50 km away. The lake bed rises gradually towards its head before tilting sharply to the shore. Small terraces can be seen almost everywhere round the lake, showing ancient lake levels.

The natural pulsations in the lake ascribed to the beating heart of the cremated giant are termed seiches and occur when wind or variations in atmospheric pressure cause the water to oscillate. The phenomenon can be observed anywhere round the foreshore simply by placing a suitably marked stick upright in a sheltered spot, but is best seen at Bob's Cove, where there is a transverse seiche across the lake, between north and south, that creates a maximum variation in level about every 4½ minutes as opposed to about 51 minutes for the fundamental seiche along the whole length of the lake. Seiches, well known on other large lakes, have been subjected to experimental and mathematical scrutiny in other parts of the world, particularly in Europe.

At the height of the goldrushes there was a fleet of about thirty boats on the lake, four steamers among them that were either brought overland from Dunedin or built on the lake itself. The paddlesteamer *Mountaineer* plied the lake for nearly sixty years before she was condemned in 1932, leaving the stately *Earnslaw* as the sole "Lady of the Lake".

The *Earnslaw* was prefabricated in Dunedin for assembly at Kingston in 1912. A twin-screw steamer 51.2 m in length and with a beam of 7.3 m, she maintained a regular service to runholders round the lake until 1969, when she was sold by the Railways Department to a private company. Under the Railways her captain enjoyed the odd rank of station master. In summer the *Earnslaw*, now a local institution, carries visitors for trips on the lake.

Wakatipu, exceeded in size in the South Island only by Lake Te Anau, ranks as the country's third largest (29,000 ha). Some 84 km in length and less than 5 km across at its widest point, the elongated lake has a depth that extends to well below sea level.

## POINTS OF INTEREST ON THE LAKE

*Clockwise, starting from Queenstown.*

**Frankton** (pop. 574): Named after Rees' wife Francis, the alternative name of Francestown has recently been suggested to eliminate confusion with the Hamilton suburb of the same name. *See "A Drive to Frankton", below.*

**Kingston** (pop. 36): In summer the quaint old *Kingston Flyer*, a veteran train, runs between here and △Lumsden (*which see for description*). The small settlement, at the railhead and with a wharf, stands on a terminal moraine where, before it cut its present exit, the lake flowed out down the Mataura Valley. Kingston's name complements Queenstown, both Irish placenames presumably bestowed by Irish goldminers. *46 km from Queenstown.*

**Halfway Bay** (*water access only*): The Lochy River here is good for brown and rainbow trout. A track leads up the river and its left-hand branch to cross the Eyre Mountains by Billy Saddle to reach the headwaters of the Mataura River. From there one may either swing north to cross the Mataura Saddle and return down the right-hand branch, or bear east to meet Robert Creek before turning north to cross the Lambies Saddle and return to Halfway Bay.

**Cecil Peak** (*water access only*): The peak itself was named Te Taumata-a-Haki-te-kura (the peak of Haki-te-kura) after the girl who swam the chilly lake by night to light a fire here. Cecil Peak Station shows visitors the activities of a high-country run. (*See "Organised Excursions" below*).

**Walter Peak** (*water access only*): The homestead block, where von Tunzelmann settled, entertains visitors. There are plans for a large-scale tourist village here.

**Elfin Bay** (*water access only or walk from Kinloch*): A short walk from the bay leads to **Rere Lake** along the start of the **Greenstone Valley** tramp.

**Kinloch** (*80 km from Queenstown*): At the present end of the road from Queenstown, crossing the recently-completed Dart River bridge. The road is proposed to continue through to the Te Anau-Milford road. Once a wayport on the lake, and like Glenorchy named after a Scottish resort, Kinloch (Gaelic for head of the lake) is the starting point for tramps along the Routeburn and Greenstone Valleys.

**Paradise** (*62 km from Queenstown*): Long believed to be named not for its tranquillity which is considerable, but for a proliferation of Paradise duck. Nearby Diamond Lake is stocked with brown and rainbow trout. From here starts a good round tramp along the Dart and the Rees river-valleys.

**Glenorchy** and **Bob's Cove** (*see "Some Other Drives" below*).

---

For local information and history, read *Out and About in Queenstown* by Florence Preston (Reed).

---

## ARROWTOWN ROUND TRIP

*41 km. The trip can be expanded to 65 km with detours to Coronet Peak and Thurlby Domain. Start at the Post Office, travelling up Ballarat St to turn left at the Old Library along Stanley St. Turn right up Shotover St and follow Gorge Rd.*

**Coronet Peak** comes into view at about 1 km to close a vista. The peak is easily identified by its coronet-bedecked silhouette.

**Arthurs Point Hotel** (*4.8 km*), first built in 1862, is the last of the seventeen hotels and twenty-three general stores that flourished between Arthurs Point and Skippers. Rebuilt after a fire in 1880, the hotel preserves much of its original character.

**Edith Cavell Bridge** (1875) (*5.4 km*) spans the Shotover River to give a view into a gorge lined with cliffs of schist. The bridge, now named after a heroine of the 1914–18 war, was originally known as the Upper Shotover Bridge until an admirer, rebuffed by officialdom in his effort to rename the structure after the British nurse, simply took a paintbrush and decorated the bridge with her name. His persistence has since been rewarded. Across the bridge, a jetboat service runs visitors to see relics of goldmining activity but primarily for a thrilling run through the gorge. The river beach here is littered with stones of every colour.

**Thomas Arthur Memorial** (*at 5.5 km*): Just over the bridge, a modest cairn marks the vicinity of the shearer's fabulous find of gold.

**View of dredge remains** (*at 6.4 km*): In the river below, on the far bank, may be seen the metallic remains of one of the Shotover's last gold dredges.

**Packers' Arms**\*\* (*7 km*): The stone inn, built in the 1860s to refresh travelling prospectors, has been restored from a makeshift haybarn to a quality restaurant. For the twenty-three years up to 1896 the inn was simply Gantleys, after Patrick Gantley who had resigned his position as Queenstown's gaoler to accommodate more willing guests. The stone walls of the original building have been largely retained. Photographs within show how its character has been preserved. *Continue to the turnoff to Skippers and Coronet Peak. On the corner, just before the junction, stands:*

**Bordeau's storehouse** (*c. 1865*) (*at 7.4 km*): The venerable old stone storehouse of the French-Canadian storekeeper Julien Bordeau now serves as a crib. Renowned for his hardiness, the packer reputedly would not do up his shirt until icicles rattled on the tails of his horses. *Here one may detour to the Coronet Peak chairlift\*\*\*, that operates all the year round and is run out-of-season at half speed to afford visitors a more leisurely look at a view of unsurpassed alpine splendour. (Note: Check running times at Queenstown before leaving.) Those not wishing to make the full detour may wish to visit the Observation Point\*\* opposite the divergence of the routes to Skippers and to Coronet Peak. There a plane table identifies points of interest in a wide view of mountain and riverflat.*

*Continuing towards Arrowtown, on the left is the:*

**Ben Lomond homestead** (*at 8.5 km*): A farmyard museum is planned to be established here.

**Malaghan Memorial** (*11.9 km*): A stone monument marks the approximate site of the Malaghan Hotel and Post Office, a building that from 1873–1906 served as the Millers Flat School. The nearby poplar grew from a stake erected by children to celebrate the relief of Mafeking during the Boer War. *A detour may be made at 13.7 km right down Hunter Rd and, right again along Speargrass Flat Rd to reach, after a detour of 2.9 km, the stone stables, barn and tiny smithy of:*

**Thurlby Domain** — once the home of Bendix Hallenstein, founder of the nationwide chain of HB menswear stores. About 30 m farther on are the iron gates to his two-storeyed, once-stately mansion (1864), now crumbling to ruin. The stonework was carried out by German masons. (*On private property. Ask permission to visit at the farmhouse beside the barn.*) *Return to Malaghan Rd. Continue further along Malaghan Rd to reach at 19.4 km the main route from Queenstown to Arrowtown. Just before the junction, on the left, is the tiny:*

**Powder magazine:** A tiny stone hut built at a safe distance from the township to accommodate explosives needed in some goldmining enterprises. *Turn left to reach:*

△**Arrowtown**\*\*\* (*19.9 km*): A mellow old mining village that merits an unhurried visit. *Return to Queenstown by the direct route, via:*

**Lake Hayes**\*\*\* (*into view at 21.9 km*): An enchanting stretch of water, known to the Maori as Wai-whaka-ata (water that reflects objects) as it occasionally perfectly mirrors its surroundings. The exotic trees that fringe the lake make the scene one much favoured by landscape artists. The lake derives its *Pakeha* name not from the nefarious pirate "Bully" Hayes, but from the European explorer of Lake Wakatipu, Donald Hay. Its waters afford excellent trout fishing, with a limit bag well in excess of those elsewhere. Brown trout were liberated in about 1870 into the lake's wood-rich waters. Gaff poaching in the spawning season from streams round the lake prompted the local acclimatisation society to auction netting concessions. For twelve years from 1896 the lake furnished most of the district's fresh fish, the surplus being sent to Dunedin. The biggest single haul was of 147 trout with a dressed weight of 223.8 kilos—the whole catch selling for 8c per kilo. The most notable, however, was of only six trout, of which the smallest was a modest 5.5 kilos and the largest a full 11.4 kilos in weight. *At 22.3 km the road passes the turnoff to:*

**Waterfall Park:** A privately-owned commercial picnic park. *Detour 900 m.*

**Picnic Area**\*\*\* (*24.9 km*): The grassed foreshore, with its gentle beach and boat-launching area, is towered over by poplars. Across the lake may be seen the venerable stone homestead on the property once owned by Robert Lee (d. 1911). He bought the property in 1910 and built the country's largest private irrigation scheme to bring water some 6.5 km from Boundary Creek on the Remarkables, a pipeline being suspended by steel cables to cross the Kawarau River. A valve by his property supplied water to teams of up to sixteen horses. *At 25.7 km the route joins Highway 6. Turn right. Almost immediately on the left is a pair of century-old stone buildings, one a barn-turned-crib, and at 26.4 km is a:*

**Fish smoker** (*c.* 1896): On the left, perched close to the road, stands an odd stone box about 4 m high and 1.5 m square. Here over a twelve-year period thousands of trout were smoked. All three walls seen from the road give the misleading impression of an enclosed structure, but the fourth side is open. *At 27.9 km on the right, is the:*

**Robert Lee Memorial Water-trough** (1911): "Erected by his friends", the trough recalls the water freely made available by Lee for passing teams of horses. *As the Lower Shotover bridge is crossed, upstream is seen a distinctive aspect of Coronet Peak. Continue on to Queenstown, passing at 36.9 km:*

**Golden Terrace Mining Village:** A recreation of the atmosphere and appearance of the goldmining village of a century ago. *Open daily from 8.30 am–5.30 pm.*

## A DRIVE TO FRANKTON

*22 km.* The settlement at Frankton, now almost a continuation of the sprawl of Queenstown round the lake's edge, lies on Frankton Arm, the shallowest corner of the lake and so the warmest for swimming. Delayed by negotiations with Rees, in 1863 the Government decided to move Queenstown to Frankton, building a police station and a post office here. The project was dropped in the face of vocal opposition, and in recognition of the fact that Queenstown Bay was a better anchorage for steamers. Enclosing the arm are Kelvin Heights, on whose slopes are the houses of a Bavarian-style development and whose tip is a perfect setting for a golf course. *Drive round the lake to Frankton, turning off where signposted for 1.5 km to reach the:*

**Zoological gardens:** On the banks of the Kawarau, flowing swiftly as it drains Lake Wakatipu, is a small area of gardens and an assortment of birds and smaller animals, among them a variety of deer. *Open daily. Return to the road along the foreshore, turning left to pause at the:*

**Lake Outlet:** Formerly known as Kawarau Falls, as there were once rapids here where the lake spills out as the Kawarau River, this was where Vogel's vision of gold galore proved illusory (*see above*). The road crosses the control structure built in the hope of recovering a rich harvest of gold. On a knoll to the right, immediately before the control bridge, is the venerable low pressure turbine from Robertson's and Bendix Hallenstein's flourmill, dismantled when the control structure was built. Beside it, a stone store, once part of the mill complex, has been built into a home. *Immediately over the bridge, to the right, is:*

**Kawarau Falls homestead:** Rees moved to Kawarau Falls when he lost his run at Queenstown in 1863 (*his cottage still stands, by itself and slightly extended, on the right by the roadside 1.6 km beyond the control bridge*). It was Rees's successors, Charles and Frank Boyes, who built the nucleus of the homestead (1879) here in an idyllic lakeside setting and who planted the trees now massive with age. The old homestead (and about 10 ha) is now a church holiday camp that offers visitors the cheapest accommodation in the area (*guests welcome*). *A short distance further on turn right and continue to reach:*

**Deer Park Heights\*\*\*:** A variety of wildlife (deer, tahr, chamois, wapiti and mountain goats among them) is seen in a natural setting. The hillside gives splendid views of the lake, the mountains, the Shotover and Kawarau Rivers, Lake Hayes and Coronet Peak. In April the stags are heard roaring their challenge to each other, and from December to February they are seen in velvet, when their offspring appear as spotted, well-camouflaged fawn. Their antlers later harden and are shed altogether in October. *Signposted. Admission by token or by five 20-cent coins per car. Automatic entrance.*

## SKIPPERS

Of all the fabulous Wakatipu diggings, it was Skippers that gave the most regular returns, with each square foot of its bed said to hold almost an ounce of gold. Miners willingly tolerated extraordinary hardships in the crowded ravines here as they toiled to win rich rewards. In this wild and bleak spot, thousands feverishly scarred the terraces and struggled with the elements in their quest for gold. Some did not return and lie buried in the old Skippers cemetery. A single Chinese grave is there, too, left behind when others were exhumed for planned reburial in their native land.

The diggers believed that the Shotover gold came from a reef at the base of Mt Aurum (the golden mountain) which from 1866 was worked as the Bullendale mine. In 1885 the country's first hydro-electric generator was installed here to drive a powerful crushing plant. Though an immense amount of gold was won, working expenses were so heavy that the concern never managed to show a profit. By the time the mine closed in 1907, more than £200,000 had been lost by its various promoters. Gold remains, but the cost of extraction, as in the past, is the barrier.

Access to Skippers was by a frightening bridle track and today by no less awesome a road. Narrow, fenceless, winding and giddy in the extreme, the road should be attempted only in good summer weather and then only by the most experienced of drivers. There are few turning or passing places, and drivers must be prepared to reverse for considerable distances, particularly when encountering the buses that run for the less intrepid. *The buses regularly make the trip when conditions allow (not from about June to September). The bus trip provides an entertaining commentary, but the trip does not at present extend as far as the site of the deserted Skippers township, nor even to the famed Skippers bridge (over 100 m long and the same height above the Shotover River).*

## SOME OTHER DRIVES

**Towards Glenorchy\*\*\*:** The drive should be made at least part of the way along the road to Glenorchy. The way follows the Wakatipu shoreline, sometimes at the water's edge, sometimes high above the lake, with the mountain scenery towards the head of the lake unfolding all too slowly. At 3.7 km the road passes pleasant **Sunshine Bay,** and at 7 km a detour leads 6.4 km to tiny **Lake Kilpatrick** and the brown trout of **Moke Lake,** two stretches of water incongruous in bleak treeless valleys (*detour not recommended in winter*).

A track leads into **Lake Dispute** at 10.4 km (*signposted: allow 1 hr*), and a shorter track plunges down to **Bob's Cove** at 15.1 km (*signposted: allow 15 mins*). The cove, reached by the Puna-Tapu track, still has the twisted piles of a jetty that once shipped out burnt lime to Queenstown — lime used in the courthouse, the old library and the County building. Dressed stone, too, was cut out and is included in the Robert Lee Water-trough memorial. Under the tall, slender beeches are the remains of three stone kilns in which the lime was burnt. The seiche action of the lake is best observed here.

**Glenorchy** (pop. 98) is reached at 44 km where a ranger for the △ Mount Aspiring National Park is stationed. Near here are deposits of scheelite on which a local industry may be based. The road continues to Paradise, to cross the Dart River and reach Kinloch. It is proposed to link eventually with the Te Anau-Milford road.

## OTHER ENVIRONS

**Coronet Peak chairlift:** In winter crowded with skiers, the cableway operates in summer at half-speed to enable visitors to enjoy a splendid view. In an unsurpassed panorama of alpine splendour, the farflung giants of Cook, Earnslaw, Aspiring and Tutoko are all in view. *15 km. Note: Check running times at Queenstown before leaving.*

*The chairlift stops briefly for an annual overhaul in the late autumn. In the skiing season the lift operates at full speed and is more expensive to travel on.*

**Tucker Beach:** A beach on the Shotover, named not after someone of that name but after a cagey Chinese miner who, when questioned as to how his claim was panning out, would only allow that he was "Making tucker, just making tucker." Here, on a rare stretch of readily accessible riverbank, one may picnic and pan for gold. *Turn left from Highway 6 immediately before the Lower Shotover bridge and follow Tucker Beach Rd for 4 km.*

## ORGANISED EXCURSIONS

*Queenstown as the most highly organised of all the country's resorts, offers a wide range of scheduled excursions. Several agencies in Queenstown Mall handle bookings for trips which include:*

**Boat trips:** The lake's veteran steamer, TSS *Earnslaw*, plies a variety of routes in summer. Other passenger craft also run on the lake. Self-drive powerboats and rowboats are available. Jetboats operate in the depths of the Kawarau Gorge and on the rapids of the Shotover River. A 2-hour raft trip on the lower Shotover passes through some exciting scenery.

**Sheep stations:** Regular boat trips operate across the lake to the runs at **Cecil Peak** and **Walter Peak.** Both feature museums, sheepdog demonstrations and tea. There are plans to further develop the Cecil Peak station by restoring the homestead, building youth hostels and arranging hikes to the back country.

**Bus trips:** Paramount is the bus trip through giddy Skippers Canyon towards the old goldtown of Skippers, along a road which deters all but the most experienced of drivers. *The halfday trip runs at least twice daily (not from June to September).*

A regular day-long excursion leads to △Milford Sound, with time allowed for a launch trip on the fiord. Other tours visit △Arrowtown, Coronet Peak, and skirt the lake to Glenorchy, Kinloch and the start of the Routeburn Track.

**Scenic flights:** Short scenic flights run up to the head of the lake, up Paradise Valley, and over the scheelite mines to Mt Earnslaw and the Dart River to return by way of Skippers Canyon. Flights leave regularly for △Milford Sound, over superb alpine and fiordland scenery. These can allow time for a launch trip on the sound before returning. Alternatively, one may enjoy the best of both worlds by flying one way and travelling by bus the other.

**Fishing and hunting:** New Zealand Safaris run escorted hunting and fishing expeditions. *Tel. 540 Queenstown.*

**Routeburn Walk:** An easy 4-day guided walk along the Routeburn takes in virgin bush, lakes and alpine scenery. Accommodation and meals are provided and, as much of the route is above 900 m, sandflies are mercifully scarce. The walk, more a tramp than a tourist excursion, may be made in either direction, from the Te Anau or the Wakatipu side. *Routeburn Walk Ltd, Box 271 Queenstown, tel. 1006 during Nov.–April.* The walk may also be made independently (*see* △ *Fiordland National Park*).

**Trail rides:** Rides of varying lengths, including campouts, lead over the romantic old Moonlight goldworkings. *Moonlight Stables, tel. 838D.*

## TOURING NOTES

**CROWN RANGE ROAD TO** △**WANAKA:** *70 km. This route (closed in winter) can be attempted only in good weather as it climbs over the highest main road in the country. Leave Queenstown by Highway 6, to run past Lake Hayes. Turn left at 18.8 km up Highway 89 to traverse the:*

**Crown Range:** The road zigzags up to Crown Terrace, affording a splendid view of the Arrow Valley stretching back to Arrowtown, before it follows the level terrace. The road rises steeply to switchback through the snowgrass until at 29.9 km the highest point is reached, 1,119.7 m above sea level. By then Frankton, a curl of Wakatipu and Queenstown have all come into view. The impressive aspect from the summit may be enhanced by walking some 200 m up the track here to see the end of the Carrick Range sliding into the Kawarau Gorge. This is the scene enjoyed by Rees and von Tunzelmann when they first approached the lake. *From the summit the road begins its generally gentle descent down the:*

**Cardrona Valley\*:** The valley bears the imprint of the goldminers — heaps of tailings, occasional pieces of twisted pipe, the odd stone cottage crumbling to ruin and, lower down, the water-carved cliffs of the sluicing claims. In fine weather mica schist reflects the sunlight to give an alluring glitter to the valley. *At 44.1 km, hard by the roadside, leans the:*

**Cardrona Hotel** (*c.* 1870)\*: The historic goldtown hotel finally lost its licence in 1961, and now stands as a sad, silent relic of the gold era in the company of a brace of cottages, an old hall and a forgotten, miniscule cemetery. (*See* △*Wanaka*, "Gold at

*Cardrona" for the history of the settlement). The near-level run continues to pass (at 64.5 km) the signposted:*

**View of Mt Aspiring** *(3,033.6 m):* Through a cleft in the nearer mountains towers the perpetually snow-covered peak that gives its name to the Mount Aspiring National Park. *Soon the road reaches:*

△**Wanaka*** *** (70 km):* A settlement on the shores of Lake Wanaka, swollen to metropolitan dimensions in summer, whose lack of commercialisation contrasts with the industry of Queenstown.

**HIGHWAY 6 TO** △**CROMWELL.** The route through the Kawarau Gorge is described under △Cromwell, "Touring Notes".

---

△ indicates a place with its own entry.

---

## RAKAIA      Mid-Canterbury.   Map 3.   Pop. 759.

*59 km S from Christchurch; 32 km N from Ashburton.*

THE FARMING CENTRE straddles the railway on the south bank of the Rakaia River. A ribbon of service buildings close by, lines Highway 1 just before it crosses the country's longest bridge, 1.75 km long.

The meaning of Rakaia (or *Rangaia*, to arrange in ranks) is obscure. One explanation is that it refers to the custom whereby a line of men would form across the ford to break the flow and so render it less hazardous for the women and children to wade through downriver. A principal greenstone route to Westland lay up the river valley.

### SOME HISTORY

**The trans-Rakaia desert:** For some years after the settlement of Christchurch the mile-wide Rakaia River was a barrier to close settlement further south. In any event land between the Rakaia and the Ashburton Rivers, which enjoyed the not inaccurate title of "the trans-Rakaia desert", was either too dry or too damp. Early travellers experienced all manner of difficulty in crossing the river. George Rhodes and his family, on their way from the Levels to Christchurch, once had to wait fully three weeks before the river was safe to cross, running out of food in the meantime. Sir John Hall (1824–1907), later to be premier and still later to spearhead the move for women's franchise, bought a canoe for use as a ferry here. He was so discouraged by his very first trip that he abandoned the canoe and settled on the north side of the river. Eventually a regular ferry was established.

For a time it seemed that Rakaia, or South Rakaia as it was then known, might become the principal centre for mid-Canterbury, but in the late 1870s Ashburton forged ahead to its present position of prominence.

### ENVIRONS

**Barrhill** is a fragment of a feudal village planned by John Cathcart Wason, who took up the 8,100-ha Lendon run he renamed Corwar, in 1870. He had a passion for trees and combined this with his wish to recreate the style of living he knew in Scotland — with himself as squire in his manor, and his employees comfortably housed in a nearby village. At Barrhill he built everything from cottages to an inn, a school and a church. For a time his wish came true but the village perished when Corwar was broken up. In 1900 Wason sold the balance of his estate and returned to Scotland. The cement-plastered church (1876), old school house and teacher's house (now a residence) stand under the boughs of massive elms and oaks as a peaceful legacy of more populous times. *16 km from Rakaia.* The Corwar homestead block, still so named, is 2 km farther up the road towards Methven.

**Rakaia Huts** *(30.5 km)* and **Rakaia River Mouth** *(22.5 km).* Fishing localities on opposing banks of the Rakaia River, a favoured stretch of salmon water.

---

## RANFURLY      Central Otago.   Maps 25 & 28.   Pop. 939.

*80 km NW of Palmerston; 90 km ENE of Alexandra.*

RANFURLY, the natural centre of the Maniototo, lies in the middle of a vast inland plain broken only by sporadic clumps of pinetrees and poplars; the town's railway station underlines its key communications role. If it lacks a history comparable with the early mining towns, it serves a fascinating district that includes Naseby — whence the Maniototo County Council decided in 1924 to shift both its offices and the hospital "owing to the regrettable decadence of Naseby and its distance from the railway". An objector retorted "A mental hospital is what is required at Ranfurly, to house eight or ten advocators who urge the change." The move took place, but not as quickly as had been suggested.

The centre was first called Eweburn as the locality was settled by farmers who took up 81-ha blocks of the Eweburn run in the 1880s. It was renamed Ranfurly after Lord Ranfurly (donor of the Ranfurly Shield) had visited the town as Governor-General. Maniototo is probably a corruption of Mania-o-toto (plain of blood), presumably a reference to the hardfought battles that took place during the conquest by Ngaitahu.

## ENVIRONS

**Hamiltons:** The Hamiltons goldfield opened at the end of 1863 to draw heavily on Naseby's population. Fickle miners were notorious for their readiness to believe that the unknown of a new find promised greater returns than the established yield of a working field. Hamiltons was indeed rich, but only in parts. The field faded more quickly than that of Naseby, but held a peak population of some 3,000. Virtually all that remains of the booming town that saw 80,000 ounces of gold recovered in eighteen months is a tiny cemetery on the foothills of the Rock and Pillar (note the headstone of Edward Barber). Part of the diggings is now flooded, and the small lake serves as a water reservoir for the nearby Waipiata detention centre. Off the roadway caution is essential as vertical shafts are obscured by scrub. *17.5 km S of Ranfurly.*

The Hamiltons run on which the strike was made was taken up in 1860 by a partnership that included one Captain Hamilton. In India he had learnt the art of building mud cottages that were both warm in winter and cool in summer. The woolshed (*c.* 1860) on the homestead block, possibly the first cob building to be erected in Central, still stands and is still in use. The cob homestead, stables and men's quarters are falling into ruin. However the impressive pigeon loft, with its shingled roof, is still intact near the outdoor oven in which bread was baked for runholder and digger alike. All date from about 1861. *15 km SE of Ranfurly. Now The Beeches. Private property. Interested visitors are welcome.*

**Puketoi station,** one of the most attractive in the Maniototo, was applied for in 1858 by the young Murison brothers. They were backed by Johnny Jones (*see index*), presumably on the basis of the usual "thirds" whereby Jones would provide the necessary stock while the runholders were permitted to retain as their own one third of each season's lambs. In time the bed-sheets the brothers used for a tent were replaced by Moa Cottage, so named as there were many *moa* bones lying on the run. This in turn, in about 1867, gave way to the homestead that still stands. The run saw the first public meeting in Central, when runholders gathered to discuss the need to upgrade roads. Present was Watson Shennan (*see index*), who years later acquired the run and here built his Puketoi Merino stud into one of the country's finest. *25.8 km SW.*

**Patearoa** (pop. 153) on the edge of the plain, had its rushes at the same time as Hamiltons but survives as a farming centre with picturesque cottages from goldrush times. An hydraulic sluicing nozzle is beside the town hall with gearing used to automatically swing the stream of water to and fro across the working face. The old Sowburn diggings are near the bridge. *17 km S of Ranfurly.*

**Creamery Bridge:** A popular Maniototo picnic spot on the Taieri River. *8 km S of Ranfurly on the way to Patearoa.*

**Styx (Paerau)\*:** The hotel and stables (1861) at now deserted Styx, a pretty picnic spot, became an overnight stop for the gold escort from the Dunstan and Wakatipu diggings on the Old Dunstan Road (*see index*). The gaol nearby, where leg-irons remain, was used to hold prisoners being taken to Dunedin for trial. Both the hotel, now roughcast, and the old school are used as holiday homes. The origin of the name Styx is uncertain. Some attribute it to the surveyor John Turnbull Thomson; others to the practice that gave rise to an identical name elsewhere, namely the placing of upright sticks to mark crossings in rivers and creeks. Paerau means a hundred ridges. *39 km SSW of Ranfurly. Beyond Patearoa. After crossing the Taieri River turn sharp left to the river's edge.*

## TOURING NOTES

**Highway 85 to △Alexandra:** Interest is added if either section of the round trip is followed suggested under △Alexandra as "A Tour of Some Old Gold Towns".

**Highway 85 to △Palmerston:** Described under △Pigroot.

Readable accounts of Central's past include *Gold Trails of Otago* by June Wood and *Gold in the River* by F. W. G. Miller while areas of interest are portrayed in *Beyond the Skippers Road* by Terri McNicol and *The Road to Skippers* by D. A. Knudson. The Remarkables Station of Queenstown, the individuality of its life and problems is described by D. G. Jardine in *Shadows on the Hill*. All the above are published by A.H. & A.W. Reed.

## RANGIORA    North Canterbury.    Map 7.    Pop. 5,991.

*33 km N of Christchurch; 13 km NNW of Kaiapoi.*

RANGIORA IS SET in sheep and dairying country, with orchards and the expanse of Ashley Forest nearby. The market town's comfortably mature atmosphere is due to its having been established only two years after Christchurch. In recent years the town has been swollen by those who work in Christchurch but prefer to live in a more rural atmosphere. Rangiora's name has been given many literal translations, such as place of rest, place of health, and day of peace. Fanciful associations have been advanced to connect the name with the Maori's legendary Hawaiki homeland.

### POINTS OF INTEREST

**The Red Lion:** The present hotel (1874) is the third on the site, the original being an iron shed (1857) built when Rangiora was a bush settlement and High St simply part of a dray track that wandered from Woodend to Oxford. It was James Bassingwaite who built the present hotel, shortly thereafter filing in bankruptcy to the surprise of his creditors, who considered him well off—which is precisely where a large number of sovereigns were found — in the well. Bassingwaite died in gaol, awaiting trial on a charge of attempted fraud. The remodelled Red Lion is still red, but its original heraldic lion rampant has given way to a neon replacement. *Corner High and Ivory Sts.*

**Anglican Church of St John the Baptist** (1859–60)*: One of the largest and most beautiful of Canterbury's wooden churches was designed by B. W. Mountfort, architect for Christchurch's Provincial Council Chambers. The original plan, since added to, included a steeple, but instead a separate belfry was erected in 1879. Most interesting of the memorials is a scroll emblazoned with the names of the building committee, who modestly arranged for it to be stored until the last of their number had die˙ ˙he west window commemorates the Leech family, George Leech settling here in 1853 and taking up Brooklands to become the patriarch of the district. *High St.*

**Rangiora and Districts Historical Museum:** A local museum includes a two-roomed cob cottage (1869) furnished in period style. The museum building was the upper floor of the local Bank of New Zealand (1878). *Good St. Open Sun., Wed., and school holidays from 2–4 pm, otherwise by arrangement with Farmers Travel Dept., Rangiora. Signposted. The cob cottage may be seen at all times.*

**Victoria Park** is a pleasant picnic place. *Percival St.*

---

MOBIL NEW ZEALAND TRAVEL GUIDE
NORTH ISLAND

The companion volume to this Guide is available from bookshops everywhere. To make the most of your travels you should carry with you the book of Mobil road maps.

---

## REEFTON*    Buller.    Maps 37 & 38.    Pop. 1,456.

*81 km SSE of Westport; 79 km NE of Greymouth.*

REEFTON LIES in a cradle of forested hills by the Inangahua River where roads from △Greymouth and △Westport converge on their way to the △Lewis Pass and Canterbury. Born in a rash of speculation engendered by the deposits of quartz that gave the town its name, Reefton's mining activity is now directed towards the deposits of coal that were so often found along with the gold-rich ore. In recent years coal production has declined. Among other local activities are timbermilling and farming.

    By reason of its sheltered location, the principal centre of Inangahua County is remarkably free from winds, a situation that results in soaring summer temperatures at the price of intensified cold and mist in winter. There is river swimming, trout fishing and hunting, and good walks to abandoned goldworkings in the hills.

**Viewpoint:** There is an excellent view of the locality from Lookout Point. *Turn left off the Reefton-Greymouth highway about 500 m from the Inangahua riverbridge. Follow Soldiers Rd for about 1 km and turn left where signposted to follow a forestry road to the lookout. 5 km.*

### SOME HISTORY

**Quartzopolis:** Some alluvial gold had been won in the district, but Reefton (or Reef Town as it was for a time occasionally known) blazed to life in 1870 after the discovery of rich goldbearing quartz reefs in the hills above Black's Point. Despite enormous transport difficulties, within a year crushing plants were operating on the ore. Leases for mining rights were taken up in every direction, and as companies were formed to provide the necessary capital, a riot of speculation broke out. Shares in untested claims boomed, though not all were as fortunate as the investor who bought a quarter-share in the Hopeful claim for £50 and soon began to receive dividends of hundreds of pounds every few weeks:

The linking of Reefton to the rest of the country by telegraph in 1872 heightened the interest of investors, so that by the end of the decade the country was in a fever over Reefton shares. Telegrams poured in by the thousand to "the most brisk and businesslike place in the Colony" to keep Reefton's stock exchange — the only one on the Coast and one of few in the country — seething with excitement day and night, every day bar Sunday. "Scrip mania" gripped the town, then nicknamed Quartz-opolis, as discoveries were made by such companies as the Imperial, the Golden Fleece and the Golden Point. The established bonanzas of the Welcome and the Keep-It-Dark struck fresh lodes at deeper levels; the town could talk of gold and nothing else.

Euphorious speculators could not flock the pavements of Broadway for ever. Share prices had parted company with reality and 1883 was the year of reckoning. In that year, of the sixty-six operating companies all but three made calls on shareholders. These exceeded dividends and many companies failed in the ensuing crash.

If the bust convinced many New Zealanders that Reefton mining shares were a ruinous investment (it even bred opposition in Hokitika to Reefton's agitation for a rail link with Christchurch), nonetheless by the end of the century the quartz lodes had yielded over £2 million, paying almost £700,000 in dividends. The continuing riches once the companies had been sorted out meant there was still room for the enterprising fraud to float a company on the strength of an unproven claim.

**Electrical firsts:** As the boomtown of the period, it fell to Reefton to become the first in the country to be lit by electricity, perhaps even the first in the southern hemisphere. The town's electric lights were shining about six years after Thomas Edison's company had first begun to light the streets of New York.

Walter Prince, a British engineer, had been brought to New Zealand by a Dunedin firm and had supervised the construction of a hydro-electric plant for a mining claim on the Shotover River (perhaps a world first) before he brought his 1-kilowatt demonstration dynamo to Reefton in 1886. Here he installed it in Dawson's Hotel to make it the first building in the hemisphere to be permanently illuminated by electricity. Public interest soon quickened into action; a public utility company was registered and early in 1888 Reefton was being fed by hydro-electric power. *Only the foundations of the early powerhouse building and parts of the plant remain. Cross the swing bridge to the east of the town and walk 200 m downriver. A plaque in Buller Rd opposite the Reefton Borough Council chambers records the event. Dawson's Hotel still stands in Broadway, and is now the Masonic.*

## A SHORT TOWN WALK

A 15-minute walk leads past several interesting buildings. Start in Broadway, the town's main street, at the foot of Walsh St. Walk up Walsh St past Shiel St to a pair of churches, **Sacred Heart** (1878) and **St Stephen's** (1878). Turn right up Church St to see the old, now-disused **courthouse** (1872) and at the end turn right down Bridge St, passing the two impressive, two-storeyed bank buildings (one now occupied by Westland Safaris) that flank the foot of Bridge St, each built with its manager's quarters over the banking chambers.

Turn left along Shiel St to pass the **School of Mines**\*\*, still in its building of 1886, with a mineral sample collection that includes specimens from most of the local quartz mines and of locally-found uranium ores. The school holds equipment to crush rocks and assay their mineral content. Opened to serve the educational needs of the gold-fields, the school gradually moved into the area of coalmining. It continued until 1970, being the last of the country's several schools of mines to close. One local graduate was Harold Evans, whose discovery of deposits of bauxite at Weipa on the North Queensland coast led to the establishment of the Comalco aluminium smelter at △ Bluff. (*Beside State Coal Mines District Office. Open by arrangement with the office.*)

Follow Shiel St back to Broadway. Turn right to return to the foot of Walsh St, passing the two impressive two-storeyed bank buildings that flank the foot of Bridge St, each built with its manager's quarters over the banking chambers.

## ENVIRONS

**Blacks Point Museum**\*\*: Housed in a former church (1876) of pitsawn timber, the collection centres on Reefton in the days of the quartz mines. Photographs, equipment, maps of claims and a model of a typical shaft quartz mine are all displayed. At the end of the side road by the museum, a water-powered gold battery has been rebuilt (basically with the remaining parts of two separate batteries), and is in working order. Quartz can be seen being pounded to powder by the five stamps. *2.3 km E on Highway 7. Generally open daily from 2–4 pm. Extended hours during holiday periods.*

**Wealth of Nations gold battery (Crushington):** The rust and rubble of the battery stand forlornly by the roadside where the riches of the curiously-named Wealth of Nations mine were once hammered from the quartz. The mine was so called as its discoverer bore the same name as the economist author of the treatise by that title, Adam Smith.

Crushing plants were not very efficient, much gold being lost in tailings often sluiced away into rivers and streams. The manager here had the foresight to stack his tailings, a move that proved profitable in later years when with the introduction of the cyanide process gold extraction methods became more efficient. The Wealth of Nations mine itself became the deepest in the district at almost 610 m. *3.7 km E on Highway 7.* Farther on (*at 4.9 km*), on the opposite side of the river may be seen the concrete foundations of the old **Globe battery** which at one time had 65 head of stamps. This was first driven by a waterwheel almost 2 km distant, power being transmitted by a continuous wire rope. The two batteries, with a now-vanished third, the Keep-It-Dark, earned for the town that once stood here the official title of Crushington.

**Garvey Creek\*:** A short drive leads up Garvey Creek to the State coalmine where "peacock" coal is won. The play of colours on the flat selvedges of the coal is probably due to the refraction of light by a film of oil distilled from the coal during its formation. The phenomenon occurs only in low-moisture high-ranking bituminous coals. Smoke is seen rising from a coal seam that has been burning for over a decade. *17 km. Turn off Highway 7 at 9 km E.*

**Waiuta\*,** a ghost town that as recently as 1951 had a population of about 150, has the most spectacular relics of the goldmining era accessible by car. At the once well-appointed town site, only a few derelict buildings and a swimming pool remain. The former mine offices and strongroom, the skeleton of the ball mill that crushed the quartz, bins, mullock heaps and odd equipment litter the site. The remains of the cyanide tanks are far below by the banks of the Snowy River. 38 km. *Turnoff signposted 21 km SW on Highway 7.*

   The Birthday reef here was discovered by four prospectors in 1906, who sold their rights to a speculator for £2,000. He did no more than prove its value and within a year sold the claim for £30,000 to the company that worked it. The plant comprised a 30-stamp mill, a tube mill in which crushed ore was ground to a mixture of sand and slime, a cyanide plant, and a furnace. The mercury amalgamation process was also used. In 1951 the mine was producing up to 800 ounces of gold a month when its ventilation shaft suddenly caved in. The decision was then made to abandon workings that reputedly included the deepest shaft in the southern hemisphere, extending down some 1,000 m. A $30,000 project to retap the seam died with its financier in 1971.

## SOME WALKS TO OLD GOLDMINING AREAS

*Some of these tracks cross private property or Forestry land, in which case permission should be sought. Some of the tracks are not well defined, and those intending to follow them should discuss directions and track conditions locally. It is prudent to advise someone of your intended route and expected time of return. The directions here are no more than a general outline and should not be regarded as a precise guide. Beware at all times of unmarked prospecting shafts.*

**Lankeys Creek:** A relatively easy hour-long walk leads up Lankeys Creek. Stoney Creek is crossed, a source of shell fossils from the Devonian Fossilbed, and old coalbins are passed before the track zigzags to the right up a scrub-covered area. From here the track arcs back to the creek and a 5-stamp battery not far from the mine mouth. One of the last batteries in use on the field, it was built of parts from other claims, including the wellknown Globe, Wealth of Nations and Inkerman mines. The metal here was not in quartz but a stone akin to a conglomerate, known locally as "cement". Colour is often found by those who pan in the creek. *Signposted 4.9 km E on Highway 7.*

**Big River\*\*\*:** For the more energetic a full day's walk of 32 km passes the site of Merrijigs and rambles on to Big River. Here, in a fascinating and remote area, are the remains of a battery, a poppet head (near collapse and one of few to survive) and a winding engine. There was an aerial tramway to bring ore down from the mine mouth whose terminal and cages remain. As the tramway had insufficient fall to enable it to operate on a gravity principle, a horse whim was used to wind gearing that may still be seen. About midway between Big River and Merrijigs, a steep track branches to the left to the Golden Lead battery of ten stamps, one that has not suffered unduly at the hands of salvagers.

**Murray Creek\*:** The walk passes the site at the head of the creek where the prospector Shiel in 1870 discovered and pegged one of the first quartz reefs to be found in the South Island. Little equipment is to be seen. The walk (which starts just west of the Blacks Point Museum) leads up Murray Creek and passes an old burnt-out opencast coalmine before swinging left at the top of the ridge. The right branch leads to the old Defiance coalmine. The track threads through attractive bush to reach the Inglewood goldmine and a now-wrecked battery about 200 m down a creek.

   "Silver" coal is found in the area, a graphite shale produced when a large coal seam in Murray Creek caught fire. In the intense heat, coal in the shale was converted to graphite. Many other thermal metamorphic rocks were formed round the artificial metamorphic circle, making the area one of special interest to rock collectors. *Allow ½ day. The start of the track is signposted at 2.2 km E on Highway 7.*

**Kirwans Reward** lies in wild high country on the Victoria Range between the head of Boatmans Creek and the Montgomerie River. It is reached only by the more experienced tramper. The deposit is a "floater" outside the main gold-and-coal belt. At about 1,200 m above sea-level the rich auriferous quartz found here was reward indeed for the prospector, William Kirwan, who in 1896 was working some distance to the north of the established mineral belt in an area subject to snow. The still-erect 15-head battery was built in 1898 (five of the stamps were added later), and an aerial tramway, now lying on the forest floor, was constructed to ferry the ore a full 2 km down from the minehead. Most of the equipment was taken in by packhorses — a remarkable feat as even the continuous wire rope to hold the ore buckets was probably taken up in one piece. The remains of a sleigh also used to transport equipment lie in the bush at the mouth of Kirwan's Creek. Snow occasionally interrupted operations, but £11,200 was paid in dividends in 1901–03 on a capital of only £3,092. Some 27,850 tons of quartz were milled from which 12,136 ounces of gold were obtained. *Allow a full day. Start at the head of Boatmans Valley. Ask directions locally. Note: There is no drinking water on the last 11 km. The track on from the mine down to the battery drops over 600 m in 3 km. A Forestry hut at Waitahu River Forks may be used by arrangement.*

The track was originally constructed as a 14 km packtrack, and passes the site of the Just In Time goldmine before it reaches the Lord Brassey claim, an open-cut goldmine unique in the area.

**Quigleys Track,** starting on Soldiers Road, crosses a low spur and then follows a branch of Devils Creek. It is marked for some distance as it passes alluvial gold workings and rocks removed from the creeks and meticulously stacked by Chinese as they searched for gold. After about an hour old workings at the head of Maori Gully are reached, beyond which the trail, often ill defined, extends for a further 13 km.

**Caledonian Mine** (**Larrys Creek**): Logging roads have made this area, formerly seen only by experienced trampers, accessible by vehicle or on foot. The route passes through bush and over riverflats. At the mine site is a 10-head battery (1874), water-powered and with parts of its pipeline still in place. On the north bank of Larrys Creek, opposite the vanished town of Collinton, a donkey engine is still crouched over a shaft, with sinking and bailing buckets nearby. *Obtain permission and directions from N.Z. Forest Service. Start from Larrys Creek Bridge (18 km SE).*

## ORGANISED EXCURSIONS

**Coalmines:** The State coalmines in the district may occasionally be visited. As the underground workings are hydraulic, visits there are frequently uncomfortable and cannot always be arranged. *Enquire at the State Mines Office, Shiel St, tel. 863.*

When looking for a placename, first consult the Index at the back of the book.

**RIVERTON\*\***     Southland.   Map 18.   Pop. 1,578.

*38.5 km WNW of Invercargill; 94 km SW of Gore.*

A MELLOW CHARM pervades Riverton that befits the oldest established settlement in Southland and Otago, as in a picturesque setting buildings freckle the green shores of the expansive estuary of the Aparima and Pourakino Rivers. Now a seaside resort and farming town, the former whaling station maintains its links with the sea. Scores of fishing boats and pleasure craft string along the jetties lining the south bank of the river whose shelter once bid to win the shipping role now played by Bluff. The estuary, still known as Jacobs River Estuary (though the river itself is called the Aparima), is dotted with occasional *maimai* that betray its fatal attraction for wild duck.

## SOME HISTORY

**Old Jacob:** Riverton's claim to be the oldest established settlement in either Southland or Otago can be projected back to before 1820, to times when there lived here a chief the whalers named Old Jacob. It was he who earned the area its first European name, Jacob's River, and a vague tradition also tells of his once fleeing inland to protect his splendidly tattooed specimen from sealers bent on acquiring it for the grisly trade in preserved heads. Aparima, as the Maori settlement was known, supported a considerable population and was noted as a centre from which to visit the Titi Islands to harvest muttonbirds.

**The Uncrowned King of Jacob's River:** Captain John Howell (1809–74) came to Riverton in about 1835 to establish a whaling station for Johnny Jones, (*see index*) later of Waikouaiti, to replace Jones's abandoned station at Preservation Inlet. As a boy in Sussex, Howell had run away to sea and had later stowed away on a migrant ship to Australia. Sailing out of Sydney he learned the whaling trade and came here after service on Kapiti Island, where he had gained an insight into Maori custom.

So well did Howell prosper that before long he was able to buy out Jones's share in the station and to trade on his own account. It was then that he prudently took as wife a Maori of high rank and with her acquired possession of the large areas of land he so quickly built into a vast holding. Howell was a man of persuasion and induced not only his half-brothers and sisters from Sydney to join him, but also weaned many whalers away from the sea and on to the land. Stock was imported from Australia so that by 1840 the settlement at Jacob's River was thriving. Edward Shortland described it as "the most smiling and refreshing aspect imaginable . . . one of the loveliest spots in New Zealand".

Howell added ships to his mercantile interests, building the 130-ton schooner *Amazon* (1848) here which on her maiden voyage ferried French settlers from Akaroa to Tahiti before briefly prospecting the riches of the Californian goldfields.

By 1850 whaling was giving only a precarious living to the few who engaged in it but by then the *Pakeha* residents of Jacob's River had their roots firmly in the soil.

Howell lived to see the area transformed from the whaling station of Jacob's River into the sawmilling and farming centre of Riverton, and the development of a busy little port. He represented Riverton in the Southland Provincial Council and is buried in the local cemetery. Howells Hills, on which South Riverton stands and which form Howells Point, together with a memorial remember the name of the man who at his death in 1874 left an estate that included 44,550 ha of pastoral country and over 25,000 sheep.

**Death of a port:** The port generated its own harbour board, pilot station, lifeboat, customs house and a busy waterfront but it was the opinionated harbour board that, in the end, killed the port. In 1878 a large bridge across the estuary restricted the use of the old jetty and there was a sharp division of opinion on whether the new wharf should be on the northern or the southern bank. Against the advice of seafarers the board, by three votes to two, elected to build on the northern side, nearest the town, with catastrophic results. The new jetty caused the scour to alter and ruined what some had (albeit extravagantly) called "the finest harbour this side of Australia". By the century's end the harbour was little more than a small fishing port — one that had seen the comings and goings of the whalers and the feverish activity generated by the goldfields of Longwood, Orepuki and Wakatipu, and had even for a time bid fair to become the premier port of Southland. A solitary dolphin, a relic from the days of sail, protrudes from the tide just upstream from the town end of the road bridge.

**Music to digest by:** It must have taken some courage for Captain John Howell to choose the site of Jacob's River for his whaling station, as the Maoris here had a reputation for unfriendliness nurtured, no doubt, by a tale that it had been the scene of the cannibal feast of an itinerant German. W. H. Pearson, Commissioner of Crown Lands under the Southland Provisional Government, related: "A foreign violinist in the early days, discovered by some young braves on the beach near the Waimatuku, was deported to the kaik as treasure trove, and being in fair condition was incontinently roasted and devoured with much apparent relish. Whether the feasters had chopped up the catgut strings as a condiment to flavour the delicacy, history does not recount, but not long after the gorge it is credibly asserted in Maori tradition that sounds of unearthly music proceeded from the cavernous interiors of the feasters, much to their consternation. The tohunga, on consultation, pronounced that the white flesh was unworthy of the honour of mastication by a Maori, and consequently it was struck out of the menu of the cuisine of the noble savage."

## THINGS TO SEE AND DO

**Riverton Museum*** contains portraits of the Howell family. Also held is a valuable collection of watercolours of Riverton and district executed in the 1870s by C. Aubrey. An appealing artist, Aubrey is a mystery among the early New Zealand artists so that not even his Christian name (probably Charles) is known for certain. A sledge held here was provided by local schoolchildren for Sir Edmund Hillary's Antarctic expeditions of 1956–58. *Palmerston St. Open daily from 2–4 pm.* To the left of the museum is the town's old customs house, which later served as an Athenaeum.

**Howell Memorial*:** A stone memorial flanked by trypots and an anchor stands on a grassed plateau near but high above the rivermouth. It looks down to the river that saw so much of the founder of Riverton. To the right may be seen waves breaking on the river bar, and upstream the view is of the myriad of jetties and boats that line the south bank. *1 km. From the south end of the bridge turn downriver. The memorial is at the end of David St.* Howell's first house (c. 1840s), much added to, is still standing (*cnr Napier and Leader Sts; opp. the school*).

**Observation Point**:** A rough road and a short walk lead to the second of several isolated rocks up which one may clamber to obtain a wide view — of Riverton spread out round the estuary, of the expansive plains beyond, and to the west out across Colac Bay. *1.5 km. On the road towards The Rocks turn right at 0.5 km up Richard St where signposted. Continue straight through a gate and up to the signposted start of the walk to Observation Point.*

The more energetic may walk about 2 km on from the top of the hill down to isolated Balancing Rock Beach. The rather unremarkable rock after which the beach is named may be seen at the back of the beach from a short distance down the track.

## ENVIRONS

**The Rocks\*\*\*,** as Riverton Rocks are more usually called, lie by the open sea on the peninsula beyond the rivermouth. There is safe bathing for children in Taramea, Mitchell's and Henderson's Bays. Howells Point concludes in a wide domain. There are many picnic spots along the way, on sandy stretches between rocky outcrops. *8.9 km to end of Howells Point.*

**Colac Bay** sweeps in a broad and shadeless arc pivoting on the low lighthouse raft of Centre Island. To the west a handful of cribs is scattered along a foreshore safe for swimming, and to the eastern end of the beach one may camp in the sand dunes and enjoy good bathing. It is on the bay's eastern shore that a tilted upthrust of argillite breaks the sweep of sand — a deposit once used by Maoris as a quarry and "workshop" for the making of implements. There is no sign of any permanent Maori habitation, the inference being that groups would only camp here temporarily from villages at places such as Ruapuke and Centre Island. The area has been well searched but very occasionally a part-worked adze may still be found on the beach. A decade ago some were discovered on the rocks themselves, shapen but still attached to their parent rock.

A further deposit of argillite is on a farm that runs to the west, from Colac to the next bay, Kawakapuka Bay, which seems to have been used principally for the fashioning of ornaments and fish-hooks. A pile of flint chips, now mostly covered by sand, extends down some 4 m. (*On private property. Those with a special interest may visit. Enquire locally*). *11 km W of Riverton.*

Offshore from Colac lies **Centre Island,** windswept and guarding the western approach to Foveaux Strait. The island, about 16 km off shore, was acquired by the Government in 1853 but when the construction of a lighthouse station began some local Maoris disputed title and occupied one of the newly-completed dwellings. The light, which was first shown in 1878 and was electrified in 1955, is manned by two keepers who are supplied by air from Invercargill. Flashing twice each 12½ seconds, the light is visible for some 37 km.

Carry your library card with you. Most public lending libraries extend lending rights to each other's members.

## ROSS*     South Westland.   Maps 17 & 37.   Pop. 368.

*30.5 km SW of Hokitika; 141.6 km E of Fox Glacier*

THE PRETTY BUSH-BACKED township of Ross, at the very end of the West Coast railway, lies across some of the richest of the country's alluvial goldfields. In spring a chain of cherry blossom marks the line of the main street at a time of year when the nearby Totara River can run thick with whitebait. A surprise too, is the size of the town's rhododendrons. Timberworkers still live in the town, whose mill has closed in favour of Ruatapu, and a limeworks supplies much of Westland's needs.

The town is named after George Arthur Emilius Ross (1829–76), at the time treasurer for the Canterbury Provincial Council.

## SOME HISTORY

**The Ballarat of Westland:** The goldfields of Ross contained "the goldmining world in miniature . . . The deep ground at Ross was a piece of Victoria, the high gravels of the Mont d'Or a little California, the dredging claims were Otago, and the bush and rain—those ubiquitous elements which governed local mining—were peculiarly Westland."

Once the silence of the Coast had been broken by the rush to the Greenstone, prospecting parties were soon to come to the Ross region to find metal in both the Totara River and its main branch, Donnelly Creek. Suitably it was a party led by Michael Donoghue, which included one McGoldrich, that opened a claim on Donoghues (now Clearwater) Creek. A succession of rich streams quickly unfurled; they were prospected, picked and panned, and before long about 4,000 were on the diggings.

As shallow creek-leads began to wane the diggers turned to ground-sluicing, and then to the sinking of shafts to tap the deep leads—a succession of overlaid-levels where alluvial gold was to be found on old riverbeds (*a model of the deepest shaft is in the museum at Hokitika*). These were unique to Ross and gave the area a permanence uncharacteristic of an alluvial field. Lifting and pumping gear was needed and soon "whims", and "whips" (horse-powered windlasses) and poppet heads were dotted over a field where, wrote a reporter in 1866, there were "as many holes as in a nutmeg grater". Bishop Harper found "winding gear visible everywhere; some steam engines at work; work going on day and night; the busy hum of machinery and labour filling the valley, which two years [earlier] had never been trodden by white man's foot."

With a steady output of gold the field enjoyed a stability and a sustained prosperity rare by any standards. It was water, the bane of the Coast, that spelt the end to the deep sinking. Large hydraulic companies were formed in the 1880s, when many ambitious schemes returned sizable profits to shareholders, many of whom were resident in Britain. A drive was put in from the Totara River to drain the flooded underground shafts but the bold Ross United Gold Mining Company succeeded only in contributing handsomely to the £200,000 that was spent to win about £26,000 in gold.

The Government helped quartzmining on Mt Greenland by subsidising a drive. There, a battery of ten stamps was built on Cedar Creek, but the lode soon dissipated. From 1891 the pattern was of steady decline. Even though the country as a whole was to win more gold in the next two decades than at any time before, Ross was not to share in it. The early dredges on the West Coast, designed for the finer gravels of Otago, broke down both too seriously and too frequently to be economic in the glacial rock and the heavier riverboulders of Westland.

Ever since, there has been a variety of attempts to tap the undoubted riches that remain. The most promising was a plan in 1907 to harness waterpower from Lake Kaniere to generate electricity for the pumps needed to drain the deeper levels. The company failed — but gave birth to the Westland Power Board — yet not before considerable hope had been raised, hope magnified by the chance finding of the Honourable Roddy nugget.

**The Honourable Roddy:** Just when the scheme to generate power at Lake Kaniere was getting under way came news the Company might have prayed for. Two diggers working on the east bank of Jones's Creek, not far from the town's centre, came across a gold nugget as large as a man's hand and weighing as much as 99 oz 12 dwt 12 grains. It was the largest authenticated find ever made in the country. The town, quite predictably, went more than a little mad. From bar to bar the nugget was swept with deliriously happy crowds until the licensee of the City Hotel pooled resources with a friend to buy it for £400. In his bar the nugget was cleaned and, with the permission of the Minister of Mines, the Hon. Roderick McKenzie, the Mayor of Ross solemnly baptised it in champagne as "the Honourable Roddy".

Visitors flocked to Ross and to the City Hotel, where for variation the nugget was playfully used as a doorstop. Later a "hospital committee" bought the nugget and took it on a tour of the country as first prize in a raffle. Enough tickets were sold to build the front rooms of a hospital in Gay St (*now used as a temple by the Masonic Lodge*). Eventually "Roddy" was bought by the Government who, in a fit of patriotic fervour, gave it to George V as a Coronation gift. The nugget was later converted into tableware for Buckingham Palace.

The size of the nugget coupled with its being slightly impregnated with quartz suggest that it was found not far from its parent rock, yet the most meticulous search failed to find a trail. It is debatable, too, as to whether the lucky pair of Scott and Sharp were working "old" or "new" ground. It was rumoured that a miner in the 1880s had overbalanced and broken his neck there, with the result that other diggers superstitiously avoided his claim. Others aver that the ground had been carefully picked over by patient Chinese. (*The site of the find is near the Empire Hotel in Aylmer St.*)

## THINGS TO SEE AND DO

**Museum**\*\*: Neat models illustrate goldmining techniques beside a facsimile of the Honourable Roddy. Tahr, chamois and deer comprise a section on the Coast's wildlife. Honey from an intriguing glass-walled apiary is sold when available. *Moorhouse St. Open Mon.–Fri. Extended hours in summer and at holiday periods.*

**St Patrick's Catholic Church** (1866– extended 1869)\* has a floor of baltic pine, said to have been purchased by Irish miners when an importer proved unable to pay for the shipment. There is also a fine *totara* altar. Outside stands a venerable maple, a jewel in autumn. Just up from the church is the township's old fire bell (1874). *Aylmer St.*

**City Hotel** (1865): Renovated but still the oldest on the Coast, the City once had the Honourable Roddy as a doorstop. Its bars saw the hilarity that followed the find. *Moorhouse St.*

**Ross cemetery:** The bush is slowly reclaiming the old cemetery, which tells of deaths by drowning and by accident. *Ask direction locally.*

**Mt Greenland** (904.3 m): An all-day return walk leads to the summit of Mt Greenland whose slopes saw the town's quartzmining activities. The old mine is a short distance down the far side of the mountain, where several shafts and the disintegrating remains of a quartz battery may be inspected. The track was upgraded in a recent bid to reopen the mines. *The track starts below the old convent. Ask directions locally.*

*Note: Points of interest both north and south of Ross are given under the entry △ West Coast Road.*

The fool wanders, the wise man travels. — Thomas Fuller (*Gnomologia*).

**ROXBURGH**   Central Otago.   Maps 1 & 14.   Pop. 760.

*158.5 km WNW of Dunedin; 58 km S of Alexandra.*

THE RIVERFLATS both north and south of Roxburgh are for some 30 km marshalled with orchards which produce much of the country's crop of peaches and apricots. Fruit dominates the town's activities, as does the annual influx of seasonal pickers. But important too are the surrounding sheepfarms, the lignite coal won from opencast mines at Coal Creek, and the massive hydro-electric power dam that pens back the waters of the Clutha not far above the town.

Hemmed by the orchards, Roxburgh spreads evenly on a level site between a precipitous hillside and the Clutha, hurrying on its way once more. Not orientated towards the river, it lacks an obvious viewpoint from which to appreciate the charm of its setting. However the traveller may detour to the bluff above the motorcamp or climb to the War Memorial in the main street.

Roxburgh is named after an ancient ruined town on Scotland's Teviot River and many of its streets bear the names of Scottish border towns (e.g. Cheviot, Melrose, Kelso, Till, Hawick).

A key to area maps appears on page 2.

## SOME HISTORY

**A bare prospect:** That Moa-hunters visited the area in search of game was vividly demonstrated in the discovery of the remains of hundreds of *moa* in a small area near Ettrick. Possibly they had fled into a swamp when fire was used to hunt them out. A well-preserved Maori feather box, now in the Otago Museum (Dunedin) was found in the Millers Flat district.

The first recorded European to see the area was the ailing Nathaniel Chalmers in 1853 as he made his hair-raising trip by *mokihi* raft down the Clutha River (*see* △ *Wanaka*).

Runs were taken up in the Teviot district (as it was then known) in 1857 and 1858. Gabriel Read made his gold discovery near Lawrence in 1861 and in the following year Frank and James Woodhouse, Andrew Young and George Cordon left Gabriels Gully to try their luck in the Dunstan region. After crossing the Teviot River (a Clutha tributary opposite the town) they did some prospecting while their clothes were hung out to dry. They did so well that they went no further. Others joined them as the river, with its rocky gorges and gravelly beaches for riffle bars, proved to have been an age-old gold trap.

A succession of miners worked the area — the early diggers took the coarse gold and the later, more patient Chinese extracted the finer gold before in 1904 the dredging boom saw some eighteen dredges working the river between Island Block and Coal Creek. The township of Roxburgh had first taken shape on the east bank, where Young and Woodhouse had made their find, but as activity grew on the west bank a settlement sprang up there as well, and finally most of those left on the east bank migrated across the river to establish Roxburgh firmly on its present site.

The dredging boom had its counterpart in the coalpits, as lignite was quarried to fuel their boilers. By the 1920s both the dredges and the hydraulic sluices had almost disappeared, but in Depression years many unemployed men fossicked along the beaches of the gorge above Coal Creek Flat.

1955 saw a final fling. When the floodgates closed the river behind the Roxburgh Dam, hundreds of sightseers swarmed downriver to try their luck on the beaches from which the waters had receded. The sightseers came no closer to success than had the investors in the Vogel's Vision scheme on the Kawarau (*see* △ *Queenstown*). Behind the dam the waters rose to flood banks that had seen generations of goldmining activity, and stone huts, rock caves, odd fruit trees and other relics disappeared beneath the newly-formed lake.

**Two bridges:** The flood of 1878 accounted for the first bridge across the Clutha at Roxburgh when the river bore the bridge from Clyde downstream. Here the bridges embraced and they were later seen "linked lovingly together" as they passed Balclutha on their way to the sea. The stone piers on the western bank are, however, those of the suspension bridge which replaced the 1878 original and was itself replaced in 1974.

**Fruitgrowing:** Some early goldminers, realising that good wages could be made from the precious metal but that the chances of making a fortune were remote, established small orchards that they worked in times when the river was high. Joseph Tamblyn is said to have planted the first fruit trees, two wild cherries purchased from a swagger. Within two years he had imported two apricots, two peaches and a plum from Australia. Tamblyn, as the district's foremost fruitgrower, established the first nursery to meet a local demand. Many growers were complaining that unscrupulous Australian nurserymen were sending over worthless trees described as new and improved varieties. The tables were turned when Tamblyn lost the name of an excellent early red apricot he had imported from New South Wales, so called it Roxburgh Red. Under its new name it found its way back to Australia.

Coal Creek has been called the finest apricot-growing district in the world. Dumbarton and the lower end of the district favour apples. Strawberries do well to the east of the river. Local orchardists have built a large cooperative packhouse at Ettrick. Heavy late frosts can savage a season's returns. When frosts threaten in spring and firepots are lit, the entire countryside can disappear under a cloud of black, sooty smoke.

*The Roxdale Cannery may be visited on one day a week between mid-January and mid-March. Tel. 96. Allow ¼ hr.*

## THINGS TO SEE AND DO

**Chinaman's Rock:** The chair-shaped slab of conglomerate in which the first pocket of gold was found in the Roxburgh district was punted across the river by John Beighton, the town's first mayor. *Main street (Scotland St), by the Civic Centre.*

**St James's Anglican Church** (1872) is the work of Peter Campbell, the stonemason who later worked on the elegant piers of the former Alexandra riverbridge. The first wedding in the much-photographed church was that of Jabez Burton, then beginning his term of over forty years as church organist. The stone for the church was quarried about 200 m from the site. *Main street (Scotland St).*

**Teviot Union Church** (1880): Built as the Presbyterian church, the stone Teviot Union Church provides the tall, iron-tipped spire that rises above surrounding trees to unify elevated views of the town. A marble plaque records the remarkable achievement of its first minister, the Rev. Robert Telford, who spent his entire thirty-eight-year ministry in this, his only pastorate. An unusual feature of the building is its sloping floor. *Scotland St.*

**Roxburgh Museum:** The tiny stone Methodist church (1872), completed some months before St James's, has been restored for use as a museum. The Methodist church gained its strength from the number of Cornishmen on the diggings. *Top end of Abbotsford St off Scotland St.*

**Roxburgh cemetery:** As with other goldfield cemeteries, this has the occasional evocative inscription and the simple marble headstones of Chinese (*far left*). *Cross to Roxburgh East and turn left. Keep bearing left. 2.6 km.*

On the way the Teviot River is crossed (*at 1 km*) where a plaque marks the first discovery of gold in the area. Looking upstream from the bridge are the powerhouse falls as they cascade some 60 m down a sheer rock face. These are occasionally illuminated by night by the district's power board, which operates small generating stations here.

## ENVIRONS

**Roxburgh hydro-electric power station:** When completed in 1962 this was the largest in the country. A straight gravity dam is 365.6 m long and 76.2 m high. Triple spillways can cope with a flood of 4,220 m$^3$/s as against the average flow of the river of 500 m$^3$/s. Behind the dam a long, narrow lake extends back some 32 km to provide good boating. Eight steel penstocks feed 56,000 hp vertical Francis-type turbines from a head of 45.1 m.

Because the Clutha is snow-fed it carries its greatest volume during the heavy thaws of spring and early summer. To store water during summer for use in winter months, control gates have been installed on the outlet to Lake Hawea. At Lake Wakatipu, control gates built by an overly optimistic goldmining company are still in existence and are used to provide further limited storage. *Turnoff signposted on Highway 8 at 10.4 km north to an observation point high above the dam. One may drive along the crest of the dam and then both north and south along the east bank of the river. The powerhouse may be visited between 10.15–11.45 am; 1–6 pm and 7–9 pm.*

**Teviot Woolshed** (*c.* 1870)\*\*: Massive stone ruins are all that remain of an enormous woolshed that must have ranked with the world's largest. The rounded facade, with twin arched doorways topped by three narrow windows, faced a building no less than 137 m long by 47.3 m wide. The shed was mysteriously destroyed by fire in 1924.

The Teviot run was the first to be applied for in Central Otago, but the lessees, Walter Miller and John Cargill (son of the leader of the Dunedin settlement) found the area a burnt-out wilderness and so were given extra time to stock their 25,900 ha. In 1861 Miller's interest was acquired by E. Anderson, an ex-officer of the British Army and John Cargill's brother-in-law. Anderson reputedly poured £100,000 into the run before, like others, he succumbed to the ravages of the rabbits and, a broken man, was found drowned in the Mataura. Oddly, the station had the first telephone in New Zealand, and perhaps in Australasia, for Anderson in the course of a world trip met Alexander Bell who, on learning of the isolated existence of the back-country runholder, presented him with two of his newly-invented devices. Anderson installed one at his homestead and the other at the Roxburgh post office. There are now scores of farms and orchards where once there was a single run. *11.5 km. Cross to Roxburgh East and turn right. At 10.6 km turn left up Three Brothers Rd. Almost at once turn left again and the woolshed ruins are on the right.*

**The Lonely Graves:** A touching tale surrounds the discovery in 1865 of a shivering dog beside the body of a goodlooking young man. After the inquest, one William Rigney asked that he might give the unknown victim a proper burial, and this he did with a large crowd in attendance, near the river that had claimed the young man's life. For years Rigney regularly tended the grave. When he died his wish was granted that he be interred beside the man he had found and buried as "Somebody's Darling". Rigney is himself described as "the man who buried 'Somebody's Darling' ". *26.3 km. Signposted S of Millers Flat on the east bank of the river.* The original headboard was glassed over when a more durable stone was provided by public subscription in 1902.

**Pinders Pond:** A dredge anchor is mounted at the entrance to the Pinders Pond reserve where there are shaded picnic spots and a lakelet safe for swimming — the hurrying Clutha, not far away, is not. The basin was the site of an hydraulic sluicing claim worked by John Ewing (*see index*). *5 km S on the east bank. Cross to Roxburgh East and turn right.*

## TOURING NOTES

**Highway 8 to △Alexandra:** The route is described under △Alexandra, "Road to Roxburgh".

## RUAPUKE ISLAND    Southland.  Map 31.

*20 km SE of Bluff. Private property.*

THE LOW CONTOURS of Ruapuke Island lie like a sleeping sentinel at the eastern approach to Foveaux Strait. It is difficult to imagine how in the times of Tuhawaiki parts of the South Island as far distant as North Canterbury could have been effectively controlled from here. The island that once supported the largest Maori population in southern New Zealand is today farmed by its Maori owners. It covers about 14,200 ha and, though of low relief, is named "two hills" for the rises of North Head and West Point. Some bush remains but most of the area is now either covered with scrub or open land used for grazing sheep. The German missionary the Rev. J. F. H. Wohlers    blished a Lutheran mission station here in 1843.

Transport to the island is difficult to arrange and permission must first be obtained from the owners.

## SOME HISTORY

**Bloody Jack:** Hone Tuhawaiki (1805? -44), because of his fondness for the adjective dubbed Bloody Jack by the whalers, was born near the mouth of the Clutha River. His uncle was Te Wakataupuka who, in 1832, sold to Peter Williams for sixty muskets the land from Dusky Bay to Preservation. When his uncle died of measles three years later, Tuhawaiki succeeded him as paramount chief of Ngaitahu and so of much of the South Island.

Handsome, intelligent, enterprising, courageous and an expert sailor, Tuhawaiki led a *taua* to exact *utu* after Te Rauparaha's assaults on Kaiapohia (*see △Kaiapoi*). After he had successfully ambushed the invaders as they returned from duckhunting on Lake Grassmere, Tuhawaiki was worsted in an encounter at Cape Campbell (on the eastern entrance to Cook Strait) but returned to the warpath to inflict further losses on Te Rauparaha at Port Underwood. He very nearly captured the great Ngati Toa chief himself and induced him to release his Ngaitahu prisoners.

Twice more Tuhawaiki invaded the northern reaches of the South Island, but failed to make contact with Te Rauparaha, who in 1839 concluded a peace treaty. Three years earlier, at Tuturau (*near △Mataura*) Tuhawaiki had overwhelmed Te Rauparaha's relative, Te Puoho, who had led a warparty down the West Coast and over Haast Pass.

A lifelong friend of the "*Pakeha* chief" James Caddell (*see index*), Tuhawaiki had a reputation for honesty and straightforwardness in his dealings with the *Pakeha* but earned a bizarre name for his wholehearted acceptance of some European customs. On a visit to Sydney he was given military uniforms by Governor Gipps, and took delight in drilling his dressed-up bodyguard on the beaches here. The missionary James Watkin noted: "He has got quite a military air." In 1840, splendidly bedecked in the regalia of a British aide-de-camp, Tuhawaiki boarded HMS *Herald* to sign the Treaty of Waitangi here.

Once converted to Christianity, Tuhawaiki came to dislike his nickname. Yet he had earned it in ways other than with expletives. When Te Rauparaha had tried one final time to free prisoners whom "Bloody Jack" was holding here, Tuhawaiki "forgot his *Pakeha* manners and dealt with the captives in the old way".

Tuhawaiki, with other South Island chiefs, in 1844 negotiated the sale of the Otago Block for £2,400, Tuhawaiki signing as "Towack, King of the Bluff". Only months later the intelligent chief, whom Edward Shortland regarded as living proof of the whalers' civilising work, was dead, accidentally drowned off the coast near Timaru.

## ST BATHANS**    Central Otago.  Maps 1 & 25.  Pop. 24.

*61 km NE of Alexandra; 39 km NW of Naseby.*

THE TINY HAMLET of St Bathans lies tucked in a hollow at the foot of the Dunstan and Hawkdun Ranges, beneath the looming hulk of Mt St Bathans. Since the goldminers moved on, their huge excavations have flooded to form a fantastic lake that daily varies in colour from dazzling blues to milky greens. Round the lake rise cliffs of many colours, heavily sluiced and adding further to the kaleidoscopic nature of the landscape.

Overlooking the scene is a string of Victorian buildings, among them the long, low Vulcan Hotel, sole survivor of thirteen, and proud that in the 1967 referendum on drinking hours not a single vote was cast in favour of six o'clock closing. All 22 votes were for later hours, a verdict that would have cheered the miners who lie buried in the hamlet's two cemeteries.

The locality takes its name from the mountain, named by the surveyor John Turnbull Thomson for his mother's home town of Abbey St Bathans.

### SOME HISTORY

**An unfortunate fortune:** The immense crater that holds Blue Lake was created by decades of hydraulic elevating to win the golden riches of a very deep drift. The technique was introduced at Gabriels Gully in 1879 by the Thames engineer J. R. Perry, who sank a shaft to the rock bottom and then installed a nozzle that drove goldbearing spoil to the surface where it was washed through sluiceboxes. The method could raise spoil over 21.5 m in a single lift, and well over 30 m in a double lift.

John Ewing (1848-1922), a lifelong miner and self-taught engineer, improved on the system at his St Bathans claim, where he could elevate paydirt a full 33 m in a single lift, and St Bathans was reputed to have the world's deepest hydraulic elevating claim, of 46.4 m in two lifts. In one fabulous year Ewing won no fewer than 3,000 ounces here, a bonanza that was to prove his undoing. Convinced that he had the Midas touch, he acquired a number of large mining properties, so overcommitting himself that when the Colonial Bank collapsed, he too became bankrupt. When another company then tried to jump his St Bathans claim, Ewing succeeded where his lawyers had failed. He appeared in person in the Court of Appeal, there to persuade three of the five judges to reverse the decision of the lower court, so preserving the claim for his creditors.

Work at St Bathans by the Kildare Consolidated Company (founded by Ewing) continued until it began to undermine the settlement's main street. The Maniototo County Council — of which Ewing had once been chairman — served a writ on the company to stop its operations, and in 1948 the claim was abandoned. Mining is at a standstill, though the lead remains as rich as ever and awaits only a profitable method of working it. *A photograph of the elevating machinery is in the hotel.*

### THINGS TO SEE AND DO

**Blue Lake\*\*\*:** The remarkable lake fills an enormous rift about 800 m long and over 50 m deep. The lake itself has a depth of over 20 m. In summer months many come to swim and to water-ski in this unique setting.

For years a deep blue in colour, the lake suddenly turned a milky green in 1968 when a stream burst through into it. Until surface water stops draining into the lake it is unlikely to permanently regain its former hue.

**The buildings of St Bathans:** The **Vulcan Hotel** (*c.* 1869), typical of its period, still wears the shamrock that betrays its allegiance in the perennial feuds of the past between Catholic and Protestant Irish. The deserted offices beside it include a door that still professes to belong to the Registered Office of the Scandinavian Water Race Company Ltd. Farther up the street is the two-storeyed combined **post office-and-postmaster's residence,** now a weatherbeaten crib. A little beyond the post office is the simple, iron Anglican **Church of St Alban the Martyr** (1882), a church whose predecessor was formally opened in 1865 only to be wrecked in a gale the next day. In London Mr F. G. Dalgety, owner of Hawkdun station, heard of the fate of the church and despatched a prefabricated iron replacement, "felt and timber-lined . . . in fact complete in every respect . . . and I have also sent chairs, cocoanut (*sic*) matting, bibles, prayer books, maps, etc.", he wrote to his manager. There is no record that the church has ever been dedicated, and it seems never to have been consecrated, perhaps because it was on private property until Dalgety & Co. finally transferred the land to diocesan trustees. Its predecessor was rebuilt at Oturehua where it still houses machinery.

Diagonally opposite the hotel, all alone, stands the former **billiards saloon.** Down the street the **stone schoolhouse** is collapsing into ruin, the old baker's oven nearby. Beside it stands immaculate **St Patrick's Catholic Church** (1892), built of sundried mud bricks, a building material common enough in the region but rare in a church.

### TOURING NOTE

**Loop Road:** For the traveller on Highway 85 the detour to St Bathans round Loop Road involves only an additional 12.4 km. The road passes through worked ground on both sides of St Bathans, particularly as it runs south to follow the fabled Dunstan Creek. Extensive mining was carried on at Vinegar Hill, named after the many fights that occurred there which led to comparisons with the 1798 Battle of Vinegar Hill in Wexford, Ireland. The nearby Cambrian diggings were as Welsh as St Bathans' were Irish — church services were held in Welsh and the first hotel was entitled the Welsh Harp. Here, too, gold remains, though a later attempt by deep sinking to strike a rich lead which had previously been worked by hydraulic elevating proved a failure.

# STEWART ISLAND

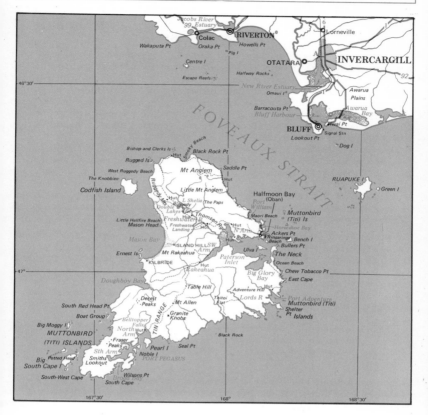

## 31

## STEWART ISLAND***    Southland.    Map 31.    Pop. 336 (Oban).

*32 km SSW of Bluff. The small guidebook* Stewart Island *by N. S. Seaward and Sheila Natusch (Pegasus) is recommended.*

ONLY AN INFINITESIMAL stretch of Stewart Island's 1,600 kilometres of coastline is touched by human habitation, where the tiny settlement of Oban sprinkles its houses through the bush and round the crescent of Halfmoon Bay. The initial impression as one crosses Foveaux Strait is of the island's magnitude. Steep, bushed promontories rise clear from a clear sea, sheltering numerous golden beaches tucked into endless successions of rock-girt coves.

The pace of life is unhurried. Sawmilling has long since ceased, most of the island is now covered by reserves for the preservation of scenery and of flora and fauna, and activity centres round the island's fishing fleet. The scene is unruffled except by the arrival several times a week of the *Wairua* from Bluff, which deposits day-trippers on the foreshore for about four hours.

With barely 20 km of road, the island is a haven for a car-free holiday; for walking, tramping, fishing, boating, and for collecting unusual seashells. No scheduled launch trips are run round Paterson Inlet, so that to see the island to advantage one should plan a stay of several days.

Sprinkled off the east and south-west coasts are the Muttonbird Islands.

To the Maori the island was Rakiura (heavenly glow), referring perhaps to the aurora australis, the "southern lights" which are very occasionally seen streaking the

Visitors to Stewart Island may find it of value to acquire knowledge from such books as *Birds in New Zealand* by C. J. Robertson, *Seashore Life in New Zealand* by R. K. Dell and Eric Heath, *New Zealand Seashells in Colour* by J. R. Penniket and C. J. H. Moon and *Ferns and Fern Allies of New Zealand* by R. J. Chinnock and Eric Heath; the island has an abundance of flora and fauna.

The definitive history of the island is *Rakiura* by Basil Howard. All the above are published by A.H. & A.W. Reed.

southern sky, as well as to the superb sunsets for which the island is famed. Such names as Chewtobacco (named for a local Maori), Big Moggy (a corruption of big *moki*), Doughboy Bay, Hellfire (a dangerous lee shore), Potted Head, and Three-Legged Woodhen add further colour.

## SOME NOTES

The island tilts from west to east, so that streams rising comparatively near the west coast meet the sea to the east. Two near-land-locked harbours gash the eastern shoreline to form Paterson Inlet and Port Pegasus. Though much of the island is steep and rugged, two almost contiguous narrow necks of lowland divide the hill formations into two distinct areas of differing geologies. To the north, complex peaks of coarse igneous rock rise to Mt Anglem (*974.9 m*), in winter dusted with snow; farther south, in an area basically comprised of granitites, the peak Rakeahua rises to 675 m above the western end of Paterson Inlet.

Foveaux Strait, about 30 km wide, is comparatively shallow. During the last Ice Age the island was probably as Cook tentatively plotted it — a peninsula joined to the mainland. Shallow though it is, the strait is still capable of being a wild and turbulent stretch of water.

Average rainfall at Halfmoon Bay is 1450 mm, evenly spread throughout the year. If summer temperatures are rarely very high, neither are they very low in winter. Warm waterproof clothing may be needed at any time of year.

**Access:** Access to the island is by the ferry *Wairua* (627 tons), which carries cargo and up to 287 passengers. In addition, the vessel periodically services manned lighthouses round the coast. The ferry is a vital link for the island, as virtually every comfort is imported from the mainland, from milk and newspapers to timber. *The ferry sails three times a week, usually on Mondays, Wednesdays and Fridays, with increased sailings over the holiday periods. It leaves Bluff at 8 am to arrive at Oban at 10 am; and leaves Oban on the return journey at 1.45 or 3 pm. Timetable varies. Details from travel agents everywhere or Ministry of Transport, tel. BLF 8119.*

The 9-passenger Britten-Norman Islander aircraft of Stewart Island Air Services shuttles between Invercargill airport and Ryans Creek airstrip on the island. *Scheduled 20-min passenger flights generally run daily and the aircraft is also available for charter.*

**Accommodation:** The limited accommodation at Oban, which is not commercialised for visitors, comprises one licensed hotel and (at present) a few motel units. By advertising in Invercargill newspapers it is occasionally possible to rent a crib (ask whether there is electricity and a water supply).

## SOME HISTORY

**The finding of Foveaux Strait:** Stewart Island's place in Ngaitahu folklore extends back to the catching of Te Ika-a-Maui (the Fish of Maui—the North Island). In their version of the legend the South Island was Maui's canoe and Stewart Island, Te Punga-o-te-waka-a-Maui (the anchor of the canoe of Maui).

To the European it first emerged as a peninsula when Cook made his second major misjudgment (drawn from the coast by claims that land had been sighted to the east, he also misjudged Banks Peninsula, naming it Banks Island). Less understandable is how he came to chart an island as a peninsula barely three weeks later. Certainly others aboard *Endeavour* on that day in March 1770 demurred. Even Sydney Parkinson, whose experience could not be compared with Cook's, noted: "The land we then saw at a considerable distance seemed to be an island, having a great opening between it and the land which we had passed before." Cook, too, shared this initial impression, but after sailing south round the island (and nearly foundering on The Traps) he wrote: "But when I came to lay this land down on paper from the several bearings I had taken, it appeared that there was little reason to suppose it an Island. On the contrary I hardly have a doubt but that it joins to and makes part of the mainland." Perhaps his thoughts were more on the question of whether the new land might be the legendary Unknown Southern Continent and so he pressed on to resolve the shipboard debate rather than turn back to check a comparatively minor detail. Cook tentatively penned the land mass on his map as a peninsula and it so remained for nearly four decades.

Cook, therefore, did not discover Foveaux Strait, but just who did, it is now not possible to say. Some claim that the passage was not discovered until 1809, but it was certainly known of by that year. Further, it is named after Lieutenant-Governor Foveaux, who did not arrive in New South Wales until 1808. But, in the historian McNab's words, "When we consider the length of time — no less than 39 years . . . and the continuous trade which shipping had carried on to Dusky Sound, Solander Island, the South Cape and the Snares . . . it passes comprehension that the existence of the strait should have so long remained unknown."

**The naming of Stewart Island:** With knowledge of the strait's discovery in doubt, the discovery that Stewart Island was indeed an island is also shrouded in mystery. Some suggest that a Captain Paterson sailed round the island in 1790 and named it after his wife's clan. Others credit the discovery to William Stewart (1767–1851) who in 1803 was on the *Pegasus* when it brought a sealing gang here. Certainly in 1809 Stewart took observations and made an excellent chart of Port Pegasus, which was published in 1816 and still in use in 1840. Stewart went to Britain in 1824 to float a flax and timber company which established a shipyard settlement on Port Pegasus, but the venture failed. The small group of sawyers he had brought from the Bay of Islands completed work on a schooner later named *Joseph Weller*, the first vessel known to be built on the island. In the course of time Stewart returned to act as pilot to HMS *Herald* on her visit to proclaim sovereignty in 1840.

**A buried bottle:** Somewhere on the shores of Port Pegasus a bottle may lie buried which contains the original document declaring the island a British possession. The proclamation ceremony took place in 1840 on "the apex of a small island which becomes a peninsula at low water" on the uninhabited harbour shore. Captain Nias hoisted the Union Jack, the guns of the *Herald* fired a salute, and Major Bunbury read the proclamation which was then placed in a bottle and buried. But where? Attempts to locate the historic trove have been several, even including in 1936 an expedition headed by an historian and assisted by a naval cruiser with more than 200 officers and ratings. (The historian Basil Howard, author of the definitive history of Stewart Island, *Rakiura* (Reed), believed that in 1950 he located the spot where the bottle had been — from which it had apparently been taken many years earlier.)

The *Herald,* as it completed the formal annexation of New Zealand by Britain begun at Waitangi, was supposed to visit Stewart Island and there obtain the signatures of chiefs to the Treaty of Waitangi. But the vessel bypassed Ruapuke and Port William, where there were chiefs, and British sovereignty over the island by right of discovery was proclaimed at Port Pegasus, where there was none. Only then did the *Herald* call at Ruapuke for Tuhawaiki's signature and those of other chiefs there.

**An island for sale:** British the island had become, but it was still, of course, Maori owned. Under the Treaty of Waitangi only the Government could purchase land from the Maori and, in 1864, Commissioner Clarke was sent south to negotiate terms for the sale and purchase of Stewart Island — which had not been included in Mantell's earlier Murihiku purchase (*see index*). Clarke's report tells how he met with 120 Maoris, representing *hapu* in Otago, Southland and Ruapuke. The group had already settled the question of title, but "I wished to satisfy myself that no undue pressure had been brought to bear on any of the claimants". The cases of both Ngaitahu and Ngatimamoe were argued before him, and "The Ngaitahu established indisputably their right . . . so that at the close of the discussion [the Ngatimamoe] were quite satisfied . . . [to] claim through their Ngaitahu ancestry."

The next day, 24 June 1864, they met again to discuss terms. Clarke offered £6,000; Ngaitahu countered with £50,000, then £22,000, and finally £12,000. "But I told them I could not, and would not, depart from my first offer, because I believed it was a liberal payment for an island which was of little or no value to themselves. . . . After some further discussion, they consented to the terms offered by me, provided that I paid the £6,000 at once. They also wished that the £2,000 reserved for education and other purposes should be paid over to them. Their reason for making this request was that all promises of a like nature made by former commissioners had never been fulfilled. I told them I would provide against any such contingency by entering the stipulation in the text of the deed." By the deed, certain Maori reserves were declared on the main island, together with some twenty-one "muttonbird islands", breeding grounds of the much-sought *titi*.

**Muttonbirds:** The muttonbird, or *titi*, has long been a delicacy prized by the Maori of Murihiku and beyond. A member of the order of seabirds known as petrels, their European name may refer either to their taste or to the woolly down of their young. The migratory New Zealand muttonbird (*Puffinus griseus*) is also known as the Sooty Shearwater. Their Australian equivalent, found in Victoria, Tasmania, Bass Strait and South Australia, is the Short-Tailed Shearwater. After spending the southern winter in the north Pacific, huge numbers fly south, along the New Zealand coast, to their main breeding grounds — bleak islands, scruffy with muttonbird scrub, to the north-east and south-west of the island. The birds return to mate in the same burrows year after year, a single white egg being laid in each burrow by the end of November. Hatching begins in January and by the end of April the chicks are ready to fly.

Until April, those whose rights were reserved under the deed are careful to avoid landing on the islands, not wishing to frighten the *titi* until the young birds are nearly fledged, for the young depend on their parents for food. But in April and May those so entitled to descend on the islands as their forefathers have for generations, to harvest chicks so fat they cannot fly nor even run very far. Care is taken not to damage the burrows so that the parent birds may return to breed in them again the following summer. Later, when the chicks have begun to fly, "torching" is used, to catch the birds when they come in to rest for the night. Up to 250,000 chicks are taken from the islands each year, to be dispatched to shops throughout the country and for use as a source of oil and feather down. The birds were traditionally stored in bags of bull kelp, the plant's large leathery sheet being split to form a bag capable of holding a dozen or so birds. The kelp, however, tends to taint the birds, giving them a blubbery flavour, and the preference now is for large tins. The birds are very fatty and must be boiled in several changes of water before they are roasted.

**A "Pakeha chief":** There are several, generally fictitious, accounts of early *Pakeha* being adopted into Maori families to live as chiefs of the tribe. The earliest authenticated case is that of James Caddell (*fl.* 1823), a boy with a sealing gang which was captured in the vicinity of Stewart Island. The rest of the party were eaten by the Murihiku Maoris; the youth, it seems, was spared only by the action of a chief's daughter, who threw a mat over his shoulders to claim him for herself. (Another account, that he touched a chief's cloak and was rendered to a degree *tapu,* is inconsistent with Maori custom.) Caddell quickly accepted his fate, whole-heartedly adopting the life-style of the tribe. In time he grew to marry a chief's daughter, and by sheer force of character established himself as a leading member of the tribe. Some say he established a reputation as a warrior whose special victims were the sealers. One writer asserted that the Maoris here "hunted the sealers even more industriously than the sealers hunted the seals"; another suggestion is that he visited Sydney, whence he returned to dramatically reduce the mortality rate among sealers. The latter version is nearer the truth. For the twelve years that followed Caddell's seizure there was little hostility between Maori and *Pakeha* in Southland, at times when in Otago several acts of savagery were taking place. Exceptions were gangs from an American vessel whom Caddell helped harass after they had perpetrated a number of outrages on the Maoris of Murihiku. Certainly his influence with Tuhawaiki (*see index*) must have contributed to the Ruapuke chief's welcome acceptance of the *Pakeha.*

When the *Snapper* visited Ruapuke in 1823, Caddell served as both pilot and interpreter, and warned Captain Edwardson in good time of a planned attack. His so-called "capture" by *Pakeha* traders was in fact a friendly excursion to Sydney on the *Snapper,* where his fair and tattooed countenance, and the company of his wife Toki-toki and his friend, "Jacky Snapper" (presumably Tuhawaiki), attracted considerable attention. After a few months they returned to New Zealand on the *Mermaid,* at which point Caddell fades from history.

**Exploitation:** After the sealers (*c.* 1820) and the whalers (*c.* 1840) had passed on, for many years from 1860 sawmills worked various parts of the island. About the turn of the century the Government hesitated to renew timber rights as the feeling had grown that the bush should be preserved. Both tin and gold were won at Pegasus, and a quartz reef was found some 8 km from Halfmoon Bay. Tin mining boomed at Pegasus from 1880–90, but the principal business lay not in gaining the precious metal but in floating companies and selling shares. More gold than tin came out of Pegasus, but not much of either. Farming on the island has never proved overly successful. Today the mills have long since fallen silent (1925), the bush is regenerating, and Stewart Islanders draw their living from the sea. Traces remain of the old tin workings, and of the whaling base at Price's Inlet.

### THINGS TO SEE AND DO AT OBAN

**Oban** (pop. 336) sits snugly in Halfmoon Bay on the north-east corner of the island, by the entrance to Paterson Inlet. The west coast of the island is warmed by a sea current from the Australian coast and the little village is sheltered from prevailing westerlies by Mt Anglem and its forested ranges. Quiet and unhurried, the settlement has a tranquillity at night broken only by the gentle *put-put-putting* of diesel motors as they generate electricity.

**Rakiura Museum (Oban)**\*\* reflects the island's fascinating history. Giant crabs, coral-like growths from the island's South Cape, Stewart Island *weka* and *kiwi,* and Little Blue Penguins are exhibited with the mollymawk and shag. Samples and a plan of tin mining claims at Port Pegasus record a brief era of mineral exploitation. Seafaring relics include an 1816 globe (still showing the island as a peninsula), items from the whaling trade, aging biscuits from a castaways depot on The Snares, and shoes fashioned from sealskin by survivors from the *Dundonald* on the Auckland Islands. Oddly out of place is a bust carved from *kauri* gum of Potatau II, Te Wherowhero Tawhiao, (1825–94), the second Maori king. *Near the foreshore at Oban. Open on boat days from 10 am to 1.30 pm while the ferry is in. Allow ½ hr.*

**Wohlers grave and memorial (Ringaringa Beach):** On the far extremity of Ringaringa Beach lie the grave of and a memorial to the remarkable German missionary of Ruapuke, Johann Friedrich Heinrich Wohlers (1811–85). Wohlers arrived at Nelson with the German settlers. However after finding there were only a few local Maoris for the mission he helped establish, he made his way south, finally establishing a mission (1844) on △Ruapuke Island under Tuhawaiki's protection. There, with perhaps the largest Maori population of any centre in southern New Zealand, he managed to induce the Maori to grow wheat until they found it more sensible to barter muttonbirds for flour. The island's population slowly declined, Wohlers ultimately moving to Stewart Island. A man of infinite patience, Wohlers did not subscribe to the belief that the Maori could be "civilised" within a few years by the influence of the Gospel. His faith and courage gave him the will to persist with what he knew would be a very slow advance. Wohlers' harmonium is in the museum at Oban. Out from Ringaringa Beach lies Native Island, largely bushclad and once the site of Maori settlement. *2 km. Signposted.* (A readable biography is *Brother Wohlers* by Sheila Natusch (Pegasus).)

**A minibus tour** of the island's roads passes a number of delightful beaches and visits Observation Point and a house moved to Oban from the Norwegian whaling base at Price's Inlet. Though designed for day-trippers from the ferry, it serves as a useful familiarisation trip for those with some time to spend on the island. *Run by Stewart Island Travel and Hamilton Gold Coach Tours on boat days and at other times by arrangement.*

**Ulva Island** (*260 ha*) was for many years the bushclad home of the naturalist Charles Traill (1826–91), who combined the running of a general store with a passion for botany, birdlife and the study of shells. Charles was appointed postmaster for "the most southerly post office in the world" (an inaccurate claim as even on Stewart Island there had been a more southerly post office, at Port Pegasus in the tin years of the 1890s). The raising of a flag signalled the arrival of mail to settlers and sawmillers, who would converge on the island to collect their letters. However those at Oban found the office too distant and that without climbing to high ground the flag was out of sight. A postal service at Oban drew away many of the customers of Ulva, but long after the Traills had died the little post office remained open, its main custom being from visitors who would mail as "postcards" letters written on the underside of *puheretaiko* leaves. The island was proclaimed a bird sanctuary in 1922, the post office closing the following year.

An hour's launch trip separates Ulva from Oban, but the water between Ulva and the shore has not deterred deer, who have swum across to cause considerable damage, though this is not apparent to the untrained eye. *Rimu, rata, miro* and *totara* stretch skywards from a floor of moss in some of the region's most delightful bush. The birdlife is prolific. Sandy beaches ideal for a day's picnic, old buildings and the graves of the Traills add further interest. *Launches run periodically from Halfmoon Bay. By arrangement visitors may be left on Ulva by launches travelling up Paterson Inlet, there to spend the day before being collected on the return journey. Generally the trip to Ulva cannot be made by the day-tripper visiting Stewart Island by the ferry.*

**Other launch trips** from Oban run up Paterson Inlet to Price's Inlet and to the South-West arm of Paterson Inlet. Surveyors Bay in Price's Inlet was the site of a Norwegian shore whaling base of which there are still relics to be seen.

Of growing popularity is the one-hour trip in the open sea north-west to Port William, where a short walk across the northern promontory leads to Sawyers Beach and an excellent view of Mt Anglem.

**Fishing trips** run periodically. The principal quarry is the cod for which the region is renowned.

## SOME WALKS FROM OBAN***

With relatively few cars and little roading, but numerous tracks and beaches, the island is essentially for the walker and the tramper. Even day-trippers will want to walk to some points of interest within easy reach and savour fully the island's perfect fusion of land, forest and sea.

**Observation Rock** (*15 mins*): Walk up the hill and along a short signposted track to reach the observation point. Below, a jetty marks Golden Bay, in the middle distance are the three islands of Faith, Hope and Charity; in the far distance the South-West arm of Paterson Inlet curls out of sight, below the outline of Rakeahua (*675.4 m*). An outstanding view in almost any weather, it is charged with dramatic intensity at sunset. By the police station at the start of the walk is a brown house whose gables have a nordic flavour. It was built in about 1925 by an engineer engaged with the Norwegian whaling venture.

**Other walks:** Another easy walk extends north from Halfmoon Bay through to Horseshoe Bay and beyond to the bush track up Garden Mound or to Lee Bay, site of the cable landing. Alternatively one may stroll along Halfmoon Bay's southern shore, passing Lonnekers, Leasks, and Harrolds Bays to reach the shipping beacon on Ackers Point (*allow at least 4 hrs*). A favoured half day walk is to Golden Bay and Ringaringa Beach, returning over the peninsula to Lonnekers Bay and so back to Oban. The route leads past excellent anchorages, attractive beaches and a number of homes tucked away in the bush almost out of sight.

**Mt Anglem:** The view from the tip of the island's tallest peak is superb. From an elevation some 978.9 m above Foveaux Strait, it takes in both coasts and the scattered islands of the strait. *Launches can by arrangement ferry parties to the mountain's coastal foot whence the return tramp can be made in a day.*

## TRAMPING AND HUNTING

**Tramping:** Tracks are being upgraded and extended by the New Zealand Forest Service, with huts to accommodate ten or so trampers planned for every four-hourly section. Tracking is virtually confined to the area north of Doughboy Bay, leaving the southerly portion (which includes Port Adventure and Port Pegasus) as a wilderness area. A favoured four-to-five day route is to follow the coastline northwest from Halfmoon Bay, perhaps detouring to walk up Mt Anglem, and returning to Paterson Inlet by way of Freshwater Landing. *Full details of routes, tracks and huts are available from the New Zealand Forest Service ranger at Oban, who should also be advised of trampers' plans.*

293

**Hunting:** It is quicker to reach distant coastal hunting areas by launch (*arrange at Oban*) or plane (*charter from Stewart Island Air Services, Invercargill*). Spread over the island's coastal regions is the last accessible herd of whitetail deer in New Zealand (the other, in the lower Routeburn-Sylvan Lake area near Lake Wakatipu, is extremely remote). An attractive deer with delicate facial features, the whitetail (or Virginian) deer (*Odocoileus virginianus*) is named for its habit of holding its large tail erect when alarmed. Lined underneath with long white hair, the tail and its splash of white are believed to act as a guide for the young when parents flee through dense undergrowth. Considerably smaller than the red deer (also found on the island), the whitetail is similar in size to the sika. His rut is some three to four weeks earlier than that of the red deer and is usually at its peak by Mid-May. In contrast with the red deer, the whitetail buck neither roars nor wallows, nor does he mob up the does. The whitetail's elusive qualities have earned him the description of "the little grey ghost" — cunning, quiet, quick, and with finely honed senses of sight, smell and hearing, he makes the red deer seem cumbersome. A trait that can give him away is an unexplained habit of stamping a forefoot on the ground. The gesture is almost silent, but the sudden movement is sometimes the first indication of his presence. *Hunting permits are available from the Forest Service ranger at Oban.*

**TAKAKA\*\*     Nelson.   Maps 26 & 32.   Pop. 939.**

*57 km NW of Motueka; 28 km SE of Collingwood.*

ISOLATED by the looming mass of the modestly-titled Takaka Hill, the dairying town of Takaka lies between the "marble mountain" and the splendid beaches of Golden Bay. Picturesque at all times of year, the district has a large number of exotic trees which are particularly colourful in autumn. As the principal point of entry for △ Abel Tasman National Park, there is a park information office here. Close by are inviting beaches such as Pohara, Tata and Patons Rock.

Takaka means bracken. The name comes from the Society Islands together with the name Motueka and the legend of the *taniwha* of Parapara Inlet (*see* △ *Collingwood*).

### SOME HISTORY

**Murderers Bay:** It was off the coast here that Abel Tasman had his only contact with the Maori — when four of his crew were killed (*see* △ *Nelson*).

**A varied role:** Today Golden Bay is primarily concerned with dairying, but it was coal and the promise of other minerals that in 1842 first drew settlers from Nelson. Coal and lime were both shipped to Nelson until the district's character changed dramatically in 1857, when thousands rushed to the goldfields in the bay. As people flowed in, timber began to pour out, shipped from wharves at Motupipi and Waitapu to markets as far afield as San Francisco. As the land was cleared, interest switched to dairying. The region remains rich in a variety of virtually untapped mineral resources. Some quarrying takes place on Takaka Hill, and at nearby Tarakohe a massive cement works exploits vast deposits of limestone. Less enduring have been gold, asbestos, paintworks (at Parapara), ironworks (at Onekaka), and coal (at Pakawau and Puponga). The hinterland is periodically prospected and the bay itself has held the promise of petroleum reserves.

As late as 1882 Bishop Suter prayed that his vicar in Golden Bay "be preserved amidst frequent dangers of rivers which abound in that bridgeless country. It is perfectly astonishing that Governments professing to rule for the people should, by the of neglect bridges, allow so much loss of life . . . half of life's energy is exhausted in replies to anxious enquiries: 'How are the rivers?' "

**The roading of a mountain:** For generations Takaka's principal mode of communication was by sea, though as early as 1856 some timber was being taken out by a bridletrack that wound over the marble mountain to Riwaka and Motueka. All were unanimous about the need for a road, but the valley split over whether it should follow the inland route or whether it should go round the coast — a route three times as long. The local member of the Nelson Provincial Council was adamant that it would be an utter impossibility to make a coach road over the rough, high, rock-bound hills. Notwithstanding, the inland route prevailed, so preserving the coastline that was to become the Abel Tasman National Park. After much painstaking surveying, first a bridletrack and finally a coach road ended the valley's era of isolation.

The building of a bridge over the Motueka River was an essential forerunner to the formation of the coach road. This proposal, too, split the population of Riwaka, but delays as the arguments raged proved beneficial. In 1877, just as tenders were being called, a flash flood occurred; the most disastrous the district has known, it would undoubtedly have swept the bridge out to sea. Plans were revised — the flood had raised the riverbed fully 3 m — and the bridge opened without incident the following year.

# GOLDEN BAY

## 32

**Takaka marble:** The best-known occurrence of marble, a hard and crystalline form of limestone, runs almost continuously from the crest of the Pikikiruna Range in Abel Tasman National Park nearly to Mt Arthur. Generally the marble is coarsely crystalline, with greyish veins caused by microscopic flakes of graphite. Occasional red and yellow veins are due to small amounts of oxide of iron.

A wide formation of the rock has been shattered by the forces that produced the mountain structure, but at Kairuru (where most of the quarrying has been done) the outcrop is solid. It has the lasting qualities of the best marble and is a light-grey with irregular veins of a darker colour. Stone from here was used in the construction of Wellington's Parliament Buildings. The stone often shows an attractive tint of pink which renders it excellent for internal ornamentation (also used in Parliament Buildings). A wide bed at Kairuru is perfectly white. Delicate dove-grey stone was used in Nelson Cathedral and for monuments throughout the country. Some 100 tons were exported to Scotland for the construction of a memorial at Kirkintilloch.

*Outcrops are seen by the roadside as one drives over Takaka Hill. Even more impressive are the weathered marble slabs and dead trees that litter the Canaan Road (turn left at 35 km from Takaka).*

> The New Zealand Forest Service has offices throughout the country which issue permits for hunting in State Forests and in Forest Parks. They also advise as to the best hunting areas.

## THINGS TO SEE AND DO NEARBY

**Beaches\*\*\*:** Nearby are inviting beaches such as Pohara, Tata, Totaranui *(for all, see below)* and Patons Rock *(11 km).*

**Pupu Springs\*\*\*:** More correctly known as Waikoropupu (bubbling waters) the springs have a daily outflow of approximately 2,160,000,000 litres, among the largest in the world. There are two main springs which can be seen at close quarters from a platform. Numerous small springs well up in the surrounding pools. The area was the scene of extensive gold workings when it was known to the miners by the even less palatable corruption of Bubu. *5 km. Turn off 2 km N on Highway 60. Signposted. Allow 30 mins.*

**Anatoki Eels\*\*:** Tame eels are fed by hand in the Anatoki River. As they hibernate in cold weather, they are not seen from May through to August. *5 km. Turnoff signposted immediately south of Takaka. Hours vary and depend on river conditions.* After seeing the eels and the tame trout that often join them, one may drive up the picturesque Anatoki River Valley.

**Takaka Rivermouth:** Rangihaeata Head, the western extremity of the rivermouth and probably named after the Ngati Toa chief, is said to have been the place of execution for no fewer than 600 Golden Bay Maoris. The invaders from Kapiti simply hurled their captives down to their deaths. *7.5 km. Turn off Highway 60 at 5.4 km N.*

**Cobb power station** (1944): The giddy road up the narrow Cobb Valley passes through rugged, spectacular scenery. The power station, with six turbines and a capacity of 32,000 kW may be visited. Shortly after leaving the power station the transmission lines cross Barrons Gorge with a single span of over 1.3 km, the longest in the country, as they carry power to Nelson and to the South Island grid. The dam, 38.1 m high and 204.1 m long, is by road 13 km beyond the powerhouse. Water is dropped 592.7 m down to the powerhouse, giving the station the highest gross head in the country and enabling considerable amounts of power to be generated from a small flow.

The scheme, undertaken by a private company in 1935, was taken over by the State before it became operational. *The powerhouse is 40 km S of Takaka (1½ hrs driving time); the dam and lake are 53 km S (2½ hrs driving time). Turn off Highway 60 at Upper Takaka.* Though well-surfaced, the road is not for the nervous motorist.

## DRIVE TO TOTARANUI

*76.5 km.* The route follows the only road access to △Abel Tasman National Park. After winding round a delightful coastline, where symmetrical sweeps of golden sand contrast with contorted cliffs of weather worn limestone, the road climbs through the forest of the park before descending to Totaranui. *Leave Takaka by signposted route from pioneer memorial to pass:*

**Pohara Beach\*\*\*** *(8.8 km):* A magnificent safe beach much favoured by summer holidaymakers. There is a museum display, open to the public, at the Golden Bay Motel. *The coast assumes dramatic qualities as the road passes under jutting crags and by a curious house perched on a sea girt rock and reaches:*

**Golden Bay Cement Works\*** *(11 km):* Dairying apart, the town's major industry. Here cement is manufactured and blown down an enormous shute to fill the holds of specially-constructed ships. (*Visits to the plant by arrangement, tel. 123*). *A little further on is the:*

**Tasman Memorial:** Erected in 1942 to mark the tercentenary of Abel Tasman's visit is a modest obelisk, a memorial to the navigator as well as to the four Dutchmen who lost their lives in the bay below. Tasman's ships were anchored near Tata Islands, to the right as one looks across Golden Bay to Cape Farewell. (*For an account of the stay, see* △*Nelson.*) *The road drops to pass* **Ligar Beach** *and* **Tata Beach\*\*** *before skirting the Wainui Inlet (where boats may be hired).*

**Wainui Falls Track** *(20.5 km):* Signposted is the start of a 2 hours return walk to the Wainui waterfall. *Gradually the bush closes in. Through an avenue of beech and punga the Park is entered at Pigeon Saddle.*

**Lookout Rock Walk** *(31.8 km):* The view from the rock extends only over the forest to Golden Bay (*1½ hrs return*). For wider views, over both Golden Bay and much of Tasman Bay, one must walk on to Gibbs Hill (*allow a good half day*). On the right is the track up to Canaan (*8 hrs*). *The road ends at:*

**Totaranui\*\*\*** *(38.2 km):* Here one may camp beside a splendid beach, reputedly the place where the Ngaitahu first landed in the South Island. There is limited accommodation, a park information office, and launching ramps for those who would explore the park's fascinating coastline. Short walks lead south to Skinners Point (*15 mins*), Goats Bay (*30 mins*) and to Waiharekeke (*1¾ hrs*), another beautiful beach. North, a track leads to Anapai Bay (*¾ hr*). *See also* △*Abel Tasman National Park.*

## ORGANISED EXCURSIONS

**Trips to Farewell Spit Lighthouse, Kahurangi Point** and other inaccessible places of interest are run by Collingwood Motors. *For details, see* △*Collingwood.*

## TOURING NOTES

**Highway 60 to △Collingwood:** At 16.6 km the road passes the locality of Onekaka, where an ironworks was established based on the area's ironsands and the coal of Puponga. A derelict wharf juts seaward, and inland the plant and buildings of the works that produced 40,000 tons of pig iron between 1922 and 1935 have all but vanished. Onekaka means hot sands.

Parapara Inlet, lair of the legendary *taniwha*, is at 19.7 km (*see* △*Collingwood for legend*).

A memorial at 24 km indicates the area of the first South Island discovery of payable gold (1856).

**Highway 60 to △Motueka:** The road winds over the marble mountain of Takaka Hill (*see above*). One may detour along the crest of the range to Canaan and walk in to Harwood's Hole (*see* △*Motueka, "Suggested Drives"*). Another variation is to leave Takaka by the road to East Takaka, to follow the eastern side of the attractive Takaka River valley and rejoin Highway 60 near Uruwhenua, a little distance north of Upper Takaka.

A metric conversion chart appears at the end of the book.

## TAPANUI   West Otago.   Maps 4 & 14.   Pop. 934.

*38 km NE of Gore; 71 km NW of Balclutha.*

TAPANUI remains as it began, very much a timber town spread out at the foot of the Blue Mountains, a range which lost much of its hue when it was stripped of native bush. Today the lower reaches are clothed with varieties of exotic pine, and bush covers its intermediate slopes. To the north-west lie the Dusky plantations, and to the south those of Conical Hill. The surrounding undulating sheep country is in fertile contrast with the parched and rock-strewn hillsides of neighbouring Central Otago. There is good hunting in the vicinity, and excellent trout fishing, particularly in the Pomahaka River.

Tapanui (the great edge) may be a reference to the edge of the forest.

## SOME HISTORY

**Second or last?** Three McKellar brothers figure in the history of Otago and Southland — David and Peter, who pioneered the Gore and Waikaia districts, and John McKellar (d. 1883) who married the daughter of William Pinkerton, original holder of the Brooksdale run, acquiring his father-in-law's property when Pinkerton moved on to New Mexico. A keen sportsman, John McKellar bred, reared and raced thoroughbreds, though a racemeeting at Tapanui in the early 1870s did little to help his reputation. A £100 purse attracted nominations from leading South Island stables, but most of the luckless thirteen who entered were attacked by strangles just before the meeting. The winner was never again to repeat his triumph, and the horse that came second also finished last.

**Mayor McKellar:** Tapanui was laid out in 1868, as runholders made way for the sawmillers, who cut out much of the bush, founded the town and ushered in closer settlement. Gold, found elsewhere nearby, generated only flutters of excitement. When a minor rush occurred in the Pomahaka, just below Tapanui, the *Tuapeka Times* could soon comment: "Some few have done well, others are making wages, but the majority have given up." Dredges were put on the rivers during the dredging boom, but too little was won to render operations economic. When one dredge began to colour the Pomahaka, angered anglers went to court to obtain an injunction to protect the Pomahaka from further pollution.

John McKellar served as Tapanui's first mayor, and the district greatly deplored his eventual departure for New Mexico from his Brooksdale estate, which had become one of the colony's social pivots. Neighbouring Heriot (originally Herriot) was named after McKellar's mother-in-law.

## POINTS OF INTEREST IN THE AREA

**Vintage farm machinery:** A local club stores some of its equipment behind the Forest Lodge Hotel where it may be seen through wire netting doors. The club gives demonstrations to visiting farming groups and at local celebrations. *Northumberland St.*

**Black Gully Domain\*\*:** On the Blue Mountains foothills are camping and pic-nicking in the most tranquil of surroundings, beside a dense stand of silver beech and shallow Black Gully Creek. From the top of the domain the prospect extends over rolling country to the Dusky plantations and beyond. *10.7 km. Leave Tapanui by Highway 90 north, turning right at 8.6 km up Black Gully Rd.* On the corner of Highway 90 and Black Gully Rd is a small private aviary, kept as a hobby by Mr R. Cook. It may be visited by those interested.

**Leithen picnic and swimming area**\*\*: A gracious, spacious picnic and barbecue area on the banks of the picturesque Pomahaka has been created on the fringe of the Dusky plantations by the N.Z. Forest Service. One enters by a narrow road canopied by the branches of exotic trees of varying depths of green. *17.1 km. Drive by way of Kelso. Signposted.*

On the way a detour may be made up Wooded Hill to a former fire-lookout, from which the cyclorama is of plantations, bush and well-wooded plains. In exceptional conditions the tip of Stewart Island's Mt Anglem may be seen (*at 4.9 km turn right and follow road for 2.1 km to summit*).

**Blue Mountain nurseries:** The commercial nurseries annually produce thousands of container-grown trees and shrubs, and grow large areas of narcissi, irises and tulips for sale as cut flowers. The nursery is known for its introduction of new and improved varieties. *99 Bushy Hill St. Open daily except Sun. tel. 16M*

**State nurseries:** With those at Whakarewarewa (near Rotorua), these nurseries, now being phased out, were in 1897 the first to be established by the state. The original nursery stables, together with an early office, are still standing. Some 200 different species of exotic trees about the nursery site make this a particularly delightful spot in autumn. *2.1 km. Proceed up Northumberland St, skirt the forestry settlement and turn left at the cemetery gates.*

**Conical Hill State mill:** Visitors may be shown over one of the country's most modern sawmills, the largest in the South Island. *11.5 km S on the Tapanui-Waipahi Rd.*

## TOURING NOTES

**Alternative route to** △**Roxburgh:** A slower but more interesting route to Roxburgh is by way of Moa Flat. The green and undulating sheeplands of West Otago and Southland quite suddenly give way first to the tussock of the Moa Flat Downs, then to the parched, rocky outcrops of Central Otago.

**Alternative route to** △**Balclutha (via Rankleburn and Clydevale):** Turn left at Pomahaka to pass through the Conical Hill plantations and meet the Pomahaka River at Rankleburn. Continue on to Clydevale where one may cross the Clutha River and follow its east bank to Balclutha.

---

## TE ANAU (Lake)\*\*\*　　　Fiordland.　　Maps 12 & 33.

*292 km WNW of Dunedin; 158 km NW of Invercargill; 167 km SW of Queenstown. Fiordland National Park headquarters provides details of walks, tramps and things to see and do in the park, and issues hunting permits.*

ENIGMATIC LAKE TE ANAU sprawls at the feet of high rugged mountains, its South, Middle and North Fiords probing fingerlike deep into the ranges. The mountains have their secrets and keep them well. In the Murchison Range were rediscovered in 1948 the remarkable *takahe*, flightless birds for half a century considered extinct. There, too, were rediscovered after generations of searching the fascinating honeycomb of caves, Te Ana-au, that gave the lake its name.

The puzzle lies in the contrast between the lake's very different shorelines: to the east, where lies the Te Anau township (pop. 2,384), trees are few; yet to the west looms the dense, seemingly impenetrable rainforest of the △Fiordland National Park. Accounting for the abrupt visual contrast is a remarkable discrepancy in rainfall, the western shoreline being drenched in some 1700 mm each year, as against the 1130 mm of the east.

The glacier-gouged lake, 417 m deep and some 214 m below sea level, yields trout and landlocked salmon. The outflow of the country's second largest lake (34,200 ha) is being controlled as part of the Manapouri power project, as it flows down the Waiau River into △Lake Manapouri.

The township is the focal point of the vast Fiordland National Park, the country's most rugged, most remote, and to many its most enticing. Excursions include trips into Milford Sound, by plane, by bus and by the much-acclaimed △Milford Track.

The visitor should allow a minimum of three full days at Te Anau.

## SOME MYTHOLOGY

**Lake of infidelity:** Close to a *kainga* (village) where now spreads Lake Te Anau was a spring, believed bottomless and known only to a *tohunga* (priest) and his wife. The spring was indeed magical for not only did it supply pure water, but fish could be caught by the netful and its very existence shielded the *kainga* from harm. Rumours of war on the Otakou Peninsula led the *tohunga* to journey to the east coast, first making his wife swear to preserve the secrecy of the spring. But she had a lover who coaxed her to show him its whereabouts, and as he was leaning over the pool the spring suddenly and silently welled up to overwhelm the lovers and with them the whole village. It flooded the entire valley and reached out with long arms into the hills.

The *tohunga*, looking back, was startled to see a great inland lake where none had been before. He hurried homeward but could find no trace of his wife or people, who had disappeared beneath the waters of the lake, Te Anau. Dismayed, he retreated to

# LAKE TE ANAU

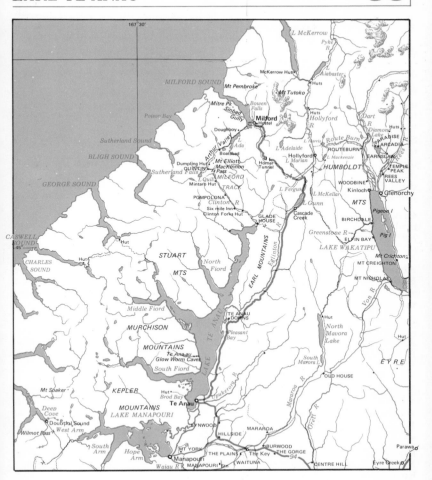

## 33

Piopiotahi (Milford Sound) to end his days in loneliness as he could not bear to see again the waters that evidenced his wife's infidelity. His name, Te Horo, was given to a cliff on the sound, at Anita Bay.

## THE TAKAHE

Long thought extinct, the *takahe (Notornis mantelli)* was rediscovered in 1948 by Geoffrey Orbell, an Invercargill medical practitioner. His finding of a colony of the flightless birds, which had not been seen for half a century (and only rarely before that), created worldwide interest. About the size of a hen, the *takahe* has feathers that range in colour from indigo to olive green; its legs and beak are scarlet. As it feeds on snowgrass, it tends to be found above the snowline, in winter descending into the heavy bush for cover. Careful watch is now kept on the birds, which extend in sparse numbers to the west of the lake, over much of the Murchison Mountains and part of the Kepler Range. Attempts are being made to breed the birds in captivity in the North Island, at Mount Bruce, near Masterton.

To minimise disturbance, a large area within the National Park has been closed, taking in the range that divides the Middle from the South Fiord of Lake Te Anau. Entry is permitted for a distance of 500 m up any stream. The rediscovery of the *takahe* reinforced speculation that the remote areas of Fiordland National Park may hold further secrets that await finders sufficiently alert as to recognise their significance.

## EXCURSIONS FROM TE ANAU

△**Milford Track*****: "The finest walk in the world." *Advance booking for the 4-to-5 day walk is essential.*

△**Milford Sound*****: The road into Milford ranks with the most magnificent of all alpine drives and is described under △Milford (Road to). For those without transport a daily bus service runs to Milford from Te Anau, leaving at 8.15 am. It allows time for lunch and a boat trip on the sound before returning at 5.45 pm. *Booking is essential at holiday periods.*

**Te Ana-au Caves\*\*\*:** Geologically young (less than 15,000 years ago the area was locked in ice), the caves lack the delicate statuary of some other limestone systems but possess instead qualities of raw power that render a visit an awesome experience. From a low entrance visitors are taken by boat to the foot of an underground waterfall and then by boat again into a glow-worm grotto. The occasional round boulder of dark granite is seen as oddly out of place, the product of lateral moraine from the departed glacier being washed into the cave system from above.

The 2-hour excursion begins with a 30-minute launch trip across the lake to the foot of the Murchison Range, the fringe of the closed *takahe* area. *Trips leave regularly from the Fiordland Travel pier.*

Te Ana-au (the cave of rushing water) is presumably the system that gave the lake its name. Many attempts to find it failed and it was not until 1948 that it was located on the Tunnel Burn stream.

**Lake Manapouri — West Arm underground powerhouse — Doubtful Sound\*\*\*:** A full day trip crosses Lake Manapouri, winds down into the bowels of the mountains to the powerhouse, and finally traverses the Main Divide to visit a fascinating fiord. *Described under △ Manapouri (Lake).*

**Lake trips:** A variety of trips are run on the lake, including excursions to Glade House (at the head of the lake and the start of the △ Milford Track). As well as taking scheduled trips, parties may arrange to be dropped off at points round the lake and be collected later in the day. *Arrange through Fiordland Travel.*

**Scenic flights\*\*\*** by floatplane lend fresh perspective to the lake-littered landforms and can include a low swoop over Lake Quill to see the 580.3 m plunge of Sutherland Falls (*see index*). Following the line of the Milford Track, flights lead to Milford Sound where a stopover may be made to allow time for a launch trip. An alternative flight takes one over Lake Manapouri's West Arm and the Wilmot Pass. The shortest flight gives a view of the township, the lake and seventeen "hidden" lakes. *Mount Cook Airlines.*

## OTHER THINGS TO SEE AND DO

**Fiordland National Park headquarters:** The park headquarters mount displays of the region's flora, fauna and natural history. Information on things to see and do in the park, including walks and the Milford Rd, is readily available. During the Christmas holiday period special group activities are organised. *Open daily.*

**Blue Gum Point:** There is swimming, waterskiing and a boat harbour at the point, where a plaque records that the first Europeans to see the lake, C. J. Nairn and W. H. Stephen, came from Jacobs River (Riverton) in January 1852.

**Nature Walk:** A 30-minute walk which leads by a small lake is named the Richard Henry Memorial Nature Walk in honour of a prominent naturalist and the first ranger in New Zealand. *Begins 2.6 km on the road to Manapouri and leads back to Te Anau.* There is a small collection of fish and native birds which may be visited, opposite the start of the walk.

**Wapiti Park:** Red deer, fallow deer, chamois, and tahr are to be seen as well as wapiti. *5 km on the road to Manapouri.*

## SOME TRAMPING

Brief details of some of the many tracks in the region appear under the entries for Fiordland National Park, Lake Hauroko and Lake Monowai. Full information is available from the Park Headquarters and from *Moir's Guide Book* (*Southern Section*).

## SOME WALKS

Short walks at Te Anau township are the Lake Shore Walk, the Richard Henry Memorial Nature Walk (*see above*) and in Ivon Wilson Park (*near camping ground*). Other short walks are combined with trips on the lake e.g. at Glade House.

> To travel hopefully is a better thing than to arrive, and the true success is to labour — Robert Louis Stevenson (Virginibus Puerisque, *El Dorado*).

## TOURING NOTES

**Highway 94 to △Lumsden:** At Mossburn a detour may be made to the West Dome Deer Ranch. *See △Lumsden.*

**Alternative route to Southland:** Leaving Te Anau south on Highway 94 one may turn off at The Key down the Blackmount Road to follow the Waiau River. The route lies through a large area that is being brought into production by the Department of Lands and Survey. Detours may be made to △ Lake Monowai and, at △ Clifden, to △ Lake Hauroko. Continue south through △ Tuatapere to follow the coast of Foveaux Strait through △ Orepuki and △ Riverton to reach △ Invercargill. *196.5 km* (*exclusive of detours*).

# MACKENZIE COUNTRY

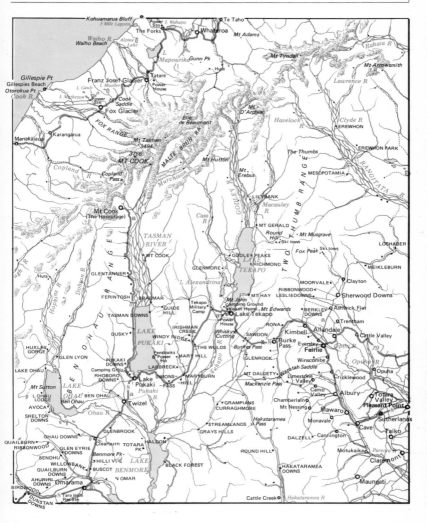

## TEKAPO (Lake)***   South Canterbury.   Maps 34 & 35.   Pop. 361.

*43.5 km NW of Fairlie; 87 km NE of Omarama.*

BATHED IN A LIGHT of extraordinary clarity, a glorious vista extends up the turquoise lake to a sliver of the Southern Alps. The waters of Lake Tekapo stretch from its dam-controlled outlet at the village, due north for almost 20 km, to where the braided Godley and Macaulay Rivers debouch their glacial waters. Framing the view are tawny tussockland and the almost treeless slopes that surround the lake.

The lake has an enigmatic charm which draws admirers back year after year. It is given its intense milky-turquoise hue by fine rock-flour, dust ground by glacial movement and held in suspension by the lake's waters. Tekapo, and more particularly its smaller neighbours, Alexandrina, McGregor and Conway, are good for brown and rainbow trout.

The name, possibly more correctly Taka-po (*taka*=sleeping mat; *po*=night) refers to an incident in which members of an exploring party sleeping here took fright in the night, rolled up their mats, and fled.

**Geology:** The lake, similar in character to the other Mackenzie country lakes, Pukaki and Ohau, occupies the lower end of a glaciated valley and is hemmed in by moraine that dates back about 20,000 years. Because of the many glaciers from which Tekapo receives its waters, the lake itself is generally too cold for swimming — though some is done at its most shallow points. Its outflow is controlled by a dam, seemingly only a road-bridge, which can vary the water level between 703.8 m and 709.9 m above sea level.

---

Consult the Index when looking for a name in this Guide.

---

## SOME HISTORY

**Karekare's return:** Tradition tells of peaceful inhabitants living here about 250 years ago, who were attacked by a raiding party from the north. In the skirmish the invaders made off with the wife of a Tekapo chief, carrying her back to Kaiapoi. When she became pregnant to the Kaiapoi chief, Waewae, she was allowed to return home. On reaching the eastern side of the lake she kindled a fire which her husband, Tukete, saw and came by raft to investigate. He accepted her back despite her condition, and when the child was born she was named Te Hoki (the return). One of the creeks feeding the Waitaki was named after her, and her mother's name, Karekare, was given to two streams in the Geraldine district.

When the first Europeans arrived, however, there was no trace of permanent Maori occupation here.

**The Mackenzie country:** It was the capture of the sheepstealer, James McKenzie, (*see index*) that brought the vast inland tussock plains to the notice of would-be runholders. Led by McKenzie's capturer, Sidebottom, a number applied for runs and were soon undergoing the trying experience of driving mobs of sheep over the wide Canterbury plains, across the broad rivers and into the Mackenzie basin.

Vegetation on the plains included *matagouri* no less than 6 m tall, which with speargrass formed "an often impenetrable thicket, which, when they had to be passed, often punished severely both man and horse".

The first act of a new runholder was to fire his run, not only to clear the land initially but repeatedly, to render tussock more palatable to sheep. Fanned by steady nor'westers, fires not infrequently spread to neighbouring runs, with stock occasionally being driven in to swamps for safety. With the diminishing vegetation and the draining of swamps, birdlife dwindled so that the seasonal migrations of Maoris from Temuka and Waimate steadily declined, to cease altogether about 1890.

## THE CHANGING MACKENZIE

The Mackenzie country covers two regions — the lower-rainfall area of the basin and the higher-rainfall region of the gorge runs. The basin is prone to regular summer droughts but sees little snow in winter months; the gorge runs, however, are generally free from drought but can suffer from the severe snows typical of the winter.

The region has been dominated by the extensive pastoral farming of fine-wool Merino sheep on thirty-seven properties, ranging in size from 600 to 42,000 ha. Wethers range over the harder, high altitude blocks. On the easier, lower properties the emphasis is on increasing ewe numbers and per-head production, so that wether flocks are disappearing. On the easier properties, too, the Merino is replaced by the halfbred (Merino × English Longwool) and Hereford and Angus cattle.

The basin, with its easy contours and typical summer drought conditions, has considerable potential for irrigation. In spite of the high altitude, production with irrigation can equal that of most other areas of New Zealand. With irrigation development, oversowing and top dressing, the Mackenzie country may in future carry over one sheep to the hectare, a total of 500,000 stock units. On the gorge runs, the potential, though great, is limited by the small areas suitable for cultivation, and by the relatively large proportion of the runs at very high altitudes.

Power development will improve the distribution of water for irrigation, but the raising of Lake Pukaki will have significant effects on the production of properties round the lake's edge. The rising waters of the lake will drown out many of the areas of developed paddocks and six homesteads, so that hay paddocks and farm buildings will have to be re-established at higher altitudes.

In the past the region has been symbolised by tussock and the Merino, but with recent development and a change in emphasis from fine wool to meat production, the symbols of the Mackenzie must also include the beef cow and the power pylon.

The runs are mainly held under pastoral leases with a permanent right of renewal, but in many cases small areas of freehold land surround the homestead area and hold the key to the running of the property. This system of freeholding only key areas was carried out by the early run-holders and is known as grid-ironing.

The area and its stations are among those described in detail by R. Pinney in *Early South Canterbury Runs* (Reed).

## THINGS TO SEE AND DO

**Church of the Good Shepherd** (1935)**, whose cool grey stone walls grow from the foreshore, is a memorial to the pioneer runholders of the Mackenzie. Built of stone gathered near the lake, and of shingle and sand from the lake's shore, the modest building stands as a simple silhouette against the mountains. The church faces out over the lake, its grey and wood-brown interior taking colour from the aspect of lake and mountain seen through its plain east window. The much-photographed scene is viewed to best advantage in early morning and late afternoon, when the interior is dull with shadow but the lake and ranges are caught in brilliant light. *On the lakefront, immediately east of the outlet. Signposted.*

A short distance away, also by the lake, is a **bronze sheepdog**, sculpted by a Mackenzie farmer's wife. Though sometimes described as commemorating McKenzie's dog Friday it in fact marks a spot called Dog Kennel Corner where boundary dogs were kept.

The district owes much to the sheepdog in general "without the help of which the grazing of the mountainous country would be impossible." Boundary dogs were tethered at strategic points along the outskirts of unfenced runs, with perhaps small kennels for shelter, there to turn back straying flocks and thus protect the runs from contamination by scab. The dogs were sometimes ill fed, ill cared for and seldom exercised, but tales are legion of the devotion shown by the personal dogs of the boundary riders. One man who broke his leg as he patrolled an unfenced boundary was kept alive through a freezing night by the snuggling warmth of his several dogs. Another, less fortunate, died, and when his body was discovered, guarded by his ever-loyal dog, beside him laid a number of *weka* which the faithful dog had killed and brought back as food for his master. So proud of their dogs were the Mackenzie shepherds that competitive dog trials were held at Haldon (near Lake Benmore) in 1869 — perhaps the first of what have developed into a national sport. Boundary dogs are still used occasionally, perhaps tethered to guard a weak place in a fenceline, but are alternated, exercised and cared for at least every other day.

**Mt John:** The region's cloudless skies and clear atmosphere have brought Tekapo an international observatory and a United States satellite tracking station, both of which are seen from the village, perched on the summit of Mt John, high above the lake. The university-operated observatory, quite separate from the tracking station, may be visited by day (the equipment works only at night) to see the country's largest telescopes, both cassegrain reflectors, and photographs taken while studying such subjects as quasars and eclipsing binary stars. (*There are no regular visiting times; generally between 1.30 and 2 pm. Tel. 813*).

The satellite tracking station may be visited, if arrangements are made in advance, to see the camera room where the Baker-Nunn camera is housed — a camera capable of recording space debris no bigger than a basketball some 5,000 km out in space. In tracking it has an accuracy of from 3 to 30 m at a range of 32,000 km. *Tel. 863. Entrance 6 km from Tekapo. Turnoff signposted at 2 km W on Highway 8.*

**Tekapo A power station** (1938–46): Highway 8 crosses a control dam, built over the outlet of the lake to enable the spring and summer snow-melt from the mountains to be stored until the following winter, when electricity demand is at its peak. The power station, on the banks of the Tekapo River, is fed by a 1.6 km tunnel from the lake. It has a generating capacity of 25,200 kW. Below the dam is the start of the extensive canal system for the Upper Waitaki power scheme (*see* △ *Twizel*) *Detour at 2.4 km W of Tekapo. The powerhouse may be visited. The canal on its way to Pukaki is crossed by Highway 8 at 14.8 km W.*

**Lakes McGregor and Alexandrina\*,** both bird sanctuaries, form an attractive camping and fishing area. The stream-fed lakes' orthodox colouring is in contrast with that of Lake Tekapo. Both smaller and shallower, they are very much warmer for swimming — even if in the freeze of 1895 Alexandrina froze solid and supported the 300 head of cattle that were driven across it. *10.7 km. Turnoff signposted on Highway 8 at 2 km W.*

**Balmoral military camp:** The camp's use is not confined to the military, serving also for Education Department get-togethers for pupils taught by correspondence and for the DSIR to train scientists destined for Antarctica *6.2 km W on Highway 8.*

**Lilybank,** at the head of Lake Tekapo is one of several high country runs whose life is ruled by a river — in this case by the braided and unpredictable Macaulay. The unbridged river sprawls between the station's 28,500 ha and the road to civilisation. The approach road ends at the riverbank, though there is a public right of access across the Macaulay and on to Mount Cook National Park. (*Those unfamiliar with the river should not attempt the treacherous crossing.*) In recent years Lilybank has also served as a skiing base for the slopes at nearby Round Hill and as a lodge for overseas hunters, some to have helicopters whirl them up to the tahr and chamois on the heights. The run was named because of the abundance of Mount Cook lilies it once had. *38 km up the east bank of the lake.*

**Scenic flights** cover Mt Cook and the glaciers, including the Fox and the Franz Josef on the West Coast; also Milford Sound and the Southern Lakes. *Air Safaris, Box 21; tel. 880.*

## TOURING NOTES

△ **Fairlie via** △ **Burkes Pass (Highway 8):** At 9.5 km Mt Cook may be seen across the waters of Lake Tekapo (*signposted*). △ Burkes Pass is crossed at 16.7 km, marked by Burnett's memorial to Micheal Burke.

△ **Timaru via Mackenzie Pass** (*109 km*)*:* At Dog Kennel Corner (*14 km E on Highway 8*) one may turn off to cross the Mackenzie Pass between the Rollesby and Dalgety Ranges to rejoin Highway 8 at Albury. At 33.5 km is a monument erected near the place where some believe James McKenzie (*see index*) was apprehended. (As on most McKenzie matters, opinions differ.) The inscription is in English, Maori and Gaelic, reflecting the origins of those involved in the incident.

**Winter Sports:** Tekapo Ski Field has all the usual facilities, plus cross-country skiing, which is not widely available elsewhere in New Zealand. Helicopters and ski planes provide access to some of the runs. *33 km. Coach leaves Tekapo Village daily at 9 am. Prior booking essential. Air Safaris, Box 21; tel. 880.*

*18.5 km N of Timaru; 59 km SW of Ashburton.*

TEMUKA HAS DEVELOPED on the South Canterbury plain so close to Timaru that it is a tribute to the wealth of the region that Temuka has become so large and so patently prosperous. From old bottle kilns producing bricks, pipes and tiles has evolved the country's principal manufacturer of insulators, ceramic components and other electrical accessories. For this reason the town's name is appropriate — a contraction of *Te umu kaha*. The name refers to the large earth ovens of the Maori, a feature commented on by early European visitors.

The town is an ideal centre for freshwater fishing, with salmon and sea-run trout in the Opihi and excellent dry-fly fishing in its tributaries. Salmon usually run from early January to the end of April.

## SOME HISTORY

**Visitors from Kapiti:** The principal *pa* of local Ngaitahu was near here, at Waiateruati. Well fortified, it had heavy palisades and extensive earthworks to reinforce the natural barrier presented on three sides by the moat-like Waiateruati Stream. The unity of Ngaitahu here was split by the *Kai-huanga* (eat relation) feud (*see index*) that so laid the tribe open to the devastations of Te Rauparaha.

In an attempt to end the feud, the Akaroa chief Te Maiharanui travelled to the Otago Peninsula to make peace with Taiaroa. On their return northwards, Te Maiharanui and his party were entertained here and given such a liberal quantity of potted birds that the visiting chief asked for the hosts' help in carrying their bounty back to Akaroa. Help was willingly given, but as soon as they reached Akaroa Harbour, Te Maiharanui with his own hands slew the men from Waiateruati and the feud erupted once more.

After Te Rauparaha had raided △ Kaiapoi in 1831, his scouts came south as far as the *pa* here, but found the South Canterbury Ngaitahu not only ready to defend themselves but daring the invaders to attack. The scouts' leader cooly parried: *"He aha te rawa a te Kaikoareare raua ko Rakiwhaka-atia ki au?"* (What business have Te Kaikoareare and Rakiwhaka-atia with me?) before his party discreetly withdrew.

**Three sites:** Temuka's development mirrored in microcosm that of Timaru. For here, as at Timaru, the surveyors left an area between the Government's town reserve and the main traffic route. Learning his lesson from the Rhodes's activities at Timaru, Samuel Hewlings, who surveyed the reserve, bought up the key area, subdivided it, as Wallingford, and watched it develop as Temuka's principal business centre. In capitalising on his position as surveyor, Hewlings was not alone, as many surveyors took advantage of the opportunities with which their profession presented them. The Rhodes brothers, too, had seen a future in subdividing near Temuka and had earlier cut up a 10.1 ha block in the fork of the Opihi and Temuka Rivers. However they could not repeat their Timaru success as floods devastated the block, putting paid to the hopes they had held for their village of Georgetown.

To the growing settlement came John Hayhurst, who for a time fought to win for Temuka the role of principal centre for South Canterbury.

**A battle over harbours:** The versatile John Hayhurst (1827–89), who had been the first to sow English grasses in the Mackenzie country and built the first flourmill in the area which gave the nearby Milford locality its name, for a time bade fair to capture the Timaru shipping trade for Temuka. A successful shepherd-turned-squatter, Hayhurst, like John Grigg at Ashburton, had recognised the potential of coastal swampland and was living here in his twenty-roomed mansion, the showplace of Green Hayes — one of the first homes in the country to be lit by electricity. He had already, in 1870, established a successful boiling-down works at Milford to eliminate the waste he himself had witnessed when surplus sheep on overstocked runs were simply driven over cliffs to get rid of them.

Hayhurst was on several local bodies and was Timaru's representative in the Canterbury Provincial Council when his chance came and he was elected to the newly-formed Timaru Harbour Board as a founder member. For ten years he had cherished the thought that the Milford Lagoon might be turned into a harbour, and had had the lagoon surveyed in 1867 by one J. S. M. Jacobsen, who declared the scheme both feasible and inexpensive.

The *Timaru Herald* fumed that it had never heard of Jacobsen, and branded the notion "a crude scheme of an ignorant, irresponsible visionary who knows nothing whatever about the subject". Hayhurst was undeterred, and ten years later the same newspaper was cautioning the Harbour Board that unless prompt action was taken Milford Harbour would be an established fact while the Timaru breakwater remained a pipedream. In 1879 the conflict was resolved when Sir John Coode, a British consultant, came down firmly in favour of Timaru.

The ambitious Hayhurst sought one final prize, and stood for the House of Representatives as a Liberal against the thirty-year-old Edward Wakefield (son of Felix and nephew of Edward Gibbon Wakefield), the editor who had so vigorously opposed his harbour scheme. The voters of the newly-constituted electorate of Geraldine divided equally between the two protagonists. A recount confirmed the tie, and it was left for the returning officer, the Timaru magistrate, to exercise his casting vote — in favour of Wakefield.

A plaque marks the site of Hayhurst's boiling-down works, just behind the cheese factory and before the end of Boiling Down Road, the eastern extension of Richard Pearse Drive. Hayhurst's Green Hayes homestead still stands in Milford Road, in use as a Salvation Army children's home.

**The first man to fly?** It is surely extraordinary that a pioneer aviator whose feats if anything outrank those of the immortal Wright brothers, who almost certainly was airborne nine months before them, could have died in obscurity at Sunnyside Psychiatric Hospital near Christchurch as recently as 1953 — unsung, and virtually unknown. Such was the fate of Richard William Pearse (1877–1953), who for some years farmed at nearby Waitohi where his experiments with flying machines in the first years of this century earned for him the reputation of an eccentric from the more charitable of his neighbours.

On 31 March 1903 the young Waitohi farmer wheeled his home-made monoplane out on to the road passing the local school and, before a group of sceptical locals, prepared it for takeoff.

Before that date, four men in other parts of the world had been briefly airborne in powered aircraft, but Pearse's effort was to eclipse them all. He taxied down the road and was airborne for about 100 m, finishing up ignominiously on a gorse hedge some 4 m high. He was slightly injured, but made several more "flights" at Waitohi and, later, on an Otago farm.

Pearse himself did not claim to have "flown" because to him "flying" meant a sustained and controlled flight. In a letter to a newspaper some fourteen years later, he dated his first attempt as being in 1904, which confused the issue until Gordon Ogilvie, in his *The Riddle of Richard Pearse* (Reed), published his well-researched analysis of Pearse's life and achievements and produced cogent evidence to support 1903 being the true date.

In many respects Pearse's aeroplane was years in advance of its time. Though flimsily built of bamboo, linen and farmyard scrap-metal, it had ailerons, a steerable tricycle undercarriage, and a home-made engine with direct drive to an adjustable-pitch metal propeller. In the 1930s, in Christchurch, he built a "Utility Plane" designed for vertical takeoff and horizontal flight, using a more powerful and highly original tiltable engine and a tail-rotor to correct torque. Though he ran the engine often enough, he never attempted to fly this later machine — and in all probability would have killed himself if he had. The "Utility Plane" and fragments of the first one are displayed at the Museum of Transport and Technology, Auckland.

Pearse also constructed motorised farm equipment, a hydro-electric generator, designed a pedal-cycle with an extraordinary ingenious transmission, and built a successful powercycle for his own use, as well as sound-recording equipment, and, later, three bungalows. He had only perfunctory primary education, no technical training of any sort, and had to make his own tools and equipment from scrap-metal. As a farmer he was a failure, and in later life he became a recluse, dying in Sunnyside Psychiatric Hospital, Christchurch, in 1953.

Given a better start in life he might have been New Zealand's Thomas Edison; as it was, his powered takeoff preceded Orville Wright's better-known flight by nine months, and earns him, if nothing else, an honoured if long-postponed place in the annals of pioneer aviation.

*The site of Pearse's first takeoff (to be marked by a memorial) is on Main Waitohi Road at 13.5 km from Temuka on the way to Hanging Rock Bridge. He took off from the road and came to grief in a hedge, since removed, that followed the fence line along the roadside west from the junction with Galbraith Road.*

**Arowhenua station:** Arowhenua, originally a run of 12,150 ha along the north bank of the Opihi, was the first station after the Levels to be taken up in South Canterbury — by William Hornbrook, as manager for his brother, in 1853. Within a year the brothers had 3,000 sheep on the property, and 5,500 by 1857. Dating from this time is a venerable wooden woolshed, one of the oldest in the country still in use. On the roofboards have been daubed sketches by an artist of some talent. It is possible that they may be the work of Edmund Norman (1820–75), an alcoholic draughtsman-turned-shepherd-and-shearer who carried a sketchbook wherever he went, but this has not been substantiated. The whole complex of station buildings in the vicinity all date from about 1853, but the homestead is of more recent origin.

The story is related of one of the early workers at Arowhenua who, during the inquest into the drowning of a man in the river, removed the corpse while the coroner and his jury were having lunch. He took its place beneath the shroud and when they lifted the sheet to solemnly view the body, greeted them with loud guffaws.

## THINGS TO SEE AND DO

**St Peter's Anglican Church** (1899), built of contrasting stone, was under construction even before its predecessor was burnt to the ground. The vicar ran into the blazing old wooden building and rescued both the lectern and the Bible now in the present church; he noted, "but as sparks were then falling from the roof I did not venture in again". The east window is dedicated to John Talbot (1845–1923), who settled at Woodlands in the Rangatira Valley, in 1869. All but one of his twelve sons became farmers, and his family name is woven through South Canterbury's farming and public life. Talbot was a stalwart on local bodies, aggregating 160 years of service. His lath-and-plaster homestead, enlarged and roughcast since it was built in about 1870, still stands and is still in the family (*in Talbot Rd, off Waitohi Rd*). The sanctuary windows are memorials to sisters, Christiana and Elizabeth, each the wife of John Talbot. The stone pulpit is in memory of the wife of John Hayhurst. *Cnr King and Dyson Sts.*

**Domain\*:** Sportsfields are pleasantly surrounded by trees and gardens liberally dotted with memorials. A celery-pine tree, the only souvenir brought back by the first conquerors of Mt Cook, has been transplanted to the native section here. (*For a description of the climb, see* △ *Mount Cook National Park*). For years it grew in the nearby garden of Jack Clarke's sister, where Clarke and his two companions stayed both before and after their successful ascent. *Off Domain Rd.*

**New Zealand Insulators Ltd:** Visitors are welcome to see the manufacture of electrical wiring devices, insulators and stoneware. *Thomas St. Tel. 565 to arrange a convenient time. Allow up to 1½ hrs.*

**Pottery:** There are numerous cottage potteries in Temuka. *For details enquire locally or contact Timaru Public Relations Office, Box 194, tel. 86-163.*

## ENVIRONS

**Arowhenua Ratana Memorial:** The arched gateway to a reserve at Arowhenua was erected by members of the Ratana movement (a Maori sect of Christianity) as a memorial to the 1914–18 war. The symbols of the movement are incorporated in the gateway along with the names of T. W. Ratana's sons. (*For details of the Ratana Movement and its symbolism, see* △ *Ratana in the North Island volume.*) The oldest building in the Arowhenua Pa area was the mission church, Holy Trinity (1866), opened by the Rev. J. Stack. Probably the first church to be built in the district, it has been demolished, but friezes of the beatitudes from the mission church line the nave of its replacement (1913). The font is inscribed with Christ's exhortation to his disciples, "Suffer the little children to come unto me", translated into Maori. A Ngaitahu meeting-house here was destroyed by fire in 1902. *The Ratana memorial and Holy Trinity Church face each other by Highway 1 at 1.2 km S.*

**Hanging Rock bridge\*:** A delightful picnicking and swimming spot. *21 km. Signposted from Post Office. At 13.5 km the route passes, on the right immediately beyond Galbraith Rd, the scene of Pearse's aeronautical experiments.* Hanging Rock bridge is described under △ Pleasant Point.

A Glossary of Maori Words appears on page 343.

**TIMARU\*\*\***     **South Canterbury.**   **Map 35.**   **Pop. 29,267.**

*164 km SW of Christchurch; 202 km NNE of Dunedin; Public Relations Office, 7 The Terrace, tel. 86-163.*

THE CITY OF TIMARU wears a sturdy, substantial look as it folds over the gently sloping hills that mark the southern end of Canterbury's gravel plains. Below, in the lee of an artificial port, curves the apron of Caroline Bay, the scene of an annual summer carnival. A natural break in an otherwise shelterless stretch of coastline formed a point on to which the port was grafted. The interruption is caused by a slab of Upper Tertiary basalt (chlorite known as Timaru bluestone) which extends under the city and also juts slightly out to sea. Inland, the limestone outcrops that stud the river valleys, shelter large numbers of ancient rock drawings.

Symbolic of the city's bright future in the broadening of its processing activities is a tannery, recently established to process up to four million pelts each year.

The name of Timaru probably began as Te Maru (the place of shelter) as this was the only haven for the Maori canoes voyaging between Oamaru and Banks Peninsula. The alternative version of Timaru, sheltering cabbage tree, is explained by the "murderous spelling by the earliest Europeans".

## SOME HISTORY

**Rhodes of the Levels:** A whaling station was operated here briefly by the Weller Bros. from about 1838 before the firm failed. Edward Shortland, the first European to cross overland from Moeraki to Banks Peninsula, described the scene in 1844: "Many forlorn-looking huts were still standing there; which, with cables, rusty iron hoops, and decaying ropes lying about in all directions, told a tale of the waste and destruction that so often falls on a bankrupt's property."

It was one of the whalers, Samuel Williams, who first interested the Rhodes brothers in the possibilities of South Canterbury and who returned to become the first permanent resident of Timaru.

# TIMARU AND ENVIRONS

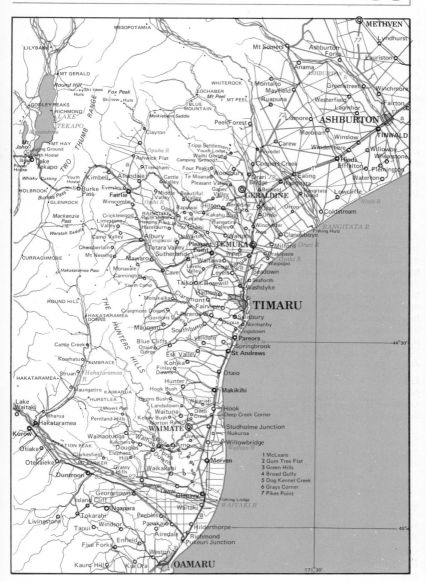

## 35

The Rhodes brothers, four of fourteen children, came to New Zealand before organised settlement began; by dint of shrewd judgment, determination and hard work, each amassed a considerable fortune. The oldest, William Barnard Rhodes (1807–78), was the first to arrive, as commander of a whaling vessel. Quickly recognising the possibilities, he urged his brothers to follow — cautioning that they "must be enterprising, obliging, and not afraid of hard work". In 1839 he landed cattle at Akaroa to establish the first cattle station in the South Island. He also founded trading stations in Hawke's Bay and Poverty Bay before basing himself in Wellington. There he became involved in politics, serving as a member of the House of Representatives (1853–66), of the Wellington Provincial Council (1861–69), and of the Legislative Council (1871–78). In later life, too, he helped found the New Zealand Shipping Company, the New Zealand Insurance Company, and the Bank of New Zealand.

It fell to George Rhodes (1816–64), the second to arrive, and Robert Heaton Rhodes (1815–84), to extend their operations from the Banks Peninsula into South Canterbury, driving sheep across the plains to take up the Levels run in 1851. The commercial heart of Timaru stands on 50 ha of the run which the brothers shrewdly freeholded, anticipating the site as being better for settlement than the neighbouring area to the south already reserved by the Government. The fourth brother Joseph (1826–1905), had interests in Hawke's Bay.

Collectively the brothers played key roles in the colony's early pastoral and commercial development. If William and Robert (both with close political ties) have been accused of profiting from their connections, the same cannot be said of the reticent George. He managed the Levels, quietly working the flock up to over 100,000 and freeholding much of the run in an era more noted for grasping opportunism than for industry. As well as in history, the Rhodes brothers have their place in folklore, as theirs were the stolen sheep recovered in the possession of James McKenzie; it was Robert Heaton Rhodes who personally charged the Gaelic shepherd with their theft. A plaque at the foot of George St, by the railway station, marks the approximate site of the first house in Timaru, built by George Rhodes in 1852. A later Rhodes' cottage still stands at the Levels.

**McKenzie — the myth:** James McKenzie (?1820–?) seems to have spent as little as two years in New Zealand — there is no record of his arriving in the country and there is none of his leaving. Born in Scotland, he materialised in Southland, South Canterbury and Otago in 1854. Described as being about 1.8 m tall with a spare, muscular body and a face long and thin, he spoke English with a strong Gaelic accent. He exploded into history in March 1855, when 1,000 sheep that had disappeared from the Levels run (*NW of Timaru*) were recovered in McKenzie's possession on the fringe of what is now the Mackenzie Country, by the pass that also bears his name (but with slightly altered spelling).

McKenzie, some say, had stolen the sheep to stock a run he had taken up in Otago, and was driving the sheep single-handed with the aid of his dog, Friday. She was a remarkable bitch, the story runs, whose tongue had been slit to prevent her barking and who could understand an order in Gaelic to move selected sheep even hours after the event and after McKenzie had left her to establish for himself an alibi elsewhere.

Captured by the Levels overseer, Sidebottom, and two Maori shepherds, McKenzie yet escaped and made his way to Lyttelton, where he was found by one Police Sergeant Edward Seager, hiding in a loft. Within a month he was on trial for sheep-stealing, and after a hearing during which he remained "mute of malice" and pretended to be unable to understand what was going on, was convicted and sentenced to five years' imprisonment. The dog, the tale continues, after being brought into court to rush to her master (so identifying him and innocently sealing his fate) was ceremoniously either hanged or shot as a witch.

The legend gives no explanation for McKenzie's subsequent pardon — beyond that he frequently escaped from gaol and was proving an expensive prisoner to hold. But it does add that the pardon was conditional on his leaving the country, never to return.

**McKenzie — the man:** Only in comparatively recent times have serious attempts been made to lift the veil of legend and reveal the facts of the McKenzie affair.

McKenzie, who refused to plead either guilty or not guilty at his trial and was described as being "mute of malice", undoubtedly had Gaelic as his mother tongue. No less a person than James FitzGerald was to note that he spoke and understood English only "with great difficulty when under any excitement".

Moreover, though silent at his trial, McKenzie subsequently explained his possession of the sheep by saying that he had been hired by one James Mossman for £20 to drive the sheep, an explanation borne out by the £21 11s found on McKenzie at his committal. It was only when Sidebottom and his helpers were close at hand that Mossman (or possibly *mossman*, Gaelic for cattle-thief) fled, telling McKenzie to stay and assuring him that "You did not steal the sheep, neither did you know I stole them." The explanation he gave to his gaoler is reinforced by Sidebottom's own evidence at the trial that he saw the prints of at least two men while giving chase to the missing sheep.

The suggestion that McKenzie was trying to stock a run is also not borne out by official records. There is no trace of any application being made by him (though he claimed to have applied to Mantell for 400 ha), let alone any grant ever being made to him. The myth that he discovered the pass through to the Mackenzie country is exploded by Torlesse's map of 1849, which shows the pass and names it Manahouna. The Maoris knew of it also. Dog Friday's dramatic introduction to the courtroom to clinch the Crown's case, too, is almost certainly fictitious, and the product of Seager in his old age embellishing an oft-told tale. It is inconceivable that such an occurrence could have escaped the attention of the newspapers of the time, even given that the Judge would have allowed it in the first place. Nor may Friday have come to a shameful end, as she is now believed to have been for years afterwards a favourite of George Rhodes.

Nine months after his trial McKenzie was granted a free pardon. His gaoler, Henry Tancred, urged that this course be taken, and when forwarding McKenzie's petition for clemency on to the governor, the Superintendent of Canterbury, James FitzGerald, noted that "I am inclined to believe his story." Nowhere in the Governor's pardon of 11 January 1856 is there any requirement that McKenzie leave the country.

The charitable view is that McKenzie probably did not steal the sheep, and certainly ought not to have been convicted of the crime. At the very most (and this is unlikely) he was an accomplice. But perhaps to suggest this is only to add further to the mystique of McKenzie — pathfinder, master drover, and social rebel. (*There is a memorial near where "Mackenzie the freebooter" was first captured, by Sidebottom and the Maoris Taiko and Seventeen on the Mackenzie country side of the Mackenzie Pass (see △ Tekapo), an alternative route to the inland lakes from Timaru. Another memorial, on Taiko Flat, marks the place from which the sheep were taken that were later found with McKenzie.)*

**A costly error:** "A miserable apology for a shipping place, without wood or water. Nothing will ever spring up there but a public house, a store and a woolshed." So did Henry Sewell dismiss the site of Timaru in 1856. If time has proved the magnitude of his miscalculation, the Provincial Government, too, joined him in error by selecting only a small area for the settlement, anticipating that any future port would be under the lee of Patiti Point. But the Rhodes brothers knew better, for they had been able to study the effects of wind and tide, and shrewdly freeholded 50 ha immediately to the north for only £60. This they enterprisingly subdivided to so overshadow the official township that when the *Strathallan* dropped anchor in the roadstead in January 1859 with the first shipload of migrants, there were sixty houses in Rhodes Town and only three in Government Town. Jealousy between the two settlements, fanned by vitriolic letters to newspapers, was intense, but as they progressed the two merged round their common interest, the port. Only nine years after he had roundly condemned the place and its prospects, Henry Sewell had the temerity to seek nomination as Timaru's representative on the Provincial Council.

However for the first two decades, progress was slow. Perhaps as well, for in 1868 a disastrous fire swept through forty buildings in little more than an hour, destroying property worth £60,000. Nearly every place of business in the main street was gutted, leading the council to require all future buildings to be constructed of stone or brick — a result of which is the number of solid older buildings in the city's centre.

**An artificial port:** For years small coasters traded to the roadstead, cargo being ferried to and from the shore by surfboats. Temporary moorings were installed in the roadstead, but the marine engineer for Otago, J. M. Balfour, ruled out both a solid breakwater, as it would trap shingle swept to the coast by the Waitaki and turned northwards by the current, and an open jetty, which would afford no shelter. An experimental groyne was constructed with a gap of about 50 m from the shore to allow the shingle to travel through. The shingle immediately blocked the opening, swept up higher than the groyne itself and, just when there was agitation for its removal, a big sea carried the whole affair away. The *Lyttelton Times* remarked that Timaru could and would never have a harbour. Balfour's experiment failed, but not before the engineer himself had been drowned in the roadstead he was working to eliminate.

While controversy was never far away, in just over twenty years no fewer than twenty-eight wrecks or strandings occurred in the vicinity of the roadstead, to give the port an unenviable reputation. The casualties included the great chief Tuhawaiki, who perished near the point that now bears his name. All the while the harbour board was not permitted to undertake any construction work without the approval of a Government-appointed commission of engineers — an unusual state of affairs that persisted until 1936.

Yet in a triumph of common sense over theoretical expertise, the city successfully created an artificial harbour, turning to advantage the steady drift of shingle up the coast. Blocked by breakwaters, the shingle reclaimed over 41 ha and the highwater mark was driven 400 m seawards. Curiously, even the construction of the Benmore dam on the Waitaki has not checked the flow of shingle up the coast, much of which is removed from the foreshore for crushing and sale. Sand from the pulverised shingle is still carried north by the sea and dropped in Caroline Bay as the current is checked. The port today ranks among the country's busiest.

**Struggle for a say:** Timaru was implacably opposed to the Canterbury Provincial Council's spending of land revenue on beautiful buildings for Christchurch and on the Christchurch-Lyttelton railway. As clamour for secession grew, the New Provinces Act was repealed, leaving the disgruntled South Cantuarians at the mercy of the Provincial Council they so distrusted. The only remedy lay in legislation in the General Assembly that would entitle local boards to collect and spend a quarter of the revenue from the sale of Crown land in their areas. In Christchurch, the Provincial Superintendent, William Moorhouse, fought desperately to maintain his domain, even threatening the General Assembly with riots and the seizure of Government property should the measure be carried. But carried it was in 1867, and in Timaru businesses declared a holiday, bands paraded, bells were rung, flags were flown — and Superintendent Moorhouse was burned in effigy by the aggrieved and triumphant community. (Such an expression of public opinion was common in Timaru at the time: when in 1880 a Government marine engineer recommended that the town's long-awaited harbour breakwater be abandoned and blown up to protect the railway line, he too was carried in effigy through the streets. But the engineer's dummy received more novel treatment. It was carried to the end of the precious breakwater, where it was blown up and its fragments scattered in the bay.)

> A traveller without knowledge is a bird without wings.
> —Sa'di.

**Home of champions:** Robert Fitzsimmons (1862–1917), son of a Timaru black-smith, joined his father at the forge to develop the physique that brought him the world middleweight boxing title when he defeated Jack Dempsey in 1891. In 1897 he beat Jim Corbett over fourteen rounds to win the world heavyweight crown, which he held until 1899. Four years later he captured the world light-heavyweight champion-ship. Flamboyant and a born showman, Bob Fitzsimmons led a colourful life outside the ring. Four expensive incursions into matrimony and a compulsion for gambling saw him die only three years after the last of 350 odd bouts with little to show for his strenuous career in the ring.

As well as the country's greatest boxer, Timaru has produced its most famous racehorse, the legendary Phar Lap, who in the late 1920s and early 1930s beat all comers and carried the fame of New Zealand bloodstock abroad. In Australia the Melbourne Cup inevitably fell to the huge stallion (he was one of the biggest horses of all time) and in America he proved himself against the best the United States had to offer. It was there that his career was cut short, as he died, poisoned, soon after winning the richest race in America. Despite his racing through the Depression era, Phar Lap was for many years among the greatest stake winners in the world.

The third of the city's champions was the Rhodes Scholar, Dr John Edward Lovelock (1910–49), world record holder for the one mile, who broke the world record for the 1,500 m in front of a crowd of 120,000 to take the gold medal at the Berlin Olympics (1936). (*In common with other gold medallists, Lovelock was presented with an oak tree by Adolf Hitler. Believed to be the only one of those presented to be still flourishing, it grows in the grounds of his old school, Timaru Boys' High School, in North St. The school library exhibits the trophies he won.*)

The world professional billiards champion for two decades, Clark McConachy (born 1895), learned the game at the tables of his father's saloon in Timaru. His best break in billiards was 1,943; against the Australian champion, Walter Lindrum, he had a break of 1,927. At snooker he scored more than 300 "centuries", in the final of the world snooker championships of 1952, scoring the maximum possible, 147.

**The Downland water supply:** Irrigation for the South Canterbury downlands area was mooted for half a century before the energetic Thomas Burnett (1877–1941) finally brought a scheme to fruition as Member of Parliament for the Temuka district. The scheme carries water to houses and farms in underground pipes instead of open races, and provides not only for stock and farmland but also for domestic use. Water is drawn from a dam at the mouth of the Te Ngawai Gorge. From six huge reservoirs pipelines fan out over 60,000 ha of agricultural country. The scheme, which has some 5,000 supply points and 1,500 km of piping, was virtually completed in 1941.

## THINGS TO SEE AND DO

**Caroline Bay\*\*\***, overlooked by the city, is the focal point for the carnival that for three weeks each Christmas fills Timaru to capacity. The bay's parks, gardens, and sandy beach are frequented by picnickers the year round. To the north of the bay, the promontory tipped by the Benvenue Cliffs (under which a ship of that name died) is Maori Park, a reserve set aside in the first survey for Maori use and now owned by the city.

When the first settlers arrived, there was a tiny indentation on Caroline Bay, made by Whales Creek, where the whalers had landed their catches. The site has been obliterated by the accretion in the lee of the harbour installations that unwittingly created the beach. The creek was back from the beach at the foot of the terrace, the whalers living on the site now taken up by the tennis courts.

**Pioneer Hall Museum\*\*:** Housed in an octagonal shaped building which mirrors the outline of the chapter house of neighbouring St Mary's church, is a wide-ranging collection of items relating to South Canterbury. Of special interest are Maori artefacts discovered locally and a series of photographs and diagrams that portray the development of Timaru's artificial port. Ominous are paintings and photographs of wrecks, and a chart showing how freely the coastline hereabouts claimed visiting vessels. *Perth St. Open daily (not Monday or Saturday) from 1.30–4.30 pm.*

Opposite the museum stands an obelisk dedicated to the memory of those who lost their lives in the 1882 *Benvenue* and *City of Perth* disaster. In exceptional conditions portions of the *Benvenue* are revealed at low tide when they are seen from the top of the Benvenue Cliffs (*end of Benvenue Ave above northern end of Caroline Bay*). In the disaster, the *Benvenue* was swept by rollers, her cargo of coal from Newcastle, NSW, shifted, her cables parted and she was swept against the cliffs by Caroline Bay to become a total loss. At the same time the *City of Perth* was seen to be drifting and was abandoned. A number of crew and would-be rescuers were lost. The *City of Perth* was later refloated and renamed *Turakina*.

**St Mary's Anglican Church** (1880–86)**: Beside the museum rises the crenellated square stone tower of St Mary's, built in the early English style of the twelfth century on the site of the city's original church. The east window commemorates Archdeacon Henry Harper, the Bishop's son, who was responsible for the building of the church. The west window was given by the family of Edward Elworthy, an early runholder. The interior has a lofty, spacious feeling whose unity overshadows individual features, such as the elaborately carved altar (flanked by Bishop Selwyn and Archbishop Julius) and the panelling of the choir, where native birds and flowers abound. Introduced birds join in the organ's silent chorus. *Perth St.*

**Aigantighe Art Gallery**\*\*\*: The gallery stages touring exhibitions as well as works from its carefully chosen permanent collection, among the best of the provincial galleries. Of interest is Sapper H. Moore-Jones's wellknown painting of *Murphy and his Donkey*. Other originals exist of this portrayal of an ambulance man at Gallipoli bringing a casualty back from the front. "Murphy's" identity is still debated, despite the New Zealander dedicating his painting to his "comrade" Simpson. Aigantighe (pronounced Egg-an-tie) is Gaelic for welcome to our home. *49 Wai-iti Rd. Open daily (not Monday or Friday) from 2–4.30 pm. Allow 1 hr. Also closed on some public holidays.*

**Botanical Gardens:** The pleasant gardens include a statue of Robert Burns, here in a district more English than Scottish in outlook. It was the gift of a former mayor and local Member of Parliament, James Craigie, devoted both to Burns and to his own Scottish origins. *Queen St, off King St, on the main route south.*

**Catholic Basilica** (1910)**: A majestic building, with twin towers and a large, impressive dome, the Basilica dominates the southern aspect of the city. Within are an array of fine stained glass and a noteworthy altar that incorporates a variety of stone. *Craigie Ave.*

**The Landing Service:** The original landing service (1867) was below the terrace (on which the old lighthouse (1877) stands) at the foot of Strathallan Street on the corner opposite the classical Customs House (1902). Reclamation for harbour and railway works has covered the site. A second service was begun in 1868 a block away, at the foot of George Street, with the beach and the highwater-mark where the railway now runs. This second service did not prosper and in 1870 was sold to Captain Cain for £975. The bluestone two-storeyed store (1867), now part of the Dalgety complex, is the only surviving relic. (*At the foot of George St, round the corner facing the railway*).

The boatmen achieved remarkable results, the schooner *Spray* loading 170 bales of wool in a single day. But boats capsized and goods were frequently drenched. In time the old whaleboats gave way to surfboats and then to iron boats hauled by steam engines. The craft were pulled between ship and shore by surf cables attached to buoys anchored offshore. The cables ran through chocks on the landing craft and first men and later machines pulled the boats along them by hauling on a rope. This was hazardous work, and because the boatmen would tend to serve first the vessels that were closest to the shore, captains were tempted to take risks in anchoring closer to the coast than was prudent in the hope of a quick turn round — a practice that inevitably inflated the number of ships lost in the roadstead.

**Hadlow Game Park:** Wallabies, llamas, African barbary sheep, emus and antelopes are some of the creatures living in a controlled natural environment. Picnic and barbecue facilities, and a gallery displaying paintings, pottery, prints and antiques provided for their human visitors. *Open daily until dusk. Hadlow Rd, off Glen-iti Rd.*

**Museum of Childhood:** An excellent display includes antique dolls, toys and animated figures. *Open 10 am–4.30 pm, Mon.-Sat.* Near Mt. Junction turnoff on Hilton Highway N of Timaru.

**Washdyke:** The area takes its unusual name from the stream in which the Levels sheep were washed before shearing, according to the custom of early days. The disposal of surplus stock and aging ewes took time, and before a boiling-down works opened here 5,000 sheep were simply driven over a nearby cliff to drown in the sea. In recent years the locality has developed as the city's main industrial area. *Washdyke. North on Highway 1.*

**Industrial tours:** A number of local industries welcome visiting groups, among them a brewery, Alliance Textiles and the Timaru Milling Company. *Details from the Public Relations Office.*

## SOME MAORI ROCK DRAWINGS

The region has a large number of early Maori rock drawings which date back to times when the itinerant Moa-hunter stalked his prey in the district. Some of these are not accessible to the public; others are physically difficult to get to. A complete list of sites in South Canterbury is held by the South Canterbury Regional Committee of the New Zealand Historic Places Trust. *Further information is available from the Pioneer Hall Museum. For general notes on Maori rock drawings, see "Introduction".*

**Craigmore shelters:** Fairly faint, the drawings in the two shelters here are of lifelike *moa* and certainly of the *kuri* (Maori dog). There are numerous drawings in shelters of greater or lesser accessibility along this impressive valley, but the paramount shelters are identified on the right, above the road, both by their protective fences and by a small sign. *At the end of Craigmore Homestead Rd, off Limestone Rd, pass through the gate and continue for 350 m. 34 km from Timaru; 17 km from Cave.*

Speculation is that the Moa-hunters may have captured *moa* here by driving their quarry over the cliffs. The subjects of the drawings suggest they at least pre-date the extinction of the *moa*.

**Frenchmans Gully drawings:** The curious drawing here of a birdman with outstretched wings on which five fledglings are poised has been variously interpreted as Tane-mahuta (god of the birds), as a bird-headed man similar to those of Easter Island, and as an embodiment of birdlife rather humanly rendered. *Frenchmans Gully Rd (linking Gordons Valley Rd and Craigmore Valley Rd).*

See also △ *Cave and Pioneer Park (see index).*

## OTHER ENVIRONS

△ **Cave\*:** Originally an outstation on the Levels, the township has an interesting boulder church. *35 km WNW.*

△ **Temuka:** A town of memorials. *18.5 km N.*

△ **Pleasant Point:** There is a railway enthusiasts' museum here. *19 km NW.*

**Rhodes cottage, The Levels\*\*:** One of the oldest buildings in South Canterbury and among the oldest of its type in the country is the simple little Levels Hut in which George Rhodes and his wife were living by 1856. Built of vertical timber slabs, the one-storey cottage is thatched with wheat straw. *10 km NW of Timaru on Highway 8. On private property opposite the old Levels railway siding. The building can be seen from the road, on the hillside by the tennis court to the right of the homestead.*

**St Mary's Anglican Church, Esk Valley** (1880): A limestone church standing on the ridge between the Otaio and Esk Valleys was built by Charles Meyer in memory of his wife and according to her wish. The site was chosen so that the church could be seen from their homestead at Blue Cliffs. There are windows given in memory of Charles Meyer, Robert Heaton Rhodes (a later owner of Blue Cliff) and his wife Jessy. *24 km.*

## ROUND TRIPS

Many pleasant trips can be planned in the district. One such trip is to leave Timaru by Highway 8, passing The Levels and △ Pleasant Point to reach △ Cave. After seeing the memorial church and the Maori rock drawings, return toward Pleasant Point, turning left to follow the signposted route to Hanging Rock bridge, a pleasant picnic and swimming spot on the Opihi River. On crossing the river turn right to pass the site of Richard Pearse's aeronautical experiments before reaching △ Temuka, where turn south to Timaru by Highway 1. *88 km.*

Other trips can be planned by referring to the entries for △ Temuka *(18.5 km).* △ Pleasant Point *(19 km),* △ Cave *(35 km),* △ Geraldine *(36 km),* △ Peel Forest *(57 km),* △ Mesopotamia *(105 km)* and △ Waimate *(46 km).*

## TOURING NOTES

**Roads from Timaru:** From Timaru roads lead inland to the Mackenzie country (through △ Pleasant Point, △ Cave, △ Fairlie and △ Burkes Pass), south (past △ Waimate, across the △ Waitaki River and through △ Oamaru) and north, (through △ Temuka and △ Ashburton). An alternative route to Christchurch is by way of △ Geraldine, or △ Methven and the Rakaia Gorge *(see index).*

△ **Tekapo via Mackenzie Pass** *(105 km):* Turn left off Highway 8 towards Fairlie, at Albury, to follow the pass used by McKenzie and see a monument near the place where some consider he was apprehended by Sidebottom.

**TUATAPERE      Southland.    Maps 12 & 18.    Pop. 836.**

*88.5 km NW of Invercargill.*

STANDING BY THE WAIAU RIVER on the very brink of primitive Fiordland, Tuatapere instantly impresses as a timber town. Farming on the rich Waiau plain has now surpassed timber in importance, but Tuatapere remains the principal timbermilling centre for the Otago/Southland market and beyond. Axemen from around the country converge on the town each New Year's Day to take part in woodchop carnivals.

For the visitor the town is an important access point to the forests, lakes and rivers of △ Fiordland National Park. The Waiau River hereabouts was once renowned for its fishing, particularly for Atlantic salmon. But the diversion of its Mararoa River tributary and the loss to the Manapouri hydro-electric power scheme of the combined waters from Lakes Te Anau and Manapouri has resulted in a reduced and irregular flow along what was once among the swiftest rivers in the country.

Tuatapere's meaning has not been satisfactorily explained (*tua* = sacred ceremony preliminary to a gathering of the people; *tapere* = an assembly for songs and amusements).

**Domain\*\***: A fragment of the bush that otherwise fell to the sawmillers as they worked their way gradually westward is preserved as a noble skirt to the simple domain, a recreational and camping spot on the banks of the Waiau. *Signposted to the right immediately over the Waiau River Bridge.*

## SOME HISTORY

**Outpost of civilisation:** Settlement dates from the arrival at nearby Papatotara of Hugh Erskine, about 1885, where he settled on the west bank of the Waiau. He carved out a home and proved the agricultural prospects of the country once bush was cleared. The sawmillers were not far behind, as they worked west from Orepuki, through Waihoaka, Te Waewae, Te Tua and so to Tuatapere which, with the arrival of the railway in 1909, soon became a major sawmilling centre. Some farmers cleared their own land, but others chose to follow the millers into cut-over areas. Until the river was finally bridged, the punt now on the Clutha at Tuapeka Mouth was a familiar landmark here.

Some years ago the author of a university thesis chose the title, *Tuatapere: Outpost of Civilisation.* Today the town prefers: "Tuatapere; Capital of the prosperous South-West Country."

## ENVIRONS

**Port Craig:** Near the western extremity of Te Waewae Bay once stood one of the largest timbermills in the hemisphere. Timber was shipped out from a settlement that boasted dozens of huts, with reticulated water and electricity. Today there is comparatively little to mark the site of a once-busy community, for after output had reached a peak in 1928 the venture failed with the Depression. All that remains is a deserted schoolhouse and traces of both the mill and the wharf. There is good crayfishing hereabouts. *An all-day walk (return) round the shore.*

**Preservation Inlet:** The site of early sealing activity in the Strait and of a short-lived gold rush. The usual mode of access to this historically interesting and geographically remote region is by foot; however those with less time to spare may fly in by amphibian from Invercargill, to camp and fish here before tramping out. *Charter flights arranged through Mount Cook Airlines at Invercargill. Tramping routes should be discussed with the Fiordland National Park ranger at Clifden.*

△**Fiordland National Park\*\*\*:** The largest, most remote and least accessible of the country's national parks.

△**Clifden:** An interesting limestone area. *13 km N.*

△**Lake Hauroko\*\*:** A bush girt lake, typical of the Fiordland National Park. *31 km NW.*

△**Lake Monowai:** Regarded by conservationists as an object lesson to hydro-power planners, the lake still bears the scars of being raised in 1924. *36 km NNW.*

## TOURING NOTES

**Road to Invercargill (Highway 99):** The route passes through △Orepuki and △Riverton, both with pleasant beaches and fascinating pasts.

**Monowai–Blackmount Road to** △**Te Anau:** This alternative route to △Te Anau has been upgraded to bring the major lakes of Fiordland National Park within easy reach. *108 km.*

---

**TWIZEL     South Canterbury.   Map 34.**

*56 km SW of Tekapo; 30.5 km NNE of Omarama. Project Information Office mounts displays and provides details of the power scheme (open daily).*

THE CONSTRUCTION TOWN for the Upper Waitaki power development scheme sprang to life by the Twizel River on the demise of △Otematata as a hydro town. Within three years it had achieved a population in excess of 4,000 and is still close to its 1976 maximum of 6,000. A complete and substantial town, built and controlled by the Ministry of Works and Development, Twizel has more than ninety different clubs.

The once monotonous skyline of roofs of identical pitch is now broken by trees. More than 90,000 have been planted in and around the town and by the time the scheme is finished some 1.5 million will be growing in the bleak Mackenzie basin. Rigorous winters necessitate special protection for water pipes and extra insulation for buildings.

Twizel takes its name from the nearby river, so called by the surveyor John Turnbull Thomson after Twizel bridge in Northumberland. The bridge, well known to the surveyor, was where in 1513 the English outflanked King James IV of Scotland by crossing the bridge to cut him off from the north.

**Twizel Inn:** The inn's painted signboard, depicting McKenzie (*see index*) and his faithful dog, originally hung at a hotel at Pukaki which was moved here with its licence to make way for the raising of the lake.

## UPPER WAITAKI POWER DEVELOPMENT SCHEME

In the huge alpine catchment of the Waitaki River are three large lakes which can produce a constant and controlled waterflow ideal for major power development. Under the scheme Lake Tekapo's waters, after passing through the existing Tekapo A power station, are conveyed by a 25-km canal to a second station, Tekapo B, on the shore of Lake Pukaki and discharged into that lake. Apart from flood flows, ground water, and some small contributory streams the Tekapo River will be dry. The Pukaki High Dam, completed in 1977, will result in the lake being raised 36.6 m, trebling its storage capacity. From Pukaki a second canal leads to the Ohau A power-house some 13 km away. Merging with the Pukaki canal is a 9 km canal from Lake Ohau. The combined waters from Lakes Tekapo, Pukaki and Ohau will thus flow through Ohau A, sited on the Ohau River.

Downstream from Ohau A, the Ruataniwha Dam is being built to raise the water-head for Ohau B. In the process it will create a new, small artificial lake, Ruataniwha. A fourth canal will feed the Ohau B station, and a fifth will lead its tailrace waters a further 7 km downstream to Ohau C, on the upper reaches of Lake Benmore. These last two stations will each have a generating capacity of 212,000 kW.

Further development in the Lower Waitaki could follow, with a series of as many as ten stations, each with a head of 18.3 m and each with an installed generating capacity of about 68,000 kW. This would complete a total of eighteen stations on the river, with an annual capacity approaching 2.5 million kW. (*See also* △ *Waitaki Valley.*)

**Canals:** In some areas the canals resemble a huge channel dug from ground level; in others they slice through hills, and elsewhere they are encased in huge ramparts. A typical section of the first canal, from Tekapo, is 11.9 m wide at its base and 5.5 m deep — sufficient width and depth to float the inter-island ferry *Aranui*. The next canal, however, with the outflow from two lakes, could float both the *Aranui* and *Aramoana* side by side. Not only do the canals increase power production but they provide the means of irrigating large areas of the Mackenzie basin.

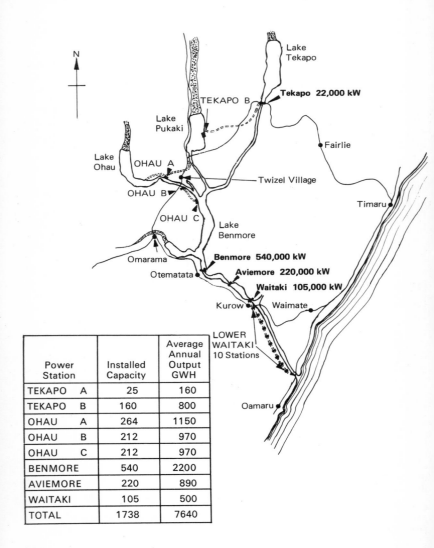

| Power Station | | Installed Capacity | Average Annual Output GWH |
|---|---|---|---|
| TEKAPO | A | 25 | 160 |
| TEKAPO | B | 160 | 800 |
| OHAU | A | 264 | 1150 |
| OHAU | B | 212 | 970 |
| OHAU | C | 212 | 970 |
| BENMORE | | 540 | 2200 |
| AVIEMORE | | 220 | 890 |
| WAITAKI | | 105 | 500 |
| TOTAL | | 1738 | 7640 |

## WAIAU    North Canterbury.    Maps 20 & 21.    Pop. 356.

*22 km NE of Culverden; 44 km NW of Cheviot; 85 km SW of Kaikoura.*

A SCATTERING of Victorian buildings lends charm to the village on the north bank of the wide Waiau River. Surrounding are the comfortable farmlands of North Canterbury, where rich riverflats cover basins between bands of undulating country. Roads from Waiau lead to Culverden and to Kaikoura, both by way of the inland and the coastal routes. Waiau means river of swirling currents.

### POINTS OF INTEREST

**Cob Cottage Museum:** The original portion of the cottage (1878) in its earliest years housed a succession of butchers and bakers. About the turn of the century a small wooden building was apparently dragged to the site and joined to the cottage. As well as pioneering relics, the collection features the agitation for a road over the Lewis Pass route. Documents include caterers' lists for the celebrations that followed the eventual opening. *Open Sunday 2–4 pm. Also open by arrangement. Enquire locally.*

**Waiau Presbyterian Church** (1888) is on the site of the first church to be built in the area north of Kaiapoi. Behind, an earlier church building (1877) now serves as a Sunday school. *By Highway 70.*

## WAIHOLA (Lake)*    East Otago.    Maps 4 & 9.    Pop. 150.

*39 km SW of Dunedin; 16 km N of Milton.*

LOW-LYING AND ENCLOSED by gentle hills is Lake Waihola, for generations a popular aquatic venue — for yachting, power boating, sculling and waterskiing. Over the years the lake has seen a diversity of craft from Maori canoes to log rafts bound for sawmills, and from rowboats to paddle-steamers. There is no longer the steam launch that at the turn of the century was available "for the convenience of ailing or convalescent tourists".

The lake's name, more properly Waihora (water spread out) as there is no "l" in Maori, is appropriate as the lake covers an area extensive for one so shallow. A short tidal river links Waihola with Lake Waipori to the north and thence via the Waipori and Taieri Rivers to the sea. The access to the Taieri River proved a boon to carters in 1862, when there was heavy traffic to the goldfields. Coastal steamers from Dunedin could reach the lake by way of the Taieri River even to the southern tip of Waihola, where stood the busy little port of Clarendon. In the harsh winter of 1862 the lake froze so solidly that one could skate all over it. *There is a small charge for car-parking and a boat-launching fee in the Waihola Domain, where there are facilities for picnicking, for camping and for water-sports.*

### TOURING NOTES

**Coast route to Dunedin via Taieri Mouth:** A 12 km drive from Lake Waihola over rolling country leads to picturesque **Taieri Mouth**** where the local fishing boats may be seen strung along the riverbank. Off shore, like a cork almost in the river's mouth, is Moturata (*rata* island) which can be reached on foot when tides and sandbars allow. The Weller brothers and, later, Johnny Jones had shore-whaling stations on a tiny beach on the island's western shore. A cave on its landward side can be explored.

Various accounts name various rocks on the Taieri River as Maori Leap. Some tell of a girl who leapt to her death when trying to jump into her lover's canoe as he fled from his enemies. Another relates that a Maori chief from a local *hapu* leapt from a high perpendicular rock on the river's north bank to escape his enemies, only to be transfixed in mid-air by a spear. A large number of *umu* (ovens) were found on Mona Hill, bearing testimony to the slaughter.

Another rock some distance upriver is named Governor's Rock as it was there that Sir George Grey once lit a fire. From Taieri Mouth the way to Dunedin lies along the coast, passing through Brighton, a seaside centre that had its heyday in the early days of the motorcar, being about as far from Dunedin as one could then comfortably visit in a day.

**Road to △Milton:** A 3.8 km detour may be made just south of the lake to Horseshoe Bush to see from the road the fine Victorian stables (1884) built for Henry Driver — an American who prospered on the Australian goldfields and came to Otago to farm, to trade and for some years to represent Roslyn in the House of Representatives. *Turn right towards Berwick at 6 km and then turn left at 7.2 km down Drivers Road to reach its end at 7.9 km.* Off to the right, at 9.3 km S of Waihola, may be seen littering the distant hillside the derelict limeworks of New Zealand Cement Holdings, abandoned in 1966.

**Coastal route to △Milton:** An alternative to Highway 1 is to drive over to Taieri Mouth and then swing south to pass through interesting country before rejoining Highway 1 by way of the Milton-Bull Creek Rd. *Adds 8 km to the direct route.*

*52.5 km NNW of Gore; 47 km E of Lumsden.*

WAIKAIA, "the stream where the *keha* burr grew" survives today as a tiny farming settlement by the hills that build to form the mountain barrier separating Southland from Central Otago. As Switzers, it once saw boom and bustle when a series of fabulous finds drew fortune-seekers to its goldfields from all over Otago and Southland.

West of Waikaia, in a substantial afforestation scheme, the Southland County Council has a plantation of over 1 million trees, predominantly *Pinus radiata* but with small areas of Oregon and *macrocarpa*. Sawn timber is produced as well as logs for the paper mills at △Mataura.

## SOME HISTORY

**The brothers Tibbetts:** The first to take up land in the district were Captain Tibbetts and his brother, Charles. The captain, apparently the victim of sunstroke contracted in India, soon illustrated his unpredictable disposition when he built his hut straddling a creek to ensure that water could be had without stirring from his bed. Ever unorthodox, when he found difficulty in mustering cattle from thick scrub he simply invested in a mortar and tried to frighten the beasts out with exploding shells. Finally he seems to have become completely insane. In a row which followed a neighbour's horse kicking his own white mare, Tibbetts shot and killed his neighbour's German cook. Walking home, unsuspecting roadmen asked the armed captain how his hunting had fared to which he replied: "Not very well. Only bagged a German." Police arrived with his brother Charles, to encounter a hail of gunfire. Charles, urged to return his brother's fire, refused and it was only when a shot severed one of his fingers that Charles fired back, hitting and killing his brother. Distraught, Charles turned his gun on himself but was saved from harm by an alert police sergeant.

Just before the fatalities John Switzers acquired the immense run here where the very next year, in 1862, gold was found in considerable quantities.

**The rush to Switzers:** Within a year of the discovery of gold the township of Switzers boasted a population of perhaps 2,000 to serve a goldfield that had both firewood and coal to remove the acute discomfort that cold caused on the nearby goldfields of Central Otago. Goldbearing creeks were found everywhere and bands of miners faced death as they struggled south "over the hill" (the 1,828 m Old Man Range) to reach the diggings. Dozens are known to have perished. A cairn (*SE of Alexandra*) was erected in 1928 in memory of those who died in the fearful snowstorm of 1863. By the next winter snow poles and wires stretched over the Old Man Range to reduce if not eliminate the hazards of the "snowpole track".

Diggers came from Tuapeka, the Clutha and from Dunedin to win their share of the £4-to-£5 million yielded by the Waikaia district, first with dish and cradle, then by ground and hydraulic sluicing. Finally some twenty dredges turned over hundreds of hectares in their two decades of operation up to 1910.

There were many fabulous finds. The Canton claim, the richest on the Waikaia River (*beyond Piano Flat*) was owned by Chinese who bought it from a group of feuding *Pakeha*. With patience and care the Chinese worked the claim 6.7 m under the riverbed, barrowing out paydirt for washing. Many won their fortunes until, with the big flood of 1878, the claim became only a memory.

The settlement originally stood on Frenchman's Hill (or Old Hill as it is now known) but eventually came to stand on a level site that had been noted as being sufficiently above the river to have escaped the big flood of 1878. The moves were for one simple reason — gold, and the need to sluice the town site to win it.

Precisely why the name of Switzers fell from favour is uncertain, but gradually the town adopted the name of the river.

**The King Solomon mine:** The best-known of the claims was the King Solomon mine. This yielded handsome returns before it finally closed in 1937. In its last eight years of operation 19,462 ounces were won to a then value of £142,178. The mine provided much-needed employment during Depression years. Until a few years ago the odd digger could be seen at work in the locality, still managing to extract a living from his labours.

**The spectre of McKellar:** The Waikaia Plains station (since fragmented into many separate holdings) was acquired by David McKellar (d. 1892) — who with Alexander McNab had pioneered the Gore district and who thereafter in 1868 met and married the daughter of a wealthy Australian squatter. The unsuspecting bride landed at Bluff complete with carriage, crates of silver, a one-hundred guinea piano and a St Vincent negro to act as footman. It is to be believed that she burst into tears when first she saw her New Zealand home — a minute sod cottage with an earth floor. Happily she made the most of her circumstances and in time a mansion of twenty rooms was built of local stone. There, in the appropriate setting of the "big house", her silver could at last be unpacked.

By 1877 the run had been sold to Duncan Gillanders and some few years later the McKellars moved on to New Mexico. There David McKellar was creating a modern ranch when he was shot and killed by natives after he had fenced off a disputed boundary. For many years McKellar is said to have haunted the upper rooms of the "big house" — others say the spectre was that of a Chinese who hanged himself here. Certainly the upper storey, which was left unoccupied, was for years too rotten to support anything more substantial than a ghost.

The stone homestead built by McKellar still stands, somewhat modernised. Two-storeyed and backed by trees, it is near the brow of a hill-line overlooking the billiards-flat Waikaia Plains. Some short distance from the homestead are the ruins of the sod cottage to which McKellar brought his bride. *On private property. 19.6 km SW from Waikaia. At Freshford, 7.3 km S, turn right. Follow road to end where bear left at 17.2 km. The homestead is a short distance on, on the right.*

## ENVIRONS

**King Solomon mine:** The site of the mine (*see above*) is marked by extensive heaps of mullock, about 400 m from the road to the left of the Awatere station homestead. The shaft has been filled in for safety. Along the hillside opposite runs the near-level line of the substantial Argyle water-race. Now dry, it once carried a considerable volume of water. It begins some distance away, to draw water from the Argyle Burn, by this point on a level well below that of the water-race. *8.3 km on the direct route to Waikaka.* Leaving Waikaia one passes through the broken country that marks the sluiced-out site of the first town.

**Piano Flat:** A pleasant picnic and camping spot on the site of diggings which extended well on from the end of the usable road. There is excellent fishing in the Waikaia River. *23 km N.*

---

**WAIKARI     North Canterbury. . Maps 20 & 21.   Pop. 342.**

*14 km NNW of Waipara; 25 km SSW of Culverden.*

OVERLOOKED BY the marble figure of Dr Charles Thomas Wilson Little MD (1866–1918), the township of Waikari nestles by the railway a sheltered distance from the main highway. The doctor, a much loved local medical practitioner, did not spare himself in the influenza epidemic of 1918 — nor was he spared by the virus.

Limeworks quarry the region's deposits so evident in nearby Weka Pass and in the worn outcrops of Pyramid Valley which runs off the Waikari-Harwarden road. Moa bones were discovered in this valley in 1937 and between 1939 and 1941 some fifty skeletons were recovered. Waikari means ditch or trench.

### TIMPENDEAN ROCK SHELTER

The shelter contains some of the most famous examples of early Maori rock art (*see "Introduction"*). Discovered by shepherds in the earliest days of European settlement, they were visited by Sir Julius von Haast in 1876. Until 1946 this was the only known shelter with drawings in the Weka Pass district, but a systematic survey has yielded many more, if none as spectacular. Some of the more striking figures were painted over in 1930 by National Museum staff, anxious to prevent further deterioration. Some others have been disfigured by sightseers. *The shelter is on an historic reserve set in farmland. Obtain permission and directions from the Timpendean homestead, the second farm on the right south of Waikari on Highway 7.*

### OTHER POINTS OF INTEREST

**Waipara County Historical Museum:** The display includes a house furnished with Victoriana, a typical country store and early photos of the area. *High St, Hawarden, 7 km NW of Waikari.*

**Lake Sumner Forest Park:** The state plantations at Lake Sumner are being developed as a recreational area. *Hunting permits, track and hut details from the New Zealand Forest Service at Christchurch.* En route the road passes Horsley Down (*12 km*) almost opposite whose Anglican church is the Horsley Down homestead, one of the earliest in the area.

### TOURING NOTE

△**Lewis Pass Road**\*\*: Highway 7 through △Culverden and over the Lewis Pass to Springs Junction, △Reefton and △Murchison is described under this entry.

---

## WAIKOUAITI*     North Otago.     Map 9.     Pop. 885.

*42 km NNE of Dunedin; 14.5 km SSW of Palmerston.*

WAIKOUAITI DRAWS its heritage from the sea. For although the oldest European settlement in Otago is now orientated to the main road it was, on the arrival of Dunedin's first settlers, the Province's principal port. Here were landed immigrants, goldseekers, goods and livestock and from here were shipped out the first wool-clips. Once the main road south was passable, wagoners no longer loaded goods for the goldfields here but went on to Dunedin. At this time many businesses moved away from the beach to the main road. A safe sandy beach attracts holidaymakers. At the bird sanctuary of Waikouaiti Lagoon, home to a variety of wading birds, very occasionally the white heron may be seen.

The generally accepted meaning of Waikouaiti is water which has become less, perhaps a reference to a drought, perhaps to the level of the lagoon at low tide.

### SOME HISTORY

**The remarkable Johnny Jones** (1809–69): Merchant, whaler, pioneer farmer, Johnny Jones's controversial figure overshadows the first years of European settlement in Otago.

He began work as a sixteen-year-old sealer in New Zealand waters and continued as an enterprising boatman plying for hire on Sydney Harbour; it has never been satisfactorily explained how at the age of twenty he had already acquired sufficient capital to hold a share in no fewer than three whaling ships off the New Zealand coast. Success led to his entry into shore whaling. He acquired George Burns's whaling station at Preservation Inlet in 1834 and built up a chain of whaling stations from Foveaux Strait to as far north as Karitane. His growing fleet serviced several others as well. By 1839 his six ships were well known and he claimed to own seven whaling stations and to employ 280 men.

With the slump in whaling Jones looked to land, buying up large areas and sharing in a Sydney-based syndicate that seriously claimed to have purchased the entire South Island. In 1839 he bought the land from Karitane to Matanaka and inland for 16 km, paying, it is said, "one tierce of tobacco and ten dozen shirts". He even conveyed three chiefs, Taiaroa, Tuhawaiki and Karetai, to Sydney to sign the deed of sale. He then proceeded to organise migrants, the *Magnet* in 1840 bringing ten families to settle at Waikouaiti on terms that would pay them £38 a year, entitle them to free rations and to 24 hectares each at the end of two years. However the first settlement disintegrated; the families suffered from a shortage of food, a fear of Maori hostility and fire; moreover they soon fell out with Jones's farm manager and moved on. Jones was not discouraged and recruited others to take their place. To give added importance to his settlement he imported a resident missionary, James Watkin, a Wesleyan whose pessimistic commentaries on the malpractices of Maori and *Pakeha* alike made his departure after almost four years predictable.

Jones's land claims were, in the main, rejected — he considered his holdings extended inland to Lake Wanaka — the award being 1,000 ha. Later negotiations brought him an additional 3,500 ha of unsold land within the Otago Province. Later he was to add to this considerably by taking up several sheep runs.

Anticipating the arrival of the Dunedin settlers, Jones ensured that he would be an established trader and intensive farmer, well able to supply the newcomers with what they would need. So from the start he dominated the Dunedin commercial scene. His shipping concern prospered to become today's Union Steamship Co., and at one time he had £20,000 in circulation of his own private banknotes — accepted without question, such was his mercantile standing. As Dr Hocken wrote: "He could make a corner in grain, determine plenty or scarcity, and disarrange the small money market. A law unto himself and to other people, he was always ready in time of need to support his will by force of fist. Yet he was generous and ever ready to help any scheme to advance the settlement." Another described him as "a son of Tom Jones, a notorious convict of Botany Bay, [and who] ruled the town of Dunedin by dint of moneybags and fisticuffs", and described how Jones was once lightheartedly outbid by a group when he sought to buy at auction "an easy chair in which to repose his squat gorilla-like frame". In retaliation he took revenge on the miscreants and indeed on the whole population of Dunedin by promptly increasing the price of sugar by 2d per pound. In his old age he sought respectability by wearing a suit, silk tie and top hat. His generosity is reflected in a number of church sites and endowments, made without discrimination to a variety of denominations, which may be regarded as atonement for his undoubted sins.

## THINGS TO SEE AND DO

**Waikouaiti Early Settlers' Museum:** A collection of local items spreads over both floors of the old barred banking chambers and manager's residence (c. 1900). Included are a pair of 12 m whaleboat oars, one of Jones's trypots, a replica of his personal £1 banknote, his portrait, and an Australian slate fireplace from his Matanaka home. Also displayed are poems and writings by the paranoiac Lionel Terry (see index) who for half a century was an inmate at Seacliff Hospital. *Main Rd (Highway 1). Open daily 3–4 pm.*

**Churches:** The old settlement has several venerable churches all built on land given for the purpose by Johnny Jones. Unpretentious **St Anne's Catholic Church** (1871) is perhaps the oldest in the Dunedin Catholic diocese still regularly used for worship (*Thomas St*). The **Waikouaiti Presbyterian Church** (1863), a wooden structure, has been relegated to the role of Sunday school beside its brick successor (*Kildare St*). **St John's Anglican Church** (1858)** is the most picturesque of the three. Of pitsawn timber and nestling in old trees, St John's was designed by B. W. Mountfort and, when it opened, was welcomed by the *Otago Witness*, which enthused "[it] is built after the Gothic style, and is altogether we believe a very neat erection. The church and parsonage have been erected entirely at the expense of Mr J. Jones, Waikouaiti." A plaque within acknowledges the parish's debt to Jones, and the east window is a memorial to one of his settlers, Henry Orbell, who lies in the shaded graveyard. By the road a short distance beyond the church, just past the domain, is a stone column dedicated to Jones and the settlers he brought here. (*Beach St.*)

**Waikouaiti Beach:** A sheltered stretch of beach with safe swimming. The dunes are anchored with marram grass planted in 1906 at the suggestion of Dr Truby King. It successfully checked the sand's inland drift. Later plantings of *Pinus radiata* have had the added effect of financing local projects. *Follow Beach St to its end.*

**Matanaka homestead*:** When Johnny Jones came to live in New Zealand he settled on the volcanic Matanaka Peninsula at the northern end of Waikouaiti Bay, where several wooden buildings from his era survive. The homestead (1846), much added to and still lived in; a cottage; the two-storeyed stable with a pigeon loft, as shown by circular holes under the northern gable; a granary and old schoolhouse; and last but not least a three-holed privy. All these buildings, other than the homestead which is private property, have been vested in and restored by the Historic Places Trust. They form the oldest surviving complex of farm buildings in New Zealand. *4 km. Leave Waikouaiti towards Matanaka Beach. Turn left up road signposted Gun Club and follow it to the end.*

---

**WAIMATE**     South Canterbury.   Maps 28 & 35.   Pop. 3,378.
*46 km S of Timaru; 46 km NNW of Oamaru.*

A WHITE HORSE, a tribute to the Clydesdale horses that drew ploughs to tame the land hereabouts, is outlined in paving stones on the slopes of the Hunters Hills. Within the town rise a series of white-painted concrete silos that tower above the many majestic trees so much a feature of the hub of southernmost South Canterbury. The town serves local farmers and has a flourishing berry-fruit industry. Hyacinth and tulip bulbs are propagated for markets throughout New Zealand, Australia and the United States. Wild wallabies are hunted in the hills. Waimate's name (stagnant water) relates to times when, between floods, there were many stagnant pools in the stream that meandered through the original swampland.

## SOME HISTORY

**Te Huruhuru** (d. 1861), chief of the Taoka *hapu* of Ngaitahu, lived at various *pa*, among them those on the south bank of the Waitaki River, at Waikouaiti and at Waimate, his headquarters in later years. When he met Studholme in 1854 he was paralysed below the waist; "He could only move his arms, but he ruled the Pah and was very clear headed." Paralysis had come with old age, for Te Huruhuru was no young man when in 1836 he went with Tuhawaiki to attack and defeat Te Rauparaha in Marlborough. However, at the year's end he only narrowly escaped from Hawea when Te Puoho's *taua* unexpectedly emerged from the Haast Pass.

Edward Shortland met the chief on the banks of the Waitaki, and while the Protector of Aborigines waited for flood waters to abate, Te Huruhuru told him of the interior and drew him a surprisingly accurate map of the inland lakes. "I took leave of this friendly family with much regret," said Shortland, who left to make his chance encounter with Bishop Selwyn, travelling south. Selwyn considered the chief's manners "particularly charming, though he has scarcely ever seen more polished models amongst our countrymen than the whalers on the coast . . . He entertained us with eels, which I returned with a present of books." In 1849 Charles Torlesse recorded camping with Te Huruhuru "the old Hunter, who has a place at [Waitaki] but hunts the country round for ducks, eels etc." It is this reference that probably explains the naming of the Hunters Hills behind Waimate. In 1973 the highest peak on the Hunters Hills was named Te Huruhuru, an event marked by a pilgrimage to the hills by descendants both of the chief and of Michael Studholme.

The chief lies buried with other members of his family in the Maori Cemetery (*2 km. Signposted from Point Bush Road*). A memorial on the junction of Queen St and Gorge Rd (where Studholme and Te Huruhuru are thought to have met) commemorates the eightieth anniversary of their meeting. Plaques in a carved shelter in Seddon Square honour both the Maori chief and the *Pakeha*.

**The Studholmes of Te Waimate:** Anyone less optimistic or any less enterprising than twenty-year-old Michael Studholme would surely not have reached Te Waimate in 1854. Setting off from Christchurch in the slush of midwinter, he spent about six weeks making the journey. Time and again his companion and bullock driver, the despondent and superstitious Saul Shrives, would come to a halt by a river or creek, declaring it to be utterly impossible to cross, but by 18 July 1854 the unlikely pair had reached their destination. Studholme met with the paralysed chief Te Huruhuru and came to an understanding that the boundaries of his run would be respected. For his part, Studholme would not interfere with the activities of the *pa*. This meeting laid the basis for the future community of Waimate.

The youthful Studholme brothers, John, Paul and Michael, had arrived at Lyttelton in 1851 to take up a block of land at Governors Bay. This they sold and for a year tried their luck on the Australian goldfields, which proved adventurous if unprofitable, for their tent was attacked and they were twice robbed of their horses. After returning to New Zealand Paul went back to Britain but John and Michael devoted themselves to squatting, taking up runs at Hororata, Riverton and in Central Otago. It was as the pair journeyed to Otago that they were struck by the country here and decided to take it up as well. At first 14,175 hectares were leased, but these were added to until Te Waimate finally spread from the sea to the Hakataramea watershed — nearly 40,500 ha. With their other holdings, including runs in the North Island, the partnership held almost 400,000 ha. Financially the brothers were over committed — annual outgoings on Te Waimate alone were £26,000 — and the depression of the 1880s forced the sale of much of their land. Indeed John Studholme, who in 1879 took over Raglan in his own right, actually offered £7,500 to anyone prepared to accept the £14,000 liability of a one-third share in that run. To economic necessity was added Governmental policy in the breaking up the Waimate run.

At its zenith, Waimate was noted for its cattle and horses, the Bell brand of the Studholmes being known throughout the country and even in Melbourne and Sydney, where many Waimate horses were used in the trams. Today, Studholme descendants still farm about 800 ha at Te Waimate. *The Cuddy, a slab hut built by Michael and John Studholme and George Brayshaw, is still standing and may be visited (see below).*

**The end of the bush:** The European settlement at Te Waimate developed as a timbertown, milling *totara*. By the time the railway arrived in 1877 there were five sawmills, cutting furiously yet quite unable to meet demand. Just when prosperity seemed assured, the growing community was overwhelmed in the exceptionally dry spring of 1878. A strong nor'wester fanned a grass fire to frightening proportions. Eight days later, when the fire was out, seventy families were left homeless, many more had lost their possessions, and one of the country's finest *totara* forests had been destroyed. Claims totalling £28,000 were filed against Michael Studholme, who managed to refute the suggestion that the fire had been caused by his employees burning off tussock, by arguing that the fire originated in the mills' ever-smouldering heaps of sawdust. He won the case but was left with legal expenses of £6,000.

The timber industry was finished, as was the Maori settlement whose *whare* had been burnt. The Maori village was not rebuilt, as much of the birdlife on which the Maoris had depended for food either perished in the fire or vanished with the forest. The disaster could not have come at a worse time, for the country as a whole was entering the grips of economic depression. In the twenty-five years between the census of 1881 and that of 1906, the population of Waimate increased by fully thirty-two souls.

**First woman doctor:** The second woman to graduate in medicine and the first to practise actively in New Zealand was Dr Margaret Barnett Cruickshank (d. 1918), a graduate of Otago University in 1897. In the twenty-two years she practised at Waimate she did much to break down the prejudice against her sex as she won the complete confidence of the district. During the world-wide influenza epidemic of 1918 Waimate was particularly hard hit, and Dr Cruickshank found herself not only ministering to the sick but also attending to their household chores. When her driver fell victim to the virus she took to her bicycle to make her rounds, but finally she too contracted influenza and died. Her epitaph, "The beloved physician — faithful unto death" was earned in a literal sense. *Her white marble statue stands in Seddon Square, Queen St.*

---

Consult the Index when looking for a name in this Guide.

## THINGS TO SEE AND DO

**The Cuddy** (1854)***: Te Waimate is one of only four properties in South Canterbury to have remained in the uninterrupted possession of the family who first took it up. In the homestead garden still stands the mud-floored slab cuddy, on its original site, but with the original snowgrass roof thatching, the work of Saul Shrives, now replaced by wheat straw. Built from a single *totara* tree, the first European dwelling in the district has split slab walls lined with lath and plaster, and a front door still held securely by hand-forged nails. Only the chimney is a later addition; in the 1870s sundried bricks replaced the original chimney of stakes and sod. The uneven clay floor today reflects the observation made by Effie Studholme, Michael's bride of 1860: "The floor was of beaten clay which had worn into depressions here and there, so that in setting a chair there was trouble in arranging the legs so as to stand firmly." Effie did not live in The Cuddy, but the sidesaddle she used when she travelled down from Christchurch on horseback after her marriage is in one corner. The enchanting cottage escaped the fire that swept through the imposing old homestead (1860) in 1928, and survived falling trees in the *Wahine* storm of 1968.

From the same era as The Cuddy is the woolshed of pitsawn *totara* on the hill behind the present homestead. At the height of Te Waimate's fortunes it handled 100,000 sheep on its twenty-two stands. The shed, still used and still containing an original Ferriers woolpress, can hold 1,050 sheep and covers a quarter of a hectare. *2 km Gorge Rd, on Kurow exit from the town. Turn up the first driveway on the left after crossing the Centennial Bridge. Private property. Telephone 8737 Waimate before visiting.*

**St Augustine's Anglican Church** (1872)**: The feature of the church, built of roughsawn timber from the Waimate Bush, is its distinctive lantern tower. Designed by the then-vicar, the Rev. C. Coates, it was added above the crossing when the church was enlarged in 1880. If not unique, the tower is at least most unusual in a New Zealand church and at various times it has been pronounced unsafe. Over fifty years ago it was gloomily noted that "the borer has got a good grip", but most would echo Archbishop West-Watson's plea that it be not removed unless absolutely essential. He commented "I think it is delightful, unusual and distinctive." The side sanctuary windows are by William Morris & Co., produced by their leading designer, Sir Edwin Burne-Jones. His windows are rare in this country, and that to the left — depicting Sir Galahad's vision of the Holy Grail, the Cup used at the Last Supper — is a particularly fine specimen of his work. The chancel was rebuilt in 1923, the former chancel remaining in the grounds as a hall.

The lychgate (1902) is a memorial to Michael Studholme and two of his sons, and the belltower (1903) nearby is dedicated to his youngest daughter. Within the belltower, notes have been made of occasions when the bell has been rung in jubilation through two world wars — "Peace 11/11/1918", "Paris and Marseilles liberated", "Victory over Europe", etc. *John St.*

The first church built at Waimate was at Point Bush in about 1860. It was near the *pa,* but for some reason the area became *tapu* and the Maoris deserted the site, abandoning the church complete with furnishings and prayer books. Some years later the building was removed to the grounds of the vicarage, where it was used as a school and later as Coates's study before it was included in a home. (*It can still be readily identified as part of 20 Augustine St, off Parsonage Rd. The stained glass from its cloverleaf window is in the local museum.*)

**Waimate Historical Society Museum**\*: The collection includes a massive plaster statue of a *wahine* and child sculpted for the Christchurch Exhibition (1906–07). Behind the museum building is the original Waimate gaol (built of *totara* in 1879), and a variety of farming and other early implements. *Harris St. Open Sunday 2–4 pm, other times by arrangement with K. S. Stewart, tel. 7168 or N. M. Bailey, tel. 8091. Allow 30 mins.*

**Seddon Square:** A small park close to the town's centre spreads around a band rotunda curiously encircled by cabbage-trees. In one corner, a carved shelter commemorates Te Huruhuru and Michael Studholme, and in another stands the white marble statue of Dr Margaret Cruickshank. By the park stand the Waimate County Council Chambers (1877–78). *Queen St.*

**Knottingly Park**\*: A spacious, tree-shaded park of over 30 ha is given a rural atmosphere by grazing sheep. An early bush cottage (1864), built of slabs split in the Waimate Bush, has been moved here. *Signposted off Gorge Road. 4 km.*

## ENVIRONS

**Centrewood Park**\*\*: From the summit of Mt John, a low ridge of the Hunters Hills, is a superb panorama over the plains of South Canterbury. North and South the coastline stretches for as far as the eye can see. A cairn commemorates the Clydesdale as does the white horse beneath it, a mosaic of more than 1,200 concrete slabs. *Signposted 6.5 km.*

**The Hunters Hills:** A delightful spot in the foothills is at **Kelcy's Bush**\* with walks to Sanders Falls, and to the Divide (*883.5 m*) for a view over much of South Canterbury and North Otago (*7.5 km; Signposted from Queen St. Southern exit from the town.*) More distant is **Hook Bush,** with forested stream and a rewarding walk up

Mt Studholme (*1,112 m*). From here in clear conditions both the Port Hills of Christchurch and Dunedin's Otago Peninsula are visible. (*15 km; signposted.*)

The Hunters Hills are variously said to have been named after the ferocity of their pigs and the multiplicity of their wallabies. However the name appears on early charts that pre-date the region's European settlement so that it is more likely that the hills are named after chief Te Huruhuru, described as "the old hunter" by Charles Torlesse. Recently its second highest and previously unnamed peak (*1,574.8 m*) was named after the chief.

**Lower Hook Beach Monument:** A small cairn marks the approximate position of a remarkable meeting which took place on 16 January 1844. A party led by Edward Shortland, Sub-Protector of Aborigines and engaged in compiling the first census of South Island Maoris, was making north on the first overland crossing from Waikou-aiti to Banks Peninsula when to their very great surprise they met a group travelling south, headed by Bishop Selwyn. In the course of his second episcopal journey (the first was throughout the North Island), Bishop Selwyn covered about 5,000 km to visit all the settlements in the South Island, Stewart Island, Ruapuke and the Chathams. He once remarked that he averaged about one confirmation for every mile of travel.

The broad, unbroken plain stretches north and south, and one can imagine the astonishment with which the groups must have met as each followed the shinglebank between surf and swamp. *10.8 km north on Highway 1, turn right down Hook Swamp Rd immediately after crossing Hook River. Bear right again. The memorial is 2.9 km from the highway, at the road's end.*

### TOURING NOTE

△**Kurow via Highway 82:** At Waihao Downs (*13.6 km*) on the right is a pioneer memorial. A short distance down the road to the right stands a stone homestead which has suffered from paint but whose golden stone outbuildings are particularly attractive. At 45 km on the left, almost opposite the entrance to Glen Mac station, is a cob building, which was until recently assumed to be a notable accommodation house of this area but which, it now appears, may have a different history.

△**Waitaki Valley:** Points of interest in the valley are given under this entry. Excellent boating and fishing.

> The symbol △ indicates a place with its own entry in the Alphabetical Section of this Guide.

---

**WAIPARA**     **North Canterbury.**   **Maps 20 & 21.**   **Pop. 294.**

*9 km N of Amberley; 14 km SE of Waikari; 58 km SW of Cheviot.*

THE HAMLET OF WAIPARA marks the junction both of Highways 7 and 1, and of the branch rail line to Waiau. Early finds of *moa* were made in the district. To the north is a large brick church, a conspicuous as well as an unexpected landmark built as a memorial to George Henry Moore. Waipara means river with a thick, muddy sediment.

**"Scabby" Moore of Glenmark:** George Henry Moore (1812–1905) amassed one of the country's largest fortunes on his Glenmark estate, in his day perhaps the most valuable property in Canterbury. He once described his 92,000 sheep, mustered for shearing: "They covered in a close mass a hill 500 feet high and looked from a distance like a mass of maggots on a piece of rotten meat, continually on the move." Moore was a curiously contradictory character. He allowed his sheep to remain thick with scab, in one year alone paying fines of £2,400, yet would walk to Christchurch with a tent on his back to save the cost of a night's accommodation. He was also otherwise regarded as a progressive farmer. When the "Doomsday Book" of 1885 was published he was listed as the wealthiest settler, ahead even of his near neighbour, the affluent "Ready-Money" Robinson.

The mansion Moore built in the seven years from 1881 cost £78,000. Complete with high stone walls, battlements and fixtures imported from Europe, the castle-like homestead overlooked an artificial lake where Moore's daughter would each week feed to ducks, swans and peacocks fully 300 home-baked loaves of bread. The homestead was gutted by fire in 1890, not two years after its completion; the artificial lake has ceased to be, but the spacious outbuildings still stand near the manager's delightful old house. So, too, does the elaborate gravestone, a dog sculpted in Italy and placed here "In loving memory of our pet Dashie, died 3rd Sept. 1887." By the formal entrance is a picturesque gatekeeper's cottage, completed before the mansion and built in an appropriate style.

Moore's daughter received a vast inheritance on her father's death. She owned Mona Vale (Christchurch) and in turn died a millionaire. She endowed St Pauls Church here with £30,000, a liberality reflected in the proportions not only of the brick church itself but also in the capacious dimensions of the former vicarage (now with glebe land leased to a neighbouring farmer). The church is complete with carillon, pipe organ, stained-glass windows, altar hangings, plate and furnishings. A window commemorates her husband, Dr Townend. Moore's brougham is held locally. *The church is by Highway 1 at 3.3 km N of the junction of Highways 1 and 7. The Glenmark homestead block is 8 km from Waipara. At the church turn left and take the first turning on the right (at 5 km). The entrance is on the right. Private property. Visits by prior arrangement only.*

## TOURING NOTE

**Timpendean Shelter:** Just south of Waikari, Highway 7 north passes the entrance to the farm on which is the renowned Timpendean shelter of Maori rock art. *See* △ *Waikari.*

---

---

**WAITAKI VALLEY**\*\*     **South Canterbury/North Otago.     Map 28.**

THE BROAD WAITAKI RIVER, as it drains the snowfields and glaciers of the Southern Alps, marks the boundary between Canterbury and Otago. It has a number of major tributaries but is basically the culmination of the three major rivers that emerge from Lakes Tekapo, Pukaki and Ohau to unite before escaping to the coast from the upland basin of the Mackenzie country. The river's catchment of 11,822 km² ranks second only to the Clutha and among the country's most valuable sources of hydro-electric power. Its headwaters are presently being developed in the Upper Waitaki Scheme (*described under* △ *Twizel*).

Dams on the river, Benmore, Waitaki and Aviemore, have created a series of lakes. Stocked with brown and rainbow trout and with land locked salmon, these attract boatowners and fishermen. Below the Waitaki dam the river is renowned for its quinnat salmon, ocean-dwelling fish that ascend the river each autumn to spawn, when they are fished by anglers. Full of fight, in a good season fish of over 20 kilos are taken. Waitaki (weeping waters) is a southern form of Waitangi, for a time the spelling used for the river's name.

## SOME HISTORY

**A remarkable prophecy:** For centuries the river valley formed a trail to the Mackenzie and (over the Lindis Pass) to Central Otago. Coastal Maoris would trek each summer to the inland lakes on fishing and fowling expeditions, preserving some of their catch for the winter.

Edward Shortland, in the course of his remarkable overland journey from Moeraki to Banks Peninsula in 1844, camped on the banks of the Waitaki while the Maoris with him gathered fernroot. "It must not be supposed," he wrote "that the fernroot, wherever it grows, is fit for food. On the contrary, it is only that found in rich loose soils. . . . A great deal of discrimination was used in selecting the best roots, which were discoverable by their being crisp enough to break easily when bent: those which would not stand this test being thrown aside." There they roasted the fernroot, bruised it with flat stones and drew the long fibres out. The remainder they pounded to the consistency of tough dough, the "taste being very like that of cassava bread. Sometimes it is sweetened with the juice of the *tutu*."

He crossed the river on a *mokihi* (raft) before speculating — "We may, however, carry on the imagination to another century — when this now desert country will no doubt be peopled — when the plains will be grazed by numerous flocks of sheep, and the streams, now flowing idly through remote valleys, will be compelled to perform their share of labour in manufacturing wool."

Today, of course, the Waitaki's hydro-electric power is fed to the whole country as well as to Oamaru's woollen mills, in a form of energy which had not begun to be utilised at the time of Shortland's remarkable prophecy.

**A bad boundary:** In times of provincial government the Waitaki River was designated as the boundary between Canterbury and Otago. But while the Waitaki River proper presented a swift-flowing and effective barrier, it was left for the Provincial Governments to squabble as to which of the Tekapo, Pukaki and Ohau Rivers formed the inland boundary. Each was anxious to have the land between the Tekapo and the Ohau. Each purported to let runs, and each tried to exercise control before the issue was decided in Canterbury's favour when the Central Government proclaimed the Ohau as the boundary.

## POINTS OF INTEREST ON THE RIVER

*In geographical order, proceeding upriver from the coast.*

**Glenavy** (pop. 245) and **Waitaki** (pop. 178): Twin fishing villages near the mouth of the river, at either end of the river bridges. The rail bridge (1876) was built close to the rivermouth as the saving in building a shorter bridge upstream would have been outweighed by the cost of a long detour. The bridge, 1,105.9 m long, when built was claimed to be more than twice the length of any bridge in England. For eighty years road traffic shared the bridge with trains. The present traffic bridge was opened in 1956.

△**Duntroon:** Rock drawings may be seen by the roadside here, presumably executed by Moa-hunters as they travelled the valley. From this point the △Dansey Pass lifts over the ranges to Central Otago. Some 17.5 km towards Kurow an isolated homestead may be seen high up on the Canterbury side of the river that was the home of Lord Kitchener's sister, Mrs H. Parker. Lord Kitchener visited here in 1910.

△**Kurow:** Only the second point at which the river is bridged, giving access to the Hakataramea. The bridge (1881) served both road and rail traffic until the railway was closed in 1930.

**Waitaki power station** (1928–34) was the first power station to be built on the river. With a dam 354.6 m long and 36.6 m high, the scheme now has seven generators with a capacity of 105,000 kW, driven from a head of 21.9 m. Unlike others in the series, the Waitaki has no spillway as such: excess water simply pours in a picturesque crescent over the whole length of the dam.

**Aviemore power station** (1968), the fourth to be built on the river, is also the South's fourth largest — exceeded only by △ Manapouri, Benmore and △ Roxburgh. The Waitangi Fault passes through the site, creating a steep terrace on the Canterbury side of the river. Because of this a portion 336.3 m long, with five spillway gates, was built of concrete over the Fault area, and an earth dam, 427.7 m long, over the remainder. The dam's headwaters are level with Benmore's tailwaters, and its own tailwaters are level with the headwaters of the Waitaki station. In this way a continuous series of three lakes has been created.

The station has four 55,000 kW generator rotors, the largest in New Zealand, but its hydraulic head of 37.5 m is considerably lower than Benmore's, with a consequential limit on their power output (*The powerhouse may be visited*). The lake has an area of 3,108 ha, exceeded only by Benmore's 7,900 ha.

*A variation of the route up the valley is afforded by driving across the Aviemore dam to follow the river's Canterbury bank as far as Benmore, where one recrosses the river along the crest of the country's largest dam to return to Otago and to Highway 83 just beyond △ Otematata.*

△**Otematata:** Built as a construction town for the Lower Waitaki scheme, the village still houses maintenance staff. Many homes now serve as cribs, handily placed to enjoy the chain of lakes.

**Benmore power station** (1956–65) is the third and largest of the series on the river. A giant earth dam, compacted with 28 million tons of impermeable clayey gravel overlaid with porous river gravel, spans the valley between two natural prominences, one accommodating the spillway and the other the intake block and penstocks. It holds back New Zealand's largest manmade lake, covering 7,900 ha and containing one-and-a-half times as much water as Wellington Harbour. A head of 94.1 m is created by the country's largest dam, which has a maximum height of 109.7 m, a maximum width of 487.2 m and a volume of 12.2 million $m^3$.

Six 90,000 kW generators are driven by an equal number of 125,000 hp turbines to give Benmore an installed generating capacity of 540,000 kW. Until Manapouri became operational, Benmore was the largest station in service in New Zealand. *Detour 5 km at Otematata to see the powerhouse (visitors may be shown over the installations), to visit the elevated Observation Point and to drive along the crest of the country's largest dam.*

Sightseeing and fishing trips are run by jetboat on Lake Benmore. These can be arranged at the Observation Point tearooms, where photographs of the dam under construction and samples of power-cables are displayed. Immediately below the dam, where rock fill was excavated to build the dam, is a sheltered recreation area suitable for waterskiing and shallow, so warmer for swimming.

**WAKATIPU (Lake)***      *See △ Queenstown.*

**WANAKA***     **Central Otago.**    **Maps 16 & 36.**    **Pop. 1,160.**

*120 km NW of Queenstown (via Cromwell), 70 km (via Crown Range); 57 km N of Cromwell; 273 km SSW of Fox Glacier. Information from Mount Aspiring National Park Headquarters (on eastern exit from township) and from Dunn's Travel Ltd, Ardmore St, tel. 859.*

THE TOWNSHIP OF WANAKA smiles north across the lake to an incomparable alpine scene. In every shade of blue lift the surrounding peaks, in a tableau often mirrored in

# WANAKA AND DISTRICT

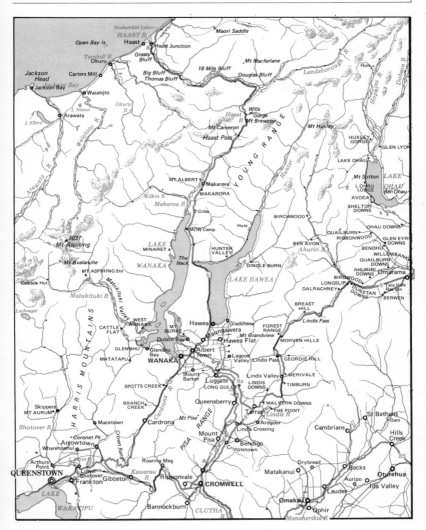

the lake's deep, glistening waters. Compared with Wakatipu, Wanaka's disposition is softer, more gentle; here the glaciers have more successfully done their work, yielding a planed and rounded landscape contorted only occasionally where harder rocks have obstructed their progress.

As elsewhere in Central, poplars and willows round the lake's edge render autumn a colourful time for a visit. Large grounds accommodate thousands of summer campers who come to boat, to fish and to swim and to waterski as well as to explore the Mount Aspiring National Park whose headquarters are in the town. Winter visitors are drawn by the developing skifields of Treble Cone. There is good fishing in Lakes Wanaka and Hawea as well as in many rivers, among them the Makarora and the Matukituki.

## SOME MYTHOLOGY

**The floating island of Lake Hawea:** Two boys, Ono and Ruia, were flying kites by the shore of neighbouring Lake Hawea when the kites entangled and crashed. Insults flew between the two families. Ono's father was musing as to how he might rid himself of Ruia's family when a *patupaiarehe* (fairy) came to him and taught him a song that, when sung, would detach a portion of land, sending it floating far out to sea. Soon Ono's father was singing loudly, and soon the land where Ruia's family was sleeping had broken away and was floating out across the lake. A storm drove the "island" aground on a shelving beach—a new land more wild yet more beautiful than any they had ever seen, and plentiful with berries, birds and fish. There Ruia's family built a new village and prospered as their descendants spread throughout the land. The floating island moved off again, to where it is not known. Perhaps it is floating still. The legend may have evolved from an occurence when Taki-Karara was fishing by the lake's outlet and the clump of earth on which he was standing drifted out into the water.

**The digger of lakes:** With other inland South Island lakes, Hawea and Wanaka were in mythology dug by the chief Te Rakaihautu who, with his followers, had arrived on the *Uruao* canoe. With him he brought a mighty *ko* (digging stick) with which he gouged out the inland lakebeds, forming mountains from the spoil. Hawea (doubt) was named by the chief as he was in doubt as to which route to take. Wanaka (more correctly Oanaka) is a corruption of the name of a chief who once came here to fish. The township was called Pembroke up to 1940.

## SOME HISTORY

**Visitors from the north:** The itinerant Otago Maoris used several routes to the West Coast, particularly the Haast Pass, to reach the greenstone country. Later Maoris tended to settle on the coast and the rivermouths, but in summer came inland to the lakes on fishing and fowling expeditions. There were small villages at Wanaka and Hawea, but they were essentially camping places.

Then came the raid in 1836 by Te Puoho, Te Rauparaha's lieutenant, who in an inspired outflanking manoeuvre brought his *taua* (war party) down the West Coast and over the Haast Pass to take the settlements here completely by surprise — "the first indications that the local Maoris had of the presence of the invaders was the swish of the *mere* and the savage cries of a band athirst for the taste of blood." Small *kainga* round the lake were overwhelmed and Te Puoho's men, starved of protein during their arduous trek, slew and ate two plump girls, Rumuri and Pipiki. One boy escaped from his captors to warn his relatives living at the outlet to Hawea, some of whom ambushed the party coming to attack them, while the others made good their escape over the Lindis Pass and down to the east coast. Triumphant, Te Puoho continued south only to encounter first victory and then disaster at Tuturau (*see* △ *Mataura*). For the *Pakeha* the raid had favourable consequences. The Maoris who had fled their *kainga* never returned, leaving the land deserted for the settlers to claim without dispute.

**Chalmers visits:** Looking for sheep country and guided by the ageing Reko, chief at Tuturau, the twenty-three-year-old Nathaniel Chalmers in 1853 became the first *Pakeha* to see the lakes. From the Nokomai he saw the distant waters of Lake Wakatipu; he crossed the Kawarau by way of the "natural bridge", and he followed the Pisa flats up to Wanaka and Hawea. Chalmers, stricken with dysentery, had little energy with which to enjoy or even take note of his achievements. Reko wanted to take him on over the Lindis Pass, but the *Pakeha* was too weak and so the little group returned to the coast on a *mokihi* (rush raft) which they sailed down the Clutha to the sea. Even in his old age Chalmers could still vividly remember sweeping through the awesome gorges on either side of Cromwell.

**A grand view:** It was left for John Turnbull Thomson to be the first recorded European to come through the Lindis Pass. In December 1857 he stood on the summit of the mountain he named Grandview. From there he marvelled at the prospect, and named, among others, Mt Aspiring (which a later surveyor renamed Perspiring, a joke that for some years was perpetuated on maps) and Mt Pisa (as a rock on the ridge reminded him of the leaning tower).

Not long after, Thomson was followed to the crest of Grandview by John McLean (*see index*) who viewed the classic scene not for its splendour but for its grazing potential. "Big" McLean claimed his vast Morven Hills run and others were quick to follow. The Wanaka runs were taken up before the end of 1858.

With the Central Otago goldrushes came an insatiable demand for timber. The lake was a source of timber rare in Central so that bushmen were quick to cut its trees and float sawn lengths down the Clutha to the embryonic townships of Cromwell and Clyde — a journey as perilous as it was profitable.

**Gold at Cardrona:** Rumours of Fox's party working secretly led many fortune-seekers to join in the sport of "hunting the Fox" (*see* △ *Arrowtown*). It was such a group that stumbled on gold in the Cardrona Valley in 1862. Though the Cardrona was at once overshadowed by the rushes to the Shotover and then to the Arrow, hundreds of diggers were ferried across the Clutha by whaleboat at Albert Town, a busy little ferry with several stores to serve the prospectors who swarmed over Central.

There were no sensational returns in the Cardrona Valley, which was as often used simply as a stopping-place by prospectors travelling from Cromwell to the diggings on the Arrow and the Shotover. The principal claims, the Gin and Raspberry (the party's favourite drink), the Pirate and the Homeward Bound, were all worked by shafts some 10 m below the surface, and each paid good wages. Some made their homes here until in 1867 there was a major exodus to the newly-opened diggings on the West Coast. Chinese filled the vacuum, but by the late 1870s both European and Chinese were drifting away.

Of those who remained was one Joe, a tunneller. One day in 1877 a trooper rode over Mt Pisa and asked for him, an incident that gave rise to rumour that Joe, known to have rich relations in Britain, had inherited £500. By the end of the week the sum had grown to £500,000 and that Saturday night Joe and his friends (comprising most of the town) drank the town dry — in anticipation and all on credit. When the truth finally dawned it transpired that Joe was to be a deputy returning officer at the local election booth, and the trooper had only been trying to deliver a document to this effect from the Registrar at Clyde. The revellers in their frenzy seem to have celebrated the departing glories of a dying town, for the spring of 1878 brought a flood that dealt a final deathblow to the community.

In the dredging boom, dredges worked both the Cardrona and the Clutha almost to the lake. (*The now-closed Cardrona Hotel stands by the road to the Crown Range. See "Suggested Drives", below.*)

## THINGS TO SEE AND DO

**Viewpoints\*\*\***: A pleasant aspect of the lake is from the **Lookout** above the town, in front of the white war memorial obelisk. A plaque identifies various points of the landscape (*Chalmers St*).

**Mt Iron** (*527.1 m*) affords a wide panorama of lake and plain. The mountain itself well illustrates the effect of glacial action. Its northern and western slopes are planed smooth and its southern face plucked by the moving ice (*1¼ hrs return; track signposted 1.3 km E on Highway 6*).

To walk up **Mt Roy** (*1,585.2 m*) is to rise further above the surrounding countryside (*5 hrs return; signposted 7 km on road to Glendhu Bay. The road up to the television translator is closed to vehicles.*)

The view from the summit of **Mt Criffel** (*1,281.7 m*) may be considered as even better (*4 hrs return; route lies across private property. Enquire locally for directions and for permission.*)

△**Mount Aspiring National Park Headquarters\*\*\***: The headquarters have information on all aspects of the park and issue hunting permits. Displays cover various facets of the park's flora, fauna and history. *Imm. E on Highway 6. Open daily.*

**Trout Hatchery\*** is an ova-collecting and "eyeing" station for salmon, rainbow and brown trout. Eggs are taken from females, fertilised, and developed to the stage where the eye is visible. Eggs from here are also distributed to other parts of New Zealand and to countries overseas. *Stone St. Visitors welcome. The hatchery operates from about May to mid-December.*

**The Maze:** Those who successfully find their way through some 3,000 m of passageways arrive at a refreshment garden. Emergency gates provide quick exits for those who fail. *1.6 km on main highway. Tel. 489.*

**Criffel Game Park:** A drive through the park, located on the northern face of Mt Criffel, provides views of the Hawea and Wanaka basins as well as sightings of deer from the 1,000-strong herd. *7 km on Cadrona River, signpost on Ballantyne Rd.*

## POINTS OF INTEREST ON THE LAKE

**Glendhu Bay\*\*\*** looks north across still water to the Alps that enclose the head-waters of the lake. The exotics here that in summer shade the bay's peaceful beaches turn in autumn to create an even more colourful scene. A favoured camping spot. *11 km NW.* The road to the bay passes through country planed by glaciers into distorted contours. There is a glimpse of Mt Aspiring (*signposted at 10 km*) and views of Ruby Island. Some 2 km beyond Glendhu Bay the lake occasionally mirrors the landscape. From here, too, a side road leads 5 km up Jack Halls Creek to the spectacular ravine of Motatapu Gorge. From there starts a tramping track to Arrowtown. (*Enquire at Motatapu station for permission.*)

**West Wanaka:** A pleasant beach here looks out to the hump of Ram Island. *22.5 km NW. Continue past Glendhu Bay to cross the deep Matukituki River.*

**Lake outlet:** Birthplace of the mighty Clutha River (*see index*). From no small streams does the Clutha grow, as broad and swift she flows from Lake Wanaka. A good fishing spot. *Signposted.*

**Dublin Bay\*:** A sheltered corner of the lake, perfect for picnics and shallow enough to be warm for swimming. *18 km NE via Albert Town.*

## LAKE HAWEA

Neighbouring Lake Hawea is without the beaches and gentle shoreline of Lake Wanaka. These were drowned when in 1958 the lake was raised some 20 m. Water is stored in spring and early summer to be released in winter down the Hawea and so to the Clutha to feed the △Roxburgh power station, when freezing temperatures in the Clutha's catchment area check its natural flow. Water for irrigation is an important byproduct of the scheme. A proposal that Wanaka be raised has been abandoned.

The vivid blue of the lake betrays its enormous depth (*410 m*), which extends to some 64.6 m below sea-level. Rainbow trout and land locked salmon are caught and many boatowners come in summer to escape the numbers on Lake Wanaka. Mt Grandview (*1,396.6 m*) is aptly named for the prospect its summit presents. (*Enquire locally for directions at Hawea Flat.*) *On the way to the lake are passed:*

**Albert Town** (*at 4.6 km*): Now a fishermen's retreat, this was the hub of the Wanaka district from early in 1863. As hundreds of diggers and packers arrived daily from the port of Oamaru by way of the Lindis Pass, the whaleboat ferry of George Hassing here across the Clutha River proved a most profitable one. Once the road opened between Cromwell and Queenstown through the Kawarau Gorge the route was deserted, and in the 1870s the settlement conceded slowly if reluctantly to Pembroke (now Wanaka township).

**Pioneers' Memorial** (*at 5.2 km*): Just after crossing the Clutha bridge is a table made of river boulders which, rough-etched with simple inscriptions, served as headstones for settlers who died between 1861–83. *Signposted. 150 m from the road.*

## OTHER SUGGESTED DRIVES

**Matukituki Valley**\*\*\* (*92 km return*): The road leads round the lake past Glendhu Bay before swinging west to fall in with the Matukituki River beyond Cattle Flat. The further one progresses into the mountains the more exciting becomes the sweep of peaks above the bush that includes Mt Aspiring and Mt Avalanche (*2,589.4 m*). Beyond 46 km the road veers left up the river's West Branch, but beyond here vehicles are occasionally marooned by the rising river or by scouring. The road ends at Raspberry Creek (*54 km*) where a 10 km track leads mainly over grassy flats to Aspiring Hut (*2½ hrs one way*).

On the way, at 18.8 km from Wanaka, is the start of a track in to Diamond Lake (*allow ½ hr return*). At 20.5 km are Twin Falls, where 60 m tall twin cataracts have cut parallel grooves into the rock face.

**Cardrona Valley:** The 25 km run up the Cardrona Valley leads through sluiced areas to the disused Cardrona Hotel, a sad, silent relic from the gold era kept company by a brace of cottages, an old hall and a miniscule cemetery. (*see △ Queenstown: "Touring Notes — Crown Range Road to Wanaka".*)

## OTHER ENVIRONS

**Treble Cone Ski Field:** Officially opened in 1976, the Treble Cone ski field has a variety of slopes and magnificent scenery. *29 km on Glendhu/Mt Aspiring Rd. Tyre chains must be carried for use on mountain road if road signs indicate.*
See also the entries for △ Haast Pass Road and △ Mount Aspiring National Park.

## ORGANISED EXCURSIONS

**Trips on the lake:** Jetboat and launch services explore the lake's possibilities. Picnic parties can be dropped off in secluded bays, to be collected later in the day. One such popular spot is Pigeon Island, a bushed island with a walking track leading to its own lakelet. Water skiing and fishing trips can also be arranged. *Run on demand by T. K. Little, tel. 414; daily Christmas–March, other times on demand by T. Clapperton, tel. 493 and 495.*

**Scenic flights** operate over a magnificent stretch of lake and alpine scenery. *Aspiring Air Ltd, tel. 427.*

**Landrover trips:** High Country Safaris run a variety of scenic tours to meet demand, and provide transport for climbers and trampers. *Tel. 860.*

Each day (except Sunday) one may take the NZR bus that leaves at 10.50 am for Franz Josef, to travel by way of Lake Hawea and The Neck to Pleasant Flat, 102 km along the △ Haast Pass Road. There one changes buses to return to Wanaka at 3 pm. *Book at NZR Depot, c/- Jacksons Gift Shop, tel. 885.*

## TOURING NOTES

**Crown Range Road to** △ **Queenstown:** *69 km.* A shorter but slower route over the highest main road in the country, and one susceptible to snow and ice in winter. *Described under △ Queenstown, "Touring Notes."*

△ **Haast Pass Road**\*\*\*: *Highway 6 to Fox Glacier.* An easy stretch of road for all that it was forged through majestic mountains and some of the country's most difficult terrain.

**Highway 6 to** △ **Cromwell** passes through **Luggate** (pop. 126.) (*at 13 km*) where the old stone buildings of a long-closed flourmill stand behind Upper Clutha Transport. A new plant processes lucerne into dehydrated pellets and stockfoods for export. Thousands of hectares in the Upper Clutha area have been sown in lucerne to supply the factory. Sawmilling and venison processing are other local industries.

## WEST COAST ROAD\*\*\*      Buller/Westland.    Map 37.

*From Westport to Haast Junction 435 km.*

THE WEST COAST ROAD stretches along the rugged Tasman shoreline, offering a widely diverse landscape. Fertile farmland and scrubby *pakihi;* cheerful towns and deserted gold settlements; the lush green of the indigenous forests and the snow of the Southern Alps, tinged pink in the aftermath of day. The Coast, drenched by a generous rainfall (which fortunately tends to occur at night) is essentially a multitude of greens, in contrast with the browns, the greys and the yellows of Canterbury and Otago. The rain, too, gives the Coast its refreshing atmosphere and clean, fragrant bush. Winters are suprisingly mild and a time of year when the peaks are least often obscured by cloud. In spring the large rivers can be a ready source of whitebait.

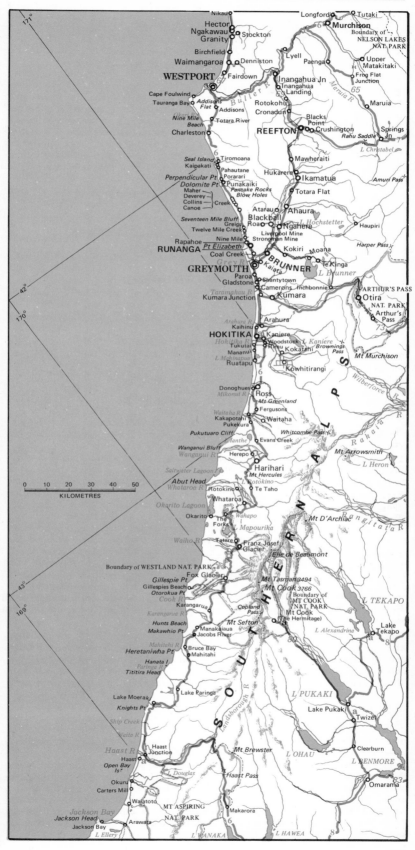

**The Wild West Coast:** The West Coast has a special niche in the folklore of the nation, doubtless as a consequence of the large contingent of Irish who came for gold and later settled here. The Coast is accepted as a place where nothing is too outrageous to have occurred; where the improbable is commonplace — the hotel that served a long beer instead of an early morning cup of tea; the mare that foaled during a race and still managed to come second — to the foal; the police who raided illegal hotel Sunday drinkers only to find them kneeling in prayer; and race courses where drink flowed so freely that a visitor could complain, "I've backed seven winners in a row, and if I'd had any money left I'd have backed the eighth!"

Most of the stories surround the Coaster's drinking habits, deriving from the era of six o'clock closing, an hour which suited neither digger nor coalminer, and a restriction the Coast cheerfully ignored. Generations have been weaned on stories that surround the efforts (?) of local police to bring the Coaster into line with the rest of the nation, but even today the Coast continues to lead the country towards more civilised drinking hours, and drunkenness is less common among Coasters than elsewhere in the country.

Certainly no other area in New Zealand is stamped with such individuality nor given such identity. From North Cape to Bluff the area is simply known as The Coast.

> Greenstone and gold, two of the more tangible assets for which the coast is known are discussed in *New Zealand's Last Gold Rush* by W. F. Heinz, and *Jade Country* by Theo Schoon (both are Reed books).

## FROM WESTPORT TO HOKITIKA

△**Westport*** (*145 km from Hokitika*): Born of gold and nourished by coal, the riverport is the chief centre of the Buller. (*Places on Highway 67 to the north are described under* △*Westport and* △*Karamea*.) *Bear right at 6.2 km to follow the coastal route over*:

**Marys Creek** (*10.8 km from Westport; 134.2 km from Hokitika*): Marys Creek wound through the now-vanished goldtown of Addisons Flat and was from 1867 to 1906 known to miners as Dirty Mary's Creek. Mary Boyle was a young girl when her mining father was killed on his claim, and rather than become a dancehall girl she elected to open her own grog-shop. With the waters of the creek she kept her shanty scrupulously clean so that great was her indignation when a group under Daniel Moloney began to work a claim upstream, discolouring the creek's clear waters. She objected to the muddying of "my creek" so vociferously that Moloney referred to it as "Mary's Dirty Creek". The name became twisted to "Dirty Mary's Creek", but finally justice was done to Miss Boyle when the title was corrected.

The immigrant Irish brought with them their grievances against England, which were nourished with reports from home of further troubles. Odd skirmishes broke out. At Okarito new arrivals who were either English or Orangemen were for a time beaten up, and a fracas at Ahaura in 1867 resulted in nearly the whole male population being sworn in as special constables. In less rumbustious moments collections were taken up for the relief of the families of Irish prisoners in British hands. The Fenian troubles were at their worst at Addisons: a protestant girl's acceptance of her compatriots' wager that she ride through the guests at a Celtic Ball as they emerged into the street was the signal for open battle between groups of orange and green armed with axe- and pick-handles. Word of the riot quickly spread, and reinforcements for both sides flocked into town. As the day progressed the Orangemen were slowly driven into a swamp, but the riot continued unabated as the groups slugged each other in the slush. Then Warden Kynnersley arrived. Alone and undaunted he rode his horse into the middle of the fray and became a legend in his own lifetime by securing an end to hostilities.

**Charleston*** (*25.7 km from Westport; 119.3 km from Hokitika*): The European Hotel holds the sole surviving licence of the reputed 101 that served the crowded town that mushroomed in the three heady years from 1866. Much of the surrounding *pakihi* is raised beach, and this was worked in times so prosperous that the postmaster from Wellington was transferred here — it is said, on promotion. The scrub now conceals most of the workings, but coal is still won behind the hotel, which contains a collection of informative early photographs. Until recent years the original European was still standing, a painting of which is in the hotel. A scattering of baches has joined the hotel and the tiny post office to return a semblance of substance to the hamlet. The hotel licence has outlived the gaol — whose first inmate was one of its builders, arrested for drunkenness after celebrating its completion.

The town was reputedly named Charlie's Town in gratitude to Captain Charles Bonner, skipper of the ketch *Constant*. He braved death and destruction to bring food to the thousand or so here who, despite their gold, were marooned by gales and by high rivers and were close to starvation. His vessel, owned by Reuben Waite, the founder of Westport, is remembered in the name of Constant Bay (*detour seaward for 0.4 km just south of the hotel*). No haven, the bay served as an overseas port into which squeezed ships that not uncommonly left their hulls on the gold-flecked sand. The only moorings were heavy iron rings, set into rocks on either side of the bay and into the large rock near the centre of the beach. Curiously, the bay declined as a port because of mining operations, which poured immense tailings into the sea to render the bay so shallow that by 1879 it could no longer be used as a port.

Both the Protestant (*north of the hotel, on Nile Hill*) and the Catholic (*400 m south*) cemeteries have headstones that tell of early and often violent deaths. Constant Bay is a good picnic and swimming spot. On the shore here are the rusting remains of the stamps from a gold battery. **Limestone caves** on the nearby Nile River are planned to be opened to the public. These form an intricate labyrinth with delicate limestone structures extending some 8 km into the north bank of the Waitakere (or Nile) River. *Moa* bones were found recently in one of the caves' four entrances. (*At present access is difficult, but the caves may soon be opened to the public and easy access provided. A permit should be obtained from the Department of Lands and Survey, Westport.*)

**Seal Island** (*offshore: 45.1 km from Westport; 100 km from Hokitika*): The seals have gone. The island, locally called Woodpecker, is good for crayfishing.

**Perpendicular Point*** (*52.4 km from Westport; 92.6 km from Hokitika*): The point was a notorious hazard for early explorers and goldseekers alike. When Charles Heaphy encountered it in 1846 he wrote: "The perpendicular cliff of Te Miko appears to debar further progress. It is almost 150 feet in height and its descent was first effected by a war party, the natives composing which let down a ladder made of the *rata* vine of the forest above. There are now two stages of ladders, made of short pieces of the ropy *rata,* lashed together with steps of irregular distance, the whole very shaky and rotten . . . the dog had to be hoisted up by a flax rope. . . . As several of the rotten steps gave way under our feet, our position was far from being pleasant."

With the influx of miners in 1865 the Nelson Provincial Government substituted a chain, through whose links saplings were forced, and this kept the access open until the track that is now the road was constructed high on the cliff side. A number of those who made the perilous climb felt compelled to carve their names at the foot of a nearby cliff, where some inscriptions may still be seen. (*Access is over private property. Ask directions locally.*)

**Punakaiki Pancake Rocks and Blowholes*** (*56.4 km from Westport; 88.6 km from Hokitika*): A feature of the Coast is a combination of stratified limestone stacks and blowholes whose main orifices in heavy weather throw up columns of dazzling spray to the accompaniment of shuddering booms. The settlement caters for visitors and has a motorcamp as well as a good swimming beach, Porari, rare on an exposed stretch of coastline. There is good river swimming under the Punakaiki River bridge (*1 km S of the rocks*).

**Barrytown** (*71.3 km from Westport; 73.7 km from Hokitika*): The lone All Nations Hotel marks the site of a departed goldtown. The beach here, good for gemstones, was the scene of extensive dredging. Very large deposits of ilmenite sand may give rise to a titanium industry. The hotel's name, a legacy of gold days, indicates that nationals of all countries were welcome.

**Ten Mile Creek** (*83.5 km from Westport; 61.5 km from Hokitika*): Here a narrow side-road curls inland up a spectacular gorge to serve a number of privately-owned coalmines. Not recommended on weekdays.

**Strongman Mine** (*85.4 km from Westport; 59.6 km from Hokitika*): Signposted is the turnoff to one of Greymouth's best-known coalmines.

**Rapahoe** (*88.5 km from Westport; 56.5 km from Hokitika*): Seven Mile Beach here is good for bathing.

**Runanga** (*91.8 km from Westport; 53.2 km from Hokitika*): A coaltown above which rises the ridge known as Old Baldy. (*See △ Greymouth.*)

**Payclerk monument** (*92.8 km from Westport; 52.2 km from Hokitika*): Raised by local residents to two mine payclerks, murdered here in 1917.

**△ Greymouth**** (*99.4 km from Westport; 45.6 km from Hokitika*): The principal town on the West Coast stands where the Grey River has sliced through a massive barrier to reach the sea.

**Paroa** (*107.5 km from Westport; 37.5 km from Hokitika*): Detour here to Shantytown. (*Described under △ Greymouth.*)

**Taramakau River** (*113.7 km from Westport; 31.3 km from Hokitika*): The scene of gold dredging by the *Kanieri.* Inland, tailings both venerable and recent are piled high. It was near here that John Henry Whitcombe (1830–63) was drowned. Tired, exhausted, and famished to the point of desperation after his traverse of the Main Divide by way of the pass now named after him, the young Canterbury Provincial Surveyor died while trying to cross the river. He now lies buried in the cemetery at Greymouth.

The river has long been a highly regarded source of greenstone. The explorer Charles Heaphy in 1846 encountered a *pa* here, preoccupied with the working of the stone.

**Kumara junction** (*117.6 km from Westport; 27.4 km from Hokitika*): Detour here to see △ Kumara. Also the turn off for Highway 73, the △ Arthur's Pass route to

Canterbury. *An alternative route from here via the 1865 trail to Hokitika is given under* △ *Greymouth "Touring Notes".*

**Arahura River** *(131.6 km from Westport; 13.4 km from Hokitika):* A fabled source of treasured greenstone.

△ **Hokitika\*\*** *(145 km from Westport; 290 km from Haast Junction):* Once "capital" of the goldfields and still Westland's administrative centre.

## FROM HOKITIKA TO HAAST JUNCTION

*The scenery becomes increasingly more grand, and population centres progressively dwindle. From Hokitika south there is only scanty accommodation outside Fox and Franz Josef and Haast Junction.*

**Kaniere** *(4.8 km from Hokitika; 285.2 km from Haast Junction):* A district heaped high with tailings and once a major goldfield. By the roadside the Kaniere Hall incorporates a window and a plaque as memorials to the victims of the Kowhiterangi tragedy *(see* △ *Hokitika).*

△ **Ross\*** *(30.5 km from Hokitika; 259.5 km from Haast Junction):* An appealing old goldtown at its best in the cherry blossom of spring.

**Lake Ianthe** *(60.4 km from Hokitika; 229.6 km from Haast Junction):* A beautiful forest-fringed lake, typical of the region.

**Harihari** (pop. 543) *(79 km from Hokitika; 211 km from Haast Junction):* A growing settlement of substance, with timbermill and Ministry of Works depot. New farms are being created in the district, among them the State Development Block at La Fontaine, where the twenty-one-year-old Sydneysider Guy Lambton Menzies ended the first solo flight across the Tasman in 1931 — upside down. In a blaze of publicity Sir Charles Kingsford Smith and his crew in 1928 had made the first crossing in the three-engined *Southern Cross,* but Menzies left Sydney secretly in his single-engined Avro Avian, it was thought for Perth — until letters he left behind revealed his true intention. After 11 hours and 45 minutes, more than 2½ hours less than Smith, he landed in the swamp here. His aircraft turned over, and when he undid his straps he fell head first into the mud. Accorded a hero's reception, he was lost in wartime flying operations in the Mediterranean in 1940. The little plane he flew had only weeks earlier been used by Kingsford Smith to reduce the Britain-to-Australia record to less than ten days.

**Mt Hercules** *(between the Poerua and Whataroa Rivers):* The task of crossing the "mountain" is not as herculean as it once was.

**Whataroa** (pop. 219) *(114 km from Hokitika; 176 km from Haast Junction):* Hospital school and timbermill give importance to this farming centre.

**Lake Wahapo** *(124 km from Hokitika; 166 km from Haast Junction):* The road follows this pretty lake for nearly 2 km. Water is led from here to feed a power station on the banks of the Okarito River. Brown trout provide good sport, and salmon have been re-establishing themselves.

**Okarito** *(detour 13 km; turn off 127 km from Hokitika; 163 km from Haast Junction):* An old goldmining town littered with iron huts, now baches. A superb view from the Okarito trig. White heron are frequently seen on the tidal reaches of the Okarito Lagoon. *(See* △ *Franz Josef Glacier.)*

**Lake Mapourika** *(132 km from Hokitika; 158 km from Haast Junction):* Described under △ *Franz Josef Glacier.*

△ **Franz Josef settlement\*\*\*** *(147 km from Hokitika; 143 km from Haast Junction):* A minute settlement not far from the glacier where stand the headquarters of the △ Westland National Park and the much-visited St James's Church.

△ **Fox Glacier\*\*\*** *(172 km from Hokitika; 118 km from Haast Junction):* The more substantial of the glacier settlements has a number of splendid walks, including to renowned Lake Matheson.

**Cook River** *(178 km from Hokitika; 112 km from Haast Junction):* Looking up the gold bearing river gives a splendid vista of river, bush and alp. Many of the rivers hereabouts offer such striking views. The river rises under the La Perouse glacier which, like Cook and Tasman, is named after a famous Pacific navigator.

**Copland Track** *(signposted):* The track leaves the highway to lead past a hot pool at Welcome Flat and up over the Main Divide to the Hermitage. *(See index.)*

**Hunts Beach** *(detour 1.2 km signposted at 209 km from Hokitika; 81 km from Haast Junction):* The beach is named after and was for a time worked by Albert Hunt, perpetrator of "Hunt's Duffer" *(see Bruce Bay, below).*

**Jacobs River** (pop. 47) *(210 km from Hokitika; 80 km from Haast Junction):* A tiny settlement on alluvial riverflats backed by forest and mountains.

**Bruce Bay** (*224 km from Hokitika; 66 km from Haast Junction*): On the mouth of the Matakitaki River. The true Bruce lies to the south of the rivermouth. The portion of coast here is an excellent source of white quartz, polished by river, sea and sand into smooth stones suitable for paperweights and doorstops. The bay was the scene of the famous "Hunt's Duffer" rush.

Albert Hunt, who had won gold at the Greenstone two years earlier, still enjoyed a prospector's reputation in 1866 with the result that his comings and goings as he roamed the Coast were watched with keen interest. On 23 March his party was granted a claim some 10 km south of Bruce Bay and 15 km inland. The diggers at Okarito refused to believe Hunt's modest assertion of four grains to the dish, at which point hysteria seems to have taken hold of the mob. Hunt was forced to lead them to the claim, at times with firearms held to his back. He set a cracking pace, and with 3,000 or so at his heels left Okarito like a latter-day Pied Piper. At Bruce Bay a township blossomed overnight, and the next day the mob again lunged on through the bush.

Suddenly Hunt disappeared. Stranded in unfamiliar forests, the enraged men searched for the elusive prospector, but to no avail. Back at Bruce Bay the mob exacted its fury on the storekeepers, who had lost no time in poising themselves here for the riches they hoped were to come. In an orgy of destruction, stores and shanties were looted for their liquor, food carried away, and the makeshift buildings of sapling and calico literally torn to pieces.

No one has satisfactorily explained what happened; whether Hunt perpetrated a cruel hoax in revenge for his not being accorded a reward for his Greenstone find, or whether (as seems more likely) he unwittingly became the target of the suspicion and greed that was so much a feature of the early days on any goldfield.

The riot was without parallel. Even so, its ringleaders went unpunished, escaping conviction on a technicality. Albert Hunt later reappeared, involved in a court case near Riverton, the result of a fresh hoax. His brother William was one of a party of four to claim the reward for discovering the Thames goldfield on Coromandel Peninsula.

**Paringa River bridge** (*236 km from Hokitika; 54 km from Haast Junction*): This was about as far as the explorer Thomas Brunner reached on his epic West Coast expedition of 1846–48, a feat recorded by a roadside marker. Unaware of the huge glaciers awaiting discovery to the south he recorded his decision to "turn my face homewards; first to rejoin my own natives, and then to endeavour once more to see the face of a white man, and hear my native tongue".

**Lake Paringa**\*\* (*243 km from Hokitika; 47 km from Haast Junction*): A lakeside motel serves as a fishing lodge. The lake has plentiful brown trout. In recent years quinnat salmon (presently protected) have been re-establishing themselves here. The lake's access to the sea is a good source of whitebait.

**Lake Moeraki**\*\*\* (*258 km from Hokitika; 32 km from Haast Junction*): An idyllic trout fishing spot. Rods and boats may be hired and whitebait nets are available in season for campers and guests at the fishing lodge to catch their breakfasts. Those with a penchant for salt water may surfcast from the beach, about 30 mins walk through the bush. From the bridge across the Moeraki River, the lake's outlet, is a magnificent view of the mountains looming above the forests, occasionally perfectly reflected in the waters of the lake.

**Knights Point**\*\* (*266 km from Hokitika; 24 km from Haast Junction*): The coast hereabouts forms a series of magnificent seascapes, with bush sloping steeply almost to the sea, with pinnacled rocks scattered at the bases of the points, and with the occasional twist of golden sand. A tablet records the opening of the final section of the Haast Pass route in 1965. Local tradition is that the gods resented the completion of the road, for within hours of the official opening a landslide had closed it again. The point is named after the dog of a surveyor who worked on the road.

**Ship Creek** (*275 km from Hokitika; 15 km from Haast Junction*): So named as occasionally the sandbar drops to reveal a wreck, believed to be part of the 2,600 ton clipper *Schonberg*, which went ashore off the Victorian coast in 1855 on her maiden voyage. Cynics suggest that her captain had run the vessel ashore deliberately — it was insured for £300,000 — as he had failed to make good his widely-publicised boast of making the Liverpool-to-Melbourne voyage in sixty days "with or without the help of God". In the event the sandbar on which the sailing ship perished proved to have been uncharted.

**Haast River bridge** (*289.6 km from Hokitika; 0.4 km from Haast Junction*): The country's longest single-lane bridge — of Callander-Hamilton steel trusses extending some 732.4 m — spans the river. Completed in 1964 at a cost of $552,000 it stands 3 m above the highest known flood-level and is designed to accommodate a flood flow of 11,200 m$^3$ secs. The bridge was an integral part of the final leg of the Otago-Haast Highway.

**Haast Junction** (*290 km from Hokitika; 146 km from Wanaka*): The township is some 4 km further south. The highway here leaves the coastal road to follow the Haast River and climb over the Haast Pass to Central Otago and △Wanaka. (*See* △*Haast Pass Road*.)

## FROM HAAST JUNCTION TO JACKSON BAY

**Haast township** (pop. 193) (*4 km from Haast Junction*): A Ministry of Works and timbermilling settlement near the mouth of the Haast River. There is fishing, both in surf and river, and good hunting hereabouts.

**Arawata River** (*35.3 km from Haast Junction*): The river lends its name to "Arawata Bill", William O'Leary (1865?–1947), who spent a lifetime prospecting and exploring the region. Immortalised by Denis Glover's sequence of poems *Arawata Bill*, O'Leary would, when he could afford it, embark on enterprises such as endeavouring to relocate a lost ruby mine, and trying to find a seaboot reputedly full of gold and hidden by shipwrecked sailors in a cave near Cascade Point. He claimed to have found the mine — his watch-chain was adorned with uncut rubies — but nothing more was heard of it.

**Jackson Bay** (*47.8 km from Haast Junction*): A tiny huddle of fishing buildings tucked snugly in the curl of the south Westland Bight marks the site of the "Special Settlement" that failed. Planted here in 1875 as a timbermilling and fishing village with potential for agriculture, the town rapidly collapsed. "A very bad class of immigrants" was how the populace, made up of an extraordinary mixture of nationalities, was scathingly described by a Royal Commission set up in 1878 to examine charges of embezzlement, favouritism, and sundry other malpractices made against the Resident Agent. The Commission considered the charges unfounded, but its report did hint of sabotage from other quarters: "The scheme has from the beginning had its enemies. . . . Some people supposed that Jackson's Bay would become the port of call for the Melbourne steamers, and that the trade and business of Hokitika would be injured as a result."

The much-needed wharf, used by fishermen and to ship out timber, was built for road construction in 1937, too late to save the settlement. Cleared land returned to bush and fishermen now provide a transitory population.

By the beach lies the grave of Claude Ollivier, who visited here in 1862 aboard the *Ada* while searching for grazing land and gold; weakened by privations, he died of pneumonia and was buried by his brother "on that dreary, inhospitable shore". In the bush, shortly before the road's end, is the overgrown cemetery of the little community (*signposted*).

## WESTLAND NATIONAL PARK***     Westland. Map 13. Area: 88,631 ha.

*Park headquarters at △Franz Josef and visitor's information office at △Fox Glacier. Both offices give details of walks and tramps, help with queries of all description and can assist with accommodation problems.*

ABEL TASMAN'S first sight of New Zealand in 1642 of "a great land uplifted high" was probably of the peaks of Westland National Park, so that this would have been the first area of New Zealand to be seen by European eyes. The area Cook dismissed as "wild, craggy and desolate" was long declared a scenic reserve before in 1960 it was formally constituted a national park. The park is unique for its twin glaciers of Fox and Franz Josef and in extending from sea level to 3,496 m.

The weather tends to be unpredictable — annual rainfall increases with altitude to 7,620 mm on the peaks. Visitors at all times must be prepared for rain in large quantities, in recognition that on such rain depend the snowfields, the glaciers, the waterfalls and the luxuriant vegetation. *For details of things to see and do, see the entries △Fox Glacier and △Franz Josef Glacier.*

## THE ECOLOGY OF THE PARK

The park's ecology ranges from the complexities of the lowlands to the nothingness of the snowlocked peaks. Its area falls into four principal zones. The coastal area, with lower rainfall and warmer temperatures, is littered with glacier-borne debris from the massive advances of the past. This has since been eroded by the sea, now at a higher level than it was during the last Ice Age. Even the shingle of the beaches supports an insect population, in the main comprising amphipods (beach hoppers), osipods (lice, etc.) and beetles.

In the piedmont zone (at the foot of the mountains) the annual rainfall rises from a coastal 2,540 mm to 5,080 mm by the time the foothills are reached. Over this area the soils vary in age, from pre-20,000 BC to about 12,000 BC, differences reflected in their vegetation. In the main the zone comprises farmed riverplain and undulating moraines which support vigorous podocarp and broadleaf forests. These forests cannot withstand the soils of the ill-drained hollows, where grow *manuka, toatoa* and silver pine.

In the third zone, the lower alpine slopes, sharp transitions occur as the climate becomes more severe, from dense well-ferned forest (up to 150 m), through forests without tree-ferns (up to 825 m) and through subalpine scrub (up to 1,200 m) to snowgrass, giant buttercup and daisy.

In the high alpine zone, which varies widely on either side of 1,500 m, the lower alpine vegetation gives way to herbs and low, turfy grasses. These dwindle as altitude increases until above 2,100 m only lichens are to be found, colonising sunwarmed rock. For all this, the ubiquitous sandfly and mosquito are to be found at 2,590 m, at Pioneer Hut. Wind-borne, they do not breed here nor do they survive for long.

# WESTPORT AND DISTRICT

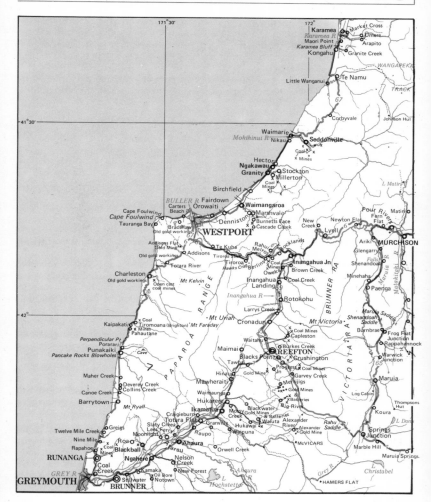

**WESTPORT\***    Buller.    Maps 24, 37 & 38.    Pop. 4,988.

*104.5 km NNE of Greymouth; 232 km SW of Nelson. Information Centre, Buller Motorways Ltd, 135 Palmerston St, tel. 8318 (after hours 27-808).*

BEHIND THE LIP of sea-washed level land on which stands the town of Westport rises the abrupt Paparoa Range, the country's principal source of bituminous coal. The town itself is marshalled by the mouth of the Buller River, the natural anchorage that gave it birth. Cement carriers are frequently in the port, to ship the output of New Zealand's largest cement works, an industry based on the ease of access to harbour, limestone and abundant coal slack. Westport, whose name is appropriate to its situation, is said to be called after a locality in Connaught, Eire.

**A salubrious setting:** Prepared to extol the virtues of Westport, a booklet published in 1907 earnestly proclaimed: "Owing to the porous nature [of the alluvial flat] Westport enjoys a very healthy existence. By the rise and fall of the tide, its sewerage system is flushed twice in twenty-four hours, with the result that its death-rate is the lowest in the world."

**Pakihi soils:** The Coast's soils are potentially its most important asset, yet to the visitor the often unkempt appearance of farmland suggests either impoverished or badly-managed land. In fact it is neither.

The mild, humid and wet climate encourages growth where plant nutrients are available, but the decomposition of vegetable material in some areas is retarded by the high moisture content of the soils, limiting the kinds and numbers of soil organisms. Thus organic matter tends to accumulate in a peaty layer above the mineral soil. This

△ indicates a place with its own entry.

335

encourages both acid leaching (as water trickles through the soil, dissolving such constituents as calcium, magnesium, phosphorus, nitrogen, iron and cobalt from the upper layers) and waterlogging (as water is trapped on compact older subsoils) to create what is locally known as *pakihi* (barren soil).

Conventional farming methods are unable to cope with the extensive *pakihi* wastelands of fern, mosses and rushes. Excessive water and soft surfaces handicap grazing, even though heavy topdressing can produce excellent growth. The high-silt composition of the soil makes mole draining unstable and the structureless subsoil renders channel drains ineffective.

The Department of Lands and Survey has a number of experimental farms where techniques are being developed to bring the *pakihi* into production. Several of these are in the vicinity of Cape Foulwind.

---

If in doubt about road conditions, contact the nearest Automobile Association office. In holiday periods, listen for the Mobil Holiday Bulletins which are broadcast regularly from most commercial radio stations.

---

## SOME HISTORY

**The madman from Victoria:** When a group of Maoris from the Coast paid in gold for goods at Nelson, the storekeeper Reuben Waite (*see index*) resolved to investigate the prospects. To the scorn of Nelsonians he chartered the ketch *Jane* in 1861, to drop diggers off at "the Buller" (as the area of Westport was known) and to sell provisions to local Maoris, again for gold. His second trip passed without criticism; Waite recalled: "Nothing was then said of the madman from Victoria." The small number of prospectors justified the opening of a store on the mouth of the Buller River, on a spot now covered by the river's waters.

For two years Waite enjoyed a monopoly. Indeed, the Orowaiti River is sometimes said to have been named after him as Maoris would herald his arrival with a joyous, "*Kia ora, Waite*" (Welcome, Waite). Without spectacular finds (the country was then gripped by the riches unfolding on the Otago goldfields) the settlement grew only gradually to service the slowly swelling number of diggers. Before the first of the West Coast rushes, to Greenstone, had induced Waite to move on to help found the second settlement of △Greymouth, the "mad Victorian" was apprehended by Westport's sole constable, not only with customers in his billiards room on Good Friday, but drunk as well.

**The town sails away:** Westport's role as a distribution centre was confirmed by the goldrushes to Charleston, Brighton and Addisons Flat, even though smaller ships could sail directly into harbours elsewhere on the coast. However the river proved a mixed blessing to the infant community, which had first established itself on the North Spit. Heavy storms and huge floods regularly inundated the township. A land agent variously described sections for sale as "amphibious", as "having breakers on the surface" and as being "navigable by ocean steamers". Finally, after weeks of heavy rain, the river abruptly changed its course, boring through the heart of the town. Four hotels sailed away on the tide; one, an eyewitness averred, crossed the bar with its lights still burning. A new site was laid out on firmer ground and the general enthusiasm engendered by the goldrushes helped the townspeople to forget their tribulations.

**Black gold:** The real wealth of Westport lay in its coal. To ship it out the harbour was developed along lines conceived by Sir John Coode, who advocated the construction of breakwaters which would confine the river to a definite channel and procure by natural scour a depth of some 4 m at low water. Westport became the largest coalport in the country, and by the end of 1903 over 5 million tons of coal had been shipped out from deposits noted by the explorers Heaphy and Brunner, and subsequently by Rochfort and Haast.

First hopes for the coal trade were unduly optimistic, as mines were developed and coal exported direct to Melbourne. When HMS *Calliope* in 1889 steamed out of the tropical storm that wrecked warships of other navies anchored at Apia, (Samoa) an official report gave credit to the good steaming qualities of Westport coal. In 1876–77 a railway was built to Ngakawau, solely to rail to the port coal brought down from the ranges above—from Denniston, Millerton and Stockton. Production reached a peak from 1909–18, with an annual output in some years of over 820,000 tons. With a marked reduction in demand, output decreased.

Gold brought an initial prosperity that coal maintained for nearly a century. Local coal resources are considerable, and their future life would seem to be governed less by their size than by the combined economics of production and utilisation.

---

A table of distances between major centres appears on page 363.

---

## COAL IN THE BULLER

The West Coast, principally Buller, provides the country's only source of bitumi- nous coal, a category of coal second only to anthracite, of which there is none in New Zealand. Usually shiny black in colour and more dense than either lignite or sub- bituminous coal, bituminous coal burns with a long smoky flame and a distinctly bituminous odour. Its heating properties are greater than those of sub-bituminous coals and there are varieties suited for gas production and for the making of metallur- gical coke.

The coals originated perhaps 60 million years ago as vegetation died and fell to forest floors. Through millions of years great layers of vegetation were formed and compressed to begin the process of "coalification". Vegetable matter feeds by a process of photo-synthesis, so that coal reserves represent stored sunlight. Burning releases heat absorbed by plants many millions of years earlier.

Coal found near the surface is mined by opencast methods — overburden is stripped and coal quarried with heavy machines. In this much cheaper way, more coal can be won by fewer men, transport is easier, and no timbering is needed. As there are no gases in confined spaces, there can be no explosions or fire hazards. Over- burden can be saved, to be replaced when a mine has been worked out, so restoring land for agriculture. Deeper coal is mined underground, using cutting machines and fast conveyor belts. Water, too, can be used to wash coal out from the mine face. Underground, shafts are driven, at times on grades as steep as 1 in 4, dividing the coal seam into blocks, or "pillars". Once a shaft has reached its extremity in any direction, the miners work back towards the entrance, removing the pillars as they go. With the supports gone, the rock above often falls into the shafts, at times causing subsidences on the surface. After it has been "pillared", a mine is sealed off to prevent the escape of poisonous and inflammable gasses and to prevent the entry of fresh air which could cause the no-longer ventilated area to erupt in flames.

Early mining attempts at Mokihinui and Ngakawau foundered because of trans- port difficulties. In 1878 the first serious attempts were made to mine the high-level coal that lies at altitudes above 600 m atop the precipitous escarpment that rises sharply behind the coastal plain north from Westport. The Denniston Incline, a self-acting haulway, with a maximum slope of 1 in 1.34, began to convey the first of 13 million tons of coal from the bins above to the railway below. As an engineering feat, the Incline attracted world-wide acclamation.

The coal industry, presently in a depressed state, awaits more large industrial users (such as the cement works at Cape Foulwind), a coalfired power station, or exports, possibly to Japan. The outlying coaltowns high on the windswept ridge have closed as, with improved transport, the miners have been able to live on the more equable coast. *Mines may be visited. See "Organised Excursions", below.*

## THINGS TO SEE AND DO

**Coaltown\*\*:** A brewery dating from the 1890s forms the nucleus and main premises for a developing community project museum. In addition to presenting themes from colonial life and natural history, it uses audio-visual techniques to give visitors the sensation of being in an underground mine. The Denniston Incline (*see below*) is also featured. *Queen St. Open daily. 9.45 am–noon, and 1.15– 4.30 pm.*

**Westport Domain:** A densely-wooded domain and pleasant picnic spot. *Cnr Palmerston and Roebuck Sts.*

**Carters Beach\*\*:** A long, safe surfbeach lies towards Cape Foulwind. *5 km W.*

## THE COALTOWNS

*92 km. Half a day or longer may be spent visiting coaltowns past and present. There are spectacular views on the drives up to Denniston, Millerton and Stockton, town sites abandoned by the miners in favour of the warmer coastal settlements when transportation removed the need for them to live atop the cold, bleak and windswept ridge. Leave Westport north on Highway 67:*

**Waimangaroa** (pop. 236) (*16.4 km*): A township that grew at the expense of coal- mining settlements that nestled on the tips of the hills that rise sheer behind it. *Here turn off to writhe up the hillside to the abandoned coaltown of:*

**Denniston** (*8.8 km from Waimangaroa*): Shattered buildings scatter the now-derelict site of a town that once had a population of 2,000. From here the famous Incline led down the precipitous hillface to the railway. From 1880 over a period of eighty-eight years 30 million tons of coal were trucked down a slope at times as great as one in one. When established the Incline was acclaimed as an engineering feat of world standing. For some years before the road was put in, all goods traffic also went up and down the precipitous cableway in coal trucks that used the weight of the descending loaded trucks to lift the empties back up the hillside. The town was named after the dis- coverer of the coalfield and engineer/surveyor for the cableway, R. B. Denniston. Coal is still mined and screened locally. It is carried by road to Waimangaroa and then railed. From the hill road are splendid views of Westport, of Cape Foulwind and of the flanking coastal plain. Seams of coal may be seen in cuttings on the road. *Return to Waimangaroa. Turn right and continue to:*

**Granity** (pop. 336) (*28.7 km*): A second coastal coalmining centre, Granity was named by early goldminers after the large number of granite blocks found in the locality. The township is a loading centre for coal from the mines to which men from Granity and neighbouring Ngakawau are transported each day. There is good surfcasting here, and gemstones may be found on the beach. *At 29.3 km turn off right to climb the range, enjoying a sweeping seascape to the north. Pass through Millerton and reach:*

**Stockton** (*6.4 km from Granity*): The overhead cableway seen at the site of departed Stockton is the largest in the country, extending 8 km to carry coal down to Ngakawau. It is possible to visit the opencast mine near here, where there is a cliff of bituminous coal in places nearly 12 m high. (*For permission contact the State Coal Mines Office, Westport.*) A 5 km walk to the north-east leads to the lip of the Ngakawau Gorge, some 396 m at its deepest point. Stockton was probably named after an English town, for about 2 km away was a second settlement, Darlington. The choice of names may have been influenced by the fact that it was between Stockton and Darlington that the first public railway in England ran; New Zealand's first electric train ran between the two local settlements.

A barren patch on the hillside to the south has been bleached by the heat of a burning underground mine that flared in minor outbreaks in 1905, 1910 and 1911 before breaking out again in 1926; it has since defied every attempt to put it out. Eventually the fire will extinguish itself, when a thick band of coke has finally formed to deny the flames oxygen. The sight is most spectacular after rain has dampened the hillside, but even on fine days a drifting column of smoke may be seen from far away. *Return to Highway 67 and continue north to reach:*

**Ngakawau** (pop. 113) (*31.5 km from Westport*): Stockton coal is brought here by aerial cableway for screening and for railing on to the port. A large briquette factory stands idle, a political white elephant of the 1960s built to process "waste" coal into bricks held together with pitch. The bricks' smokiness when burning, their high price and the fact that there was no waste coal (industrial users buy all the slack produced) saw the scheme fail dismally.

---

The traveller will in both town and country encounter the plaques and notice-boards of the New Zealand Historic Places Trust, whose role is to preserve such physical links with the past as still remain. To a great extent the Trust relies on its individual members, whose small annual subscription also entitles them to copies of the Trust's publications.

---

## A DRIVE TO CAPE FOULWIND

*33 km (excluding detours).* The drive leads out to the knuckle of land that protrudes into the Tasman Sea, sheltering Westport from prevailing westerlies. The peninsula contains much *pakihi* which is the subject of experimental farms run by the Department of Lands and Survey. The Cape was first named by Abel Tasman, who in 1642 with simple accuracy called it Clyppygen Hoeck (Rocky Point). It was Cook who gave it its present undeserved title after he encountered adverse winds in 1770. Inland from the Cape, the area known as Addisons Flat saw one of the last of the major goldrushes on the Coast, when in May 1867 an American negro named Addison made a good strike. *Leave Westport and bear right after crossing the narrow Buller Bridge (originally built as a railbridge to the Cape) to pass the:*

**Guardian Cement Works\*** (*10.2 km*): The modern plant's 45 m smokestacks are a feature of the cape. The industry is based on limestone quarried on the cape and local coal (slack coal being trucked here to be pulverised to allow instant combustion before being fed to the furnaces). As more limestone than coal is used, it is for the coal to be trucked the farthest. In the works, clay is mixed with limestone and suddenly heated to fuse the two into a burnt clinker which, once ground with gypsum, forms finished cement. The product of the country's most modern cement works is trucked and then shipped out through Westport to nationwide markets and to Pacific islands. When the third kiln is established the plant will be the country's largest. *Visitors welcome. Call first at the office. Features are the automatic instrument panels that control and illustrate the kiln process. Allow ½ hr. Beyond the works the Cape Foulwind lighthouse comes into view, with The Steeples offshore. At 11.9 km the road forks. First bear left to reach:*

**Tauranga Bay\*\*** (*14.8 km*): A delightful dune-backed beach of considerable character is almost locked by a low, craggy island, the home of a seal colony. In exceptional conditions in low neap tides one may walk across to the island, but seals, particularly young seals, may generally be seen on the northern tip of the beach. This can be reached at low tide; alternatively one may walk up on to the small hill and look down on the colony. Swimmers should treat the beach with caution. Once a railway reached the cove to rail stone for harbour works, but all that remains is a tunnel back from the beach (*now unsafe, this should not be entered*). *One may drive on south along the beach to cross the isthmus and reach Nine Mile Beach for a dramatic view of the coast and ranges to the south. From Tauranga Bay return to the fork, turning left to reach:*

**Cape Foulwind Lighthouse** (*19.8 km*): The cape has witnessed only one recorded loss, when in 1825 the *Rifleman,* en route from Hobart to Britain, went down. None survived; but local tradition is that the cargo was plundered by Maoris at Westport and the survivors despatched in the traditional manner. A track leads down to a cliff-backed sandy cove beneath the lighthouse, a favoured picnic and swimming spot. Offshore lie The Steeples. Near the lighthouse a waterfall, seen at its best after rain, plummets into the ocean. *Return towards Westport, turning left where signposted towards Carters Beach; bear left and turn right opposite the motor camp to follow:*

**Carters Beach\*\***: A lengthy stretch of sandy, gently shelving beach. Good for swimming. *Follow the beach north for 3 km to reach:*

**South Head:** Two rock fingers contain the waters of the Buller River to lead them some distance out from the shore. *Turn right to drive along the brink of the rock wall, between river and airport, and so return to Westport.*

## ROAD TO KARAMEA

*196 km (return). Allow a full day.* The road leads north up the coast to "winterless △ Karamea", passing a variety of coalmining towns and threading through bush over the Karamea Bluff. *Leave Westport north on Highway 67 to pass through Waimangaroa (16.4 km), Granity (28.7 km) and Ngakawau (31.5 km) (for all, see above). Beyond Ngakawau the road continues between steep hill and sea, past flax, nikau and cabbage trees, before turning up the south bank of the Mokihinui River.*

**Seddonville** (pop. 75) (*detour 2.5 km*): A timbermilling and coalmining hamlet at the railhead, named after Richard John Seddon. Two burning mines here flare occasionally after lying dormant for lengthy periods. There is good river swimming and fishing hereabouts. At Charming Creek a private company is the last in the area to use hydraulic sluicing to raise coal. There are excellent walks (*ask particulars locally*). *The highway crosses the river and winds slowly through the bush of the* **Karamea Bluff.** *A particularly large matai tree is signposted. 500 m beyond is a view back down the coast to the burning mine at Millerton. Little* **Lake Hanlon** *is passed, tucked away in bush yet close by the road, before the road descends to:*

**Little Wanganui** (pop. 89) (*79.5 km*): A farming and sawmilling hamlet on the mouth of the Little Wanganui River. A track leads up the river and over the Wangapeka Saddle to emerge on Highway 61. (*Described under* △ Nelson). *The road runs on through dairy land to:*

△ **Karamea\*** (*98 km*): If time allows one may drive a little distance beyond the township to the road's end by the Kohaihai River, there to cross the footbridge and walk the first few kilometres of the magnificent coastal section of the renowned △ Heaphy Track.

## OTHER ENVIRONS

**Charleston:** A shadow of the roaring gold town it once was, with but one of its reputed 101 hotels still trading. *25.7 km S on Highway 6. Described under* △ *West Coast Road.*

**Punakaiki Rocks\*\*\***: A drive south along the splendid coastline passes the curious stratified limestone rocks and the booming blow-holes of Punakaiki. *56.4 km S on Highway 6. Described under* △ *West Coast Road.*

## ORGANISED EXCURSIONS

**Stockton mines:** A half-day trip runs through Granity to Stockton, where both underground and open-cast coal mines are visited. *Weekdays only. Departs 9 am and 1 pm. Lemons Coaches, Palmerston St, tel. 7177.*

**Denniston mine:** A half-day trip climbs up to Denniston, now virtually a ghost town but brought to life with old photographs and a lively commentary. A visit to an underground mine is made and operations of the famous "incline" explained. *Buller Motorways Ltd, Palmerston St, tel. 8318. Tour leaves at 12.45 pm. Other tours by arrangement.*

**Cape Foulwind:** The rural mail delivery can be joined to visit Cape Foulwind, Tauranga Bay and the Okari River, and to inspect the cement works. *Weekdays only. Leaves at 10.30 am. Lemons Coaches. Other trips by arrangement.*

## TOURING NOTES

△ **Greymouth via Highway 6:** Points of interest along the intriguing coast road are described under △ West Coast Road.

△ **Inangahua via Highway 6:** The route upriver is described under △ Buller River.

The New Zealand Forest Service has offices throughout the country which issue permits for hunting in State Forests and in Forest Parks. They also advise as to the best hunting areas.

339

*30 km N of Invercargill; 51 km S of Lumsden.*

A TALL WATERTOWER rising from the plains is the first one sees of the solid farming centre of Winton. The town was named after Tom Winton, a stockman who found lost stock grazing here, and thereafter occasionally camped with his charges on the banks of what came to be called Winton's Creek. Winton helped with the survey of the town site in 1862 and his name triggered a surveyor's recollection of the Eglinton Tournament, a "mediaeval" jousting tournament staged some twenty-three years earlier on the Earl of Eglinton's (also the Earl of Winton) Ayrshire estate. A number of streets are named after members of the Scottish and English nobility who took part, among them Eglinton, Home, Grange, Bute and Brandon.

## SOME HISTORY

**Winton's wooden railway:** One of the first acts of the newly-formed Southland Provincial Council in 1863 was to embark on the building of a railway from Invercargill some 32 km to Winton so to reach the well-drained gravel plains of the interior — essential if Invercargill was to gain a share in the Otago goldfields bonanza. From a railhead here wagoners would have been able to take goods on to Wakatipu without suffering the ordeal of the morass of mud to the south that was the "Great North Road".

A newcomer from Australia, J. R. Davis, enthusiastically argued for a wooden railway, a concept which had been rejected by the Victorian Government. The plan was to lay square wooden rails so that they could be turned to be used on all four sides. Special rolling stock was to be built, with each wheel on its own axle, without flanges but kept on the rail by a small guide wheel placed at an angle of 45°. The cost was estimated at less than a quarter of that of iron. Further, added adhesion to the rails was expected to increase engines' pulling power and so save on the construction of cuttings and embankments.

An experimental track was laid on which Davis used his little engine, *Lady Barkly*, with great success. "The motion was found pleasant," reported the *Invercargill Times*, "and quite free from that oscillation and concussion which distinguish travelling on iron rails with the ordinary engine." The £110,000 scheme proceeded.

The Provincial Government was in financial difficulties long before the first 13 km were completed to Makarewa, and when the first section finally opened, in October 1864, the public were livid at being excluded from the successful opening ceremony. To placate the populace several excursions were run a week later, but the 2,000 who went returned chastened by the experience, for in the afternoon rain rendered the rails so slippery that the engine wheels spun helplessly. It was midnight before the only trip back was completed; the many who were left behind were forced to trudge thirteen wearying kilometres back to Invercargill, or to camp out in the wet.

The track lay idle, used only by drays who found the broad rails an attractive alternative to the roadway's sea of slush. The little *Lady Barkly*, a lighter engine, returned to the scene, carrying mail and a limited amount of cargo. She, however, had not been designed for the gauge, and her wheels projected over the outer edges of the rails, so causing excessive wear. Another engine of twice her power was built, but still the service was slow, intermittent and unsatisfactory. Those in a hurry still preferred to walk. Maintenance costs on the decaying and warping rails spiralled to three times the line's gross revenue. The experiment was a dismal failure. Iron rails were essential and eventually the impecunious Provincial Government managed to extend the railway, in iron, to Winton. It was then late 1870. The goldfields traffic was but a memory and Southland had been driven to shed her independence.

The line had taken six years to progress a further 19 km, but under Vogel's nation-wide free-spending public works policy only seven more years were to pass before the line was completed right through to Kingston, on Lake Wakatipu. Winton had been a busy township during the construction of the wooden railway as many of the sleepers and rails were cut from nearby forests. After the line's failure it took nearly half a century for Winton to recover its lost population and to develop as a focal point in Central Southland.

**The Winton baby farmer:** Winton was the last town where lived Minnie Dean, the only woman ever to be executed in New Zealand. A young Scottish widow, she arrived in Southland from Tasmania to marry a Mossburn farmer who, when bankrupt, moved his family here. His wife began a children's home, accepting illegitimate children for adoption in return for payments of £20 or £30. She first fell foul of the law when a magistrate fined her a princely 4d (3c) for keeping an unregistered home, but the extent of her nefarious activities was revealed only when an alert railway guard noticed her on the Lumsden train with a baby and a hatbox, but alight with only the hatbox. He alerted the police who found witnesses who had carried the box to the train — when it was light — and from the train — by which time it was heavy. Likely spots were dug up and finally in the garden of The Larches (more imposing in name than in appearance) the bodies of two infants were found buried. Convicted and executed in 1895 on a single charge of murder, Minnie Dean had probably accounted for over twenty children in this way. She was a woman of contradictions — capable of demonstrating warmth and affection to her wards.

Letters she wrote to women with children for adoption are charged with religious and benevolent concern. Her dull and feckless husband, Charles, was jointly prosecuted, but at the preliminary hearing it became obvious that he had had no idea of his wife's activities. Charles claimed his wife's body after the execution and it lies in an unmarked grave in the Winton cemetery. Most assume that Minnie Dean was both insane and money-orientated. For many years it has been illegal for parents to pay a premium when adopting a child out.

*The unmarked grave is in the cemetery 1.4 km N of the town. Those who wish may enter by the second of the two entrances and proceed straight through the cemetery. The plot is the last on the left, faced by those of James Fitzgerald and John Spowart.*

## ENVIRONS

**Some picnic places:** In the vicinity are several excellent picnic places. There are two areas within the **Forest Hill Scenic Reserve — Tussock Creek** (*19.5 km*) where one of several tracks leads to a giant southern *rata*, and **Lochiel** (*13 km*) from which a track leads to a point where a stream disappears underground in a limestone cavern. With the added attractions of both fishing and river swimming are **Taringatura** (*6 km; cross the river at Limehills and turn right*) and **Otapiri Gorge** on the edge of the Hokonui Hills (*20 km; turn right off Highway 6 at 11 km N*).

**Lady Barkly:** The locality of Lady Barkly, once a rail siding, acquired its unusual name not from an aristocratic sojourner but from the little locomotive, one of the first to be built in Ballarat, Victoria. After service on the wooden railway the engine was rendered redundant and ended her days here, powering a flourmill. *5 km N on Highway 6.*

A Glossary of Maori Words appears on page 343.

**WYNDHAM**      Southland.    Maps 14, 18 & 19.    Pop. 216.

*32 km S of Gore; 44 km ENE of Invercargill.*

SHELTERED FROM the traffic, both road and rail, that passes through nearby Edendale, the quiet dairying centre of Wyndham lies on riverflat, near the Mataura River.

Like △Edendale, Wyndham was seen as a likely dairying centre, and when the enterprising Thomas Brydone in 1882 erected the country's first significant dairy factory there, Wyndham itself soon followed suit with the establishment of a cooperative. The cooperative sold the whole of its initial output to Joseph Ward's Association, which cost money when a Sydney buyer failed to meet the £600 bill.

At the turn of the century the locality experienced a boom in flaxmilling which lent impetus to settlement in the area.

The town is named after General Wyndham who, during the Crimean War, won fame for his heroism during an unsuccessful assault on Redan, after which a stream and nearby locality are also named. To the Maori the area was Mokoreta (clear or sweet water), a reference to Wyndham Stream. Both the Wyndham Stream and the Mimihau offer good fishing.

# A BRIEF MAORI VOCABULARY

THE MAORI LANGUAGE belongs to the Polynesian sub-family of languages, a fact which enabled Captain Cook's Tahitian interpreter, Tupaia, to translate for him on his initial voyage of discovery to New Zealand in 1769.

The language was first reduced to writing by the early missionaries, but they simply used English letters to represent Polynesian sounds and only comparatively recently have appropriate techniques been evolved to establish the significant sound contrasts in the Maori language. These are not yet in common use.

The alphabet is restricted to fifteen letters—h, k, m, n, p, r, t, w, a, e, i, o, u, wh, and ng. Every syllable ends in a vowel, and the quantity of the vowel may vary, so changing the meaning of a word. Such subtle differences are beyond the capacity of most *pakeha*.

In general:
A is pronounced as in "rather"
E is pronounced as in "ten"
I is pronounced as in the "ee" in "seen"
O is pronounced as in the "oa" in "board"
U is pronounced as in the "oo" in "bloom".

When two vowels come together each is given its proper sound: e.g. Aotea is pronounced "A-o-te-a". (Longer Maori names are occasionally hyphenated to assist with pronunciation.)

WH is usually pronounced as f, although the correct sound has been likened to an f but without the top teeth touching the lower lip. NG is pronounced as in "singing" (in the South Island the letter "ng" often becomes a distinct "k").

Words which commonly form part of Maori place-names are as follows:

| | | | |
|---|---|---|---|
| AHI | fire | O | of, or the place of |
| AO | cloud | ONE | mud, sand or beach |
| ARA | path or road | PA | fortified village |
| ATA | shadow | PAE | ridge, or resting place |
| ATUA | god | PAPA | broad, flat, or ground covered with vegetation |
| AWA | river, channel, gully, valley | PO | night |
| HAKA | dance | PUKE | hill |
| HAU | wind | PUNA | spring of water |
| HUA | fruit, egg | RANGI | sky |
| IKA | fish | RAU | hundred, many or leaf |
| ITI | small | RIKI | small or few |
| KAI | food, or eat | ROA | long or high |
| KINO | bad | ROTO | lake |
| MA | white or clear | RUA | cave, hollow or two |
| MA | (short for *manga*) tributary or stream | TAHI | one, single |
| | | TAI | sea, coast or tide |
| MANGA | tributary or stream | TAPU | forbidden or sacred |
| MANU | bird | TE | the |
| MATA | headland (also many other meanings) | TEA | white or clear |
| MAUNGA | mountain | WAI | water |
| MOANA | sea, lake | WAKA | canoe |
| MOTU | island | WHANGA | bay, inlet or stretch of water |
| MURI | end | WHARE | house |
| MUTU | ended, finished | WHATA | raised platform for storing food |
| NUI | big, or plenty of | WHENUA | land or country |

The standard reference Maori dictionary, *A Dictionary of the Maori Language* by H. W. Williams, had its origins in a dictionary and grammar compiled by the missionary, Bishop William Williams (*see index*) and issued by the Mission Press at Paihia in 1844.

Members of the Williams family saw the work through its first five editions and three reprints, and the dictionary now bears as author the name of Bishop Herbert W. Williams, William's grandson.

# GLOSSARY OF MAORI WORDS

*In this glossary the meanings are given of Maori words used in the text. Most have more than one meaning, and those given here are the meanings appropriate to the contexts in which the words appear. Readers are referred to* A Dictionary of the Maori Language *(7th edition 1971) by Herbert W. Williams (Government Printer), the dictionary originally compiled by the missionary Bishop William Williams and first published in 1844. A "Brief Maori Vocabulary" appears at page 33 in the North Island volume of this guide.*

*Translations of place names, which appear throughout the text, are not repeated here.*

**a**   of; belonging to

**amo**   upright supports for lower end of **maihi** on front gable of house

**atua**   god; supernatural being

**auhunga**   pale variety of greenstone

**awarua**   cloak

**haka**   dance

**hapu**   pregnant; section of tribe; clan; secondary tribe

**hautu**   give the time (for rowers in a canoe)

**Hawaiki**   legendary homeland of **Maori**

**hei-tiki**   greenstone ornament worn suspended from the neck

**heke**   migrate; party of emigrants

**hinau**   *Elaeocarpus dentatus*—a tree

**huanga**   relative; member of same hapu

**ika**   fish

**inanga**   *Galaxias attenuatus* and *Retropinna retropinna*—whitebait

**iwi**   bones; nation; people (i.e. tribe)

**kahikatea**   *Podocarpus excelsum*—white pine

**kai**   consume; eat

**kaik**   southern variant of **kainga**

**kainga**   unfortified village

**kaka**   *Botaurus poeciloptilus*—bittern

**kakapo**   *Strigops habroptilus*—ground parrot

**kamahi**   *Weinmannia racemosa*—a tree

**kanakana**   *Geotria australis*—lamprey

**karakia**   charm; spell; incantation

**kauri**   *Agathis australis*—forest tree

**kauru**   edible stem of **ti-para** (*Cordyline*)

**kea**   *Nestor notabilis*—alpine parrot

**kereru**   *Hemiphaga novaeseelandiae*—wood pigeon

**kiekie**   *Freycinetia banksii*—a climbing plant

**kiwi**   *Apteryx* of various species—wingless bird

**ko**   wooden implement for digging or planting

**kohoperoa**   *Eudynamis taitensis*—long-tailed cuckoo

**kokowai**   red ochre

**konini**   fruit of *Fuschia excorticata*

**korero**   tell; say; discussion

**kotuku**   *Egretta alba modesta*—white heron

**koura**   *Jasus lalandii, J. hugeli* and *Paranephrops planifrons*—crayfish

**kowhai**   *Sophora tetraptera* and *S. microphylla*—trees

**kumara**   *Ipomoea batatas*—sweet potato

**kuri**   dog

**kuriawarua**   dogskin cape

**maeroero**   fabulous monster

**makomako**   *Anthornis melanura*—bellbird

**makutu**   bewitch; spell; incantation

**mana**   prestige; influence; psychic force

**manga**   *Thyrsites atun*—barracuda

**manuka**   *Leptospermum scoparium* and *L. ericoides*—shrubs or trees; so-called "tea-tree"

**maori**   normal; usual; ordinary (hence: man of Polynesian race, i.e. not a foreigner)

**maoritanga**   explanation; meaning (hence: lore and customs of the **Maori**)

**matai**   *Podocarpus spicatus*—a tree

**mere**   short flat stone weapon for hand-to-hand fighting

**miro**   *Podocarpus ferrugineus*—a tree

**moa**   *Dinornis gigantea* and other species—extinct birds of order Dinornithiformes

**mokihi**   raft (made of bundles of rushes or flax)

**moko**   tattooing (on the face or body)

**motu**   anything isolated, e.g. island

**ngiru-ngiru**   *Petroica toitoi* and *P. macrocephala macrocephala*—white or yellow-breasted tomtit

**niho**   tooth

**nikau**   *Rhopalostylis sapida*—New Zealand palm

**nui**   large; great

**o**   of; belonging to

**pa**   stockade; fortified place

**pakeha**   foreign; imported (hence: person of predominantly European descent)

**pakihi**   barren land

**paoa**   downward stroke

**paraerae**   sandal of leaves or flax twisted into a pad

**patu**   strike; beat; weapon

**patupaiarehe**   sprite; fairy (malign or beneficent)

**paua**   *Italiotis* of several species—univalve molluscs

**pipi**   cockle (in general)

**pohutukawa**   *Metrosideros excelsa*—a tree

**pounamu**   greenstone

**poutahu**   post supporting end of ridge-pole of a house

**rata**   *Metrosideros robusta*—a forest tree

**raupo**   *Typha augustifolia*—bulrush

**rimu**   *Dacrydium cupressinum*—a tree

**riroriro**   *Pseudogerygone igata*—grey warbler

**roa**   long; tall

**rua**   pit; hole; two

**ruru**   *Ninox novaeseelandiae*—owl; morepork

**takahe**   *Notornis hochstetteri*—large and rare flightless bird

**tangata**   man; human being

**tangi** lamentation; mourning (hence: funeral)

**tangiwai** transparent variety of greenstone

**taniwha** fabulous water-monster

**tapu** under religious or superstitious restriction (hence: sacred)

**taua** hostile expedition; army

**te** the (definite article)

**tika** just; fair; correct

**tipua** demon; object of terror

**titoki** *Alectryon excelsum*—a tree

**titi-pounamu** *Ancathisitta chloris*—rifleman (a bird)

**toatoa** *Phyllocladus trichomanoides* and *P. glaucus*—trees

**toetoe** grass, sedge etc. of various species

**toheroa** *Amphidesma ventricosum*—a bivalve mollusc

**tohunga** skilled person; wizard; priest

**totara** *Podocarpus totara*—a forest tree

**tuatara** *Sphenodon punctatus*—reptile like a large lizard

**tui** *Prosthemadera novaeseelandiae*—parson bird

**tutae-koka** discoloured flaw in greenstone

**tutu** *Coriaria arborea*—a shrub

**umu** earth oven

**utu** satisfaction; ransom; compensation

**waiata** song

**wairua** spirit

**waka** canoe (in general)

**weka** *Gallirallus australis* and *G. hectori*—woodhen

**whare** house; habitation

**wheke** squid; octopus

**whenua** land; country

**whetu** star

*New Zealand's South Island in Colour;* K. & J. Bigwood and Jim Henderson picture the South Island at its best, and in *Unspoiled South Island* L. W. McCaskill presents the varied South Island national parks with an interesting text and fifty full-page colour plates. Both are Reed books.

# METRIC CONVERSION CHART

As this book is appearing in the period during which metric measurements are being introduced, the following conversions are provided as a guide.

*Length*

| | | | | | |
|---|---|---|---|---|---|
| 1 inch | = 25.4 millimetres (mm) | | 1 mm | = 0.039 inch |
| 1 inch | = 2.54 centimetres (cm) | | 1 cm | = 0.394 inch |
| 1 foot | = 30.5 centimetres (cm) | | 1 m | = 3.28 feet |
| 1 yard | = 0.914 metre (m) | | 1 m | = 1.09 yards |
| 1 mile | = 1.61 kilometres (km) | | 1 km | = 0.621 mile |

*Weight (Mass)*

| | | | | | |
|---|---|---|---|---|---|
| 1 ounce | = 28.3 grams (g) | | 1 g | = 0.035 ounce |
| 1 pound | = 454 grams (g) | | 1 kg | = 2.20 pounds |
| 1 ton | = 1.02 tonnes (t) | | 1 t | = 0.984 ton |

*Volume (Fluids)*

| | | | | | |
|---|---|---|---|---|---|
| 1 ounce | = 28.4 millilitres (ml) | | 1 ml | = 0.035 ounce |
| 1 pint | = 568 millilitres (ml) | | 1 l | = 1.76 pints |
| 1 gallon | = 4.55 litres (l) | | 1 l | = 0.220 gallon |

*Area*

| | | | | | |
|---|---|---|---|---|---|
| 1 square inch | = 6.45 square centimetres ($cm^2$) | | 1 $cm^2$ | = 0.155 sq. inch |
| 1 square foot | = 929 square centimetres ($cm^2$) | | 1 $m^2$ | = 10.8 sq. feet |
| 1 square yard | = 0.83 square metre ($m^2$) | | 1 $m^2$ | = 1.20 sq. yards |
| 1 acre | = 0.40 hectare (ha) | | 1 $km^2$ | = 0.386 sq. mile |
| 1 square mile | = 2.59 square kilometres ($km^2$) | | 1 ha | = 2.47 acres |

*Temperature*

| °F | °C | | °C | °F |
|---|---|---|---|---|
| 32 | 0 | | 0 | 32 |
| 40 | 4.4 | | 5 | 41 |
| 50 | 10.0 | | 10 | 50 |
| 60 | 15.6 | | 15 | 59 |
| 70 | 21.1 | | 20 | 68 |
| 80 | 26.7 | | 25 | 77 |
| 90 | 32.2 | | 30 | 86 |
| 98.4 | 36.9 | | 35 | 95 |
| 100 | 37.8 | | 40 | 104 |

**Places and features appear in bold type.**

*Ships, canoes, trains, and Maori words other than place names and proper nouns appear in italics.*

For subjects of a general nature, refer to the Table of Contents on page 6.

# INDEX

# INDEX

# NOTES

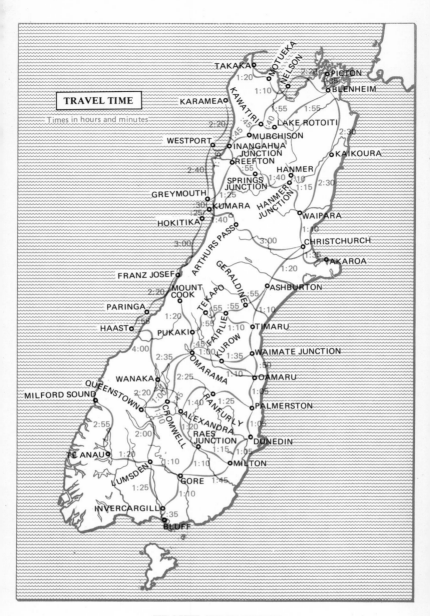

## TRAVEL TIME GUIDE
(supplied by the Ministry of Transport)

The times, in hours and minutes, represent:
(a) Driving time for a driver who travels at 80 to 90 km/h on open stretches of road plus a safety factor of 5 to 10 minutes per hour for traffic delays (and short stops for petrol, refreshments etc.).
(b) Driving time *only* for a driver who travels at about 70 km/h on open stretches of road or who is using a low-powered car. These drivers should allow another 5 to 10 minutes per hour for safety.

### Holiday time
In heavy holiday or Sunday traffic allow an extra 15 to 20 minutes on roads approaching main centres or important holiday centres.

### Long trips
Share the driving if you have another driver as a passenger. Normally don't plan a trip of more than 8 hours' driving in one day if you do it all yourself.

### Meals and rests
During trips of over 4-5 hours allow an extra hour for a rest or a meal. Make a practice of stopping for a short rest every couple of hours, at least on long trips. This will reduce fatigue and inattention.

Tired drivers have accidents—avoid rushing—plan your trip and enjoy a safe holiday.